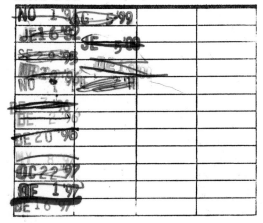

The Shanidar Neandertals

The Shanidar Neandertals

ERIK TRINKAUS

Department of Anthropology
Peabody Museum
Harvard University
Cambridge, Massachusetts

1983

ACADEMIC PRESS

A Subsidiary of Harcourt Brace Jovanovich, Publishers

New York   London
Paris   San Diego   San Francisco   São Paulo   Sydney   Tokyo   Toronto

ACADEMIC PRESS, INC.
111 Fifth Avenue, New York, New York 10003

United Kingdom Edition published by
ACADEMIC PRESS, INC. (LONDON) LTD.
24/28 Oval Road, London NW1 7DX

Library of Congress Cataloging in Publication Data

Trinkaus, Erik.
    The Shanidar Neandertals.

    Bibliography: p.
    Includes index.
    1. Neanderthal race.   2. Shanidar Cave (Iraq)
I. Title.
GN285.T74 1983   573.3   83-2488
ISBN 0-12-700550-1

PRINTED IN THE UNITED STATES OF AMERICA

83 84 85 86   9 8 7 6 5 4 3 2 1

To T. Dale Stewart

To honor DR. SAUL JARCHO, distinguished paleopathologist and anthropologist, Mr. Morris Feld donated funds to the Department of Anthropology, Harvard University. This publication has been made possible in part by this contribution. I am grateful for this generosity and hope that this volume, especially the discussion of the paleopathology of the Shanidar Neandertals, will form a worthy tribute to Dr. Jarcho's interests in and contribution to anthropology and paleopathology.

Contents

Figures

Tables

Preface

In the spring of 1973, as a graduate student beginning doctoral research, I wrote to Dr. T. Dale Stewart at the Smithsonian Institution to inquire whether it would be possible to study the postcranial remains from the Shanidar Neandertals. He promptly replied that I would be welcome to study the materials at his disposal in Washington, which included the Shanidar 3 original specimen, casts of several of the Shanidar 1 and 2 limb bones, and various unpublished notes and photographs. That spring and during the spring of 1974, I visited Dr. Stewart at the Smithsonian and collected the Shanidar data that were to form part of my dissertation on Neandertal pedal morphology.

As I was completing my study of Neandertal foot remains, it became increasingly apparent that an adequate understanding of the functional morphology of the Neandertals and their place in human evolution would only be achieved if the largest possible samples could be made available for analysis. At that time, one of the largest known samples of Neandertals was that from Shanidar Cave. The numerous publications of Dr. Ralph S. Solecki of Columbia University on the excavations and fossil discoveries at Shanidar and of Dr. Stewart and the late Dr. Muzaffer Şenyürek on the fossil human remains were more than adequate to indicate the size and completeness of the specimens. Yet, many of the partial skeletons had received only preliminary descriptions or had had only select aspects of their remains described in detail. It was evident to many, including Dr. Stewart, that there was more work to be done on the Shanidar fossils and that considerably more paleontological data could be obtained from them.

With these thoughts in mind, I wrote in March 1975 to Dr. Stewart and offered to assist with the paleontological study of the Shanidar fossils. He had previously been generous with information about and access to the Shanidar material, and I hoped that he might be receptive to such an offer. To my surprise, he suggested that I assume full responsibility for the completion of the reconstruction, study, and eventual publication of the Shanidar Neandertal sample. He was at that time completing a summary of his own work on the Iraqi fossils and planned only to finish the description of the fragmentary Shanidar 3 remains, then in Washington. Subsequently, with the support of Drs. Stewart and Solecki, I made the contact with Dr. Isa Salman, then Director-General of Antiquities of the Republic of Iraq, during the fall of 1975 and made the first of three trips to the Iraq Museum, Baghdad, in June 1976.

The majority of the cleaning and reassembly of the Shanidar fossils in the Iraq Museum had been done by Drs. Stewart and Şenyürek. Only the Shanidar 5 partial skeleton had not been worked on, and it was toward its cleaning and reassembly that I directed my attention in 1976. It was also possible at that time to study most of the other Shanidar remains in Baghdad and to continue the reassembly begun by Dr. Stewart of the Shanidar 4, 6, 8, and 9 multiple burial. It was primarily this additional work on the Shanidar 4, 6, 8, and 9 remains that was continued during my 1978 and 1980 trips to the Iraq Museum. Some additional minor reconstruction was done on the Shanidar 1, 2, 5, and 7 specimens, but most of the remaining time spent working in the Iraq Museum was devoted to collecting the qualitative descriptions, quantitative data, and a photographic record of the Shanidar fossils that form the core of this work.

Following my trip to the Iraq Museum in 1976, Dr. Stewart transferred the fragmentary Shanidar 3 remains to me for the completion of their study. During 1976 and 1977, I continued the cleaning and reassembly begun by Dr. Stewart and, with the assistance of Dr. Stewart, prepared the description that was eventually published in Sumer.

It was apparent from the beginning of my studies of the Shanidar fossils in the Iraq Museum that the material warranted monographic treatment. The descriptions by Stewart, Şenyürek, and me of partial skeletons or select aspects of the anatomy were useful for presenting individual specimens. Yet, few of the articles were exhaustive, and many had become out of date as a result of additional reassembly of the bones. This book is the result of that decision to describe all of the Shanidar Neandertals in a single volume in order to present both the characteristics of the individual specimens and the patterns of the entire sample. It is hoped that it will provide both some insight into these prehistoric peoples of the region around Shanidar and the data necessary for additional analyses of Neandertal morphology.

Acknowledgments

Even though I assume all responsibility for what is contained within these pages, it should be apparent to all who have dealt with human fossil remains that I have only picked up where others have left off. The first of the Shanidar Neandertals was discovered 20 years before I had my first glimpse of one of the original Shanidar specimens, and the last of them was excavated 16 years before I began my studies of the Shanidar sample. In those years, a number of individuals laid the groundwork for my studies: Drs. Ralph and Rose Solecki and their assistants, both Iraqi and American, were responsible for the discovery, excavation, and safe transport to the Iraq Museum of the fragile Neandertal skeletons; the late Dr. Muzaffer Şenyürek and Dr. T. Dale Stewart performed the major part of the cleaning, consolidation, and reassembly of the fragmentary fossils and wrote a number of articles on which I have relied for my discussions of the remains; and the staff of the Iraq Museum maintained the specimens in excellent condition over the years. To all these individuals I am grateful.

Through all my work on the Shanidar Neandertals there have been two individuals who have provided the extra assistance and support that have made it all possible. They are Dr. Ralph S. Solecki and, especially, Dr. T. Dale Stewart. It is they who provided the archaeological and paleontological background for my work with Shanidar specimens. But mostly it is they who willingly allowed me to take over the paleontological study of these important fossils and provided every assistance to make my work productive. I greatly appreciate the opportunity they provided and the encouragement they furnished along the way.

The Shanidar Neandertals are national antiquities of the Republic of Iraq and I was able to study them with the permission of the State Organization of Antiquities and Heritage. Dr. Isa Salman, Director-General of Antiquities during my visit to the Iraq Museum in 1976, and Dr. Muayed Sa'id al-Damirji,

xxi

Director-General of Antiquities during my 1978 and 1980 work in the Iraq Museum, were very kind in allowing me to work with the Shanidar fossils in Iraq. In addition, the Directors of the Iraq Museum while I was working in Baghdad, Dr. Fausi Rashid (1976), Dr. Subhi Anwar Rashid (1978), and Dr. Abdul Qadir al-Takriti (1980), greatly facilitated my research in the Iraq Museum. Dr. Ali Nakabendi, director of the laboratory of the Iraq Museum, provided me with the materials I needed for the cleaning and reassembly of the Shanidar specimens. Finally, Mr. Donnie George, whose interest in the Shanidar Neandertals was always a pleasure, helped my studies of them in a variety of ways that made my work in the Iraq Museum more productive than it otherwise could have been. I am extremely grateful to all these individuals and to the members of the Iraq Museum staff for their hospitality, assistance, and interest in the Shanidar Neandertals.

The paleontological study of the Shanidar remains has involved extensive comparisons with other Upper Pleistocene fossil human specimens, primarily from the Near East and Europe. Many of the comparative data on these fossils have been published, but many of the measurements employed here are new or have been published for only a small percentage of the known specimens. As part of both the Shanidar study and my ongoing analyses of Neandertal morphology, I have had the opportunity to study a number of archaic and early anatomically modern *Homo sapiens* fossils. Like the Shanidar remains, these specimens are national antiquities and reside, for the most part, in public museums. The individuals in charge of these remains have been universally generous in letting me study, measure, and publish findings on these fossils. I am indebted for their hospitality and kindness to: Prof. Jesus Altuna (Sociedad de Ciencias Naturales Aranzadi, San Sebastián); Prof. Yves Coppens (Musée de l'Homme, Paris); Prof. Ivan Crnolatac (Geološko-Paleontološki Muzej, Zagreb); Prof. Henri Delporte (Musée des Antiquités Nationales, St. Germain-en-Laye); Dr. Avi Eytan and Mr. Joseph Zias (Rockefeller Museum, Jerusalem); Prof. Jean-Louis Heim (Musée de l'Homme and Institut de Paléontologie Humaine, Paris); Prof. Hans Joachim (Rheinisches Landesmuseum, Bonn); Prof. André Leroi-Gourhan (Musée de l'Homme, Paris); Profs. Henry de Lumley and Marie-Antoinette de Lumley (Musée de l'Homme and Université d-Aix-Marseille, Marseille); Prof. Mirko Malez (Jugoslavenska Akademija Znanosti i Umjetnosti, Zagreb); Dr. Michel Philippe (Muséum d'Histoire Naturelle, Lyon); Dr. L. Pradel (Châtellerault); Dr. C. B. Stringer (British Museum [Natural History], London); Profs. François Twiesselmann and André Leguebe (Institut Royal des Sciences Naturelles de Belgique, Brussels); and Prof. Bernard Vandermeersch (Université de Paris VI, Paris).

Several individuals have kindly provided unpublished data from their own studies of recent or fossil human remains. They are Prof. William W. Howells (Harvard University), Dr. Jonathan H. Musgrave (University of Bristol), Dr. C. B. Stringer (British Museum [Natural History]) and Prof. Milford H. Wolpoff (University of Michigan). In addition, Prof. Bernard Vandermeersch (Université de

Paris VI) has been especially kind in allowing me to study unpublished fossil remains in his care and to include measurements of them in this work. I would like to express my sincere thanks to these individuals.

During my years of work on the Shanidar sample, I have profited from many conversations with other human paleontologists, especially those interested in the Neandertals. It is not possible to list all who have made valuable suggestions, but there are a few individuals who deserve special mention in this respect: Prof. William W. Howells (Harvard University); Prof. Alan E. Mann (University of Pennsylvania); Prof. Fred H. Smith (University of Tennessee); Dr. T. Dale Stewart (Smithsonian Institution); Dr. C. B. Stringer (British Museum [Natural History]); Prof. Bernard Vandermeersch (Université de Paris VI); and Prof. Milford H. Wolpoff (University of Michigan). In addition, Dr. Michael R. Zimmerman (Jeanes Hospital, Philadelphia) assisted me with the diagnoses of the numerous abnormalities on the Shanidar skeletons (Chapter 12). I am very appreciative of their suggestions and criticisms.

A few of these individuals have also performed the arduous task of critically reading the manuscript to rid it of inconsistencies, factual errors, and lapses of coherency on my part. They are Profs. Howells, Smith, Stringer, and Wolpoff, and it is thanks to them that there are as few errors in the final version as there are. Those remaining are, of course, my own responsibility.

Although most of the illustrations in the book are from my personal work on the Shanidar fossils, Drs. Solecki and Stewart and the photographic department of the Iraq Museum kindly provided photographs of the site and the specimens. Most of the photographs of the Shanidar fossils were printed by Mr. Hillel Burger and his assistants in the Peabody Museum, and several of the drawings were done by Ms. S. Whitney Powell of the Peabody Museum. In addition, Mrs. Olga Masse of the Department of Anthropology, Harvard University assisted with many aspects of manuscript preparation. I am grateful to these individuals for their assistance.

During the 1980 research trip to the Iraq Museum, Mr. Mario Chech of the Université de Paris VI molded a large percentage of the Shanidar specimens and subsequently produced excellent casts of them. These casts have been very useful for verifying observations during the final analysis of the Shanidar sample, and I am appreciative of his efforts in this respect.

None of this work would have been possible without the financial support that I have received from several sources. The National Science Foundation Anthropology Program made possible the three research trips to the Iraq Museum and one trip (1978) to Europe for the collection of the Shanidar and comparative paleontological data (National Science Foundation grants BNS76-14344, BNS76-14344 A01, and BNS-8004578). Additional funds for portions of the research at Harvard University were kindly provided by the Harvard University Graduate Society Fund (1977 and 1978). Finally, the generosity of Mr. Morris Feld, who kindly contributed funds to the Department of Anthropology, Harvard University in the name of Dr. Saul Jarcho, has made possible in part the publication of this monograph; I am thankful to Prof. W. W. Howells for making the Jarcho Fund available for this purpose. All these foundations and individuals have been very generous, and I am grateful for their support of my research on the Shanidar Neandertals.

There is one last individual who deserves more thanks than I can express here: my wife, Dr. Kathryn Maurer Trinkaus. It is she, more than anyone else, who has seen me through the long and, at times, seemingly interminable task of describing and analyzing the Shanidar sample. Her experience working in the Near East prepared me in invaluable ways for my trips to Iraq. Her general knowledge of anthropology, combined with abundant patience, provided me with feedback on my innumerable ramblings about the details of this bone or that aspect of morphology. Her assistance with a number of aspects of the work made the task much easier, and her encouragement through it all is in large part responsible for its completion.

The Shanidar Neandertals

CHAPTER 1

Introduction

The large cave that overlooks the Shanidar Valley in northeastern Iraq has provided shelter to human groups intermittently during the past 100,000 years. During that time, the various tenants of Shanidar Cave left behind considerable cultural debris and, among the various sediments on the cave floor, the remains of their dead. We can never know precisely who those people were, but through careful studies of what they left behind, including their own skeletal remains, we can attempt to reconstruct their physiques, adaptive patterns. and roles in human evolutionary history.

Through circumstances of preservation and discovery, the skeletal remains of nine individuals from the Mousterian levels of Shanidar Cave have become known to us. These are the Shanidar Neandertals. They consist of the partial skeletons of seven adults and two infants, which range in completeness from a few limb bones to a largely intact skeleton. As such, they comprise one of the largest samples of Neandertals. They are thus a major addition to the human paleontological record and a prime source of information concerning late Pleistocene human evolution in the Near East.

The Shanidar Neandertals are paleontologically important for several reasons. They greatly enlarge the quite small sample of Neandertal remains from the Near East. They are the only reasonably complete fossil human remains from the Near East outside the Levant. Perhaps most important, the Shanidar Neandertals retain portions of all anatomical regions. They thus provide data for a variety of paleontological studies of the Neandertals. Through the integration of the morphological data from the Shanidar fossils into studies of the Neandertals, our understanding of these extinct populations as part of late Pleistocene human evolution should be measurably enriched.

The field of human paleontology has advanced over most of the past century as each new discovery of fossil human remains has shed additional light

1

upon the morphological patterns of prehistoric humanity. For many years, the paucity of reasonably complete specimens meant that most new finds forced scholars to reevaluate previous conceptions and to adjust evolutionary schemes to accommodate the latest discovery. In this situation, many individual fossils acquired an exaggerated importance and evolutionary reconstructions were made to revolve around them. The course of human evolution was therefore seen as an ordering in space and time of individuals, fragments of which have been passed on to us, rather than a sequence of changing morphological patterns and associated adaptive patterns through time.

In recent years, paleontologists have increasingly moved away from this particularistic approach, trying to form samples from the collections of known fossils and to view human evolution more in terms of shifts in patterns of variation through time. This approach has been most successful for recent time periods, from which there are sufficiently large samples, and for which it is possible to assign specimens reliably to specific samples. As a result of this research, new insight has been gained into the morphological patterns of fossil hominids. Furthermore, it has been possible to reformulate the relevant questions whose answers should lead to the eventual elucidation of the evolutionary origins of living humans.

Despite this change in emphasis from the specimen to the sample, the individual fossil remains important in any study. Available samples are still small, extremely so for several anatomical regions, and known ranges of variation can be significantly altered by the addition or deletion of single specimens. What is needed is a populational approach in which carefully defined samples are systematically compared, never losing sight of the relative contributions of the individual pieces that make up the samples.

Two types of paleontological work follow from a populational approach to the hominid fossil record. One consists of detailed description of individual fossil specimens and discussion of the features that are unique to the specimens in question. This form of treatise provides the information necessary for careful evaluation of the relevance of each specimen to the greater scheme of human evolution. It also focuses on any aspects of a fossil that may be unique to that specimen. Furthermore, such descriptions make available detailed paleontological data to the profession and thus provide the basis for the second type of study. The last feature is especially important because most fossil human remains, including those from Shanidar, are national antiquities and seldom leave their countries of origin.

The other type of paleontological work consists of comparative and functional analyses of specific anatomical regions that attempt to delineate and interpret anatomical similarities and differences among samples. It is these analyses that form the basis for the reconstruction of human evolutionary history.

This discussion of the Shanidar Neandertal sample is primarily the first form of paleontological work. It is a detailed description of the fossil human remains from the Mousterian levels of Shanidar Cave. As such, it is a discussion of those aspects of their morphology that place these remains within the greater Neandertal sample and those that make them unique.

Because all description is necessarily comparative, data are provided where appropriate to permit the adequate evaluation of the morphological patterns exhibited by the Shanidar fossils. In addition, because the data from the Shanidar sample and the comparisons of their morphologies to those of later Pleistocene and recent humans furnish insights into both the functional anatomy and phylogenetic affinities of these Upper Pleistocene humans, interpretations of their morphological patterns are included where relevant. Functional interpretations are provided in the chapters that describe and discuss the individual fossils and are summarized in Chapter 13. The phylogenetic implications of the Shanidar specimens are dealt with as well in Chapter 13. These discussions are followed in the final chapter with some thoughts on the evolution of the Neandertals.

The information presented here should enable the integration of the paleontological data from the Shanidar fossils into our knowledge of the Upper Pleistocene hominid fossil record. It should also provide some new insights into the evolution of the Neandertals and their role in the origin of anatomically modern humans.

CHAPTER 2

Shanidar Cave and the Discovery of the Shanidar Neandertals

The important archaeological and paleontological discoveries in Shanidar Cave have received considerable publicity. This is due to the efforts of Dr. Ralph S. Solecki and his associates, especially Dr. T. Dale Stewart, who have produced a number of works since the site was first explored in the early 1950s (see References). These publications detail the history of work at Shanidar and the circumstances of the various discoveries that have been made there, of which the Neandertal finds have been the most spectacular. I will not attempt to summarize all the details of the exploration of Shanidar Cave and the discovery of the nine Neandertal partial skeletons; this has been done by Solecki and others (see especially Solecki 1963, 1971b; Stewart 1977). However, there are aspects of the history of the excavations in Shanidar Cave and the discoveries of the Neandertals that relate to our appreciation of the Neandertal remains.

THE SITE OF SHANIDAR CAVE

Shanidar Cave is located in the Zagros Mountains of northeastern Iraq, in the middle of Iraqi Kurdistan. As such, it is close to the point where Iraq meets Iran and Turkey (Figure 1). The region is one of high limestone bluffs and rolling

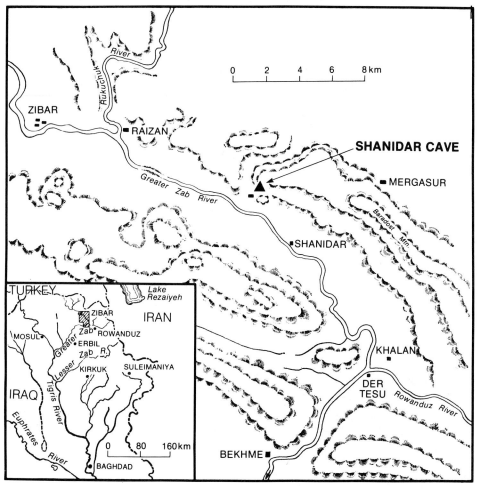

Figure 1 Northeastern Iraq with the location of Shanidar Cave. Redrawn with permission from Solecki (1963). (Copyright 1963 by the American Association for the Advancement of Science.)

terrain. The limestone contains numerous caves, of which Shanidar Cave appears to be one of the largest.

The site itself is in the Shanidar Valley, which leads off to the north from the larger valley formed by the Greater Zab River, not far from the village of Shanidar (36° 50′ N, 44° 13′ E). It is about 13.5 km northwest of the junction of the Greater Zab River with the Rowanduz River, about 400 km north of Baghdad. The cave is 765 m above sea level, about two-thirds of the way up the side of the Shanidar Valley, close to where the lower, more level part of the slope meets the nearly vertical upper portion of the limestone bluff (Figure 2). The cave thus has a commanding view of the Shanidar Valley and is not far

Figure 2 View across the Shanidar Valley, with Shanidar Cave (lower right). Photo courtesy R. S. Solecki.

from the Greater Zab Valley. In prehistoric times, under cooler and wetter conditions, it must have been a welcome retreat.

Inside the broad triangular entrance to the cave is a large space, approximately 50 m wide and almost 45 m deep (Figure 3). At the time of excavation, the cave was occupied by several families of Barzani Kurds, and the excavation showed that the cave was well used by peoples in both the recent and prehistoric past (Solecki 1971b, 1979).

The excavated portion of Shanidar Cave contains archaeological deposits that are nearly 14 m deep (Figure 4). The majority of the remains are from the Middle Paleolithic, but the sequence extends, with some breaks, to the present. Although the site contains a large number of discernible stratigraphic levels, it was not possible to identify clearly every one during excavation because many grade into each other, are discontinuous within the excavated area, and/or were disturbed by a number of rockfalls within the cave that left large limestone

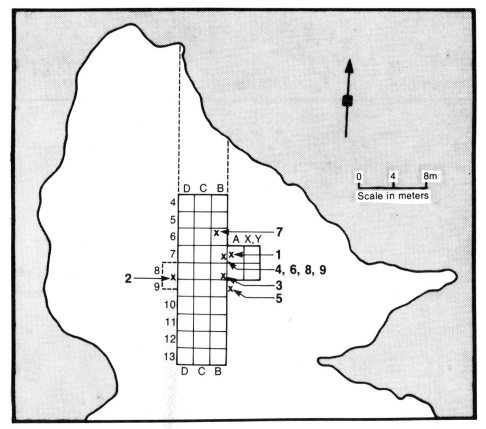

Figure 3 Schematic floorplan of Shanidar Cave, indicating the area excavated, the excavation grid, and the horizontal locations of the Neandertal partial skeletons. Redrawn with permission from Stewart (1977).

blocks in the deposits. The Shanidar deposits were therefore divided into five strata, or *Layers*, which were identified on the basis of both natural stratigraphy and inclusive cultural material. The different layers are, as far as can be determined, separated from each other by chronological breaks.

The uppermost stratum, Layer A, includes material from the Neolithic to the present, including innumerable hearths, artifacts, and organic material. Below Layer A is a Proto-Neolithic level, Layer B1, that has yielded considerable amounts of cultural material and 28 human burials. Layer B2, which was originally thought to be continuous with B1 and was later shown to be distinct stratigraphically and culturally, is typically Mesolithic, with numerous microliths and lacking the grinding tools of the overlying Neolithic and Proto-Neolithic. These three upper levels are relatively shallow, but they nonetheless have yielded considerable cultural material (Solecki 1952–1953, 1963).

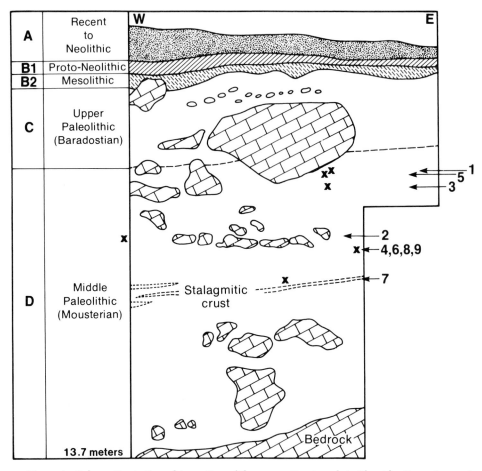

Figure 4 Schematic stratigraphic section of the excavation trench in Shanidar Cave. Approximate vertical positions of the Neandertal partial skeletons are indicated. Redrawn with permission from Stewart (1977).

Layer C contains a lithic assemblage that bears many resemblances to the Levantine Aurignacian, especially its earlier phases. It contains high frequencies of burins, end scrapers, *rabots* (utilized blade cores), and notched pieces (Garrod 1957; Solecki 1952–1953; 1958a). These characteristics have led Solecki (1958a) to refer to it as a new industry, the Baradostian, which is known only from the Zagros Mountains. The typological characteristics of the industry may, however, be due in part to the scarcity of large flint nodules in the Zagros and the need to reutilize many tools and cores (Jelinek 1975).

Layer C is as much as 4 m deep in places and appears to have spanned a considerable period of time. Not surprisingly, there are noticeable frequency changes in tool types within Layer C; several type classes, such as side scrapers and burins, decrease through time, whereas end scrapers and denticu-lates–notched pieces increase through the deposits (Edens 1980; Solecki 1958a). However, the general characteristics of the assemblage are consistent with the interpretation that it represents an early Upper Paleolithic phase with-in the Zagros Mountains.

These typological inferences are supported by a series of radiocarbon deter-minations from different depths within Layer C (Table 1). These radiocarbon dates place the beginning of Layer C around 34,000 years B.P. and its end about 28,000 years B.P. No human remains were discovered in Layer C.

The Middle Paleolithic levels, Layer D, make up the majority of the Shanidar deposits, being approximately 8.5 m deep. Hearths, animal remains, and stone tools are distributed continuously throughout Layer D, but there appear to be two concentrations of occupational debris. The upper concentra-tion is near the top of Layer D, immediately below the depositional disconfor-mity between Layers C and D. It is within this material that three Neandertals—Shanidar 1, 3, and 5—were discovered. The lower concentration of debris is near the middle of Layer D, between 9.8 and 8.5 m below datum. It contains a distinct stalagmitic lens, indicating a brief period of high humidity. Six of the Neandertals—Shanidar 2, 4, 6, 7, 8, and 9—were found slightly above this lower occupational concentration.

The Mousterian assemblage from Shanidar Cave has been described by Solecki (1963) as relatively homogeneous throughout Layer D, and all the de-scriptions of the industry treat the tools as though they derive from a single lithic industry (Akazawa 1975; Skinner 1965; Solecki 1952–1953). Any trends through time within the Shanidar Layer D Mousterian are therefore obscured, if such existed.

Quantitative data on the Shanidar Layer D assemblage have been published by Skinner (1965) and Akazawa (1975). Skinner's sample included a sample of all the excavated implements and cores (N = 618) in the Iraq Museum, the Smithsonian Institution, and Solecki's laboratory at Columbia University. Akazawa only studied the material in the Iraq Museum, yet he obtained a sample size similar to that of Skinner (714 implements, 672 of which can be fitted into Bordes's Mousterian typology). It is evident from the published data that a number of pieces included in his sample by Akazawa, especially in the miscellaneous types (Bordes's types 38–62), were not considered to be imple-ments by Skinner. Yet despite some marked differences in type frequencies, which are undoubtedly due to both their different samples and personal varia-tion in type identification, the frequency distributions of Skinner and Akazawa are generally similar, especially for types 1–37. The type frequencies of Skin-ner and Akazawa are provided in Table 2.

The Shanidar Layer D assemblage contains predominantly Mousterian ele-ments, with a preponderance of Mousterian points and side-scrapers, es-pecially single edge side-scrapers. It is possible that many of the implements that have been classified as Mousterian points are in fact side-scrapers that

TABLE 1
Radiocarbon Determinations from Layers C and D of Shanidar Cave

	Depth below datum (m)	Years before present (B.P.)	Laboratory number	Comments	References
Upper Layer C	2.35	28,700 ± 700	W-651		Rubin and Alexander (1960)
	3.05	26,500 ± 1,500	L-335H	portions of the	Broecker and Kulp (1957)
	3.05	29,500 ± 1,500	W-178	same sample	Rubin and Suess (1955)
Middle Layer C	—	33,900 ± 900	GrN-1830	"bone" fraction	Vogel and Waterbolk (1963)
		34,000 ± 420	GrN-1494	"rest" fraction	
Lower Layer C	3.30	33,300 ± 1,000	W-650		Rubin and Alexander (1960)
	4.57	32,300 ± 3,000	L-335I	portions of the	Broecker and Kulp (1957)
	4.57	>34,000	W-180	same sample	Rubin and Suess (1955)
	—	35,440 ± 600	GrN-2016	"bone" fraction	Vogel and Waterbolk (1963)
		34,590 ± 500	GrN-2015	"rest" fraction	
Upper Layer D	5.10	46,900 ± 1,500	GrN-2527		Vogel and Waterbolk (1963)
	—	50,600 ± 3,000	GrN-1495		Vogel and Waterbolk (1963)

TABLE 2
Typological Characteristics of the Shanidar Mousterian Assemblage[a]

Bordes's type number	Type	Skinner (1965) N = 571		Akazawa (1975) N = 672	
		Count	%	Count	%
Levallois					
1, 2	Levallois flake	5	0.88	5	0.74
3	Levallois point	1	0.18	0	0.00
4	Retouched Levallois point	4	0.70	0	0.00
Mousterian					
6	Mousterian point	68	11.91	41	6.10
7	Elongate Mousterian point	43	7.53	49	7.29
8	Limace	3	0.53	5	0.74
Side-scraper					
9	Single straight	77	13.49	24	3.57
10	Single convex	88	15.41	62	9.23
11	Single concave	6	1.05	6	0.89
12	Double straight	39	6.83	1	0.15
13	Double convex	27	4.73	0	0.00
14	Double concave	3	0.53	0	0.00
15	Double biconvex	5	0.88	14	2.08
16	Double biconcave	0	0.00	4	0.60
17	Double concave–convex	6	1.05	5	0.74
18	Straight convergent	22	3.85	3	0.45
19	Convex convergent	14	2.45	21	3.13
21	Déjété	16	2.80	9	1.34
22	Transverse straight	4	0.70	0	0.00
23	Transverse convex	1	0.18	5	0.74
25	Bulbarly retouched	2	0.35	5	0.74
26	Abrupt retouched	21	3.68	0	0.00
28	Bifacially retouched	3	0.53	0	0.00
29	Alternate retouched	5	0.88	8	1.19
Upper Paleolithic					
30, 31	End-scraper	21	3.68	11	1.64
32, 33	Burin	11	1.93	32	4.76
34, 35	Perforator	16	2.80	43	6.40
36, 37	Backed blade	1	0.18	18	2.68
Miscellaneous					
38	Naturally backed blade	17	2.98	35	5.21
40	Truncated piece	0	0.00	26	3.87
42	Notched piece	16	2.80	46	6.85
43	Denticulate	16	2.80	42	6.25
44	Burinate	0	0.00	3	0.45
45	Retouched flake: bulbar surface	0	0.00	10	1.49
46, 47	Retouched flake: thick	4	0.70	50	7.44
48, 49	Retouched flake: thin	4	0.70	87	12.95

(continued)

TABLE 2 *Continued*

Bordes's type number	Type	Skinner (1965) N = 571		Akazawa (1975) N = 672	
		Count	%	Count	%
51	Tayac point	1	0.18	0	0.00
54	End-notched flake	0	0.00	2	0.30
62	Miscellaneous	1	0.18	0	0.00
ILty	Levallois types index		1.75		0.74
IR	Side-scraper types index		59.37		24.85
IAn	Backed blades index		0.18		2.68
	Mousterian type tools index		79.33		38.99
	Upper Paleolithic type tools index		8.58		15.48
	Denticulate tools index		2.80		6.25
IL	Levallois débitage index		3.0		
IF	Faceting index		43.2		
ILam	Blades index		12.7		
	Discoidal cores	27	57.45		
	Prismatic cores	10	21.28		
	Informe cores	10	21.28		

*a*Data from Skinner (1965:105) and Akazawa (1975:5–7). The type names are preceded by Bordes's (1954–1955) type numbers. Typical and atypical types have been pooled.

were retouched so as to resemble points. Although the Levallois technique was employed, it was relatively rarely used in manufacturing the Shanidar implements. These characteristics of the assemblage are reflected in the typological and technological indices that can be computed from the available data (Table 2).

In addition to the 672 tools that Akazawa classified according to Bordes's technique, he identified 42 "retouched rods" (as defined by Hole and Flannery [1967]). These implements are usually associated with Baradostian or Zarzian assemblages, but they appear to come from the lower Mousterian levels at Shanidar and are therefore clearly associated with the Mousterian.

These characteristics of the Shanidar Layer D assemblage are similar to those of other Zagros Mousterian assemblages, such as those from Bisitun E+ to F− (Coon 1951; Skinner 1965), Hazar Merd C (Garrod 1930; Skinner 1965) and Kunji (Hole and Flannery 1967; Skinner 1965). They all contain high frequencies of Mousterian points and side-scrapers, the tools tend to be extensively retouched, and the flake production strategy resulted in disc cores, whereas the Levallois technique was rarely employed (Skinner 1965). Indices of Levallois débitage (IL) are 4.8, 7.0, and 4.5 for Bisitun E+ to F−, Hazar Merd C, and Kunji, respectively (Skinner 1965).

These typological characteristics of the Shanidar Mousterian and the other

Zagros Middle Paleolithic industries have suggested to Skinner (1965:197) that there was a "cultural area" within the Zagros during Middle Paleolithic times and that the typological differences between these industries and the contemporaneous Levantine industries can be considered to be the products of stylistic traditions. On the other hand, it may be that the differences between the Zagros and Levantine Mousterian assemblages are due to the nature of available raw material (Jelinek 1975; Solecki 1963). Most of the raw material available in the Zagros is in the form of stream pebbles rather than large nodules or tabular layers and, as a result, tools at Shanidar and the other Zagros sites tend to be small and were extensively retouched before they were discarded (Jelinek 1975). Because the Levallois technique is rather wasteful of raw material, it was probably seldom used so as to get the maximum use out of the available siliceous rock.

The faunal remains from Layer D were analyzed preliminarily by Reed (Reed and Braidwood 1960) and Perkins (1964) and have been studied in detail by Evins (1981). All the species represented are currently extant, although some of them have become extinct locally in historical times. The dominant species in the sample are wild goat (*Capra aegagrus*), tortoise (*Testudo graeca*) and, to a lesser extent, wild boar (*Sus scrofa*), red deer (*Cervus elaphus*), roe deer (*Capreolus capreolus*), and red fox (*Vulpes vulpes*). It is not known to what extent the faunal sample reflects solely human predation or a combination of human and nonhuman carnivore predation. There appears to be relatively little variation in either the species represented or their relative proportions through the levels of Layer D (Evins 1981), even though there was considerable climatic fluctuation in the region during the Upper Pleistocene (Wright 1962). The faunal profile probably reflects primarily the rugged topography of the area around Shanidar because more open-country animals, such as sheep, are rare until they are introduced through domestication in the post-Pleistocene (Evins 1981; Perkins 1964).

Solecki and his colleagues have used several techniques to date the deposits in Layer D. Two samples of charcoal from the top of Layer D have yielded radiocarbon dates that suggest an age of at least 45,000 years B.P. for the end of the Shanidar Mousterian (Table 1). On the basis of palynological analyses of nine samples and trace-element analyses of five samples distributed through the uppermost 8.5 m of the Shanidar deposits, Solecki (1963) reconstructed a climatic sequence for the deposits. The climatic sequence, with the aid of the radiocarbon determinations, was correlated with estimated climatic sequences from elsewhere in the Near East and the eastern Mediterranean. In addition, a constant rate of deposition in the cave was assumed to assist in the dating of the earlier levels of the site. Using all these estimates in concert, an age of about 60,000–70,000 years B.P. was suggested for the middle of Layer D, and the bottom of Layer D was placed at about 100,000 years B.P.

These age estimations are extremely tenuous and need to be substantiated by independent means. They are all dependent upon the two radiocarbon determinations from the top of Layer D. These dates are beyond the range within which standard radiocarbon dating techniques produce reliable finite dates (Henry and Servello 1974) and they therefore may be only minimum ages. Furthermore, the Upper Pleistocene Near Eastern climatic sequence is considerably more complex than was previously believed (Farrand 1971, 1979), and it is difficult to accept a constant rate of sedimentation within Shanidar Cave.

These age determinations for the different portions of Layer D nonetheless provide a general chronological framework for the Shanidar Mousterian deposits. They show, most importantly, that the Shanidar Mousterian deposits and the Neandertals they contained span considerable geological time. The Shanidar fossils were probably roughly contemporary with the other Near Eastern Neandertals from Amud and Tabūn (Jelinek 1982; Chapter 13) and with many of the European early last glacial Neandertals (Vandermeersch, 1965; Wolpoff, 1980b).

HISTORY OF EXCAVATIONS

The site of Shanidar Cave was first explored by R. S. Solecki in 1951 while he was engaged in an archaeological survey of northeastern Iraq. The large cave was occupied then, and during much of the time that the cave was being excavated, by a group of Barzani Kurds; this limited the area that Solecki could excavate to a portion of the middle of the cave. During the 1951 reconnaissance, Solecki dug a test pit and recovered sufficient material to encourage him to return later in 1951 for more extensive excavations (Solecki 1952). In his sounding late in 1951, Solecki established the basic four-part stratigraphic sequence, Layers D–A, that has remained, with refinements, the stratigraphic scheme for Shanidar Cave (Solecki, 1952–1953).

Solecki returned for 10 weeks of excavation in 1953. He completed the sounding begun in 1951 and enlarged the area of excavation. It was during this season that he was able to outline in considerable detail the stratigraphic sequence within the cave (Solecki 1955a, 1955b). It was also in 1953 that the first Neandertal remains to be discovered in Iraq were found. On 22 June, deep within the Mousterian levels, the fragmentary skeleton of an infant (Shanidar 7) was unearthed (Solecki 1953, 1954, 1955c). The remains were turned over to the late Dr. Muzaffer Şenyürek for study.

During 1956 and 1957, Solecki returned to Shanidar for excavations within the cave and elsewhere in the valley. The little work that was done in the cave during the fall of 1956 was concentrated in Layer A (Solecki 1957a). But during the spring of 1957, significant work was done in Shanidar Cave, much of it in Layer D (Solecki 1957d, 1958b). During the months of April and May, three adult Neandertal skeletons (Shanidar 1, 2, and 3) were discovered (Solecki 1957b, 1960). Shanidar 3 was the first of these to be discovered, on 16 April 1957, but due to its fragmentary nature it was not recognized as hominid until after the excavations. Shanidar 1 was discovered shortly afterward, on 27 April, close to the top of Layer D. It was the discovery of the Shanidar 1 skeleton (Figure 5) that firmly established the presence at Shanidar Cave of humans morphologically similar to the other Near Eastern and European Neandertals. Almost a month later, on 23 May, human remains, which became Shanidar 2, were encountered slightly above the level at which the child was found in 1953, near the middle of Layer D. These and subsequently discovered Neandertal remains were turned over to Dr. T. Dale Stewart for study.

Given the successes of the 1956–1957 season at Shanidar, there was every reason to believe that Shanidar Cave would yield more archaeological and paleontological material. So in 1960, with an expanded crew, Solecki returned to Shanidar. Archaeologically, the 1960 season served to expand greatly the cultural remains from Shanidar Cave; paleontologically, it added five more Neandertal partial skeletons to the Shanidar sample (Solecki 1961, 1971b).

Initially, portions of Shanidar 2 and 3, which could not be recovered in 1957 due to large overburdens, were recovered. Then on 3 August 1960, the largely complete, although damaged, skeleton of a large individual, Shanidar 4, was revealed slightly above the level of the Shanidar 2 remains. Soil samples from around this skeleton yielded surprisingly high concentrations of wildflower pollen, suggesting that offerings of flowers were placed around the grave (Leroi-Gourhan 1968, 1975; Solecki 1971b, 1975, 1977); this is the well-known "flower burial" from Shanidar Cave. Shortly after the discovery of Shanidar 4, on 7 August, another skeleton was uncovered near the top of Layer D at the same level as Shanidar 1. This became Shanidar 5. Then, as Shanidar 4 was being excavated and prepared for removal, bones of a second individual were found mixed with those of Shanidar 4. These bones duplicated ones already identified for Shanidar 4 and were considerably smaller; this Neandertal became Shanidar 6. To add further to the confusion, several bones of an infant were noticed among the loose bones collected when Shanidar 4 and 6 were removed in a block from Shanidar Cave, and while Stewart was cleaning and restoring Shanidar 4 and 6 in the Iraq Museum in Baghdad he realized that there were portions of a third adult preserved with Shanidar 4 and 6. This totaled seven adults and two infants from the Mousterian levels of Shanidar Cave, the largest sample of Neandertal partial skeletons known from a single site.

Numbering of the Fossils

The history of excavation of the Shanidar Neandertals has led to confusion over the numbering of the individuals. The first child to be discovered, in 1953, was referred to only as the *Shanidar child* (Solecki 1953). When, in 1957, three adults were unearthed, they were referred to as Shanidar I, II, and III, in the order of recognition of their hominid status (Solecki 1957d, 1960). The same procedure was followed for the discoveries in 1960 of Shanidar IV, V, and VI.

TABLE 3
Numbering of the Shanidar Individuals

Original designation	Catalogue of Fossil Hominids number	Current number
I or 1	1	1
II or 2	2	2
III or 3	3	3
IV	4	4
V	5	5
VI	6	6
"child"	7	7
VII	—	8
VIII	—	9

When Stewart realized that there was another adult with Shanidar IV and VI, he tentatively called it Shanidar VII (1963), pending further determination of which pieces belonged to this individual and which belonged to Shanidar IV and VI. Subsequently, Solecki (1971b, 1977), accepting the identification of a seventh adult and calling it Shanidar VII, referred to the second Shanidar child, the one discovered with Shanidar IV and VI, as Shanidar VIII.

This system of numbering, Shanidar I–VIII plus the Shanidar child, was confused by the publication of the *Catalogue of Fossil Hominids: Part III* (Stewart and Solecki 1975). In the *Catalogue of Fossil Hominids*, the editors labeled Shanidar I–VI as Shanidar 1–6, referred to the Shanidar child as Shanidar 7, and omitted Shanidar VII and VIII. Although it may lead to some confusion initially, I believe that the *Catalogue of Fossil Hominids* should be followed as a standard reference. In this, every specimen is given a number; there is only one numbering system for each site (rather than, for example, the two systems used by McCown and Keith [1939], one for partial skeletons and one for isolated bones, for the hominids from Mugharet es-Skhūl and Mugharet et-Tabūn), and only arabic numerals are used. For the Shanidar Neandertals, therefore, Shanidar I–VI become Shanidar 1–6, the "Shanidar child" (the first child) becomes Shanidar 7, Shanidar VII of Stewart and Solecki (the seventh adult) becomes Shanidar 8, and Shanidar VIII of Solecki (the second child) becomes Shanidar 9 (Table 3). This is the numbering system I have used previously (Trinkaus 1977b) and I employ it in this monograph.

THE NEANDERTAL PARTIAL SKELETONS

The Shanidar 1, 2, 3, 5, and 7 partial skeletons were discovered as isolated burials, and therefore the attribution of their remains by individual has been clear. The Shanidar 4, 6, 8, and 9 remains, however, have been considerably more difficult to sort by individual.

Shanidar 4, 6, 8, and 9 were discovered superimposed on each other. They represent either a single multiple burial or a series of single burials closely spaced in time. The order of burial seems to have been Shanidar 9 first and then Shanidar 8, 6, and 4, in that order (Solecki 1977). Most of their remains were removed in a block, to be sorted later in the Iraq Museum. Loose bones that became separated during removal of the block from the cave were collected and placed with the other remains in Baghdad. In 1962, Stewart unpacked the remains, restored many of the pieces, and sorted the bones by individual (Stewart 1963). Subsequently, in 1976 (Trinkaus 1977b), 1978, and 1980, I continued the sorting and restoration to achieve the present arrangement.

During burial and the subsequent excavation, many of the Shanidar 4, 6, 8, and 9 remains became mixed. The Shanidar 9 infant remains are readily separable from the others. The adult remains have been sorted primarily on the basis of size and, in the case of Shanidar 4, with the aid of the *in situ* photographs. The Shanidar 4 remains are significantly larger than those of Shanidar 6, and larger than most of those of Shanidar 8. The Shanidar 8 remains, however, are only slightly larger than those of Shanidar 6, and for many of the bones it is simply impossible to determine whether they belong to Shanidar 6 or 8. Because Shanidar 6 was discovered first, and appears to have been more complete, many of the bones that could belong to either Shanidar 6 or 8 have been assigned to Shanidar 6. This probably accounts, in part, for the paucity of remains from Shanidar 8. Most of the Shanidar 4 pieces are probably accurately assigned.

The circumstances of discovery and excavation of the individual Shanidar Neandertals have been dealt with in detail by Solecki and Stewart in a number of publications (e.g., Solecki 1953, 1960, 1971b; Stewart 1963, 1977). It is not necessary to repeat all the details here, but summaries of this information may provide additional insight into the Shanidar remains.

Shanidar 1

During excavations along the east wall of the trench in square B7 on 27 April 1957, workmen encountered bone at 4.34 m below datum (the depth figures indicate the position of the first bone encountered). This level is slightly below the boundary between Layers C and D. The bone turned out to be the top of the cranium of an individual presenting clear Neandertal features (Figure 5). Further excavation around the cranial vault revealed the facial skeleton, slightly displaced anteriorly, and the mandible and cervical vertebrae, considerably removed to the left and front of the cranium. The postcranial skeleton extended to the east from the cranium, into the side of the excavation beneath about 4 m of sediment containing a number of limestone blocks, some of them

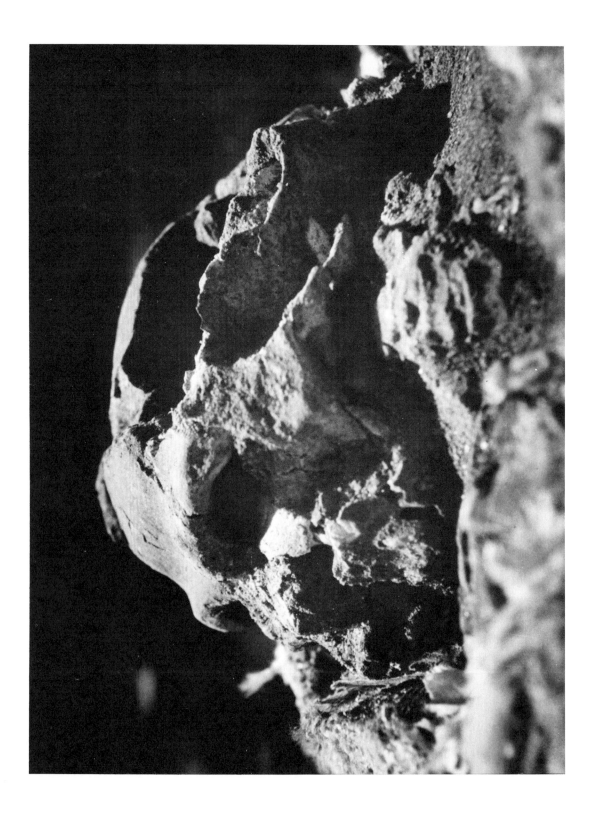

large enough to require blasting before removal. The skull and vertebrae were removed as a unit encased in plaster. Then the deposits above the postcranial skeleton were excavated to expose the skeleton fully. The postcranial skeleton was removed in two sections: a larger one containing the trunk, arms, and upper legs, and a smaller one containing the lower legs and feet.

Shanidar 1 had been lying on his back, turned slightly onto his right side, with his arms across his chest and his legs fully extended. The head had been displaced from the trunk. The remainder of the bones, except for the tibiae that had been disturbed after interment, were close to their original anatomical positions. Based on the arrangement of the bones and the position of the body between large limestone blocks and under a layer of small rocks, Solecki suggested that Shanidar 1 died in a rockfall and was subsequently covered with a layer of small pieces of limestone by the other members of his social group.

The Shanidar 1 remains, like all the Shanidar Neandertal specimens, were not mineralized, usually quite fragmentary, and always fragile to the touch. This applies mainly to the larger bones and especially to the bones with thin cortical surface bone and underlying trabeculae. Therefore, many of the smaller bones, long bones with narrow shafts, and areas of solid cortical bone, such as much of the facial skeleton, survived well, whereas the femoral and tibial shafts, the cranial vault, and much of the axial skeleton were quite fragmentary.

Shanidar 1 was reconstructed by Stewart (1958, 1959) during 1957 and 1958. He concentrated his efforts on the skull and selected portions of the postcranial skeleton (Stewart 1977). The reconstruction of the facial skeleton, both cranial and mandibular, was straightforward and provided an accurate restoration. Much of the cranial vault bone had lost its internal table and portions were missing. Also, there is no solid contact between the left temporal and the rest of the cranial vault. Therefore, it was necessary for Stewart to approximate the positions of the left temporal and portions of the parietals and occipital. Although there is some warping of the posterior cranium in the final reconstruction, it is minor and can easily be corrected in measurements of the cranium. Despite Stewart's original reservations about his restoration (Stewart 1958), it is probably as accurate a restoration as is possible, given the condition of the fossil; it is undoubtedly close to the original shape of the cranium.

The cleaning and restoration of most of the postcranial skeleton presented few difficulties. A number of the bones, such as the ilia, ischia, sacrum, and right femoral shaft, were crushed in situ and could not be disassembled and restored to their original conditions without loss of information. On these bones and parts of others, the fracture lines contained variable quantities of bone meal that would be lost in disassembly and cleaning of the pieces, so that gaps would remain between the fragments when they were reassembled. There-

Figure 5   The Shanidar 1 cranium as it was discovered in situ. Photo courtesy R. S. Solecki.

fore, a number of pieces were left in their original state after surface cleaning and chemical impregnation to provide some solidity.

Sometime prior to his death, Shanidar 1 sustained injuries to his right frontal and left orbit and a massive injury to his right side that resulted in arthritic degenerations of the right knee, ankle, and first tarsometatarsal joint, a fracture of the right fifth metatarsal, and extreme atrophy and/or hypotrophy of the right clavicle, scapula, and humerus with fractures and a possible amputation of the distal humerus. These abnormalities are discussed in detail in Chapter 12. However, reference is made to them where they bear upon the morphological interpretations of the Shanidar 1 remains. It is not clear to what extent these lesions may have affected the morphology of anatomical regions that are not clearly abnormal. It will be assumed that the influence was minimal, unless there is evidence to suggest otherwise.

SHANIDAR 1

Cranium	Clavicles	Ossa coxae
Mandible	Scapulae	Femur (right)
Maxillary dentition: 16	Humeri	Patellae
Mandibular dentition: 14	Radius (left)	Tibiae
Cervical vertebrae: 4	Ulna (left)	Fibulae
Thoracic vertebrae: 10–11	Metacarpals: 3	Tali
Lumbar vertebrae: 5		Calcanei
Sacrum		Anterior tarsals: 8
Ribs: ≥ 14		Metatarsals: 8
		Proximal phalanx: 1

Shanidar 2

Toward the end of the 1957 season, one of the workmen cleaning the west wall on 23 May encountered teeth along the western boundary of square D8. On further examination, the teeth were recognized to be those of an adult human, Shanidar 2. The teeth were found at 7.25 m below datum, close to the middle of the Shanidar deposits and well within the Mousterian levels. The rest of the skull, when exposed, revealed the cranium and mandible of an adult Neandertal that had been flattened from side to side so that its breadth was only 5–6 cm. Apparently it had been buried between two rocks that, with the weight of the overlying sediment, had crushed the soft bone. Because Shanidar 2 was discovered late in the season, it was decided to remove the skull with the attached postcranial bones (two scapulae and the cervical vertebrae) in two blocks, each jacketed in plaster. The rest of the postcranial skeleton, several thoracic and lumbar vertebrae, and a tibia and fibula were left deep in the west wall of the excavation under more than 7 m of deposits; they were excavated early in the 1960 season.

The cervical vertebrae and scapulae of Shanidar 2 were pressed up against the occipital, suggesting that the head had been forced strongly backwards at the time of death. Because little of the postcranial skeleton survived, the burial position of Shanidar 2 is unknown. Yet a rockfall either at time of death or shortly thereafter undoubtedly influenced the final resting position of the individual.

The Shanidar 2 skull was considerably more damaged than that of Shanidar 1, but its poor condition was exacerbated by its treatment in the Iraq Museum. By the time Stewart began his restoration of the fossil in 1960, it had been soaked, in its *in situ* position, in preservative (Figure 6). Stewart was able to disassemble the skull and to reassemble some portions of it, but it was not possible to provide a full restoration of the cranium (Stewart 1961b). More recently (1978), I added slightly to Stewart's restoration, primarily using the teeth and the preserved fragments of alveoli to reconstruct the dental arcade. Stewart completely restored the mandible, replacing the missing portions with filler. His reconstruction is reasonable. However, if the reconstruction of the maxillary dental arcade is accurate, the mandibular reconstruction is too wide posteriorly. Yet since the symphyseal region of the mandible is absent and the central portions of the maxillae are fragmentary, it is not possible to determine conclusively which reconstruction is closer to the original condition.

The restoration of the postcrania presented no difficulties. Although portions are missing from the preserved bones, none of them appears to have been significantly distorted.

SHANIDAR 2

Cranium	Cervical vertebrae: 7	Scapulae
Mandible	Thoracic vertebrae: 8	Tibia (left)
Maxillary dentition: 16	Lumbar vertebrae: 4	Fibula (left)
Mandibular dentition: 15		

Shanidar 3

The first fragments of Shanidar 3 were uncovered on 16 April 1957 during cleaning of the east wall of the main excavation trench. They were found in the northeast corner of square B9 at approximately 5.40 m below datum. Hence, Shanidar 3 was not far from Shanidar 1 but was probably slightly older, being a meter deeper in the deposits. The remains were between rocks in the wall of the trench, and only vertebrae and ribs were still in anatomical position. The individual appears to have been lying on his right side between the rocks.

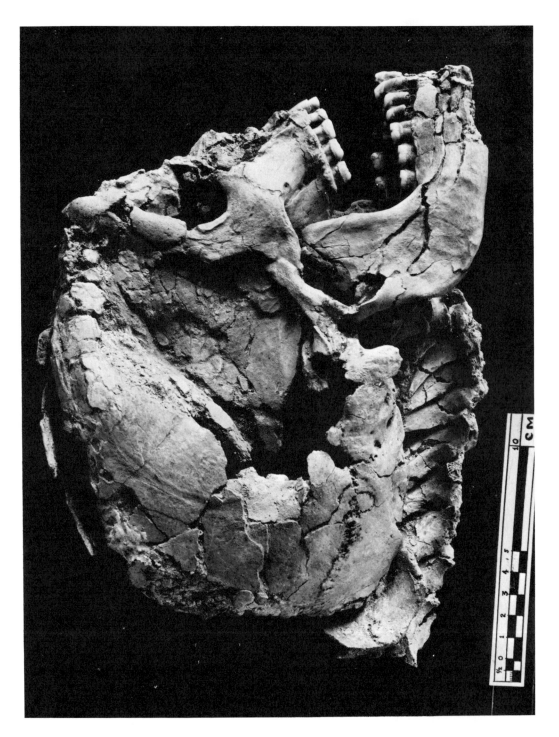

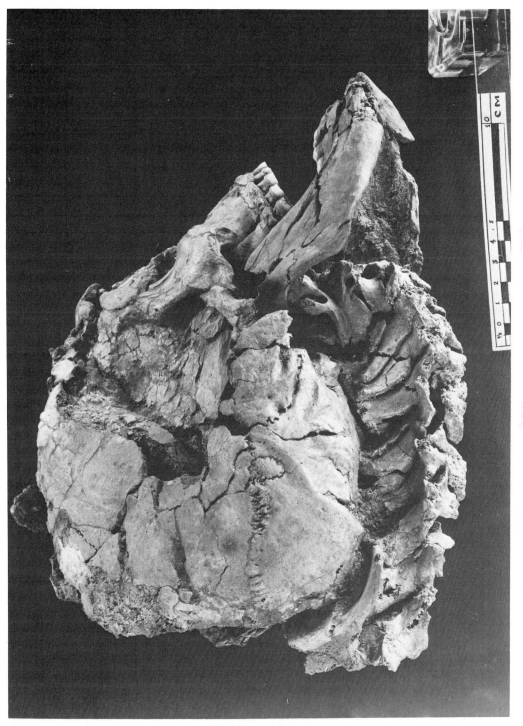

Figure 6 Two views of the Shanidar 2 skull and cervical vertebrae in their crushed *in situ* position. This was the condition of the specimen after initial cleaning and impregnation in the Iraq Museum and prior to the reconstruction by Stewart. Photos courtesy the Iraq Museum.

23

During the 1957 season, portions of the ribs, thoracic and lumbar vertebrae, sacrum, innominate bones, a clavicle, hand bones, and foot bones were recovered, along with four isolated teeth. In 1960, further excavation was undertaken in the vicinity of the discovery, and portions of thoracic vertebrae, ribs, clavicles, scapulae, humeri, ulnae, radius, and hand bones were retrieved. These remains have been combined to provide our current knowledge of the anatomy of Shanidar 3.

The analysis of Shanidar 3 was begun by Stewart after the 1957 season, but circumstances prevented him from completing it and integrating the 1960 discoveries. In 1976, I resumed the reconstruction of the fragmentary pieces and, with Stewart, completed the preliminary analysis of the partial skeleton (Trinkaus 1982f; Trinkaus and Stewart 1980). Almost all the Shanidar 3 bones, with the exception of some of the smaller hand and foot bones, are damaged, some considerably. However, there has been little or no warping of the bones, and it has been possible to reassemble most of the preserved pieces.

SHANIDAR 3

Maxillary dentition: 2	Clavicles	Ossa coxae
Mandibular dentition: 2	Scapulae	Femur (side indet.)
Thoracic vertebrae: 12	Humeri	Tibiae
Lumbar vertebrae: 5	Ulnae	Fibulae
Sacrum	Radius (left)	Tali
Ribs: ≥ 20	Carpals: 6	Calcanei
	Metacarpals: 4	Anterior tarsals: 9
	Proximal phalanges: 3	Metatarsals: 6–7
	Middle phalanges: 4	Sesamoids: 2
	Distal phalanges: 3	Proximal phalanges: 2

Shanidar 4

On 3 August 1960, Solecki decided to remove a number of large limestone blocks near the middle of the Mousterian deposits that were protruding from the east wall of the trench to square B7. During this process, bone was encountered between the rocks, at 7.49 m below datum. The bone turned out to be human tibia and fibula. Excavation continued between the rocks, and most of the skeleton of a large individual was revealed lying on his left side with the right arm across the body and the legs partially flexed (Figure 7). This individual became Shanidar 4, the Shanidar "flower burial" (Solecki 1971b, 1975, 1977). Although most of the bones could be identified and appeared relatively intact in situ, it was soon realized that all of them were extremely fragile, contained numerous breaks, and tended to fall apart if removed. After considerable effort (see Solecki 1971b; Stewart 1963), the skeleton was removed in a block to be unpacked in the Iraq Museum.

As mentioned earlier, during the preparation of Shanidar 4 for removal from Shanidar Cave and subsequently in the Iraq Museum, the remains of two adults

Figure 7 The Shanidar 4 partial skeleton *in situ* in Shanidar Cave. The right scapula, humerus, radius, ulna, ribs, innominate bone, femur, and proximal tibia are evident, as are the left radius and ulna above the right forearm bones. The cranium and mandible had been removed prior to the taking of this photograph. The remains of Shanidar 6, 8, and 9 were underneath the semiflexed remains of Shanidar 4. Photo courtesy R. S. Solecki.

(Shanidar 6 and 8) and an infant (Shanidar 9) were found associated with the Shanidar 4 partial skeleton. Their particular circumstances are discussed later. There may be some mixing of the Shanidar 4 bones with those of Shanidar 6 and 8. If any exists, it is probably minimal and should not adversely affect the morphological consideration of the Shanidar Neandertals as a sample.

The Shanidar 4 skeleton was unpacked in 1962 by Stewart and the more complete pieces were restored and studied by him at that time (Stewart 1963). In 1976 (Trinkaus 1977b), 1978, and 1980, I continued this work, which appeared at times to be interminable. Not only were the Shanidar 4 bones more fragmented than those of Shanidar 1 or 2, but they were mixed with those of two other adults and few of the breaks presented clean edges for reassembly. For example, of the 184 pieces of cranial vault preserved for Shanidar 4, none has all of its edges unworn and many lack portions of the internal or external tables. Also, Shanidar 4 is the only one of the Shanidar Neandertals to have significant calcareous encrustations, which are many times harder than the friable bones and cannot be removed in many cases without damage to the bone. Although it appears at the moment as though the reassembly of the Shanidar 4 (and Shanidar 6 and 8) remains has proceeded as far as is possible, a considerable number of unidentified fragments remain and it may be possible to add pieces on to some of the existing bones. However, I doubt significant new morphological data will be obtained through additional reconstruction.

Some of the Shanidar 4 bones are in extremely poor condition. However, there is relatively little distortion in the pieces because in most cases bone fragments without reliable joins have been left apart.

SHANIDAR 4

Cranium	Scapulae	Ossa coxae
Mandible	Humeri	Femora
Maxillary dentition: 3	Ulnae	Patella (left)
Mandibular dentition: 9	Radii	Tibiae
Cervical vertebrae: ≥ 4	Carpals: 10	Fibulae
Thoracic vertebrae: ≥ 7	Metacarpals: 10	Tali
Lumbar vertebrae: 4	Proximal phalanges: 8	Calcanei
Sacrum	Middle phalanges: 6	Anterior tarsals: 5
Coccygeal vertebra: 1	Distal phalanges: 5	Metatarsals: 6–7
Ribs: ≥ 20		Sesamoid: 1
		Proximal phalanges: 9
		Middle phalanges: 5
		Distal phalanges: 5

Shanidar 5

Four days after the discovery of Shanidar 4, on 7 August 1960, Solecki began exploring along the east wall of the Shanidar excavation near where

Shanidar 1 and 3 had been found, largely with the hope of finding more pieces of Shanidar 3. Instead, he found another Neandertal skeleton about 4.48 m below datum. This became Shanidar 5 (Solecki 1961). As with the other Shanidar adults, Shanidar 5 was wedged between rocks and appears to have been killed by a rockfall. In fact, the Shanidar 5 remains were quite disturbed, yet close enough to an original articulated position to establish firmly that he was crushed and bent by a rockfall. The legs were in a semiflexed position with the anterior surface facing down. The pelvis, or what little remains of it, was beneath a medium-sized rock, the other side of which supported the cranium. The upper limb and trunk bones that have survived were found out of context. It therefore appears that the trunk of Shanidar 5 was bent backward so that the head was next to the pelvis, and then the body was buried in this position.

The cranium of Shanidar 5 was pressed up against the rock between it and the pelvis, so that the cranium, rock, and pelvis were removed as a unit. The limb bones were removed in pieces to be reassembled later. Although it was found in 1960, Shanidar 5 was not unpacked until 1976, when I cleaned and restored the specimen (Trinkaus 1977d, 1978f).

The Shanidar 5 cranium had been greatly compressed in situ, so that the face, left temporal, and left parietal were folded underneath the frontal. Most of the breaks were clean, so that it has been possible to reassemble the maxillae, zygomatic bones, frontal bone, left parietal bone, and left temporal bone with minimal difficulty.

The upper limb bones from Shanidar 5, although incomplete, are in excellent condition. The femora and tibiae, however, lost considerable portions of their shafts where the bone turned to bone meal in situ. However, the joins between the fragments are, for the most part, reliable.

SHANIDAR 5

Cranium	Scapula	Os coxae (side indet.)
Maxillary dentition: 3	Ulnae	Femora
Cervical vertebra: 1	Radius (right)	Patellae
Ribs: ≥ 8	Carpals: 3	Tibia (left)
	Metacarpals: 3	Fibula (left)
	Proximal phalanges: 2	
	Middle phalanges: 2	
	Distal phalanges: 3	

Shanidar 6

The circumstances of discovery of Shanidar 6 were discussed previously with respect to Shanidar 4. Suffice it to say that on 9 August 1960, Stewart realized that another, smaller individual was present below Shanidar 4. Because Shanidar 5 had been discovered in the meantime, this new individual was given the number of Shanidar 6. The Shanidar 6 remains were already mixed with those of Shanidar 4 *in situ*, and became more so during the process of excavation and unpacking of the block containing the bones in Baghdad. Based on the position of the arm bones, Shanidar 6 appears to have been buried in a position similar to that of Shanidar 4, semiflexed on the left side, slightly to the southwest and below Shanidar 4.

Most of the remains of this individual are in good condition, frequently better than those of Shanidar 4. Although few of the bones are complete and many of the long bones lack significant portions, almost all of the joins are clean and leave no doubt as to the reconstruction. A few of the Shanidar 6 remains, in particular the dentition and femora, were originally assigned to Shanidar 4 (Stewart 1963). However, size differences and duplication of parts have made it possible to assign correctly most of the pieces.

SHANIDAR 6

Cranium	Humeri	Os coxae (side indet.)
Maxillary dentition: 11	Ulnae	Femora
Mandibular dentition: 5	Radii	Patella (right)
Sternum	Carpals: 2	Tibiae
Lumbar vertebrae: 4	Metacarpals: 5	Fibulae
	Proximal phalanges: 3	Talus (right)
	Middle phalanges: 4	Anterior tarsals: 2
	Distal phalanges: 2	Metatarsals: 4
		Proximal phalanx: 1
		Distal phalanx: 1

Shanidar 7

The first discovery of Neandertal remains in Shanidar Cave occurred on 22 June 1953. During excavation, first the skull and then the whole body of an infant was found at a depth of 7.87 m below datum in square B6. It was therefore slightly above the stalagmitic level in the middle of Layer D and below the Shanidar 4, 6, 8, and 9 multiple burial. This makes it the most ancient of the Shanidar individuals.

The infant was lying on its right side in a tightly flexed position. All of the bones were crushed, so that the maximum vertical thickness of the skeleton was about 4.5 cm. Yet it appears as though most of the skeleton was preserved, despite its extreme fragmentation.

The remains were cleaned and studied by Şenyürek in 1956 and 1957. But he concerned himself almost exclusively with the largely complete deciduous dentition and only mentioned briefly the other pieces (Şenyürek 1957a, 1957b, 1959). Although the cranial and postcranial pieces are incomplete, they provide information on the growth and development of Neandertal morphology.

SHANIDAR 7

Cranium	Ulna (right)	Femur (right?)
Maxillary dentition: 8	Metacarpals: 9?	Tibia (side indet.)
Mandibular dentition: 8	Proximal phalanges: 3	Metatarsals: 10?
Cervical vertebra: 1?	Middle phalanges: 4	Proximal phalanges: 3
Lumbar vertebrae: 3	Distal phalanx: 1	
Ribs: 2		

Shanidar 8

During the packaging and removal in a block of Shanidar 4 and 6 between 4 and 15 August 1960, a number of bones and fragments were dislodged. They were collected and placed with the other remains in the Iraq Museum. In 1962, when he began his study of the Shanidar 4 and 6 remains, Stewart soon realized that a second adult of small size was represented, mostly by the loose bones (Stewart 1963). The new adult became Shanidar VII (now Shanidar 8).

It is hard to describe Shanidar 8 as a partial skeleton because it is primarily a collection of extras from Shanidar 4 and 6. However, the bones appear to go together, on the basis of size and morphology, and they should therefore properly be considered as part of an individual. Except for the isolated scaphoid bone and the foot bones, most of the Shanidar 8 bones are extremely incomplete.

SHANIDAR 8

Cranium	Fibula (right)
Humeri	Anterior tarsal: 1
Radius (right)	Metatarsals: 6
Carpal: 1	Sesamoid: 1
	Proximal phalanges: 4
	Middle phalanx: 1

Shanidar 9

The infant discovered in association with Shanidar 4, 6, and 8 was first noticed in August 1960, when the multiple burial was being removed from Shanidar Cave. The remains, which consist of parts of nine vertebrae, became separated from the adult skeletons, and their exact *in situ* location was lost.

The Shanidar 9 vertebrae were found articulated and encased in semibrecciated sediment in two sections. One section contained C-5–C-7 plus T-1; the other contained five thoracic vertebrae. It is assumed that the two pieces fit together, which would make the five thoracic vertebrae T-2–T-6. This assumption cannot be substantiated.

SHANIDAR 9

Cervical vertebrae: 3
Thoracic vertebrae: 6

CHAPTER 3

Morphometric Considerations

A substantial portion of the paleontological data from the Shanidar Neandertal sample consists of linear and angular measurements of the fossils. Although the measurements alone would give a very incomplete description of the sample, morphometrics permit the systematic comparison of the Shanidar Neandertals to each other, a consideration of the ranges of variation in size and proportions within the Shanidar sample, and an evaluation of the position of the Shanidar specimens within ranges of variation of the Neandertals and other Pleistocene hominid samples. For this reason, an effort has been made to provide as complete a set of measurements as possible for the Shanidar remains.

Most of the morphometrics provided were determined personally on the original fossil remains. A few of the measurements have been taken from the work of T. D. Stewart. These consist of *in situ* measurements of several long bones, particularly those of Shanidar 4, and several determinations that were not repeated. There are differences in a number of measurements between the determinations previously published by Stewart and those presented here. These differences are due either to personal differences in measuring techniques or to reconstructions of the specimens done subsequent to the work of Stewart that have altered the dimensions of the fossils.

A number of the morphometrics provided are estimates of the original dimensions of the fossils (indicated by enclosing the measurements in parentheses in the tables). In a sample as fragmentary as the Shanidar one, it is necessary to approximate measurements that would otherwise be unobtainable. If this were not done, the available morphometric data would be a fraction of what it is. The various estimates consist of four general types.

The most frequent approximation is the reconstruction of damaged margins

31

of bones, usually when most of the bone is present but the edges have become abraded. On a number of the bilaterally symmetrical bones, such as the cranium, mandible, and vertebrae, only one side is preserved; in such cases, they have been measured from the midline to the preserved side and the figure has been doubled to obtain the total dimension. For such measurements, the side that has provided the value is indicated in the tables. It has also been possible to estimate values, such as long bone lengths, by combining the preserved portions of the right and left bones, aligning them according to anatomical landmarks. These last two methods assume strict bilateral symmetry, which is not necessarily valid (LeMay 1976; Ruff 1979), but the error so introduced should be minimal.

A number of the long bones preserve major portions of their diaphyses and epiphyses but are too incomplete to permit direct measurement of standard lengths. Also, several of the forearms and lower legs retain most of one of the long bones but little of the other. For each of these, I have computed least squares regressions, based on samples of recent human limb bones, to estimate the lengths of the bones from either their preserved portions or the length of the accompanying forearm or lower leg bone. To minimize error, regressions were used only when the correlation coefficient was greater than .90. This technique may underestimate the lengths of some of the bones because Neandertal epiphyses tend to be relatively larger than those of recent humans (Endo and Kimura 1970; Patte 1955; Trinkaus 1980). Yet the margins of error should be within a few percent, and the additional data provide a considerably expanded sample for a variety of comparisons.

The measurements provided follow, in large part, the definitions of Howells (1973) for the cranium and Martin (1928) for the mandible and postcrania. Those measurements defined by Howells (1973) are followed in the tables by his three-letter abbreviations, and those listed by Martin (1928) are accompanied by "M=#" to indicate the number of his equivalent measurement. However, in order to characterize fully the Shanidar Neandertals metrically, it has been necessary to take definitions of measurements from a variety of published sources and to define a number of new ones. All the measurements that do not derive from Martin (1928) or Howells (1973) have their definitions provided in the footnotes to the tables.

Several measurements, particularly from Shanidar 1, were taken on clearly abnormal bones. They are provided to indicate the amount of alteration that has taken place secondary to the pathology in that bone. These are labeled with a p preceding the measurement.

All the linear measurements in the tables are in millimeters unless otherwise indicated. All the angular measurements are in degrees.

Although this work is primarily descriptive, it is necessary to provide data from other hominid samples for a proper evaluation of the morphology of the Shanidar Neandertals. Given the relatively large number of Upper Pleistocene human remains now known, it would be difficult, and beyond the scope of this work, to list the primary measurements for all the specimens that would make up comparative samples, as has been the custom in monographs on Neandertals (e.g., Heim 1976; Suzuki and Takai 1970). Therefore, comparisons of the Shanidar specimens to other hominid samples will contain only summations of the data from the other samples, unless there is a reason to refer to particular specimens.

Recent research in later Pleistocene human paleontology has shown that many traditional groupings of specimens are inaccurate reflections of the morphological patterns evident in the fossil record. Some sample definitions are too broad, geographically and temporally, and tend to obscure potentially important regional and temporal patterns of variation, whereas others are too narrow and tend to produce very small samples with limited ranges of variation. This has been especially true for definitions of the Neandertals. One set of definitions of the Neandertals (e.g., Boule 1911–1913, 1921; LeGros Clark 1964; Vandermeersch 1972) have seen them as a homogeneous group restricted to Europe, primarily western Europe. Another set of definitions (e.g., Brace 1964; Brose and Wolpoff 1971; Hrdlička 1927, 1930) have seen them as a heterogeneous group of later Pleistocene archaic *Homo sapiens* fossils from all regions of the Old World.

It is now apparent that the Neandertals are best defined, for the purposes of interpreting their anatomy and phylogenetic position, as a group of archaic *Homo sapiens* from Europe and western Asia who lived from the end of the last interglacial to the middle of the last glacial and shared a set of morphological characteristics that have been traditionally termed *Classic Neandertal* (Howells 1975, 1978; Santa Luca 1978; Stringer 1974a, 1974b, 1978; Stringer and Trinkaus 1981; Trinkaus 1976a, 1976b, 1977a, 1981; Trinkaus and Howells 1979). Lists of morphological features of the Neandertals have been provided recently by Vandermeersch (1972), Heim (1978), LeGros Clark and Campbell (1978), and others. Although these lists indicate the general pattern of Neandertal morphology, it should be kept in mind that there is considerable variation around these ideal types.

If the Shanidar fossil human remains are indeed those of Neandertals, as various assessments of their morphology have indicated (Stewart 1958, 1960, 1961a, 1961b, 1962a, 1962b, 1963, 1977; Stringer and Trinkaus 1981; Trinkaus 1976a, 1976b, 1977d, 1978b, 1980, 1981, 1982f), they should be most closely related to the other Near Eastern Neandertals and more distantly related to the European Neandertals. In order to permit the evaluation of this question, the Neandertals have been divided into two geographical samples, a European one and a Near Eastern one. The European sample includes all the Neandertal specimens from Europe as far east as the Crimea. The Near Eastern sample includes individuals from three sites in Israel—Amud (Suzuki and Takai 1970), Kebara (Smith and Arensburg 1977), and Tabūn Layers B and C (McCown and Keith 1939)—the Bisitun 1 radius from Iran (Coon 1951), and the Teshik-Tash 1 immature skeleton from Uzbekistan (Gremyatskij and Nesturkh 1949; Ullrich

1955). In addition, comparative data are provided for the last interglacial (Early
Neandertal) Zuttiyeh 1 anterior cranium (Keith 1927) and Tabūn E1 femur
(McCown and Keith 1939), both of which come from sites in Israel. (Few useful
comparative data are available for the apparently Early Neandertal Azykh 1
mandible, and the Tabūn E2 mandibular molar (McCown and Keith [1939] is of
little comparative value across samples of Upper Pleistocene humans.) The
other Mousterian human remains from this region are either anatomically modern (e.g., Darra-i-Kur 1 [Angel 1972]) and individuals from Qafzeh and Skhūl
(see below), or are of uncertain morphological affinity to the Neandertals (e.g.,
Shukbah D1 and D2 [Keith 1931] and Dzhruchula 1 [Gabuniya et al. 1961]).
(The incisor from Bisitun and the femur from Tamtama, reported as hominid by
Coon [1951, 1975], are nonhominid.)

The various archaic H. sapiens remains from Africa and eastern Asia, many
of which have been called Neandertaloid or Neandertal-like, are best considered as archaic H. sapiens of an evolutionary grade similar to that of the Neandertals but of uncertain phylogenetic relationship to the Neandertals. However,
the sample of European and Near Eastern H. sapiens remains that antedate the
Neandertals appears to provide a good ancestral group for the Neandertals
(Hublin 1978a; Stringer 1974b; Trinkaus 1976a, 1982c), and they are referred to
here as the Early Neandertals. It has been difficult to determine whether certain
specimens, which derive from late last interglacial deposits, should be placed
in the Neandertal or Early Neandertal samples (e.g., some of the Krapina specimens [Smith 1976a, 1976b; Wolpoff, 1979]); they have, in a number of cases,
been included within the Neandertal sample.

The immediate successors of the Neandertals, whatever their evolutionary
origins may be, are the Skhūl and Qafzeh samples in the Near East and the Early
Upper Paleolithic hominids in Europe. Although the Skhūl and Qafzeh hominids are associated with late Levantine Middle Paleolithic industries, their
morphology aligns them primarily with recent humans and separates them
from the Neandertals (Howell 1957; Howells 1970; McCown and Keith 1939;
Santa Luca 1978; Stewart 1960; Trinkaus 1976a, 1976b; Vandermeersch 1972,
1978b, 1981a). Additionally, because there has been significant human evolution since the beginning of the European Upper Paleolithic (Billy 1972; Frayer
1977, 1978, 1980, 1981), comparisons of the Neandertals to later European
hominids will be with Early Upper Paleolithic human remains, primarily those
associated with Aurignacian industries.

In light of these considerations, comparisons of the Shanidar remains to
other human fossil samples will be in reference to Near Eastern Neandertals,
European Neandertals, Early Neandertals, Skhūl–Qafzeh hominids, and Early
Upper Paleolithic hominids. In addition, reference will be made to data from
various samples of recent human skeletal remains and to samples of earlier
hominid species, particularly H. erectus.

Whenever possible, fossils will be referred to by their designations in the
Catalogue of Fossil Hominids (Oakley et al. 1971, 1975, 1977). The Krapina

specimens are identified by the catalog numbers of Gorjanović-Kramberger and, for the associated dentitions, the letter designations of Gorjanović-Kramberger (1906) and Wolpoff (1979). The numbers of the Chou-kou-tien *H. erectus* specimens are those of Weidenreich (1941, 1943) rather than the more complicated system of the *Catalogue of Fossil Hominids* (Limbrey 1975).

The comparative paleontological data have been taken from a number of publications and from personal investigations of original specimens. Much of the cranial and mandibular data have been tabulated by Morant (1927, 1930), McCown and Keith (1939), Suzuki (1970), Lumley (1973), Sergi (1974), Thoma (1975), Heim (1976), F. H. Smith (1976a), Santa Luca (1980), and Vandermeersch (1981a). Additional unpublished data have been kindly provided by C. B. Stringer. Most of the comparative dental metrics are listed by Twiesselmann (1973), Smith and Arensburg (1977), Trinkaus (1977c), Frayer (1978), Tillier (1979), and Wolpoff (1979). The postcranial data come primarily from personal studies of the original fossils, but a large proportion of the data has been presented in a variety of publications (e.g., Endo and Kimura 1970; Heim 1974; Lovejoy and Trinkaus 1980; Matiegka 1938; McCown and Keith 1939: Musgrave 1973; Rhoads and Trinkaus 1977; Stewart 1962a, 1962b; Trinkaus 1975a, 1975b, 1976a, 1976b, 1978c, 1978d, 1980, 1981; Twiesselmann 1961; Vandermeersch 1981a). The comparative data for samples of recent humans, unless indicated otherwise, come from personal studies of skeletal samples.

Whenever the comparative samples are sufficiently large (usually a minimum of five individuals), the comparative metrics have been summarized using means and standard deviations. Although these statistics are frequently taken to describe normally distributed samples, they are not meant to indicate the shapes of the distributions here. At any rate, most of the fossil samples are too small to determine the shapes of the distributions of the variables in the populations from which the samples have been drawn.

In addition, shape, as well as size, is of interest and frequently of more concern than absolute size. Therefore, a number of ratios have been computed to provide indications of skeletal proportions. These ratios have been converted in most cases to indices by multiplying them by 100. These indices have also been summarized for sufficiently large comparative samples using means and standard deviations. Simple ratios potentially contain distortions of the data because they assume that the relationships between pairs of variables are linear and have an intercept of zero. However, for limited ranges in size, these assumptions are not necessarily inaccurate. Furthermore, the insights gained from using ratios to assess proportional similarities and differences outweigh potential disadvantages.

These considerations of the morphometric data provided in this monograph for the Shanidar fossil remains and various comparative samples should indicate the nature of the data and possible sources of distortion in the data.

CHAPTER 4

Age and Sex
of the Shanidar
Neandertals

The determination of the age and sex of fossil hominids has been one of the most subjective aspects of human paleontology. No one method has proven to be universally applicable, largely because so few specimens preserve in common the same anatomical regions. And, perhaps more important, there is disagreement as to the degree to which scales of reference, derived from extant humans, can be applied to prehistoric hominids (Genovés 1954, 1969; Skinner 1977: Smith 1980; Trinkaus 1980; Vallois 1961).

It is nonetheless valuable to know, within reasonable margins of error, the sex and age at death of specimens under consideration. At present, fossil samples of archaic *Homo sapiens* are not of sufficient size nor restricted enough temporally and geographically to enable the computation of reliable paleodemographic statistics. But size and morphology are influenced by both age and sex, so that whenever possible they should be taken into account. In this way potential biases due to sampling can be weighed. It is primarily for this reason that the sexes and ages at death of the Shanidar Neandertals have been estimated.

AGE

The ages at death of the Shanidar individuals have been estimated by a variety of methods, each one of which possesses a certain margin of error. For reasonably complete individuals, such as Shanidar 1, it is possible to use several age indicators, but the less complete individuals, such as Shanidar 6 and 8, permit the use of fewer methods with a correspondingly greater possible error. Because reference populations of Neandertals do not exist for establishing scales for developmental and degenerative processes, scales based on recent humans have been used. The age estimates provided here should therefore be considered primarily as relative ages for the Shanidar Neandertals. Yet, they still furnish an indication of the longevity of these prehistoric humans relative to other samples of Pleistocene humans.

Shanidar 1

Shanidar 1 retains substantial portions of the skeleton, so that several sources of information can be used for age determination. In particular, cranial suture closure, dental wear, arthritic degenerations, and pubic symphyseal morphology have been used.

The endocranial surfaces of the Shanidar 1 cranial sutures are almost completely lost because much of the cranial vault bone separated along the diploë and the inner table did not survive. On the external surface, it is possible to observe part of the coronal suture to the right of bregma, most of the sagittal suture, most of the left side of the lambdoid suture, and the lateral half of the right side of the lambdoid suture. The coronal and sagittal sutures were completely fused, although neither was obliterated externally. The lambdoid suture appears to have been completely open. This suggests an age of at least 25–30 years, and probably one slightly older (Olivier 1960). Given the variation in sutural closure among recent humans (Genovés and Messmacher 1959; Singer 1953), and the possibility that it occurred at earlier ages among prehistoric humans (Vallois 1960), a more precise age estimate would be unreasonable.

The teeth of Shanidar 1 exhibit extensive occlusal wear, in which the crowns have been completely removed from the anterior teeth and only the upper second and third molars preserve enamel on their occlusal surfaces (Table 16; Figure 26). Because rates of occlusal wear vary considerably among populations, depending largely upon the amount of grit in the food and whether they use their anterior teeth for paramasticatory purposes, this can provide little more than a rough estimate of age at death without a reliable reference sample (Miles 1963). However, it is clear that all of the Shanidar 1 teeth are extensively worn, far more so than those of Shanidar 2 and 6 (Tables 16, 17, and 21; Figures 26, 27, and 30). Because Shanidar 2 and 6 are both adults with fully erupted and worn third molars, the wear on the Shanidar 1 teeth suggests a considerably greater age, probably at least 30 years.

It is extremely difficult to assess the age dependency of arthritic degenerations because the rate of degeneration is related to activity patterns, possible trauma, and infection, as well as age. Shanidar 1 exhibits exostoses on practically every part of the skeleton. Much of the degeneration appears to have been promoted by an extensive injury to the right side of the body (see Chapter 12), and some of the exostoses, such as on the tendinous surfaces of the patellae and the proximal left ulna, can be ascribed to irritation of the tendinous insertions from high levels of muscular activity. Yet the pervasiveness of degenerative joint disease, even between the vertebrae, implies that there was a considerable amount of time for some of the exostoses to form.

Shanidar 1 is one of the few Neandertals for whom the symphyseal surfaces of the pubic bones are largely preserved. The right bone retains the inferior two-thirds of the dorsal half and portions of the ventral margin of the symphysis, whereas the left bone preserves most of the ventral half and the inferior half of the dorsal portion of the surface (Figure 8). Following the system of pubic symphysis age changes of McKern and Stewart (1957), Shanidar 1 exhibits: Component I: Stage 4; Component II: Stage 4 or 5; Component III: Stage 3 or 4. This suggests a probable age range of 23 to 39 and a mean estimate of about 29. (These age estimates assume that the pubic symphysis age changes parallel those of modern Euroamericans.)

Taken together, these data imply that Shanidar 1 was at least 30 years old at

(a)   **(b)**   **(c)**

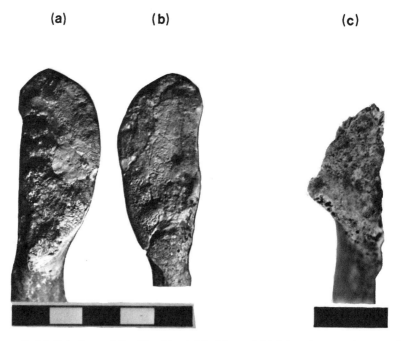

Figure 8 Medial views of the Shanidar 1 (a) right and (b) left pubic symphyses and of the Shanidar 3 (c) left pubic symphysis. Portions of the Shanidar 1 symphyseal surfaces have been reconstructed with plaster. Only the inferior corner of the Shanidar 3 symphysis is preserved. Scales in centimeters.

the time of death. Although the pubic symphyseal morphology suggests a slightly younger age, the evidence of the dental occlusal wear in particular supports an age closer to 35 or 40 years. The age at death of Shanidar 1 was therefore probably at least 30 years but probably not more than 40 or 45 years.

Shanidar 2

The age of Shanidar 2 has been estimated largely from the dentition. The Shanidar 2 teeth (Table 17; Figure 27) all exhibit some wear, but only the anterior teeth show significant wear. The wear on the cheek teeth, especially the later erupting second and third molars, is minimal; little or no dentin has been exposed on them. If one assumes conditions of rapid dental attrition, as suggested by the wear on the Shanidar 1 dentition, no more than several years would be necessary to produce the observed wear on the third molars. This would place Shanidar 2 in his early 20s. A slower rate of wear would imply a slightly older age, probably in the middle or late 20s.

Additional evidence for the age of Shanidar 2 is provided by his coronal and lambdoid sutures. The external surfaces of the coronal suture have been preserved on each side near stephanion; the suture is not fused, at least externally. The lambdoid suture, which is preserved along its lateral half on the right side, is largely open. The sutural evidence therefore also suggests a relatively young age.

The rest of the Shanidar 2 skeleton provides no data that would contradict these age estimations. Except for some minor exostoses along the vertebral column, what remains of the postcranial skeleton is free from degenerative disease. Therefore, it seems reasonable to ascribe to Shanidar 2 an age at death between 20 and 30, and probably closer to 20 than 30.

Shanidar 3

Shanidar 3 provides evidence for age estimation in the form of dental wear, pubic symphyseal morphology, sacroiliac morphology, and degenerative joint disease. The Shanidar 3 teeth (Table 18; Figure 28) were all extensively worn. The anterior teeth lost most or all of their crowns prior to death and the upper third molar retains only a ring of enamel around dentin. This wear is among the most extensive among the Shanidar Neandertals; an advanced age is therefore suggested.

A small inferior portion of the left pubic symphysis has survived. Although it is only a fraction of the symphyseal surface, it is sufficient to indicate the general morpholgy of the surface (Figure 8). Following the system of pubic symphyseal age changes of McKern and Stewart (1957), Shanidar 3 exhibits: Component I: Stage 5; Component II: indeterminate; Component III: Stage 5.

This suggests a minimum age of about 36 years and a mean estimate of about 41 years, if one assumes that Component II was also Stage 5, which is usually the case once Components I and II have reached stage 5 (McKern and Stewart 1957).

Shanidar 3 also preserves part of the anterosuperior right auricular surface. Because the auricular surface undergoes age-related changes similar to those of the pubic symphysis (Kobayashi 1967), it is possible to use its morphology to give an estimate of age at death. Using the scale of Kobayashi (1967), the Shanidar 3 auricular surface suggests an age of at least 40 years, probably between 40 and 50 years.

Shanidar 3, like Shanidar 1, exhibits pervasive degenerative joint disease. Some of it was undoubtedly due to trauma (Chapter 12), but much of it is activity and/or age related. Although the amount of arthritis would not exclude a young adult age, it would agree more with an advanced age.

These data suggest that Shanidar 3 died at an age slightly older than that of Shanidar 1. Therefore, an age estimate between 35 and 50 years, and most likely between 40 and 50 years, would be reasonable.

This estimate is supported by an age determination based on the histological structure of a fragment of femoral diaphysis of Shanidar 3 (Thompson and Trinkaus 1981). Because the degree of cortical bone remolding and secondary osteon formation in the femoral diaphysis is age related, it is possible to use a quantification of the histological structures observed in a cross section of the cortical bone to estimate the age of the individual (Thompson 1978). For Shanidar 3, the relative areas of secondary osteon lamellae and haversian canals (0.287 and 0.046 mm^2, respectively), the densities of secondary osteons and haversian canals plus primary osteons (19.0 and 20.25/mm^2, respectively), and the perimeters of the secondary osteons and haversian canals (0.394 and 0.127 mm, respectively) provide an age estimate of 42 $\pm$ 8.2 years.

Shanidar 4

The Shanidar 4 partial skeleton, being quite fragmentary, provides few sources of data for age determination. But those that are available imply an advanced age.

Small sections of sutures are evident on the cranial vault fragments. Those that are, or appear to be, either coronal or sagittal sutural sections are largely fused but are still evident at least on the external surface. It appears that the lambdoid suture was still partly open, but there is too little of it preserved to substantiate this observation.

The teeth of Shanidar 4, like those of Shanidar 1 and 3, were worn down almost to the roots anteriorly and had most of the occlusal enamel removed from the molars (Table 19; Figure 29). The amount of wear more closely approximates that of Shanidar 1 than that of Shanidar 3. Furthermore, Shanidar 4 suffered extensive alveolar resorption in the molar region and some ante-mortem tooth loss (Table 15; Figure 21).

Various articulations of Shanidar 4 on the upper and lower limbs and the vertebral column show evidence of degenerative joint disease. Much of it was probably due to stress from activity patterns, but some of it may indicate an advanced age.

These data, but in particular the dental wear, suggest an age similar to that of Shanidar 1, between 30 and 45 years.

Shanidar 5

The evidence for the age of Shanidar 5 comes almost exclusively from the cranium and teeth. The postcrania preserve few articulations, and most of them are normal.

The Shanidar 5 cranial vault retains most of the coronal, sagittal, and left lambdoid sutures. The coronal and sagittal sutures were entirely fused, oblite-rated on their endocranial surfaces, and still apparent on the external surface. The lambdoid suture is open, but it experienced some remolding prior to death. It is possible that it was partly fused and became separated during fossilization. In addition, the cranial vault bones, where broken, exhibit thin internal and external tables and a considerable thickness of diploë with fine trabeculae. This condition is characteristic of vault bones of elderly individuals. It may even be possible that the exceptional thickness of the Shanidar 5 frontal squama (10.0–10.2 mm) is partly due to old age thickening of the bone.

The few preserved teeth indicate a pattern similar to those of Shanidar 3, anterior teeth with the crown removed by wear and posterior teeth with only a ring of enamel around dentin (Table 20; Figure 29). Furthermore, as with Shanidar 4, Shanidar 5 lost several teeth antemortem and experienced consid-erable alveolar resorption (Table 15; Figure 30).

This information implies that Shanidar 5 was similar in age to Shanidar 3. Therefore, a probable age range of 35 to 50 would be most appropriate.

Shanidar 6

The only reliable age indicator preserved for Shanidar 6 is its quite com-plete dentition. The teeth show slightly more wear than those of Shanidar 2 but none of the extensive wear of Shanidar 1, 3, 4, and 5 (Table 21; Figure 30). This would suggest an age slightly older than that of Shanidar 2.

The postcranial skeleton of Shanidar 6 supports an early adult age. None of the lines of fusion of the long bone epiphyses is discernible and, except for some minor exostoses on the patella and acetabular rim, the articulations are free from degenerative joint disease.

Therefore, Shanidar 6 was probably between 20 and 35 years old at death. If it is assumed that Shanidar 2 died in his early 20s, the actual age at death of Shanidar 6 may have been closer to 25 years.

Shanidar 7

Shanidar 7 is the one individual for which an accurate age can be determined. Although most of its fragmentary skeleton indicates no more than that it is a very young infant, the partially erupted decidous dentition permits a more precise estimate. The estimate is based entirely on the degree of calcification of the teeth, for neither the maxillary nor the mandibular alveoli survived to provide an indication of the degree of eruption.

The crowns of the central deciduous incisors are completely formed, and the maxillary central deciduous incisors show development of about half of the root. The first deciduous molars and the second deciduous incisors have completely formed crowns, but the roots are only beginning to show below the neck. The crowns of the deciduous canines are complete but there is no evidence of roots, and the second deciduous molar crowns are about three-quarters developed. This degree of calcification suggests an age between 6 and 9 months, probably close to 8 months (Lunt and Law 1974; Moorrees *et al.* 1963; Ubelaker 1978). This age estimate is slightly lower than the 9 months estimated by Şenyürek (1957b, 1959), but given the margin of error in such estimates (± 2–3 months), the two determinations are not contradictory.

Shanidar 8

It is extremely difficult to give an age to the remains that have been grouped together as Shanidar 8. The remains are fully adult because all of the epiphyseal lines are obliterated, and there is no evidence of degenerative joint disease. This suggests that it represents a young adult, but the incomplete nature of the partial skeleton does not permit a more precise estimate of its age at death.

Shanidar 9

The vertebrae that make up the remains of Shanidar 9 are clearly those of a young infant. All of the bones are highly porous, especially the centra. Most important for age assessment, all of the centra and several of the neural arches had not yet fused to their adjacent elements in the vertebrae. The separation of all of the preserved centra from their neural arches places a maximum age of about 3 years on the remains. At least one of the two surfaces of each dorsal cartilaginous joint between the neural arches is preserved on C5 to T1 and on the vertebrae that are probably T3–T6 (Chapter 10). The neural arches of the C6, C7, and the T4?–T6? were partially joined dorsally. Those of the C5, T1, and T3?, however, were still unfused. Because the neural arches of the upper thoracic and cervical vertebrae unite dorsally during the latter half of the first year (Warwick and Williams 1973), Shanidar 9 appears to have been between 6 months and 1 year at death. Shanidar 9 was therefore about the same age as Shanidar 7.

SEX

Sex determination among fossil hominids has been considerably more difficult than age estimation. Whereas it is possible to estimate reliably the sex of about 90% of recent human skeletal material using a variety of indicators (Krogman 1962), it is uncertain how many of the traits used for sexing modern human skeletal material can be applied to fossil hominids (Genovés 1969). Early attempts to assign sex to incomplete fossil remains led to a disproportionate number of specimens being called male (Genovés 1954; Weiss 1972). This probably resulted from paleontologists' using the general level of robusticity of the skull as a sexual indicator, and because early hominids are more robust than recent humans, most were referred to as male.

Not only are Neandertal and other early hominid crania generally more robust than those of recent humans, but most of the qualitative characteristics traditionally used to discriminate male and female crania (e.g., Krogman 1962) are inapplicable. For example, the various sexually distinct features of the orbits listed by Krogman (1962) and others are obscured by the presence on the Neandertals of supraorbital tori.

Recent attempts to assign sex to Neandertal specimens (e.g., Smith 1980; Trinkaus 1980) have shown that although a variety of morphological features can be used to indicate sex, it is primarily pelvic morphology that provides a secure sex determination. In particular, it is the morphology of the sciatic notch and of the ischiopubic ramus that furnishes the best indications of sex. The border of the "typical" male sciatic notch forms an almost complete semicircle, whereas the "typical" female notch is open posteriorly, becoming almost horizontal from the middle of the notch to the posterior inferior iliac spine. The "typical" male ischiopubic ramus is relatively robust and has a straight inferior margin, whereas the "typical" female ischiopubic ramus is thinner, inferomedially concave just below the pubic symphysis, and flares anteriorly along its inferior margin (Phenice 1969; Poulhés 1947).

It is unfortunately not possible to use the mediolateral length of Neandertal pubic bones as an indication of sex because both male and female Neandertals have elongated pubic bones (Stewart 1960; Trinkaus 1976b, 1978c; Chapter 9). As a result, the classic sexually discriminating measurements, such as the subpubic angle (Olivier 1960) and the ischiopubic index (Washburn 1948), are inapplicable.

If pelvic remains alone are employed to determine the sexes of known Neandertals, 10 individuals—four males (Amud 1, La Chapelle-aux-Saints 1, La Ferrassie 1, and Neandertal 1), three females (La Ferrassie 2, Krapina 209, and Tabūn C1), plus Shanidar 1, 3, and 4—could be sexed. There have therefore been several attempts to sex Neandertal remains using cranial and mandibular dimensions (Smith 1980; Thoma 1975; Wolpoff 1980a), dental dimensions (Wolpoff 1976), and postcranial dimensions (Trinkaus 1980). These studies have shown that Neandertal postcranial dimorphism is similar to that of recent humans (females about 10% smaller than males, on the average, in linear skeletal dimensions [Trinkaus 1980]), but that Neandertal cranial and mandibular dimorphism may have been slightly greater than that of recent humans (Smith 1980). These studies have also shown that there is relatively little overlap in many skeletal dimensions between Neandertal males and females that can be sexed by pelvic morphology. It may therefore be possible to use absolute size to indicate the sexes of those Shanidar adults (Shanidar 2, 5, 6, and 8) for whom diagnostic pelvic bones have not been preserved.

Even though it is possible to use cranial, mandibular, and appendicular dimensions to assign sex to Neandertal specimens such as the Shanidar fossils, there are difficulties involved. There was undoubtedly overlap in size between males and females in any one population, even though the preserved pelvically sexable Neandertals show little overlap in size between the sexes. Furthermore, there were probably population differences in mean stature; the pooling of individuals from many populations to form a Neandertal sample would tend to increase the amount of overlap in size between the sexes to a greater extent than would be present in any one Neandertal population. For these reasons, the reliability of a sex determination based solely on size is greatest when that individual approaches the lower or upper limits of the known Neandertal ranges of variation. The reliability decreases rapidly as the size of the individual in question approaches the range of male–female overlap.

The use of absolute size to indicate sex must assume that the mean body dimensions for each sex of the population from which the specimens in question derive are close to the means for each sex of the reference sample. The overall size range of the Shanidar 1–6 individuals, as indicated by their stature estimates (Chapter 11), are within the known range of variation of Near Eastern and European Neandertals, with Shanidar 1 close to the upper limits of the Neandertal range, Shanidar 6 at the lower limit of the range, and Shanidar 2, 3, 4, and 5 close to the overall Neandertal mean stature estimate (Tables 97 and 98). It therefore appears reasonable to assume that the mean statures of each sex for the Shanidar populations were close to those of the overall Neandertal sample.

In addition to overall size, it is possible to use mastoid process height to determine the sex of a Neandertal specimen (Smith 1980), much as it can be employed for recent human material (Giles and Elliot 1963). Although many Neandertals have quite small mastoid processes (Smith 1980; Vallois 1969), a pattern of sexual dimorphism comparable to that of recent humans appears to have been present.

Unlike indicators of overall body size and mastoid process height, it does not appear to be possible to use Neandertal dental dimensions to assign sex to fossil specimens. Neandertal canines, the teeth that should show the greatest sexual dimorphism (Gonda 1959), have breadths that approximate a normal distribution, whether one uses a large and heterogeneous sample (Wolpoff 1976) or a small and geographically restricted one. Furthermore, there are relatively few Neandertal teeth associated with sexually diagnostic sexual remains, and those that are do not appear to follow a consistent pattern of sexual dimorphism. As with recent humans, there appears to have been an extensive overlap in dental dimensions, such as canine breadth, between male and female Neandertals, making the dimensions of any one canine sexually undiagnostic.

It may be possible, on the other hand, to determine the sex of an infant if the deciduous dentition is preserved, as it is for Shanidar 7, because recent human male deciduous teeth are usually larger than those of females (Black 1978; Margetts and Brown 1978). However, as with permanent teeth, overlaps in size between males and females within populations and interpopulational size variations (Lukacs 1981) require that any one fossil specimen has dental dimensions that are at the limits of the known Neandertal ranges of variation before its sex can be ascertained reliably.

The Shanidar 1, 3, and 4 partial skeletons preserve sufficient portions of their pelves to provide indications of their sexes. In addition, they retain skull and/or postcranial remains whose dimensions can be compared to those of other Neandertals for substantiation of their sex attributions. The other four adults preserve little or none of their pelves, so that they must be sexed strictly on the basis of size in relation to the Shanidar 1, 3, and 4 specimens and other Neandertals. Data for the Shanidar adults, the Amud 1 male and Tabūn C1 female Near Eastern Neandertals, and European Neandertal males and females are presented in Tables 4 and 5, which allow comparisons of their sexually diagnostic cranial, mandibular, and postcranial dimensions.

Shanidar 1

The pelvis of Shanidar 1 consists of largely intact and undistorted pubic bones (Figure 55), crushed and fragmentary portions of both ilia and ischia, and a slightly crushed sacrum (Figure 35; Chapters 7 and 9). The ilia and ischia were fragmented *in situ* and were removed in sections following impregnation with preservative. It is impossible to disassemble the preserved sections and reconstruct them to their original shapes because the extreme fragmentation of portions of them and the friable nature of the bone preclude forming a series of joins without considerable new distortion. However, it is possible to reconstruct visually some portions of the ilia and ischia.

The left innominate retains a portion with the anterior and superior margins of the sciatic notch intact, but the posterior margin of the sciatic notch extending down to the posterior inferior iliac spine has been damaged and displaced. It appears from the portions preserved that the sciatic notch curved strongly inferiorly posterior to the middle of the sciatic notch. Although no reconstruction of the preauricular area can be fully substantiated, the remains appear to be most compatible with a male morphology in this region.

The ischiopubic rami of Shanidar 1 are sufficiently preserved to indicate their total morphology. They subtend a very large subpubic angle (125°), which is hyperfemale (Olivier 1960). This, however, is a product of the pubic elongation that is characteristic of the Neandertals (Trinkaus 1976b). Despite this elongation, the ischiopubic rami are typically male in morphology. They lack the subpubic concavity characteristic of females (Phenice 1969; Figure 55); the inferior margins of the rami are relatively flat without the anterolateral flaring characteristic of females, and the rami are thick in cross sections as are those of males but rarely females (Poulhés 1947). These features support the reconstruction of the sciatic notch in indicating a male pelvis.

The dimensions of the Shanidar 1 skull and limb bones also indicate that it was probably male. The Shanidar 1 cranial capacity, maximum cranial length, maximum cranial breadth, nasion–lambda arc, maximum frontal breadth, bifrontal breadth, and nasion–prosthion height are all above the known ranges of variation for European and Near Eastern Neandertal females and well within the known ranges of variation for Neandertal males (Table 4). Furthermore, several of the Shanidar 1 cranial dimensions are extremely close to those of the male Amud 1 specimen; only cranial capacity and maximum cranial length are appreciably larger for Amud 1. The right and left mandibular corpus heights, as measured at the mental foramina, are similarly comparable to those of male Neandertals and distinct from those of Neandertal females. In addition, the heights of the Shanidar 1 mastoid processes are in the middle of the European Neandertal male range of variation, slightly below that of Amud 1, but well above those of Tabūn C1 and European Neandertal females.

The dimensions of the Shanidar 1 limb bones provide further support for the interpretation that Shanidar 1 was male. The three long bone lengths available for Shanidar 1, those of the radius, femur, and tibia (Table 5), are at the top of the European Neandertal male ranges of variation, although they are slightly less than those of Amud 1. The talus and metatarsal 4 lengths are not as high relative to those of other Neandertal males, but they are still within Neandertal male ranges of variation and separate from those known for Neandertal females. The cubital articular dimensions of Shanidar 1 are less diagnostic but are still within Neandertal male ranges of variation.

TABLE 4
Sexual Differences in Skull Dimensions (mm)[a]

	Shan. 1	Shan. 2	Shan. 4	Shan. 5	Amud 1	Tabūn C1	European Neandertals[b]		
							Males	Females	Males & Females
Cranial capacity (cc)	1600	—	—	—	1740	1271	1550–1681(4)	1305–1350(2)	1305–1681(6)
Maximum cranial length (M-1)	207.2	—	—	—	215.0	(183.0)	193.0–209.0(5)	190.0–205.0(3)	190.0–209.0(8)
Maximum cranial breadth (M-8)	(154.0)	—	—	—	154.0	(141.0)	147.0–158.0(5)	139.0–146.0(3)	139.0–158.0(8)
Nasion–lambda arc	250.0	—	—	(255.0)	255.0	224.0	242.0–255.0(5)	221.0–231.0(3)	221.0–255.0(8)
Maximum frontal breadth (M-10)	128.0	—	—	(128.0)	124.0	121.5	121.0–127.0(5)	108.3–114.0(2)	108.3–127.0(7)
Bifrontal breadth (FMB)	(115.0)	(123.0)	(118.0)	115.8	114.0	107.0	110.0–119.0(5)	104.0–113.0(3)	104.0–119.0(11)
Nasion–prosthion height (M-48)	86.0	—	—	94.0	(89.0)	(79.0)	83.0–90.0(3)	78.5 (1)	78.5–90.0(4)
Mastoid height (MDH)	27.5 & 28.1	(32.0)	—	23.2	32.0	17.5	25.4–30.5(3)	18.5–24.2(3)	18.0–32.5(18)
Mandible corpus height at mental foramen (M-69[1])	35.8 & 36.9	34.8 & 34.5	(37.0)	—	34.0	27.5	33.5–38.0(2)	26.0–31.5(3)	26.0–38.0(19)

[a]For the Shanidar individuals, Amud 1, and Tabūn C1, the dimensions are provided (right and left where appropriate). For the European Neandertal samples, the range is provided with the sample size.

[b]Numbers in parentheses indicate sample size.

TABLE 5
Sexual Differences in Postcranial Dimensions (mm)[a]

	Shan. 1	Shan. 2	Shan. 3	Shan. 4	Shan. 5	Shan. 6	Shan. 8	Amud 1	Tabūn C1	European Neandertals[b]		
										Males	Females	Males & Females
Humerus total length (M-2)	—	—	(314.5)	(301.0)	—	(289.0)	—	—	284.5	306.0–333.0(3)	283.0(1)	283.0–333.0(7)
Humerus distal articular breadth (M-12a)	45.3	—	(47.0)	(45.0)	—	38.2	—	—	38.0	45.0–50.3(7)	38.9–45.7(6)	38.9–50.3(16)
Radius articular length (M-2)	(235.5)	—	—	(225.0)	(218.5)	(206.5)	—	(245.0)	211.5	223.0–233.0(3)	194.0–211.5(3)	194.0–233.0(7)
Radius head dorsoventral diameter (M-5(1))	23.2	—	25.0	22.1	—	20.0 & 19.0	18.2	—	19.6	22.4–24.8(5)	18.0–22.7(7)	18.0–24.8(14)
Femur bicondylar length (M-2)	(458.0)	—	—	(422.0)	(447.0)	(384.0)	—	(482.0)	410.0	423.5–458.0(5)	407.0(1)	407.0–458.0(6)
Femur head diameter (M-19)	—	—	—	49.2	47.5	—	—	(48.3)	43.0	52.0–54.3(5)	44.0–47.0(4)	44.0–54.3(9)
Tibia maximum length (M-1a)	(355.0)	337.5	—	—	(350.0–360.0)	(300.0)	—	(386.0)	319.0	331.0–370.0(4)	311.0(1)	311.0–370.0(5)
Talus length (M-1)	52.8	—	55.8	—	—	—	—	51.3	46.2	51.7–57.4(5)	45.9–48.8(3)	45.9–57.4(10)
Metatarsal 4 articular length (M-2)	(71.0)	—	—	—	—	65.4	64.0	—	65.1	71.5–75.6(4)	62.6–66.0(2)	62.6–75.6(6)

[a]For the Shanidar individuals, Amud 1, and Tabūn C1, the dimensions are provided (right and left where appropriate). For the European Neandertals, the range is provided with the sample size.

[b]Numbers in parentheses indicate sample size.

These data, taken together, should be sufficient to establish that Shanidar 1 is male.

Shanidar 3

The pelvic remains of Shanidar 3 are quite incomplete. They consist of nine identifiable pieces of the innominate bones (Figure 56) and two sections of the sacrum (Figure 36; Chapters 7 and 9). They are insufficient to reconstruct the overall shape of the pelvis, and even the preservation of the sciatic notches is not adequate to indicate their shapes. Yet the various pieces provide information on several sexually diagnostic regions.

The pubic bones of Shanidar 3 exhibit the same mediolateral elongation as Shanidar 1 and other Neandertals (Trinkaus, 1976d; Figure 56). This is reflected in, among other things, a subpubic angle of about 104° (reconstructed from a fragment with the left inferior symphyseal surface and the ischiopubic ramus), which is well within the modern female range of variation and separate from that of modern males (Oliver 1960). However, the ischiopubic ramus (Figure 56) exhibits neither the subpubic concavity nor the anterolateral flaring of the inferior margin seen in recent female pelves (Phenice 1969). In addition, the ischiopubic ramus of Shanidar 3 is robust, similar to those of Shanidar 1 and other Neandertal and recent human males.

The pelvic surface of the right ischium exhibits a moderately concave surface with a strongly medially projecting and large ischial spine. This configuration suggests a characteristically male morphology with the ischial spine encroaching upon the pelvic aperture. This arrangement is not strictly limited to male pelves, but it is found among males more than among females.

The right preauricular surface possesses a smooth surface with slight ligamentous roughening but without the pitting or sulcus usually associated with pregnancy in the female (Houghton 1974; Kelley 1979). Because Shanidar 3 reached advanced adulthood, it is assumed that Shanidar 3, if female, would have given birth at least once or twice. One would therefore expect to find some scarification of the preauricular surface if the remains were female; the absence of such scarification, although negative evidence, supports the diagnosis that Shanidar 3 is male.

Only one of the Shanidar 3 long bones, the right humerus, is sufficiently intact to provide a reasonable length estimate; its length is in the middle of the Neandertal male range and well above those of the two Neandertal females with intact humeri (Table 5). Furthermore, the Shanidar 3 talus length and humeral distal articular breadth are in the middles of the respective Neandertal male ranges of variation, and its radial head diameter is the largest known for a Neandertal.

These data, and in particular those from the pelvis, strongly support a conclusion that Shanidar 3 is male.

Shanidar 4

The innominate bones of Shanidar 4 were crushed *in situ* to such a degree that significant restoration is impossible. The remaining pieces of the ilium and ischium are held together by matrix and preservative, and all exhibit some distortion. Yet an inferior portion of the left ilium has been preserved with the sciatic notch intact. The Shanidar 4 sciatic notch is a tightly curved semicircle similar to those of males and quite distinct from the posteriorly more open notches of females.

The two measurements from the Shanidar 4 skull that provide an indication of its sex, the bifrontal breadth and mandibular corpus height, are both close to the upper limits of the Neandertal male ranges of variation, clearly separate from those of Neandertal females, and even above those of Shanidar 1 (Table 4). The Shanidar 4 postcranial dimensions are less diagnostic sexually because its humeral and femoral lengths and humeral, radial, and femoral articular dimensions are in the zones of overlap between Neandertal males and females (Table 5). Only the Shanidar 4 radial length is clearly more within the Neandertal male range of variation than within that of Neandertal females.

Even though the postcranial dimensions of Shanidar 4 are largely inconclusive as to its sex, the configuration of its inferior ilium and its large skull dimensions suggest that it should be considered male.

Shanidar 2

None of the Shanidar 2 pelvis has survived, so that any determination of its sex must be based on the sizes of those regions that are preserved, the cranium, mandible, and left lower leg.

The most sexually diagnostic feature of the Shanidar 2 cranium, the height of its mastoid process, clearly aligns it with male Neandertals. The Shanidar 2 mastoid height is greater than those of Shanidar 1 and all European Neandertal males and is matched only by those of Amud 1 and Krapina 38.14 (Table 4). In addition, Shanidar 2 has the largest bifrontal breadth measurement known for a Neandertal (this measurement may be slightly overestimated for Shanidar 2; Chapter 5), and the Shanidar 2 mandibular corpus heights are most similar to those of Neandertal males such as Amud 1, even though they are slightly less than those of Shanidar 1 and 4.

The Shanidar 2 tibial length (Table 5) is not exceptional for a male Neandertal and is below those of Shanidar 1 and Amud 1. Nonetheless, it is within the European Neandertal male range of variation and well above those of La Ferrassie 2 and Tabūn C1.

Although the tibial length of Shanidar 2 only suggests that Shanidar 2 was male, the dimensions of its skull, and particularly of its mastoid process, strongly support a diagnosis of male.

Shanidar 5

Only a few fragments of an iliac blade with none of the margins survive from the Shanidar 5 pelvis. Therefore, sex determination must be based on an assessment of the relative sizes of its cranium and limb bones.

The Shanidar 5 cranium is one of the largest known Neandertal crania. Its nasion–lambda arc is matched only by that of Amud 1, and it is greater than those of Shanidar 1 and all European Neandertals (Table 4). Its maximum frontal breadth is equaled only by that of Shanidar 1 and exceeds those known from Levantine and European Neandertals. Also, its nasion–prosthion height is well above those of all other known Neandertals. Only its bifrontal breadth, among overall cranial dimensions, is more modest, being only slightly above that of Shanidar 1 and exceeded by those of Shanidar 2 and 4 and Spy 2.

In contrast to its enormous overall cranial dimensions, the Shanidar 5 mastoid process is quite small. Its height is well below those of Shanidar 1 and 2 and Amud 1, slightly below the known range for European male Neandertals, and within the European Neandertal female range of variation (Table 4). This association of such a small mastoid process with so large a cranium is unusual.

The Shanidar 5 postcrania present a similar mixture of dimensions with regard to male and female Neandertals. Its radial length and femoral head diameter fall between the ranges of variation of Neandertal males (including Shanidar 1, 2, and 4) and Neandertal females. Yet, its femoral and tibial length estimates are in the middle of the European Neandertal male ranges of variation, close to those of Shanidar 1 and above those of Shanidar 4 and 2, respectively (Table 5).

Even though the height of the Shanidar 5 mastoid process and the dimensions of its radius and femoral head may cast some doubt on a sexual diagnosis of male for Shanidar 5, the dimensions of its cranium and the lengths of its femora and tibia can only indicate a male. Shanidar 5 will therefore be considered a male.

Shanidar 6

The Shanidar 6 pelvis and cranium are each represented by small fragments, none of which provides significant information as to size or sexually diagnostic morphology. Therefore, a determination of its sex must depend upon its postcranial size relative to those of other Neandertals. Yet, Shanidar 6 is the only Shanidar specimen that provides a length estimate for all four limb segments, as well as several articular dimensions.

The Shanidar 6 femora and tibiae are the shortest of the currently known Neandertal lower limb bones, and its humeri and radii have lengths close to the lower limits of the European and Near Eastern Neandertal ranges of variation (Table 5). Similarly, its cubital articular dimensions are close to those of the

Neandertals with the smallest known distal humeri and proximal radii and clearly separate from those of known Neandertal males. Furthermore, for all the postcranial dimensions that are available for both Shanidar 6 and the contemporaneous Shanidar 4, Shanidar 6 is considerably smaller. These data therefore indicate that Shanidar 6 is female.

Shanidar 7

On the basis of comparisons of the Shanidar 7 deciduous dental dimensions to those of other Neandertals, Şenyürek (1957b, 1959) and Smith and Arensburg (1977) concluded that the Shanidar 7 remains are female. However, a comparison of the Shanidar 7 deciduous dental dimensions to those of a larger sample of Near Eastern and European Neandertals (Tables 91 and 92) shows that the Shanidar 7 dental dimensions, although relatively small, are not exceptionally so. Only the lengths of the di^2 and di_1 and the breadth of the dm^2 are noticeably below the values of most other Neandertals, and the dimensions of the dc^- are toward the upper end of the Neandertal ranges of variation. This suggests that the Shanidar 7 teeth fall in the size range where males and females overlap, a range that can easily include a third of the individuals in a recent human population (Black 1978). It therefore seems best to consider the Shanidar 7 partial skeleton as unsexable.

Shanidar 8

There are few bones preserved for Shanidar 8 that can provide an indication of its sex. Little remains of the skull, nothing has been preserved from the pelvis or dentition, and none of the long bones is sufficiently complete to permit an estimate of its length. Yet it is possible to compare its radial head diameter and fourth metatarsal length to those of other Neandertals (Table 5).

The Shanidar 8 radial head diameter is very close to the lower limit of the known Neandertal female range of variation and separate from those of Neandertal males. It is below those of Shanidar 1, 3, and 4 and even less than those of Shanidar 6. Similarly, the Shanidar 8 metatarsal 4 length is most similar to those of Neandertal females, including Shanidar 6 and Tabūn C1, and significantly less than those of Neandertal males, including Shanidar 1.

These two comparisons are reasonably definite in indicating that Shanidar 8 was female, even though they measure only a small part of the anatomy.

Shanidar 9

It is not possible to determine the sex of the Shanidar 9 infant's vertebrae. Infant vertebrae are not sexually dimorphic, especially when a reference sample of same age infants of known sexes is absent.

SUMMARY

The Shanidar Neandertal sample therefore consists of two infants (Shanidar 7 and 9), three young adults (Shanidar 2, 6, and 8), and four older adults (Shanidar 1, 3, 4, and 5). It is difficult to tell exactly how old each of the adults was at death, but it is possible to rank the Shanidar partial skeletons in terms of age. The best arrangement would be, in ascending order: 7 & 9; 2; 6 & 8; 1 & 4; 3 & 5. The age of Shanidar 8 is highly uncertain, so that its position in the ranking could be considerably different. It is unlikely that the rest of the arrangement would be significantly altered by additional information.

Among the Shanidar adults, three of the individuals appear, on the basis of pelvic evidence, to be male (Shanidar 1, 3, and 4). Two other individuals are probably male, largely on the basis of the large size of their skulls (Shanidar 2 and 5). Only two of the adults (Shanidar 6 and 8) appear to be female. This provides a sample with 71.4% males, which appears to be considerably greater than an expected frequency of 50.5% if there were equal numbers of males and females in the population. However, given a sample of only seven, this frequency of males is not significantly different from an expected P equal to 50.0% if the distribution were random ($P = 0.164$). It may therefore be assumed that there is not necessarily a systematic bias in the sexing of the Shanidar Neandertals.

The Shanidar fossil sample thus preserves males and females, infants, young adults, and old adults. However, it is clearly dominated, in numbers and degree of preservation, by elderly males. Even though there are other sites that have yielded the remains of adult Neandertals of similarly advanced ages at death (Boule 1911–1913; Heim 1976; Nemeskéri and Harsányi 1962), Shanidar is the only site that has provided the remains of several elderly male Neandertals. This should be kept in mind with respect to the evaluation of their morphologies since males tend to be larger and more robust than females among the Neandertals (Smith 1980; Trinkaus 1980), and many of the abnormalities present on the Shanidar specimens (Trinkaus and Zimmerman 1982; Chapter 12) are undoubtedly correlated with the advanced ages of these individuals.

CHAPTER 5

The Cranial
and Mandibular
Remains

The Shanidar Neandertal sample is noteworthy for the amount of cranial and mandibular material it preserves. Most of the cranium and virtually all of the mandible of Shanidar 1 remain. Shanidar 2 retains much of the maxillae and mandible and major portions of the orbital region and posterior cranial vault. Substantial portions of the Shanidar 4 skull exist, but it has been possible to reassemble only parts of its frontal bone, maxillae, and mandible. Shanidar 5 retains most of his maxillae, orbits, and frontal bone as well as most of the left parietal and temporal bones. Shanidar 6 preserves only a small piece of its left maxilla and zygomatic bone and right alveolus, and Shanidar 8 retains its left infraorbital foramen. Although only Shanidar 1 presents a largely complete skull, it is possible to obtain an accurate picture of the overall cranial morphology of three of the individuals—Shanidar 1, 2, and 5—as well as significant information from Shanidar 4.

The cranial and mandibular remains of each of the six individuals are described separately. The morphological patterns evident in the sample are discussed at the end of the descriptions. The morphometric data for all of the crania are listed in Tables 6–13, and the mandibular data are in Table 14.

SHANIDAR 1

Inventory

CRANIUM

The Shanidar 1 cranium is largely complete, although portions of it have been damaged. The various pieces were reassembled as close as possible to the original shape, and several portions of it were reconstructed with filler (see Table 6 for overall dimensions).

Os Occipitale   The squamous portion is largely complete. It sustained minor abrasion along the edges and loss of bone on the medial right lambdoid suture. Large sutural bones are present in the lambdoid suture and on the right side near asterion. The basal portion is intact, but it has been damaged and reconstructed in the regions of the left mastooccipital crest and occipitomastoid suture and of opisthion.

Os Sphenoidale   The body is represented only by small fragments of bone in filler, and most of the left greater wing is absent. The right greater wing is intact, as are the beginnings of the pterygoid plates. Little of the pterygoid plates remains.

Os Temporale: Right   The bone is largely complete. There has been some minor loss of bone along the squamous suture, loss of the styloid process, and some abrasion near the internal acoustic meatus.

Os Temporale: Left   Laterally it is a virtually complete bone, with minimal abrasion along the sutures. The medial portion of the petrous bone is absent.

Os Parietale: Right   Most of the bone is present, but the several fragments from which it is formed are joined in places by reconstruction. The outer table is present along the coronal suture and along the sagittal suture from bregma to about 10 mm above lambda. Bone is also preserved along the lateral lambdoid suture and all of the squamous suture, as well as in the region of the parietal tuber. Much of the inner table is absent because the bone separated postmortem along the diploë. Some distortion has resulted from the postmortem fragmentation of the parietal.

Os Parietale: Left   The bone consists of fragments joined to the neighboring bones along the sutures. The majority of the bone is lacking. It is present for about 30 mm along the coronal suture extending laterally from bregma, for about 28 mm along the sagittal suture extending posteriorly from bregma, and for about 20 mm along the lambdoid suture extending laterally from lambda. There are also several fragments at the anterior end of the squamous suture.

Os Frontale   The supraorbital region is virtually intact externally, and internally it lacks only portions of the orbital plates and the endocranial wall of the frontal sinus. The squamous portion is reconstructed from a number of pieces that provide a reasonable representation of the shape. The left orbit is pathologically deformed, and healed scars are present on the right frontal squamous.

Os Nasale: Left   The central portion is present with the nasomaxillary suture. The remaining portions of the left nasal bone and all of the right nasal bone have been reconstructed.

Maxilla: Right   The external surface is virtually intact, including the molar and premolar alveoli. The canine and incisor alveoli are fragmentary, and the internal surfaces of the nasal cavity and maxillary sinus are absent. Most of the palate is intact, but it reaches the midline only anteriorly.

Maxilla: Left   The bone consists of several pieces joined to neighboring bones and to each other. Most of the anterior maxillary surface has been reconstructed. The alveolar bone is present for its entire length, but the edges are damaged. The alveolar piece includes the subnasal region with the inferior nasal margin and the palate anterior to P^4. Also present are the frontal process with the superior third of the nasal margin and several pieces along the zygomaticomaxillary suture.

Os Zygomaticum: Right   Complete bone.

Os Zygomaticum: Left   The bone is complete, but the lateral aspect was flattened by an injury.

MANDIBLE

The mandible is virtually complete and undistorted. The only damage had been to the tips of the coronoid processes, the labial anterior alveoli, and 36 mm of the left inferior margin extending anteriorly from gonion (See table 14 for overall dimensions).

Morphology

The Shanidar 1 skull was discovered with the cranium appearing largely intact, although the left side of the neurocranium had been crushed by a rock, and the mandible apparently complete. This is in part an illusion because all of the bones were cracked *in situ* and were held in position by the surrounding matrix. Many of the more porous bones, such as those of the cranial vault, had separated and portions had turned into bone meal.

During his reconstruction of the Shanidar 1 skull, Stewart (1958, 1959) had the usual problems of reassembling pieces of a cranium that are incomplete and friable. By using the pieces that were still relatively solid, the reliable contacts between the pieces, and a reasonable amount of aligning pieces by eye, Stewart achieved a reconstruction that is undoubtedly close to the original shape.

The impression of completeness (Figures 9 and 10) comes from Stewart's decision to restore some of the missing portions with a commercial crack filler (Savogran). It has the advantage of giving great solidity to the specimen so that it can be handled easily. However, it is considerably harder than the bone itself and is not easily removed for alterations in the reconstruction.

The small amount of distortion present in the reconstruction is readily

Figure 9   The Shanidar 1 skull in (a) *norma facialis*, (b) *occipitalis*, and (c) *lateralis* right. The mandible has been articulated with the cranium by placing the right premolars and molars in centric occlusion. Scale in centimeters.

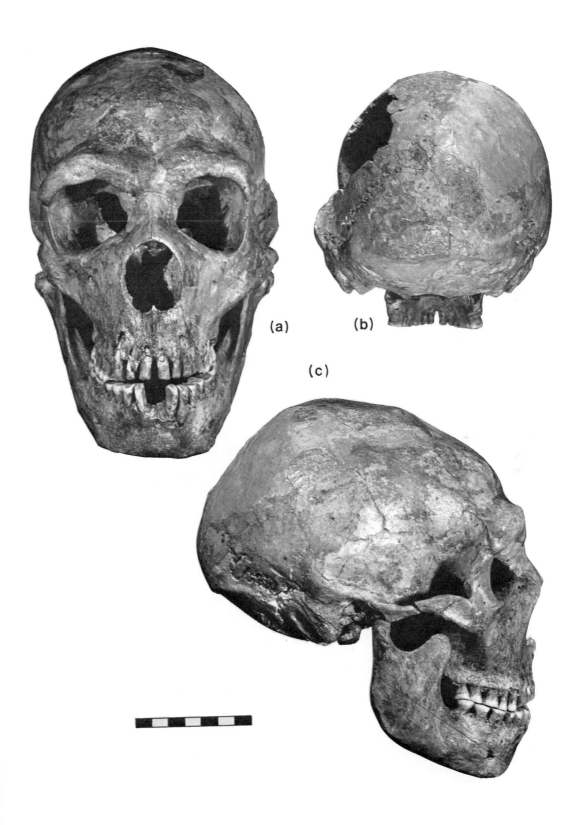

(a)

(b)

(c)

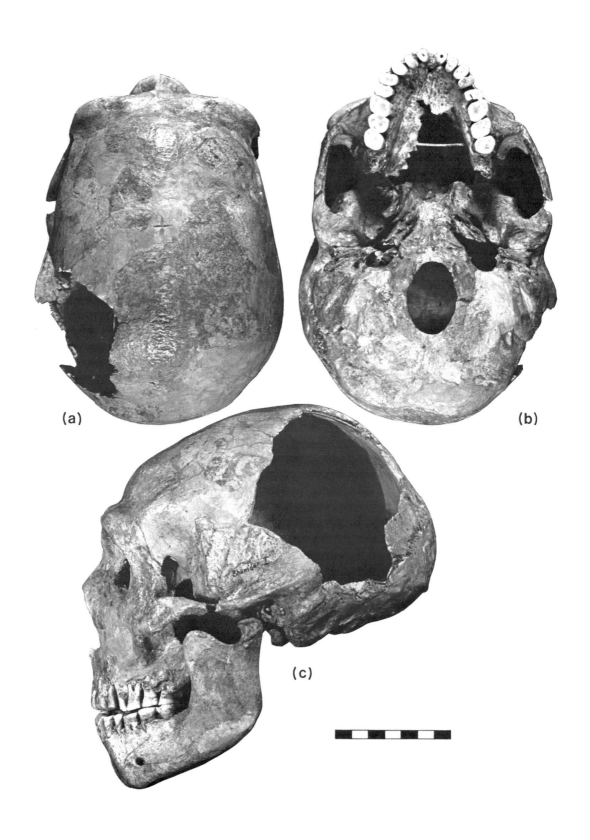

(a)

(b)

(c)

apparent, and affected measurements can be adjusted to compensate for any effect it might have. The facial skeleton is too far forward, as evidenced by small gaps of 2.5 and 7.5 mm, respectively, in the right and left zygomatic arches. The prosthion–basion length and the relevant cranial radii (Tables 7 and 10) have been adjusted accordingly (5.0 mm for midline measurements, 2.5 and 7.5 mm, respectively, for right and left side measurements. The left temporal bone is twisted slightly laterally, but it does not appear to alter any of the morphometrics. Additionally, there is a small amount of filler along the sagittal suture just above lambda, where there is a tenuous contact between the right parietal and the occipital. The reconstruction in this region may slightly lengthen the parietal (bregma–lambda) arc and chord and increase the degree of parietal curvature, but it is unlikely that the increase is more than 2 mm (and therefore less than 2.0% of the bregma–lambda length). However, there is a large sutural bone at lambda (maximum median sagittal length = 16.0 mm), which makes the location of lambda uncertain (Figures 9–11). The point at which the sagittal suture meets the sutural bone is clearly too high, and the midpoint of the suture along the inferior margin of the sutural bone would be too low. Therefore, the lines formed by the two halves of the lambdoid suture have been extended medially to the point where they meet on the midline, a point that is approximately in the middle of the sutural bone. This point has been used as lambda in all of the relevant measurements.

The overall impression of the Shanidar 1 skull (Figures 9 and 10) is one of a large skull with a number of features commonly considered to be characteristic of Neandertals (Boule 1921; Howells 1975; LeGros Clark 1964; Vandermeersch 1972). These features include the large rounded supraorbital torus, the long and low cranial vault, the prognathic midfacial skeleton, the elongated mandible lacking a chin, as well as a number of details of the facial sekelton and cranial base. Detailed consideration of the various anatomical regions of the Shanidar 1 skull show that although it is Neandertal in its total configuration, there are a number of aspects in which it is slightly different from the majority of the Neandertals.

THE CRANIAL VAULT

The overall shape of the Shanidar 1 cranial vault is similar to those of other Neandertals in being long and relatively narrow (Tables 6 and 7). Its cranial index (maximum cranial breadth/glabellooccipital length) of 74.3 falls in the middle of a European Neandertal range of variation (74.8 ± 3.1, N = 9). It is between those of Amud 1 (ca. 71.6) and Tabūn C1 (ca. 77.0) and well within recent human ranges of variation (range of means for 53 recent human samples: 68.8–90.8 [Weidenreich 1945]). The Shanidar 1 height–length index (ba-

---

Figure 10 The Shanidar 1 skull in (a) *norma verticalis*, (b) *basalis*, and (c) *lateralis* left. Scale in centimeters.

TABLE 6
Measurements of the Crania (mm)

	Shanidar 1	Shanidar 5
Maximum cranial length (M-1)	207.2	—
Nasion–occipital length (M-1d)	205.5	—
Glabella–lambda length (M-3)	193.5	(202.0)
Nasion–lambda length (M-3a)	194.0	(204.0)
Glabella–inion length (M-2)	198.0	—
Nasion–inion length (M-2a)	196.5	—
Height subtense over glabella–inion length (M-22a)	102.0	—
Height subtense over nasion–lambda length	63.5	(54.5)
Basion–nasion length (M-5)	116.4	—
Basion–bregma height (M-17)	135.0	—
Basion–lambda length	125.0	—
Prosthion–lambda length	231.0	(257.5)
Prosthion–inion length	207.0	—
Prosthion–bregma length	183.5	203.4
Prosthion–bregma subtense[a]	33.0	31.7
Prosthion–bregma fraction[a]	77.3	89.5
Maximum cranial breadth (M-8)	(154.0)r[c]	—
Maximum frontal breadth (M-10)	128.0	(128.0)r[c]
Bistephanic breadth (M-10b)	126.5	109.0
Bistephanic arc	160.0	138.0
Biauricular breadth (M-11)	134.2	(155.0)l[c]
Biasterionic breadth (M-12)	118.2	—
Anterior temporal breadth[b]	110.3	103.5
Nasion angle (basion–bregma) (NBA)	73°	—
Basion angle (nasion–bregma) (BBA)	52°	—
Bregma angle (nasion–basion) (BRA)	55°	—
Nasion angle (basion–prosthion) (NAA)	69°	—
Prosthion angle (basion–nasion) (M-72(5))	68°	—
Basion angle (nasion–prosthion) (BAA)	43°	—

[a]Subtense from the prosthion–bregma length to nasion, and the distance along the prosthion–bregma length from prosthion at which the subtense to nasion falls.

[b]The breadth between the right and left temporal lines, measured at the point of the minimum cranial breadth.

[c]Measurement estimated by doubling distance from right (r) or left (l) side to midline.

sion–bregma height/glabellooccipital length) equals 65.1, which matches the highest known value for a Neandertal (Amud 1: ca. 64.7; Tabūn C1: ca. 62.8; La Chapelle-aux-Saints 1: 61.5; Circeo 1: ca. 60.3; La Ferrassie 1: 65.1; Gibraltar 1: ca. 61.6). This vault height is further indicated by its calotte height index (maximum height over glabelloinion line/glabelloinion length) of 51.5, which is approached only by that of Amud 1 (51.0) and is above the range of a European Neandertal sample (40.2–47.8, 44.4 ± 2.3, N = 8). Yet both of these height indices for Shanidar 1 are near the lower ends of the ranges of variation of more recent human samples (Martin 1928; Morant 1930; Suzuki 1970; Vandermeersch 1981a). The Shanidar 1 cranial vault thus appears to be intermedi-

TABLE 7
Radii from the Transmeatal Axis (mm)

	Shanidar 1		Shanidar 5	
	Right	Left	Right	Left
Vertex radius (VRR)	127.0		—	
Nasion radius (NAR)	109.0		102.0	
Bregma radius	120.0		116.0	
Lambda radius	114.0		(133.0)	
Inion radius	91.5		—	
Temporal line radius[a]	86.0	—	—	—
Subspinal radius (SSR)	115.0		117.0	
Prosthion radius (PRR)	119.0		126.0	
Dacryon radius (DKR)	(94.5)	(93.3)	—	—
Zygoorbitale radius (ZOR)	85.3	—	84.5	84.5
Frontomalare radius (FMR)	82.5	—	78.6	85.3
Ectoconchion radius (EKR)	76.8	—	74.6	78.7
Zygomaxillare radius (ZMR)	71.7	(70.0)	80.5	—
Molar alveolus radius (AVR)	97.7	95.0	—	(102.0)
Canine alveolus radius[b]	110.0	110.0	—	(117.5)

[a]The perpendicular from the transmeatal axis (Howells 1973) to the highest point on each temporal line.
[b]The perpendicular from the transmeatal axis to the middle of each canine alveolus.

ate between most other Neandertals and recent humans in terms of cranial vault height.

The height of the Shanidar 1 cranium appears to be largely the product of an expansion of its parietal bones, an inference that is supported by a consideration of its median sagittal contour (Figure 11). The frontal appears to be quite flat, despite a slight bulge immediately posterior to the supratoral sulcus. The occipital bone appears to have a curvature similar to those of other Neandertal occipital bones, but the parietal arc is considerably more arched than those of other Neandertals.

The straightness of the frontal profile is illustrated by a frontal curvature index (chord/arc) of 93.5, which is above those of all other Neandertals (85.9–93.1, N = 11; Amud 1: 88.9; Tabūn C1: ca. 89.7; European Neandertals: 90.3 ± 2.2, N = 9; a lower index indicates a greater curvature for the bone). It is even above that of Shanidar 5 (91.5). This index is 90.4 for the Zuttiyeh 1 frontal bone. The Shanidar 1 index is even further removed from those of an Early Upper Paleolithic sample (86.3 ± 1.7, N = 13) and a Skhūl–Qafzeh sample (88.2 ± 1.6, N = 5). Additionally, its frontal angle (144°) is greater than those of the vast majority of recent humans (range of male means for 17 recent human samples: 124.3° ± 3.4° to 137.1° ± 4.0° [Howells 1973]) and all other Neandertals (131–143°, N = 11; Amud 1: 139°: Tabūn C1: ca. 131°; European Neandertals: 139.0° ± 2.3°, N = 9) except Shanidar 5 (147°); the angle increases as the degree of curvature decreases (Howells 1973); Zuttiyeh 1 has a frontal angle of 140°. An

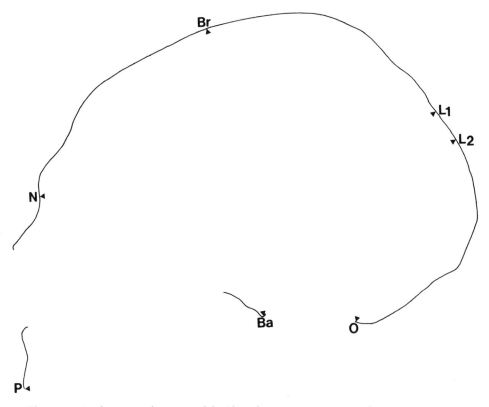

Figure 11   Median sagittal contour of the Shanidar 1 cranium. P = prosthion, N = nasion, Br = bregma, L_1 and L_2 = superior and inferior margins of the ossicle at lambda, O = opisthion, and Ba = basion.

Early Upper Paleolithic sample is indistinguishable from the recent human samples with respect to this angle (129.1° ± 4.5°, N = 17), whereas a Skhūl-Qafzeh sample has slightly higher angles (132.2° ± 1.6°, N = 4).

   The occipital contour of Shanidar 1, in contrast to the frontal arc, is fairly strongly curved. Its occipital curvature index (chord/arc) of 76.2 is small, but not unusually so, for a Neandertal (Amud 1: ca. 80.8; Tabūn C1: ca. 83.3; European Neandertals: 80.1 ± 4.7, N = 4). However, it is 2.81 standard deviations below the mean index of an Early Upper Paleolithic sample (82.1 ± 2.1, N = 12). Its occipital angle (113°) falls in the middle of the known Neandertal range (La Chapelle-aux-Saints 1: 108°; La Ferrassie 1: 118°; Gibraltar 1: 101°), which is below the mean for Early Upper Paleolithic hominids (116.2° ± 5.7°, N = 11) and towards the lower end of the range for recent humans (range of male means for 17 recent human samples: 113.9° ± 5.3° to 125.9° ± 5.8° [Howells 1973]).

   In contrast to the frontal bone, the Shanidar 1 parietal bones are markedly curved. The parietal curvature index (chord/arc) of 90.7 for Shanidar 1 is below

TABLE 8
Measurements of the Cranial Vaults (mm)

	Shanidar 1		Shanidar 5	
	Right	Left	Right	Left
Nasion–bregma chord (FRC, M-29)	111.3		118.0	
Nasion–bregma subtense (FRS)	17.7		17.0	
Nasion–bregma fraction (FRC)	49.3		71.0	
Nasion–bregma arc (M-26)	119.0		129.0	
Bregma–lambda chord (PAC, M-30)	118.8		(112.5)	
Bregma–lambda subtense (PAS)	25.4		(22.5)	
Bregma–lambda fraction (PAF)	63.8		(56.0)	
Bregma lambda arc (M-27)	131.0		(126.0)	
Bregma–asterion chord (BAC)	143.5	146.7	—	—
Lambda–opisthion chord (OCC, M-31)	101.3		—	
Lambda–opisthion subtense (OCS)	33.4		—	
Lambda–opisthion fraction (OCF)	45.4		—	
Lambda–opisthion arc (M-28)	133.0		—	
Lambda–inion chord (M-31(1))	68.4		—	
Lambda–inion arc (M-28(1))	75.0		—	
Inion–opisthion chord (M-31(2))	55.7		—	
Inion–opisthion arc (M-28(2))	58.0		—	
Lambda–asterion chord (M-30(3))	98.5	—	—	—
Lambda–asterion arc (M-27(3))	115.0	—	—	—
Frontal angle (FRA, M-32(5))	144°		147°	
Parietal angle (PAA)	134°		(136°)	
Occipital angle (OCA)	113°		—	

the lower limits of the Levantine and European Neandertal range of variation (91.7–94.5, N = 12; Amud 1: 93.3; European Neandertals: 93.4 ± 1.1, N = 11); only Shanidar 5, with an index of ca. 89.3, has a lower index. The Shanidar 1 index is nonetheless close to the means of an Early Upper Paleolithic sample (90.4 ± 1.1, N = 17) and a Skhūl-Qafzeh sample (91.2 ± 1.8, N = 4). And the parietal angle of Shanidar 1 (134°) falls well within recent human ranges of variation (range of male means for 17 recent human samples: 129.2° ± 2.7° to 136.1° ± 3.6° [Howells 1973]) and slightly below the means of an Early Upper Paleolithic sample (137.0° ± 3.5°, N = 19) and a Skhūl–Qafzeh sample (136.9° ± 3.6°, N = 4). It is considerably below those of Levantine and European Neandertals (140–152°, N = 10; Amud 1: 144°; European Neandertals: 144.8° ± 3.8°, N = 9), but it is approached by that of Shanidar 5 (ca. 136°).

These data indicate a characteristically Neandertal degree of curvature for the median sagittal occipital arc, a very flat frontal arc, and a highly curved parietal arc. This combination of a flat frontal and curved parietals is exceptional for a Neandertal, as well as for most more recent humans. This can be illustrated by the ratio of their frontal and parietal angles; this ratio, expressed as a percentage, ranges from 93.2 to 100.2 among European Neandertals (96.4 ±

2.6, N = 7), equals 96.0 on Amud 1, but is 107.5 for Shanidar 1. The Shanidar 1 value is 4.67 standard deviations from the overall Neandertal mean (including Amud 1). Early anatomically modern humans have ratios similar to those of most Neandertals (Skhūl–Qafzeh sample: 96.7 ± 2.7, N = 4; Early Upper Paleolithic sample: 93.8 ± 3.7, N = 16), and those of recent humans, although more variable, cluster around those of Upper Pleistocene hominids (Howells 1973).

Additional information on the Shanidar 1 cranial vault is provided by the relative proportions of the median sagittal arc that are formed by the frontal, parietal, and occipital bones. The frontal arc of Shanidar 1 (119.0 mm) is only slightly below a European Neandertal mean (125.0 ± 8.4 mm, N = 9) and within the range of other Near Eastern archiac human frontal arcs (Amud 1: 135.0 mm; Tabūn C1: ca. 107.0 mm; Zuttiyeh 1: 125.0 mm). However, its parietal and occipital arcs (131.0 and 133.0 mm, respectively) are greater than those of European Neandertals (114.4 ± 5.3 mm, N = 10 and 114.7 ± 5.0 mm, N = 4, respectively) and Near Eastern Neandertals (Amud 1: 120.0 and 130.0 mm, respectively; Tabūn C1: ca. 108.0 mm for the occipital arc). As a result, the frontal arc of Shanidar 1 makes up only 31.1% of the sagittal arc, whereas its parietal arc is 34.2% of the total arc, and its occipital arc is 34.7% of the total arc. By comparison, the frontal arc is usually the longest among European Neandertals (35.5 ± 1.3%, N = 4), and the parietal and occipital arcs are shorter and usually subequal (32.1 ± 1.6%, N = 4 and 32.4 ± 1.4%, N = 4, respectively). These three percentages are 35.1, 31.2, and 33.8%, respectively, for Amud 1, which are closer to those of the European Neandertals than to those of Shanidar 1. In a sample of Early Upper Paleolithic crania, it is the frontal and parietal arcs that are subequal (34.1 ± 1.0%, N = 15 and 34.9 ± 1.8%, N = 15, respectively), whereas the occipital arc is slightly shorter on the average (31.0 ± 1.1%, N = 15).

The relative shortness of the Shanidar 1 frontal arc is more dramatically illustrated by the index from the ratio of its frontal arc to its parietal arc. This index is only 90.8 for Shanidar 1, which is 1.97 standard deviations from the mean of a European Neandertal sample (111.5 ± 10.5, N = 7) and is approached only by that of Spy 1 (95.0); Amud 1 has an index of 112.5. Yet this index for Shanidar 1 is within the ranges of variation of a Skhūl–Qafzeh sample (96.6 ± 8.8, N = 4) and an Early Upper Paleolithic sample (99.9 ± 8.6, N = 18).

It should be kept in mind that there is considerable variation within all samples as to the relative lengths of the frontal and parietal arcs, and that Shanidar 1, although extreme, is not outside the expected ranges of variation of any Neandertal or more recent human sample. In addition, the significance of this variation in the position of the coronal suture is uncertain. It is the product of the relative growth patterns of the frontal and parietal bones (Hoyte 1966; Young 1959), which are related to the rate and timing of cerebral growth patterns (Trinkaus and LeMay 1982). There is a gross correlation between the position of the coronal suture and the central cerebral sulcus (Horsley 1892; LeMay, personal communication, 1981), but it is not sufficient to predict the relative sizes of the frontal and parietal lobes from the position of the coronal suture. Furthermore, there is relatively little variation in the size of the frontal lobe relative to that of the whole cerebrum (Kochetkova 1978), so that it would be difficult to draw any inferences about cerebral lobe proportions from variations in the frontal arc/parietal arc index.

It has been possible to obtain measurements of the vault thickness at the frontal and parietal tubers only on the right side (Table 9). Both of the thickness measurements for Shanidar 1 (frontal: 8.5 mm; parietal: 8.0 mm) are above the means for these measurements in a sample of European Neandertals (frontal: 6.9 ± 1.0 mm, N = 10; parietal: 7.6 ± 1.1 mm, N = 27). These measurements of thickness, however, are similar to those of Amud 1 (9.0 and 8.0 mm, respectively) but above those of Tabūn C1 (5.0 mm) and Zuttiyeh 1 (6.0 mm) for the frontal bone. Yet if the Shanidar 1 thickness measurements are compared to those of four male specimens (Amud 1, La Chapelle-aux-Saints 1, La Ferrassie 1, and Neandertal 1), whose frontal and parietal thicknesses are 8.3 ± 0.5 mm and 8.5 ± 1.4 mm, respectively, the Shanidar 1 values appear close to what would be expected for a male Neandertal.

THE OCCIPITOMASTOID REGION

The occipitomastoid morphology of Pleistocene hominids has recently been investigated in detail by Hublin (1978a, 1978b) and Santa Luca (1978). In these works they have shown that, although the occipital and posterior temporal bones of the Neandertals exhibit many of the features seen in other members of the genus *Homo,* there is a morphological configuration that appears to be distinctive of the Neandertals and their immediate predecessors. Because most of the Shanidar 1 occipitomastoid region is well preserved on both sides, it is possible to evaluate the morphology of this region in relation to those of other Neandertals.

The lambdoid suture is preserved along most of its extent on the left side and for most of its lateral half on the right side. There is a large sutural bone (maximum height = 16.0 mm) located at lambda. The presence of such a large

TABLE 9
Thickness Measurements of the Cranial Vault Bones Measured at the Tubers (mm)

	Frontal thickness		Parietal thickness	
	Right	Left	Right	Left
Shanidar 1	8.5	—	8.0	—
Shanidar 2	—	—	8.2	—
Shanidar 4	9.0	8.8	8.1	
Shanidar 5	10.2	10.0	—	9.0

ossicle at lambda is not unusual in recent humans, occurring between 11.1 and 28.0% in eight recent human samples (Berry and Berry 1967), and it is known to occur in Neandertals (e.g., La Chapelle-aux-Saints 1 [Boule 1911–1913] and Circeo 1 [Sergi 1974]). In addition, there is a small sutural bone approximately 28.0 mm posteromedial from asterion on the right side (Figure 9).

The occipital plane of the Shanidar 1 occipital curves gently from lambda to inion (Figures 9 and 10). The slight posterior projection of the bone at lambda gives the impression of a moderate occipital bun, or *chignon*. It is not possible to determine conclusively whether a bun was present because the reconstruction of the parietal bones just above lambda distorts the contour slightly. However, it appears as though Shanidar 1 did possess an occipital bun, but it was a relatively small one. The posterior crania of Amud 1 and Tabūn C1 were also damaged, but it appears as though Amud 1, like Shanidar 1, possessed a weakly expressed bun, whereas Tabūn C1 appears to have lacked one. Among European Neandertals, 100% (N = 9) exhibit buns (Trinkaus and LeMay 1982). At any rate, the curvature of the occipital plane is variable among the Neandertals, as indicated by their lambda–inion chord/arc indices (Amud 1: 86.2; European Neandertals: 86.7 ± 5.2, N = 8). Shanidar 1, with an index of 91.2, has a relatively flat occipital plane, similar to those of La Ferrassie 1 (92.8) and Neandertal 1 (93.7).

Even though the Shanidar 1 occipital is exceptionally long, its occipital plane does not occupy a larger proportion of the median sagittal arc. The index of the lambda–inion arc to the lambda–opisthion arc is 56.4 for Shanidar 1, which is slightly below a European Neandertal mean of 62.5 (SD = 6.0, N = 4) and that of Amud 1 (66.9), but well within the Neandertal range of variation and close to that of Tabūn C1 (ca. 55.6). Yet the portion of the nasion–opisthion arc occupied by the inion–opisthion arc (the length of the nuchal plane) is 15.1% for Shanidar 1, which is slightly above the range of a small European Neandertal sample (9.8–14.4%, 12.0 ± 1.9%, N = 4) and that of Amud 1 (11.2%). Therefore, the nuchal plane of Shanidar 1 is relatively large, suggesting well-developed nuchal muscles.

The transverse occipital torus of Shanidar 1 is prominent from inion to about 10.0 mm posterior of asterion on both sides. In *norma basalis* (Figure 12) it can be seen to arc posteriorly to each side of inion without forming an external occipital protuberance at inion, thus resembling all other Neandertal and many recent human occipital bones (Fenner 1939; Hublin 1978a). The nuchal surface is slightly excavated just anterior to the transverse nuchal torus, where *M. trapezius* inserts, but most of the surface between the inferior nuchal lines and the superior nuchal lines (or transverse occipital torus), the attach-

Figure 12 The mastooccipital region of Shanidar 1. Lateral views of the mastoid regions of the (a) right and (b) left sides; (c) inferior view of the occipital and temporal bones. The left mastoccipital crest has been reconstructed in plaster, as have portions of the nuchal plane. Scale in centimeters.

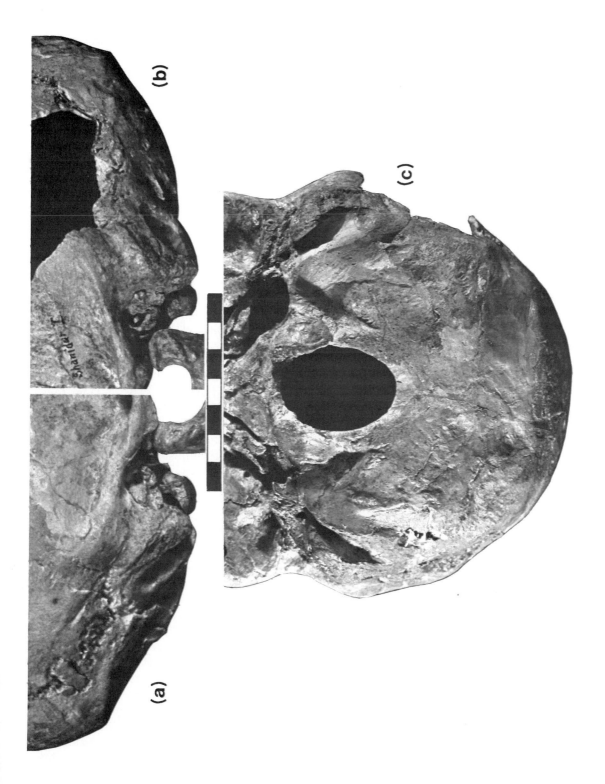

ment area of M. *semispinalis capitis*, is smooth and slightly concave. This configuration appears to be characteristic of the Neandertals (Hublin 1978a).

There is a large shallow suprainiac fossa (fossa supratoralis of Weidenreich [1940]) located above the central portion of the transverse occipital torus (Figure 9). It is approximately 20.0 mm high and between 40.0 and 50.0 mm wide and is bordered by the transverse occipital torus inferiorly and by a slight elevation of the external table superiorly and laterally. The floor of the fossa is slightly porous and rugose. Suprainiac fossae are found on all European Neandertals (N = 16), Amud 1, and all European Early Neandertals (N = 7), and Shanidar 1 conforms to the Neandertal pattern with respect to this feature. However, the Shanidar 1 suprainiac fossa is larger and less discretely separated from the adjacent surface bone than are those of most European Neandertals. Because suprainiac fossae are rare in samples of recent humans, Upper Paleolithic hominids, the Skhūl–Qafzeh hominids, and fossil hominids from Africa and eastern Asia (Hublin 1978a, Santa Luca 1978), its presence on Shanidar 1 aligns him most closely with the Early Neandertals and Neandertals.

The inferior nuchal lines and external occipital crest are only moderately marked on Shanidar 1. The inferior nuchal lines arise from the external occipital crest about 40% of the distance from opisthion to inion and lead, gently laterally and then anteriorly, into the well-formed occipitomastoid crests. Only the right occipitomastoid crest is preserved on Shanidar 1; it is a large, prominent crest that projects beyond the mastoid process (Figure 12). Its height, measured from the floor of the digastric sulcus, is 136.1% of the height of the mastoid process similarly measured (Table 12). And the occipitomastoid crest extends posteriorly beyond the mastoid process almost to asterion. The precise function of the occipitomastoid crest is uncertain, but it probably provides additional attachment area for M. *digastricus* and possibly M. *rectus capitis posterior major*. At any rate, a large occipitomastoid crest appears to be characteristic of the Neandertals as well as of other archaic *Homo sapiens* fossils (Hublin 1978b; Santa Luca 1978; Stewart 1961a; Weidenreich 1943). Although it is found on recent human crania, it is seldom developed to the extent seen on Shanidar 1 and other Neandertals (Stewart 1961a).

Both of the Shanidar 1 mastoid processes are well preserved. They are wide at the base and then taper distinctly towards their tips. This morphology is the result of the processes being formed by two confluent elements. The anterior part of each process, which descends vertically just posterior to the external auditory meatus, is the equivalent of the mastoid process in recent humans. The posterior portion of each process, which provides the large breadth to the base and extends it posteriorly towards asterion, is an expansion of the mastoid air cells.

This configuration of the mastoid process and retromastoid regions gives the impression that the processes themselves are small. In fact, the presence of a small mastoid process has been considered characteristic of the Neandertals (Boule 1921; LeGros Clark 1964; Vandermeersch 1972). However, the heights of the Shanidar 1 mastoid processes, measured from the Frankfurt plane (27.5 &

28.1 mm) are within the ranges of variation of recent human males (range of means for 17 recent human samples: 25.9 ± 2.4 to 30.9 ± 3.1 mm [Howells 1973]). The Shanidar 1 mastoid processes are shorter than that of Amud 1 (32.0 mm), but their heights are much greater than that of Tabūn C1 (17.5 mm). They are also above the mean of a European Neandertal (both sexes) sample (23.8 ± 3.6 mm, $N = 18$), but still well within the range of that sample (17.5–32.5 mm, $N = 18$).

The large size of the occipitomastoid crest among the Neandertals, including Shanidar 1, dwarfs the mastoid process. In addition, the mastoid notch appears to be relatively shallower than it is among recent humans. Thus, although the Shanidar 1 and other Neandertal mastoid processes are not particularly short when measured from the Frankfurt plane, their height measurements from the mastoid notch (Shanidar 1: 8.3 & 9.3 mm; European Neandertals: 3.0–10.4 mm, 6.6 ± 2.2 mm, $N = 15$) are somewhat less than a recent human mean of 12.6 mm provided by Vallois (1969).

The lateral surfaces of the Shanidar 1 mastoid processes exhibit well-developed mastoid crests, extending from just anterior of each asterion to the midanterior margins of the processes (Figure 12). These crests indicate strong insertions for each M. *sternocleidomastoideus*. There is a swelling on each mastoid crest, especially on the right side, which appears to be an anterior mastoid tubercle, one of the features that has been described as characteristic of the Neandertals by Hublin (1978a, 1978b) and Santa Luca (1978). If these swellings on the superoanterior surfaces of the Shanidar 1 mastoid processes are indeed anterior mastoid tubercles, they differ from those commonly seen on European Neandertal mastoid processes, where the anterior mastoid tubercle is largely separate from the mastoid crest.

Above the mastoid crests there are smooth supramastoid sulci, which are bordered superiorly by strongly developed supramastoid crests (Figure 12). The supramastoid crests extend posteriorly to about asterion, where they blend into the posterior temporal lines.

The occipitomastoid region of Shanidar 1 thus conforms generally to the configuration characteristic of other Neandertals, especially in the form of the transverse occipital torus, the development of the occipitomastoid crests, and the shape and size of the mastoid processes. It differs from other Neandertals in its weak development of an occipital bun, the large size and shallowness of the suprainiac fossa, and the merging of the anterior mastoid tubercles with the mastoid crests.

THE ANTERIOR TEMPORAL AND ZYGOMATIC BONES

The temporal bones of Shanidar 1 preserve most of both external acoustic meatuses along with their tympanic parts. The right bone is complete medially to the inferior lateral opening of the carotid canal, but the left bone is broken off medially at the medial end of the tympanic part. In addition, fragments of the medial ends of each petrous bone are preserved attached to the body of the sphenoid bone and the basilar part of the occipital bone. Neither styloid process remains, but the stylomastoid foramina are both evident. Unfortunately, both external acoustic meatuses are partially filled with exostoses so that their original morphologies have been obscured (Chapter 12).

Even though the auditory exostoses have altered the morphology of the external acoustic meatuses, including the lateral margins of the tympanic portions, they have not affected the basal surfaces of the temporal bones. The right tympanic portion is well preserved, and the left tympanic region sustained only minor damage.

The long axis of the right tympanic portion forms an angle of about 78° with the median sagittal cranial plane, being oriented anteromedial to posterolateral. Amud 1 has an angle of about 84° for this feature, and three European Neandertals—La Chapelle-aux-Saints 1 (82° & 82°), La Ferrassie 1 (74° & 76°) and La Quina 5 (84° & 84°)—have angles on either side of that of Shanidar 1. The orientation of the Shanidar 1 tympanic portion appears to be intermediate between the strictly transverse orientation seen in some Neandertals and the more oblique orientation of many recent humans.

The tympanic portions of Shanidar 1 exhibit prominent crests extending mediolaterally along the middle of the tympanic portion, especially on the right side where the region is well preserved. These crests have been referred to as *petrotympanic crests* by Vallois (1969), but they appear to be neither a continuation of nor homologous to the petrotympanic crest defined by Poirier and Charpy (1931). These crests will be referred to here merely as *tympanic crests*.

On the right temporal bone (the left side appears to have been similar prior to postmortem damage) there is a thick and moderately prominent tympanic crest, which extends laterally from the vaginal process of the styloid process, along the middle of the basal surface of the tympanic portion, to the middle of the inferior margin of the external acoustic meatus. Although this feature should probably be called a crest, it appears more as a distinct swelling or thickening of the tympanic bone, and it is probably homologous to the tympanic thickening seen in *H. erectus* (Rightmire 1979; Weidenreich 1943). In addition, there is a small crest, which extends laterally from the middle of the foramen for the styloid process and curves slightly posteriorly to abut against the anterior margin of the mastoid process. The presence of crests along the basal surface of the tympanic portion appears to be characteristic of the Neandertals (Guth 1963; Vallois 1969), even though there is considerable variation in the precise disposition of the crests.

Neandertal temporal bones are also characterized by a mediolateral broadening of the tympanic portion, which is reflected in greater distances between the stylomastoid foramen and the lateral margin of the tympanic portion (Schwalbe 1914; Vallois 1969). This distance is about 13.5 and 11.8 mm, respectively, for the right and left sides of Shanidar 1; these values are close to that of Amud 1 (13.2 mm) and the mean of 12.7 mm (SD = 2.2 mm, N = 5) of a small western European Neandertal sample (Vallois 1969). They are considerably above means of 7.0 mm (range = 5.0–9.0 mm) and 6.0 mm provided by Vallois (1969) and Schwalbe (1914) for small samples of Europeans. However, a recent Amerindian sample provided higher values (10.9 ± 1.7 mm, N = 27), so that the Shanidar 1 and other Neandertal tympanic breadths appear to fall merely at the upper limits of recent human ranges of variation.

The tympanic regions of the Shanidar 1 temporal bones are thus similar to those of other Neandertals, especially in the disposition of the tympanic crests.

The mandibular fossae of Shanidar 1 are relatively large and shallow. The left one has been slightly altered by degenerative joint disease, but the right fossa is apparently normal. Contrary to the pattern described for the Neandertals (e.g., Vandermeersch 1981a), the anterior tubercles on the Shanidar 1 zygomatic processes are large and prominent. They extend below the relatively flat anterior margins of the mandibular fossae, forming rugose projections below the zygomatic processes. Because the anterior tubercle provides attachment for the fibrous capsule of the temporomandibular joint and part of the lateral temporomandibular ligament, its prominence in Shanidar 1 suggests high levels of stress through the mandible.

The rugosity indicated by the anterior tubercles is extended anteriorly into the attachment for *M. masseter*. However, the masseteric attachment on the right side (the left side was altered following trauma) is only moderately marked, and it is not particularly long. The length of the *M. masseter* insertion is 35.0 mm, which falls in the middle of the means of three recent human samples of varying robusticity measured by Carlson and Van Gerven (1977) (43.1 ± 5.2 mm, N = 8; 33.8 ± 3.4 mm, N = 52; 31.8 ± 3.2 mm, N = 188.

The superior margin of the right zygomatic arch is only mildly marked by the temporal fascia. However, the posterolateral margin of the frontal process of the zygomatic bone exhibits a distinct crest descending from the frontozygomatic suture. This crest appears large as a result of the notch that forms between the frontal and temporal processes of the zygomatic bone (Figure 9). It is an anteroinferior extension of the temporal crest that is present along the anterior 45.0 mm of the temporal line. It is therefore an indication of a strong origin for the anterior portion of *M. temporalis* and the temporal fascia.

The remainder of the temporal line across the frontal bone and the right parietal to where it meets the supramastoid crest is low and weakly marked. The inferior and superior temporal lines are distinct across most of the parietal, but neither is salient. And stephanion is almost at the level of the maximum frontal breadth, so that the bistephanic breadth is 98.8% of the maximum frontal breadth. Thus only the anterior portion of *M. temporalis* appears to have formed distinctive markings on the Shanidar 1 cranium.

THE UPPER FACIAL SKELETON

The upper facial skeleton of Shanidar 1 is virtually complete on the right side. Only the right nasal bones, orbital walls, and anterior alveoli have been damaged. The left side is less complete. A major portion of the middle of the left maxilla has been restored with filler, and most of its alveoli are abraded. Furthermore, the lateral margin of the left supraorbital torus and the left zygomatic bone sustained trauma, which healed over, remodeling the left orbit and zygomatic bone in the process (Chapter 12). It appears as though the right side of the face and most of the left maxilla were not affected by the injury to the left orbit. Therefore, most of the observations will refer to the normal right side. It is assumed that the left side, if it had not been injured, would be close to a mirror image of the right side.

The supraorbital torus of Shanidar 1 consists of two even arches, which form rounded superior margins for the orbits. The right torus is divided into three elements, as defined by the morphology of the superior orbital margin (Figure 9). The medial section runs from just above the frontolacrimal suture to the supraorbital notch, and it is slightly concave inferiorly. The middle section extends from the supraorbital notch to a suggestion of a notch about two-thirds of the way laterally across the orbit, and it is slightly convex inferiorly. The lateral portion extends evenly across the lateral third of the torus to the fronto-zygomatic suture. This morphology of the supraorbital region is very similar to that of the original Neandertal specimen (Schwalbe, 1901) and a number of other Neandertal crania.

Despite the partial separation of regions of the Shanidar 1 supraorbital torus, it conforms to the classic definition of a supraorbital torus (Cunningham 1908). The superciliary arch has expanded so that it has obscured any trace of the supraorbital margin or rim. Laterally, the trigonum supraorbitale is absent, and the region above the frontozygomatic suture, where it would have been, is occupied by an extension of the swelling of the superciliary arch. There is no evidence or even suggestion of the lateral torus thinning seen in some European late Neandertals (Lévêque and Vandermeersch 1981; Smith and Ranyard 1980; Wolpoff et al. 1981).

As a result of the morphology of the orbital margin, the torus thickens slightly over the middle of the orbit and then tapers to the frontozygomatic suture. The thickness of the supraorbital torus, measured in the middle of the orbit, is 14.8 mm. This measure is similar to those of Amud 1 (15.0 mm) and Zuttiyeh 1 (15.7 & 14.8 mm) and near the top of a European Neandertal range of variation (9.3–15.5 mm, 12.0 ± 2.0 mm, N = 18). It implies a heavy brow for Shanidar 1 relative to those of most Neandertals.

The supratoral sulcus above the orbits is readily apparent as a short horizontal surface extending posteriorly from the anterior margin of the torus. It does not slope inferiorly before rising onto the frontal squamous. The depth of the supratoral sulcus is greatest over the lateral half of the torus and decreases to a minimum at supraglabellare. This decrease in the supratoral sulcus above glabella and an apparent flattening of the supraorbital torus at glabella is not due to a decrease in the size of the torus at the midline. As can be seen in *norma verticalis* (Figure 10), glabella remains largely within, if not slightly anterior to, the coronal plane defined by the supraorbital torus. The flattening is caused by

TABLE 10
Measurements of the Upper Facial Skeletons (mm)

	Shanidar 1		Shanidar 2		Shanidar 4		Shanidar 5	
	Right	Left	Right	Left	Right	Left	Right	Left
Basion–prosthion length (M-40)	117.1	—	—		—	—	—	—
Nasion–prosthion height (M-48)	86.0	—	—		—	—	—	94.0
Bijugal breadth (JUB, M-45[1])	(124.0)r	—	(123.0)r		—	—	—	132.5
Bimaxillary breadth (ZMB)	104.0	—	(115.0)r		—	(116.0)l	—	(120.0)l
Bimaxillary subtense (SSS)	40.0	—	(30.0)		—	(31.5)	—	(38.0)
Bifrontal breadth (FMB)	(115.0)r	—	(123.0)r		—	(118.0)l	—	115.8
Nasiofrontal subtense (NAS)	—	—	—		—	—	—	21.5
Bizygomatic breadth (ZYB, M-45)	140.0	—	(140.0)r		—	—	—	(160.0)l
Subnasal height[a]	(29.0)	—	—		—	—	—	(31.0)
Nasal height (NLH)	62.2	—	—		—	—	—	68.5
Nasal breadth (NLB, M-54)	30.2	—	—		—	—	—	(38.5)
Nasal aperture height[b]	(36.0)	—	—		—	—	—	41.0
Orbital height (OBH, M-52)	36.0	36.1	—	—	—	—	36.7	38.0
Orbital breadth (OBB)	47.9	p44.4	—	—	—	—	46.0	47.0
Biorbital breadth (EKB)	—		(118.0)r		—	—	—	116.0
Interorbital breadth (DKB, M-49a)	23.1		(36.6)l		—	—	—	(28.0)
Nasiodacryal subtense (NDS)	(10.0)		—		—	—	—	—
Simotic chord (WNB, M-57)	(16.3)		(16.0)l		—	—	—	15.8
Simotic subtense (SIS)	5.9		—		—	—	—	6.8
Inferior zygomatic length (IML)	32.0	—	40.4	—	—	—	—	—
Maximum zygomatic length (XML)	47.9	—	58.9	—	—	—	—	51.5
Zygomatic subtense (MLS)	9.1	—	16.0	—	—	—	—	9.5
Cheek height (WMH)	25.5	p28.0	26.5	—	—	(27.0)	32.5	—
Masseter attachment length[c]	35.0	—	35.5	—	—	—	—	—
Glabella projection (GLS)	4.3		—		—	—	—	5.0
Supraorbital torus thickness[d]	14.8	—	(15.0)	(14.0)	—	13.6	12.8	11.5
Zygomaxillary angle (SSA)	105°		(125°)		—	(123°)	—	(115°)
Nasiofrontal angle (NFA)	—		—		—	—	—	139°
Nasiodacryal angle (NDA)	(98°)		—		—	—	—	—
Simotic angle (SIA)	(108°)		—		—	—	—	99°

Note: p = specimen altered by pathology. Also, measurement estimated by doubling distance from right (r) or left (l) side to midline.

[a] Direct distance from prosthion to the anterior nasal spine.

[b] Direct distance from the anterior median sagittal margin of the nasal aperture on the nasal bones to the most inferior margin of the nasal aperture on the anterior maxillae.

[c] Maximum anteroposterior length of the tuberosity for the attachment of M. masseter on the temporal and zygomatic bones and, when present, on the maxillae. Measurement from Carlson and Van Gerven (1977).

[d] Superoinferior thickness of the supraorbital torus measured at the middle of the superior orbital margin perpendicular to the orbital plate.

the anterior position of the midline of the frontal squama above, and by the noticeable anterior projection of nasion and the whole of the nasal bridge below (Figures 11 and 12). As a result of the relatively forward positions of supraglabellare and nasion, the glabellar projection measurement for Shanidar 1, as measured from the chord between nasion and supraglabellare, is only 4.3 mm. This is within the ranges of variation of recent human males (range of means for 17 samples: 1.5 ± 0.8 to 5.6 ± 1.1 mm (Howells 1973)) and an Early Upper Paleolithic sample (4.8 ± 1.6 mm, N = 17); it is below the mean of a European Neandertal sample (6.8 ± 1.3 mm, N = 11) and those of Amud 1 (8.0 mm), Tabūn C1 (9.0 mm) and Zuttiyeh 1 (8.0 mm).

The anterior surfaces of the Shanidar 1 supraorbital torus show slight evidence of the "vermiculate" surface bone described by Tappen (1973). This surface texture is the product of rapidly growing fine cancellous bone during growth and development, which then becomes slowly remodeled during adulthood (Oyen et al. 1979). The advanced state of remodeling seen in the Shanidar 1 brows, which largely obscures the vermiculate pattern, is in aggreement with the advanced age at death attributed to this individual.

The frontal sinuses were exposed through the loss of most of the orbital plates and the endocranial surface of the sinuses. Stewart molded the anterior surface of the sinuses; a drawing of the resultant cast (Figure 13) shows the size and shape of the sinuses. As with other Neandertals (Heim 1978; Tillier 1974; Vlček 1967), the Shanidar 1 frontal sinuses fill most of the supraorbital torus near glabella, extend laterally to above the middle of the orbits, and do not extend up into the frontal squamous. Measurements of the sinus cast provide a maximum breadth of 74.0 mm and a height of about 28.0 mm (the inferior extent of the sinuses is uncertain). These figures place Shanidar 1 well within European Neandertal ranges of variation (breadth: 52.0–91.0 mm, 66.0 ± 1.2 mm, N = 9; height: 25.0–42.0 mm, 32.9 ± 5.6 mm, N = 9). The Shanidar 1 frontal sinus is similar in size to that of Amud 1 (breadth: 62.0 mm; height: 32.0 mm) and larger than that of Tabūn C1 (breadth: 52.1 mm; height: 24.2 mm). (Tillier [1974] provides a frontal sinus depth measurement of about 10.0 mm

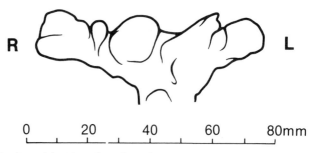

R   L

0   20   40   60   80mm

Figure 13 Outline of the Shanidar 1 frontal sinuses, drawn from a mold of the frontal sinuses by Stewart. Redrawn with permission from Stewart (1977).

for Shanidar 1; given the absence of the posterior wall of the sinus, such a measurement cannot be considered reliable.)

Neandertal orbits are typically described (e.g., Heim 1976) as rounded compared to those of recent humans, which are usually subrectangular. The Shanidar 1 right orbit (Figure 9) is slightly more rectangular than those of European Neandertals. Its medial border, which is partially restored, gives the impression of being rounded, but the inferior and lateral margins are quite straight. The superior border, however, is moderately curved. The orbit is noticeably higher laterally than medially, giving it a trapezoidal shape.

The dimensions of the Shanidar 1 right orbit place it in the middle of the Neandertal range of variation with regard to absolute size and proportions. The product of its orbital height and breadth (1724 mm^2) is virtually the same as the mean of a variable European Neandertal sample (1727 ± 152 mm^2, N = 5) and above those of Amud 1 (1570 mm^2), Tabūn C1 (1386 mm^2) and Zuttiyeh 1 (ca. 1628 mm^2). Its orbital index (height/breadth) of 75.2 is moderately below those of Amud 1 (80.9), Tabūn C1 (78.6) and Zuttiyeh 1 (ca. 84.1), and a European Neandertal mean (84.5 ± 7.6, N = 5). The combination of a relatively large orbital breadth and a small orbital height on Shanidar 1 is responsible for its low orbital index; the Shanidar 1 orbital breadth (47.9 mm) is above those of Amud 1 (43.0 mm), Tabūn C1 (42.0 mm) and Zuttiyeh 1 (44.0 mm), and a European Neandertal mean (45.5 ± 4.1 mm, N = 5), whereas its orbital height (36.0 mm) is similar to those of Amud 1 (36.0 & 38.0 mm) and Zuttiyeh 1 (ca. 37.0 mm), above that of Tabūn C1 (33.0 mm), and slightly below a European Neandertal mean (38.1 ± 0.8 mm, N = 6).

The large orbital breadth of Shanidar 1 may also be responsible for its small interorbital breadth (ca. 23.1 mm). It is at the bottom of the known European Neandertal range of variation (23.0–32.0 mm, 29.0 ± 2.7 mm, N = 10) and below those of Amud 1 (≥31.5 mm), Tabūn C1 (32.0 mm), and Zuttiyeh 1 (28.0 mm). The Shanidar 1 interorbital breadth is nonetheless towards the top of recent human ranges of variation (range of male means for 17 recent human samples: 18.6 ± 1.8 to 24.4 ± 2.4 mm [Howells 1973]).

The nasal bones of Shanidar 1 are incomplete, but enough remains of the left nasal bone, the right side of the nasal aperture, and the inferior margin of the nasal aperture to reconstruct the missing portions reliably. The most striking aspect of the Shanidar 1 nose is the small size of its aperture in the context of a large face and projecting nasal region. Its nasal height is 72.3% of the nasion–prosthion height, which is in the middle of a limited Neandertal range of variation (Amud 1: ca. 73.0%; Tabūn C1: ca. 73.4%; European Neandertals: 72.7 ± 1.7%, N = 4). However, its nasal index (breadth/height) is only 48.6, which is more than three standard deviations below a European Neandertal mean (56.0 ± 2.0, N = 4) and well below those of Amud 1 (ca. 52.3) and Tabūn C1 (ca. 58.6).

Despite the small size of the Shanidar 1 nasal aperture, the volume of the nasal cavity is large. The nasal floor descends sharply within the inferior nasal margin, and the sides of nasal cavity appear to have sloped away laterally from the sides of the aperture. It is impossible to determine how much of the space within the maxillae was occupied by the nasal cavity and how much by the maxillary sinuses because little of the internal nasal skeleton remains. But the combined space was voluminous.

All of the Shanidar 1 nasal region and maxillary alveoli project markedly anteriorly (Figures 9 and 10). At the same time, the zygomatic bones remain relatively posterior, in the same coronal plane as the lateral margins of the orbits. This gives the Shanidar 1 face the pronounced midfacial prognathism and retreating zygomatic profile characteristic of the Neandertals (Brose and Wolpoff 1971; Howells 1975; Stringer 1974a, 1974b). In Shanidar 1, this morphology is reflected in several ways.

The nasal bones project for a considerable distance from nasion, almost horizontally relative to the coronal plane of the nasal aperture. The roots of the zygomatic processes on both sides of the maxilla are at the level of the M^2–M^3 interdental septum, as they are on the La Chapelle-aux-Saints 1 and La Ferrassie 1 crania, rather than anterior to M^2 as in most recent humans (Europeans: P^4–M^1: 3.6%; M^1: 47.3%; M^1–M^2: 45.5%, M^2: 3.6%; N = 55; Amerindians: P^4–M^1: 1.5%; M^1: 56.7%; M^1–M^2: 40.3%; M^2: 1.5%, N = 67). In addition, the alveoli extend 14.8 mm posterior from the distal margins of the third molars. Among recent humans, in contrast, the alveoli usually extend only slightly behind the distal margins of the third molars (Europeans: 7.3 ± 1.5 mm, N = 102 [Twiesselmann and Brabant 1967]; Australians: mean: 8.9 mm, range: 4.0–15.0 mm, N = 135 [Campbell 1925]). This elongation of the alveoli can also be shown by the ratio of the alveolar length to the dental arcade length; it is 128.5 in Shanidar 1, as compared to 112.2 for an index of the means for a recent human sample (alveolar length = 54.3 ± 1.9 mm; dental arcade length = 48.4 ± 1.9 mm; N = 107 [Twiesselmann and Brabant 1967]). The only other Neandertal that provides both measurements, La Ferrassie 1, has an index of 124.0. These figures show that the dentition of Shanidar 1 is positioned anteriorly.

The midfacial prognathism of Shanidar 1 can be further illustrated metrically in two ways, by its zygomaxillary angle and by a comparison of its zygomaxillare and molar alveolus radii. The zygomaxillary angle (the angle at subspinale formed by the right and left lines from subspinale to each zygomaxillare anterior), which measures the projection of the lower maxillae in front of the zygomatic bones, is 105° for Shanidar 1. This value is significantly lower, indicating more facial projection, than those of recent human males (range of male means for 17 samples: 120.3° ± 6.6° to 138.9° ± 4.7° [Howells 1973]), Early Upper Paleolithic hominids (127.3° ± 8.8°, N = 6), and a small Skhūl–Qafzeh sample (ca. 124°–133°, N = 3). It is even slightly below those of most other Neandertals (Amud 1: ca. 115°; La Chapelle-aux-Saints 1: 105°; Circeo 1: 114°; La Ferrassie 1: 109°; Gibraltar 1: 114°). (The 8–10-year-old Teshik-Tash 1 cranium has a zygomaxillary angle of 113°, which Alexeev [1981] estimates would have become about 111° if the individual had reached adulthood.)

The difference between the Shanidar 1 right zygomaxillare and molar alveolus radii equals 26.0 mm, which is slightly above a European Neandertal mean (22.1 ± 3.0 mm, N = 4; La Chapelle-aux-Saints 1: ca. 21.0 mm; Circeo 1: ca. 21.0 mm; La Ferrassie 1: 26.5 mm; Gibraltar 1: 20.0 mm), and is equaled only by that of La Ferrassie 1. It is well above that of Amud 1 (ca. 17.0 mm). Moreover, it is completely outside the range of variation for recent human male means (range of means for 17 samples: 4.6–11.6 mm [Howells 1975]) and a small Early Upper Paleolithic sample (4.7 ± 3.2 mm, N = 7). A small Skhūl–Qafzeh sample is quite variable with respect to this measurement of midfacial prognathism (3.0–21.0 mm, N = 3). The higher values for the Shanidar 1 and other Neandertal zygomaxillare and molar alveolus radii differences are not due to larger overall size of the specimens; the zygomaxillare radii of Shanidar 1 (71.7 and ca. 70.0 mm) and other Neandertals (Amud 1: ca. 81.0 mm; European Neandertals: 75.8 ± 2.9 mm, N = 4) are similar to those of Early Upper Paleolithic hominids (81.6 ± 4.0 mm, N = 7) and recent human males (range of means for 17 samples: 66.6 ± 1.9 to 82.6 ± 3.2 mm [Howells 1973]). Thus, the Shanidar 1 midface is, along with those of most other Neandertals, highly prognathic.

Non-Neandertal archiac *H. sapiens* from Europe and Africa tend to be variable with respect to these two indicators of midfacial prognathism. The last interglacial Saccopastore 2 cranium and the Middle Pleistocene Arago 21 and Petralona 1 crania have zygomaxillary angles between those of most Neandertals, including Shanidar 1, and more recent humans (117°, ca. 114° and 121°, respectively); Petralona 1 has a very low molar alveolus–zygomaxillare radii difference (ca. 9.5 mm), whereas that of Saccopastore 2 (ca. 20.0 mm) is comparable to those of Neandertals. The Upper Pleistocene Irhoud 1 cranium shows little midfacial prognathism; its zygomaxillary angle (123°) and molar alveolus–zygomaxillare radii difference (16.0 mm) are largely distinct from those of Neandertals. However, the Broken Hill 1 specimen, which exhibits considerable lower facial prognathism, has values for these measurements (116° and 26.0 mm, respectively) closer to those of the Neandertals.

The anterior projection of the Shanidar 1 midface is associated with a retreating zygomatic profile. The anterolateral surface of the right zygomatic bone forms a continuation of the anterior maxillary surface without any angulation in the region of zygomaxillare anterior or the middle of the zygomatic bone. This is illustrated by a zygomatic curvature index (zygomatic subtense/ maximum zygomatic length) of 19.0 for Shanidar 1. This index is at the bottom of recent human ranges of variation (range of male means for 30 samples: 19.6 ± 2.6 to 23.2 ± 2.2 [Howells, personal communication, 1982]). It is also in the middle of a Neandertal–Early Neandertal range (Amud 1: ca. 18.2; La Chapelle-aux-Saints 1: 15.3; Circeo 1: 21.1; La Ferrassie 1: 18.6; Saccopastore 2: 21.0), and below those of early anatomically modern humans (Cro-Magnon 1: 21.0; Mladeč 1: 22.0; Předmostí 3: 21.9; Skhūl 5: 22.8). This retreating profile combines with the midfacial prognathism of Shanidar 1 to give the impression of a highly projecting nasal and alveolar region.

In *norma facialis*, Shanidar 1 appears to lack the highly inflated maxillae considered typical of the Neandertals (Coon 1962; LeGros Clark 1964). The anterior surfaces of the maxillae are slightly concave but do not exhibit canine fossae. In addition, the lateral margins of the maxillae are concave laterally between the zygomatic bones and the alveoli, suggesting the morphology described by Sergi (1947) and Heim (1978) as present among Early Neandertals but absent from the Neandertals. It is possible that this morphology may be due to the relatively narrow palate of Shanidar 1, as suggested by a comparison of its external palate breadth of 71.5 mm with those of Shanidar 2 (ca. 78.5 mm) and Shanidar 5 (ca. 78.0 mm). However, its external palate breadth is not especially small for a Neandertal (see below) and is 51.1% of its bizygomatic breadth. This percentage of the bizygomatic breadth is between those of Shanidar 2 (ca. 56.1%) and Shanidar 5 (ca. 48.8%) and in the middle of the Neandertal range of variation (Amud 1: 51.4%; Tabūn C1: ca. 53.8%; European Neandertals: $49.3 \pm 1.1\%$, $N = 4$). It is also insignificantly above the range of male means for recent humans (range of means for 17 samples: 47.1–50.3% [Howells 1973]). Therefore, despite the similarity of the Shanidar 1 midfacial skeleton to those of other Neandertals in terms of midfacial prognathism, it appears to have slightly less inflation of the maxillae, which cannot be explained as a product of relative palate breadth.

On the anterior surface of the right maxilla there are two separate infraorbital foramina. There is a large, readily apparent one, and slightly medial and superior to the large one is a smaller foramen (Table 11). Double foramina are relatively common in some, but not all, recent human groups (2.9–33.1% in 33 recent human samples; mean frequency = 15.8% (Berry and Berry, 1967; Riesenfeld 1956), and they are known to occur in other Neandertals (e.g., La Chapelle-aux-Saints 1).

The Shanidar 1 palate (Figure 26) is sufficiently complete to permit a consideration of its overall proportions. Most of the palatine process of the left maxilla is absent posterior to P^4, but a sufficient amount of the right side and the left alveoli survives to enable a reconstruction of the missing portions.

TABLE 11
Number, Presence of Bifurcation, Dimensions, and Position of Infraorbital Foramina (mm)

	Shanidar 1	Shanidar 4	Shanidar 5		Shanidar 6	Shanidar 8
	Right	Left	Right	Left	Left	Left
Number	2	2	2	1	1	1
Bifurcation	absent	absent ?	absent	present	present	absent
Foramen height	4.5, 1.6	4.0, 1.6	2.5, 2.7	6.1	2.2	4.8
Foramen breadth	2.6, 2.0	—, 2.8	2.4, 3.0	3.0	5.7	8.0
Foramen to orbital margin distance	13.7	10.9, 10.6	19.3	16.2	12.8	—

There has been considerable alveolar resorption in the molar region, largely as a result of the extensive dental occlusal wear; this may affect some of the measurements slightly.

The overall sagittal length of the dental arcade (prosthion to the M^3 distal surfaces) is 52.0 mm (Table 12), which is close to the mean of a small Neandertal sample (Amud 1: 53.0 mm; La Ferrassie 1: 50.0 mm; Gibraltar 1: 54.0 mm; Tabūn C1: 55.5 mm) and slightly above the mean of a recent human sample (48.4 ± 1.9 mm, N = 108 [Twiesselmann and Brabant 1967]). Similarly, its external palate breadths measured at the distal margins of the canines and first molars (45.2 & 64.3 mm, respectively) are close to the values for other Neandertals (Amud 1: 44.0 & 69.2 mm; La Ferrassie 1: 46.0 & 70.5 mm; Gibraltar 1: 43.5 & ?? mm; Tabūn C1: 48.0 & 67.0 mm). Its external palate breadth of 71.5 mm is also very similar to those of other Neandertals (Amud 1: 77.0 mm; Tabūn C1: ca. 69.3 mm; European Neandertals: 71.8 ± 3.6 mm, N = 4), most of which are above those of many but not all recent humans (range of male means for 17 recent human samples: 60.1 ± 3.2 to 68.9 ± 3.9 mm [Howells 1973]). Despite the similarity of palatal dimensions among the Neandertals, their palatal indices (external breadth/length) are quite variable (Amud 1: 145.2; La Ferrassie 1: 150.0; Gibraltar 1: 124.1; Tabūn C1: ca. 124.9), and Shanidar 1 falls in the middle of that range of variation (137.5).

The depth of the Shanidar 1 palate, measured at M^1, is about 15.0 mm; it may have been slightly greater prior to the alveolar resorption in the molar region. The only available measurements for other Neandertals are ca. 12.0 mm and ca. 15.5 mm for La Ferrassie 1 and Amud 1, respectively. These values are towards the top of, but well within, recent human ranges of variation because recent human sample means vary from 9.0 to 15.0 mm and individuals vary from 6.0 to 21.0 mm (Martin 1928).

The Shanidar 1 upper facial skeleton thus exhibits a number of Neandertal characteristics, which in turn serve to distinguish it from more recent human samples. It possesses a large, rounded supraorbital torus with a moderate supratoral sulcus, large orbits that are not quite as rounded as those of most other Neandertals, and a midfacial prognathism associated with a retreating zygomatic profile that projects the whole nasal region and the dental arcade anteriorly. Its facial skeleton appears to differ from European Neandertals only in its minimally inflated maxillae, which gives the maxillary walls a slight concavity. But the total morphological pattern has its closest affinities with the Neandertals.

THE ENDOCRANIAL CAST

During his study of the Shanidar 1 cranium, Stewart made an endocranial cast of the largely preserved right side (Stewart 1977:133). This was achieved by marking the midline on the endocranial surface, and then fitting a latex mold to the right endocranial surface through the opening in the left parietal.

TABLE 12
Measurements of the Palates and Cranial Bases (mm)

	Shanidar 1		Shanidar 2		Shanidar 5	
	Right	Left	Right	Left	Right	Left
External palate breadth (MAB, M-61)	71.5		(78.5)		(78.0)l	
Bicanine external breadth[a]	45.2		—		(52.0)l	
Bipremolar external breadth[b]	44.1		(59.0)		—	
Anterior bimolar external breadth[c]	64.3		(70.3)		—	
Posterior bimolar external breadth[d]	71.2		(78.0)		—	
Bicanine internal breadth[a]	29.5		(32.0)		—	
Bipremolar internal breadth[b]	33.5		(37.5)		—	
Anterior bimolar internal breadth[c]	38.9		(41.0)r		—	
Posterior bimolar internal breadth[d]	44.2		(51.0)r		(46.0)l	
Palate height (M-64)	15.0		—		—	
Dental arcade length[e]	52.0		(53.0)		(49.5)	
Alveolar length[f]	66.8		(64.0)		(66.0)	
Foramen magnum length (M-7)	41.9		(41.0)		—	
Foramen magnum breadth (M-16)	28.5		(27.0)r		—	
Mastoid height (MDH)	27.5	28.1	(32.0)	—	—	23.2
Mastoid width (MDB)	16.1	19.0	25.0	—	—	20.7
Digastric mastoid height[g]	8.3	(9.3)	10.6	—	—	8.0
Digastric crest height[h]	11.3	—	6.6	—	—	—
Acoustic meatal height[i]	7.4	8.3	—	—	—	10.8
Acoustic meatal breadth[j]	p(6.3)	p(7.0)	—	—	—	6.4
Temporal squamous height[k]	40.0	—	—	—	—	44.5
Temporal squamous arc[l]	(123.0)	—	—	—	—	128.0
Temporal line height[m]	79.0	78.5	—	—	—	—
Occipital condyle length	23.5	22.0	(25.0)	—	—	—
Occipital condyle breadth	11.0	13.0	(13.0)	—	—	—

Note: p = specimen altered by pathology. Also, measurement estimated by doubling distance from right (r) or left (l) side to midline.

[a]External and internal alveolar breadths measured at the distal margins of the canines.

[b]External and internal alveolar breadths measured at the distal margins of the first premolars.

[c]External and internal alveolar breadths measured at the distal margins of the first molars.

[d]External and internal alveolar breadths measured at the distal margins of the third molars.

[e]Direct distance in the median sagittal plane from prosthion to the line tangential to the distal margins of the third molars.

[f]Direct distance in the median sagittal plane from prosthion to the line tangential to the posterior margins of the maxillary alveolar bone.

[g]Height of the mastoid process measured from the deepest point in the digastric sulcus.

[h]Height of the mastooccipital crest measured from the deepest point in the digastric sulcus.

[i]Maximum dimension (usually superoinferior) of the external acoustic meatus.

[j]Maximum dimension of the external acoustic meatus measured perpendicular to the height.

[k]Direct distance from the Frankfurt plane to the highest point on the squamous suture of the temporal bone.

[l]The superior arc of the temporal bone along the squamous suture from the parietal incisure to the intersection of the infratemporal crest with the temporosphenoidal suture.

[m]Direct distance from the Frankfurt horizontal to the highest point on the temporal line.

He subsequently modeled in the portions of the right hemisphere that were incomplete due to loss of the internal tables of the vault bones or damage to the cranial base. Then, assuming bilateral symmetry of the endocranium, Stewart modeled the left hemisphere in plasticene as a mirror image of the right side.

This process produced an endocranial cast (Figure 14) that provides an accurate impression of the overall size and shape of the Shanidar 1 endocranial cavity. It does not, however, permit detailed morphological studies of the endocranial surfaces. Much of the internal surface bone was lost or damaged so that details of the surface texture, such as the meningeal vessel patterns, are absent. Because human and nonhuman primate brains are consistently asymmetrical (LeMay 1976, 1977), both in surface detail and relative proportions, patterns of asymmetry cannot be assessed from the essentially hemispheric endocranial cast of Shanidar 1.

Once Stewart had modeled a complete endocranial cast, he determined by water displacement that the endocranial volume of Shanidar 1 is about 1600 cc (1977:133). This value for Shanidar 1 is slightly below that of Amud 1 (1740 cc), well above that of Tabūn C1 (ca. 1271 cc), and slightly above a European Neandertal mean (1510 ± 150 cc, N = 6). However, it is identical to the mean of

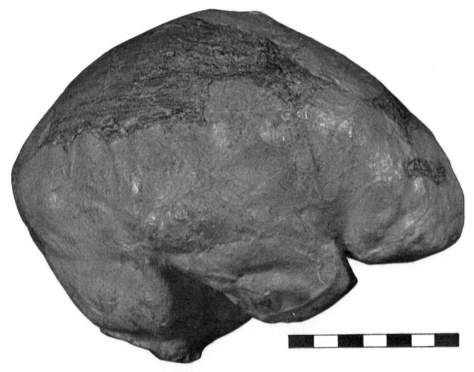

Figure 14   Right lateral view of the Shanidar 1 endocranial cast made by Stewart. The darkened areas indicate reconstruction necessitated by the absence of the internal table. Scale in centimeters.

TABLE 13
Measurements of the Shanidar 1 Endocranial Cast (mm)[a]

Frontooccipital length	(180.0)
Maximum breadth	(141.0)
Maximum frontal breadth	(131.0)
Height at mid-frontooccipital length	(119.0)
Lateral horizontal length	181.0
Insular vertical	72.0
Parietal vertical	93.0
Occipital vertical	25.0
Vertical occipital pole-protrusion	46.0
Parietal length	88.0

[a]Measurements from Ogawa et al. (1970).

the four male European Neandertal endocranial capacities (La Chapelle-aux-Saints 1, Circeo 1, La Ferrassie 1, and Spy 2: 1601 ± 62 cc, N = 4). All of these values are insignificantly different from the average cranial capacities known for Skhūl–Qafzeh hominids (1545 ± 27 cc, N = 5) and Early Upper Paleolithic hominids (1577 ± 135 cc, N = 11).

The relative size of the brain can be assessed by an index that compares the cube root of the cranial capacity to the bicondylar femoral length (as an indicator of body size). This index is about 2.55 for Shanidar 1, which is within the known Neandertal range of variation (Amud 1: ca. 2.50; La Chapelle-aux-Saints 1: ca. 2.73; La Ferrassie 1: ca. 2.60; Spy 2: 2.73; Tabūn C1: ca. 2.64). This index, although more variable, is on the average very similar in an Early Upper Paleolithic sample (2.60 ± 0.17, N = 10). A small sample of Skhūl–Qafzeh specimens has an average index of 2.35 ± 0.11 (N = 3), a result that is produced more by their long femora (490.8 ± 22.9 mm, N = 3, versus 440.7 ± 29.0 mm, N = 5 for the Neandertal sample) than by their cranial capacities (see previous discussion). Shanidar 1 therefore had a cranial capacity very much in keeping with its status as a later Pleistocene large male human.

The endocranial cast from Shanidar 1 was studied by Ogawa et al. (1970) in conjunction with their analysis of the Amud 1 endocranial cast. Their measurements of the Shanidar 1 endocranial cast are provided in Table 13.

The length of the Shanidar 1 endocranium (ca. 180.0 mm) is between that of Amud 1 (187.0 mm) and a European Neandertal mean (176.0 ± 5.9 mm, N = 7). Its maximum breadth (ca. 141.0 mm) is very close to both that of Amud 1 (ca. 140.0 mm) and a European Neandertal mean (140.3 ± 6.7 mm, N = 7). These dimensions produce a breadth/length index of ca. 78.3, which is above that of Amud 1 (ca. 74.9) but is minimally below a European Neandertal mean (79.7 ±

Figure 15 The Shanidar 1 mandible: (a) superior view; (b) inferior view; and (c) posterior view. Norma lateralis (d) right and (e) left. Norma medialis (f) right and (g) left. The lateral and medial views are in the planes of the premolar–molar regions and rami. Scale in centimeters.

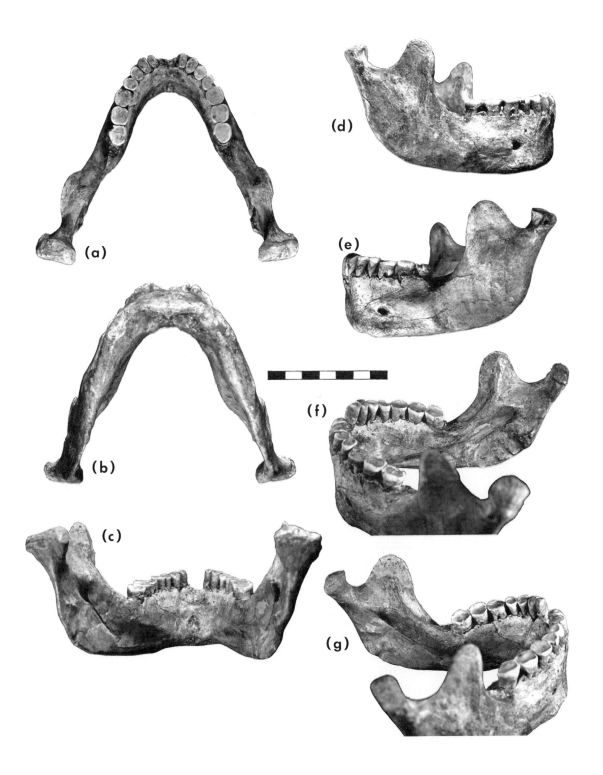

2.6, N = 7). The value for this index for Shanidar 1 and most other Neandertals is above the means of an Early Upper Paleolithic sample (74.1 ± 2.8, N = 9), but there is considerable overlap between the Neandertals and Upper Paleolithic hominids with regard to this index (Vlček 1969; Ogawa et al. 1970).

The endocranial cast of Shanidar 1 is relatively high in addition to being broad. Its index of parietal height over the lateral–horizontal (P) to the lateral–horizontal length (LH) is 51.4. This value is equal to that of Amud 1 and above those of La Chapelle-aux-Saints (47.2), Neandertal 1 (46.5), and La Quina 5 (46.5). The P/LH index tends to increase in more recent hominids, being 50.9 ± 1.7 (N = 5) in a small Early Upper Paleolithic sample. The relatively high values for Shanidar 1 and Amud 1 reflect the heights of their parietal regions.

These endocranial proportions for Shanidar 1 correspond closely to the cranial vault dimensions as measured on the exocranial surface. Both indicate relatively large and high parietal regions.

THE MANDIBLE

Shanidar 1 possesses one of the most complete Neandertal mandibles known (Figure 15; Table 14). The body is complete and undistorted except for minor damage to the alveoli and along the posterior inferior border of the left side. The rami lack only the tips of the coronoid processes, which have been restored with filler.

In conjunction with the relatively large size and prognathism of the Shanidar 1 cranium, its mandible is large, comparable in size to those of other large Neandertals. Its superior length (115.0 mm) is in the middle of a European Neandertal range (100.0–122.0 mm, 113.8 ± 8.2 mm, N = 6) and a Near Eastern Neandertal range (Amud 1: ca. 111.0 mm; Tabūn C1: 102.0 mm; Tabūn C2: 122.0 mm). Most of these Neandertal mandibular lengths, including that of Shanidar 1, are above the ranges of variation for two recent European samples (95.3 ± 2.3 mm, N = 107 [Twiesselmann and Brabant 1967]; 91.3 ± 5.5 mm, N = 50). Furthermore, they are largely above the known values for a European and Near Eastern early anatomically modern human sample (92.5–107.0 mm, 100.3 ± 6.2 mm, N = 7).

If these values for mandible length are normalized for overall body size using femoral bicondylar length, the resultant index for Shanidar 1 (ca. 25.1) is between those of Amud 1 (ca. 23.0) and Tabūn C1 (24.9) and those of La Chapelle-aux-Saints 1 (ca. 26.7) and La Ferrassie 1 (ca. 26.6). All of these values, except that of Amud 1, are above those for more recent humans (Caviglione 1: ca. 20.2; Dolní Věstonice 3: 22.1; Předmostí 3: 21.4; Qafzeh 9: ca. 22.8; Skhūl 4: 21.7; Skhūl 5: ca. 20.7; recent European sample: 21.0 ± 1.1, N = 50). Shanidar 1, along with most Neandertals, clearly had a long mandible, both absolutely and relative to body size.

The mandibular bicondylar maximum breadth of Shanidar 1 (142.8 mm) is toward the top of the Neandertal range (Amud 1: ca. 145.0 mm; Tabūn C1: ca.

TABLE 14
Measurements of the Mandibulae (mm)

	Shanidar 1		Shanidar 2		Shanidar 4	
	Right	Left	Right	Left	Right	Left
Dental arcade length[a]	51.0		(56.0)		(55.0)	
Superior length[b]	115.0		(112.0)		(111.0)	
Inferior length (M-68)	90.0		(96.0)		—	
Bicondylar maximum breadth (M-65)	142.8		(154.5)		(135.0)r	
Bicondylar articular breadth[c]	123.5		(138.5)		—	
Bicoronoid breadth (M-65[1])	(109.5)		(128.0)		(126.0)l	
Bigonial breadth (M-66)	104.4		—		—	
Bicanine external breadth[d]	37.0		(39.0)		(35.0)l	
Bicanine internal breadth[d]	27.4		(29.0)		(25.0)l	
Anterior bimolar external breadth[d]	66.3		(66.0)		(60.0)l	
Anterior bimolar internal breadth[d]	49.4		(48.5)		(39.0)l	
Posterior bimolar external breadth[d]	73.1		(76.0)		—	
Posterior bimolar internal breadth[d]	56.2		(60.5)		(58.0)l	
Symphyseal height (M-69)	37.2		(37.3)		(36.6)	
Symphyseal breadth	17.6		—		17.5	
Corpus height at foramen (M-69[1])	35.8	36.9	34.8	34.5	—	(37.0)
Corpus breadth at foramen (M-69[3])	17.5	17.6	(17.6)	17.8	—	17.4
Corpus height at canine[e]	35.0	35.3	—	34.3	—	(35.5)
Corpus breadth at canine[e]	18.7	18.2	—	(16.8)	—	16.5
Corpus height at molars (M-69[2])	34.5	35.5	34.4	—	—	—
Corpus breadth at molars	17.7	17.4	(19.2)	(18.8)	—	17.2
Ramus height (M-70)	59.4	—	63.0	64.5	—	—
Ramus breadth (M-71a)	41.7	40.2	44.0	43.7	(45.5)	—
Anterior symphyseal angle[f]	78°		—		(72°)	
Symphyseal angle[g]	65°		—		(60°)	
Gonial angle (M-79)	81°	80°	74°	69°	—	—
Mental foramen position	P_4–M_1	M_1	M_1,M_1	C_-,M_1	P_4–M_1	M_1
Mental foramen number	1	1	2	2	2	1
Digastric fossa depth[h]	10.4	9.9	—	—	—	11.1
Digastric fossa breadth[h]	18.2	16.3	—	—	—	16.5

[a]Direct distance in the median sagittal plane from infradentale to the line tangential to the distal margins of the third molars.

[b]Direct distance in the median sagittal plane from infradentale to the line across the middles of the mandibular condyles. Measurement from Twiesselmann and Brabant (1967).

[c]Distance between the midpoints of the mandibular condyles.

[d]See footnotes a–d in Table 12.

[e]Height and breadth of the corpus measured at the canine–first premolar interdental septum.

[f]The angle in the median sagittal plane between the occlusal plane and the anterior margin of the symphysis.

[g]The angle in the median sagittal plane between the occlusal plane and the midline of the symphyseal cross section.

[h]The anteroposterior (depth) and mediolateral (breadth) maximum dimensions of the insertion area for M. digastricus on the inferior surface of the mandibular corpus.

133.0 mm; Tabūn C2: 130.0 mm; European Neandertals: 136.0 ± 8.7 mm, N = 7). All of these breadth measurements are above those of a recent European sample (122.7 ± 2.6 mm, N = 106 [Twiesselmann and Brabant 1967]) and samples of recent Australians (112.4 ± 5.0 mm, N = 33) and Melanesians (112.1 ± 5.2 mm, N = 54 [Keiter 1934]). When the bicondylar maximum breadth is compared to the superior length to provide a mandibular index (length/breadth), Shanidar 1 has an index of 80.5. This index is between the mean of a variable European Neandertal sample (82.7 ± 6.1, N = 5), and the ratio of the means of a recent human sample (77.7 [Twiesselmann and Brabant 1967]). Other Neandertals from the Near East (Amud 1: ca. 76.6, Tabūn C1: ca. 76.7, Tabūn C2: 93.8) have variable indices.

The breadth of the Shanidar 1 mandible is evident as well in the dimensions of the dental arcade. Although the external alveolar breadth measured at the M_1 posterior alveolus is not particularly large (66.3 versus 63.1 ± 1.8 mm, N = 7 for a European Neandertal sample and 65.6, 62.5, and 60.5 mm, respectively, for Amud 1 and Tabūn C1 and C2), the length of its dental arcade (51.0 mm) is slightly less than the mean of a European Neandertal sample (53.6 ± 2.7 mm, N = 7), similar to that of Amud 1 (50.9 mm), and below those of Tabūn C1 and C2 (54.0 and 59.0 mm, respectively). This gives a length/breadth index of 76.9 for Shanidar 1, which is below those of Tabūn C1 and C2 (86.4 and 97.6, respectively) and a European Neandertal mean (84.5 ± 6.1, N = 6) but similar to that of Amud 1 (77.6). The apparent shortness of the Shanidar 1 mandibular dental arcade may be in part a product of the extensive interproximal wear on its molars (Figure 26). Because teeth migrate anteriorly as they wear (Hylander 1977; Wolpoff 1971a), the Shanidar 1 dental arcade may have been longer when the third molars first attained full occlusion.

The body of the Shanidar 1 mandible is similar to those of other Neandertals. Its corpus heights, measured at the mental foramina (35.8 & 36.9 mm), are slightly above that of Amud 1 (34.0 mm) and a European Neandertal mean (31.5 ± 3.7 mm, N = 19), but they are quite separate from the low Tabūn C1 mandibular height (27.5 mm) and the high Tabūn C2 mandibular height (42.5 mm). Moreover, its robusticity indices (breadth/height at the mental foramen; 48.9 & 47.7) are very close to a European Neandertal mean index (50.3 ± 5.4, N = 19) and in the middle of the large Levantine Neandertal range of variation (Amud 1: 44.1, Tabūn C1: 54.5, Tabūn C2: 38.6). Similarly, its symphyseal height (37.2 mm) is slightly above a European Neandertal mean (34.7 ± 3.9 mm, N = 14), similar to that of Amud 1 (37.0 mm), and between those of Tabūn C1 (30.3 mm) and Tabūn C2 (42.0 mm). Its symphyseal robusticity index (47.3) is marginally higher than those of most European Neandertals (43.6 ± 3.8, N = 14), Tabūn C1 (43.6) and Tabūn C2 (40.5).

The lateral surfaces of the Shanidar 1 mandibular corpus exhibit one large mental foramen below the mesial root of each M_1. In addition, there is one very small foramen on the right side about halfway between the large foramen and the alveolus below the P_4–M_1 interdental septum. The location of the mental foramina below the first molars is also found on the Amud 1 and Tabūn C2 mandibles, although Tabūn C1 has it below the P_4-M_1. Among European Neandertals, 65.0% have it below M_1, 25.0% have it below P_4-M_1, and 10.0% have it below P_4 (N = 20). In contrast, most recent humans have the mental foramina below the premolars, usually around the P_4 (Keiter 1934; Larnach and Macintosh 1966, 1971; Liau 1956; Simonton 1923). In only 2 of 11 samples of recent humans, one Afroamerican (N = 42; Simonton 1923) and the other Australian (N = 134; Larnach and Macintosh 1971), does the frequency of mental foramina below the M_1 exceed 10%, and in both of these cases the frequencies (14.3 and 12.7%, respectively) are below 15%. The posterior positioning of the mental foramina among most Neandertals is probably a secondary reflection of the anterior placement of the dentition, but the developmental relationship between the two features is not apparent.

Extending posteriorly from the mental foramina are moderately strong lateral superior tori, which lead into the lateral prominences and the anterior margins of the rami. The lateral superior tori are bordered by wide, but not particularly deep, submolar sulci and by shallow intertoral sulci. The marginal tori are weak, although they are roughened by platysmatic striae and lead posteriorly from large anterior marginal tubercles. This degree of development of lateral corpus features is similar to other Neandertal mandibles (e.g., La Ferrassie 1 [Heim 1976]) and slightly less than that of earlier *H. sapiens* and *H. erectus* mandibles (Billy and Vallois 1977; Lumley 1973; Lumley and Lumley 1971; Weidenreich 1936).

The symphyseal region of Shanidar 1 is slightly retreating, clearly lacking a prominent mental protuberance. The angle between the horizontal plane of the alveoli and the anterior surface of the symphysis is 78°, which is similar to those of other Near Eastern Neandertals (Amud 1: 82°; Tabūn C1: 72°; Tabūn C2: 80°), slightly below a European Neandertal mean (83.4° ± 7.3°, N = 8), and considerably below those of a recent human sample (94.1° ± 2.0°, N = 109 [Twiesselmann and Brabant 1967]). The angle between the horizontal plane of the alveoli and the incision–gnathion line of the symphysis is only 65° on Shanidar 1; this angle measurement is below those of most other Neandertals but still well within their ranges of variation (Amud 1: 74°; Tabūn C1: 61°; Tabūn C2: 72°; European Neandertals: 70.3° ± 5.9°, N = 10).

The symphyseal region exhibits a prominent symphyseal tuberosity, as well as less protruding lateral tubercles (Figure 9). In conjunction with relatively deep right and left anterior mandibular incisures, these features form a clear mental trigone. However, the mental trigone remains largely within the plane of the anterior surface of the mandible, so that it cannot be legitimately referred to as a chin. There is a suggestion of considerable alveolar prognathism in the incisor region (Figure 15), but the damage to the incisor and canine alveoli precludes any estimate of how much there might have been.

The posterior surface of the symphysis exhibits a smooth and relatively short alveolar plane, a moderately developed superior transverse torus and a prominent inferior transverse torus (Figures 15 and 16). Between the transverse tori there is a deep genioglossal fossa with a pair of distinct mental spines. Unlike the pattern described by Heim (1976) for European Neandertals, the genioglossal fossa is well above the inferior margin of the symphysis rather than immediately above the inferior margin.

Along the inferior surface of the symphysis are distinct digastric fossae. Each one consists of a slightly excavated area bordered anteriorly and laterally by small muscular crests (Figure 15). Although they are quite prominent, suggesting well-developed digastric muscles, they do not form a large depression across the symphysis as in a number of fossil hominids. Interestingly, the fossae are asymmetrical; the right one is slightly larger (Table 5). This may be simply normal variation, or the smaller size of the left muscular attachment may be due to a reduction of the left masticatory musculature following the injury to the left zygomatic region.

The medial surfaces of the mandibular corpus are sharply divided into sublingual and submandibular fossae by prominent mylohyoid lines (Figure 15). The sublingual fossae are relatively shallow and only show a suggestion of mandibular tori in the region of M_3. The submandibular fossae, however, are quite deep, forming clear sulci immediately below and parallel to the mylohyoid lines. As with the lateral surfaces, the marginal tori are weak, so that the submandibular fossae are largely flat as they approach the inferior margins of the corpus.

Between the distal edges of the third molars and the anterior margins of the rami are large retromolar spaces. These are evident in lateral views by the approximately 10.0 mm of horizontal bone distal to the third molars (Figure 15). In superior view, this bone appears porous, as though it were covered by

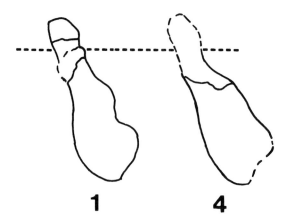

1   **4**

Figure 16 Mandibular symphyseal cross sections of Shanidar 1 and 4. The horizontal line indicates the occlusal plane of the mandible (approximated for Shanidar 4). Redrawn from Stewart (1961b: fig. 13; 1963: fig. 3).

gingival tissues during life. The presence of this retromolar space has been used by Howells (1975) as a characteristic Neandertal feature. It is found on all known European Neandertals (N = 16) except La Quina 9 (Martin 1926a), and it is present on the Amud 1, Tabūn C1, and Tabūn C2 mandibles. However, it also exists among more recent fossil hominids (Matiegka 1934; McCown and Keith 1939), as well as among recent humans. As with the extension of the maxillary alveoli posterior to the upper third molars, the mandibular retromolar spaces are probably a reflection of the pronounced midfacial prognathism of the Neandertals combined with moderate-sized dentitions and rami.

The lateral surfaces of the Shanidar 1 mandibular rami are relatively smooth. One can easily discern the lateral eminences, masseteric fossae, and ectocondyloid crests, but all of them are minimally developed. This agrees with the moderate markings seen on the right zygomatic bone for M. masseter. The one feature that is prominent on the lateral ramal surfaces is the subcondylar tubercle (Figure 14). This tubercle provides attachment for the fibrous capsule of the temporomandibular joint and for the lateral temporomandibular ligament. The origins of these ligaments are well developed on the cranium (see previous discussion), and therefore it is to be expected that they would also be well developed on the mandible.

The medial surfaces of the rami exhibit much clearer morphology. There are prominent pharyngeal crests extending posterosuperiorly from the large mylohyoid lines, and then dividing into reasonably large endocoronoid crests and slightly smaller endocondyloid crests (Figure 15). Whereas the masseteric surfaces are virtually smooth, the medial pterygoid surfaces show pronounced rugosity all along the inferoposterior margins of the rami. These roughenings for medial pterygoid muscles extend superiorly almost to the point where they would merge with the tuberosities for the lateral pterygoid muscles just below the condyles.

There is no lateral flaring of the gonial angles. The gonial angles extend almost directly inferiorly from the superior portion of the rami and, if anything, they turn slightly medially. This morphology is supported by the index derived from a comparison of the bigonial breadth to the maximum bicondylar breadth. The index is 73.1 for Shanidar 1, which is within the range of variation for other Neandertals (Amud 1: 71.7; La Chapelle-aux-Saints 1: 67.4; La Ferrassie 1: 72.8; Krapina J: 75.5; Tabūn C1: 69.9; Tabūn C2: 67.7) and considerably less than the range of 83.5–124.7 provided by Weidenreich (1936) for recent human mandibles.

The mandibular foramen of Neandertals has been described by Kallay (1970) and F. H. Smith (1978) as frequently exhibiting a morphology known as the horizontal–oval type. In this, a large, flat area of bone extends posteroinferiorly from the lingula across the mylohyoid sulcus, changing the inferior margin of the mandibular foramen from a V-shape to a horizontal, slightly curved border. This enlargement of the lingula is apparently produced by an expansion of the sphenomandibular ligament (F. H. Smith 1978). The horizontal–oval pattern occurs in 61.5% of adult European Neandertals (N = 13) and on Tabūn C2, but not on Amud 1 or Tabūn C1. It is present between 0.0 and 3.7% in five recent human samples studied by F. H. Smith (1978).

The mandibular foramina of Shanidar 1 lack the horizontal–oval pattern, exhibiting the morphology more commonly seen in recent human mandibles (Figure 15). There are prominent, slightly medially directed lingulae forming a V-shaped inferior margin to the mandibular foramina. Leading anteroinferiorly from the mandibular foramina are deep, distinct mylohyoid sulci, which are open along their entire lengths.

Both of the Shanidar 1 coronoid processes were damaged *in situ*, and they have been restored with filler. After studying the Shanidar 2 mandible, which has relatively high coronoid processes, Stewart (1961b) suspected that the Shanidar 1 processes were reconstructed too short. Although this may be true, there is an insufficient amount of the processes preserved to determine accurately their original heights. At any rate, the relatively large sizes of the bases of the coronoid processes, combined with the well-developed endocoronoid crests, imply that they were strongly built.

Both of the mandibular condyles are preserved for Shanidar 1. The left condyle suffered minor degenerative joint disease (Figure 15), possibly as a result of the injury to the left orbit and zygomatic region, so that morphological considerations will be limited to the right condyle. The right condyle is evenly cylindrical from medial to lateral, with distinct anterior and posterior borders. The shape of the mandibular condyle changes during an individual's life, largely as a result of changing masticatory stress as the dentition wears down (Mongini 1975). The right condyle of Shanidar 1 corresponds to Category 5 of Mongini (1975), which is associated with the highest level of dental occlusal wear, particularly anterior dental wear. Because Shanidar 1 suffered extensive occlusal wear, especially of the anterior teeth (Figure 26; Table 16), it is to be expected that its mandibular condyles would assume this configuration.

Shanidar 1 therefore possesses a large, typically Neandertal mandible. It is a robust bone with moderate to strong markings for the masticatory musculature and ligaments and for various architectural features on the surface bone. Its most prominent aspect is the elongation of the mandibular corpus, which places the dental arcade considerably anterior of the rami.

SHANIDAR 2

Inventory

CRANIUM

The Shanidar 2 cranium is in numerous pieces, of which eight are identifiable and provide morphological information. The eight pieces consist of (1) a facial piece with portions of the right supraorbital torus, right zygomatic and temporal bones, and both maxillae joined so as to reconstruct the dental arcade (maximum dimension [superoinferior] = 128.5 mm); (2) a major portion of the right posterolateral vault with parts of the frontal, parietal, temporal, and occipital bones (maximum dimension [anteroposterior] = 169.3 mm); (3) a left frontal and parietal piece near stephanion (maximum dimension [anteroposterior] = 101.2 mm); (4) a portion of the left nasal and orbital margins with the frontal bone and the left maxillary, nasal, and lacrimal bones (maximum breadth = 82.3 mm); (5) a median section of the right supraorbital torus (maximum breadth = 32.7 mm); (6) a piece of the left temporal squamous with portions of the adjacent greater wing of the sphenoid bone and frontal squamous (maximum dimension [anteroposterior] = 82.5 mm); (7) the right petrous bone (maximum dimension = 41.7 mm); and (8) the right and left pterygoid plates (maximum dimension [superoinferior] = 43.0 mm).

Os Occipitale   The right third of the squamous is preserved along with the right margin of the foramen magnum. The right condyle is present, and it exhibits exostoses on its margins. The midline is approached only at opisthion and basion, but at those points the bone is damaged so that the precise locations of the landmarks are uncertain.

Os Sphenoidale   The sphenoid bone consists of the posterior half of the left greater wing with portions of the sphenofrontal and sphenosquamosal sutures and of the right and left pterygoid plates and fragments of the body between them. The superior half of the right plates is preserved, as are most of the left plates.

Os Temporale: Right   The zygomatic process is complete from the temporozygomatic suture to the attachment with the body of the temporal. The mastoid process is also intact along with a portion of the occipitomastoid suture. Preserved separately is a fragmentary petrous bone with part of the external acoustic meatus and a crushed glenoid fossa.

Os Temporale: Left   The majority of the squamous portion of the temporal bone, which extends from the sphenosquamosal suture anteriorly to the supramastoid region, is preserved. None of the squamous or occipitomastoid sutures is preserved.

Os Parietale: Right   The bone is present from the coronal suture to the lambdoid suture, but it lacks portions of the internal table and retains none of the sagittal or squamous sutures.

Os Parietale: Left   A small fragment of the external table with parts of the coronal suture and left temporal line is preserved.

Os Frontale   The frontal squamous consists of a small piece on the right coronal suture, a section of external table along the left coronal suture near stephanion, a small piece near the left pterion, and crushed and distorted bone near the right lateral margin of the supraorbital torus. A small portion of the supraorbital torus is preserved along the right frontozygomatic suture, and there is a fragment of anterior surface of the right mid-supraorbital torus. In addition, the left supraorbital region preserves the anterior and inferior surfaces of its medial two-thirds with the supratoral sulcus surface preserved along its lateral half.

Os Lacrimale: Left   A small fragment is preserved along the lacrimal fossa.

Os Nasale: Left   A middle section of the nasal bone is present, with portions of the nasomaxillary and internasal sutures.

Maxilla: Right   The major portion of the right maxilla consists of the anterior and lateral surface bone from the zygomaticomaxillary suture to the premolar and molar alveoli. The anterior two-thirds of the palate and the nasal floor are preserved with the posterior margins of the incisor alveoli. In addition, there is a fragment of the anterior subnasal surface bone with the anterior margins of the incisor alveoli, which is joined to the palate by the roots of the incisors.

Maxilla: Left   The left maxilla retains the frontal process with most of the nasomaxillary suture and the medial orbital border, the anterior two-thirds of the palate and nasal floor with the I^1 alveoli, a fragment of the anterior subnasal surface bone with the I^1 alveoli, and the external surface bone between the molar alveoli and the zygomaticomaxillary suture. The frontal process is joined to the piece of left supraorbital torus, whereas the other three pieces form part of the reconstructed superior dental arcade.

Os Zygomaticum: Right   The bone is complete, but the frontal process is partly crushed and distorted.

MANDIBLE

The mandible as reconstructed appears complete, but major portions consist of filler. The right corpus is largely present, but only the external surface of the left corpus is intact. The symphyseal region is largely reconstructed, and bone-on-bone contact between the right and left portions of the corpus may not exist. Both rami are present, but the left coronoid process is absent, and all of the left condyle and part of the right condyle are reconstructed. The molar and premolar alveoli are present, but most of the anterior alveoli are absent and have been reconstructed. The rami and the posterior dentition may be too far apart because the mandible does not occlude properly with the reconstructed maxilla (Figure 17). However, because both the maxillary and the mandibular dental arcades are reconstructed after extensive damage along the midline, it is difficult to determine the extent to which either, or both, is distorted. Maximum dimensions are provided in Table 14.

Morphology

The Shanidar 2 skull suffered extensively during its depositional history. It was buried between two rocks, leaning toward its right side, and the two sides were pushed together so that the breadth of the skull was approximately half its original breadth (Figure 6). In the process, much of the bone, especially on the left side and along the midline, turned to bone meal and small fragments, thereby making a restoration of the skull to its original shape virtually impossible.

This damage was exacerbated when, after the skull was removed to the Iraq Museum in 1957, a technician soaked the whole skull, in its *in situ* position, in an acetate chemical. In 1960, when Stewart began the restoration of Shanidar 2, he carefully disassembled the pieces and reassembled those that had reasonable contacts (Stewart 1961b).

Stewart began by reassembling the mandible, much of which remained. The lateral portions of the corpus and the rami presented little difficulty, but virtually all of the symphyseal area was reduced to bone meal. Using the anterior teeth as a guide, Stewart modeled the symphysis in filler (Savogran) and joined both sides of the mandible. As he stated (1961b:99), the posterior dentition and the rami are probably too far apart and inclined too far laterally, but the overall arrangement of the mandible should be close to its original form.

The various portions of the cranium presented considerably more difficulty. In 1960, Stewart assembled two main pieces. The first is a posterior lateral portion of the right cranial vault, which is undistorted but preserves few craniometric landmarks. The other piece is the lateral third of the right side of the facial skeleton. In addition, there were several pieces which could not be readily joined to the two large ones.

In 1976, 1978, and 1980, I attempted to fit together additional pieces of the Shanidar 2 cranium. I had little success with the cranial vault, but it was possible to reassemble several pieces of the maxillae. By using an anterior piece of the palate with the incisor alveoli, interproximal wear facets on the anterior teeth, and measurements from the midline to each side, I reconstructed most of the inferior maxillae and maxillary dental arcade (Figure 27). The reconstruction is based on several tenuous contacts between teeth, especially around the canines, and a small contact between the right side of the palate and the right M^1 lingual alveolus. Although the overall shape and proportions of the palate appear to be the most reasonable possible, the posterior breadth of the dental arcade may be too small. Because the posterior alveolar breadth of the mandible is considerably larger than that of the maxilla (Figure 17), the mandible is too wide posteriorly, the maxilla is too narrow, or both. Given the fragmentation of both jaws along the midline, it is impossible to determine which is the more accurate reconstruction.

Despite these deficiencies in the reconstruction of the Shanidar 2 skull, there is considerable information to be obtained from the specimen. Many of the data consist of qualitative morphological observations rather than detailed osteometric determinations. However, because two of the more diagnostic areas for Neandertals—the occipitomastoid region and the facial skeleton—are reasonably well preserved on the skull, it is possible to place the Shanidar 2 skull morphologically with respect to Neandertal ranges of variation.

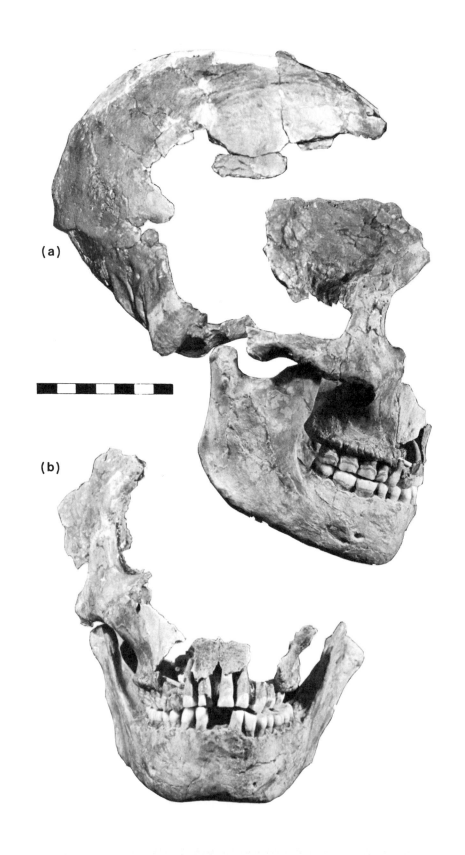

(a)

(b)

THE CRANIAL VAULT

The cranial vault of Shanidar 2 is too incomplete to determine any of the standard osteometrics. The only craniometric landmarks preserved are opisthion, basion, and stephanion, and none of the midline is preserved above opisthion. Those portions of the right parietal that remain suggest that the parietals were relatively high and rounded, apparently similar to those of Shanidar 1 (compare Figures 9 and 17). The occipital bone indicates a fairly strong angulation of the bone at inion and a marked curvature of the occipital plane. It is not possible to assess accurately the curvature of the frontal bone, but if the alignment of the facial skeleton and posterior cranium in Figure 17 is accurate, the curvature of the Shanidar 2 frontal bone may have been greater than that of Shanidar 1.

The thickness of the right parietal bone can be measured near the parietal tuber. Its thickness of 8.2 mm is similar to that of Shanidar 1 (8.0 mm) and Amud 1 (8.0 mm), and all of these measurements are slightly above a European Neandertal mean (7.6 ± 1.1 mm, N = 27) and close to the parietal thickness measurements of other large Neandertal males (see earlier discussion).

THE OCCIPITOMASTOID REGION

The occipital bone is complete to the midline only around the foramen magnum, but enough of the right side of the occipital bone and the right mastoid region on the temporal bone is preserved to permit a detailed assessment of their morphology (Figure 18). Both the lambdoid suture and the transverse occipital torus are broken off 10.0–30.0 mm lateral of the midline. Despite this, there appears to be a sufficient portion of the transverse occipital torus to indicate the morphology of the region around inion, even if the configuration of the sutures around lambda is indeterminate.

The lambdoid suture is relatively straight along its course from the medial break of the occipital bone to asterion. It is not possible to determine whether a sutural bone was present at lambda, but there is a moderate-sized sutural bone about 20.0 mm posteromedial of asterion. In this, Shanidar 2 resembles Shanidar 1 and 25.9–54.0% of the individuals in eight recent human samples (Berry and Berry 1967).

Figure 17 The Shanidar 2 skull in (a) *norma lateralis* right and (b) *norma facialis*. The mandible and facial portion have been articulated by placing the right premolars and molars in centric occlusion, which results in the left maxillary molars' being too far medial with respect to the left mandibular molars. The orientation of the posterior and superior cranial vault piece relative to the facial skeleton was determined by approximating the distance between the mandibular condyle and the anterior mastoid margin and the distance between the preserved coronal suture and the supraorbital torus, using the contours of the temporal crest and temporal line as a guide. The posterior cranial piece may be rotated too far anteriorly. The section of cranial vault approaches the midline only at opisthion, and the bone posterior of frontomalare is crushed and distorted. Scale in centimeters.

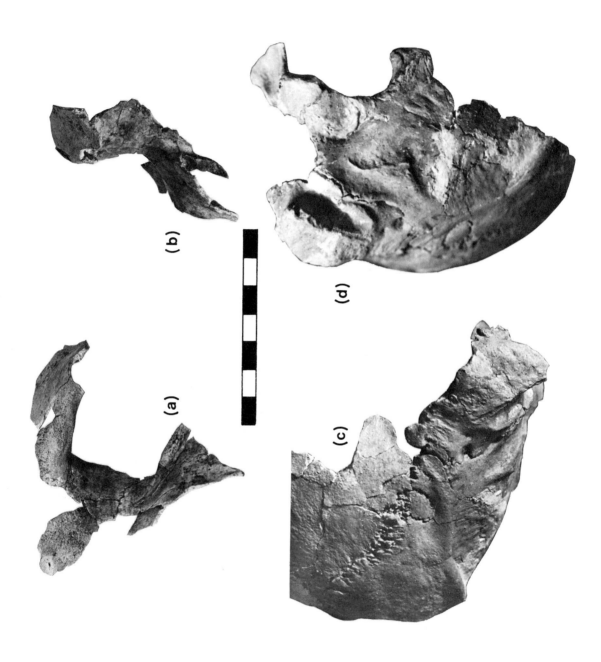

The transverse occipital torus is well developed between asterion and inion, forming a distinct inferiorly directed lip. It is divided into two inferiorly convex sections by a notch in the middle of the torus. This notch may indicate the division of the torus into a medial section for M. *semispinalis capitis* and a lateral section for M. *obliquus superior*. The surface between the inferior nuchal line and the transverse occipital torus is quite rugose, suggesting that these muscles were powerfully developed.

The region above inion and the central portion of the transverse occipital torus, where a suprainiac fossa might be found, is incomplete. However, there is a distinct depression, as seen in norma *lateralis*, just above the torus towards the midline. This depression forms the beginning of a hollow that increases in size medially along the most medial 10.0 mm of the preserved torus. It is not possible to determine conclusively if this is the beginning of a suprainiac fossa, but it is extremely similar to the lateral portion of the suprainiac fossa seen on Shanidar 1. Most probably there was a broad suprainiac fossa on Shanidar 2 similar to that of Shanidar 1.

On the inferior portion of the nuchal plane is a distinct crest, which is the dividing line between M. *rectus capitis posterior major* and M. *rectus capitis posterior minor*. This cresting suggests a development of these muscles beyond the usual extent because this region is commonly only moderately rugose. Bordering these muscular attachments laterally is an occipitomastoid crest, which is quite modest by Neandertal standards. Although it appears clearly behind the mastoid process in norma *lateralis* (Figure 18), its height from the mastoid notch is only 6.6 mm, as compared to 11.3 mm for Shanidar 1. The Shanidar 2 occipitomastoid crest is also dwarfed by the large size of its mastoid process.

The Shanidar 2 mastoid process is one of the largest known for a Neandertal. Its height, as measured from the Frankfurt plane, is about 32.0 mm. This is equal to that of Amud 1 (32.0 mm) and is considerably greater than that of Tabūn C1 (17.5 mm). It is almost at the top of a European Neandertal range of variation (17.5–32.5 mm, 23.8 ± 3.6 mm, N = 18). It is even slightly greater than the highest male mean for a series of recent human samples (range of means for 17 samples: 25.9 ± 2.4 to 30.9 ± 3.1 mm [Howells, 1973]) and above those of Shanidar 1 (27.5 & 28.1 mm). The height of the mastoid process, as measured from the mastoid notch (10.6 mm), is at the top of a European Neandertal range (3.0–10.4 mm, 6.6 ± 2.2 mm, N = 15), slightly larger than those of Shanidar 1 (8.3 & 9.3 mm) and close to a recent human mean of 12.8 mm (Vallois 1969).

On the lateral surface of the Shanidar 2 mastoid process, there is a moderately developed mastoid crest. It is evident as a rugose line along the middle of the mastoid process, but it does not extend posteriorly from the process itself.

Figure 18 (a) Anterior and (b) left lateral views of the Shanidar 2 left orbital piece; (c) right lateral and (d) basal views of the Shanidar 2 mastooccipital region. The orientations of the pieces are approximate. Scale in centimeters.

There is thus a distinct vertical sulcus between the posterior margin of the mastoid process and asterion. Consequently, the continuity between the mastoid crest and the transverse occipital torus seen in Shanidar 1 and other Neandertals (Hublin 1978a) is absent. The lateral surface of the mastoid process below the mastoid crest is relatively rugose, but there is no evidence of an anterior mastoid tubercle such as appears to be present on the Shanidar 1 mastoid processes and those of many other Neandertals.

The occipitomastoid region of Shanidar 2 thus shows Neandertal features in the development of its transverse occipital torus and suprainiac fossa. However, it has one of the largest Neandertal mastoid processes and lacks an anterior mastoid tubercle.

THE ZYGOMATIC ARCH AND THE TEMPORAL FOSSA

The right zygomatic arch is complete from the middle of the articular tubercle on the zygomatic process of the temporal bone to the body of the zygomatic bone (Figure 17). The portion remaining of the articular tubercle suggests that Shanidar 2, like Shanidar 1, has a large tubercle. This implies well-developed temporomandibular joint ligaments, particularly the fibrous capsule of the joint.

On the inferior margin of the zygomatic arch, near the temporozygomatic suture, there is a depression. This is caused by the inferior projection of the articular tubercle posteriorly and of a tubercle formed by the attachment of M. masseter anteriorly. The attachment for M. masseter along the zygomatic bone and onto the maxilla is highly rugose. Its length (35.5 mm) is similar to that of Shanidar 1 (35.0 mm), both of which are within the ranges of variation of several recent human samples (43.1 ± 5.2 mm, N = 8; 33.8 ± 3.4 mm, N = 52; 31.8 ± 3.2 mm, N = 188 [Carlson and Van Gerven 1977]). However, the strength of the M. masseter attachment on Shanidar 2, as indicated by the tubercle development on the zygomatic arch and the area covered along the zygomatico-maxillary suture (Figure 17), is considerably greater than that of Shanidar 1 and most recent humans.

Shanidar 2 lacks the tubercle along the posterolateral margin of the frontal process of the zygomatic bone that is present on Shanidar 1. Yet the anterior temporal line is still visible extending posteriorly from the frontozygomatic suture, despite the extreme crushing of that region. The superior and inferior temporal lines are clearly visible from stephanion to a short distance above asterion.

These patterns on the Shanidar 2 cranium suggest well-developed masticatory muscles. This conclusion is supported by the study of the Shanidar 2 mandibular rami (see following discussion).

THE UPPER FACIAL SKELETON

The Shanidar 2 upper facial skeleton consists primarily of the right side from the molar alveoli to the frontozygomatic suture, plus the palate (Figures

17 and 27). In addition, there is a piece with the medial margins of the left orbit, including parts of the supraorbital and nasal regions (Figure 18) and a fragment of the right supraorbital torus. It is not possible to join these pieces or orient them accurately relative to each other.

The fragment of supraorbital torus preserved on the right side and the left supraorbital region indicate a large, robust brow. Its estimated thicknesses at midorbit (15.0 & 14.0 mm) are similar to those of Shanidar 1 (14.8 mm), Amud 1 (15.0 mm) and Zuttiyeh 1 (15.7 & 14.8 mm), and toward the top of a European Neandertal range of variation (12.0 ± 2.0 mm, N = 18). The anterior and superior surfaces of the torus are covered with partially remodeled fine cancellous bone, indicating rapid torus growth during development (Oyen et al. 1979).

It is not possible to reconstruct the shape of the Shanidar 2 orbits. What remains of the medial and superior sides of the left orbit and the lateral side of the right orbit suggests that they were more subrectangular than round (Figures 17 and 18). Yet it is primarily the superior and inferior margins of the orbits that determine their configurations, and these areas are the least complete of the Shanidar 2 orbital margins.

It is possible to estimate the interorbital breadth of Shanidar 2 from the distance between the left dacryon and the midline indicated by the internasal suture; the resultant value is about 36.6 mm. This value is considerably larger than that of Shanidar 1 (ca. 23.1 mm) and those of many other Neandertals (Amud 1: ≥ 31.5 mm; Tabūn C1: 32.0; Zuttiyeh 1: 28.0 mm; European Neandertals: 29.0 ± 2.7 mm, N = 10) and well above values for recent human males (range of means for 17 samples: 18.6 ± 1.8 to 24.4 ± 2.4 mm [Howells 1973]). This large interorbital breadth suggests a wide upper face, an inference that is supported by the estimate of bifrontal breadth determined on the right facial and palatal piece (ca. 123.0 mm). This bifrontal breadth is high for a Neandertal (Amud 1: 114.0 mm; Tabūn C1: 107.0 mm; Zuttiyeh 1: 113.0 mm; European Neandertals: 110.7 ± 4.2 mm, N = 11). It is exceptionally large compared to recent humans (range of male means for 17 recent human samples: 92.0 ± 4.2 to 102.4 ± 3.6 mm [Howells 1973]). Shanidar 2 apparently had an exceptionally wide upper face.

Even though the breadths of the Shanidar 2 upper face are quite large, the interorbital–bifrontal breadth proportions are within Neandertal ranges of variation. The index formed by these breadths is about 29.8 for Shanidar 2. It is well above those of Shanidar 1 (ca. 20.1) and 5 (ca. 24.2) and Zuttiyeh 1 (24.8), but it is close to those of Amud 1 (≥ 27.6) and Tabūn C1 (29.9). The Shanidar 2 index is marginally greater than those of known European Neandertals (21.3–28.6, 26.5 ± 2.4, N = 9) but well within their expected ranges of variation. Most, but by no means all, of the Neandertals have values for this index above those of most recent humans (range of the ratio of the male means for 17 samples: 18.8–24.4 [Howells 1973]).

The nasal aperture of Shanidar 2 is represented only by a section of the superior left margin on the maxilla extending inferiorly from the nasomaxillary suture (Figure 18). It is nonetheless possible to obtain an impression of the degree of projection, if not the size, of the nasal region. The left orbital piece in *norma lateralis* shows that the nasal bridge projects anteriorly from the orbital plane at a prominent angle.

Associated with this suggested anterior placement of the nasal aperture is a rather modest degree of midfacial prognathism. Although conforming to the Neandertal pattern of midfacial prognathism, the Shanidar 2 midface is less projecting than those of Shanidar 1 and other Neandertals.

This is indicated by the position of the right zygomatic root; it is above the M^2, rather than posterior to the M^2 as in Shanidar 1, La Chapelle-aux-Saints 1, and La Ferrassie 1. It overlaps the range of variation of recent humans (see discussion of the Shanidar 1 upper facial skeleton), but is still more posterior than the zygomatic roots of most more recent humans. In addition, the posterior extensions of the maxillary alveoli beyond the third molars (11.0 mm) are intermediate in size between that of Shanidar 1 (14.8 mm) and those of most more recent humans (recent Europeans: 7.3 ± 1.5 mm, N = 102 [Twiesselmann and Brabant 1967]). Furthermore, the index formed from its alveolar and dental arcade lengths is about 120.8, which is midway between that of Shanidar 1 (128.5) and the index of the palatal lengths means (112.2) for a recent European sample (Twiesselmann and Brabant 1967).

It is possible to estimate the difference between the zygomaxillare and molar alveolus radii. The lengths of the radii can be estimated by placing the mandibular dentition in centric occlusion with the right maxillary dentition and then using the position of the right mandibular condyle to approximate the location of the external acoustic meatus. Zygomaxillare anterior and the P^4–M^1 alveolus are well preserved on the right side of the facial piece. As long as only the difference between the radii, and not the radii themselves, are used in the comparisons, any error introduced by using the condyle rather than the meatus should be minimal. (A change in the estimated position of the external acoustic meatus by as much as 10.0 mm would change the lengths of the radii, but it would not alter the angle between the radii significantly. It is only angular changes that are of concern, because an increase or decrease in the radii lengths would affect both equally and would be eliminated through subtraction. The lengths of the radii relative to each other will change slightly if the angle between them changes, as it will if the position of the external acoustic meatus is moved superiorly or inferiorly relative to the facial skeleton. Yet any such angle change would be small, and the lengths of the radii relative to each other will change only as the sine of the angle between them. Because the sine of small angles is very small, the introduced error should be insignificant.)

The difference between the two estimated radii for Shanidar 2 is only about 15.0 mm. This value is considerably below those of Shanidar 1 (26.0 mm) and European Neandertals (20.0–26.5 mm, 22.1 ± 3.0 mm, N = 4). This low value for Shanidar 2 is approached only by that of Amud 1 (ca. 17.0 mm) among the Neandertals, and it is not very far from the range of male means for recent human samples (range of means for 17 samples: 4.6–11.6 mm [Howells 1975]).

The moderate midfacial prognathism of Shanidar 2 is further indicated by its zygomaxillary angle. The estimates of this angle, computed from the bimaxillary breadth of about 115.0 mm and the estimated subspinale subtense of 30.0 mm, is 125°. This value is markedly greater than that of Shanidar 1 (105°), those of European Neandertals (105°–114°, 110.6° ± 4.3°, N = 4) and even that of Amud 1 (ca. 115°), indicating a much flatter midfacial region. It is well within the ranges of variation of recent human males (range of means for 17 samples: 120.3° ± 6.6° to 138.9° ± 4.7° Howells 1973]) and Early Upper Paleolithic hominids (127.3° ± 8.8°, N = 6), and among archiac H. sapiens it is approached only by the Middle Pleistocene Petralona 1 cranium (121°) (Stringer et al. 1979). Shanidar 2 therefore appears to have had the least prognathic midface currently known for a Neandertal.

The modest midfacial projection of Shanidar 2 may be a product in part of the massiveness of the zygomatic bones. In Shanidar 1, the zygomatic bone is moderately developed and exhibits a retreating profile. In Shanidar 2, in contrast, the whole bone, but especially the anterior margin, is heavily built and projects anteriorly and laterally. This is reflected in part by its zygomatic curvature index of 27.2; it is well above those of Shanidar 1 (19.0) and other Neandertals (Amud 1: ca. 18.2; La Chapelle-aux-Saints 1: 15.3; Circeo 1: 21.1; La Ferrassie 1: 18.6) and even above those of most more recent humans (early anatomically modern humans: 21.0–22.8, N = 4; range of male means for 30 recent human samples: 19.6 ± 2.6 to 23.2 ± 2.2 [Howells, personal communication, 1982]).

This anterior projection and curvature of the zygomatic bone places the right zygomatic root above the M^2 rather than above the M^2–M^3 interdental septum as in Shanidar 1. In addition, it produces a slight concavity below the zygomaticomaxillary suture; it is this that gives the impression of a more convex zygomatic region in Shanidar 2 than Shanidar 1 (Stewart 1961b).

The slight concavity below the zygomaticomaxillary suture and around the infraorbital foramen gives the imporession of a small canine fossa. However, this is not a true canine fossa because the remainder of the anterior maxillary surface is either flat or slightly convex. The overall impression is of a maxilla that is slightly more inflated than that of Shanidar 1.

The apparent inflation of the Shanidar 2 maxillae implies large maxillary sinuses and nasal cavity. It is not possible to determine how large each of these was because all of the internal nasal skeleton is lacking. But the nasal floor descends steeply posterior to the inferior nasal aperture margin to reach the level of the palate near the incisive canal. This pattern is seen in Shanidar 1, and it implies that the nasal cavity was indeed large.

The profile of the maxilla between the zygomaticomaxillary suture and the alveoli, as seen in norma facialis, is concave. However, rather than being a smooth curve as in Shanidar 1 (Figure 9), it consists of an angular curve in the bone just above the alveoli and then a straight or even slightly convex profile up to the zygomatic bone. In this respect, it approaches the morphology described by Sergi (1947) and Heim (1978) for the Neandertals more than that

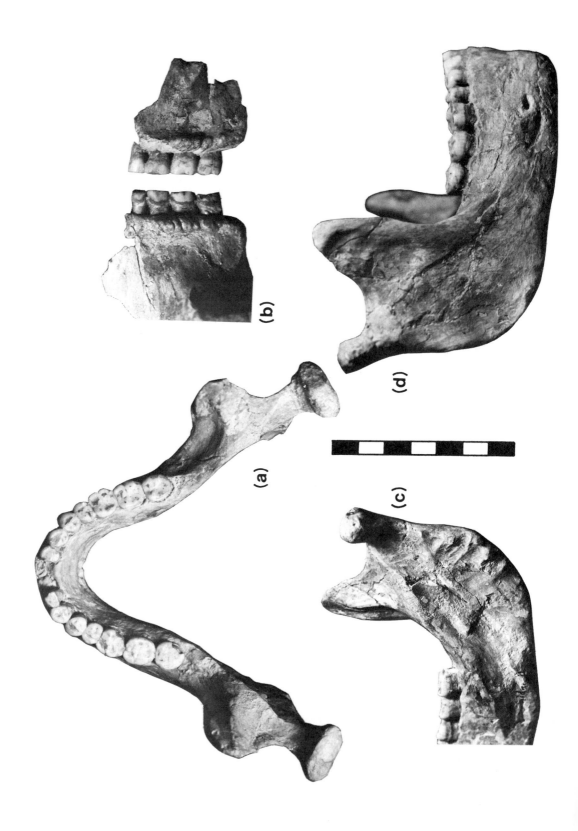

depicted for the Early Neandertals. This is in agreement with Shanidar 2's having a slightly more inflated maxilla than is present on Shanidar 1.

The Shanidar 2 maxillae possess bilateral exostoses on the buccal alveoli (tori *alveolares*), which are small above M^1, become prominent above M^2 and M^3, and then taper off above the retromolar alveoli (Figure 19). Similar exostoses are present but rare among recent humans (Hrdlička 1940). They have variously been considered as the products of inflammation of the subgingival alveolus (Alexandersen 1967), part of a functional hypertrophy of the alveolar bone (Hrdlička 1940), and genetically determined discrete traits (Moorrees 1957). Because there is no pronounced periodontal inflammation on the Shanidar 2 maxillae, one of the latter two interpretations appears to be more probable as an explanation here.

The palate of Shanidar 2 is missing most of the bone posterior to the first molars, but the alveoli are complete posterior of the third molars, especially on the right side (Figures 17 and 27). The overall length of the palate (prosthion–M^3 distal surfaces) is about 53.0 mm. This measure is the same as a Neandertal mean of 53.1 mm (Amud 1: 53.0 mm; La Ferrassie 1: 50.0 mm; Gibraltar 1: 54.0 mm; Tabūn C1: 55.5 mm) and slightly above a recent human mean (48.4 ± 3.7 mm, N = 108 [Twiesselmann and Brabant 1967]). However, its external palate breadth measured at the distal margins of the first molars (ca. 70.3 mm) is toward the top of the known Neandertal range (Amud 1: 69.2 mm; La Ferrassie 1: 70.5 mm; Tabūn C1: ca. 67.0 mm), and its external palate breadth (ca. 78.5 mm) is similarly large, even for a Neandertal (Amud 1: 77.0 mm; Tabūn C1: ca. 69.3 mm; European Neandertals: 71.8 ± 3.6 mm, N = 4). This makes the Shanidar 2 palate one of the broadest of the known Neandertal palates, most of which are wider than those of recent humans (range of male means for 17 samples: 60.1 ± 3.2 to 68.9 ± 3.9 mm [Howells 1973]). Because the Shanidar 2 palate is not particularly long, its large breadth gives it a large palatal index (external breadth/alveolar length) of about 148.1. This index falls in the upper half of the Neandertal range of variation (Amud 1: 145.2; La Ferrassie 1: 150.0; Gibraltar 1: 124.1: Tabūn C1: ca. 124.9) and above that of Shanidar 1 (137.5).

The upper facial skeleton of Shanidar 2 is therefore more robust than that of Shanidar 1, but it exhibits a number of similar characteristics. It has a robust supraorbital torus with apparently large orbits, a projecting nasal bridge, and an anteriorly placed dentition. It does not, however, show as much midfacial prognathism as Shanidar 1 does.

Figure 19 Views of the Shanidar 2 maxillae and mandible. (a) Superior view of the reconstructed mandible; (b) lateral views of the right and left maxillae in the premolar and molar regions (taken prior to the reassembly of the maxillae) showing the development of the alveolar exostoses; (c) medial view of the right mandibular ramus; (d) right lateral view of the mandible. The symphyseal region and portions of the rami have been restored with filler. Scale in centimeters.

THE MANDIBLE

As noted, the Shanidar 2 mandible was seriously damaged *in situ*, and its appearance of completeness (Figure 19) is due to Stewart's restoration of many of the missing portions. The mandibular breadths across the rami and posterior dentition are probably too large, but because any other attempted restoration would probably also contain distortion, the current alignment will be used for comparisons. It should be kept in mind that the breadths of the mandible should probably be slightly less than those listed in Table 5.

The superior length of the Shanidar 2 mandible (ca. 112.0 mm) is similar to those of other Neandertals (Amud 1: ca. 111.0 mm; Tabūn C1: 102.0 mm; Tabūn C2: 122.0 mm; European Neandertals: 113.8 ± 8.2 mm, N = 6), and Shanidar 1 (115.0 mm). Furthermore, the index of the mandibular length and the tibial maximum length for Shanidar 2 is about 33.2, which is close to those of Shanidar 1 (ca. 32.4), Tabūn C1 (32.0), La Chapelle-aux-Saints 1 (ca. 33.8), and La Ferrassie 1 (ca. 33.0) and slightly above that of Amud 1 (ca. 28.8). It is well above those of more recent humans (Caviglione 1: ca. 23.1; Předmostí 3: 24.7; Skhūl 4: 24.5; Skhūl 5: ca. 25.8; recent European sample: 25.0 ± 1.5, N = 50), although this large difference is due in part to its long mandible and in part to its probably relatively short tibia (assuming that Shanidar 2 had a low crural index similar to those of other Neandertals; Chapter 11). However, the similarity of this index for Shanidar 2 to those of other Neandertals indicates that it did indeed have a relatively long mandible, as do Shanidar 1 and other Neandertals.

The reconstructed bicondylar maximum breadth of Shanidar 2 equals about 154.5 mm, which is more than two standard deviations from a European Neandertal mean (136.0 ± 8.7 mm, N = 7). It is also greater than those of Amud 1 (ca. 145.0 mm), Tabūn C1 (ca. 133.0 mm), Tabūn C2 (130.0 mm), and even Shanidar 1 (142.8 mm). This breadth for Shanidar 2 is well outside the ranges of variation of samples of recent Europeans (122.7 ± 2.6 mm, N = 106 [Twiesselmann and Brabant 1967]), Australians (112.4 ± 5.0 mm, N = 33 [Keiter 1934]), and Melanesians (112.1 ± 5.2 mm, N = 54 [Keiter 1934]). It should be emphasized, however, that the Shanidar 2 bicondylar breadth may be too large, given the problems associated with its reconstruction (see previous discussion).

The mandibular index (length/breadth) of Shanidar 2 is about 72.5. This value is 1.9 standard deviations below a European Neandertal mean of 82.7 ± 6.1 (N = 5) and somewhat below those of Shanidar 1 (80.5), Amud 1 (ca. 76.6), Tabūn C1 (ca. 76.7), and Tabūn C2 (93.8). Shanidar 2 may therefore have had an extremely wide mandible. If, on the other hand, the bicondylar maximum breadth were reduced by 5% to 146.8 mm so as to compensate for possible distortion in the reconstruction, the mandibular index would increase to 76.3. This value would be close to those of Amud 1 and Tabūn C1 and, although still relatively low, would not be unusual for a Neandertal.

The corpus of the mandible is that of a large and robust bone. Its symphyseal height (ca. 37.3 mm) is similar to those of Shanidar 1 (37.2 mm) and Amud 1 (37.0 mm), slightly above a European Neandertal mean (34.7 ± 3.9 mm, N = 14), and between those of Tabūn C1 (30.3 mm) and Tabūn C2 (42.0 mm). Its corpus heights, measured at the mental foramina (34.8 & 34.5 mm) are between those of Shanidar 1 (35.8 & 36.9 mm) and Amud 1 (34.0 mm), distinct from those of Tabūn C1 (27.5 mm) and Tabūn C2 (42.5 mm), and slightly above a European Neandertal mean (31.5 ± 3.7 mm, N = 19). The associated robusticity indices at the mental foramina (50.6 & 51.6) of Shanidar 2 are slightly above those of Shanidar 1 (48.9 & 47.7). They are thus close to a European Neandertal mean (50.3 ± 5.4, N = 19) and in the midst of the values for other Near Eastern Neandertals (Amud 1: 44.1, Tabūn C1: 54.5, Tabūn C2: 38.6).

These measurements of the corpus at the mental foramina have been taken at what would probably have been the location of the mental foramina if there had been only one on each side. Both of the mandibular canals bifurcated to form two mental foramina on each side. The foramina on the right side are subequal in size; the superior one is directly under the mesial root of the M_1, whereas the inferior one is beneath the distal root of the M_1. On the left side there is a large foramen below the mesial root of the M_1, and a slightly smaller foramen is located underneath the C_-. The location of the mental foramina, or at least the principal one, beneath the M_1 is the same as those of Shanidar 1, Amud 1, and Tabūn C2, and the same as those of 65.0% of other Neandertals (N = 20). Among recent human samples, most of the mental foramina are below the premolars (Keiter 1934; Larnach and Macintosh 1966, 1971; Liau 1956; Simonton 1923), and less than 15%, and usually less than 10%, are below M_1.

The Shanidar 2 mandible exhibits small retromolar spaces between the distal margins of the third molars and the anterior margins of the rami (Figure 17). These retromolar spaces are noticeably smaller than those of Shanidar 1 and many other Neandertals. This is probably due in part to the broad rami of Shanidar 2 (minimum breadths = 44.0 & 43.7 mm). These ramus breadths are above those of Shanidar 1 (41.7 & 40.2 mm), Amud 1 (40.0 mm), Tabūn C1 (38.0 mm), and Tabūn C2 (40.0 mm) and above a European Neandertal mean (40.1 ± 4.0 mm, N = 9). They are considerably greater than those of almost all recent humans (Europeans: 33.1 ± 1.6 mm, N = 108 [Twiesselmann and Brabant 1967]; Europeans: 31.9 ± 2.9 mm, N = 50; Amerindians: 36.2 ± 1.3 mm, N = 50; Australians: 32.6 ± 1.8 mm, N = 33 [Keiter 1934]; Melanesians: 33.1 ± 2.1 mm, N = 54 [Keiter 1934]), an Early Upper Paleolithic sample (36.3 ± 1.3, N = 8), and most of a Skhūl–Qafzeh sample (38.3 ± 4.4 mm, N = 5). However, the Shanidar 2 ramus breadths are not exceptional for a Neandertal because several European Neandertals (e.g., La Chapelle-aux-Saints 1: 44.9 & 45.5 mm; La Ferrassie 1: 43.5 & 44.1 mm; La Quina 5: 44.3 mm) have minimum ramus breadths similar to those of Shanidar 2.

However, if the minimum ramus breadths of the Shanidar 2 mandible are compared to its superior length of about 112.0 mm, the resultant indices are about 39.3 and 39.0. These values are above those of Shanidar 1 (36.3 & 35.0), Amud 1 (ca. 35.6), Tabūn C1 (37.3), Tabūn C2 (32.8), and those of most European Neandertals (La Chapelle-aux-Saints 1: ca. 39.0 & ca. 39.6; La Ferrassie 1: 35.7 & 36.1; Krapina J: 33.4; La Quina 5: ca. 36.2; Régourdou 1: 37.2). Only that of La Chapelle-aux-Saints 1 among the Neandertals is equal to those of Shanidar 2. Among European and Near Eastern archaic hominids, only Mauer 1, with its exceptionally wide rami, and Shanidar 4 (see later discussion) exceed Shanidar 2 in their relative ramus breadth indices (Arago 2: 38.0; Arago 13: ca. 37.9; Bañolas 1: ca. 37.3; Mauer 1: 43.4, Montmaurin 1: 36.6; Shanidar 4: ca. 41.0). The mandibular rami of Shanidar 2 were therefore quite wide, both absolutely and relatively. Because the mandibular alveolar length of Shanidar 2 (ca. 56.0 mm) is not exceptionally large for a Neandertal (see later), the large breadths of his mandibular rami relative to total mandible length were probably responsible for the small sizes of his mandibular retromolar spaces.

The large relative breadths of the Shanidar 2 rami indicate that the amount of projection of the dental arcades anterior to the rami, and by extension the zygomatic bones with which the anterior ramal margins are closely associated, was less than that of Shanidar 1 and most other Neandertals. Therefore, the amount of midfacial prognathism that is indicated by the Shanidar 2 mandible is less than that of Shanidar 1. The degree of midfacial projection suggested by the Shanidar 2 mandible is thus in agreement with the configuration evident in the maxillae.

The lateral surfaces of the corpus exhibit relatively weak superior lateral tori extending posteriorly from the mental foramina. On the right side particularly, the superior lateral torus forms a tubercle just posterior of the superoanterior mental foramen, but then tapers off to a low swelling before it reaches the lateral prominence. Both inferior margins are damaged and partially restored with filler so that the development of the marginal tori is uncertain. However, the intertoral sulci are barely discernible. The marginal tori therefore must have been quite modest. The submolar sulci are large and flat but not particularly deep. The lateral surfaces of the Shanidar 2 mandibular corpus are, if anything, remarkable for their minimal relief.

Because the symphysis has been largely reconstructed in filler, it is not possible to assess its morphology. There is bone preserved on the left external surface anterior to the I_2. The resulting lateral profile (Figure 19) suggests that the symphyseal angle, as determined between the horizontal alveolar plane and the anterior surface of the symphysis, was close to 90°. It was probably less retreating than that of Shanidar 1 (compare Figures 14 and 19).

The region below the left C^- and I_2 exhibits a large and relatively deep anterior mandibular incisure with a strong tubercle (lateral tubercle of the mental trigone?) inferior to it. These remaining features suggest that Shanidar 2 had a mental trigone at least as prominent as that of Shanidar 1. However, the incomplete state of the specimen precludes any definite conclusion as to this morphology.

The medial surfaces of the mandibular corpus are sharply divided into sublingual and submandibular fossae. Both of the sublingual fossae are largely restored so that their detailed morphology is indistinct. The mylohyoid lines are apparent as muscular lines on raised crests extending anteroinferiorly from prominent triangular tori and pharyngeal crests. The development of the bone underlying the mylohyoid lines creates sulci along the anterosuperior margins of the submandibular fossae, similar to those of Shanidar 1.

The posterior margins of the submandibular fossae blend into markedly rugose insertion areas for the medial pterygoid muscles, insertions that extend from the inferior surfaces below the pharyngeal crests to midway up the posterior margins of the rami. These insertions for the medial pterygoid muscles are considerably more robust than even those of Shanidar 1, a pattern which is in agreement with the extra development of the masticatory musculature attachments on the cranium of Shanidar 2.

Corresponding to the strong musculature for the Shanidar 2 mandible are prominent developments of architectural reinforcements of the rami. The medial surfaces of both superior rami were damaged and have been restored. However, much of the medial surface of the right ramus is intact, and the lateral surface of the right ramus is largely preserved to the tip of the coronoid process and the lateral margin of the condyle (Figure 19). As mentioned, the right triangular torus is strongly built, and extending superiorly from it is a large endocondyloid crest and the remains of what appears to have been a large endocoronoid crest. These features, which supply strength to the bone to resist forces generated by the masticatory musculature, either directly on the mandible or through reaction forces at the temporomandibular joint (White 1977), would be expected to be accentuated in an otherwise reasonably robust mandible.

The mandibular foramina of Shanidar 2 are preserved on both rami. Each one possesses a medially projecting lingula, which tapers inferiorly along its posterior margin into a deep, V-shaped mandibular foramen (Figure 19). There is no evidence of bridges across the mylohyoid sulcus so as to form a horizontal–oval type of mandibular foramen. The mylohyoid sulci appear to have been open along their entire lengths. Therefore, Shanidar 2 agrees with Shanidar 1 in having the morphology usually present in recent humans (96.3–100.0% in five recent human samples [F. H. Smith 1978]), but less frequently among Neandertals (Amud 1 and Tabūn C1 but not Tabūn C2, 38.5% of European Neandertals, $N = 13$).

On the lateral surfaces of the rami, features are again more apparent than on the Shanidar 1 mandible. The lateral eminences are distinct, although not especially prominent. But there are clear masseteric fossae, which are bordered posteroinferiorly by raised ridges around the gonial angles. The ectocondyloid crests are not particularly prominent, but they lead—on the right side where it is preserved and on the left side by inference—into strong subcondylar tubercles. The prominence of the subcondylar tubercle on the right ramus corresponds with the large size of the anterior tubercle on the zygomatic process of the right temporal bone because both provide attachments for the fibrous capsule of the temporomandibular joint, an articulation that bears stress during mastication (Hylander 1975).

Only the lateral half of the right mandibular condyle remains, and it is too incomplete to provide data on the form of the condyle. It implies a relatively large size for the articular surfaces, although it cannot be properly measured.

Although the Shanidar 2 maxillary dental arcade is noticeably wider than those of most other Neandertals, its mandibular dental arcade is not particularly wide. Its external alveolar breadth measured at the M_1 posterior alveolus (ca. 66.0 mm) is similar to those of Shanidar 1 (66.3 mm) and Amud 1 (65.6 mm), and slightly above a European Neandertal mean (63.1 ± 1.8 mm, N = 7) and those of Tabūn C1 and C2 (62.5 and 60.5 mm, respectively). Its alveolar length of about 56.0 mm is similarly toward the top of the known Neandertal ranges of variation (Shanidar 1: 51.0 mm; Amud 1: 50.9 mm; Tabūn C1: 54.0 mm; Tabūn C2: 59.0 mm; European Neandertals: 53.6 ± 2.7 mm, N = 7). These provide a length/breadth index of about 84.8 for Shanidar 2. This index is very close to the mean index of a European Neandertal sample (84.5 ± 6.1, N = 6) and that of Tabūn C1 (86.4), above those of Shanidar 1 (76.9) and Amud 1 (77.6), and below that of Tabūn C2 (97.6).

The discrepancy between the maxillary length/breadth index indicating a wide palate and the mandibular length/breadth index suggesting an average breadth to the dental arcade could not be due to biases from the reconstructions. If anything, the maxilla is too narrow and/or the mandible is too wide. The differences must be due to differences in the Neandertal reference samples, both of which are small and contain different sets of individuals. The Shanidar 2 dental arcades are probably similar in relative breadth to those of most other Neandertals.

The Shanidar 2 mandible provides the impression of a relatively large, probably wide, and robustly built Neandertal mandible. As with the Shanidar 2 cranium, its mandible is strongly marked for the attachments of the masticatory muscles, and the medial and lateral surfaces of the bone exhibit prominent surface relief. Moreover, as with the cranium, the degree of midfacial prognathism appears to be less than that of Shanidar 1 and other Neandertals.

SHANIDAR 4

Inventory

CRANIUM

The Shanidar 4 cranium was extensively crushed and abraded *in situ* so that reconstruction has been limited. The remaining portions consist of 19 identifiable pieces of facial skeleton, cranial base, and vault plus 74 pieces of cranial vault, few of which are identifiable as to bone. It is possible to gain an impression of the original facial and frontal morphology, but the cranial base and posterior cranial vault pieces are too fragmentary to permit any reliable reconstruction of those regions.

Os Occipitale The bone preserves a piece of the right squamous with 30.0 mm of the lambdoid suture (maximum breadth = 33.7 mm) and a portion of the left occipital torus with 17.5 mm of the lambdoid suture (maximum breadth = 23.0 mm).

Os Sphenoidale The left medial and lateral pterygoid plates are preserved without the hamulus. Maximum height = 37.0 mm.

Os Temporale: Right The bone retains the zygomatic process from just anterior of the articular tubercle to the temporozygomatic suture (maximum length = 34.8 mm) and most of the squamous portion with the anterior and superior squamous suture, the supramastoid crest, and the superior margin of the mastoid process (maximum length [anteroposterior] = 65.7 mm).

Os Temporale: Left The bone retains most of the zygomatic process anterior of the articular tubercle (maximum length = 34.4 mm) and an anterior section of the squamous portion with the sphenosquamosal suture and part of the squamous suture (maximum length [anteroposterior] = 35.5 mm).

Os Parietale: Right? A posteromedial section of the right (?) parietal bone is preserved with about 30.0 mm of the posterior sagittal suture and the medial end of the lambdoid suture (maximum length = 49.5 mm).

Os Parietale: Left A small section of the bone along the sagittal suture (maximum breadth = 25.0 mm) is present, as are an anteromedial piece with bregma and about 20.0 mm of each of the coronal and sagittal sutures extending out from bregma (maximum breadth = 27.0 mm).

Os Parietale: Side Indeterminate A large portion of a parietal bone near the tuber is preserved. Maximum dimension = 48.9 mm.

Os Frontale The frontal bone consists of four pieces. There is a major portion of the left half of the frontal bone, with the lateral half of the left supraorbital torus, the left frontozygomatic suture, most of the temporal crest, the region around the tuber, a section of the frontal crest about midway between glabella and bregma and a small section of the coronal suture just lateral from bregma (maximum length = 100.0 mm; maximum breadth = 91.1 mm). A major section of the right squamous portion around the tuber is preserved with part of the temporal crest and 11.5 mm of the coronal suture just lateral of stephanion (maximum length = 70.0 mm; maximum breadth = 67.0 mm). There are fragments of the superoanterior surface bone at glabella (maximum breadth = 41.0 mm) and of one orbital plate (maximum length = 36.0 mm).

Maxilla: Right The right maxilla is represented mostly by the medial third of the bone, from the superior tips of the I^2–P^4 sockets to the beginning of the nasomaxillary suture (maximum height = 58.5 mm; maximum breadth = 32.7 mm). In addition, a central portion of the palate is preserved separately (maximum length [anteroposterior] = 26.3 mm).

Maxilla: Left   Most of the anterior surface of the left maxilla is preserved, with much of the nasal margin, the nasomaxillary suture, the medial half of the orbital margin, and the superior edges of the alveoli from I^1 to M^2 (maximum height = 63.0 mm; maximum breadth = 64.8 mm). A section of the palate is also preserved (maximum length [anteroposterior] = 31.6 mm).

Os Zygomaticum: Right   The right zygomatic bone consists of the complete temporal process (maximum length = 27.6 mm) and the majority of the frontal process (maximum height = 25.2 mm).

Os Zygomaticum: Left   The bone consists of the majority of the frontal process and all of the temporal process. Maximum length = 40.5 mm.

MANDIBLE

The mandible consists of five pieces: the symphysis with the left body and ramus (maximum length = 125.3 mm), two pieces of the right body and ramus (maximum lengths = 104.2 mm and 46.0 mm), the lateral half of the right condyle (maximum dimension = 9.9 mm), and a piece of the right M^1 and M^2 alveoli (maximum length = 25.0 mm). The symphyseal and left side piece is complete from the right I_2–C interdental septum to the ramus, even though there was antemortem resorption in the molar region and postmortem abrasion to the incisor and canine alveoli. The anterior portion of the ramus with the coronoid process is complete, but the posterior margin and the condyle are absent. The right body and ramus pieces preserve the lateral surface largely intact and most of the medial surface from the premolar region to the mandibular notch. The right coronoid process is missing, and the right condyle preserves only the lateral half of the articular surface plus the subcondylar tubercle. It is possible to place the two larger pieces of the right body and ramus together, but the contacts with the molar alveoli piece are tenuous and there are no contacts between the main portion of the right ramus and the condyle.

Morphology

Shanidar 4 preserves a substantial proportion of its anterior skull and portions of the posterior cranium. Yet of the four adults with major portions of the skull preserved, Shanidar 4 provides the least information concerning cranial and mandibular morphology.

When the Shanidar 4 skeleton was uncovered, the skull was lying on its left side, flattened from side to side. As with much of the Shanidar 4 postcranial skeleton, the cranium and mandible were highly friable, broken into innumerable pieces, and abraded along all exposed edges. In addition, the cranial vault bones of Shanidar 4, of which about 80 separate pieces remain, were eroded on their internal and/or external tables, frequently split through the diploë, and usually rounded along the breaks. As a result it has been extremely difficult to reassemble much of the vault, and only the frontal bone is sufficiently complete to indicate its overall shape. The bones of the facial skeleton are less eroded, although there are few contacts between the preserved pieces.

In 1962, when Stewart cleaned and studied the Shanidar 4, 6, and 8 skeletons in the Iraq Museum, he abandoned any thought of reassembling the Shanidar 4 cranium. He devoted most of his efforts to the mandible and postcrania, largely omitting the cranium except for a few comments on the section of left supraorbital torus and the right zygomatic arch (Stewart 1963). The mandible (Figure 21) presented only a few problems in reconstruction. The left side is solid and possesses no distortion. The right side has four pieces, two of the corpus that fit approximately together, a piece of the molar alveoli, and a separate condylar fragment. There are a large number of cracks in the inferior region of the right corpus that have slightly expanded the breadth of the corpus.

The mandibular dental arcade breadths were approximated by drawing the midline of the mandible through the symphysis, measuring from the midline to the left side, and then doubling the measurement. The breadths across the ramal region were estimated by orienting the right ramus and corpus relative to the left one, using the dental arcade breadths determined from the left side, and then measuring across both coronoids and measuring from the estimated position of the right condyle to the midline and doubling the measurement. It is clear that the potential for error in these breadth measurements is high, but repeated determinations of these dimensions produced consistent results. Other metric determinations on the Shanidar 4 mandible should be reliable without qualification.

Even though a substantial percentage of the upper facial skeleton is preserved, few of the pieces fit together. Most of the pieces provide some morphological information, but only the left half of the frontal bone and the large piece of left maxilla indicate the shape of the Shanidar 4 face. It is not possible to orient accurately the left maxilla by itself because it lacks the midline below the nasal aperture and does not join with the eroded palatal piece. However, the midline can be determined on the left mandibular corpus, the size and position of the left dentitions can be reconstructed reasonably, and the distance between the left zygomaxillary region and the left coronoid process can be estimated. It is therefore possible to orient the left maxilla relative to a median sagittal plane and to estimate the amount of midfacial projection on the Shanidar 4 cranium.

Despite these deficiencies in the Shanidar 4 skull, portions of the facial skeleton provide important morphological data. Most of the information comes from the mandible, but the cranium makes its contribution.

THE CRANIAL VAULT

As a result of the extreme fragmentation of the parietal and occipital bones, most of the information on the Shanidar 4 cranial vault comes from the frontal bone (Figure 20).

The overall size of the frontal bone can be indicated by the chord between bregma and frontomalare anterior. This dimension equals 116.5 mm for Shanidar 4. This value is slightly below those of Shanidar 1 (117.5 mm), Shanidar 5 (119.0 & 120.4 mm), Amud 1 (119.9 & 118.6 mm), Zuttiyeh 1 (119.3 mm) and La Ferrassie 1 (120.5 mm), but above those of La Chapelle-aux-Saints 1 (110.5 & 114.3 mm) and La Quina 5 (110.6 & 109.0 mm). These data show that the Shanidar 4 frontal was similar in size to those of most other Neandertals.

The curvature of the Shanidar 4 frontal cannot be measured, but it appears to have been modest. There is a relatively strong curve just above the supratoral sulcus, but the posterior half of the medial sagittal contour is virtually flat. In this, the Shanidar 4 frontal resembles that of Shanidar 1 and differs from the more even curve of the Shanidar 5 frontal.

The thickness of the Shanidar 4 cranial vault bones can be measured at the right and left frontal tubers (9.0 & 8.8 mm, respectively) and at one parietal tuber of indeterminate side (8.1 mm). The frontal thicknesses are above those of Shanidar 1 (8.5 mm), Tabūn C1 (5.0 mm), Zuttiyeh 1 (6.0 mm), and most European Neandertals (6.9 ± 1.0 mm, N = 10) and are matched only by that of Amud 1 (9.0 mm) among the Neandertals. The parietal measurement, in contrast, is similar to those of Shanidar 1 and 2 and Amud 1 (8.0, 8.2, and 8.0 mm, respectively) and between a European Neandertal parietal thickness mean (7.6 ± 1.1 mm, N = 27) and the mean of a small Neandertal male sample (8.5 ± 1.4 mm, N = 4). The Shanidar 4 cranial vault fragments exhibit the enlarged diploic space and thinned tables characteristic of older individuals, and it is possible that his advanced age at death was partly responsible for his thick cranial vault bones.

THE OCCIPITOMASTOID REGION

There are two small pieces that retain portions of the transverse occipital torus. They are too small to indicate the shape of the torus or whether a suprainiac fossa was present, but they indicate a strongly built transverse occipital torus. Its degree of development most closely approximates that of Shanidar 2 and is greater than that of Shanidar 1.

The right temporal bone preserves a fragment of the mastoid crest, much of the supramastoid sulcus, and a major portion of the supramastoid crest. The mastoid crest appears to have been prominent, and the supramastoid crest was strongly built.

THE TEMPORAL FOSSA REGION

Significant portions of both zygomatic arches survive. Neither articular tubercle is preserved, but much of the *M. masseter* attachments along the inferior

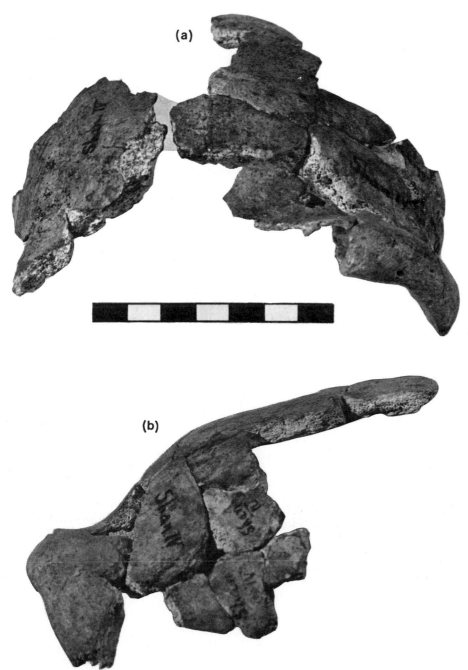

Figure 20 (a) Anterior and (b) left lateral views of the Shanidar 4 frontal bone and parietal fragment at bregma. The positions of the two pieces of frontal relative to each other and the orientations of the frontal bone relative to the Frankfurt horizontal are approximate. Scale in centimeters.

margins are present. Both exhibit a series of small notches for the muscular insertions, implying muscles that were well developed. This inference is supported by the large tubercle that formed at the left zygomaxillare anterior and by the markings of the M. *masseter* insertion on the right mandibular ramus.

The posterolateral margin of the left frontal process is vertically straight, lacking the tubercle for the anterior insertion of the M. *temporalis* fascia present on Shanidar 1. The temporal crests are preserved on both sides and are quite prominent, extending at least 40.0 mm from the frontozygomatic suture. This suggests that at least the anterior portions of the Mm. *temporalis* were well developed.

THE UPPER FACIAL SKELETON

The orbital region of Shanidar 4 is represented by two pieces of the supraorbital torus, a small portion of the frontal process of each zygomatic bone, and the anteroinferior margin of the left orbit along the maxilla. There are no contacts between these five pieces, so it is not possible to ascertain the shapes or dimensions of the orbits.

The supraorbital torus is represented primarily by a piece that extends from the middle of the left orbit to the frontozygomatic suture and retains all of the anterior and superior toral surfaces plus a small portion of the orbital plate. It is a robust torus, which tapers minimally laterally. Its midorbit thickness of 13.6 mm is slightly less than those of Shanidar 1 (14.8 mm), Shanidar 2 (15.0 & 14.0 mm), Amud 1 (15.0 mm), and Zuttiyeh 1 (15.7 & 14.8 mm). Yet it is still above a European Neandertal mean (12.0 ± 2.0 mm, N = 18).

The supratoral sulcus is long and relatively deep, at least over the lateral two-thirds of the orbit. The supratoral surface goes directly posteriorly for about 20.0 mm over the midorbit, and then it curves markedly upward. It is noticeably longer anteroposteriorly than that of Shanidar 1. The small piece near glabella suggests that the supratoral sulcus remained relatively long on the midline, but it is not possible to determine whether it flattened out medially as in Shanidar 1.

The anterior and superior surfaces of the Shanidar 4 supraorbital torus are covered with fine cancellous bone, which has become partially obscured through remodeling. In this, Shanidar 4 is very similar to Shanidar 1 and other older Neandertals.

The frontal sinuses of Shanidar 4 are evident on the inferior surface of the glabellar fragment and on the medioinferior surfaces of the left supraorbital torus. Although the sinuses are incomplete, it is apparent that they extended only to the middle of the orbit laterally, filled the supraorbital torus medially, and did not extend into the frontal squamous. They are thus similar to those of other Neandertals.

The lateral margin of the sinus is clearly evident in the left torus. Because the median sagittal plane is indicated by the frontal spine and bregma, it is

possible to estimate the sinus breadth by doubling the distance from the midline to the lateral extent on the left side. This provides a breadth estimate of
88.0 mm, which is above those of Shanidar 1 (74.0 mm), Amud 1 (62.0 mm),
Tabūn C1 (52.1 mm), and most European Neandertals (66.0 ± 12.9 mm, N = 9)
and is exceeded only by that of La Ferrassie 1 (91.0 mm) (Tillier 1974; Vlček
1967).

The Shanidar 4 maxillae give the impression of being relatively large and
robust but not especially prominent (Figure 21). By orienting the left maxilla
over the mandible, it is possible to estimate the bimaxillary breadth at 116.0
mm and the direct distance from zygomaxillare anterior to subspinale at 66.0
mm. These measurements provide a subtense from subspinale to the bimaxillary breadth of about 31.5 mm and a zygomaxillary angle of about 123°. This
zygomaxillary angle is exceeded only by Shanidar 2 (ca. 125°) among the Neandertals, and it is considerably greater than those of Shanidar 1 (105°), Amud 1
(ca. 115°), and European Neandertals (105°–114°, 110.6° ± 4.3°, N = 4). As with
that of Shanidar 2, the zygomaxillary angle of Shanidar 4 falls within the ranges
of variation of Early Upper Paleolithic hominids (127.3° ± 8.8°, N = 6) and
recent humans (range of male means for 17 samples: 120.3° ± 6.6° to 138.9° ±
4.7° [Howells 1973]). It indicates that Shanidar 4, like Shanidar 2, has an
exceptionally flat midfacial region for a Neandertal.

A further indication of this relative flatness of the Shanidar 4 midface is the
position of its left zygomatic root approximately above M^2 as in Shanidar 2,
rather than above the M^2–M^3 interdental septum as in Shanidar 1, La Chapelle-
aux-Saints 1, and La Ferrassie 1.

The anterolateral surface of the maxilla is slightly concave anterior of the
zygomaticomaxillary suture. The maxilla is not inflated as in European Neandertal maxillae, but neither does it have a canine fossa. It is similar to Shanidar
2 in having a projecting anterior zygomatic bone, which creates a concavity
between zygomaxillare anterior and the molar alveoli. When viewed in norma
facialis (Figure 21), the lateral profile of the maxilla has a contour intermediate
between the straight border of European Neandertals and the notch evident on
recent human crania (Sergi 1947).

Despite its minimal anterior projection, the Shanidar 4 midface is nonetheless large. Its estimated bimaxillary breadth of 116.0 mm is greater than that of
Shanidar 1 (104.0 mm), similar to those of Shanidar 2 (ca. 115.0 mm) and
Amud 1 (114.0 mm), but less than that of Shanidar 5 (ca. 120.0 mm). It is
slightly above a European Neandertal mean (109.4 ± 6.2 mm, N = 5) and
considerably above the means of an Early Upper Paleolithic sample (96.1 ± 5.3
mm, N = 9) and those of most recent humans (range of male means for 17
samples: 92.2 ± 4.8 to 104.3 ± 5.2 mm [Howells 1973]).

On the left maxilla there are two separate infraorbital foramina, as well as at
least four smaller foramina along the orbital margin of the frontal process of the
maxilla (Table 9). The larger of the two infraorbital foramina is along a fracture,
so that its breadth and possible bifurcation are indeterminate. The second

foramen is located slightly medial of the primary one and is considerably smaller. The presence of double infraorbital foramina is similar to Shanidar 1 and other Neandertals.

The upper facial skeleton of Shanidar 4 appears to conform most to the morphological pattern of Shanidar 2. It is a wide face with a robust supraorbital torus, little midfacial prognathism, and relatively flat or slightly concave anterior maxillae. The shape of its maxillae thus contrasts with those of Shanidar 1 and most other Neandertals.

THE MANDIBLE

Although the Shanidar 4 mandible had been reduced to five separate pieces, a sufficient amount of the bone remains to provide considerable morphological and morphometric data (Figure 21). All of the morphometrics except the estimates of superior length and ramus breadth derive from the left corpus, ramus, and symphysis piece. Qualitative observations come from the whole mandible.

A reconstruction of the mandible using the two large corpus and ramus pieces and the lateral half of the right condyle provides a superior length of about 111.0 mm. This length is minimally below those of Shanidar 1 and 2 (115.0 and ca. 112.0 mm, respectively), close to that of Amud 1 (ca. 111.0 mm) and a European Neandertal mean (113.8 ± 8.2 mm, N = 6), and between those of Tabūn C1 (102.0 mm) and Tabūn C2 (122.0 mm). The Shanidar 4 mandibular superior length is also considerably above the means of two recent European samples (95.3 ± 2.3 mm, N = 108 [Twiesselmann and Brabant 1967]; 91.3 ± 5.5 mm, N = 50). Furthermore, it is above the known ranges of European and Near Eastern early anatomically modern humans (92.5–107.0 mm, 100.3 ± 6.2 mm, N = 8), although it is within their expected range of variation.

If the Shanidar 4 superior mandibular length is normalized for body size using his femoral bicondylar length, the resultant index is about 26.3. This index is very close to those of Shanidar 1 (ca. 25.1) and 5 (ca. 26.0) and between those of Amud 1 and Tabūn C1 (ca. 23.0 and 24.9, respectively) and those of La Chapelle-aux-Saints 1 and La Ferrassie 1 (ca. 26.7 and ca. 26.6, respectively). All of these Shanidar indices and those of most of the other Neandertals are well above those of more recent humans (Caviglione 1: ca. 20.2; Dolní Věstonice 3: 22.1; Předmostí 3: 21.4; Qafzeh 9: ca. 22.8; Skhūl 4: 21.7; Skhūl 5: ca. 20.7; recent European sample: 21.0 ± 1.1, N = 50). Shanidar 4, along with the other Shanidar Neandertals, apparently had a long face relative to overall body size.

The Shanidar 4 mandibular reconstruction also provides an estimate of bicondylar maximum breadth of about 135.0 mm. This value is slightly below those of Shanidar 1 (142.8 mm), Shanidar 2 (ca. 154.5 mm), and Amud 1 (ca. 145.0 mm). Yet it is minimally above those of Tabūn C1 (ca. 133.0 mm) and C2 (130.0 mm) and almost identical to a European Neandertal mean (136.0 ± 8.7 mm, N = 7). Again, Shanidar 4 and the other Neandertals are consistently

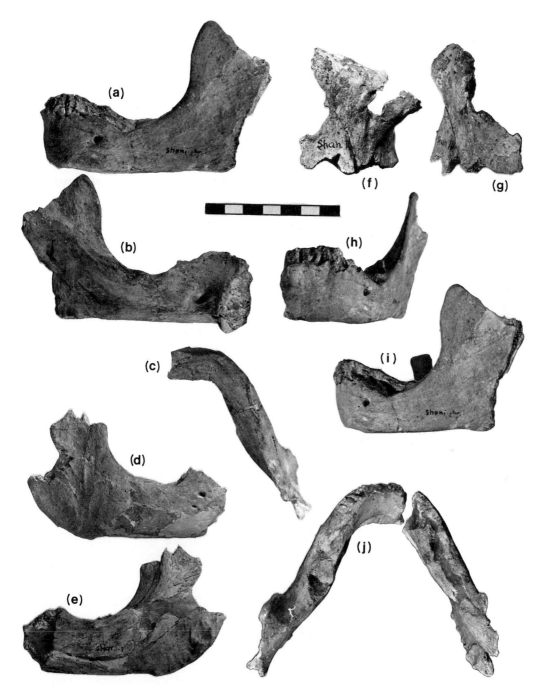

Figure 21 The Shanidar 4 left maxilla and mandible. Mandible: (a) left lateral, (b) left medial, (c) inferior, (d) right lateral, and (e) right medial views. The lateral and medial views are in the planes of the lateral corpori and rami. Left maxilla in (f) *norma facialis* and (g) *norma lateralis* left. Left mandibular piece in (h) *norma facialis* and (i) *norma lateralis* left; the position of the left M_3 alveolus is marked by the plasticene plug. (j) Occlusal view of the mandible. The two major pieces of the right corpus have been joined and the missing portions reconstructed in wax; the positions of the right and left halves relative to each other are approximate because postmortem damage and expansion of the anterior end of the right piece prevent a proper union between them. Scale in centimeters.

above recent human means (Europeans: 122.7 ± 2.6 mm, N = 106 [Twies-selmann and Brabant 1967]; Australians: 112.4 ± 5.0 mm, N = 33 [Keiter 1934]; Melanesians: 112.1 ± 5.2 mm, N = 54 [Keiter 1934]).

It is possible to compute a mandibular (length/breadth) index for the Shanidar 4 mandible of about 82.2. This index is similar to that of Shanidar 1 (80.5) and above that of Shanidar 2 (ca. 72.5). It is quite close to a European Neandertal mean (82.7 ± 6.1, N = 5); the other Near Eastern Neandertals have somewhat variable indices (Amud 1: ca. 76.6; Tabūn C1: ca. 76.7; Tabūn C2: 93.8). The Shanidar 4 mandible, as reconstructed, is therefore similar in overall proportions and size to those of other Neandertals.

The proportions of the Shanidar 4 mandibular dental arcade are similarly close to those of other Neandertals. Its external alveolar breadth measured at the distal M_1 margin is about 60.0 mm, which is slightly less than those of Shanidar 1 and 2 (66.3 and ca. 66.0 mm, respectively), but well within Nean-dertal ranges of variation (Amud 1: 65.6 mm; Tabūn C1: 62.5 mm; Tabūn C2: 60.5 mm; European Neandertals: 63.1 ± 1.8 mm, N = 7). Its dental arcade length of about 55.0 mm is also similar to those of Shanidar 1 and 2 (51.0 and ca. 56.0 mm, respectively) and other Neandertals (Amud 1: 50.9 mm; Tabūn C1: 54.0 mm; Tabūn C2: 59.0 mm; European Neandertals: 53.6 ± 2.7 mm, N = 7). The length/breadth index derived from these mandibular dental arcade dimen-sions is about 91.7 for Shanidar 4. This value is relatively high for a Neandertal (Shanidar 1: 76.9; Shanidar 2: ca. 84.8; Amud 1: 77.6; Tabūn C1: 86.4; Tabūn C2: 97.6; European Neandertals: 84.5 ± 6.1, N = 7). Shanidar 4 thus had a somewhat long dental arcade or a narrow arcade breadth.

The corpus of the Shanidar 4 mandible is otherwise very similar to those of the other Shanidar and Neandertal mandibles. Its symphyseal height (ca. 36.6 mm) is minimally below those of Shanidar 1 and 2 (37.2 and ca. 37.3 mm, respectively) and Amud 1 (37.0 mm) and slightly above a European Neandertal mean (27.7–42.3 mm, 34.7 ± 3.9 mm, N = 14); the Tabūn C1 and C2 sym-physeal heights span most of the known Neandertal range (30.3 and 42.0 mm, respectively). The Shanidar 4 symphyseal breadth (17.5 mm) is virtually the same as that of Shanidar 1 (17.6 mm), but it is above those of all other Neander-tals (Tabūn C1: 13.2 mm; Tabūn C2: 17.0 mm; European Neandertals: 15.0 ± 1.0 mm, N = 14; range = 13.2–17.0 mm, N = 16). For this reason, its sym-physeal robusticity index (breadth/height) of about 47.8 is similar to that of Shanidar 1 (47.3) but above the majority of the indices of other Neandertals (Tabūn C1: 43.6; Tabūn C2: 40.5; European Neandertals: 43.6 ± 3.8, N = 14).

Despite damage to the alveoli in the region of the left mental foramen, the height of the Shanidar 4 corpus at the mental foramen appears to be quite high (ca. 37.0 mm). This figure is slightly above those of Shanidar 1 (35.8 & 36.9 mm) and Shanidar 2 (34.8 & 34.5 mm); it is also above those of most other Neander-tals (Amud 1: 34.0 mm; Tabūn C1: 27.5 mm; Tabūn C2: 42.5 mm: European Neandertals: 26.3–38.0 mm, 31.5 ± 3.7 mm, N = 19). Yet, as with symphyseal breadth, corpus breadth at the mental foramen for Shanidar 4 (17.4 mm) is similar to those of Shanidar 1 (17.5 & 17.6 mm) and Shanidar 2 (ca. 17.6 & 17.8 mm) but greater than the mean European Neandertal value (15.7 ± 1.4 mm, N = 19) and those of Amud 1 (15.0 mm), Tabūn C1 (15.0 mm), and Tabūn C2 (16.4 mm). This provides a robusticity index of about 47.0 for Shanidar 4, which is about the same as those of most other Neandertals (Amud 1: 44.1; Tabūn C1: 54.5; Tabūn C2: 38.6; European Neandertals: 50.3 ± 5.4, N = 19) as well as of Shanidar 1 (48.9 & 47.7) and Shanidar 2 (ca. 50.6 & 51.6).

The Shanidar 4 mental foramina consist of one very large foramen on the left side, located below the M_1, and two smaller ones on the right side, located below the P_4–M_1 interdental septum. The presence of double foramina on at least one side is similar to Shanidar 2, which has two foramina on each side, and the positioning of the mental foramina below the P_4–M_1 interdental septum and below M_1 is similar to the arrangement present in the Shanidar 1 and 2 mandibles. Again, this is a typically Neandertal pattern because Amud 1, Tabūn C1, and Tabūn C2, and 90.0% (N = 20) of European Neandertals have their mental foramina below or posterior to the P_4–M_1 interdental septum. Even though 60.0% of samples of recent Australians may have mental foramina below or posterior to the P_4–M_1 interdental septum (Larnach and Macintosh 1966, 1971), most recent human samples have less than 30.0% of their mental foramina that far posterior (Keiter 1934; Liau 1956; Simonton 1923).

In contrast with Shanidar 1 and 2 and almost all other Neandertals, Shanidar 4 appears to lack a mandibular retromolar space (Figure 21). The left corpus preserves the M_3 alveolus, which has been only moderately altered by alveolar resorption, and the crown of the left M_3. If the crown is positioned above the socket, its distal margin is in the same coronal plane as the anterior margin of the ramus. The only other Neandertal mandible that exhibits so small a space between the M_3 and the ramus is La Quina 9 (Martin 1926a).

The absence of a retromolar space in the Shanidar 4 mandible is due in part to the breadth of its ramus, as the overall mandible and dental arcade lengths are similar to those of other Neandertals. The right ramus breadth is about 45.5 mm, which is slightly greater than those of Shanidar 2 (44.0 & 43.7 mm) and considerably above those of Shanidar 1 (41.7 & 40.2 mm). It is also at the upper limit of the known range of variation of other Near Eastern and European Neandertals (Amud 1: 40.0 mm; Tabūn C1: 38.0 mm; Tabūn C2: 40.0 mm; European Neandertals: 40.1 ± 4.0 mm, N = 9; range: 34.7–45.5 mm, N = 12). All of these values are considerably greater than those of recent humans (Europeans: 33.1 ± 1.6 mm, N = 108 [Twiesselmann and Brabant 1967]; Europeans: 31.9 ± 2.9 mm, N = 50; Amerindians: 36.2 ± 2.9 mm, N = 50; Australians: 32.6 ± 1.8 mm, N = 33 [Keiter 1934]; Melanesians: 33.1 ± 2.1 mm, N = 54 [Keiter 1934]), and the Shanidar 4 breadth especially is well above the breadths in an Early Upper Paleolithic sample (35.0–39.0 mm, 36.3 ± 1.3 mm, N = 8) and most of the ramus breadths in a Skhūl–Qafzeh sample (32.0–42.5 mm, 38.3 ± 4.4 mm, N = 5).

If the minimum ramus breadth of the Shanidar 4 mandible is normalized for overall size by its mandibular superior length, the large size of the ramus remains in evidence. The resultant index for Shanidar 4 is about 41.0. This index is greater than those of Shanidar 2 (ca. 39.3 & ca. 39.0) and Shanidar 1 (36.3 & 35.0) and above those of all other Neandertals (Amud 1: 35.6; Tabūn C1: 37.3; Tabūn C2: 32.8; La Chapelle-aux-Saints 1: ca. 39.0 & ca. 39.6; La Ferrassie 1: 35.7 & 36.1; Krapina J: 33.4; La Quina 5: ca. 36.2; Régourdou 1: 37.3). Among European and Near Eastern archiac humans, only the Mauer 1 mandible, with an index of 43.4, has a relatively wider mandibular ramus than Shanidar 4. Because the dental arcade length of the Shanidar 4 mandible (ca. 55.0 mm) is average for a Neandertal, it is undoubtedly the exceptionally wide ramus that is responsible for the absence of a retromolar space.

The large breadth of the Shanidar 4 mandibular ramus and the absence of a retromolar space agree morphologically with the minimal midfacial prognathism of the maxillae. The anterior placement of the anterior zygomatic bone would be necessary to fit with the broad ramus and would tend to reduce the projection of the central maxillae in front of the zygomatic region.

The lateral surfaces of the mandibular corpus exhibit prominent lateral superior tori, which arise anteriorly around the mental foramina. Posteriorly, the lateral superior tori become less distinct, although as well developed, in the region of the lateral prominences. The intertoral sulcus, on the left side in particular, appears deeper than those of Shanidar 1 and 2. This is due in part to the greater development of the lateral superior tori of Shanidar 4, but it is created primarily by the presence of a robust marginal torus. The marginal torus of Shanidar 4 arises from a large anterior marginal tubercle and extends along the inferior margin, tapering off as it approaches the M. masseter and M. pterygoideus medialis insertions. It is not possible to assess how large the submolar sulci were because alveolar resorption after antemortem loss of several molars (Table 15) caused the loss of most of the lateral surface bone to the superior margins of the lateral superior tori. The development of lateral corpus features on Shanidar 4 is considerably more than that of Shanidar 1 and 2, implying a more robust mandible for Shanidar 4.

The symphyseal region of Shanidar 4 exhibits the same slightly retreating profile present on Shanidar 1 (Figure 16). The angle between the anterior surface of the symphysis and the horizontal plane of the alveoli is about 72° on Shanidar 4. This angle is comparable to that of Shanidar 1 (78°) and those of other Neandertals (Amud 1: 82°; Tabūn C1: 72°; Tabūn C2: 80°; European Neandertals: 83.4° ± 7.3°, N = 8). However, it is relatively low for a Neandertal and extremely low compared to those of recent humans (94.1° ± 2.0°, N = 109 [Twiesselmann and Brabant 1967]). The angle between the horizontal plane of the alveoli and the midline of the symphysis is about 60° for Shanidar 4, which is not quite as low compared to that of Shanidar 1 (65°). Yet it is relatively low for a Neandertal (Amud 1: 74°; Tabūn C1: 61°; Tabūn C2: 72°; European Neandertals: 70.3° ± 5.9°, N = 10). Evidently, Shanidar 4 has a retreating symphyseal profile, although its angles are still within Neandertal ranges of variation.

The anterior surface of the symphysis is intact only on the left side. There is a definite swelling of bone on the symphysis, which is apparently a combination of the symphyseal tuberosity and the lateral tubercles (Figure 21). They do not form a triangular elevation, and so technically there is no mental trigone. But the protruding area delineated by a clear anterior mandibular incisure is certainly the equivalent of a mental trigone. Because the incisor and canine alveoli are damaged, it is not possible to determine whether there was any alveolar prognathism. Yet the bone along the superior edge of the anterior mandibular incisure turns anteriorly (Figure 21), suggesting that there might have been some alveolar prognathism.

The lingual surface of the mandibular symphysis is marked by a relatively long and flat alveolar plane with little or no superior transverse torus on its superior half and by a pronounced inferior transverse torus on its inferior half (Figures 16 and 21). The inferior surface of the inferior transverse torus has been crushed, but it appears as though this torus originally curved smoothly onto the inferior margin of the symphysis. On the superior margin of the inferior transverse torus there are two distinct mental spines, which form the inferior edge of a large, but moderately shallow, genioglossal fossa. The fossa is quite similar to that of Shanidar 1 (Figure 15).

The inferior surface of the left corpus next to the symphysis exhibits a prominent and large digastric fossa (Figure 21). As with the Shanidar 1 digastric fossae, it is delineated primarily by a muscular crest along its anterior and lateral margins, but the Shanidar 4 insertion area for M. digastricus is slightly more recessed into the surface of the mandible. Apparently the digastric muscles were as well developed on Shanidar 4 as they appear to have been on Shanidar 1.

The inferior transverse torus leads around on the medial surfaces of the mandible to form large and moderately prominent mylohyoid lines. There is no evidence regarding the configuration of the sublingual fossae, since the regions were resorbed following antemortem tooth loss, but the submandibular fossae appear deep and clearly defined. The Shanidar 4 submandibular fossae do not have sharp sulci just below the mylohyoid lines, as in Shanidar 1 and 2, but are more evenly curved between the mylohyoid lines and the marginal tori.

The mylohyoid lines lead posteriorly onto prominent pharyngeal crests and triangular tori. But most of each ridge extends beyond the triangular tori to form very pronounced endocoronoid crests. Although one can discern the endocondyloid crests, they are insignificant when compared to the endocoronoid crests. As a result of the large endocoronoid crests, the anteromedial surfaces of the rami have deep sulci running parallel to the anterior borders of the rami.

Posteroinferior from the mylohyoid line and pharyngeal crest on the right ramus is one of the most prominently marked M. pterygoideus medialis insertions known for a Neandertal (Figure 21). Not only are the markings highly rugose, they extend from well on to the inferior margin to half the way up the posterior border of the ramus. In addition, the gonial border has been extended inferiorly and posteriorly to increase the muscular attachment area. This extension is accentuated by a notch on the inferior margin between the marginal torus and the medial pterygoid surface; the notch is evident on the right and left sides in *norma lateralis* as well as *norma medialis*. This exceptional insertion area for *M. pterygoideus medialis* implies a powerful masticatory apparatus.

The mylohyoid sulci are preserved on both rami, but the mandibular foramen is intact only on the left side. Both of the mylohyoid sulci have mylohyoid bridges, which extend from slightly below the mandibular foramina for about 20.0 mm along the sulci. Mylohyoid bridges occur in variable frequencies in recent human samples (0.0–41.0% in 16 recent human samples [Ossenberg 1976]). The left mandibular foramen lacks the horizontal–oval pattern, which occurs in the majority (61.5%, N = 13) of adult European Neandertals and on Tabūn C2 but is absent from Shanidar 1 and 2, Amud 1, and Tabūn C1. As with Shanidar 1 and 2, the mandibular foramen has a distinct lingula, which descends inferiorly along its posterior margin to form a V-shaped entrance into the mylohyoid sulcus. Yet, unlike Shanidar 1 and 2, the lingula does not project medially, remaining largely within the contours of the medial ramal surface.

The lateral surfaces of the Shanidar 4 mandibular rami are strongly marked for the attachment of each *M. masseter*. There are modest lateral eminences. Extending inferiorly from the lateral eminences are distinct ridges formed by the intermuscular tendinous septa in the superficial layers of each *M. masseter*. Although such ridges are common on recent human and Neandertal mandibles, they are seldom as developed as on Shanidar 4. There is little evidence of them on the Shanidar 1 and 2 rami (Figures 15 and 17). In addition, there is a raised and rounded ridge along the gonial margin of the Shanidar 4 right ramus that sets off a masseteric fossa similar to that of Shanidar 2. The evidence from the medial and lateral surfaces of the Shanidar 4 mandibular rami suggests that Shanidar 4 had powerfully developed masticatory muscles, possibly the strongest of the Shanidar Neandertals.

In association with strong masticatory muscles, one would expect a reinforcement of the temporomandibular joint because it bears stress during mastication (Hylander 1975). Such a reinforcement is demonstrated by the presence of a large subcondylar tubercle just below the right mandibular condyle. It is larger than those on either Shanidar 1 or Shanidar 2. Because the subcondylar tubercle provides attachment for the fibrous capsule of the temporomandibular joint and for the lateral temporomandibular ligament, an expansion of it implies hypertrophy of the ligamentous stabilization of the joint.

The right mandibular condyle is too incomplete to determine its detailed morphology. It appears to have been relatively large, but if normalized for the overall size of the mandible, it may not be particularly large.

The Shanidar 4 mandible is thus a large robust bone with prominent muscular attachment markings and architectural buttressing. Its overall proportions and corpus morphology are similar to those of the other Neandertals, but it is exceptional for its wide rami and the absence of a retromolar space.

SHANIDAR 5

Inventory

CRANIUM

The Shanidar 5 cranium includes most of the upper facial skeleton, the frontal bone, the left parietal bone, and the left temporal bone. Maximum length (prosthion–lambda) = 257.5 mm.

Os Sphenoidale   The inferior half of the right pterygoid plates remains without the hamulus. Maximum height = 21.0 mm.

Os Temporale: Left   The left temporal bone is largely complete. There was some abrasion and loss of bone on the medial petrous crest near the carotid canal, and the region of the occipitomastoid suture posterior to the mastoid process proper is absent. In addition, the styloid process was lost.

Os Parietale: Right   The bone retains only a strip of bone parallel to the coronal suture from bregma to stephanion, which extends up to 40.0 mm from the coronal suture.

Os Parietale: Left   The bone consists of much of the anterior parietal margin, the center of the bone near the tuber, and the posteromedial portion near lambda. A large piece toward asterion, a small area near pterion, and a section along the sagittal suture are missing, and there has been some erosion of the internal table near the tuber. The coronal suture is present from bregma to just lateral of stephanion, the sagittal suture extends 16.0 mm posteriorly from bregma and 49.5 mm anteriorly from lambda, the lambdoid suture extends 58.0 mm laterally from lambda, and 18.0 mm of the squamous suture is present anteriorly along its superior margin.

Os Frontale   The frontal bone is largely complete. The supraorbital torus is complete, and the orbital portion lacks bone only on parts of the orbital plates, exposing the frontal sinuses. The squamous portion has been abraded laterally right and left along the sphenofrontal sutures, but it is complete along the coronal suture from about 20.0 mm below each stephanion. There has been some minor bone loss and warping along the midline due to postmortem breakage. The left squamous exhibits a healed fracture of the external table. In addition, there is a separate piece with a portion of the left orbital plate and the ethmoid air cells (maximum length = 28.0 mm).

Ossa Nasale   The right and left nasal bones are fused together. They are complete along their anterior margin and most of the nasomaxillary sutures, but the region immediately below nasion is lacking.

Maxilla: Right   The right maxilla is complete along the orbital margin from the nasomaxillary suture to the zygomaticomaxillary suture. The superior two-thirds of the nasal aperture is present, and the anterior nasal spine is largely intact. The anterior surface is complete laterally to the infraorbital foramina and the zygomaticomaxillary suture, and the anterior end of the masseteric insertion is present. The palate is complete along its medial two-thirds from the incisor alveoli to just anterior of the palatomaxillary suture, and the alveoli are preserved for I^1, I^2, C^-, and P^4.

Maxilla: Left   Two pieces make up the left maxilla, each of which is joined to neighboring bones. The superior piece includes the orbital margin from the nasomaxillary suture to the zygomaticomaxillary suture and the region around the infraorbital foramen. The other portion includes the I^1–P^3 alveoli, pieces of internal and external alveoli around the M^3, and the palate from the incisors to the region of M^3. The alveoli sustained extensive antemortem resorption.

Os Zygomaticum: Right   The remaining portion consists of the complete orbital margin and the adjacent anterolateral surface bone. Nothing remains of the temporal process.

Os Zygomaticum: Left   The bone is largely intact, lacking only a lateral portion of the zygomaticomaxillary suture and part of the orbital surface.

Morphology

The Shanidar 5 cranium was discovered with the right side of the supraorbital torus and the right frontal squamous appearing alongside a medium-sized rock. The superior surface of the left half of the frontal was up against the rock, the frontal having been folded inferiorly close to its median sagittal line. The whole facial skeleton was turned under the frontal, fragmented into innumerable pieces, but the maxillae were largely in their original configuration. In addition, the left parietal was folded inferiorly slightly posterior to the coronal suture, and the left temporal was turned medially up against the maxillae. The whole cranium therefore occupied a fraction of its original volume.

Although Shanidar 5 was discovered in 1960, it was not until 1976 that it was unpacked in the Iraq Museum. At that time I cleaned all the pieces and reassembled most of the facial skeleton and the frontal bone (Trinkaus 1977d, 1978f). The joins between the pieces of maxillae and between the maxillae and zygomatic bones were clean and introduced little or no distortion. Most of the frontal bone was reassembled without difficulty, although the two sides of the frontal are separated slightly along the midline crack near the coronal suture. The zygomaticomaxillary piece was then joined to the frontal at the two frontozygomatic sutures. Subsequently, I was able to attach the central and posteromedial portion of the left parietal to the strip of left parietal attached to the frontal bone along the coronal suture and to join the left temporal bone to the rest of the cranium. Although there may be some small distortions in the cranium as restored, it should closely approximate its original prefossilization configuration (Figures 22 and 23).

There are three regions of the Shanidar 5 cranium that contain or might contain some distortion. All of the distortion has resulted from difficulties inherent in joining the innumerable pieces of the cranium, especially where the edges along the breaks are thin or have been damaged; they are not due to warping of the bones. These regions are the midline juncture of the nasal bones and maxillae with the frontal bone, the join across the anterior left parietal, and the attachment of the left temporal bone to the remainder of the cranium.

It is apparent in *norma lateralis* that the superoposterior end of the nasal bones is displaced posteriorly relative to the frontonasal suture on the frontal bone. The frontonasal and frontomaxillary sutures are preserved only on the frontal bone, and a gap of at least 2.0 mm exists between the frontal bone and the nasal bones and maxillae. The posterior displacement of the nasal bones (ca. 2.5 mm) is the product of several small angular distortions at glue joins across the inferior orbital margins, especially around the zygomaticomaxillary sutures. On each side below zygoorbitale only a thin layer of anterior surface bone has been preserved, so that some small angular distortion is inevitable and was perceptible only after the zygomatic and maxillary piece had been joined to the frontal bone. The resultant posterior displacement of the nasal bones is minimal and does not affect either morphometrics or morphological observations.

In *situ*, the left parietal consisted of a strip about 30.0 mm wide along the coronal suture, three large pieces of the central and posteromedial parietal and several smaller pieces. The three central and posteromedial pieces join cleanly because their diploë and external tables are well preserved. The anterior strip is fused to the frontal along the coronal suture without distortion. The juncture between these two sections, however, is the break along which the parietal was folded under the frontal *in situ*; both of the edges sustained some erosion, but they probably did not lose more than 1.0 mm of bone between them. The absence of a good fit between these pieces therefore allows considerable play in the orientation of the more posterior parietal piece relative to the anterior parietal and frontal. The pieces were aligned visually, using the contours of the frontal and parietal bones and aligning the posterior section of the sagittal suture in the same median sagittal plane as the bregma, nasion, and prosthion. In *norma lateralis* (Figure 22), it appears as though the sagittal contour is uneven; this is due to the absence of a piece along the sagittal suture close to the location of vertex and not to any angulation of the preserved contours. Any distortion of the parietal bone should be minimal.

The measurements of the parietal median sagittal contour (Table 2) are given as approximates. This is done in recognition that about 1.0 mm of bone may be missing along the fracture line, making the arc and chord measurements slightly short (by less than 1% of their values), and because the region around lambda is irregular, making the precise location of lambda uncertain. It appears

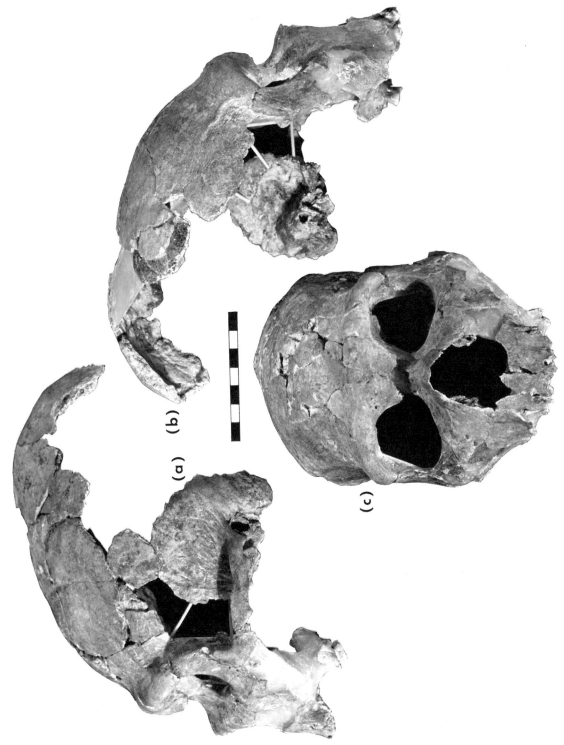

Figure 22 The Shanidar 5 cranium in (a) *norma lateralis* left, (b) *norma lateralis* right, and (c) *norma facialis*. Scale in centimeters.

Figure 23 The Shanidar 5 cranium in (a) *norma verticalis* and (b) *basalis*. Scale in centimeters.

as though a small sutural bone may have been present at lambda, as with Shanidar 1, but that observation cannot be confirmed.

The beautifully preserved left temporal bone is connected to the rest of the cranium across the temporozygomatic suture and along about 18.0 mm of the squamosal suture slightly posterior of pterion. The temporozygomatic suture is well preserved on both the temporal and zygomatic bones, but it allows some play in the orientation of the two bones relative to each other. The temporal is joined to a small piece of parietal bone, 28.0 mm high by 30.5 mm wide, located posteroinferior of stephanion. The juncture along the squamous suture is clean and contains no distortion. However, the join between the anteroinferior piece of parietal and the strip of parietal fused to the frontal bone along the coronal suture is less certain because both edges have been slightly eroded. Yet by using the contour along the zygomatic arch and the contour in the coronal plane through the two pieces of parietal bone, it is possible to orient the temporal bone visually relative to the rest of the cranium. The only measurements that would be affected by a misalignment of the temporal bone are the cranial base breadths across the temporal bone (e.g., biauricular breadth).

The angle of the facial skeleton relative to the cranial vault has been established by the joins at the frontozygomatic sutures, especially the better-preserved left suture, and by the temporal bone. It is not possible for the projection of the face to be any less and still allow sufficient space for the temporal bone to fit between the zygomatic and parietal bones.

Shanidar 5 therefore possesses the second most complete cranium of the Shanidar specimens. Its median sagittal contour is largely complete from prosthion to lambda, most of the upper facial skeleton is preserved, and several cranial breadths and heights can be estimated from the left temporal bone. The only major bone that is entirely lacking is the occipital bone.

THE CRANIAL VAULT

The Shanidar 5 cranial vault (Figures 22 and 23) is relatively narrow, as are those of most Neandertals. An index formed by the maximum frontal breadth and the nasion–lambda length (breadth/length) equals about 62.7. This value is well within Neandertal ranges of variation (Shanidar 1: 66.0; Amud 1: 61.2; Tabūn C1: 71.1; European Neandertals: 64.8 ± 3.8, N = 7). Furthermore, this measure of relative cranial breadth does not separate the Neandertals from a sample of Early Upper Paleolithic hominids (67.4 ± 2.8, N = 12) any more than the cranial index using maximum breadth and length does. Shanidar 5, along with most other Neandertals, is merely dolichocranic, as are many recent humans (Weidenreich 1945).

It is not possible to assess the height of the Shanidar 5 cranial vault using standard osteometrics because basion is not preserved. However, it is possible to determine the bregma radius at about 116.0 mm. This measurement is slightly less than those of Shanidar 1 (120.0 mm) and Amud 1 (123.2 mm) but above a European Neandertal mean (109.2 ± 5.0 mm, N = 5), suggesting that Shanidar 5 had a cranial height similar to those of other Neandertals. However, a height/length index using the bregma radius and the nasion–lambda length provides an index of about 56.9 for Shanidar 5. This value is below those of Shanidar 1 (61.9) and Amud 1 (61.7) and those of the few European Neandertals for which the data are available (La Chapelle-aux-Saints 1: 60.7; La Ferrassie 1: 60.3; La Quina 5: 65.0; Spy 1: 61.5). This index therefore suggests that Shanidar 5 had a relatively long and low cranial vault, although it was not absolutely low for a Neandertal.

The same indication of a long and low cranial vault is provided by the calotte height index, computed from the nasion–lambda length (maximum subtense from the nasion–lambda length divided by the nasion–lambda length). The index is about 26.7 for Shanidar 5, which is below the minimum of a Neandertal sample (28.1–33.5, N = 9; Amud 1: 30.1; Tabūn C1: ca. 29.8; European Neandertals: 31.5 ± 2.4, N = 7). It is considerably below that of Shanidar 1 (32.7), who has a relatively high calotte (see earlier discussion). Because Neandertal indices are consistently lower than those of an Early Upper Paleolithic sample (40.1 ± 2.1, N = 14 [Morant 1930]) and most recent human samples (range of means for 21 recent human samples: 36.2–43.4 [Morant 1927]), Shanidar 5 appears to have had an extremely low calotte.

Most of the differences in this cranial height index between the Neandertals and the Early Upper Paleolithic hominids appear to be in the height measurement from the nasion–lambda line to the vault. The mean nasion–lambda lengths for the two samples are virtually identical (185.3 ± 9.2 mm, N = 9 and 185.6 ± 6.1 mm, N = 14, respectively), but their height measurements are significantly different (57.7 ± 5.0 mm, N = 9 and 74.5 ± 5.3 mm, N = 14, respectively; t = 5.23, p < 0.01). With Shanidar 5, however, the height (54.5 mm) is only slightly below the Neandertal mean, but the nasion–lambda length (ca. 204.0 mm) is the longest known for a Neandertal. It is approached only by Amud 1 at 202.5 mm. It therefore appears that the apparent flatness of the Shanidar 5 cranial vault suggested by both cranial height indices is due in part to its extreme elongation.

The exceptional elongation of the Shanidar 5 cranial vault appears to be a product of a posterosuperior positioning of lambda. The lambda radius, which measures the posterosuperior positioning of lambda, is about 133.0 mm for Shanidar 5. This distance is approached only by Amud 1 (ca. 123.2 mm), which has the largest known Neandertal cranium (Suzuki 1970). This distance for Shanidar 5 is considerably greater than that of Shanidar 1 (114.0 mm) and is 2.95 standard deviations above a Neandertal mean (the Neandertal sample includes Amud 1; 111.5 ± 7.3 mm, N = 6). However, if the lambda radius is normalized for overall size using the bregma radius, the Shanidar 5 cranium becomes truly exceptional. The ratio of its lambda and bregma radii, expressed as an index, is 114.7, which is 4.50 standard deviations from a Neandertal mean (94.8 ± 4.2, N = 6 [including Amud 1]). Shanidar 1 has a value for this ratio of 95.0, and Amud 1 a value of 98.6.

Despite this difference between the Shanidar 5 and 1 posterior cranial vaults, the preserved portions of their median sagittal contours are generally similar because both have relatively flat frontal bones and curved parietal bones.

The Shanidar 5 frontal bone has a smooth curvature from the shallow supratoral sulcus to bregma, and it lacks the more marked anterior curvature and flatter posterior contour of the Shanidar 1 and possibly Shanidar 4 frontal bones (Figure 24). Its degree of curvature is indicated by a frontal curvature index (chord/arc) of 91.5. This figure is between those of most other Neandertals (Amud 1: 88.9; Tabūn C1: ca. 89.7; European Neandertals: 90.3 ± 2.2, N = 9) and the value of 93.5 for Shanidar 1, who has an extremely flat frontal bone. In contrast, a small Skhūl–Qafzeh sample has a mean index of 88.2 (± 1.6, N = 5) and an Early Upper Paleolithic sample has a mean index of 86.3 (± 1.7, N = 13). The frontal angle of Shanidar 5 (147°) is above the upper limit of the Neandertal range (131°–143°, N = 11; Amud 1: 139°; Tabūn C1: ca. 131°; European Neandertals: 139.0° ± 2.3°, N = 9; Zuttiyeh 1 has a frontal angle of 140°). It is also above those of virtually all more recent humans (range of male means for 17 samples: 124.3° ± 3.4° to 137.1° ± 4.0° [Howells 1973]), Early Upper Paleolithic hominids (129.1° ± 4.5°, N = 17) and Skhūl–Qafzeh hominids (132.3° ± 1.6°, N = 4). The Shanidar 5 frontal angle is also slightly greater than that of Shanidar 1 (144°), implying that its frontal bone is quite low.

The curvature of the Shanidar 5 parietal median sagittal arc is considerably greater than that of its frontal bone. The parietal curvature index (chord/arc) of Shanidar 5 about 89.3, which is slightly below that of Shanidar 1 (90.7) and the mean of an Early Upper Paleolithic sample (90.4 ± 1.1, N = 17). It is well below those of other Neandertals (Amud 1: 93.3; European Neandertals: 93.4 ± 1.1, N = 11), and it is even less than the mean of a small Skhūl–Qafzeh sample (91.2 ± 1.8, N = 4). Similarly, its parietal angle of about 136° falls in the interface between most Neandertal values (140°–152°, N = 10; Amud 1: 144°; European Neandertals: 144.8° ± 3.8°, N = 9) and those of recent humans (range of male means for 17 samples: 129.2° ± 2.7° to 136.1° ± 3.6° [Howells 1973]). It is close to the mean values of an Early Upper Paleolithic sample (137.0° ± 3.5°, N = 19) and a Skhūl–Qafzeh sample (136.9° ± 3.6°, N = 4).

Shanidar 5 therefore follows the same pattern as Shanidar 1 in having a relatively flat frontal bone and a more curved parietal arc. This is supported by the ratio of its frontal and parietal angles (ca. 108.1), which is 4.92 standard deviations from a Neandertal mean (96.3 ± 2.4, N = 8; sample includes Amud 1 [96.0]) and even above that of Shanidar 1 (107.5). It is not unknown among other Neandertals to have greater parietal curvature than frontal curvature because it occurs in Circeo 1 (at least as measured by frontal and parietal angles). However, most recent humans (Howells 1973), 95.0% of a combined Skhūl–

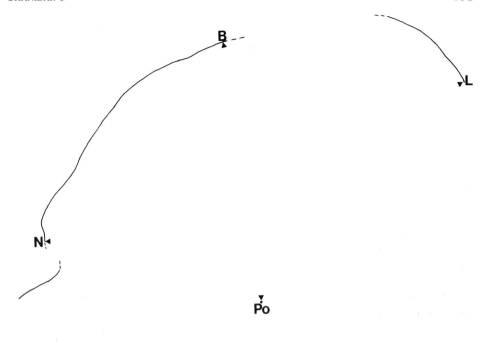

Figure 24   Median sagittal contour of the Shanidar 5 cranium. Pr = approximate position of prosthion, N = nasion, B = bregma, L = lambda, Po = left porion. The slight concavity in the posterior frontal arc is the product of the left frontal scar. The lack of alignment of the nasal bone contour with the position of nasion is due to to a slight posterior positioning of the mid-superior maxillary region produced by multiple glue joins along the zygomaticomaxillary sutures.

Qafzeh and Early Upper Paleolithic sample (N = 20), 87.5% of the Neandertals (N = 8) and even 92.3% of an East Asian *Homo erectus* sample (N = 13) (Santa Luca 1980: Weidenreich 1943) have greater curvature of the frontal bone than of the parietal bones. Furthermore, none of the other fossil hominids and few recent humans approach the combination of a very flat frontal bone and a highly curved parietal arc seen in both Shanidar 1 and Shanidar 5.

Shanidar 5, unlike Shanidar 1, agrees with 87.5% of the Neandertals (N = 8) in having a frontal arc longer than its parietal arc. The index formed by the ratio of the frontal arc to the parietal arc is about 102.4 for Shanidar 5, which is less than a European Neandertal mean (111.5 ± 10.5, N = 7) and that of Amud 1

(112.5). Yet it is considerably greater than that of Shanidar 1 (90.8). More recent hominid samples tend to have lower indices (Skhūl–Qafzeh: 96.6 ± 8.8; N = 4; Early Upper Paleolithic: 99.9 ± 8.6; N = 18), implying that their parietal arcs are usually longer than their frontal arcs. However, not only are these indices highly variable in all of the samples, but their significance is uncertain. A variety of factors, including the rates and timing of cerebral growth and the relative development of exocranial structures can influence growth patterns at sutures and hence the configuration of the cranial vault bones in the adult (Hoyte 1966; Trinkaus and LeMay 1982; Washburn 1947; Young 1959).

In addition to being relatively long and low, the Shanidar 5 cranial vault bones are among the thickest known for a Neandertal. The Shanidar 5 frontal bone is 10.2 and 10.0 mm thick at the right and left tubers, respectively. These measurements are, on the average, 3.20 standard deviations from a European Neandertal mean (6.9 ± 1.0, N = 10) and 5.38 standard deviations from the mean of a sample of recent human males (5.8 ± 0.8 mm, N = 37 [Young 1957]). They are similarly greater than those of Shanidar 1 (8.5 mm), Shanidar 4 (9.0 and 8.8 mm), Amud 1 (9.0 mm), Tabūn C1 (5.0 mm), and Zuttiyeh 1 (6.0 mm).

The thickness of the Shanidar 5 left parietal bone, measured at its tuber, is 9.0 mm. This measurement is greater than those of most Neandertals (Amud 1: 8.0 mm; European Neandertals: 7.6 ± 1.1, N = 27) and slightly above those of Shanidar 1 (8.0 mm), 2 (8.2 mm), and 4 (8.1 mm) and of other male Neandertals. The exceptional thickness of the Shanidar 5 cranial vault bones may be due in part to the advanced age at death of the individual. In cross section, the frontal and parietal bones exhibit thin external and internal tables and an expanse of diploë with fine trabeculae. This is a pattern evident in the cranial vault bones of elderly recent humans, and it is frequently associated with an increase in cranial bone thickness. It is not possible to determine what the thickness of the Shanidar 5 frontal and parietal bones would have been as a young adult, but they were probably still relatively thick for a Neandertal.

Shanidar 5 thus exhibits a heavily built cranial vault, which is characterized by its exceptional length, low frontal arc, high parietal arc, and a high position of lambda.

THE OCCIPITOMASTOID REGION

All that remains of the Shanidar 5 occipitomastoid region is the left mastoid process and supramastoid region (Figure 22). The lateral surface of the mastoid process is divided into superior and inferior portions by a prominent mastoid crest. Inferior to the crest is a continuous rugosity for the insertion of M. sternocleidomastoideus. Superior to the crest is a smooth, wide, but shallow supramastoid sulcus that extends from the posterior margin of the external acoustic meatus to the retromastoid region of the temporal bone. There is a slight swelling of the anterior end of the mastoid crest, but there is no evidence of an anterior mastoid tubercle.

The supramastoid crest arises above the external acoustic meatus to form a relatively low ridge. As it goes posteriorly, it becomes less sharply delineated, especially inferiorly, and more diffuse. And as it approaches the parietal incisure, it forms a large but low anterior supramastoid tubercle.

The mastoid process itself is modest in height for a male Neandertal, especially for one that has cranial dimensions as large as those of Shanidar 5. Its height, measured from the Frankfurt plane, is only 23.2 mm, which is considerably below those of Shanidar 1 (27.5 & 28.1 mm) and Shanidar 2 (ca. 32.0 mm). The Shanidar 5 measurement is minimally below a European Neandertal mean (both sexes) of 23.8 mm ($\pm$ 3.6 mm, N = 18), and it is somewhat below the range of means of recent human males (25.9 $\pm$ 2.4 to 30.9 $\pm$ 3.1 mm [Howells 1973]). It falls between the heights of the Amud 1 and Tabūn C1 mastoid processes (32.0 and 17.5 mm, respectively). However, the height of the Shanidar 5 mastoid process, as measured from the mastoid notch, is 8.0 mm. This value is similar to those of Shanidar 1 (8.3 & ca. 9.3 mm), slightly less than that of Shanidar 2 (10.6 mm), and greater than a European Neandertal mean (6.6 $\pm$ 2.2 mm, N = 15 [Smith 1980; Vallois 1969]).

The Shanidar 5 mastoid process is therefore not particularly large, at least in height, but it exhibits considerable rugosity.

THE ANTERIOR TEMPORAL BONE AND THE TEMPORAL FOSSA

Virtually all of the tympanic region, temporomandibular articulation, zygomatic process, and squamous portion of the left temporal bone survive, so that significant information can be derived from them. It is primarily the medial petrous portion that suffered postmortem damage.

The external acoustic meatus is perfectly preserved, and it exhibits a morphology considered to be characteristically Neandertal. It is elongated and exceptionally so, even for a Neandertal, for they are generally considered to have relatively elliptical external acoustic meatuses (LeGros Clark 1964; Vallois 1969). An index of the minimum–maximum diameters of the meatus varies from 54.3 to 90.7 in a sample of European Neandertals (73.2 $\pm$ 9.7, N = 17) and equals 56.1 for Tabūn C1; for Shanidar 5 it is 59.3. These indices, however, largely overlap those of recent humans (Eskimo mean: 71.8, N = 98; Amerindian mean: 60.4, N = 98; Euroamerican mean: 68.5, N = 98 [Schulter 1976]), and even the low index of Shanidar 5 is not particularly different from those of recent humans.

A more diagnostic aspect of the Shanidar 5 external acoustic meatus is its anteroinferior–posterosuperior orientation. This orientation is evident on most Neandertal temporal bones, but it occurs rarely in recent humans (about 7.0% in one sample [LeDouble, 1903]). The meatus is more commonly horizontally oriented in recent humans.

Vallois (1969:526) states that the positioning of the external acoustic meatus in line with the long axis of the zygomatic process is a typically Neandertal characteristic that distinguishes them from recent humans. This pattern is clearly seen on Shanidar 5 (Figure 22), in which the continuation of the long axis of the zygomatic process crosses the superior half of the meatus.

The details of the tympanic region are exceptionally well preserved on the Shanidar 5 left temporal bone, and they show similarities to the Shanidar 1 temporal bones and those of other Neandertals.

The long axis of the tympanic portion forms an angle of about 82° with the median sagittal cranial plane, being oriented anteromedial to posterolateral. This angle is similar to that of Shanidar 1 (ca. 78°) and those of other Neandertals (Amud 1: 84°; La Chapelle-aux-Saints 1: 82° & 82°; La Ferrassie 1: 74° & 76°; and La Quina 5: 84° & 84°). As with Shanidar 1, there is a thick and prominent tympanic crest that extends laterally from the vaginal process of the styloid process to the middle of the inferior margin of the external acoustic meatus. The superoinferior thickness of this crest is much greater than that of Shanidar 1 and resembles the tympanic thickening of H. erectus (Weidenreich 1943). There is also a clearly defined crest that emerges out of the posterior margin of the main tympanic crest near the stylomastoid foramen and extends laterally and slightly posteriorly to the anterolateral margin of the mastoid process. This crest is considerably more prominent and delineated from adjacent structures than the similar crest on Shanidar 1.

The Shanidar 5 left temporal bone also exhibits the mediolateral broadening of the tympanic region that has been considered characteristic of the Neandertals (Schwalbe 1914; Vallois 1969). The distance between the stylomastoid foramen and the lateral margin of the tympanic portion is 13.0 mm, which is similar to those of Shanidar 1 (ca. 13.5 & ca. 11.8 mm) and Amud 1 (13.2 mm) and close to a European Neandertal mean (12.7 ± 2.2 mm, N = 5 [Vallois 1969]). Yet these Neandertal tympanic breadths are not much greater than those of at least one recent Amerindian sample (10.9 ± 1.7 mm, N = 27).

The Shanidar 5 tympanic region therefore closely resembles those of Shanidar 1 and many other Neandertals in the orientation and configuration of the tympanic portion and tympanic crests.

The mandibular fossa of Shanidar 5 is both wide and deep, implying a large temporomandibular joint. The postglenoid process is robust but not particularly projecting, and a substantial portion of the posterior margin of the mandibular fossa is formed by the anterior surface of the tympanic portion. The tympanosquamosal fissure is evident between the postglenoid process and the tympanic portion.

Contrary to traditional descriptions of Neandertal mandibular fossae (e.g., Vallois 1969), the anterior margin of the Shanidar 5 mandibular fossa is not particularly flat. It forms a near vertical anterior wall to the fossa, which rounds onto the anterior articular surface for the mandibular condyle. The anterior half of the fossa has been slightly altered by degenerative joint disease, but it does not appear to have advanced sufficiently to alter the basic configuration of the fossa. Furthermore, the form of the mandibular fossa is closely correlated with patterns of dental function (Hinton 1979), and like the associated mandibular condyle (Mongini 1975), it changes shape during the life of the individual.

As with Shanidar 1 and 2, there is a prominent articular tubercle on Shanidar 5 for the cranial attachments of the fibrous capsule of the temporo-mandibular joint and of the lateral temporomandibular ligament. The Shanidar 5 anterior tubercle is intermediate in size between those of Shanidar 1 and Shanidar 2, implying well-developed articular ligaments.

The inferior surface of the zygomatic process is scalloped between the artic-ular tubercle and the temporozygomatic suture for the attachment of the middle layer of M. *masseter*. In this it is similar to, but less strongly marked than, Shanidar 2. In addition, there is a turning inferiorly of the lower margin of the process at the temporozygomatic suture, suggesting a tubercle similar to that present on Shanidar 2. Such a tubercle would be for the posterior end of the attachment of the superficial layer of M. *masseter*. These indications imply a well-developed muscle.

Most of the M. *temporalis* attachment is preserved on the left zygomatic bone, and there is a strong suggestion of a tubercle on the posterolateral margin of the left zygomatic bone for the anterior end of the temporalis fascia, as in Shanidar 1. In addition, there are temporal crests for about 25.0 mm posterior to the frontozygomatic sutures. The temporal lines are preserved at least as far as stephanion on each side and, although readily apparent, have been slightly effaced. The bistephanic breadth of Shanidar 5, at 109.0 mm, is only about 85.2% of the maximum frontal breadth. The bistephanic breadth of Shanidar 1, however, is 98.8% of its maximum frontal breadth, implying that the size of the Shanidar 5 temporal muscles was greater than that of the Shanidar 1 muscles. By comparison, the ratios of the means of the bistephanic and maximum frontal breadths for 17 recent human male samples range from 90.8 to 98.4% (Howells 1973) and the mean ratio of a European Neandertal sample is 95.7% ($\pm$ 3.2%, N = 7). Amud 1 and Tabūn C1 have ratios of 99.2 and 99.6%, respectively. There-fore, whereas the Shanidar 1 temporal lines have relative heights similar to those of recent humans and other Neandertals, those of Shanidar 5 are much higher.

The temporal fossae of Shanidar 5 thus imply relatively strong attachments for the masticatory muscles, slightly greater than those of Shanidar 1 but proba-bly less than those of Shanidar 2. Although these inferences cannot be con-firmed by the insertions for the muscles on the mandible, the robusticity of the left temporomandibular joint suggests a similarly strong development.

THE UPPER FACIAL SKELETON

A considerable proportion of the Shanidar 5 upper facial skeleton is pre-served. Portions of the posterior maxillae and internal facial skeleton are lack-ing, but most of the anterior facial mask is present on at least one side (Figure

22). There is certainly enough of the facial skeleton to see readily that Shanidar 5 possesses a large and typically Neandertal face.

The Shanidar 5 face is one of the largest known among the Neandertals. Its nasion–prosthion height of 94.0 mm is above the known range of variation of other Neandertals (Amud 1: ca. 89.0 mm; Tabūn C1: ca. 79.0 mm; La Chapelle-aux-Saints 1: 83.0 mm; Circeo 1: ca. 90.0 mm; La Ferrassie 1: 88.0 mm; Gibraltar 1: 78.5 mm) and that of Shanidar 1 (86.0 mm). In this, Shanidar 5 and several Neandertals are significantly larger than most Skhūl–Qafzeh hominids (74.6 ± 2.7 mm, N = 5), Early Upper Paleolithic hominids (69.0 ± 5.9 mm, N = 13), and recent humans (range of male means for 17 recent human samples: 57.5 ± 5.3 to 74.5 ± 4.3 mm [Howells 1973]). In addition, the bimaxillary breadth of Shanidar 5, at about 120.0 mm, is greater than those of Shanidar 1, 2, and 4 (104.0, ca. 115.0, and ca. 116.0 mm, respectively) and other Neandertals (Amud 1: 114.0 mm; European Neandertals: 109.4 ± 6.2 mm, N = 5). Again, many of the Neandertal specimens have considerably greater bimaxillary breadths than those of Skhūl–Qafzeh hominids (105.0–109.0 mm, N = 3), Early Upper Paleolithic hominids (96.1 ± 5.3 mm, N = 9), and recent humans (range of male means for 17 samples: 92.2 ± 4.8 to 104.3 ± 5.2 mm [Howells 1973]).

In addition to being large, the Shanidar 5 face projects noticeably in front of its neurocranium. Its molar alveolar radius of about 102.0 mm is greater than those of Shanidar 1 (97.7 and 95.0 mm), Amud 1 (ca. 98.0 mm) and Tabūn C1 (ca. 83.0 mm), and among European Neandertals it is exceeded only by that of La Ferrassie 1 (La Chapelle-aux-Saints 1: ca. 95.0 mm; Circeo 1: ca. 95.0 mm; La Ferrassie 1: 106.5 mm; Gibraltar 1: ca. 95.0 mm). By comparison, the same measurement is 77.0, 88.0, and 85.0 mm for Qafzeh 6 and 9 and Skhūl 5, respectively, and 85.2 ± 4.7 mm (N = 9) for a sample of Early Upper Paleolithic crania. Recent human male means vary between 73.7 (± 2.7) and 88.3 mm (± 3.8 mm) for 17 samples (Howells 1973). If the molar alveolar radius is normalized for overall body size using femoral bicondylar length, the large length of the Shanidar 5 and other Neandertal faces is still in evidence. The resultant index is about 22.8 for Shanidar 5. This value is between those of La Chapelle-aux-Saints 1 (ca. 22.1) and La Ferrassie 1 (ca. 23.2), slightly above those of Shanidar 1 (ca. 21.3 and ca. 20.7), Amud 1 (ca. 20.3), and Tabūn C1 (ca. 20.2). This index for early anatomically modern humans is generally lower, with only Předmostí 4 slightly overlapping the Neandertals (Caviglione 1: 18.6; Dolní Věstonice 3: 19.9; Předmostí 3: 19.5; Předmostí 4: 20.3; Qafzeh 9: ca. 18.7; Skhūl 5: ca. 16.5).

It is also possible to assess the overall length of the Shanidar 5 face by estimating the mandibular superior length from the preserved portions of the cranium. If the mandibular fossa is used to indicate the middle of the condyle and the maxillary incisor alveoli are used to estimate the position of infradentale, a mandibular superior length of about 116.0 mm can be estimated. This measure is slightly greater than those of Shanidar 1 (115.0 mm), 2 (ca. 112.0 mm), and 4 (ca. 111.0 mm), and it falls in the middle of the Neandertal range of variation (Amud 1: ca. 111.0 mm; Tabūn C1: 102.0 mm; Tabūn C2: 122.0 mm; European Neandertals: 112.5 ± 8.6 mm, N = 5). Furthermore, if this estimate of mandibular superior length is normalized for overall size by dividing it by the femoral bicondylar length, the resultant index (ca. 26.0) is very close to those of Shanidar 1 and 4 (ca. 25.1 and ca. 26.3, respectively). It is also within known Neandertal ranges of variation (Amud 1: ca. 23.0; Tabūn C1: 24.9; La Chapelle-aux-Saints 1: ca. 26.7; La Ferrassie 1: ca. 27.1) and separate from those of more recent humans (Dolní Věstonice 3: 22.1; Předmostí 3: 21.4; Qafzeh 9: ca. 22.8; Skhūl 4: 21.7; Skhūl 5: ca. 20.7; recent European sample: 21.0 ± 1.1, N = 50).

These various comparisons establish that the Shanidar 5 face is as projecting as those of other Neandertals and, in addition, is the largest Neandertal face known so far.

The supraorbital torus of Shanidar 5 consists of two evenly curved arches, with the superciliary arches extending over each supraorbital margin and trigonum supraorbitale. The superior margins of each, in *norma facialis*, are smoothly rounded. The inferior margins are more rounded, but as with Shanidar 1, the middle third of each orbital margin is flattened slightly by a swelling of bone just lateral to the supraorbital notch. The supraorbital notches themselves are not noticeable and can be located only by the slight change in direction of the inferior toral contour.

The Shanidar 5 torus is thickest near the medial side of the orbit, and it tapers gradually towards the frontozygomatic suture. In this, it resembles the Shanidar 1 and Amud 1 supraorbital tori; it differs from those of Shanidar 4, Tabūn C1, and Zuttiyeh 1, all of whose tori show little or no lateral thining. It does not, however, exhibit the constriction of the lateral third seen in some European Late Neandertals (Lévêque and Vandermeersch 1981; Smith and Ranyard 1980). The actual thickness of the Shanidar 5 torus, measured at the middle of each orbit, is only 12.8 and 11.5 mm on the right and left sides, respectively. These values are close to a European Neandertal mean (12.2 ± 2.0 mm, N = 18), but they are below those for Shanidar 1, 2, and 4 (14.8, ca. 15.0 & ca. 14.0, and 13.6 mm, respectively), Amud 1 (15.0 mm), and Zuttiyeh 1 (15.7 & 14.8 mm). The Shanidar 5 torus is surprisingly thin, given the large size of the cranium and the tendency among the Shanidar Neandertals to have relatively thick supraorbital tori.

The Shanidar 5 supraorbital torus is, nonetheless, similar to that of Shanidar 1 in having the two superciliary arches descend to a moderately prominent glabellar region. Although glabella is placed anterior to the coronal plane of the supraorbital torus, as can be seen in *norma verticalis* (Figure 23), the medial sagittal contour (Figure 24) suggests that the glabellar region is evenly rounded and not particularly projecting. This latter impression comes in part from the development of the frontal squamous directly posterior to the supraorbital torus along the midline, so that the median supratoral sulcus is shallow, although long anteroposteriorly.

In addition, nasion is positioned anteriorly with respect to glabella. This is indicated by the slightly greater nasion–lambda length than glabella–lambda length (Table 6); among the Neandertals (N = 9) and Early Upper Paleolithic hominids (N = 9), the distance from nasion to inion is always less than the distance from glabella to inion, indicating that glabella usually projects anteriorly of nasion. As a result of the anterior placement of nasion on Shanidar 5, its glabella projection value (the subtense from glabella to the nasion–supraglabella chord) is only 5.0 mm, which is slightly above that of Shanidar 1 (4.3 mm) and toward the top of a recent human male range of means (1.5 ± 0.8 to 5.6 ± 1.1 mm [Howells 1973]). However, it is below a European Neandertal mean (6.8 ± 1.3 mm, N = 11) and those of Amud 1 (8.0 mm), Tabūn C1 (9.0 mm), and Zuttiyeh 1 (8.0 mm).

As mentioned earlier, the Shanidar 5 supratoral sulcus is quite shallow near the midline, although it extends posteriorly for a considerable distance from the anterior toral margin (Figure 22). In fact, the supratoral region rises directly from the highest point of the torus on to the frontal squamous from the glabellar region laterally to about one-third of the way across the orbit. It is only as the squamous begins to descend laterally for the temporal fossa that there is a sulcus sufficiently deep to separate the torus itself from the bone of the frontal squamous. Therefore, although the supraorbital torus of Shanidar 5 is relatively prominent, it is fairly continuous superiorly with the rest of the frontal bone.

The superior and anterior surfaces of the supraorbital torus, particularly laterally, exhibit the remnants of fine cancellous surface bone. As with Shanidar 1 and 4, the fine cancellous bone on the Shanidar 5 brow has been largely obscured by remodeling since it was laid down.

During the restoration of the frontal bone, it was possible to study some aspects of the frontal sinuses. The Shanidar 5 frontal sinuses are similar to those of Shanidar 1 and other Neandertals in being limited to the glabellar region and the medial halves of the orbits. They are multichambered and largely fill the space available to them within the median half of the supraorbital torus, but they do not extend into the frontal squamous above. The anteroposterior depth of the right frontal sinus was measured as 16.5 mm near the middle of the right sinus, and therefore not on the midline where the measurement would be greatest. For a rough comparison, the maximum depth of a sample of European Neandertals has a mean of 22.7 mm (± 5.0 mm, N = 6 [Vlček 1967]) and Tabūn C1 has a sinus depth of 10.4 mm (Tillier 1974). This suggests that the Shanidar 5 frontal sinuses probably had a maximum depth close to the Neandertal mean. Although they could not be measured, the maximum breadth and height of the Shanidar 5 sinuses appear to be large, comparable to those of Shanidar 1. Shanidar 5, therefore, along with Shanidar 1 and 4, conforms to the Neandertal pattern of having large, centrally located frontal sinuses (Heim 1978; Vlček 1967).

The Shanidar 5 orbits follow the general Neandertal pattern of being quite rounded, especially along their superior margins. In addition, both the lateral and inferior margins are clearly convex, and the medial margins may well have been as well (Figure 22). The right and left orbits have areas (height × breadth) of 1688 and 1786 mm², respectively. These values are on either side of a European Neandertal mean (1727 ± 152 mm², N = 5) and the area of the Shanidar 1 right orbit (1724 mm²). They are, however, greater than those of Amud 1 (1570 mm²), Tabūn C1 (1386 mm²), and Zuttiyeh 1 (ca. 1628 mm²). The Shanidar 5 orbital indices (79.8 & 80.9) are close to those of Shanidar 1 (75.2), Amud 1 (80.9), and Tabūn C1 (78.6), but slightly below that of Zuttiyeh 1 (ca. 84.1) and a European Neandertal mean (84.5 ± 7.6, N = 5). The Shanidar 5 orbits are thus similar in size and proportions to those of other Neandertals.

The Shanidar 5 interorbital breadth estimate (ca. 28.0 mm) is toward the middle of the known European Neandertal range of variation (23.0–32.0 mm, 29.0 ± 2.7 mm, N = 10). It is between the interorbital breadths of Shanidar 1 (23.1 mm) on one hand and those of Shanidar 2 (ca. 36.6 mm), Amud 1 (≥ 31.0 mm), and Tabūn C1 (32.0 mm) on the other hand. Zuttiyeh 1 has an interorbital breadth of 28.0 mm. The interorbital breadth of Shanidar 5 is nonetheless, like those of most Neandertals, above the normal ranges of variation of recent humans (range of male means for 17 recent human samples: 18.6 ± 1.8 to 24.4 ± 2.4 mm [Howells 1973]). The biorbital breadth of Shanidar 5 (116.0 mm) is relatively large for a Neandertal (Amud 1: 112.0 mm, European Neandertals: 107.3 ± 4.2 mm, N = 6) and exceptionally so for a recent human (range of means for 17 recent human male samples: 92.7 ± 3.6 to 102.5 ± 3.7 mm [Howells 1973]).

In contrast to its orbits, which are of average Neandertal size, Shanidar 5 has an extremely large nasal region. Its nasal height and breadth (68.5 and ca. 38.5 mm, respectively) are both the largest of these dimensions known for a Neandertal (Amud 1: ca. 65.0 and ca. 34.0 mm; Tabūn C1: ca. 58.0 and ca. 34.0 mm; La Chapelle-aux-Saints 1: 61.0 and 34.0 mm; Circeo 1: ca. 66.0 and 36.0 mm; La Ferrassie 1:62.0 and 34.0 mm; Gibraltar 1: 58.5 and 34.5 mm). Shanidar 1, by comparison, has nasal dimensions close to the Neandertal means (62.2 and 30.2 mm, respectively). The nasal index (breadth/height) of Shanidar 5, however, is about 56.2, which is very close to the mean index of the same European Neandertal sample (56.0 ± 2.0, N = 4) and those of Amud 1 (ca. 52.3) and Tabūn C1 (ca. 58.6). It is well above the low index of Shanidar 1 (48.6).

The large size of the Shanidar 5 nasal region is not evident only in its aperture dimensions. The whole of the nasal region projects anteriorly from the coronal plane of the orbits (Figure 22). The nasal bridge approaches the Frankfurt horizontal, extending about 24.0 mm anteriorly from the region of nasion. Laterally from the nasal aperture, the anterolateral surfaces of the maxillae slope primarily laterally until they reach the zygomaticomaxillary sutures, indicating considerable expansion of the enclosed maxillary sinuses and nasal cavity. And, as with Shanidar 1 and 2, the floor of the nasal cavity slopes inferiorly directly posterior of the inferior nasal aperture margin, thereby further increasing the volume of the nasal cavity. This expansion of the maxillae is much greater than that seen in Shanidar 1, 2, or 4, and it is comparable to the facial expansion of western European Neandertals such as La Chapelle-aux-Saints 1 (Boule 1911–1913) and La Ferrassie 1 (Heim 1976).

Because the maxillae of Shanidar 5 are inflated, there is not even a suggestion of a canine fossae. There is a very slight concavity near the infraorbital foramina, but the majority of the maxillae, especially the more inferior region where a canine fossa would be present, is flat or gently convex. As a result, the profile of the maxillae in *norma facialis* (preserved only on the right side) is straight with only the slightest concavity (Figure 22). In this, it conforms to the morphology described by Sergi (1947) and Heim (1978) for the Neandertals. In this feature, Shanidar 5 contrasts with Shanidar 1, who has a more concave maxillary profile (Figure 9). Associated with the anterior projection of the Shanidar 5 nasal region is an anterior placement of the whole palate. There are several indications of this prognathism.

The zygomatic root on the right side is above the M^2–M^3 interdental septum, as in Shanidar 1, La Chapelle-aux-Saints 1, and La Ferrassie 1, rather than above the M^2, as in Shanidar 2 and 4. The premaxillary region shows, especially in *norma lateralis* left (Figure 22), considerable alveolar prognathism. Because this is added onto the anterior projection of the nasal aperture, it places the anterior alveoli far forward.

The midfacial prognathism of Shanidar 5 is also evident in the large retromolar portions of the maxillary alveoli. Measured on the left side, the distance between the distal M^3 margin and the posterior edge of the alveolus is about 16.5 mm, which is greater than the values of 14.8 and about 11.0 mm for Shanidar 1 and 2, respectively. The Shanidar 5 retromolar dimension is, furthermore, outside the ranges of variation of two recent human samples (Australians: 8.9 mm [4.0–15.0 mm], N = 135 [Campbell 1925]; Europeans: 1.8–12.7 mm, 7.4 ± 1.5 mm, N = 102 [Twiesselmann and Brabant 1967]). This elongation of the alveolus, which is a reflection of an anterior placement of the dental arcade within the maxilla, can be further illustrated by the index of the alveolar length to the dental arcade length; it is about 133.3 for Shanidar 5, 128.5 for Shanidar 1, and about 120.8 for Shanidar 2, as compared to 112.2 for an index of the means for a recent human sample (Twiesselmann and Brabant 1967).

One of the measures that has been used to quantify midfacial prognathism is the difference between the zygomaxillary and molar alveolus radii. Using the right zygomaxillare anterior and the estimated position of the left M^1, a difference between these radii of about 21.5 mm is obtained for Shanidar 5. This is close to those of La Chapelle-aux-Saints 1 (21.0 mm), Circeo 1 (21.0 mm), and Gibraltar 1 (20.0 mm), below those of Shanidar 1 (26.0 mm) and La Ferrassie 1 (26.5 mm), and above those of Shanidar 2 (ca. 15.0 mm) and Amud 1 (ca. 17.0 mm). As such, it is considerably greater than those of recent humans (range of male means for 17 samples: 4.6–11.6 mm [Howells 1975]) and Early Upper Paleolithic hominids (4.7 ± 3.2 mm, N = 7) and at the upper limit of a small Skhūl–Qafzeh sample (3.0–21.0 mm, N = 3).

It is also possible to estimate the zygomaxillary angle for Shanidar 5, using

the estimated bimaxillary breadth (ca. 120.0 mm) and the direct distance from
the right zygomaxillare anterior to subspinale (71.0 mm). The resultant angle,
about 115°, falls between that of Shanidar 1 (105°) and those of Shanidar 2 (ca.
125°) and 4 (ca. 123°). It is the same as that of Amud 1 (ca. 115°) and at the upper
limit of the known European Neandertal range of variation (La Chapelle-aux-
Saints 1: 105°; Circeo 1: 114°; La Ferrassie 1: 109°; Gibraltar 1: 114°). The
Shanidar 5 zygomaxillary angle is still separate from those of most more recent
humans, such as those of a small Skhūl–Qafzeh sample (124°–133°, N = 3), an
Early Upper Paleolithic sample (127.3° ± 8.8°, N = 6), and recent humans
(range of male means for 17 samples: 120.3 ° ± 6.6° to 138.9° ± 4.7° [Howells
1973]).

These data all indicate that Shanidar 5 had considerable midfacial prognathism, comparable to that of most other Neandertals. Even though its midfacial projection is slightly less than that of Shanidar 1, as indicated by both the
difference of the facial radii and the zygomaxillary angle, it is still quite separate from those of Shanidar 2 and 4 and most more recent humans.

Associated with the midfacial prognathism and anterior maxillary inflation
of the Shanidar 5 face is a flattening, or retreating profile, of the zygomatic
bones. As with Shanidar 1 and most European Neandertals, the Shanidar 5
zygomatic bones continue the same lines of curvature of the anterior maxillae
without any marked angulation. This is reflected in the zygomatic curvature
index of 18.4 for the left zygomatic bone, an index which falls in the middle of
the Neandertal range (Amud 1: ca. 18.2; La Chapelle-aux-Saints 1: 15.3; Circeo
1: 21.1; La Ferrassie 1: 18.6) and close to that of Shanidar 1 (19.0). As with
Shanidar 1, the zygomatic curvature index of Shanidar 5 is at the lower end of
more recent human ranges of variation (early anatomically modern humans:
21.0–22.8, N = 4; range of recent human male means: 19.6 ± 2.6 to 23.2 ± 2.2
[Howells, personal communication, 1982; see previous discussion]) and well
below that of Shanidar 2 (27.2).

Despite this midfacial projection of the maxillae, the region around nasion
does not protrude exceptionally. The nasiofrontal angle of Shanidar 5, which
measures the projection of nasion in front of the bifrontal chord (a lower angle
indicates greater projection) is 139°. This value falls in the region of overlap
between the Neandertals (Amud 1: 129°; Tabūn C1: 142°; European Neandertals: 122°–142°, 135.3° ± 5.9°, N = 9), recent humans (range of male means for
17 samples: 137.4° ± 4.1° to 146.9° ± 4.8° [Howells 1973]), Early Upper Paleolithic hominids (145.1° ± 7.9°, N = 15) and Skhūl–Qafzeh hominids
(139°–152°, N = 3). Among the European Neandertals, the possibly late last
interglacial Krapina C and E crania have among the highest values for this angle
(138° and 142°, respectively), and earlier European specimens tend to have
relatively high nasiofrontal angles (Arago 21: ca. 151°; Ehringsdorf 9: 151°;
Petralona 1: 142°). Similarly, the last interglacial Near Eastern Zuttiyeh 1 frontal has a high nasiofrontal (150°). African archaic H. sapiens specimens tend to
be variable in this feature (Bodo 1: ca. 143°; Broken Hill: 135°; Irhoud 1: 148°),

and the East Asian Mapa 1 specimen has a relatively high nasiofrontal angle (ca. 151°); the Dali 1 cranium appears to have had an equally nonprojecting nasion (Wu 1981). In relation to the other Neandertals, Shanidar 5 thus has a relatively high nasiofrontal angle, suggesting that his midfacial prognathism increased from the supraorbital torus to the nasal aperture to the anterior alveoli.

As with Shanidar 1 and 4 (see earlier discussion), the infraorbital foramina of Shanidar 5 (Table 9, Figure 22) are double. On the right side, there are two subequal foramina, one immediately below zygoorbitale and the other slightly inferolateral to the first one. On the left side, there is only one very large foramen, but within the foramen is a large bony septum that bifurcates the foramen on the anterior maxillary surface. Internally, it can be seen that the right and left sides each have two separate canals for the infraorbital nerve and artery.

The palate and maxillary alveoli of Shanidar 5 have undergone both ante-mortem and postmortem alterations. The alveoli are preserved, in large part, from the right P^4 to the left P^3 or P^4, but several of the teeth were lost ante-mortem (Table 13) and all of the alveoli sustained extensive alveolar resorption (Figure 30). In addition, small portions of the left M^3 internal and external alveoli survive. A major portion of the palate remains, but it is damaged as it approaches the alveoli on both sides, it is broken off posteriorly anterior of the palatomaxillary suture, and its original height had been significantly reduced by alveolar resorption.

The length of the Shanidar 5 dental arcade is about 49.5 mm, which is slightly less than those of Shanidar 1 and 2 (52.0 and ca. 53.0 mm, respectively) and other Neandertals (Amud 1: 53.0 mm; La Ferrassie 1: 50.0 mm; Gibraltar 1: 54.0 mm; Tabūn C1: 55.5 mm). It is very close to the mean of a recent human sample (48.4 ± 1.9 mm, N = 108 [Twiesselmann and Brabant 1967]), which is not surprising because the dimensions of Neandertal premolars and molars, which make up most of the length of the dental arcade, are well within recent human ranges of variation (Trinkaus 1978b; Tables 21 and 22). Its external palate breadth, measured at the C^- distal margins, however, is rather exceptional. At about 52.0 mm, it is greater than those of all other Neandertals (Amud 1: 44.0 mm; Tabūn C1: 48.0 mm; La Ferrassie 1: 46.0 mm; Gibraltar 1: 43.5 mm), including Shanidar 1 (42.5 mm). Similarly, its external palate breadth, at about 78.0 mm, is at the top of the Neandertal range of variation (Amud 1: 77.0 mm; Tabūn C1: ca. 69.3 mm; European Neandertals: 71.8 ± 3.6 mm, N = 4). It is much greater than that of Shanidar 1 (71.5 mm), but it is exceeded slightly by that of Shanidar 2 (ca. 78.5 mm). Recent human external palate breadths are all much smaller and do not approach the values of Shanidar 5 and the other large Neandertals (range of means for 17 recent human male samples: 60.1 ± 3.2 mm to 68.9 ± 3.9 mm [Howells 1973]).

As a result of the large palatal breadths of Shanidar 5, along with its modest dental arcade length, its palatal index (external breadth/length) is 157.6. This value is towards the top of a variable range for a small Neandertal sample

(Amud 1: 145.2; Tabūn C1: ca. 124.9; La Ferrassie 1: 150.0; Gibraltar 1: 124.1), well above that of Shanidar 1 (137.5), but similar to that of Shanidar 2 (ca. 148.1). The Shanidar 5 palate is therefore relatively, as well as absolutely, wide.

On the buccal alveolus next to the left M^3 there is a small alveolar exostosis (Figures 29 and 30). It is not possible to determine whether it extended anteriorly beyond the M^2–M^3 interface or was present on the right side. The Shanidar 5 alveolar exostosis is not as large as those on Shanidar 2 (Figure 19), but the morphology of the bony growth is similar. As mentioned in reference to those of Shanidar 2, alveolar exostoses have been considered to be the products of pathological inflammation of the alveolus (Alexandersen 1967), functional hypertrophy of the alveolus (Hrdlička 1940), and the individual's genotype (Moorrees 1957). With Shanidar 2, it was assumed that one of the latter two explanations must be involved because there is no associated alveolar pathology. However, with Shanidar 5, the presence of extensive alveolar inflammation and resorption associated with antemortem tooth loss makes it impossible to choose between the three hypotheses. It is interesting, nonetheless, that of the three Shanidar adults which preserve the buccal alveoli—Shanidar 1, 2, and 5—two exhibit alveolar exostoses.

Shanidar 5 thus has an exceptional upper facial skeleton. Not only is it absolutely large, the largest of the known Neandertals, but it is also one of the more prognathic. The large size of the facial skeleton may be part of the general overall large size of the Shanidar 5 cranium, but the midfacial prognathism is independent of absolute size. The rest of the details of the facial skeleton, including the orbital and nasal dimensions, the anterior maxillary morphology, and the position of the zygomatic root, all appear to be, at least in part, related to the size and projection of the midfacial region.

SHANIDAR 6

Inventory

CRANIUM
The Shanidar 6 cranium retains only a piece of the left facial skeleton, a fragment of the right palate, and part of the left pterygoid plates. Two of these pieces were originally assigned to Shanidar 4 (Stewart 1963; Trinkaus 1977b), but it has become evident that they do not articulate with the preserved portions of the Shanidar 4 cranium and must derive from Shanidar 6.

   Os Sphenoidale   The superior two-thirds of the left pterygoid plates is preserved and retains the anterior portions of the plates and most of the medial plate. Maximum height = 23.1 mm.

   Maxilla: Right   The bone fragment consists of a small piece of the palate adjacent to the P^3.

   Maxilla: Left   The bone retains a portion of the frontal process, the in-

Figure 25 Anterior views of (a) Shanidar 6 and (b) Shanidar 8 left facial fragments. Each one preserves all or part of the infraorbital foramen. Scale in centimeters.

feromedial orbital margin, and the anterior maxillary surface with the infraorbital foramen. Maximum breadth = 26.7 mm.

Os Zygomaticum: Left   A small fragment of the maxillary process remains along the zygomaticomaxillary suture. Maximum breadth = 13.8 mm.

Morphology

There is an insufficient amount of the Shanidar 6 facial skeleton preserved to indicate more than that it was a moderately robust face. It is not possible to determine what the overall shape of the maxillae might have been.

All of the left infraorbital foramen is preserved. Like those of Shanidar 1, 4, and 5 (see earlier discussion), it consists of two canals (Figure 25). Although it has only a single large aperture on the anterior maxillary surface, the foramen is divided into two bony canals by a septum just inside of the foramen.

SHANIDAR 8

Inventory

CRANIUM

A small piece of left maxilla is preserved, which is assigned to Shanidar 8 because it duplicates an anatomical region already represented by larger pieces in the Shanidar 4 and 6 facial skeletons.

Maxilla: Left   The fragment preserves the infraorbital foramen and an adjacent portion of the zygomaticomaxillary suture. Maximum breadth = 22.9 mm.

Morphology

This small fragment of the Shanidar 8 cranium does not permit any assessment of the overall configuration of the Shanidar 8 facial skeleton. It only indicates the presence of a single, large, and nonbifurcated infraorbital foramen (Figure 25).

ARTIFICIAL DEFORMATION OF THE SHANIDAR 1 AND 5 CRANIA

Only two of the Shanidar individuals, Shanidar 1 and 5, have cranial vault bones that are sufficiently intact to provide indications of their overall neurocranial configurations. Shanidar 1 has an occipital bone that is indistinguishable from those preserved for other Neandertals. Both of these individuals have quite flat frontal bones that are close to the limits of known Neandertal ranges of variation and completely outside of the ranges of variation of early anatomically modern humans. Yet, both Shanidar 1 and 5 have highly curved parietal bones that are distinct from those of other Neandertals and most similar to those of more recent humans. This combination of a flat nasion-bregma arc and a curved bregma-lambda arc is unique among Pleistocene hominids from Europe and western Asia and serves to distinguish these two Shanidar individuals from their predecessors, successors, and contemporaries. Furthermore, the Shanidar 5 cranium has an exceptionally high position for lambda, which is unknown among both Neandertals and early anatomically modern humans from Europe and the Near East.

It may be that the Shanidar 1 and 5 neurocranial morphologies merely represent the limits of the normal range of variation for Neandertal populations, which is as yet poorly sampled by the fossil record. However, among recent humans, it is primarily in populations that routinely practice artificial cranial deformation that similar patterns of frontal flattening and parietal curvature are seen (Blackwood and Danby 1955; Brown 1981; Dembo and Imbelloni 1938; Dingwall 1931). It may therefore be more likely that Shanidar 1 and 5 experienced artificial cranial deformation as infants and that their unique neurocranial configurations can be seen as products of some form of head modeling.

It is difficult to establish the presence of artificial deformation among Pleistocene hominid crania, given the difficulties in determining what is normal for a prehistoric population (Brothwell 1975; Brown 1981; Larnach 1974). Furthermore, artificial cranial deformation among recent humans is highly variable both within and between populations, and there is frequently a continuum in any one population that practices cranial deformation from non-deformed to highly deformed crania.

Among recent humans, cranial deformation is produced by binding the infant's head shortly after birth and maintaining pressure on the cranium until the desired shape is achieved or the infant rejects the binding, usually a period of several months to several years (Blackwood and Danby 1955). The most common form of binding is a band that is bound tightly around the frontal and occipital regions, either with a board (the tabular form) or just a flexible band (the annular form) (Dembo and Imbelloni 1938). Variation in the resultant deformation derives from the length of time the binding is maintained, the presence or absence of a board, the tightness of the binding, and the position of the band on the cranium. Similar deformation can be produced by head pressing, in which the mother manually applies pressure to her infant's head (Macgillivray 1852); the changes from head pressing are usually less pronounced that those produced by head binding.

Crania that experienced frontoccipital head binding or pressing characteristically exhibit frontal flattening and elongation, increased parietal curvature, and an increase in cranial height in the parietal region. Variably associated with these changes are occipital flattening combined with a superior displacement of lambda, prebregmatic eminences with posterolateral frontal depressions, and a narrowing of the biparietal breadth (Blackwood and Danby 1955; Brown 1981).

Shanidar 1 and 5 clearly exhibit the increased frontal flattening and parietal curvature and the elevation of the parietal region. Shanidar 1 does not exhibit occipital flattening or an elevation of lambda. Shanidar 5, however, has marked elevation of lambda, as is indicated by his lambda radius/bregma radius ratio, and this elevation of lambda was probably associated with occipital flattening. Even though none of the Shanidar 5 occipital bone survives, this elevation of lambda is associated with occipital flattening among recent humans. Furthermore, if a normally curved Neandertal occipital bone were placed on the Shanidar 5 cranium, the resultant overall length would be truly extraordinary.

Neither Shanidar 1 nor Shanidar 5 exhibits prebregmatic eminences or posterolateral frontal depressions, although Shanidar 1 does have a general flattening of the posterior squamous rather than the continuous curve of the frontal median sagittal arc seen in Shanidar 5 and other Neandertals. In addition, neither Shanidar specimen exhibits frontal elongation and, in fact, Shanidar 1 has a short frontal compared to its parietal bones. It is difficult to determine whether either Shanidar 1 or 5 exhibits biparietal narrowing, but the cranial index of Shanidar 1 is close to the Neandertal mean and suggests that at least Shanidar 1 does not exhibit this feature.

The Shanidar 1 and 5 cranial vaults thus exhibit several of the more prominent features associated with frontoccipital head binding in recent humans, in particular the frontal flattening, the parietal arching, and, in Shanidar 5, elevation of lambda. It appears reasonable to infer that their vault configurations were the products in part of artificial cranial deformation. Any other interpretation of their vault shapes would have to explain their rather unique configurations relative to other archiac *H. sapiens* fossils; other western Asian archaic *H. sapiens* crania (e.g., Amud 1, Tabūn C1, Teshik-Tash 1, Zuttiyeh 1) have typically Neandertal neurocranial configurations, and the early anatomically modern human crania from Qafzeh and Skhūl do not exhibit any abnormal morphology that is not clearly the product of postmortem deformation (e.g., Skhūl 9).

It is possible that some of the abnormal curvature of the Shanidar 1 and 5 cranial vaults is due to postmortem deformation, especially in the parietal region. This could have been produced by plastic deformation *in situ* or, more likely, by angular distortion during reassambly. However, this alone could not account for the differences between the Shanidar 1 and 5 neurocranial configurations and those of Upper Pleistocene hominids. An additional factor, such as artificial cranial deformation, must have been involved.

It is difficult to infer which deformation technique might have been used, but the absence of extreme flattening, except perhaps on the absent Shanidar 5 occipital bone, suggests that either flexible bands (the annular technique) or head pressing was employed. The contrasts between the Shanidar 1 and 5 cranial vaults probably reflect differences in the positioning of the head binding and the duration of its application, as well as normal individual differences in head shape.

It is not possible to determine whether Shanidar 2 and 4 were also subjected to artificial cranial deformation, given the incomplete states of their cranial vaults. The apparent flatness of the Shanidar 4 frontal bone and the relatively high parietal region of Shanidar 2 are suggestive of similar cranial deformation, but they are insufficient by themselves to indicate intentional head binding.

SUMMARY OF THE SHANIDAR SKULL MORPHOLOGY

The Shanidar crania and mandibulae provide a picture of a sample with morphological affinities to the Near Eastern and European Neandertals. This is evident primarily in the morphology of the facial skeleton and the temporal and occipital regions. However, within the context of a Neandertal morphological pattern, there are aspects that are unique to the Shanidar sample, and there is considerable variation.

The special features of the Shanidar skulls may be the products of sampling or of their geographical origin near the eastern end of the known Neandertal range. These problems are discussed in Chapter 13. The variation within the Shanidar sample may also be largely a reflection of normal individual variation with a population, since all other Neandertal sites that have yielded reasonably complete remains of more than one individual provide evidence of mor-

phological variation (e.g., Krapina [Gorjanović-Kramberger 1906; Smith 1976a],
La Quina [Guth 1963; Martin 1923, 1926a; Vallois 1969], and Spy [Fraipont and
Lohest 1887; Thoma 1975]). However, a significant amount of the variation is
probably due to the temporal separation of the earlier Shanidar 2, 4, 6, and 8
specimens from the later Shanidar 1 and 5 specimens. The actual amount of
geological time separating these two subsamples from Shanidar is uncertain,
and the estimate of about 15,000 years by Solecki (1960) may be only a
minimum.

Data on overall cranial vault shape derive primarily from the later Shanidar
1 and 5 specimens. They have relatively large cranial vaults with little frontal
curvature and exceptionally curved bregma-lambda arcs compared to other
Neandertals. The Shanidar 1 occipital bone exhibits a degree of curvature similar to those of other Neandertals and appears to have had a small occipital bun.
The Shanidar 5 occipital bone is absent, but the elevated position of lambda
implies that his occipital bone was quite flat. These unusual features of the
cranial vault, compared to both Neandertals and anatomically modern humans,
as discussed in the preceding section, are probably the products of artificial
cranial deformation and do not reflect the phylogenetic affinities of these individuals. It is likely that both Shanidar 1 and 5 would have had cranial vaults
within the range of variation of other Neandertals had they not been subjected
to head binding or pressing as infants.

The earlier Shanidar 2 and 4 cranial vaults are insufficient to indicate their
overall configurations, since Shanidar 2 preserves primarily part of the posteri-
or neurocranium and Shanidar 4 retains a portion of the frontal bone and small
fragments of the posterior vault. Shanidar 2 appears to have had a relatively
high parietal arc, and Shanidar 4 probably had a rather flat frontal bone, but it is
uncertain what the relative amounts of frontal and parietal curvature were in
these earlier Shanidar specimens.

The Shanidar occipitomastoid regions show considerable variation.
Shanidar 1 and 2 have large, diffuse suprainiac fossae and occipitomastoid
crests. Yet the Shanidar 1 mastoocipital crest is continuous with the transverse
occipital torus, whereas that of Shanidar 2 is separate from its torus. Shanidar 1
has a relatively weak transverse occipital torus, whereas those of Shanidar 2
and 4 are robust for Neandertals. Shanidar 1 possesses anterior mastoid tubercles, but Shanidar 2 and 5 lack them. There is marked variation in mastoid
process size, with Shanidar 2 having a large one and Shanidar 5 having a small
one. Those of Shanidar 2 and 5 are roughly parallel sided, similar to those of
most recent humans, whereas those of Shanidar 1 narrow inferiorly, as do those
of many European Neandertals. And there is considerable variation in the
supramastoid region. This variation appears to follow little pattern except for
the robusticity of the transverse occipital tori, which are more robust in the
earlier specimens.

Tympanic regions are preserved only for Shanidar 1 and 5, and both of them
conform to the morphological pattern seen in European and Levantine Nean-

dertals. They have relatively wide tympanic regions oriented largely perpendicular to the sagittal plane and prominent tympanic crests. And Shanidar 5 has an elongated and obliquely oriented external acoustic meatus.

Most of the temporal variation within the Shanidar skull is in their facial skeletons. All of them have relatively large supraorbital tori, which lack, or appear to lack, significant lateral thinning, even though the Shanidar 5 torus does become slightly thinner laterally. Shanidar 1 and 5 and probably Shanidar 2 possess large orbits. But whereas Shanidar 1 and 5 exhibit marked midfacial prognathism comparable to that of European Neandertals, Shanidar 2 and 4 have degrees of midfacial prognathism intermediate between those of other Neandertals and most more recent humans. This dichotomy in midfacial prognathism is reflected in their zygomaxillary to molar alveolus radii differences, their zygomaxillary angles, the positions of their zygomatic roots above M^2 versus M^2–M^3, and the sizes of their mandibular retromolar spaces. In all of these features, the Shanidar 2 and 4 premaxillae project less anteriorly from the zygomatic bone–mandibular ramus region than do those of Shanidar 1 and 5.

The contrasts in midfacial projection cannot be due to differences in overall facial size between Shanidar 1 and 5 and Shanidar 2 and 4. There is some variation in facial length, since Shanidar 1 and 5 have slightly longer faces than do Shanidar 2 and 4 (as indicated by their mandibular superior lengths). Yet when these facial lengths are normalized for overall body size using femoral and tibial lengths, any difference between the two Shanidar subsamples disappears, and they all appear Neandertal-like in their relative facial lengths.

The differences in facial projection are probably due largely to contrasts in the relative positioning of the anterior zygomatic bones. The region around zygomaxillare anterior projects anteriorly on both Shanidar 2 and 4, whereas Shanidar 1 and 5 have retreating zygomatic profiles. Furthermore, Shanidar 2 and 4 have wide mandibular rami, at the upper limits of Neandertal ranges of variation, whereas Shanidar 1 has comparatively narrower mandibular rami.

The contrast in midfacial prognathism between the earlier and later Shanidar crania appears to be a reflection of the relative positioning of the anterior zygomatic regions, with their associated anterior mandibular rami and masticatory musculature. Shanidar 2 and 4 had their masseter and temporal muscles positioned anteriorly, which would have increased their mechanical advantages relative to the bite force. This suggests that Shanidar 2 and 4 had masticatory apparatus proportions that increased their effectiveness relative to the proportions of the Shanidar 1 and 5 facial skeletons. This interpretation is supported by the greater robusticity of the Shanidar 2 and 4 facial skeletons, robusticity which is evident in the development of surface features on their mandibular corpori and of muscular insertion markings on their mandibular rami and zygomatic bones.

In addition to the variation in midfacial projection and robusticity, there are differences among the Shanidar Neandertals in anterior maxillary morphology. Shanidar 5 alone presents the "typically" Neandertal inflated maxillae without any suggestion of a canine fossa. Shanidar 1 has slightly concave anterior maxillae, whereas Shanidar 2 and 4 have flat anterior maxillae that are slightly concave just below their projecting anterior zygomatic regions. The differences between the Shanidar 5 and Shanidar 2 and 4 maxillae can be explained as secondary effects of their degrees of midfacial prognathism. The differences between Shanidar 1 and 5 are probably due to individual variation in maxillary inflation.

The Shanidar skulls thus show considerable variation, both individual and temporal, while conforming to a general Neandertal morphological pattern. The temporal variation appears to be largely one of decreasing robusticity, which results in, among other things, an increase in midfacial prognathism.

CHAPTER 6

The Dental Remains

The Shanidar adults provide considerable data on Near Eastern Neandertal dental morphology and proportions. A total of 96 permanent teeth are preserved from six of the seven adults, and two of the individuals, Shanidar 1 and 2, preserve virtually complete dentitions (Table 15).

All of the Shanidar Neandertals experienced extensive occlusal attrition and moderate degrees of interproximal wear, so that many of the morphological details of their tooth crowns have been lost. This applies particularly to Shanidar 1, 3, 4, and 5, whose anterior teeth were worn down to their cervicoenamel junctions and whose posterior tooth crowns consist of rings of enamel around secondary dentin. Even the teeth of Shanidar 2 and 6 are significantly worn, although most of the morphology of their posterior teeth and some of the morphology of their anterior teeth remain. As a result, most of the discussion of the Shanidar teeth is concerned with their dimensions rather than their discrete characteristics.

The dimensions of the Shanidar permanent teeth and their degrees of occlusal wear are listed in Tables 16 to 20. Comparative dental metrics are provided in Tables 22 to 24.

SHANIDAR 1

Shanidar 1 retains all of its teeth except the mandibular central incisors (Figure 26; Table 16). Most of the teeth are in minimally damaged alveolar bone, so that there is little question as to their position and orientation. Only the maxillary

TABLE 15
Inventory of the Permanent Teeth[a]

		I-1	I-2	C	P-3	P-4	M-1	M-2	M-3
Shanidar 1									
Maxilla	Right	+	+	+	+	+	+	+	+
	Left	+	+	+	+	(+)	+	+	+
Mandible	Right	P	+	+	+	+	+	+	+
	Left	P	+	+	+	+	+	+	+
Shanidar 2									
Maxilla	Right	(+)	+	+	(+)	+	+	+	+
	Left	+	+	+	+	+	+	+	+
Mandible	Right	−	+	+	+	+	+	+	+
	Left	(+)	+	+	+	+	+	+	+
Shanidar 3									
Maxilla	Right	−	−	−	−	−	−	−	+
	Left	−	−	+	−	−	−	−	−
Mandible	Right	−	−	+	−	−	−	−	−
	Left	−	+	−	−	−	−	−	−
Shanidar 4									
Maxilla	Right	−	−	P	−	−	−	−	−
	Left	P	−	+	(+)	(+)	P	P	P
Mandible	Right	(+)	+	−	+, P	+, P	+	A	A
	Left	+	(+)	(+)			A	A	(+)
Shanidar 5									
Maxilla	Right	(+)	P	P	P	P	−	−	−
	Left	P	A	P	A	A?	(+)	−	+
Shanidar 6									
Maxilla	Right	−	−	+	+	+	+	+	+
	Left	−	−	−	(+)	+	+	+	+
Mandible	Right	−	−	−	+	+	−	+	+
	Left	−	−	+	−	−	−	−	−

[a] + = occlusal surface present; (+) = occlusal surface present but damaged postmortem; P = postmortem loss of the tooth (as indicated by the alveolus); A = antemortem loss of the tooth (as indicated by the alveolus); − = tooth and alveolus absent.

central incisors had their roots significantly abraded and may not be precisely in their original positions.

The most impressive aspect of the Shanidar 1 dentition is its extreme occlusal attrition, especially on the anterior teeth. All of the anterior teeth except the right mandibular C have lost their crowns, and all of the posterior teeth except the maxillary second and third molars have their occlusal surfaces made up almost exclusively of secondary dentin. Associated with this occlusal attrition is considerable interproximal wear, especially around the first molars. Unless Shanidar 1 died at an age more advanced than that suggested by the other age indicators (Chapter 4), there is little question that there were considerable wear-producing agents in his diet.

Despite the extensive attrition of the Shanidar 1 teeth, no significant dental

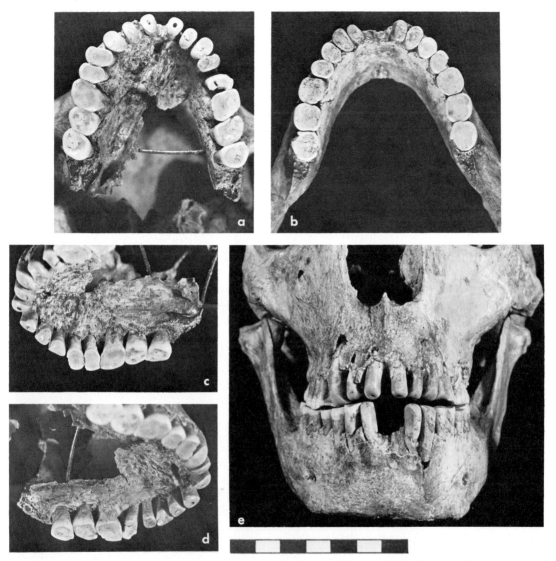

Figure 26 Views of the Shanidar 1 dentition. (a) Occlusal view of the mandibular dentition. (b) Occlusal view of the maxillary dentition. (c,d) Oblique views of the maxillary dentition. (e) Anterior view of the occluded dentitions. The I_1 were lost postmortem, and the positions of the I^1 are approximate due to postmortem damage to their alveoli. Scale in centimeters.

abnormalities are evident. Caries are absent, as they are from the other Shanidar teeth and all known Neandertal dental remains. The only teeth lost, the mandibular central incisors, were lost postmortem from damaged alveoli. The maxillary central incisors had their pulp chambers exposed through occlusal attrition, but there does not appear to have been any subsequent inflammation. The interdental septa are well preserved in the maxillary and mandibular premolar

TABLE 16
Dental Dimensions and Occlusal Wear of Shanidar 1

		Length (M–D) (mm)	Breadth (B–L) (mm)	L/B	L × B (mm²)	Wear category[a]	Labial rounding
Maxilla							
I-1	R	—	(7.7)			8	Present
	L	—	(7.5)			8	Present
I-2	R	—	(8.9)			8	Present
	L	—	(8.7)			8	Present
C	R	—	(9.5)			8	Present
	L	—	(10.0)			8	Present
P-3	R	7.0	10.4	67.3	72.8	7	Absent
	L	—	(9.6)	—	—	8	Present
P-4	R	6.8	9.7	70.1	66.0	7	Absent
	L	(6.2)	10.0	(62.0)	(62.0)	7	Absent
M-1	R	10.3	12.3	83.7	126.7	7	Absent
	L	10.7	11.7	91.5	125.2	7	Absent
M-2	R	9.1	11.8	77.1	107.4	5	Absent
	L	10.1	11.9	84.9	120.2	5	Absent
M-3	R	9.7	11.6	83.6	112.5	5	Absent
	L	9.4	11.6	81.0	109.0	5	Absent
Mandible							
I-2	R	—	(8.5)			8	Present
	L	—	(8.4)			8	Present
C	R	—	9.0			7	Absent
	L	—	(9.8)			8	Present
P-3	R	7.7	8.4	91.7	64.7	5	Absent
	L	6.5	8.5	76.5	55.3	6	Absent
P-4	R	7.5	8.1	92.6	60.8	6	Absent
	L	6.8	8.8	77.3	59.8	6	Absent
M-1	R	10.5	10.4	101.0	109.2	6	Absent
	L	10.5	10.0	105.0	105.0	7	Absent
M-2	R	11.0	11.0	100.0	121.0	6	Absent
	L	10.9	10.8	100.9	117.7	6	Absent
M-3	R	11.6	10.9	106.4	126.4	6	Absent
	L	11.5	10.8	106.5	124.2	6	Absent

[a]The wear categories are those of Molnar (1971), in which "1" indicates an unworn tooth and "8" indicates a tooth whose roots function as the occlusal surface.

and molar regions; they show a moderate degree of osteoporosis, but they are either flat or convex towards the occlusal surface. There is no evidence of infrabony pockets. This degree of deterioration of the interdental septa and the absence of infrabony pockets suggests that there was little periodontal inflammation (Costa 1977).

The maxillary and mandibular alveoli are intact on the right side (Figure 26) and exhibit resorption evenly along the molar and premolar regions. They no longer approach the cervicoenamel junctions of the teeth, and the apex between the roots of the right M_1 has been exposed. This noticeable recession of the alveoli is related to the extensive occlusal wear on the Shanidar 1 teeth. During the life of an individual, the clinical crown height (the distance between the gingiva, or alveolar margin in skeletal material, and the occlusal surface) remains virtually constant because the alveoli recede at the same rate that the teeth wear down (Alexandersen 1967; Costa 1977). Therefore, in an individual such as Shanidar 1, who lost one-half to two-thirds of his molar crowns through occlusal attrition, considerable alveolar resorption would be expected.

Given the degree of occlusal wear on the Shanidar 1 dentition, the reasonably advanced age of the individual, and the presence of extensive abnormalities elsewhere on the individual (Chapter 12), the Shanidar 1 dentition and periodontal region is remarkably healthy.

The Shanidar 1 maxilla and mandible were occluded by placing the premolars and molars in maximum intercuspation so as to best approximate centric occlusion (Figure 26). Due to some distortion in the reconstruction and uneven occlusal wear of the teeth, it is not possible to achieve an indisputable occlusion, but the one shown is probably the best possible. In centric occlusion, the anterior teeth are, or would be if less worn, in edge-to-edge occlusion. It is not possible to determine whether Shanidar 1 had edge-to-edge occlusion or an overbite prior to the wearing down of his occlusal surfaces, but at least one Neandertal with an unworn dentition (Le Moustier 1 [Weinert 1925]) had a moderate overbite. At any rate, it is normal, under conditions of high attrition, for an overbite to be transformed into edge-to-edge occlusion through a lingual tilting of the maxillary incisors and compensatory growth of the mandibular condylar region during adulthood (Hylander 1977). It is probably this normal process during adult life that produced the edge-to-edge occlusion of Shanidar 1 and many other early hominids (Brace and Mahler 1971).

SHANIDAR 2

Shanidar 2 has the most complete of the Shanidar dentitions (Figures 27 and 29; Table 17). All of the maxillary teeth are present, although the right I^1 and P^3 and the left C^- and P^3 have lost some of their crowns. All of the mandibular dentition on both sides from I_2 to M_3 is preserved with little damage. The labial and buccal three-quarters of the left I_1 remain, but the tooth has not been placed in the mandibular reconstruction. Although there has been noticeable occlusal wear on the teeth, especially the maxillary anterior teeth, much of the occlusal morphology can be discerned.

Major portions of the maxillary and mandibular alveoli remain in the premolar and molar regions, so that there is no uncertainty as to the position and orientation of those teeth. As mentioned earlier, however, the midlines of both

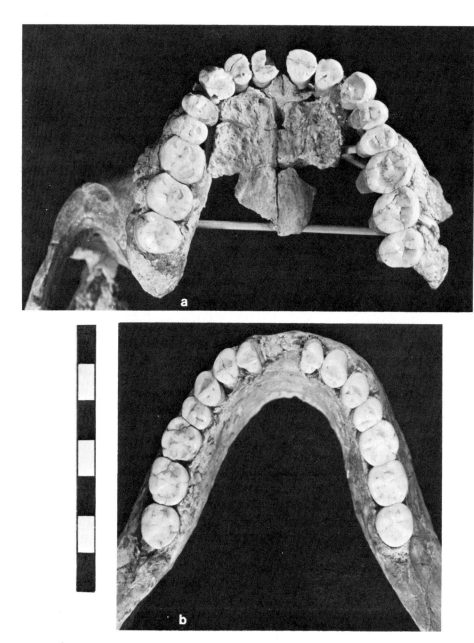

Figure 27 Occlusal views of the Shanidar 2 (a) maxillary and (b) mandibular dentitions. The left I_1 is not included in the mandibular reconstruction. Scale in centimeters.

TABLE 17
Dental Dimensions and Occlusal Wear of Shanidar 2

		Length (M–D) (mm)	Breadth (B–L) (mm)	L/B	L × B (mm²)	Wear category[a]	Labial rounding
Maxilla							
I-1	R	—	8.3			5	Absent
	L	8.2	8.2			5	Absent
I-2	R	7.1	8.2			5	Absent
	L	7.3	8.2			5	Absent
C	R	7.6	9.8			6	Absent
	L	8.0	9.9			5	Absent
P-3	R	—	—	—	—	2	Absent
	L	7.0	10.0	70.0	70.0	2	Absent
P-4	R	6.1	10.0	61.0	61.0	3	Absent
	L	7.0	10.3	68.0	72.1	4	Absent
M-1	R	10.7	12.1	88.4	129.5	4	Absent
	L	10.9	12.3	88.6	134.1	4	Absent
M-2	R	10.5	12.9	81.4	135.5	3	Absent
	L	11.3	12.7	89.0	143.5	3	Absent
M-3	R	10.0	12.9	77.5	129.0	2	Absent
	L	9.7	12.3	78.9	119.3	2	Absent
Mandible							
I-1	L	5.2	7.3			5	Absent
I-2	R	6.3	8.6			4	Absent
	L	5.9	8.1			4	Absent
C	R	7.8	9.5			4	Absent
	L	7.7	9.9			4	Absent
P-3	R	7.6	9.4	80.9	71.4	3	Absent
	L	7.2	9.5	75.8	68.4	3	Absent
P-4	R	7.1	9.1	78.0	64.6	3	Absent
	L	6.6	9.1	72.5	60.1	3	Absent
M-1	R	11.2	11.1	100.9	124.3	4	Absent
	L	11.6	10.9	106.4	126.4	4	Absent
M-2	R	11.6	11.2	103.6	129.9	3	Absent
	L	12.0	11.3	106.2	135.6	3	Absent
M-3	R	11.2	10.8	103.7	121.0	3	Absent
	L	11.7	11.2	104.5	131.0	2	Absent

[a]The wear categories are those of Molnar (1971), in which "1" indicates an unworn tooth and "8" indicates a tooth whose roots function as the occlusal surface.

jaws were damaged *in situ* and have been reconstructed using, in part, the preserved teeth to indicate the shapes of the dental arcades. Despite this, there should be little doubt that the teeth are positioned properly and are close to their original orientations.

It is not possible to assess adequately the extent to which Shanidar 2 suffered from periodontal disease because the alveoli are incompletely preserved.

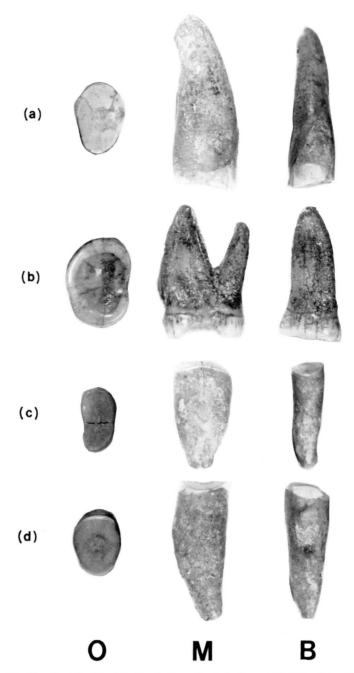

Figure 28   The Shanidar 3 isolated teeth. From top to bottom: (a) left C$^-$, (b) right M^3, (c) left I$_2$, and (d) right C$_-$. O = occlusal view; M = mesial view; B = buccal (labial) view. In the occlusal views, buccal (labial) is at the top. Scale in centimeters.

There were no caries, there does not appear to have been any antemortem tooth loss, and where preserved the alveoli lack infrabony pockets. The maxillary molar alveoli exhibit alveolar exostoses (Figure 19), which may or may not be related to periodontal inflammation (Chapter 5). Associated with the exostoses is a moderate degree of alveolar recession. In addition, there is a considerable development of calculus on the buccal molar and premolar surfaces, which is still present on the right side and can be discerned on the left side (Figure 19). There is also calculus remaining on the mandibular premolars and molars near the cervical margins of the crowns. It is not possible to determine whether the alveolar recession was due to a maintenance of a constant clinical crown height or to periodontal inflammation resulting from the calculus build up. Given the apparent lack of extensive periodontal disease, the former explanation appears more likely.

In Figure 17, the Shanidar 2 maxilla and mandible were occluded by placing the right premolars and molars in maximum intercuspation. This closely approximates centric occlusion for the right sides of the dental arcades. Due to the differences in dental arcade width in the maxillary and mandibular reconstructions, it is not possible to place both sides of the jaws in full occlusion simultaneously; the right side will be used to indicate the pattern of occlusion for Shanidar 2. In this position, the anterior teeth occlude edge to edge with a very slight overjet. Given the moderate degree of occlusal wear on the Shanidar 2 teeth, it is likely that this represents a pattern of occlusion intermediate between an overbite and full edge-to-edge occlusion (Hylander 1977).

SHANIDAR 3

The Shanidar 3 dentition consists of four isolated teeth without any of the maxillary or mandibular alveoli. The anterior teeth were extensively worn (Figure 28; Table 18) in such a way that the canines preserve only small labial

TABLE 18
Dental Dimensions and Occlusal Wear of Shanidar 3

		Length (M–D) (mm)	Breadth (B–L) (mm)	L/B	L × B (mm²)	Wear category[a]	Labial rounding
Maxilla							
C	L	(7.3)	9.8			7	Absent
M-3	R	9.6	12.8	75.0	122.9	6	Absent
Mandible							
I-2	L	—	(9.0)			8	Present
C	R	(7.2)	8.4			7	Present

[a]The wear categories are those of Molnar (1971), in which "1" indicates an unworn tooth and "8" indicates a tooth whose roots function as the occlusal surface.

and lingual sections of the enamel and the I$_2$ retains none of the crown. The M^3 retains most of a heavily worn crown, which has traces of calculus along its buccal and distal margins.

SHANIDAR 4

About a third of the Shanidar 4 teeth remain, but none of them is in place in the maxilla or mandible. The maxillary alveoli were extensively damaged, so that only the tips of a few sockets remain (Figure 21). The mandibular incisor, canine, and premolar alveoli were similarly damaged, and the mandibular molar regions sustained extensive alveolar resorption with some antemortem tooth loss (Figure 21; Table 15). The preserved teeth were all heavily worn (Figure 29; Table 19), and most of them were damaged postmortem. The metrics obtained from them are therefore approximate.

The Shanidar 6 teeth were originally assigned to Shanidar 4 (Stewart 1963), but it has become apparent that they come from a different individual. In particular, it is unlikely that the reasonably unworn right mandibular teeth assigned to Shanidar 6 (Figure 30) belong in the Shanidar 4 mandible. Furthermore, associated with the Shanidar 4, 6, 8, and 9 multiple burial are various isolated teeth, here assigned to Shanidar 4, which agree in their degree of occlusal attrition, do not duplicate one another, and show an amount of deterioration similar to that of the Shanidar 4 mandible. It is therefore likely that the Shanidar 4 teeth are correctly assigned, and that the teeth originally referred to him belong to another individual, probably Shanidar 6.

The right and left mandibular molar alveoli were largely resorbed, and several of the molars were lost antemortem (Figure 21; Table 15). Assuming that the Shanidar 4 teeth were not lost through carious decay, given the absence of caries among the Neandertals, they must have become loose as a result of periodontal inflammation and associated bone loss. The present state of the mandibular alveoli is thus probably the product of initial periodontal disease around the molars, followed by tooth loss, and finally remodeling of the alveolar bone possibly associated with further periodontal inflammation. Shanidar 4 therefore appears to have had considerably more dental disease than Shanidar 1 or 2.

SHANIDAR 5

All of the dental data for Shanidar 5 come from his maxilla because neither the mandible nor any of the mandibular dentition survived.

Only one tooth is preserved intact, the left M^3, and two others retain one-

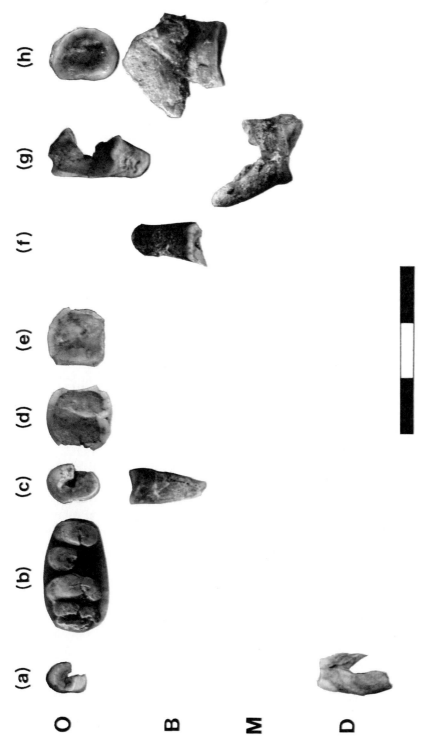

Figure 29 Isolated teeth of Shanidar 2, 4, and 5. (a) Shanidar 2 left I_1, (b) Shanidar 4 left I_2–right I_2, (c) Shanidar 4 left M_3, (f) Shanidar 5 right I^1, (g) Shanidar 5 left M^1, and (h) Shanidar 5 left M^3. O = occlusal view (buccal [labial] margin above); B = buccal/labial; M = mesial; D = distal. Scale in centimeters.

TABLE 19
Dental Dimensions and Occlusal Wear of Shanidar 4

		Length (M–D) (mm)	Breadth (B–L) (mm)	L/B	L × B (mm²)	Wear category[a]	Labial rounding
Maxilla							
C	L	—	(9.9)			8	Present
P-3	L	—	—	—	—	7	Absent
P-4	L	—	—	—	—	7	Absent
Mandible							
I-1	R	—	—			—	Present
	L	—	(8.8)			7	Present
I-2	R	—	(8.4)			7	Present
	L	—	—			7	Present
C	L	(6.7)	—			6	Absent
P-3	?	(6.6)	8.3	(79.5)	(54.8)	7	Absent
P-4	?	(7.1)	8.8	(80.7)	(62.5)	7	Absent
M-1	R	(10.6)	11.3	(93.8)	(119.8)	6	Absent
M-3	L	—	—	—	—	6	—

[a]The wear categories are those of Molnar (1971), in which "1" indicates an unworn tooth and "8" indicates a tooth whose roots function as the occlusal surface.

half to two-thirds of their crowns, the right I¹ and the left M¹ (Figure 29; Table 20). In addition, there is a broken root of a right premolar. These teeth are similar to those of Shanidar 1, 3, and 4 in being extensively worn. Only the M³ retains enamel around the entire circumference of the crown, but it preserves little of the occlusal morphology.

The maxilla retains the alveoli from the right P⁴ to the left P³ or P⁴, plus a fragment of alveolus near the left M³ (Figure 30). Unquestionably, it experienced pervasive periodontal inflammation and associated alveolar resorption. The alveolar bone either healed over subsequent to antemortem tooth loss or exhibits osteoporosis. There are no apparent infrabony pockets, but the inter-

TABLE 20
Dental Dimensions and Occlusal Wear of Shanidar 5

		Length (M–D) (mm)	Breadth (B–L) (mm)	L/B	L × B (mm²)	Wear category[a]	Labial rounding
Maxilla							
I-1	R	—	—			8	Present
M-1	L	—	13.4	—	—	7	Absent
M-3	L	9.6	13.0	73.8	124.8	6	Absent

[a]The wear categories are those of Molnar (1971), in which "1" indicates an unworn tooth and "8" indicates a tooth whose roots function as the occlusal surface.

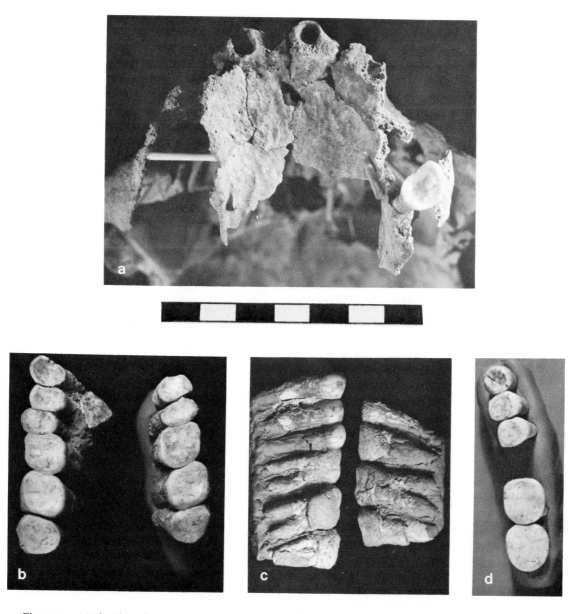

Figure 30   (a) The Shanidar 5 palate in occlusal view. (b) The Shanidar 6 maxillary dentition in occlusal and (c) buccal views; (d) the Shanidar 6 mandibular dentition in occlusal view. Note the alveolar resorption of the Shanidar 5 anterior palate and the calculus on the Shanidar 6 molars. Scale in centimeters.

dental septa are flattened or concave from remodeling. There is a small ring of calculus near the cervicoenamel junction of the left M³, and similar calculus may have been present on the other teeth. In addition, four of the anterior teeth, the right I² and C⁻ and the left I¹ and C⁻, have fenestrae at the apieces of their root sockets. And two teeth, the left I² and P³, and possibly the left P⁴, were lost antemortem, as evidenced by the complete healing over of their alveoli. Shanidar 5 clearly suffered from dental disease, probably more so than Shanidar 4.

SHANIDAR 6

Although almost nothing remains of the Shanidar 6 alveoli, her dentition provides considerable morphological and metrical data (Figure 30; Table 21). The maxillary premolars and molars are largely complete, and they are associated with two canines and two each of the right mandibular premolars and molars (Table 15). All of the teeth are worn, but most of the molar and some of the premolar occlusal morphology is evident.

TABLE 21
Dental Dimensions and Occlusal Wear of Shanidar 6

		Length (M–D) (mm)	Breadth (B–L) (mm)	L/B	L × B (mm²)	Wear category[a]	Labial rounding
Maxilla							
C	R	7.4	10.3			5	Absent
P-3	R	6.5	10.6	61.3	68.9	6	Absent
	L	(6.6)	9.9	(66.7)	(65.3)	6	Absent
P-4	R	6.5	10.5	61.9	68.3	4	Absent
	L	7.4	10.7	69.2	79.2	6	Absent
M-1	R	10.7	12.1	88.4	129.5	4	Absent
	L	11.0	12.3	89.4	135.3	5	Absent
M-2	R	11.4	12.6	90.5	143.6	3	Absent
	L	11.8	12.8	92.2	151.0	3	Absent
M-3	R	10.6	12.2	86.9	129.3	4	Absent
	L	10.0	13.0	76.9	130.0	3	Absent
Mandible							
C	R	7.8	8.5			5	Absent
P-3	R	7.2	9.3	77.4	67.0	5	Absent
P-4	R	7.3	9.1	80.2	66.4	4	Absent
M-2	R	12.6	11.8	106.8	148.7	4	Absent
M-3	R	12.8	12.2	104.9	156.2	4	Absent

[a]The wear categories are those of Molnar (1971), in which "1" indicates an unworn tooth and "8" indicates a tooth whose roots function as the occlusal surface.

Along the buccal margins of the maxillary molars are large calculus deposits (Figure 30). These concretions are similar to those of Shanidar 2, 4, and 5, but they are much larger, extending from the occlusal edge to the gingival margin. This strongly suggests, along with the less complete data from the other specimens, that the Shanidar individuals had large calculus deposits on their molars during most of their lives.

ANTERIOR DENTAL REMAINS

Data on anterior teeth are provided by six of the Shanidar adults. Yet only Shanidar 2 and 6 furnish indications of their anterior crown morphologies. The other individuals indicate patterns of occlusal wear and dental dimensions.

The maxillary incisors of Shanidar 2 (Figure 27) are quite worn, but there is little doubt that they are shovel shaped. The central incisors conform to the pattern described as slightly shoveled by Hrdlička (1920) and Carbonell (1963), whereas the lateral incisors exhibit their moderately shoveled category. The shoveling of these teeth is slightly accentuated by the formation of lingual tubercles. This pattern is present on most other Neandertal maxillary incisors (Carbonell 1963; Coon 1962; Patte 1959). Shoveling of the incisors appears to be a reliable genetic indicator (Berry 1978; Turner 1969), and it may represent an adaptation to a high attrition environment by increasing the surface area of the incisor crowns (Hrdlička 1920).

The only unworn mandibular incisors are those of Shanidar 2. The incomplete I_1 shows a moderately strong lingual tubercle, as do the two I_2 (Figures 27 and 29). In addition, the right and left I_2 are slightly asymmetrical, with longer distal shoulders than mesial ones. However, the shapes of the crowns may have been slightly altered by I_1–I_2 interstitial wear.

The maxillary canines of Shanidar 2 and 6 are large with longer distal shoulders than mesial ones and moderately strong lingual tubercles. It is difficult to determine the extent of the lingual tubercles because all of them, and expecially that of the Shanidar 6 right C^-, have been reduced in size by occlusal wear. Large and distinct lingual tubercles are present on the Shanidar 2 mandibular canines; they are set off from the rest of the crown by small sulci. However, the Shanidar 6 left C_- shows only a suggestion of a lingual tubercle. Its tubercle may have been reduced by occlusal wear, or it may never have been particularly large.

The evaluation of the Shanidar anterior teeth must include a consideration of their absolute size. It is not possible to use reliably the mesiodistal length of anterior teeth to evaluate their size because normal occlusal attrition, especially on the incisors, rapidly decreases the measurement. Therefore, metric comparisons will employ only the labiolingual breadth. This should not introduce any bias because Neandertal anterior teeth are generally similar in mesiodistal to labiolingual proportions to those of recent humans (Twiesselmann 1973).

The Shanidar specimens agree with other Neandertals in having exceptionally large anterior teeth. In fact, the incisors and canines of the Neandertals are among the largest, on the average, of those known for members of the genus *Homo* (Brace 1967, 1979; Twiesselmann 1973).

The Shanidar 1 and 2 I^1 breadths are slightly below a European Neandertal mean of 8.6 mm, close to those of other Near Eastern Neandertals and Skhūl–Qafzeh fossils, and above the means of more recent human samples (Table 22). However, the Shanidar 1 incisors were reduced to their roots by wear, so that their breadth measurements may be as much as 0.5 mm below their original crown dimensions. The Shanidar 2 I^2 breadths are also slightly below a European Neandertal mean, although they are close to the values for other Near Eastern Neandertal I^2. However, the Shanidar 1 I^2 breadths are considerably above the Neandertal mean, even though they too may have been reduced by the extensive occlusal wear. The Shanidar 1, 2, 3, 4, and 6 maxillary canine breadths are all remarkably close to the European Neandertal mean of 10.0 mm, slightly above those from Amud and Tabūn, and well above the means of more recent human samples.

In the mandibular anterior dentition, the Shanidar 2 and 4 central incisor breadths are respectively close to and considerably above those of most other Neandertals and more recent humans, whereas the breadths of the lateral incisors of Shanidar 1, 2, 3, and 4 are all noticeably above the European Neandertal mean breadth of 7.8 mm, and towards the upper limits of the Near Eastern Neandertal range of variation. The mandibular canine breadths fall on either side of the European Neandertal mean, with Shanidar 1 and 2 being above it and Shanidar 3 and 6 being below it. The Amud and Tabūn lower canine breadths are below those ofShanidar 1 and 2 and most European Neandertals, but are similar to those of Shanidar 3 and 6. All of these anterior dental breadths, except the Shanidar 2 I_1 and the Shanidar 3 and 6 C_ breadths, are well above the means of more recent human samples.

It is possible to compute a summed anterior tooth breadth for the maxillary incisors and canines of Shanidar 1 and 2. These values are approximately 26.2 and 26.4 mm, respectively. A modest European Neandertal sample has a mean of 27.4 mm, so that Shanidar 1 and 2 fall slightly below the mean. However, the Shanidar 1 and 2 values are similar to those of Amud 1 (26.2 mm) and Tabūn C1 (24.7 mm). They are within 2 standard deviations of the mean of a small Skhūl–Qafzeh sample, but they are 2.54 standard deviations from the mean of an Early Upper Paleolithic sample and at least 3 standard deviations from the means of recent human samples (Table 24).

Only Shanidar 2 retains a sufficiently complete mandibular anterior dentition to permit a direct computation of its summed mandibular anterior tooth breadths. However, it is possible to compute the labiolingual breadth of the Shanidar 4 left C_ from its mesiodistal length using a least squares regression

TABLE 22

Comparative Data for the Breadths of Incisors and Canines (mm)[a]

		Near Eastern Neandertals	European Neandertals	Skhūl-Qafzeh sample	Early Upper Paleolithic sample	Recent Melanesians[b]	Recent Europeans[c]	Recent Amerindians[b]
Maxilla								
I-1	$\bar{X} \pm$ SD	8.2–8.4	8.6 ± 0.6	8.2 ± 0.4	7.5 ± 0.3	7.6 ± 0.4	7.1 ± 0.5	7.3 ± 0.5
	N	3	21	10	13	30	98	108
I-2	$\bar{X} \pm$ SD	8.1 ± 0.5	8.5 ± 0.8	7.5 ± 0.6	6.8 ± 0.5	6.8 ± 0.4	6.2 ± 0.5	6.7 ± 0.5
	N	5	25	9	10	33	103	107
C	$\bar{X} \pm$ SD	8.8–9.5	10.0 ± 0.6	9.2 ± 0.8	9.0 ± 0.9	8.7 ± 0.7	8.3 ± 0.6	8.6 ± 0.6
	N	3	25	9	12	44	108	113
Mandible								
I-1	$\bar{X} \pm$ SD	7.0–8.0	7.3 ± 0.4	6.7 ± 0.6	6.4 ± 0.4	6.2 ± 0.4	6.0 ± 0.4	5.8 ± 0.5
	N	3	16	8	14	29	102	95
I-2	$\bar{X} \pm$ SD	7.5–9.0	7.8 ± 0.5	7.2 ± 0.6	7.0 ± 0.6	6.5 ± 0.5	6.3 ± 0.4	6.3 ± 0.4
	N	4	24	8	18	35	107	99
C	$\bar{X} \pm$ SD	8.3–9.1	9.2 ± 0.8	8.3 ± 0.8	9.0 ± 0.6	8.1 ± 0.7	7.8 ± 0.5	7.9 ± 0.6
	N	3	29	8	13	47	109	124

[a] For samples less than 5, the range of the values is provided.
[b] Wolpoff 1971b.
[c] Twisselmann and Brabant 1967.

based on a sample of Neandertal C_ (r = 0.548, N = 34). Although such regressions have characteristically low correlation coefficients (0.49, N = 109 in a recent human sample [Twiesselmann and Brabant 1967]), they can be used to provide a general indication of tooth breadth. This regression provides an estimate of 8.2 mm for the Shanidar 4 left C_ breadth.

The resultant summed anterior tooth breadths for the Shanidar 2 and 4 mandibular dentitions are each about 25.4 mm. These estimates are slightly above a European Neandertal mean of 24.7 mm, similar to that of Tabūn C2 (25.2 mm) and above those of Amud 1 (23.6 mm) and Tabūn C1 (22.9 mm). They are also near the upper limits of the expected range of a Skhūl–Qafzeh sample, and significantly greater than those of a European Early Upper Paleolithic sample and recent human samples (Table 24).

The large dimensions of the Shanidar 1 and 2 anterior teeth are further illustrated by comparisons of their summed anterior dental breadths to the square roots of their summed posterior dental areas (see below for their summed posterior dental areas). The resultant indices are 118.7 for the Shanidar 1 maxillary dentition and 114.4 and 111.8 for the Shanidar 2 maxillary and mandibular dentitions, respectively. The maxillary index of Shanidar 2 is in the middle of the known Neandertal range (Amud 1: 117.7; Tabūn C1: 114.2; Krapina D: 111.6; Krapina F: 112.0; Le Moustier 1: 109.0; La Quina 5: 115.5), whereas that of Shanidar 1 is slightly above the Neandertal range. All of the early anatomically modern human maxillary dentitions except that of Qafzeh 7 have lower indices (Qafzeh 7: 115.2; Qafzeh 9: 107.1; Skhūl 4: 106.9; Skhūl 5: 106.0; Early Upper Paleolithic sample: 105.3 ± 6.0, N = 5). The Shanidar 2 mandibular index is similarly in the middle of the Neandertal range (Amud 1: 107.3; Tabūn C1: 109.0; Tabūn C2: 111.7; European Neandertals: 105.6 + 4.6, N = 9); it is, however, well above those of early anatomically modern humans (Qafzeh 7: 97.1; Qafzeh 9: 99.2; Skhūl 4: 100.0; Skhūl 5: 91.9; Combe-Capelle 1: 93.9; Předmostí 3: 94.1; Předmostí 9: 91.6; Předmostí 10: 96.3).

The summed anterior–posterior dental index of Shanidar is probably artifically elevated. The extensive interproximal wear on the molars and premolars reduced the dimensions of those teeth, which would increase this index. This may have also exaggerated the indices of some of the other specimens. It is possible to avoid this bias by comparing only the summed breadths of the anterior (I-1 to C) and posterior (P-3 to M-3) teeth, even though less information on the posterior teeth is incorporated into these indices than with the areas. The resultant indices are 47.0 and 45.5 for the Shanidar 1 and 2 maxillary dentitions, respectively, and 48.9 for the Shanidar 2 mandibular dentition. These indices are within the ranges of variation of other Neandertals (maxilla: Amud 1: 48.0; Tabūn C1: 46.8; Krapina D: 46.1; Krapina F: 49.0; Le Moustier 1: 45.8; La Quina 5: 45.0; mandible: Amud 1: 47.7; Tabūn C1: 47.6; Tabūn C2: 49.1; European Neandertals: 47.1 ± 1.4, N = 9). The maxillary index of Shanidar 1 and the mandibular index of Shanidar 2 are above the ranges of variation of early anatomically modern humans (maxilla: 39.1–45.5, 43.4 ± 2.1, N = 9; mandible: 41.4–44.9, 42.7 ± 1.3, N = 8), as are those of all other

Neandertal mandibular and most other Neandertal maxillary indices. The maxillary index of Shanidar 2, however, along with that of La Quina 5, falls within but at the top of the early anatomically modern human range.

The Shanidar specimens thus have anterior teeth with dimensions similar to those of other Neandertals and, on the average, larger than those of more recent humans. The relative enlargement of their anterior teeth is evident especially in the mandibular dentitions, but it is present as well in the maxillary teeth.

The presence of large anterior teeth among the Neandertals has been attributed to an assumed tendency of the Neandertals to use their teeth for paramasticatory pruposes (Brace 1962, 1979; Brose and Wolpoff 1971; Ryan 1980; Wolpoff 1975). In this interpretation, it is assumed that their anterior teeth were frequently loaded nonaxially (horizontally or obliquely) while using the teeth as a vise. That the Neandertals engaged in such behavior is supported by the presence of transverse scratches (mesiodistal or distomesial) on the labial surfaces of several Neandertal maxillary incisors (Koby 1956; Martin 1923; Patte 1960); presumably the scratches were inflicted by tools used to cut meat or other matter held in the teeth. Frequent use of the anterior teeth as a vise would increase the lingual–labial stress on the teeth. An augmentation of the labiolingual diameters of the anterior teeth would provide increased resistance to such stress and would therefore be adaptive. However, although Neandertals undoubtedly used their teeth for more than chewing food, it is uncertain to what extent the dimensions of their anterior teeth can be referred to normal dietary mastication, common patterns of anterior oral food preparation and/or nondietary (paramasticatory) use of the anterior teeth (Brace et al. 1981; Puech 1981; P. Smith 1976; Trinkaus 1978b; Wallace 1975).

Only one individual from Shanidar Cave, Shanidar 2, preserves the crowns of his maxillary incisors. On the labial surfaces of the left I^1 and I^2, there are distinct horizontal scratches that angle slightly with respect to the occlusal plane, being marginally higher on the distal side. Similar scratches do not appear to be present on the right incisors or on the canines. These striations are almost identical to those described by Koby (1956) and Patte (1960) on European Neandertal central maxillary incisors; they indicate that a sharp object, probably a stone flake, was drawn across the labial surfaces of the teeth so as to cut an object held between the maxillary and mandibular incisors. Shanidar 2, therefore, probably engaged in similar activities.

All of the Shanidar Neandertals show extensive wear on their anterior teeth. This wear is at least equal to, and usually greater than, that seen on the molars (Tables 16–20). When the occlusal wear is moderate, as on Shanidar 2 and 6, the anterior teeth are planed off almost parallel to the occlusal plane. There is a slight inferolabial to superolingual slope to the wear, but it is not pronounced (Figures 27 and 30). On several of the teeth, the dentin forms a small hollow within the ring of enamel. As the occlusal surface approaches the cervicoenamel junction, as in the Shanidar 1 right C_ and the two Shanidar 3 canines, the surface becomes almost flat or even slightly convex. At this level, the enamel is thin and would wear at a similar rate as the secondary dentin (P. Smith 1976). But once the crown has been completely removed, there is no longer sufficient resistance along the edges of the tooth, and the occlusal surface becomes increasingly convex.

Shanidar 1, 3, and 5 had sufficient anterior occlusal wear on their incisors and some of their canines to eliminate all of the enamel. The secondary dentin of the roots was functioning as the occlusal surface of those teeth. All of these teeth have their margins rounded, especially the labial and lingual margins. It is natural that the tooth should become rounded as the enamel is removed because the cement is softer than the secondary dentin and wears away faster (P. Smith 1976). However, the amount of rounding seen on the Shanidar teeth (e.g., Figure 26) is exceptional. Furthermore, the Shanidar 4 mandibular incisors show similar rounding even though they retain traces of enamel.

The anterior teeth of recent humans with extensive occlusal wear frequently show rounding of the labial and lingual margins. Usually this rounding wear is lingual on the maxillary teeth and labial on the mandibular teeth, perhaps as a result of the characteristic overbite of recent humans. Among the Shanidar Neandertals there is some lingual rounding, but the majority of it is labial. This is especially apparent on the Shanidar 1 maxillary dentition and the Shanidar 5 I^1 (Figures 26 and 29). Although the edge-to-edge occlusion of Shanidar 1 and 2 might promote more even rounding of the teeth, it would not, in and of itself, produce the pattern of wear seen on the Shanidar incisors and canines.

The marked labial rounding of those Shanidar teeth that had been extensively worn suggests that some type of material was being pulled across the teeth, perhaps in a stripping manner or slowly as it was being held as in a vise by the teeth. This interpretation is supported by the microscopic wear on the labial margins of the secondary dentin of these teeth.

In the Shanidar 1 maxilla, the right I^2 and both C^- show clear striations along the labial halves of their occlusal surfaces, which are oriented predominantly labiolingually. These striations are not readily apparent on the Shanidar 1 right and left I^1 or left I^2, but they may be present but less pronounced. Similar labiolingual striations are present on the Shanidar 5 right I^1 and markedly on the Shanidar 4 left C^-. In the mandibular dentition, similar striations are seen on the Shanidar 1 left C_-, Shanidar 3 left I_2 and Shanidar 4 left I_1 and C_-. The other anterior mandibular teeth of Shanidar 1 and 4 do not appear to exhibit them, but fine striations may exist on them as well.

This form of microwear has been documented for several European Neandertals and recent human hunter–gatherers (Ryan 1980), and it suggests that the Shanidar individuals were using their anterior teeth for holding or stripping objects. Any enclosed grit would easily produce the fine striations seen on the incisors and canines. Such an inference is compatible with the hypothesis that they used their anterior teeth extensively for heavy food preparation and in nondietary activities. However, it does not explain the large dimensions of the anterior dentitions, as many recent humans engage in similar activities without the massive incisors and canines (Brose and Wolpoff 1971; Wallace 1975).

An alternative explanation for the large size of Neandertal incisors and canines invokes their large body mass. Although Neandertals, including those from Shanidar, had statures similar to those of recent humans (Chapter 11), their pronounced postcranial robustness must have given them mean body weights greater than those of most recent humans (Chapters 7–9; Endo and Kimura 1970; Loth 1938; Lovejoy and Trinkaus 1980; Trinkaus 1976a). In recent human samples, the best correlations between body size and a dental dimension are with anterior tooth diameters (Anderson *et al.* 1977; White 1974). If this relationship holds for the Neandertals, their large anterior tooth dimensions may be in part a reflection of their large body masses.

The incisors and canines of the Shanidar Neandertals are thus quite similar to those of other Neandertals. They are large and were subjected to extensive attrition. At least the maxillary incisors of Shanidar 2 were shoveled, and most of them appear to have possessed substantial lingual tubercles.

POSTERIOR DENTAL REMAINS

Three of the Shanidar adults—Shanidar 1, 2, and 6—retain complete maxillary posterior dentitions, whereas Shanidar 3, 4, and 5 together contribute two maxillary premolars and two maxillary molars. Shanidar 1 and 2 each retain all of their mandibular posterior teeth, but Shanidar 4 and 6 have far less complete mandibular dentitions, retaining two premolars and two molars each (Table 15). Most of the morphological data on the premolars and molars comes from Shanidar 2 and 6.

The maxillary premolars possess subequal cusps, with the buccal cusp being slightly larger than the lingual one. On the Shanidar 2 maxillary premolars, there is a pronounced central mesiodistal sulcus, which is delimited by thick enamel ridges mesially and distally. A similar morphology appears to have been present on the other preserved maxillary premolars. The mandibular premolars, on the other hand, have large buccal cusps and very reduced lingual cusps. There is considerable development of the cingulum along the mesiolingual and distolinqual margins of each P_3, and on the Shanidar 2 right and left P_4, the development of the cingulum on the distolingual margins forms distinct cusps of similar size to the lingual cusp. This accessory cusp is separated from the lingual and buccal cusps by sulci extending lingually and distally from the central basin of the crown. The effect of this extra cusp is to give the teeth quadrilateral outlines rather than the rounded trapezoidal shapes of the anterior mandibular premolars. The Shanidar 6 P_4 probably possessed a similar accessory cusp, and, if one can judge from outlines of the teeth, those of Shanidar 1 and 4 did as well.

All of the maxillary first and second molars appear to have possessed four full cusps. They may have had additional crenulations between the cusps, but none of the teeth is sufficiently unworn to determine whether they did. On all

TABLE 23

Comparative Data for the Areas (length × breadth) of Premolars and Molars (mm²)[a]

		Near Eastern Neandertals	European Neandertals	Skhūl-Qafzeh sample	Early Upper Paleolithic sample	Recent Melanesians[b]	Recent Amerindians[b]
Maxilla							
P-3	X̄ ± SD	77.8 ± 5.3	84.9 ± 12.3	80.1 ± 8.1	68.7 ± 9.3	77.2 ± 8.2	73.3 ± 8.0
	N	6	22	8	15	55	102
P-4	X̄ ± SD	62.4–69.8	82.0 ± 11.9	72.2 ± 7.8	68.3 ± 10.2	72.9 ± 8.4	68.4 ± 9.1
	N	3	20	9	14	58	108
M-1	X̄ ± SD	137.0 ± 13.3	140.8 ± 20.0	138.5 ± 12.2	132.1 ± 16.2	138.3 ± 13.8	128.5 ± 14.5
	N	5	28	13	24	79	140
M-2	X̄ ± SD	115.1–127.4	134.8 ± 20.8	132.5 ± 14.0	130.5 ± 18.0	126.5 ± 14.9	121.7 ± 16.6
	N	3	21	7	20	70	119
M-3	X̄ ± SD	84.7–93.5	125.7 ± 12.1	114.8 ± 15.6	108.6 ± 20.7	110.3 ± 14.6	102.2 ± 17.2
	N	2	21	6	12	52	88
Mandible							
P-3	X̄ ± SD	59.5–70.2	72.9 ± 9.0	67.6 ± 6.8	62.1 ± 8.4	62.9 ± 6.8	58.4 ± 6.4
	N	3	27	7	12	42	126
P-4	X̄ ± SD	51.3–75.1	71.1 ± 10.0	68.2 ± 7.5	65.5 ± 8.6	71.6 ± 13.9	64.7 ± 8.5
	N	3	33	7	10	52	120
M-1	X̄ ± SD	105.0–121.0	129.5 ± 17.5	136.1 ± 12.7	127.4 ± 14.9	134.0 ± 13.5	130.4 ± 12.6
	N	4	43	8	26	76	134
M-2	X̄ ± SD	124.7 ± 19.3	134.6 ± 16.4	122.7 ± 17.6	122.3 ± 19.0	123.8 ± 15.0	125.1 ± 14.9
	N	6	34	9	21	65	117
M-3	X̄ ± SD	106.8–124.6	131.1 ± 13.5	129.7 ± 17.2	120.0 ± 23.5	126.2 ± 14.3	120.2 ± 17.7
	N	3	34	7	12	60	101

[a] For samples less than 5, the range of the values is provided.
[b] Wolpoff 1971b.

TABLE 24
Comparative Data for Summed Anterior Dental Breadths and Summed Posterior Dental Areas

		European Neandertals	Skhūl–Qafzeh sample	Early Upper Paleolithic sample	Recent Melanesians[a]	Recent Amerindians[a]
Maxilla						
I^1–C– summed breadth (mm)	$\bar{X} \pm$ SD	27.4 ± 1.6	25.0 ± 1.7	23.0 ± 1.3	23.0 ± 1.0	22.7 ± 1.2
	N	11	7	8	20	85
P^3–M^3 summed "area" (mm^2)	$\bar{X} \pm$ SD	572.6 ± 49.3	556.7 ± 48.3	494.8 ± 68.3	537.0 ± 43.5	495.0 ± 50.5
	N	6	4	7	31	64
Mandible						
I_1–C– summed breadth (mm)	$\bar{X} \pm$ SD	24.7 ± 1.3	22.4 ± 1.2	21.6 ± 1.0	20.6 ± 1.2	20.0 ± 1.3
	N	12	7	6	24	84
P_3–M_3 summed "area" (mm^2)	$\bar{X} \pm$ SD	554.6 ± 54.5	537.4 ± 56.7	504.0 ± 72.9	520.0 ± 44.2	495.0 ± 49.5
	N	12	5	5	30	68

[a]Wolpoff 1971b.

of the first molars the protocone is well developed and the hypocone is exceptionally large. The hypocones on the second molars are variable in size, being large on the Shanidar 6 M^2 and smaller on those of Shanidar 1 and 2. On all five of the third molars, however, only a trace remains of the hypocones, usually just a thickening of the enamel along the distolingual margin.

As far as can be determined, all of the Shanidar mandibular molars exhibited full Y-5 morphologies with little reduction of any of the cusps. The Shanidar 2 and 6 second and third molars possess anterior and posterior foveae, and similar foveae may have been present on the Shanidar 2 first molars.

Unlike their anterior teeth, the Shanidar posterior teeth are not particularly large. As indicated by their area (length × breadth) values, their premolars are, on the average, somewhat smaller than those of most European Neandertals. However, they are similar in size to those of other Near Eastern Neandertals and more recent humans (Table 23). The areas of their first molars are similarly rather low, being well below the mean European Neandertal areas and closest to the recent human means. However, other Near Eastern Neandertals also have relatively small first molars compared to those of European Neandertals. The second molars of Shanidar 2 and especially Shanidar 6 are quite large, being respectively close to and well above the means for European Neandertal second molars and well above the mean values for other Near Eastern Neandertal and more recent human second molars. The Shanidar 1 second molars, however, are quite modest in size. All of the Shanidar M^3 are relatively large, even though those of Shanidar 1 are slightly smaller than the rest. They have areas close to the European Neandertal mean and generally above those of more recent humans. They are all much larger than those of Amud 1 and Tabūn C1, both of whom have rather diminutive M^3. The Shanidar 1 and 2 M_3 areas are modest for a Neandertal, even though they are at the upper end of the Near Eastern Neandertal range of variation. That of Shanidar 6, however, is exceptionally large; among other Neandertals it is matched only by those of Le Moustier 1.

This degree of overlap shows up as well in their summed P-3–M-3 areas. The maxillary summed posterior tooth areas are 487.3, 532.1, and 550.3 mm^2 for Shanidar 1, 2, and 6, respectively. These values are all well within the ranges of variation of other Neandertals and more recent human groups. Yet they are slightly below those of most European Neandertals and close to or above those of Amud 1 (495.2 mm^2) and Tabūn C1 (467.7 mm^2). The mandibular summed posterior tooth areas of Shanidar 1 and 2 (472.1 and 516.5 mm^2, respectively) are likewise slightly below those of most European Neandertals, close to or slightly above those of other Near Eastern Neandertals (Amud 1: 483.4 mm^2; Tabūn C1: 441.3 mm^2; Tabūn C2: 509.3 mm^2), and within the ranges of variation of more recent human samples (Table 24).

It is possible that the relatively small dimensions of some of the Shanidar premolars and first molars could be due to interproximal wear. All of the individuals with heavy occlusal wear also experienced extensive interproximal wear (e.g., Shanidar 1; Figure 26). Furthermore, although the Shanidar 1 and 2 mandibular third molars are similar in size, the Shanidar 1 mandibular premolars and first molars are considerably smaller than those of Shanidar 2. Because interproximal wear can noticeably reduce the mesiodistal lengths of teeth (Hylander 1977; Wolpoff 1971a), this may have had an effect on the dimensions of the Shanidar teeth.

The tendency of the Shanidar Neandertals to have relatively large posterior molars, particularly in the mandible, is reflected in the relative sizes of the first, second and third molar areas. In the maxillary dentition, most recent humans (> 75% [Trinkaus 1978b]) exhibit $M^1 > M^2 > M^3$. The same pattern is found exclusively in a Skhūl–Qafzeh sample ($N = 5$), but a small Early Upper Paleolithic sample ($N = 7$) is highly variable (Frayer 1978). European Neandertals, however, are split between $M^1 > M^2 > M^3$ (55.6%) and $M^2 > M^1 > M^3$ (44.4%) ($N = 9$), whereas both Amud 1 and Tabūn C1 follow $M^1 > M^2 > M^3$. Shanidar 1 has the pattern most common among recent humans, but Shanidar 2 and 6 have M^2 as the largest tooth followed by M^1 and then M^3.

In the mandibular dentition, there is considerable variation among recent humans so to which molar is largest, but in the majority of the cases (> 60%) it is the M_1 that is largest, usually followed by the M_2 (Trinkaus 1978b). Small samples of Skhūl–Qafzeh ($N = 3$) and early Upper Paleolithic hominids ($N = 5$) are highly variable, and the samples are too small to indicate a pattern (Trinkaus 1978b). In a European Neandertal sample, however, $M_2 > M_3 > M_1$ is the most common pattern (36.8%), followed by $M_1 > M_2 > M_3$ (23.7%), $M_3 > M_2 > M_1$ (21.1%), and $M_3 > M_1 > M_2$ (15.9%) ($N = 19$). Amud 1 and Tabūn C2 exhibit $M_3 > M_1 > M_2$, whereas Tabūn C1 has $M_2 > M_3 > M_1$. Shanidar 2 conforms to the most common Neandertal sequence, whereas Shanidar 1 exhibits $M_3 > M_2 > M_1$ (Tables 16 and 17). The Shanidar 6 M_3 is larger than her M_2, but without the M_1 it is difficult to determine to which size arrangement her molars conform.

The premolars and molars from the Shanidar Neandertals are similar to those of other Neandertals and more recent macrodont humans. They are not particularly large, although the second and third molars are near the upper limits of recent human ranges of variation. And in conjunction with their moderately large size, their occlusal surfaces maintain the usual full complement of cusps along with some accessory cuspules. Only the maxillary third molars show any signs of simplification of the occlusal morphology.

TAURODONTISM

The enlargement of the pulp chambers of the teeth, or taurodontism, has long been considered characteristic of Neandertal teeth (Keith 1913). Recent analy-

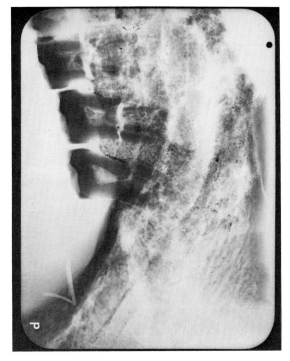

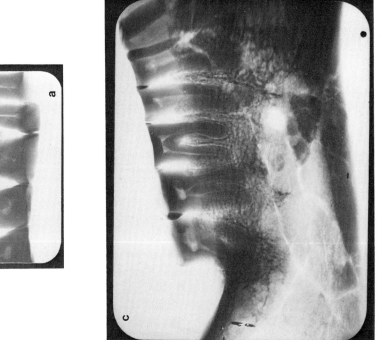

Figure 31 Lateral radiographs of the Shanidar 1 and 2 right premolars and molars. (a) Shanidar 1 P^3–M^3; (b) Shanidar 1 P^3–M^3; (c) Shanidar 1 C–M_3; (d) Shanidar 2 M_1–M_3. Photos courtesy the Iraq Museum.

ses have shown that in fact taurodontism is not found in all Neandertals (Coon 1962; Kallay 1963; Patte 1959) and may occur frequently in recent humans (Blumberg et al. 1971; Brabant and Kovacs 1961).

X rays of the Shanidar 1 maxillary and mandibular molars and of the Shanidar 3 M³ show small pulp chambers (Figure 31). However, all of these teeth were extensively worn, and concomitant remodeling of the dentin has reduced the sizes of the pulp chambers. Their pulp chambers may well have been large originally, but it is no longer possible to assess objectively whether they could be classified as taurodont.

The X rays of the Shanidar 2 molars suggest that there has been little or no alteration of the pulp chambers as a result of occlusal attrition (Figure 31). The teeth appear as though they are somewhat taurodont. If the relative dimensions of the Shanidar 2 mandibular molar crowns and pulp chambers are compared to those of recent human taurodont and nontaurodont molars using the discriminant fuctions of Blumberg et al. (1971), the M_2 and M_3 appear moderately taurodont, and the M_1 is nontaurodont.

Taurodontism has been considered an adaptation for prolonged tooth life in a high attrition environment (Blumberg et al. 1971; Coon 1962). Because an expansion of the pulp chamber of a molar would increase the distance between the occlusal surface and the apex between the roots, it would increase the time before either the apex would be exposed through normal alveolar recession as the tooth wears or the tooth was reduced to two or three root stubs through wear. If this interpretation is accurate, it is to be expected that taurodontism would be present among the Shanidar Neandertals, given their high degree of occlusal attrition.

SUMMARY

The teeth from the Shanidar adults follow a consistent pattern. This involves absolutely and relatively large anterior teeth, moderately large posterior molars, and some elaborations of the occlusal morphology, such as shoveling of the maxillary incisors and foveae on the molars. Most of the teeth show extensive occlusal wear, and the posterior teeth of the older individuals exhibit considerable interproximal wear. In those individuals with advanced dental attrition, the anterior teeth are rounded, especially on their labial margins. This anterior labial attrition appears to have been produced, or at least accentuated, by the use of the incisors and canines as a vise during food preparation and/or nondietary activities. The total pattern is one of adaptation for a high-attrition environment in which the teeth were used for a variety of purposes.

CHAPTER 7

The Axial Skeleton

The Shanidar Neandertals preserve a considerable number of vertebrae and ribs and one segment of a sternum, providing the largest sample of Neandertal axial skeletal remains from any known site. Portions of at least 71 presacral vertebrae, 3 sacra, 1 coccygeal vertebra, 1 sternal segment, and innumerable rib pieces have survived from Shanidar 1–6. Most of the remains are from Shanidar 1, 2, 3, and 4, with Shanidar 5 and 6 retaining only a few pieces each.

Even though it is difficult to reconstruct the overall configurations of the Shanidar axial skeletons because few of the vertebrae and ribs are complete, it is possible to obtain an accurate appreciation of most of the bones for at least one individual. For example, Shanidar 2 retains all of his cervical vertebrae, of which only C3 and C4 lack substantial portions, Shanidar 3 has a complete series of lumbar vertebrae, and Shanidar 1, 3, and 4 retain substantial portions of their sacra. Only for the thoracic vertebrae are there few relatively complete elements.

Each type of vertebra (cervical, thoracic, lumbar, sacral, and coccygeal) is discussed separately, followed by descriptions of the ribs and sternal segment. The vertebral morphometrics are in Tables 25–31, and the rib and sternal measurements are in Tables 32 and 33, respectively.

CERVICAL VERTEBRAE

Inventory

SHANIDAR 1

C1 Consists of the right superior facet and foramen transversarium. Maximum dimension = 37.0 mm.

178

C5 Almost complete bone with minimal damage and reconstruction. Maximum length = 61.7 mm; maximum breadth = 54.7 mm.

C6 The body, the left pedicle, the laminae, and the spine are preserved. The articular facets are damaged. Maximum length = 64.9 mm; maximum breadth = 50.0 mm.

C7 Consists of the body, pedicles, and laminae with minor damage to the edges and the articular facets. Maximum length = 42.0 mm; maximum breadth = 54.6 mm.

SHANIDAR 2

C1 Complete articular facets and right foramen transversarium are preserved. The anterior and posterior arches are largely reconstructed. Maximum breadth = 62.2 mm.

C2 Consists of the body with the dens partly reconstructed, the right pedicle, articular facets and lamina, and the left lamina and inferior articular facet. Maximum breadth = 56.8 mm.

C3 Consists of the body and right pedicle, articular facet, and lamina. Maximum breadth = 39.3 mm.

C4 Body and right pedicle are preserved. Maximum breadth = 36.1 mm.

C5 Consists of the body, the right pedicle, lamina and articular facets, and the spine with minor damage to all preserved portions. Maximum breadth = 46.8 mm.

C6 Consists of the body, laminae, and the spine, with the intermediate portions reconstructed. Maximum breadth = 43.9 mm.

C7 Most of the bone is present, but there has been damage to the anterior half of the body, the right superior and the left superior and inferior facets, and the tip of the spine. Maximum breadth = 47.5 mm.

SHANIDAR 4

C2 The spine is complete with a small part of the left lamina. Maximum length = 26.0 mm; maximum breadth = 24.4 mm.

C3? The majority of the spine is present but lacks the vertebral canal margin. Maximum length = 17.7 mm; maximum breadth = 16.8 mm.

C4? The body is largely complete (maximum breadth = 25.0 mm) with a separate complete spine (maximum length = 24.2 mm; maximum breadth = 22.5 mm).

C5? The body is largely complete. Maximum breadth = 28.7 mm.

C6? The body is largely complete. Maximum breadth = 30.2 mm.

C6 or C7 The majority of the spine is present but lacks the vertebral canal margin. Maximum length = 35.6 mm; maximum breadth = 19.5 mm.

SHANIDAR 5

C5, C6, or C7 Small fragment with the right superior and inferior articular facets and part of the right lamina. Maximum dimension = 34.3 mm.

Morphology

Neandertal cervical vertebrae have been known since the late nineteenth century with the discoveries at Spy (Fraipont and Lohest 1887) and Krapina (Gorjanović-Kramberger 1906), but the classic description of Neandertal cervical morphology was put forth by Boule (1911–1913) in reference to La Chapelle-aux-Saints 1. Boule (1913:16) described Neandertal necks as short and massive and lacking normal human curvature and their lower cervical vertebrae as archaic because they possess long, straight, and nonbifid spines.

There has been considerable criticism of Boule's reconstruction of the La Chapelle-aux-Saints 1 neck (Arambourg 1955; Heim 1976; Kleinschmidt 1938; Schultz 1955; Stewart 1962a; Straus and Cave 1957; Toerien 1957), and it has been shown that Neandertal necks were posturally indistinguishable from those of recent humans. The archaic or unique features emphasized by Boule are either within recent human ranges of variation or indeterminate from an incomplete series of cervical vertebrae (e.g., dorsoventral curvature). Yet these studies have shown that Neandertal cervical vertebrae do tend to cluster towards the robust end of recent human ranges of variation.

Most of the information on cervical vertebral morphology of the Shanidar Neandertals derives from Shanidar 2, who retains portions of all seven cervical vertebrae. Shanidar 1 and 4 provide valuable additional information (Figure 32). The Shanidar cervical vertebrae have been described by Stewart (1962a, 1963), and the discussion here derives in part from his work.

Data on the atlas come primarily from the Shanidar 2 C1 because the Shanidar 1 C1 preserves only the right lateral mass with the superior articular facet and foramen transversarium. The regions of the anterior and posterior tuberlces are absent from the Shanidar 2 atlas and have been reconstructed using the more complete C2 as a guide. The vertebral breadths (Table 25) should be accurate.

The Shanidar 2 atlas is a relatively large bone. Its vertebral canal breadth (ca. 34.0 mm) is at the tops of the ranges of recent male samples (26.0–32.5 mm, N = 20 [Stewart 1962a]; Euroamericans; mean = 29.9 mm, range = 23.5–39.0, N = 96 [Lanier 1939]; Afroamericans; mean = 28.8 mm, range = 23.0–35.0, N = 88 [Lanier 1939]). Its vertebral canal dorsoventral diameter (ca. 36.5 mm) is similarly at the top of the range (31.0–36.0 mm, N = 20 [Stewart 1962a]) of at least one recent male sample. The Shanidar 2 C1 has relatively large superior articular facets that appear slightly sinuous as a result of a small notch along each internal margin. The La Chapelle-aux-Saints 1 and La Quina 5 atlases and one from Krapina have similarly notched superior articular facets (Boule 1911–1913; Martin 1923), but Shanidar 1, like La Ferrassie 1, has an evenly bordered articular facet. The Shanidar 2 inferior articular facets for the axis are subcircular and minimally concave.

Only the medial margins of the foramina transversaria are preserved, and their anterior and posterior roots appear to be roughly equal in robustness, with

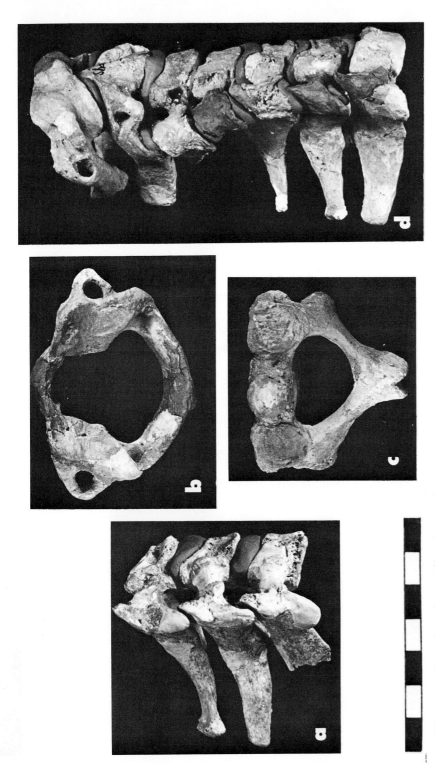

Figure 32 Cervical vertebrae of Shanidar 1 and 2. (a) Right lateral view of the Shanidar 1 fifth, sixth, and seventh cervical vertebrae. Superior views of the Shanidar 2 (b) atlas and (c) axis. (d) Right lateral view of the Shanidar 2 seven preserved cervical vertebrae. All the vertebrae have portions restored, most of which are white. The vertebrae were articulated by placing their articular facets in contact and approximating the thicknesses of their intervertebral disks, which were reconstructed in plasticene (dark gray). The curvature of the Shanidar 2 cervical region is approximate. Scale in centimeters.

TABLE 25
Measurements of the First and Second Cervical Vertebrae (mm)

	Shanidar 2 C1	Shanidar 2 C2	Shanidar 4 C2
Dorsoventral diameter[a]	—	(51.0)	—
Superior transverse diameter[b]	(51.0)	51.2	—
Inferior transverse diameter[b]	(58.4)	55.2	—
Canal dorsoventral diameter (M-10)	(36.5)	17.7	—
Canal transverse diameter (M-11)	(34.0)	(27.5)	—
Dens height (M-1a)		(18.0)	—
Body ventral height (M-1)		20.6	—
Body dorsal height (M-2)		15.7	—
Body inferior dorsoventral diameter (M-5)		16.0	—
Body inferior transverse diameter (M-8)		(19.5)	—
Spine length[c]		(17.5)	17.7

[a]Maximum dorsoventral dimension of the vertebra.

[b]Maximum transverse dimension measured to the lateral margins of the superior or inferior articular facets; measurement from Stewart (1962a).

[c]Distance from the superodorsal midline margin of the vertebral canal to the tip of the spine, measured parallel to the long axis of the spine; measurement from Stewart (1962a).

the anterior one possibly being slightly heavier. On the right side, the sulcus for the vertebral artery has been covered over by a bony arch to form a foramen; the left side is too incomplete to determine whether a foramen was present, although Stewart (1962a) believed that a partial foramen had been formed. Similar foramina occur in 12.3% (N = 81) and 11.8% (N = 102) of samples of recent Afroamericans and Euroamericans, respectively (Ossenfort 1926), and therefore are not unusual.

The only well-preserved axis from Shanidar is the Shanidar 2 C2, which is largely complete on the right side. The Shanidar 4 C2 preserves only the spinous process. As with its associated atlas, the Shanidar 2 axis is a large and robust bone. Its vertebral canal transverse diameter (ca. 27.5 mm) is toward the top of recent human male ranges of variation (Euroamericans; mean = 24.1 mm, range = 19.0–27.6 mm, N = 96; Afroamericans: mean = 23.9 mm, range = 19.9–29.6 mm, N = 88 [Lanier 1939]). However, its vertebral canal dorsoventral diameter (17.7 mm) is well within recent human male ranges of variation (Euroamericans: means = 17.1 mm, range = 13.6–21.3 mm, N = 96; Afroamericans: mean = 16.2 mm, range = 13.3–20.7 mm, N = 88 [Lanier 1939]).

The Shanidar 2 dens is largely complete and is a round and robust process. The only other sufficiently intact Neandertal dens, three from Krapina (Gorjanović-Kramberger 1906) and that of Régourdou 1 (Piveteau 1963–1965), are slightly smaller. Its height (ca. 18.0 mm) is at the top of a recent male range of variation (11.0–18.0 mm, N = 20 [Stewart 1962a]) and above those of Régourdou 1 (15.5 mm) and one of the Krapina axes (ca. 15.0 mm). The dorsoventral and transverse diameters of the dens at the base (12.5 and 11.5 mm, respectively) are similarly greater than those of the Krapina axes (10.0 and 9.0 mm, 10.0 and 9.3 mm, 10.0 and 9.0 mm, respectively); the dorsoventral diameter, however, is well within recent human male ranges of variation (Euroamericans: mean = 12.7 mm, range = 11.0–15.2 mm, N = 96; Afroamericans: mean = 12.1 mm, range = 10.3–13.8 mm, N = 88 [Lanier 1939]).

The right superior articular facet of the Shanidar 2 C2 is slightly elongated dorsoventrally and is largely flat, sloping gently inferolaterally. The inferior articular facets are of moderate size, and the complete right inferior facet slopes noticeably from superoventral to inferodorsal (contrary to Stewart [1962a:140]), forming an angle of 142° with the inferior margin of the right lamina in the sagittal plane. This value for this angle is between those of Tabūn C1 (160°) and Régourdou 1 (132°), and all of them are within recent human ranges of variation (McCown and Keith 1939; Stewart, 1962a).

The right half of the Shanidar 2 C2 spinous process is preserved; it is of moderate length, robust, and clearly bifid, as are those of most recent humans (24.3%–99.0% in 5 samples [Lanier 1939]). The complete Shanidar 4 axis spinous process is similar in size to that of Shanidar 2 (Table 23) and is also bifid, although the separation of the two halves is largely on the caudal margin of the spinous tip rather than across the whole tip, as in Shanidar 2.

The third and fourth cervical vertebrae are presented by incomplete pieces of bodies and neural arches for Shanidar 2 and by spines and one body for Shanidar 4. The bodies are all of moderate size, and the right superior articular facet of the Shanidar 2 C3 makes an angle of 50° with the horizontal midline of the body. The C3 and C4 spinous processes of Shanidar 4 are both bifid, especially the C4, which has relatively long and divergent right and left spines as do many recent humans on their fourth cervical vertebrae (Cunningham 1886; Lanier 1939).

Shanidar 1 and 2 each preserves most of its last three cervical vertebrae, and Shanidar 4 retains portions of those vertebrae (Table 26). The three cervical vertebral bodies preserved for Shanidar 4 are here identified as C4, C5, and C6, but it is possible, although less likely, that they belong to C5–C7. All of these vertebrae, especially the more complete ones from Shanidar 1 and 2, have long, relatively horizontal, straight, and nonbifid spinous processes, which appears to be characteristic of the Neandertals and less common for recent humans (Stewart 1962a; Heim 1976; Piveteau 1963–1965).

The spinal angles for the Shanidar 1 and 2 C5 (16° and 17°, respectively) are toward the lower end of a recent male range of variation (5°–56°, N = 20 [Stewart 1962a]) and are even below those of La Chapelle-aux-Saints 1 and La Ferrassie 1 (31° and 25°, respectively). The Shanidar 1 and 2 C6 spinal angles (19° and ca. 14°, respectively) are comparable to those of La Chapelle-aux-Saints 1 and La Ferrassie 1 (12° and 17°, respectively) and at the lower end of a

TABLE 26
Measurements of the Third to Seventh Cervical Vertebrae (mm)

	Shan. 2 C3	Shan. 2 C4	Shan. 4 C4	Shan. 1 C5	Shan. 2 C5	Shan. 4 C5	Shan. 1 C6	Shan. 2 C6	Shan. 4 C6	Shan. 1 C7	Shan. 2 C7
Dorsoventral diameter	—	—	—	60.0	56.0	—	64.0	59.0	—	—	(63.0)
Superior transverse diameter	(50.5)r	—	—	54.0	(50.0)r	—	(57.0)	(50.0)r	—	(54.0)	—
Inferior transverse diameter	(56.0)r	—	—	(56.5)	—	—	(56.5)	—	—	(54.0)	(54.0)r
Canal dorsoventral diameter (M-10)	14.4	—	—	15.5	13.0	—	16.8	(16.0)	—	16.0	—
Canal transverse diameter (M-11)	(28.5)r	—	—	27.3	25.0	—	28.0	23.7	—	25.0	27.3
Body ventral height (M-1)	11.0	11.0	10.0	9.5	11.0	10.1	10.4	12.0	9.7	13.0	(13.0)
Body dorsal height (M-2)	12.5	12.0	12.5	12.5	13.0	—	12.3	13.0	12.4	14.0	(14.0)
Body median height (M-3)	9.7	9.6	10.3	9.5	10.2	9.8	10.0	10.0	10.0	12.5	11.1
Body superior dorsoventral diameter (M-4)	15.5	14.3	17.3	13.0	13.0	—	13.4	12.7	15.3	14.0	(16.0)
Body superior transverse diameter (M-7)	—	22.5	—	24.7	20.0	—	(28.0)	21.8	—	(27.5)	—
Body inferior dorsoventral diameter (M-5)	16.0	16.0	15.4	13.8	14.0	—	15.5	15.5	17.3	16.2	15.3
Body inferior transverse diameter (M-8)	(18.8)	20.0	—	21.0	18.6	20.2	25.2	24.3	22.7	26.2	—
Spine length	—	—	20.0	30.0	28.0	—	35.0	29.0	—	—	(36.0)
Spine angle[a]	—	—	—	16°	17°	—	19°	(14°)	—	—	17°

Note: measurement estimated by doubling distance from the right (r) side to midline.

[a]The angle, measured in the median sagittal plane, between the long axis of the spine and the horizontal plane defined by the dorsoventral midline of the body.

recent male range of variation (5°–41°, N = 20 [Stewart 1962a]). Only the Shanidar 2 C7 spine is intact, and its angle (17°) approximates those of La Chapelle-aux-Saints 1 (15°) and some recent humans (6°–39°, N = 20 [Stewart 1962a]). The only other sufficiently preserved Neandertal C5–C7, those from Krapina and Régourdou 1, have similarly horozontal C6 and C7 spines (Gorjanović-Kramberger 1906; Piveteau 1963–1965), although the Krapina C5, but not the Régourdou 1 C5, has a more angled spine.

The lengths of the Shanidar 1 and 2 C5 to C7 spines (Table 24) are all at the upper limits of or slightly above the range of the recent human male lengths provided by Stewart (1962a) (C5: Shanidar 1: 30.0 mm; Shanidar 2: 28.0 mm; recent males: 14.0–26.0 mm, N = 20; C6: Shanidar 1: 35.0 mm; Shanidar 2: 29.0 mm; recent males: 19.0–34.0 mm; C7: Shanidar 2: ca. 36.0 mm; recent males: 19.0–40.0 mm, N = 20). The spines of the La Chapelle-aux-Saints 1 lower cervical vertebrae (C6: 28.1 mm, C7: 33.5 mm) are minimally shorter than those of Shanidar 1 and 2, whereas those of La Ferrassie 1 (C5: 32.5 mm, C6: 37.5 mm, C7: 41.2 mm) are somewhat longer. Those of Régourdou 1 (C5: 19.0 mm, C6: 25.8 mm) are the shortest known for a Neandertal.

None of the four Shanidar C5–C7 spinous processes are bifid, as is the case with all other known Neandertal lower cervical vertebral spines (Boule 1911–1913; Heim 1976; Piveteau 1963–1965). However, the C7 spine is rarely, if ever, bifid in recent humans because it provides the inferior insertion for the ligamentum nuchae, and C5 and C6 spines are variably nonbifid in recent human populations (Cunningham 1886; Lanier 1939). Bifidity of the lower cervical spines is probably related to the pattern of attachment of the ligamentum nuchae and associated musculature, all of which is influenced by the relative robusticity of the cervical region. The nonbifid nature of the Shanidar and other Neandertal C5 and C6 spinous processes is probably correlated with the length and massiveness of their spinous processes, which is undoubtedly a reflection of hypertrophy of the nuchal musculature.

It has been possible to measure the angle of the superior articular facets relative to the horizontal plane of the body for the Shanidar 1 C5 and C6. These angles are 54° and 65°, respectively, which are within recent human ranges of variation of 46°–62° (N = 20) and 41°–68° (N = 20) (Stewart 1962a). The preserved portions of the Shanidar 2 C5–C7 superior articular facets appear to have had angles similar to those of Shanidar 1, although none of the Shanidar 2 facets is sufficiently complete to be measured accurately. Clearly, these vertebrae do not have the horizontal articular facets Boule (1911–1913) described for the Neandertals.

In order to test Boule's (1911–1913) statement that Neandertal necks were short, Stewart (1962a) assembled the Shanidar 2 C2–C7 and determined a distance of 108.0 mm from the tip of the dens to the dorsoinferior margin of the C7 body. A recent human sample had a mean of 108.8 mm and a range of 98.0–121.0 mm (N = 20). A comparison of this neck length to the total length (325.0 mm) of the left tibia (the only sufficiently complete limb bone of

Shanidar 2) provided an index of 32.3. A recent human sample had a mean of 29.5 and a range of 23.0–35.4 (N = 20) (Stewart 1962a). However, because Neandertals, including those from Shanidar, tend to have low crural indices (Trinkaus 1981; Chapter 11), a comparison of the cervical vertebrae length of Shanidar 2 to its original stature should provide a ratio even closer to the recent human mean.

Further indications of the size of the Shanidar cervical vertebral columns are provided by the summed ventral heights of their lower cervical vertebral bodies. The C5–C7 of Shanidar 1 and 2 have summed ventral body heights of 32.9 and ca. 36.0 mm, respectively, which are comparable to those of European Neandertals (La Chapelle-aux-Saints 1: ca. 34.0 mm; Régourdou 1: 32.9 mm) and the Early Upper Paleolithic Předmostí 3, 4, and 9 hominids (36.0, 32,4, and 37.0 mm, respectively) and close to a range of means for 8 recent human samples (35.5–40.2 mm [Heim 1976; Matiegka 1938]). The summed ventral height of the three Shanidar 4 cervical vertebrae, assuming that they derive from C4–C6, is 29.8 mm, which is relatively, but not exceptionally, low (Shanidar 2: 34.0 mm; La Ferrassie 1: ca. 33.6 mm; Régourdou 1: 32.0 mm; Předmostí 3, 4, and 14: 35.0, 36.0, and 32.7 mm, respectively; range of means for eight recent human samples: 33.5–40.6 mm [Heim 1976; Matiegka 1938]).

The only Shanidar individual for whom cervical body heights can be compared to other segments of the vertebral column is Shanidar 1. If the summed ventral heights of the Shanidar 1 C5–C7 are divided by his summed L3 to L5 ventral heights, the resultant index is approximately 41.4. This value is close to that of La Chapelle-aux-Saints 1 (ca. 42.5) but is toward the lower end of the range of variation of one recent human sample (Japanese: 48.9 ± 3.5, N = 30 [Hasebe 1912]); two other recent male samples, however, provide slightly lower means (Euroamericans: 46.7; N = 96; Afroamericans: 45.8, N = 88 [Lanier 1939]). This suggests that Shanidar 1 may have had a relatively, but not exceptionally, short cervical region.

The same pattern is evident when the summed ventral heights of the Shanidar 1 and 4 C5 and C6 are compared to their femoral bicondylar lengths. The resultant indices (ca. 4.34 and ca. 4.69, respectively) are lower than those of the La Chapelle-aux-Saints 1 and La Ferrassie 1 Neandertals (ca. 5.05 and ca. 4.85, respectively) and those of the Předmostí 3, 9, and 14 early anatomically modern humans (4.73, 5.40, and 5.27, respectively) but above that of Skhūl 5 (ca. 3.88).

These data suggest that the neck lengths, absolutely and relatively, of the Shanidar Neandertals were within the ranges of variation of more recent humans, as are those of other Neandertals. However, it appears as though at least the lower cervical vertebrae of Shanidar 1, and perhaps also Shanidar 4, were relatively shorter than those of many more recent humans.

The Shanidar cervical vertebrae thus conform to the Neandertal pattern of being morphologically within recent human ranges of variation but relatively robust. In the Shanidar specimens, this robusticity is reflected in the large dimensions of the Shanidar 2 atlas and axis and in the long and relatively horizontal spinous processes of the C5, C6, and C7.

THORACIC VERTEBRAE

Inventory

SHANIDAR 1

T1   A damaged body is preserved and retains a fragment of the right pedicle. Maximum breadth = 28.4 mm.

T2?   The spine is complete with small parts of the laminae. Maximum length = 44.1 mm.

T12   The spine is preserved with the laminae and the left inferior articular facet.

Fragments of seven or eight Thoracic Vertebrae   Portions of vertebrae, mostly laminae and spines, are partially fused in matrix and are all very fragmentary.

SHANIDAR 2

T1   Consists of the body damaged anteriorly and on the left side (maximum breadth = 37.4 mm) and the laminae and spine, also damaged (maximum breadth = 46.3 mm).

T2   Retains the superior half of the body, right articular facets, and the anterior half of the right lamina. Maximum breadth = 47.8 mm.

T3   Consists of the right articular facets, right and left laminae, and the spine, all damaged. Maximum breadth = 42.1 mm.

T4   Consists of the right articular facets and lamina. Maximum dimension = 36.0 mm.

T5   Right and left pedicles, articular facets and laminae are present, with damage to all. Maximum breadth = 45.8 mm.

T10   Consists of right and left laminae with the damaged spine. Maximum breadth = 36.0 mm.

T11   On the right side the articular facets and lamina are present, whereas the left side retains the pedicle, the articular facets, the base of the transverse process, and the lamina. The spine is intact. Maximum breadth = 51.3 mm.

T12   Right and left articular facets, transverse processes and laminae, and the spine are preserved. There is minor damage to the left inferior facet, the transverse processes, and the spine. Maximum breadth = 42.0 mm.

SHANIDAR 3

    T1 Consists of the spine with the left lamina and the left superior articular facet (maximum length = 53.4 mm) and a left posterior fragment of the body (maximum height = 18.3 mm).

    T2 Consists of the complete spine with portions of the laminae. Maximum length = 47.0 mm.

    T3 Consists of the complete spine with the left transverse process, superior articular facet, and lamina. Maximum length = 57.0 mm.

    T4 The spine is complete with most of the right articular facets and lamina. Maximum length = 59.0 mm.

    T5 Consists of the complete spine, laminae, and inferior articular facets. Maximum length = 55.0 mm.

    T6 Consists of the complete spine, laminae, articular facets, and left pedicle with a posterior portion of the body. Maximum length = 63.3 mm.

    T7 The pedicles are largely intact with articular facets, laminae, and right transverse process (maximum breadth = 58.6 mm), and a fragment of the posterior surface of the body (maximum height = 18.4 mm).

    T8 The left pedicle is incomplete with articular facets, and lamina. Maximum length = 31.3 mm.

    T9 Consists of the right superior articular facet with most of the right pedicle. Maximum length = 21.8 mm.

    T10 Largely complete spine and left lamina, articular facets, and pedicle are preserved with a left posterior portion of the body. Maximum length = 62.4 mm.

    T11 Complete spine, laminae, articular facets, pedicles, and right transverse process are present with the posterior margin of the body. Maximum length = 50.0 mm.

    T12 The body, right pedicle, right superior articular facet, inferior articular facets, laminae, and spine are largely intact. Maximum length = 68.0 mm.

SHANIDAR 4

Fragments of vertebral bodies, laminae, articular facets, and spines Only five of the pieces are indentifiable as to vertebral number. Some of the fragments may belong to Shanidar 6 or 8. Two of the spines were identified by Stewart (1963) as cervical.

    T1 Ventral portion of the spine. Maximum length = 14.5 mm; maximum breadth = 18.0 mm.

    T2 Complete spine with the left pedicle and part of the left inferior articular facet. Maximum length = 41.3 mm; maximum breadth = 26.6 mm.

    T3 Most of the spine lacking the vertebral canal margin. Maximum length = 32.0 mm; maximum breadth = 18.0 mm.

T4 Portion of the spine lacking the vertebral canal margin. Maximum length = 23.0 mm; maximum breadth = 24.3 mm.

T12 The laminae, the ventral end of the spine, and the left inferior articular facet. Maximum length = 28.5 mm; maximum breadth = 27.3 mm.

Morphology

The thoracic vertebrae from Shanidar are fragmentary and provide little morphological data (Tables 27 and 28). Most of the vertebrae are represented by fragments of pedicles, laminae, and articular facets, with pieces of the spines and bodies. Only the Shanidar 3 T12 is largely complete, even though all 12 of the Shanidar 3 thoracic vertebrae are represented and 8 of the Shanidar 2 thoracic vertebrae are present.

There is little of note morphologically in the Shanidar thoracic vertebrae. All of the pieces appear to be well within recent human ranges of variation, as are the thoracic vertebrae of other Neandertals (Boule 1911–1913; Gorjanović-Kramberger 1906; Heim 1976; McCown and Keith 1939; Piveteau 1963–1965). The bodies and neural arches appear to be relatively robust. The relative angulation of the spines appears to follow the same pattern from T1 to T12 as in recent humans, although it is difficult to assess their orientations except for the Shanidar 2 and 3 T11 and T12. None of the spines is bifid and, as in recent humans, the upper spinous tips are flat and wide and become increasingly narrow and high as one goes caudally along the vertebral column.

Heim (1976) suggested that the La Chapelle-aux-Saints 1 and La Ferrassie 1 transverse processes were more laterally and less dorsally oriented than those of recent humans. On those few Shanidar thoracic vertebrae that preserve the orientation of the transverse process—the Shanidar 2 T11 and T12 and the Shanidar 3 T3, T11, and T12—the processes are oriented dorsolaterally as in recent humans.

The Shanidar thoracic vertebrae are thus similar to those of robust recent humans in all of the features for which they provide an indication of their morphology.

LUMBAR VERTEBRAE

Inventory

SHANIDAR 1

L1 Complete spine and a crushed body fused to L2.

L2 Crushed body and parts of the pedicles, laminae, and spine fused to L1.

TABLE 27

Measurements of the First to Fifth Thoracic Vertebrae (mm)

	Shan. 2 T1	Shan. 3 T1	Shan. 1 T2	Shan. 2 T2	Shan. 3 T2	Shan. 4 T2	Shan. 2 T3	Shan. 3 T3	Shan. 3 T4	Shan. 2 T5	Shan. 3 T5
Superior transverse diameter	—	(41.0)l	—	(50.0)r	—	—	(42.0)r	—	—	(35.5)	—
Inferior transverse diameter	(42.0)r	—	—	(48.0)r	—	—	(34.5)	—	(36.5)r	33.2	37.0
Canal dorsoventral diameter (M-10)	—	—	—	—	—	—	—	—	—	(15.0)	—
Canal transverse diameter (M-11)	—	—	—	23.2	—	—	15.3	—	—	17.5	11.6
Body ventral height (M-1)	17.3	—	—	—	—	—	—	—	—	—	14.2
Body dorsal height (M-2)	15.0	—	—	—	—	—	—	—	—	—	11.2
Body median height (M-3)	—	—	—	—	—	—	—	—	—	—	—
Body superior dorsoventral diameter (M-4)	—	—	—	—	—	—	—	—	—	—	14.5
Body inferior dorsoventral diameter (M-5)	—	—	—	—	—	—	—	—	—	—	14.6
Body inferior transverse diameter (M-8)	—	—	—	—	—	—	—	—	—	—	27.5
Spine length	—	37.0	38.0	—	40.5	34.4	—	41.7	43.8	—	44.1

Note: measurement estimated by doubling distance from right (r) or left (l) side to midline.

TABLE 28
Measurements of the Sixth to Twelfth Thoracic Vertebrae (mm)

	Shan. 3 T6	Shan. 3 T7	Shan. 2 T10	Shan. 3 T10	Shan. 2 T11	Shan. 3 T11	Shan. 1 T12	Shan. 2 T12	Shan. 3 T12
Superior transverse diameter	37.1	35.4	—	(40.0)l	33.9	42.2	—	36.0	(41.0)r
Inferior transverse diameter	35.9	36.5	33.3	—	34.3	37.7	—	(29.5)	(29.0)r
Canal dorsoventral diameter (M-10)	12.5	(13.0)	—	—	—	14.8	—	—	16.0
Canal transverse diameter (M-11)	17.8	17.0	—	(17.0)l	17.6	18.0	—	21.0	(19.0)
Body ventral height (M-1)	—	—	—	—	—	—	—	—	21.7
Body dorsal height (M-2)	—	—	—	—	—	25.1	—	—	26.6
Body median height (M-3)	—	—	—	—	—	—	—	—	20.0
Body superior transverse diameter (M-7)	—	—	—	—	—	—	—	—	—
Body inferior dorsoventral diameter (M-5)	—	—	—	—	—	—	—	—	(38.0)
Body inferior transverse diameter (M-8)	—	—	—	—	—	—	—	—	34.7
Spine length	46.7	—	—	37.7	28.4	34.0	32.4	—	46.0

Note: measurement estimated by doubling distance from right (r) or left (l) side to midline.

191

L3   Body with most of the ventral surface.

L4   Complete body fused to L5.

L5   Body crushed between L4 and S1 and a separate piece with the laminae, inferior articular facets, and most of the spine.

Isolated Lumbar Articular Facet   Superior right articular facet with large
exostosis.

SHANIDAR 2

L1   Dorsal edge of the body, pedicles, damaged transverse processes,
damaged superior articular facets, and the right inferior articular facet.
Maximum breadth = 57.4 mm.

L2   Right pedicle, transverse process, articular facets, and lamina with the
left lamina and the spine. All largely intact with minimal damage.
Maximum breadth = 57.2 mm.

L3   A right dorsal fragment of the body, complete right pedicle, articular
facets and lamina, complete spine, and complete left superior articular
facet. The remainder is absent or heavily abraded. Maximum breadth =
64.9 mm.

L4   Right and left articular facets, the laminae, and the spine are intact. The
remainder is absent. Maximum breadth = 51.6 mm.

SHANIDAR 3

L1   Complete body, pedicles, laminae, spine, and left inferior articular
facet. Maximum length = 81.3 mm.

L2   Complete body, laminae, and inferior articular facets. Maximum length
= 68.5 mm.

L3   Complete body and spine and the left pedicle, articular facets, and
lamina. Maximum length = 83.0 mm.

L4   Complete body with the left pedicle, articular facets, transverse process, and lamina plus a portion of the spine. Maximum length =
88.6 mm.

L5   Largely complete body, pedicles, transverse processes, and left articular facets. Maximum breadth = 104.0 mm.

SHANIDAR 4

Associated with the Shanidar 4 remains are three left superior articular
facets, two left inferior articular facets, nine transverse processes, four spines,
and seven fragments of vertebral bodies (some of which may be thoracic). Some
of these pieces may belong to either Shanidar 6 or 8, but most, if not all,
probably derive from Shanidar 4 because they are relatively large, definitely
larger than the lumbar spines assigned to Shanidar 6.

It is not possible to reassemble any of the pieces, but the spines and transverse processes can be sequenced to provide estimates of their vertebral numbers. In addition, one inferior articular facet appears to derive from L1.

L1   The left lamina and inferior articular facet (maximum height = 30.8 mm), the complete spine (maximum length = 25.0 mm), the tip of the right transverse process (maximum breadth = 16.8 mm), and the majority of the left transverse process (maximum breadth = 31.1 mm).

L2   The majority of the spine plus the lateral two-thirds of the right transverse process (maximum breadth = 22.9 mm) and the complete left transverse process (maximum breadth = 31.7 mm).

L3   The majority of the spine plus most of the right transverse process (maximum breadth = 37.1 mm).

L4   The majority of the spine (maximum length = 26.0 mm) plus most of the right transverse process (maximum breadth = 41.3 mm).

L5   The complete left transverse process (maximum breadth = 42.6 mm).

SHANIDAR 6

Associated with the Shanidar 4, 6, and 8 remains are four lumbar spines, which are much smaller than those of Shanidar 4. They are therefore assigned to Shanidar 6. The four spines are here assigned to L1–L4, but it is possible that one of the other lumbar vertebrae besides L5 is not represented.

L1   Largely complete spine. Maximum length = 18.9 mm.
L2   Dorsal tip of the spine. Maximum length = 14.8 mm.
L3   Largely complete spine. Maximum length = 17.5 mm.
L4   Largely complete spine. Maximum length = 17.0 mm.

Morphology

The lumbar vertebrae from Shanidar are more complete than their thoracic vertebrae (Figures 33 and 34). Yet only those of Shanidar 3 are sufficiently intact to permit a reconstruction of the lumbar region. The Shanidar 2 L1–L4 retain only the dorsal halves of the vertebrae, and those of Shanidar 1, 4, and 6 consist of separate segments of vertebrae or fragments thereof.

The Shanidar lumbar vertebrae are morphologically similar to those of robust modern humans. They have relatively large bodies, robust neural arches, and relatively large spinous processes. None of their spinous processes is bifid, but several of them—the Shanidar 2 L3 and L4, the Shanidar 3 L4 and L5, the Shanidar 4 L4, and the Shanidar 6 L2—exhibit variable amounts of bifidity of the dorsoinferior margins of their spines. However, the morphology of the dorsal margins of lumbar vertebral spines is highly variable in most samples of humans.

The transverse processes of Shanidar 3 and 4 appear relatively long and

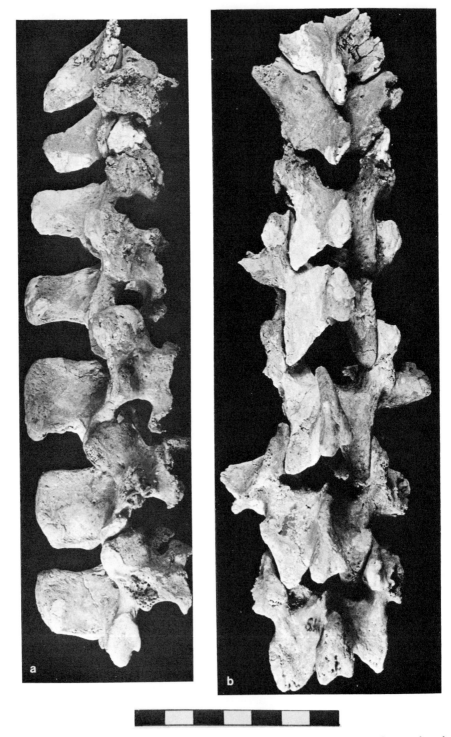

Figure 33 (a) Right lateral and (b) dorsal views of the Shanidar 2 T10–L4. The vertebrae have been articulated using their articular facets; because none of the bodies is preserved, the curvature of the region represented is approximate. Scale in centimeters.

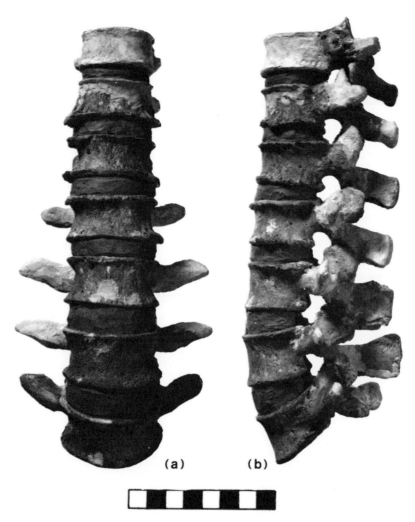

(a)   **(b)**

Figure 34   (a) Anterior and (b) left lateral views of the Shanidar 3 T11–L5. The T11 body, the cranial surface of the T12 body, the L2–L4 transverse processes, and portions of the spines and facets have been reconstructed with filler. The dimensions of the intervertebral disks are approximate. Photo courtesy T. D. Stewart. Scale in centimeters.

tapering laterally; long transverse processes would tend to increase the moment arms, and hence the effectiveness, of the erector spinae muscles for lateral bending and stability of the lumbar region.

The bodies of the Shanidar 3 lumbar vertebrae are sufficiently complete to permit an assessment of their relative ventral and dorsal craniocaudal heights (Table 29). The bodies of the L1–L3 are slightly longer craniocaudally on their dorsal margins, and the L4 has nearly parallel superior and inferior surfaces.

TABLE 29
Measurements of the Lumbar Vertebrae (mm)

	Shan. 1 L1	Shan. 2 L1	Shan. 3 L1	Shan. 4 L1	Shan. 2 L2	Shan. 3 L2	Shan. 1 L3	Shan. 2 L3	Shan. 3 L3	Shan. 1 L4	Shan. 2 L4	Shan. 3 L4	Shan. 4 L4	Shan. 1 L5	Shan. 3 L5
Dorsoventral diameter	—	—	81.6	—	—	—	—	—	(83.0)	—	—	(88.0)	—	—	(48.5)l
Superior transverse diameter	29.3	—	—	—	33.0	(33.0)l	—	29.8	(28.0)l	—	34.0	(38.0)l	—	45.5	—
Inferior transverse diameter	(31.0)r	—	28.5	—	27.9	30.4	(41.0)l	—	(33.0)l	—	36.0	(47.5)l	—	—	—
Canal dorsoventral diameter (M-10)	—	—	17.1	—	—	(16.0)	—	—	(13.5)	—	—	(20.0)	—	—	—
Canal transverse diameter (M-11)	20.0	—	20.5	—	(25.0)r	(20.0)	18.8	(25.0)r	22.2	—	26.5	24.5	—	(27.5)	31.2
Body ventral height (M-1)	—	—	23.0	—	—	24.0	25.0	—	26.1	27.0	—	29.0	—	—	31.3
Body dorsal height (M-2)	—	—	28.6	—	—	28.2	—	—	28.7	—	—	29.1	—	—	25.4
Body median height (M-3)	—	—	21.2	—	—	20.0	—	—	20.0	—	—	22.0	—	—	22.8
Body superior dorsoventral diameter (M-4)	—	—	34.5	—	—	37.8	—	—	38.1	—	—	35.3	—	—	37.6
Body superior transverse diameter (M-7)	—	—	46.7	—	—	49.8	—	—	50.5	—	—	53.7	—	—	(53.5)
Body inferior dorsoventral diameter (M-5)	—	—	38.4	—	—	36.3	—	—	35.5	—	—	36.3	—	—	38.0
Body inferior transverse diameter (M-8)	—	—	47.9	—	—	50.2	45.5	—	52.0	51.1	—	54.0	—	—	53.7
Spine length	31.0	(31.0)	34.0	25.0	35.0	—	29.5	33.0	(36.0)	35.0	33.0	(34.0)	(26.0)	30.0	—

Note: measurement estimated by doubling distance from right (r) or left (l) side to midline.

The L5, in contrast, shows a marked wedging, with the dorsal height being only 81.2% of the ventral height. Among recent humans, there tends to be, on the average, slightly less ventral wedging of the L1 to L3 bodies than those of Shanidar 3 and a very slight dorsal wedging of the L4 body (Matiegka 1938; Zito 1981). Yet the proportions of the Shanidar 3 L1–L4 bodies are well within the ranges of variation of recent humans. The ratios of the mean L5 ventral and dorsal heights for seven recent human samples vary from 79.2 to 88.0% (Matiegka 1938; Zito 1981), a range that includes the proportions of the Shanidar 3 L5 body. For comparison, this ratio is approximately 82.7% for La Chapelle-aux-Saints 1 (using Boule's reconstruction of the ventral margin) and 87.2, 86.5, and 78.2% for Cro-Magnon 1 and 3 and Předmostí 3, respectively. Shanidar 3 therefore possessed the lumbar vertebral body configurations associated with normal lordosis among recent humans. Because these shapes of the vertebral bodies develop in response to biomechanical stress during growth (Houston and Zaleski 1967), Shanidar 3 must have had a posture indistinguishable from that of recent humans.

The overall lengths of the Shanidar 1 and 3 lumbar regions can be assessed through comparisons of their summed ventral heights to those of recent humans. Their summed heights for L3 to L5 are 79.5 and 86.4 mm, respectively, both of which fall within a range of means for nine recent human samples (75.0–89.1 mm [Lanier 1939; Matiegka 1938; Zito 1981]). The summed L3–L5 ventral heights for La Chapelle-aux-Saints 1 is about 80.0 mm.

The sum of the L1–L5 ventral heights of Shanidar 3, the only Neandertal for which this value can be computed, is 133.4 mm. This value also falls well within the range of means for nine recent human samples (124.6–143.6 mm [Lanier 1939; Matiegka 1938; Zito 1981]). The absolute lengths of the Shanidar lumbar regions, at least those of Shanidar 1 and 3, are therefore comparable to those of recent humans.

The summed lumbar lengths relative to sacral length for Shanidar 1 and 3 are also similar to those of recent humans. The index of their summed L3–L5 ventral body heights to their sacral ventral lengths is about 74.0 and about 84.7, respectively, for Shanidar 1 and 3; these values are within 1 standard deviation of a recent human mean (Japanese: 79.7 ± 6.9, N = 29 [Hasebe 1912]) and fall on either side of the recent human mean. In addition, the index of the Shanidar 3 L1–L5 summed ventral heights to sacral ventral length (ca. 130.8) is very close to a recent human mean (Japanese: 129.9 ± 11.1, N = 29 [Hasebe 1912]).

It is possible to compare the summed L3–L5 ventral heights of Shanidar 1 and 3 to estimates of their femoral bicondylar lengths (the femoral bicondylar length of Shanidar 3 can be estimated from its humeral maximum length using a least squares regression based on other Neandertals [r = 0.873, N = 7] at ca. 438.5 mm). The resultant indices (ca. 17.4 and ca. 19.7, respectively) are on either side of the estimate of approximately 18.6 for La Chapelle-aux-Saints 1.

The Shanidar lumbar vertebrae thus appear to be similar in size and morphology to those of recent humans. There are very few lumbar vertebrae preserved for other Neandertals (Bartucz 1940; Boule 1911–1913; Endo and Kimura 1970; Gorjanović-Kramberger 1906; Heim 1976; Lumley 1973), all of them are quite fragmentary, and all appear to be similar to those of the Shanidar Neandertals and more recent humans.

SACRUM

Inventory

SHANIDAR 1

The sacrum is largely complete with most of S1–S5. The coccygeal articulation is not preserved. The right auricular surface retains only the inferior corner, whereas only the superior half of the left auricular surface remains. The whole bone is distorted slightly. Maximum height = 110.0 mm; maximum breadth = 100.0 mm.

SHANIDAR 3

The bone consists of two portions that have been joined with filler, one with S1 and part of S2 and the other with most of S3 to S5. S1 retains the body, the right superior articular facet and the left lateral part with the superior margin of the auricular surface; S3 to S5 are largely complete with damage to the bodies and the spinous tubercles. Maximum height (as reconstructed) = 122.5 mm.

SHANIDAR 4

S2 to S5 bodies and vertebral canal moderately complete. The right side is intact from S3 to S5 with the inferior margin of the auricular surface. The left side is preserved only on S5. Maximum height = 81.2 mm; maximum breadth = 73.0 mm.

Morphology

Shanidar 1, 3, and 4 retain substantial portions of their sacra, and those of Shanidar 1 and 3 are sufficiently complete to permit assessments of their overall sizes and proportions (Figures 35–37; Table 30). Yet none of the Shanidar sacra is undistorted, and all of them lack some regions, at least on one side. However, sacra are poorly known for other Neandertals because only five Neandertals retain sacra—La Chapelle-aux-Saints 1, La Ferrassie 1, Régourdou 1, Subalyuk 1, and an individual from Spy (Bartucz 1940; Boule 1911–1913; Fraipont 1927; Heim 1976)—and they are all less complete than those from Shanidar.

The Shanidar 1 sacrum has been slightly crushed and twisted, so that its

Figure 35 (a) Dorsal and (b) ventral views of the Shanidar 1 fourth and fifth lumbar vertebrae and sacrum. The lower lumbar vertebrae and the sacrum were crushed together postmortem and could not be separated without loss of information. Scale in centimeters.

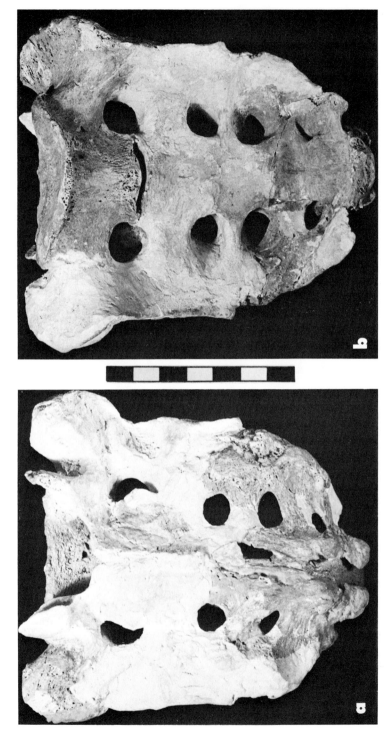

Figure 36 (a) Dorsal and (b) ventral views of the Shanidar 3 sacrum. The portions in white have been reconstructed with filler. Scale in centimeters.

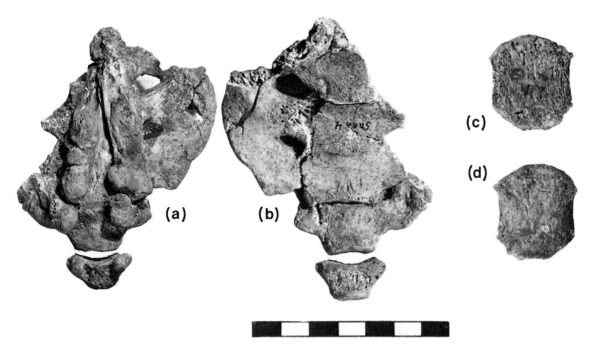

Figure 37   (a) Dorsal and (b) ventral views of the Shanidar 4 sacrum and first coccygeal vertebra, and (c) ventral and (d) dorsal views of the Shanidar 6 first segment of the sternal body. The Shanidar 4 sacrum preserves S2–S5. Scale in centimeters.

overall dimensions can only be approximated. However, because all of the pieces along the ventral midsagittal arc are largely in place, the measurements should be close to the bone's original dimensions. The two pieces of the Shanidar 3 sacrum, the S1 and the S3–S5, have been joined together with filler to approximate the original bone. As a result of these postmortem damages and reconstructions, it is not possible to assess accurately the curvatures of the Shanidar 1 and 3 sacra. Yet the ventral height and breadth measurements should be reliable.

All three of the Shanidar sacra appear to have or to have had five vertebrae. Shanidar 1 exhibits five sacral vertebrae (the L4 and L5 bodies were crushed onto the sacrum *in situ* but were separate antemortem). The two pieces of the Shanidar 3 sacrum fit together properly only if a single vertebra is reconstructed between the existing segments. Only the four caudal sacral vertebrae of Shanidar 4 survive, but the presence of the inferior margin of the right auricular surface adjacent to the S2–S3 ventral juncture makes it unlikely that there was more than one sacral vertebra above the preserved four. The Shanidar Neandertals therefore agree with the majority of recent humans (62.0–92.8% in 7 recent human samples [Schultz 1930]) in having five sacral vertebrae.

The sacral vertebrae from Shanidar were variably fused to each other

TABLE 30
Measurements of the Sacra (mm)

	Shanidar 1		Shanidar 3[d]		Shanidar 4	
	Right	Left	Right	Left	Right	Left
Ventral height (M-2)	(107.5)		(102.0)		—	
Dorsal height (M-3)	—		(121.5)		—	
Ventral depth (M-6)	—		(23.0)		—	
Position of ventral depth[a]	—		(67.0)		—	
Ventral height of S1[b]	29.7		31.7		—	
Ventral height of S2[b]	27.0		—		—	
Ventral height of S3[b]	18.0		(23.3)		17.0	
Ventral height of S4[b]	—		15.8		16.0	
Ventral height of S5[b]	—		15.3		15.3	
Sacral breadth (M-5)	(104.0)l		(117.0)l		—	
Middle breadth (M-9)	(96.0)r		(99.0)		(94.0)r	
Sacral ala breadth (M-11)	—	—	—	28.5	—	—
Auricular height (M-14)	(68.0)		—	(62.0)	—	—
Auricular breadth (M-15)	—	—	—	40.5	—	—
Biauricular angle (M-21)	—		(32°)l		—	
Base dorsoventral diameter (M-18)	—		35.1		—	
Base transverse diameter (M-19)	(47.0)r		(60.0)		—	
Canal transverse diameter (M-17)	(38.0)r		(39.0)l		—	
Cx1 surface dorsoventral diameter[c]	—		11.4		9.6	
Cx1 surface transverse diameter[c]	—		21.1		17.7	

Note: measurement estimated by doubling distance from right (r) or left (l) side to midline.

[a]Distance along the ventral height chord from its superior end at which the ventral depth subtense is located.

[b]Ventral heights of the individual sacral vertebral bodies.

[c]Dorsoventral and transverse diameters of the facet for the first coccygeal vertebra.

[d]The Shanidar 3 sacrum was extensively reconstructed in the region of S2. The accuracy of the height and curvature measurements is dependent upon the reliability of this reconstruction.

around their bodies, even though all of the lateral parts appears to have been fused together. The Shanidar 1 sacral vertebrae were probably fully fused together, even though damage, especially around the S1–S2 juncture, precludes full confirmation of that observation. The Shanidar 3 S3, S4, and S5, and probably S2 as well, were fully fused together. The S1 body, however, was separate from that of the S2 along their ventral margins, even though they were joined at least on the right side. A similar partial fusion of the S1 and S2 bodies is evident on the La Ferrassie 1 sacrum. The Shanidar 4 S3 and S4 were completely joined, but the S2 and S3 bodies were separate at least along their ventral margins and the S4 and S5 bodies were completely unfused. Neither the Shanidar 3 nor the Shanidar 4 sacra show any evidence of fusion of the Cx1 to the S5; at least partial fusion has been known to occur in 71.3% (N = 136) of a recent human sample (Dieulafé 1933).

The state of preservation of the Shanidar sacra makes assessments of asymmetries difficult, especially for Shanidar 1 and 4. The only observable asymmetry concerns the Shanidar 3 S4 and S5 sacral foramina, which are significantly larger on the right side. In addition, the S5 left dorsal foramen opens into the sacral canal and has only a pinhole foramen opening onto the dorsal surface. Similar kinds of asymmetries are reasonably common in recent human sacra (Paterson 1893).

One of the more notable aspects of the Shanidar sacra is the size of their sacral hiatuses. The Shanidar 3 sacral hiatus extends to the S3–S4 juncture, as does that of La Ferrassie 1 (Heim 1976). About a third of recent humans have sacral hiatuses that extend to the superior S4 or above (Euroamericans: 34.3%, N = 519; Afroamericans: 30.4%, N = 694 [Trotter and Lanier 1945]). On Shanidar 1, the sacral hiatus extends to the middle of the S2, whereas that of Shanidar 4, like that of La Chapelle-aux-Saints 1, goes to the S2–S3 juncture. Although similar sacral hiatuses are known for recent humans (Paterson 1893; Trotter and Lanier 1945), they are rare. Sacral hiatuses that extend to the middle of S2 or above are extremely rare (Euroamerican sample: 0.4%, N = 519; Afroamerican sample: 0.0%, N = 694 [Trotter and Lanier 1945]), and sacral hiatuses that extend to the superior S3 or above are not much more common (Euroamerican sample: 2.3%, N = 519; Afroamerican sample: 1.4%, N = 694 [Trotter and Lanier 1945]). The large sacral hiatuses of Shanidar 1 and 4 and La Chapelle-aux-Saints 1 are thus exceptional.

The ventral lengths of the Shanidar 1 and 3 sacra (ca. 107.5 mm and ca. 102.0 mm, respectively) fall in the middle of the range of means of recent human samples (93.0–116.0 mm for 23 recent human samples [Radlauer 1908]). In addition, the lengths of the Shanidar 1 and 3 sacra relative to femoral bicondylar length (used here as an indicator of overall body size) indicate that their sacra are similar in relative, as well as absolute, size to those of recent humans. The resultant index (sacral ventral length/femoral bicondylar length) is about 23.5 for Shanidar 1. The femoral bicondylar length of about 438.5 mm for Shanidar 3, estimated from its humeral maximum length using a least squares regression based on other Neandertals (r = 0.873, N = 7), provides a sacral–femoral length index of about 23.3. Both of these values are minimally above the male and female means of a recent human sample (males: 21.4 ± 1.7, N = 25; females: 22.8 ± 1.9, N = 31 [Warren 1897]).

The sacral breadth of Shanidar 1 (ca. 104.0 mm) is similarly in the middle of recent human sample means (80.0–120.0 mm for 25 recent human samples [Radlauer 1908]), whereas that of Shanidar 3 (ca. 117.0 mm) is closer to the upper limits of recent human ranges of variation. By comparison, La Chapelle-aux-Saints 1, La Ferrassie 1, Régourdou 1 and Subalyuk 1 have sacral breadths of about 102.6 mm, about 118.0 mm, 102.9 mm, and 94.0 mm, respectively. These sacral breadths provide sacral indices (breadth/length) of about 96.7 for

Shanidar 1 and about 114.7 for Shanidar 3. Both of these indices are well within recent human ranges of variation, although the Shanidar 1 index tends toward the lower end of recent human indices and the Shanidar 3 index is relatively high (Paterson 1893; Radlauer 1908). However, if the Shanidar sacral indices are compared only to those of recent human males (range of means of six recent human samples: 91.4–101.4 [Radlauer 1908]), rather than to those of recent human females (range of means of seven recent human samples: 99.1–112.6 [Radlauer 1908]), the Shanidar 1 index falls in the middle of the recent male range, whereas that of Shanidar 3 is considerably above those of most recent human males.

The relative breadths of the Shanidar 1 and 3 sacra are further illustrated by the ratios of their sacral breadths to estimates of their femoral bicondylar lengths. The resultant indices are about 22.7 for Shanidar 1 and about 26.7 for Shanidar 3 (using the estimated femoral bicondylar length of ca. 438.5 mm). These values fall on either side of those for La Chapelle-aux-Saints 1 (ca. 23.9) and La Ferrassie 1 (ca. 25.8), both of which are close to the male and female means of a recent human sample (males: 24.5 ± 1.2, N = 25; females: 25.9 ± 1.3, N = 30 [Warren 1897]). The breadths of the Shanidar sacra are therefore similar to those of other Neandertals and recent humans.

The middle breadths of the Shanidar 1, 3, and 4 sacra (ca. 96.0, ca. 99.0 and ca. 94.0 mm, respectively) are similar to each other and to that of Subalyuk 1 (95.0 mm), above those of La Chapelle-aux-Saints 1 (ca. 83.2 mm) and Régour-dou 1 (ca. 86.0 mm), and at the upper end of recent human ranges of variation (range of 26 recent human means: 70.0–96.0 mm [Radlauer 1908]). As a result, the sacral breadth indices (middle breadth/sacral breadth) of Shanidar 1 and 3 (ca. 92.3 and ca. 84.6, respectively) are relatively high for recent humans (recent human range of 26 sample means: 72.7–83.5 [Radlauer 1908]), especially that of Shanidar 1. They are below the very high index of Subalyuk 1 (101.6), but above those of La Chapelle-aux-Saints 1 (ca. 81.1) and Régourdou 1 (ca. 83.6). These data suggest that the Shanidar sacra are rather wide in their middle sections.

The auricular surfaces of Shanidar 1 and 3 extend from the top of S1 to the middle of S3, as indicated by the portions preserved on their right sides. This is the sacral vertebral distribution of the auricular surfaces of most recent humans (50.0–65.0% in six recent human samples [Radlauer 1908]). The Shanidar 4 right auricular surface, which is preserved only at its caudal end, appears to be contained entirely on its S1 and S2. This condition is rarer among recent humans (8.0–18.1% in six recent human samples [Radlauer 1908]).

The biauricular angle can be computed only for the Shanidar 3 sacrum, on which it is about 32°. This angle is at the upper end of recent human ranges of variation (range of means for 7 recent human samples: 18°–30° [Radlauer 1908]). It is, however, similar to that of La Chapelle-aux-Saints (ca. 27°) but quite different from that of Subalyuk 1 (15°).

The three sacra from Shanidar thus appear to be generally similar to those of recent humans and other Neandertals. The only features of note are their relatively large middle breadths and the large sacral hiatuses of Shanidar 1 and 4.

COCCYGEAL VERTEBRA

Inventory

SHANIDAR 4

Cx1 The complete vertebra. Maximum height = 16.0 mm; maximum breadth = 24.9 mm. Formerly attributed to Shanidar 9 (Trinkaus 1977b).

Morphology

A complete coccygeal vertebra is preserved from the Shanidar 4, 6, 8, and 9 multiple burial (Figure 37). It is the only complete coccygeal vertebra known from an archaic fossil hominid; La Ferrassie 1 retains the craniodorsal quarter of his Cx1. Because Shanidar 4 is the only individual from the multiple burial that retains significant portions of the pelvis, it is assumed that the coccygeal vertebra derives from Shanidar 4. On the basis of its morphology and the similarities in size between its cranial intervertebral surface and the caudal surface of the Shanidar 4 S5 (Tables 30 and 31), it is identified as a Cx1.

The dimensions of the Shanidar 4 Cx1 (Table 31) are similar to those of recent human first coccygeal vertebrae. Its ventral surface is gently concave craniocaudally and otherwise smooth. The dorsal surface has two fossae, one on each side between a low central ridge and the cornua. The fossae and the central ridge are extensively perforated by small foramina. The cornua are modest in size and extend cranially minimally beyond the plane of the S5 surface. In articulation, the Shanidar 4 sacral and coccygeal cornua were probably separate from each other. The transverse processes of the Cx1 are similarly relatively small.

The cranial intervertebral surface of the Cx1 is concave with a distinct fossa 4.0 mm by 11.2 mm in its middle. Similar fossae are common on recent human first coccygeal vertebrae (Dieulafé 1933), but they are seldom as large as that of Shanidar 4. There is no trace of any fusion of the Cx1 to the S5, on either the S5 or the Cx1. In a recent European sample, only 28.7% (N = 136) showed a similar absence of S5–Cx1 fusion (Dieulafé 1933); the La Ferrassie 1 Cx1 exhibits an ossification of the right lateral sacrococcygeal ligament that undoubtedly fused it to the S5, even though the body of his Cx1 was not fused to the S5 at least dorsally.

TABLE 31
Measurements of the Shanidar 4 First Coccygeal Vertebra (mm)

Superior maximum dorsoventral diameter[a]	12.1
Superior maximum transverse diameter[a]	24.9
Ventral height (M-1)	10.9
Dorsal height (M-2)	12.6
Median height (M-3)	10.6
Sacral surface dorsoventral diameter	8.5
Sacral surface transverse diameter	17.5
Cx2 surface dorsoventral diameter	8.5
Cx2 surface transverse diameter	12.2

[a]Maximum dorsoventral and transverse diameters of the superior end of the vertebra.

The caudal intervertebral surface for the Cx2 is gently convex and slightly roughened. In being convex, rather than flat or concave, it agrees in morphology with 36.2% (N = 130) of a recent European sample (Dieulafé 1933). And as with the S5–Cx1 articulation, there is no evidence that the Shanidar Cx1 was fused to his Cx2; a lack of Cx1–Cx2 fusion is the predominant pattern among recent humans (73.1%, N = 130, in a recent European sample [Dieulafé 1933]).

The first coccygeal vertebra from Shanidar 4 is therefore similar to those of recent humans in size and morphology. Its lack of fusion to the adjacent vertebrae is relatively common among recent humans.

RIBS

Inventory

SHANIDAR 1

Portions of eight right ribs and six left ribs are identifiable as to side but not as to number, and numerous small fragments are present, either fused to each other or fused to vertebrae in matrix. They cannot be sorted accurately as to number, and few are sufficiently complete to provide any morphological information.

SHANIDAR 3

All twelve right ribs and at least eight of the left ribs (numbers 1–3, 6–9, and 11) are preserved with major portions of seven right ribs (numbers 2, 3, 5–9) and four left ribs (numbers 3, 7–9) represented. One rib, 9 left, exhibits a partially healed wound.

TABLE 32
Measurements of the Ribs (mm)

	1	2	3	4	5	6	7	8	9	10	11	12
Shanidar 3												
Right												
Proximal height (M-1)		11.2	11.7	—	11.6	11.5	11.6	10.8	9.1	—		—
Proximal thickness (M-2)		7.2	—	—	10.7	10.6	10.8	10.0	8.4	—		—
Shaft height[a]		14.7	14.1	—	15.1	16.4	17.7	17.7	15.5	12.8		11.3
Shaft thickness[a]		6.8	8.4	9.7	9.1	10.0	9.7	9.1	8.7	7.9		7.4
Left												
Proximal height (M-1)			9.8					10.8	10.0		—	
Proximal thickness (M-2)			10.4					10.3	9.6		—	
Shaft height[a]			12.0					17.7	15.4		13.0	
Shaft thickness[a]			8.3					9.5	8.3		5.6	
Shanidar 4												
Right												
Proximal height (M-1)	—	12.0		12.6			—				9.9	8.9
Proximal thickness (M-2)	—	8.5		9.3			—				7.0	4.7
Shaft height[a]	4.1	13.6		15.8			16.8				10.4	—
Shaft thickness[a]	19.0	6.4		6.8			8.1				6.5	—
Shanidar 5												
Right												
Proximal height (M-1)				9.5	8.8	10.5						
Proximal thickness (M-2)				7.6	9.2	9.1						
Shaft height[a]				(16.0)	16.4	—						
Shaft thickness[a]				7.3	7.8	—						
Left												
Proximal height (M-1)		10.3							11.2			
Proximal thickness (M-2)		14.5							9.7			
Shaft height[a]		—							16.2			
Shaft thickness[a]		—							7.5			

[a] Measured at the angle of the rib where the *Mm. iliocostalis* line intersects the inferior margin of the rib.

SHANIDAR 4

A large assortment of broken ribs is preserved, many fragments of which are indeterminate as to side and number. Some of the ribs probably belong to Shanidar 6 or 8, but the majority derive from Shanidar 4. They include 18 proximal pieces with the neck and vertebral articulation, 10 distal pieces with the costal cartilage surface, the left first rib, and 7 right ribs that can be identified by number (numbers 1, 2, 4, 5, 7, 11, and 12).

SHANIDAR 5

Eight large rib fragments and numerous small, indeterminate ones remain. The large fragments consist of at least three right ribs (three of numbers 4–7) and at least two left ribs (numbers 2 and 9/10).

Morphology

The ribs from the Shanidar 1, 3, 4, and 5 Neandertals are universally incomplete and are usually quite fragmentary. Only for Shanidar 3, who retains all 12 right ribs, is it possible to assign reliably numbers to the preserved pieces. The incompleteness of the ribs makes it impossible to gain more than a very general appreciation of the size and configuration of the Shanidar thoraxes.

The ribs of other Neandertals, especially European male Neandertals, have been repeatedly described as being exceptionally robust and less curved than those of recent humans (Boule 1911–1913; Heim 1976; Loth 1938; Schaafhausen 1858). Those of the Shanidar Neandertals conform to the pattern of being quite robust, although it is difficult to determine whether they indicate more voluminous thoraxes than those of recent humans.

The Shanidar ribs are similar in height to those of recent human males, but they have relatively greater thicknesses, both proximally and near the angle (Table 32). In addition, most of the ribs have very clear markings for the Mm. intercostalis and other muscles of the dorsal and lateral thorax. This hypertrophy of the ribs and their associated musculature is in agreement with the apparent hypertrophy of the erector spinae muscles indicated by the presacral vertebrae and of the scapular muscles indicated by their scapulae (Chapter 8).

STERNUM

Inventory

SHANIDAR 6?

Complete segment of the sternum, almost certainly the second segment or first sternebra. Maximum length = 32.9 mm.

Morphology

A complete segment of the body of a sternum was discovered with the Shanidar 4, 6, 8, and 9 remains. Judging from its shape and size, it almost certainly represents the first segment of the body, or the first sternebra (Figure 37; Table 33). It is uncertain whether the segment derives from Shanidar 4 or 6. Stewart (1963) tentatively assigned it to Shanidar 6 on the basis of size, and it will be considered here as deriving from Shanidar 6; there is considerable overlap between the sexes in sternal dimensions, and there are no sexed sterni from Shanidar with which to compare it.

The superior surface of the segment, for articulation with the manubrium at the sternal angle, was not fused to the manubrium. This is the condition found in the majority of recent human sterni (Euroamerican sample: 86.9%, N = 480; Afroamericans: 90.2%, N = 397 (Trotter 1934b)). The inferior surface was apparently fused to the second sternebra, at least partially, and was broken from it postmortem. This joint usually fuses between puberty and the mid-20s, and only in a few cases (less than ca. 5%) does it remain open later in adulthood (McKern and Stewart 1957).

The ventral surface of the segment is almost perfectly flat. The dorsal surface is gently concave superoinferiorly and relatively flat transversely, except where the margins slope obliquely to meet the ventral surface at the ventrolateral margins. The inferolateral surfaces for the third costal cartilages are clearly marked, but the superolateral surfaces for the second costal cartilages blend imperceptibly with the cartilagenous surface for the manubrium.

The length of the segment (32.2 mm) is similar to that of Tabūn C1 (32.0 mm), below that of Régourdou 1 (38.0 mm), but close to means of 30.6 mm (range: 24.0–37.0 mm, N = 38) and 31.3 mm (range: 21.0–38.0 mm, N = 33), respectively, for samples of recent Europeans and Asians (Vallois 1965). The minimum breadth of the segment (27.1 mm), however, is above those of Tabūn C1 and Régourdou 1 (ca. 21.0 mm and 24.0 mm, respectively) and provides a breadth/length index of 84.2, which is considerably above those of Régourdou

TABLE 33
Measurements of the Second Sternal Segment of Shanidar 6 (mm)

Segment length	32.2
Middle breadth[a]	27.1
Middle thickness[a]	7.1
Superior costal breadth[b]	21.0
Inferior costal breadth[b]	19.7

[a]Measured at the middle of the segment as minimum dimensions.
[b]Measured across the middles of the facets for the second and third costal cartilages.

1 (63.1) and Tabūn C1 (ca. .65.6). Yet the breadth/length index of the Shanidar 6 sternal segment is close to the respective means (87.1 and 86.6) of highly variable recent European and Asian samples (ranges: 54.2–132.0, N = 38 and 60.6–200.0, N = 33, respectively [Vallois 1965]). The thickness of the segment (7.1 mm) is comparable to those of Régourdou 1 (7.5 mm) and Tabūn C1 (6.6 mm).

The Shanidar 6 sternal segment thus has overall proportions similar to recent human means and is distinct from the relatively narrow first sternebrae of the only other Neandertals that preserve this bone, Régourdou 1 and Tabūn C1.

SUMMARY

The remains of the Shanidar axial skeletons indicate a set of individuals whose trunks were similar to those of recent humans. The overall proportions of virtually all of the elements of their axial skeletons fall within the ranges of variation of more recent humans, as do those of other Neandertals. The only consistent pattern is one of pronounced robusticity that places them near the limits of recent human ranges of variation with respect to several features. These features include the size of the lower cervical vertebral spines, the lengths of the lumbar transverse processes, the size of the Shanidar 4 Cx1, and the thicknesses of the ribs. The only other feature of note is the large size of their sacral hiatuses, especially those of Shanidar 1 and 4.

CHAPTER 8

The Upper Limb Remains

A number of upper limb remains are preserved from the Shanidar Neandertals, and many of them are either well preserved or sufficiently intact to permit the reasonable reconstruction of some of their missing portions. This is especially true for the bones of the forearm and hand. As a result, it is possible to evaluate many aspects of their upper limb morphology and its implications.

Each of the shoulder and arm bones is discussed separately, followed by a presentation of the hand bones. The osteometric data are in Tables 34 to 62.

CLAVICLES

Inventory*

SHANIDAR 1

Right Abnormal and atrophied clavicular diaphysis from near the manubrial end to just distal of the conoid tubercle. Maximum length = 104.0 mm.

Left Complete diaphysis lacking the manubrial articulation and part of the acromial surface. Maximal length = 150.8 mm.

---

*An incomplete diaphyseal fragment was described as the sternal end of the Shanidar 4 right clavicle (Stewart 1963, 1977). It is not human and is probably the proximal end of a immature quadrupedal humerus. Maximum length = 77.4 mm.

SHANIDAR 3

Right Fragmentary diaphysis from the costoclavicular ligament facet to the acromial end but lacking both articulations. The diaphysis is complete only distally; only the inferior surface is preserved on the proximal two-thirds. Maximum length = 141.7 mm.

Left A proximal diaphyseal fragment with half of the costoclavicular ligament facet (maximum length = 44.0 mm), and a distal diaphyseal section with the conoid tubercle and the distal musculoligamentous attachment areas (maximum length = 65.0 mm).

Morphology

Only Shanidar 1 and 3 preserve portions of their clavicles. Shanidar 1 retains most of the left clavicle and a major portion of the right one, but the right clavicle is abnormal and is discussed later (Chapter 12). Shanidar 3 retains enough of the right clavicle to determine its overall proportions, plus two small pieces of the left one (Figure 38; Table 34).

The estimated maximum lengths of the Shanidar 1 and 3 clavicles (ca. 150.0 and ca. 149.0 mm, respectively) are large compared to those of most recent human males (range of means of 46 samples: 118.2–158.0 mm [Olivier 1951–1956]), but they are at the lower end of the European Neandertal range of variation (Krapina 142: 149.5 mm; Régourdou 1: ca. 161.0 mm; La Ferrassie 1: ca. 179.0 & 178.0 mm) and only slightly longer than the estimated clavicular length (135.0–140.0 mm) of the Tabūn C1 female. This suggests that the Shanidar clavicles, although relatively long for a recent human male, are not especially long compared to those of European Neandertals.

This inference is supported by a consideration of their claviculohumeral indices; these are approximately 46.7 for Shanidar 3 and can be estimated at about 44.8 for Shanidar 1 (using an estimated humeral maximum length of 335.0 mm for Shanidar 1, which was estimated from its femoral bicondylar length using a least squares regression based on other Neandertals [r = 0.873, N = 7]). These values fall in the middle of recent human male values (range of means for 23 samples: 42.3–49.2 [Oliver 1951–1956]) and are only slightly below the estimate of 47.2–49.0 for Tabūn C1. In contrast, La Ferrassie 1 and Régourdou 1 have claviculohumeral indexes of about 52.8 & about 53.1, and about 51.9, respectively, indicating exceptionally broad shoulders for these Neandertals. Shanidar 1 and 3 do not appear to have had this exaggerated clavicular elongation.

The elongation of European Neandertal clavicles has given the impression that they are relatively gracile (Heim 1974; McCown and Keith 1939; Olivier 1951–1956) because the standard robusticity index is midshaft circumference/maximum length (Olivier 1960). The midshaft circumference of Shanidar 1 (37.0) is toward the top of the Neandertal range of variation (Amud

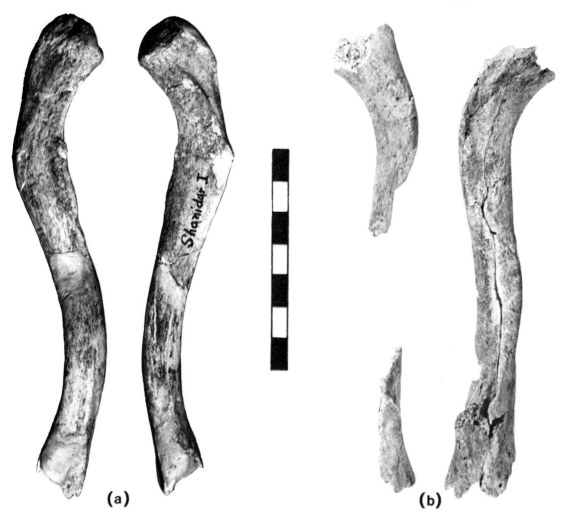

Figure 38 The Shanidar 1 and 3 clavicles. (a) Superior and inferior views of the Shanidar 1 left clavicle. (b) Inferior views of the Shanidar 3 right and left clavicles. Scale in centimeters.

1: 42.0 mm; Tabūn C1: 34.0 & 32.0 mm; European Neandertals: 33.7 ± 3.6 mm, N = 14) and in the middle of the range of variation of European Neandertals from sites other than Krapina (37.4 ± 0.8 mm, N = 6; Krapina: 31.0 ± 1.8 mm, N = 8). These values are close to the means of recent European (males: 38.3 ± 3.7 mm, N = 82; females: 32.1 ± 2.6 mm, N = 64 [Parsons 1917]) and Afroamerican (males: 40.1 ± 3.9, N = 50; females: 34.8 ± 4.1 mm, N = 50 [Terry 1932]) samples because they tend to fall between the male and female means. It is not possible to measure accurately the midshaft circumference of the fragmentary Shanidar 3 clavicle, but its midshaft estimated diameters, which are

TABLE 34
Measurements of the Clavicles (mm)

	Shanidar 1	Shanidar 3	
	Left	Right	Left
Maximum length (M-1)[a]	(150.0)	(149.0)	—
Articular length[b]	(146.0)	(145.0)	—
Vertical diameter (M-4)	8.7	(9.5)	—
Horizontal diameter (M-5)	13.8	(16.0)	—
Circumference (M-6)	37.0	—	—
Conoid height[c]	8.0	9.0	9.3
Conoid breadth[c]	19.5	19.0	16.9
Acromial height[d]	(13.0)	—	—
Acromial breadth[d]	(23.0)	—	—

[a]The maximum lengths of the Shanidar 1 and 3 clavicles were estimated from their articular lengths using a regression based on recent human clavicles (r = 0.990).
[b]The direct distance between the midpoints of the sternal and acromial ends.
[c]The height and breadth of the clavicle measured at the point of maximum development of the conoid tubercle.
[d]The height and breadth of the acromial end of the clavicle.

on the average about 12.5% greater than those of Shanidar 1 (Table 34), suggest that Shanidar 3 had a relatively large midshaft circumference (ca. 41.5 mm, if it was 12.5% larger than that of Shanidar 1).

The midshaft circumference of Shanidar 1 provides a robusticity index of about 24.7, which is at the top of the Neandertal range of variation (La Ferrassie 1: cm. 21.2 & 21.3; Krapina 142: 22.7; Régourdou 1: ca. 24.8; Tabūn C1: 23.6–24.4). All of these values are in the middle of recent human ranges of variation (range of means for 33 male samples: 21.1–27.7 [Olivier 1951–1956]).

Both of the Shanidar clavicles give the impression of being flattened superoinferiorly (craniocaudally), rather than being roughly circular in cross section. Their midshaft indices (vertical diameter/horizontal diameter) of 63.0 and about 59.4, respectively, are toward the bottom of a European Neandertal sample (77.6 ± 11.7, N = 13). There is considerable variation in the techniques of measurement of these diameters, which make comparisons with recent human samples difficult (Olivier 1951–1956). It is nonetheless apparent from the range of means for recent human male samples (79.1–97.0, for 33 samples) provided by Olivier (1951–1956) that Shanidar 1 and 3 and most of the Neandertals have relatively flat clavicular shafts.

The incomplete state of the bones makes it impossible to quantify accurately their proximal and distal curvatures. Visual inspection, however, indicates that both of them have normal distal curvatures and that the Shanidar 1 has a normal proximal curve. The proximal half of the Shanidar 3 clavicle, in contrast, is exceptionally straight (Figure 38). There may be a small amount of postmortem distortion, but it is unlikely that the original curvature was much greater than that presented by the bone in its current state.

The musculoligamentous marking on the Shanidar clavicles are strong. The Shanidar 3 costoclavicular facets are enlarged, forming broad flat surfaces on the inferior surfaces of the bones. Distally, both individuals show clear attachment areas for *M. trapezius* and *M. deltoideus*, even though the conoid tubercles are not particularly large. The overall morphology of moderately developed shafts with strong muscular markings is similar to that seen on the other Shanidar arm bones and those of other Neandertals.

SCAPULAE

Inventory

SHANIDAR 1

Right The spine, a corner of the glenoid fossa and the superior end of the axillary border. The entire bone is atrophied. Maximum breadth = 98.2 mm.

Left Largely intact bone with a complete glenoid fossa, the superior two-thirds of the axillary border, the complete coracoid process, a largely intact spine with some damage to the acromion, a portion of the vertebral border superior to the spine, and the superior border near the scapular notch. Maximum breadth = 143.7 mm; maximum height = 112.8 mm.

SHANIDAR 2

Right A portion of the vertebral border adjacent to the spine and part of the medial spine. Crushed and distorted piece. Maximum breadth = 66.4 mm.

Left Badly crushed and distorted bone with most of the spine, about half of the glenoid fossa, the superior 40 mm of the axillary border, and the supraspinal and infraspinal surface bone adjacent to the spine. Maximum breadth = 125.2 mm.

SHANIDAR 3

Right The scapula consists of two portions: a major piece with most of the infraspinatus surface including the axillary border, the vertebral border below the spine, and the spine, but missing the inferior angle, the midsection of the spine, and portions of the superior part of the axillary border (maximum height = 136.0 mm; maximum breadth = 118.0 mm);

and the ventral surface of the root of the coracoid process with part of
its lateral margin (maximum breadth = 24.0 mm).

Left The bone is represented by three pieces: a lateral portion of the infraspinatus surface with the vertebral border (maximum height = 77.3
mm; maximum breadth = 55.4 mm), the superior lateral corner of the
infraspinatus surface with the beginnings of the axillary border and
spine (maximum height = 52.7 mm), and the superior half of the
glenoid fossa with the supraglenoid tubercle (maximum height = 34.9
mm).

SHANIDAR 4

Right The bone consists of three separate pieces: a complete acromion
with most of the spine (maximum breadth = 132.6 mm), a complete
glenoid fossa with the superior end of the axillary border (maximum
height = 70.0 mm), and a portion of the inferior angle with the M. *teres
major* surface (maximum length = 56.5 mm).

Left Incomplete acromion and spine. Maximum breadth = 107.4 mm.

SHANIDAR 5

Side indeterminate Preserved are a section of the superior or vertebral
border (maximum dimension = 35.4 mm) and a portion of the infraspinatus surface (maximum length = 36.4 mm).

Morphology

Shanidar adults 1, 2, 3, and 4 retain major portions of their scapulae, although all of the bones are incomplete and some are quite fragmentary (Figures
39 and 40; Table 35). The Shanidar 1 and 3 scapulae were damaged *in situ*, but
it has been possible to assemble the preserved portions so that there is a minimum of distortion. Although it has been necessary to reconstruct missing portions, especially near the margins of the bones, to obtain some of the measurements, the degree of reconstruction is small and the estimates should be
reliable. The Shanidar 1 right scapula, along with the right clavicle and
humerus, is abnormal because it is a fraction of the size of the normal left
scapula. It is discussed separately in Chapter 12. The Shanidar 2 scapulae were
badly crushed and could not reasonably be reassembled without distortion.

Figure 39 The Shanidar 1 and 2 scapulae. (a) Lateral view of the Shanidar 1 left scapula with
the cross section of the midaxillary border viewed in a superior–inferior direction (ventral is
above). (b) Dorsal view of the Shanidar 1 left scapula. (c) Dorsal view of the crushed Shanidar 2 left
scapula. The tip of the acromion and a portion of the spine on the Shanidar 1 scapula have been
reconstructed. Scale in centimeters.

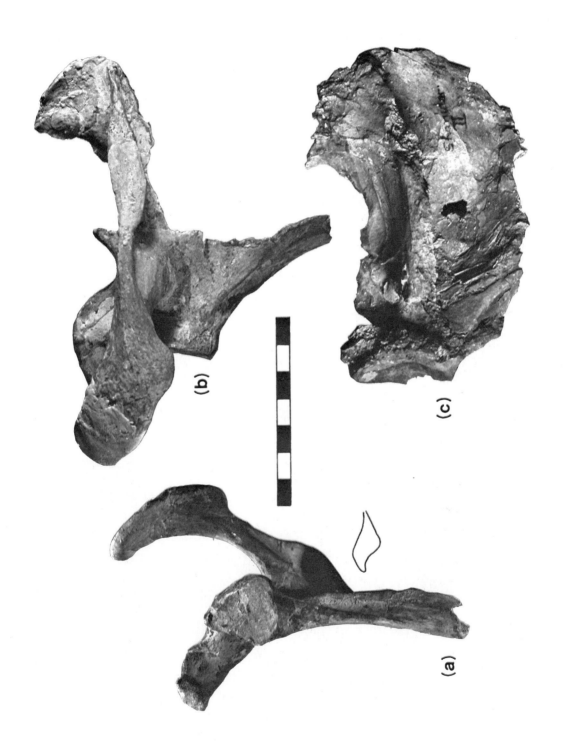

(b)

(c)

(a)

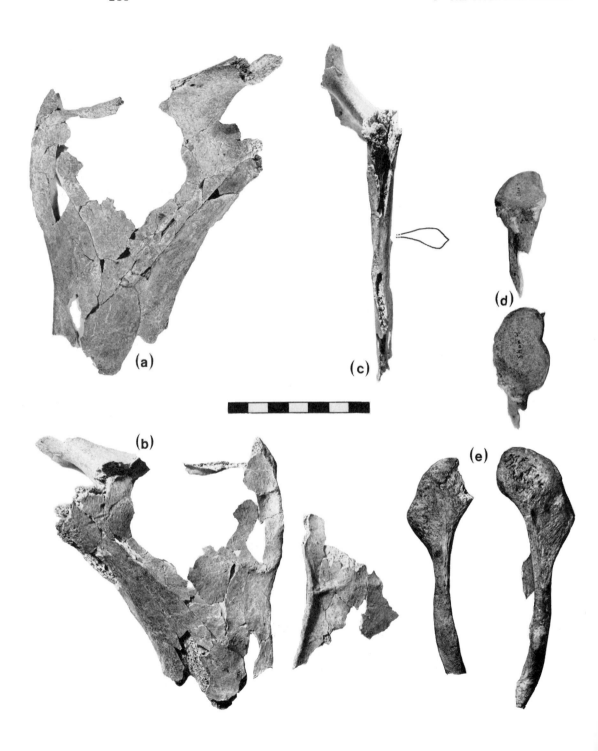

(a)

(b)

(c)

(d)

(e)

Those pieces of the Shanidar 4 scapulae that have been preserved are undistorted, but it has not been possible to assemble them into an accurate reconstruction. The Shanidar 5 scapular fragments are too incomplete to provide morphological data.

Neandertal scapulae have been shown to be similar to those of modern humans in overall morphology (Stewart 1962b; Vallois 1928–1946). The primary feature that can be employed to separate them from those of more recent humans is the morphology of their axillary borders. All of the other differences are proportional and tend to cluster Neandertal scapulae near the limits of recent human ranges of variation.

Recent human axillary borders exhibit three patterns that grade into one another: a single ventral sulcus, a single dorsal sulcus, and ventral and dorsal sulci (bisulcate). Among recent humans, the majority of the individuals exhibit the ventral sulcus pattern and most of the others possess the bisulcate pattern (Dittner 1977; Eickstedt 1925; Trinkaus 1977a). The dorsal sulcus pattern is extremely rare or absent in most samples. Among European Neandertals, 55.6% exhibit dorsal sulci, 38.9% have the bisulcate pattern, and 5.6% exhibit ventral sulci (N = 18). Amud 1 and Tabūn C1 both exhibit the dorsal sulcus pattern. However, all of the individuals from European and Levantine sites other than Krapina who preserve axillary borders (N = 8) have the dorsal sulcus pattern. All of the Skhūl–Qafzeh hominids (N = 4) and 83.3% of the Early Upper Paleolithic hominids (N = 6) possess the bisulcate pattern; the other Early Upper Paleolithic specimen, Předmostí 14, exhibits dorsal sulci.

The axillary border of the Shanidar 1 left scapula exhibits a large dorsal sulcus with the lateral margin completely on the ventral side of the axillary border, and even the atrophied right scapula has a clear dorsal sulcus. The Shanidar 3 right scapula, in contrast, has a bisulcate morphology. The superior half of its border is damaged, but the inferior half of the border exhibits dorsal and ventral sulci and the lateral margin is located in the middle of the axillary border. The Shanidar 2 and 4 scapulae each preserves only the superior 30–40 mm of the border, the portion directly below the glenoid fossa. It is therefore difficult to determine definitely what their axillary border morphologies were, but it appears that they each possessed the dorsal sulcus pattern. It is possible but less likely that one or both of them had the bisulcate morphology.

The morphology of the axillary border appears to be related to the robusticity of the individual (Trinkaus 1977a). The presence of a dorsal sulcus provides additional attachment area for M. teres minor, which is one of only two

Figure 40 The Shanidar 3 and 4 scapulae. (a) Dorsal view of the Shanidar 3 right scapula. (b) Ventral views of the Shanidar 3 right and left scapulae. (d) Lateral view of the Shanidar 3 right scapula with the midaxillary cross section viewed in a superior–inferior direction (ventral is above). (d) The Shanidar 4 right glenoid fossa and superior axillary border viewed parallel to the axillary border (above) and the glenoid fossa (below). (e) Superodorsal views of the Shanidar 4 right and left spines and acromion processes. Scale in centimeters.

TABLE 35
Measurements of the Scapulae (mm)

	Shanidar 1	Shanidar 2	Shanidar 3	Shanidar 4[f]	
	Left	Left	Right	Right	Left
Morphological length (M-2)	110.0	(116.0)	(115.0)	(115.0)	—
Axillary border length (M-3)	—	—	(125.0)	—	—
Functional length of axillary border[a]	—	—	(140.0)	(150.0)	—
Infraspinatus length (M-5a)	—	—	(127.0)	—	—
Spinoacromial length (M-7)	(151.0)	—	—	—	—
Basal spinous length (M-8)	93.0	(88.0)	90.2	—	—
Spine height[b]	38.2	—	(40.0)	—	—
Maximum acromial breadth (M-9)	28.0	—	—	28.2	28.8
Coracoid breadth[c]	14.7	—	—	—	—
Coracoid thickness[d]	8.2	—	—	—	—
Glenoid maximum length (M-12)	(37.0)	38.1	—	37.1	—
Glenoid maximum breadth (M-13)	25.6	—	—	25.5	—
Glenoid articular length[e]	(32.5)	35.5	—	32.7	—
Glenoid articular breadth[e]	23.7	—	—	21.8	—
Axillospinal angle (M-16)	(67°)	—	(60°)	—	—
Axilloglenoid angle (M-17)	(145°)	—	—	—	—
Spinoglenoid angle (M-21)	78°	—	—	—	—

[a]Direct distance from the center of the glenoid fossa to the inferior angle.

[b]Distance from the line connecting the supraspinatus and infraspinatus surfaces at the lateral margin of the spine to the most dorsal point on the adjacent spine.

[c]Maximum anteroposterior diameter of the coracoid process.

[d]Maximum superoinferior diameter of the coracoid process measured near the end of the process.

[e]Diameters of the subchondral bone of the scapulohumeral articulation, but not including the region onto which the articular capsule attaches.

[f]The morphological length and functional length of the axillary border of the Shanidar 4 right scapula were measured by Stewart while the specimen was *in situ* (Stewart 1963:9).

muscles that consistently laterally rotates the humerus. Because all of the major humeral adductors are medial rotators of the humerus, *M. teres minor* helps to maintain rotational stability of the shoulder during powerful downward movements of the arm. Because several of the humeral adductors were highly developed among the Shanidar Neandertals, especially *M. pectoralis major* (see humerus discussion), it is to be expected that they would exhibit dorsal sulci and hence strong *M. teres minor* attachments.

The proportional differences between the Neandertal and recent human scapulae involve relatively greater mediolateral scapular dimensions (lengths), larger angles between the axillary border and the spine, and relatively narrow glenoid fossae (Stewart 1962b; Vallois 1928–1946).

Morphological length can be measured directly on the Shanidar 1 left scapula (110.0 mm) and estimated for the Shanidar 2, 3, and 4 scapulae (ca. 116.0, ca. 115.0, and ca. 115.0 mm, respectively). All of these values are high compared to those of recent humans (range of means for 22 recent human samples: 83.9–102.9 [Vallois 1928–1946]). By comparison, La Ferrassie 1 has a scapular morphological length of 121.5 mm and those of the Krapina 125, 127, 130, and 132 scapulae are, respectively, ca. 115.0 mm, ca. 100.0 mm, ca. 107.0 mm, and ca. 107.0 mm. The mediolateral enlargement of the Shanidar scapulae is further illustrated by the ratios of the scapular morphological lengths to their estimated humeral maximum lengths. The values of the resultant indices for Shanidar 1, 3, and 4 are about 32.8 (using an estimated humeral maximum length of 335.0 mm), about 36.1 and about 37.7, respectively. These indices are similar to that of La Ferrassie 1 (35.8) and above those of early anatomically modern humans (Barma Grande 2: 30.0; Qafzeh 9: ca. 28.2; Skhūl 4: 28.2; Skhūl 5: ca. 27.0). Most recent humans have indices below those of the Shanidar Neandertals (e.g., North Africans: 31.0 ± 1.3, N = 27 [Warren 1897]), although the upper limits of recent human ranges of variation overlap the indices of the Shanidar and La Ferrassie Neandertals (Frey 1923). It is nonetheless clear that the Shanidar individuals had broad scapulae.

The large morphological lengths of the Shanidar scapulae do not appear to have been associated with any difference in the overall proportions of the scapulae, at least for Shanidar 3. The ratio of the Shanidar 3 infraspinatus fossa height to its morphological length, expressed as a percentage (110.4), is similar to those of a recent human sample (112.0 ± 1.1, N= 31 [Warren 1897]). The only other Neandertal scapula on which these dimensions can be measured, the La Ferrassie 1 right scapula, provides a ratio of about 123.5, indicating that it had both wide and high scapulae, even more so than Shanidar 3.

In addition to having relatively large scapulae, the Shanidar Neandertals have high axillospinal angles. This angle is 67° on the Shanidar 1 left scapula and about 60° on the Shanidar 3 right scapula. These values are above those of other Neandertals (Tabūn C1: 55°; European Neandertals: $56.7° \pm 1.5°$, N = 6), which in turn are above those of Skhūl 4 and 5 (52 and 51°, respectively) and most recent humans (range of means for 16 samples: 40.5°–47.8° [Vallois 1928–1946]).

The combination of large morphological lengths and axillospinal angles suggests an enlargement of the rotator cuff muscles, especially *M. infraspinatus* and *M. subscapularis*. The large morphological lengths of all four Shanidar scapulae would increase the muscular attachment areas along the spine. The greater axillospinal angles of at least Shanidar 1 and 3 reflect a more lateral positioning of the inferior end of the axillary border relative to the vertebral border. This would increase the breadth at the inferior angle, which would in turn increase the surface areas of the infraspinatus and subscapulae fossae.

The enlargement of the surface area for the attachment of the rotator cuff muscles on the Shanidar scapulae is further accentuated by the heights of their spines above the supraspinatus and infraspinatus surfaces. An increased distance between the supraspinatus and infraspinatus surfaces and the dorsal surface of the spine would increase the volume of muscle fibers that would be contained on the scapular dorsal surface. It would also tend to increase the moment arm of M. deltoideus around the scapulohumeral articulation by enlarging the distance between the acromion and the middle of the glenoid fossa. Because the scapula is primarily an attachment area for muscles and is responsive to atrophy and hypertrophy of those muscles (Doyle 1977; Riesenfeld 1966), these aspects of the Shanidar and other Neandertal scapulae indicate a hypertrophy of their shoulder musculature.

The acromion process is completely preserved only on the Shanidar 4 right scapula, but the Shanidar 1 and 4 left scapulae preserve the medial two-thirds of their acromion processes. All three of these bones present prominent inferior tubercles immediately above their glenoid fossae, and their superior and inferior margins are nearly parallel as they extend laterally from that tubercle. The two Shanidar 4 acromion processes have a marked dorsal rugosity of the lateral half of the acromion, which indicates a hypertrophied M. deltoideus. It is not possible to determine whether Shanidar 1 had a similar rugosity.

The maximum breadths of the Shanidar 1 (28.0 mm) and Shanidar 4 (28.2 & 28.8 mm) acromion processes are greater than that of Tabūn C1 (22.0 mm), the only other Neandertal with a largely complete acromion. These values for Shanidar 1 and 4, however, are similar to those of Skhūl 4 (26.0 mm) and a Předmostí sample (27.4 ± 3.1 mm, N = 5) and are within recent human ranges of variation (range of means of 19 samples: 22.7–30.2 mm [Vallois 1928–1946]).

The glenoid fossae of the Shanidar 1 and 4 scapulae are piriform in shape. Their breadth/length indices (ca. 69.2 and 68.7, using the maximum fossa diameters) are similar to those of other Neandertals (Amud 1: 67.6; Tabūn C1: 65.0; European Neandertals: 65.9 ± 4.6, N = 10) and below those of most Early Upper Paleolithic scapulae (73.1 ± 2.5, N = 5) and those of most recent humans (range of means for 21 samples: 71.9–81.8 [Vallois 1928–1946]). As with those of other Neandertals, the Shanidar scapular glenoid fossae are relatively long and narrow. The significance of this pattern is not clear.

The Shanidar 1 left scapula has a high axilloglenoid angle (ca. 145°) compared to those of recent humans (range of means for 15 samples: 119.5°–140.1° [Vallois 1928–1946]) and Skhūl 5 (127°), but it is only slightly above the mean of a European Neandertal sample (140.6° ± 5.3°, N = 7) and that of Amud 1 (140°). It is, however, well above that of Tabūn C1 (132°), and it lies at the top of the Neandertal range of variation (132°–150°, N = 9). This angle reflects both the orientation of the glenoid fossa and the lateral positioning of the axillary border; its high values for Shanidar 1 and other Neandertals is therefore due in part to their high axillospinal angles.

The Shanidar 1 spinoglenoid angle, however, is also at the limits of recent human ranges variation (Shanidar 1: 78°; range of means for 15 recent human samples: 82.0°–97.1° [Vallois 1928–1946]). Yet it is also at the lower end of a Neandertal range of variation (77°–93°, N = 7), is similar to that of Tabūn C1 (77°) and is below a European Neandertal mean (84.7° ± 5.0°, N = 6). This implies that its glenoid fossa may have been oriented slightly more inferiorly than those of most contemporary and more recent humans.

The Shanidar scapulae are therefore similar to those of other Neandertals and at the limits of the ranges of variation of more recent humans in having either the dorsal sulcus or bisulcate morphology of their axillary borders, absolutely and relatively large dimensions of the rotator cuff muscle attachment areas, and relatively long and narrow glenoid fossae. The first two features appear to be reflections of a hypertrophy of their scapular musculatures.

HUMERI

Inventory

SHANIDAR 1

Right Abnormal and atrophied diaphysis from the anatomical neck to the supracondylar region. Maximum length = 243.2 mm.

Left The bone consists of two pieces. The proximal piece extends from the anatomical neck, preserving the lesser tubercle but none of the greater tubercle or head, to the deltoid tuberosity; the lateral margin of the intertubercular sulcus has been reconstructed (maximum length = 134.0 mm). The distal piece retains the distal quarter of the diaphysis and all of the distal epiphysis (maximum length = 116.0 mm).

SHANIDAR 3

Right The bone consists of three portions: 13 fragments of the head and greater tuberosity, a major portion of the diaphysis that is largely complete from the surgical neck to the distal margin of the deltoid tuberosity and consists of only the anteromedial and anterolateral surfaces from the deltoid tuberosity to the supracapitular ligamentous surface (maximum length = 268.5 mm), and a distal epiphyseal piece with anterior and distal surfaces of the trochlea and medial epicondyle and most of the anterior surface of the capitulum (maximum breadth = 63.0 mm).

Left The bone consists of three identifiable portions: a proximal anterior diaphyseal section with the M. *pectoralis major* insertion, most of the intertubercular sulcus, and most of the M. *teres major* insertion (maximum length = 67.0 mm), a diaphyseal fragment with most of the deltoid tuberosity (maximum length = 61.1 mm), and the complete

medial epicondyle with the anteromedial half of the trochlea and the
medial margin of the olecranon fossa (maximum breadth = 39.8 mm).

SHANIDAR 4

Right   The bone consists of two major pieces and several smaller fragments. One major piece consists of a proximal diaphyseal section with
the surgical neck but lacking part of the intertubercular sulcus (maximum length = 76.5 mm). The other piece includes a distal diaphyseal
section (about 130 mm long) with the posterior and lateral surfaces of
the olecranon fossa and distal articular areas; it retains most of the
trochlea, capitulum, and lateral epicondyle, and part of the medial
epicondyle (maximum length = 193.2 mm).

Left   The bone is represented by three distal pieces: a section of distal
lateral diaphysis with part of the lateral supracondylar ridge (maximum
length = 95.4 mm), the medial half of the trochlea and part of the
medial epicondyle (maximum breadth = 32.1 mm), and the posterior
and lateral surfaces of the lateral epicondyle with some of the adjacent
diaphyseal surface (maximum length = 58.1 mm).

SHANIDAR 6

Right   Largely complete diaphysis from the surgical neck to just proximal
of the olecranon fossa. All surfaces are present along the distal half of
the diaphysis, but the proximal half lacks the anterior margin and medial surface. Medium length = 233.5 mm.

Left   Complete distal diaphysis and epiphysis with minimal damage to the
medial epicondyle. Maximum length = 134.7 mm.

SHANIDAR 8

Right   A largely complete trochlea, of which only the medial margin is fully
preserved (previously assigned to Shanidar 6 [Trinkaus 1977b]). Maximum breadth = 20.7 mm.

Left   Lateral half of the capitulum. Maximum dimension = 25.5 mm.

Morphology

Shanidar 1, 3, 4, and 6 preserve substantial portions of their humeri, and
Shanidar 8 preserves a couple of fragments (Figures 41 and 42). However, none
of them is complete. Yet Shanidar 1 and 6 retain largely complete distal epiphyses, Shanidar 3 and 4 retain substantial proportions of their distal epiphyses, and Shanidar 1, 3, 4, and 6 all preserve substantial proportions of their
diaphyses. There are no complete proximal epiphyses.

It has been possible to estimate the lengths of the Shanidar 3 and 6 humeri

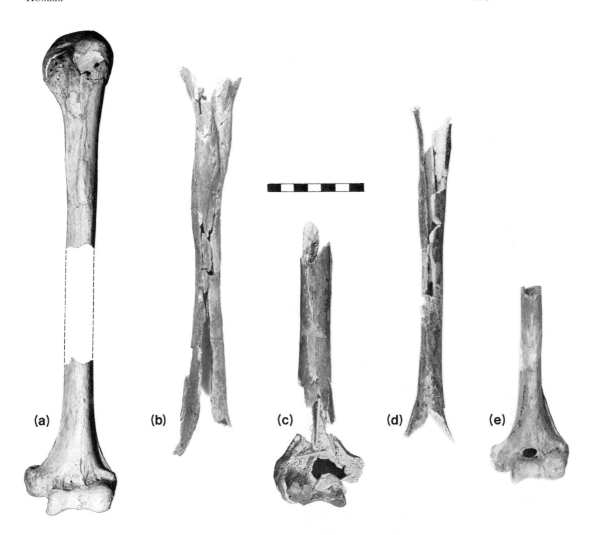

Figure 41 Anterior views of the humeri. (a) Shanidar 1 left; (b) Shanidar 3 right; (c) Shanidar 4 right; Shanidar 6 (d) right and (e) left. The head of the Shanidar 1 humerus is reconstructed in plaster, and the distance between the proximal and distal pieces is based on the estimated maximum length of 335.0 mm. Scale in centimeters.

from the preserved portions of their diaphyses and distal epiphyses (Table 36). The maximum length of the Shanidar 4 right humerus was measured *in situ* by Stewart (1963), from which a total length has been estimated (Table 34). The Shanidar 1 left humerus, however, is lacking its head and the middle third of the diaphysis, so that an accurate length estimate is not possible from the preserved portions of the bone. However, humerofemoral indices are relatively uniform for most recent and fossil *H. sapiens* (Trinkaus 1981), and it is possible

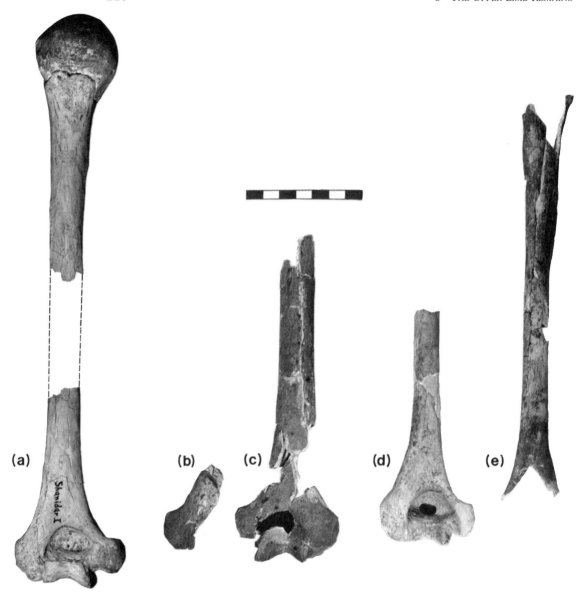

Figure 42 Posterior views of the humeri. (a) Shanidar 1 left; (b,c) Shanidar 4 left and right; (d,e) Shanidar 6 left and right. The head of the Shanidar 1 humerus has been reconstructed in plaster, and the distance between the two pieces is based on an estimated maximum length of 335.0 mm. Scale in centimeters.

to estimate accurately the bicondylar length of the Shanidar 1 right femur (Table 65). I have therefore computed a least squares regression equation using other Neandertals, including Shanidar 4 and 6 ($r = 0.873$, $N = 7$), which provides a humeral maximum length estimate of 335.0 mm for Shanidar 1. This

TABLE 36

Measurements of the Humeri (mm)

	Shanidar 1	Shanidar 3[h]		Shanidar 4[i]		Shanidar 6[j]		Shanidar 8
	Left	Right	Left	Right	Left	Right	Left	Right
Maximum length (M-1)	—	(319.0)	—	(305.0)	—	—	(293.0)	—
Total length (M-2)	—	(314.5)	—	(301.0)	—	—	(289.0)	—
Maximum diameter (M-5)	—	26.4	—	26.8	—	(20.0)	—	—
Minimum diameter (M-6)	—	17.6	—	19.0	—	14.4	—	—
Deltoid diameter (M-6a)	—	22.4	—	—	—	20.7	—	—
Circumference (M-7)	—	72.0	—	75.5	—	56.0	—	—
Minimum circumference (M-7a)	62.0	—	—	73.0	(71.0)	55.0	55.0	—
Pectoralis major length[a]	—	46.0	—	—	(45.0)	—	—	—
Pectoralis major breadth[a]	—	10.4	9.5	—	11.2	—	—	—
Cubital angle (M-16)	87°	—	—	—	—	—	84°	—
Articular cubital angle[b]	98°	—	—	—	—	—	96°	—
Lesser tubercle length[c]	27.7	—	—	—	—	—	—	—
Lesser tubercle breadth[c]	(16.4)	—	—	—	—	—	—	—
Epicondylar breadth (M-4)	64.5	—	—	(65.0)	—	—	(56.0)	—
Distal articular breadth (M-12a)	45.3	(47.0)	—	(45.0)	—	—	38.2	—
Trochlear breadth (M-11)	22.9	24.7	—	28.6	—	—	23.3	—
Capitular breadth (M-12)	22.4	—	—	—	—	—	14.9	—
Projection medial epicondyle[d]	20.0	14.5	14.0	(16.0)	—	—	(15.0)	—
Projection lateral epicondyle[e]	15.4	—	—	21.0	20.9	—	16.6	—
Trochlear depth[f]	16.7	17.1	—	(16.0)	17.5	—	13.6	14.5
Capitular depth[g]	20.7	—	—	—	—	—	17.5	—
Olecranon fossa breadth (M-14)	28.3	—	—	29.5	—	—	26.6	—
Olecranon fossa depth (M-15)	13.0	—	—	—	—	—	13.5	—

[a]Maximum length and breadth of the *M. pectoralis major* tendon insertion area.

[b]Angle between the diaphyseal axis and the line drawn across the distal capitular margin and the distal margin of the central trochlear sulcus.

[c]Maximum anteroposterior and mediolateral dimensions of the lesser tubercle; the breadth is measured from the nearest margin of the humeral head.

[d]Maximum mediolateral distance from the medial trochlear margin to the most medial point on the medial epicondyle.

[e]Maximum mediolateral distance from the lateral margin of the trochlea on the posterior surface to the most lateral point on the lateral epicondyle.

[f]Minimum anteroposterior dimension of the trochlea.

[g]Maximum anteroposterior dimension of the capitulum.

[h]The total length was estimated from the length of the preserved portion (268.5 mm) using a regression based on recent human humeri ($r = 0.977$), and the maximum length was estimated from the total length using a similar regression ($r = 0.996$).

[i]The maximum length was measured *in situ* by Stewart (1963); the total length was estimated from the maximum length using a regression based on recent human humeri ($r = 0.996$).

[j]The total length was estimated from the combined length of the aligned right and left humeri (237.5 mm) using a regression based on recent human humeri ($r = 0.938$); the maximum length was computed by adding the projection of the left trochlea beyond the left capitulum onto the articular length estimate.

estimate for Shanidar 1 is not as reliable as those for the other Shanidar humeri, and indices that employ it should be viewed cautiously.

The right humerus of Shanidar 1 is represented by a highly abnormal diaphysis, which is discussed in Chapter 12 along with its associated abnormal clavicle and scapula.

The diaphyses of the Shanidar humeri appear to be similar to those of other Neandertals and contrast in some features with those of more recent humans. The midshafts of Shanidar 3, 4, and 6 exhibit the moderate mediolateral flattening (platybrachia) characteristic of most Neandertals and some more recent humans (Figure 43). Their midshaft indices (66.7, 70.8, and 72.0, respectively) are lower than those of Amud 1 (74.5) and Tabūn C1 (81.9) and are slightly below the mean of a European Neandertal sample (72.3 ± 3.7, N = 12). Their indices are even further from the means of a Skhūl–Qafzeh sample (79.6 ± 7.4, N = 5) and an Early Upper Paleolithic sample (78.9 ± 8.1, N = 15) and from the range of means of 12 recent human samples (75.9–82.1 (Delsaux 1976; Hrdlička 1932b; Martin 1928).

The Shanidar humeral diaphyses are, like those of most other Neandertals, toward the upper limits of recent human ranges in terms of robusticity. The Shanidar 4 and 6 humeri span the Neandertal range in terms of robusticity indices (minimum circumference/maximum length) (Shanidar 4: ca. 23.9; Shanidar 6: ca. 18.8; Neandertals: 18.5–23.0, N = 7; Tabūn C1: 18.5, European Neandertals; 20.7 ± 1.4, N = 6). The Shanidar 1 robusticity index, using the estimate of 335.0 mm for maximum length, is about 18.5. Some of the Neandertal indices, and especially that of Shanidar 4, are slightly above those of most Skhūl–Qafzeh hominids (18.2 ± 1.4, N = 4), Early Upper Paleolithic hominids (18.4 ± 1.3, N = 7), and recent humans (range of means for 14 samples: 17.6–20.9 [Delsaux 1976]).

The most remarkable aspect of the Shanidar humeral diaphyses is the development of their M. deltoideus and especially M. pectoralis major attachments.

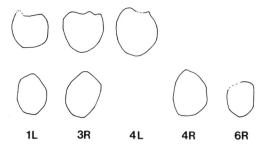

1L   3R   4L   4R   6R

Figure 43 Diaphyseal cross sections of the humeri of Shanidar 1 (1L), Shanidar 3 (3R), Shanidar 4 (4R and 4L), and Shanidar 6 (6R). Top row: at the middle of the M. pectoralis major insertions; bottom row: at the middle of the deltoid tuberosities. The sections are viewed in a proximal–distal direction, and anterior (volar) is above.

On the Shanidar 3, 4, and 6 humeri, the deltoid tuberosity is evidenced by a strongly marked, roughened, slightly raised ridge, which is sufficiently pronounced on the Shanidar 3 right humerus to produce a sulcus between it and the anterior margin of the bone (Figures 41 and 44). The formation of a sulcus alongside the deltoid tuberosity is present on several European Neandertal (Thoma 1975) and more recent human humeri (Vandermeersch 1981a).

The M. *pectoralis major* tuberosity is largely preserved on the Shanidar 3 humeri and the Shanidar 4 left humerus, and its medial half remains on the Shanidar 6 right humerus. All of these insertions have raised ridges around the tuberosity with a roughened depression in the middle. The breadths of the Shanidar 3 and 4 tuberosities (10.4 & 9.5, and 11.2 mm, respectively) are at the top of the Neandertal range of variation (4.9–10.4 mm, N = 8; Amud 1: 10.0 & 9.0 mm; Tabūn C1: 4.5 & 5.2 mm; European Neandertals: 8.7 ± 1.4 mm, N = 6), and are considerably above those of samples of European Upper Paleolithic hominids (5.1 ± 0.9 mm, N = 6) and recent humans (6.5 ± 1.4 mm, N = 36). This suggests massive humeral adductors and it conforms to the muscular development suggested by their scapulae.

The only preserved portion of a proximal epiphysis for one of the Shanidar humeri is the lesser tubercle of the Shanidar 1 left humerus. It is a relatively large and projecting tubercle, implying a strong insertion for M. *subscapularis*. This inference is in agreement with the conclusions drawn from the Shanidar 1 scapular morphology.

The distal epiphyses of the Shanidar humeri are morphologically similar to those of other Neandertals and more recent humans. There are no observable differences between the morphologies of their articular surfaces and those of other H. *sapiens* humeri. All of the notable features of the Shanidar distal humeri are features that are related to robusticity and tend to place them toward the limits of recent human ranges of variation in humeral morphology.

The cubital angles of the Shanidar 1 and 6 humeri, as measured across the distal margins of the capitulum and trochlea, are 87° and 84°, respectively. These values are similar to those of other Neandertals (Tabūn C1: 86°; European Neandertals: (84.2° ± 2.1°, N = 12), which are similar to those of Skhūl 4 and 5 (84° each), an Early Upper Paleolithic sample (82.6° ± 2.1°, N = 7), and recent humans (range of means for 7 samples: 77.0°–84.5° [Martin 1928]).

The Shanidar distal humeral articulations exhibit the moderate enlargement seen in most Neandertal humeri (Trinkaus 1980). The index formed by the ratio of the distal articular breadth to the total length is about 14.9 for Shanidar 3, about 15.0 for Shanidar 4, about 13.2 for Shanidar 6, and about 13.7 for Shanidar 1 (using an estimated total length of 330.0 mm for Shanidar 1). The indices for Shanidar 3 and 4 are close to a European Neandertal mean (14.9 ± 0.4, N = 7), whereas those of Shanidar 1 and 6 are below those of all European Neandertals and close to that of Tabūn C1 (13.4). The low value for Shanidar 6 may be due in part to sexual dimorphism because Neandertal and recent human females tend to have slightly lower indices than males from the same

Figure 44 Details of the arm bones. (a) Details of the Shanidar 3 proximal diaphyseal muscular insertions, with the prominent M. *pectoralis major* insertions evident. (b) Anterolateral view of the Shanidar 4 proximal left humeral diaphysis, with the proximal half of the M. *pectoralis major* tuberosity. (c) Anterior (volar) view of the Shanidar 3 left proximal radius. (d) Medial view of the Shanidar 3 left distal ulna, showing the M. *pronator quadratus* crest. Scale in centimeters.

samples (Trinkaus 1980); this would not explain the relatively low index for Shanidar 1, however. The Shanidar 3 and 4, but not the Shanidar 1 and 6, values for this index are above those of Skhūl 4 and 5 (13.6 and 11.3, respectively), an Early Upper Paleolithic sample (13.2 ± 0.5, N = 9), and most recent humans (Amerindians: 13.9 ± 0.7, N = 50; Europeans: 14.2 ± 0.8, N = 50 [Trinkaus 1980]). These data imply a slight increase in relative cubital articular dimensions, at least for Shanidar 3 and 4, which was probably an adaptation for higher levels of joint reaction force.

The modest enlargement of the Shanidar distal humeral articulations is associated with little or no expansion of their epicondylar regions. They have robust medial and lateral epicondyles, with strong markings for the associated muscles and ligaments, but their distal articular indices (articular breadth/epicondylar breadth) are similar to, or towards the lower end of the ranges of variation of, those of other *H. sapiens* humeri. These indices are 70.2, about 69.2, and about 68.2 for Shanidar 1, 4, and 6, respectively. They are all similar to, if slightly below the averages of, other Neandertals (Tabūn C1: 68.9; European Neandertals: 72.1 ± 2.0, N = 13), Skhūl 4 and 5 (70.8 and 71.7, respectively), Early Upper Paleolithic hominids (71.6 ± 2.5, N = 7), and recent humans (range of means for 7 samples: 68.8–81.1 [Delsaux 1976]). This suggests that the Shanidar Neandertals had slightly enlarged epicondyles compared to their distal articular breadths.

The Shanidar 1, 3, and 6 humeri, and probably those of Shanidar 4, have pronounced supracondylar crests. This implies a hypertrophy of their *Mm. extensor carpi radialis longus*. In this feature, they are similar to most other Neandertal humeri and those of many more recent humans.

The Shanidar 6 distal left humerus has a large septal aperture (9.5 mm × 6.0 mm), and the Shanidar 1 left humerus has two pinhole perforations of the olecranon fossa (Figure 41). It is not possible to determine whether Shanidar 3 and 4 possessed septal apertures. Of the European Neandertals, 42.5% exhibit full septal apertures and another 10.0% have pinhole perforations of the olecranon fossa (N = 20). However, 72.7% of the Neandertals with either size perforation of the distal humerus come from Krapina, and only 27.7% (N = 9) of the European Neandertals from sites other than Krapina exhibit holes through the olecranon fossa–coronoid fossa septum. The Tabūn C1 humerus lacks a perforation. Similar perforations are unknown in small samples of Skhūl–Qafzeh (N = 4) and Early Upper Paleolithic (N = 8) hominids, and occur in variable amounts among recent humans (range of frequencies in 55 samples: 1.5–41.5% (Akabori 1934; Hrdlička 1932a; Trotter 1934a). The frequency of septal apertures among recent humans appears to be correlated with gracility, although the etiology is not clear (Benfer and McKern 1966).

The Shanidar humeri are therefore similar to those of other Neandertals in being morphologically close to more recent human humeri and differing only in their tendencies to have greater platybrachia, larger articular surfaces (at least for Shanidar 3 and 4) and pronounced muscular attachment areas.

ULNAE

Inventory

SHANIDAR 1

Left Complete bone lacking only the styloid process. Some minor damage occurred to the diaphysis. Maximum length = 270.2 mm.

SHANIDAR 3

Right A fragment of the coronoid process with part of the humeral articular surface and the *M. brachialis* tuberosity. Maximum length = 17.5 mm.

Left A fragment of the coronoid process with all of the humeral surface and part of the radial notch (maximum length = 17.7 mm), and a complete distal epiphysis with the medial half of the diaphysis to the proximal margin of the *M. pronator quadratus* tuberosity (maximum length = 69.0 mm).

SHANIDAR 4

Right The bone preserves portions of the diaphysis from the distal margin of the *M. brachialis* tuberosity to the distal epiphysis and most of the distal epiphysis. For the proximal third of the diaphysis, only the dorsal and part of the medial surfaces are preserved. The medial margin of the head had been reconstructed. Maximum length = 197.0 mm.

Left The bone is virtually complete, lacking only small pieces from the dorsolateral diaphysis and most of the diaphysis in the region of the *M. pronator quadratus* tuberosity. The contact between the distal end and the remainder of the bone in the region of the *M. pronator quadratus* tuberosity is tenuous but is confirmed by comparisons of the resultant length with that of the left radius. Maximum length = 257.5 mm.

SHANIDAR 5

Right Complete bone lacking only a small section of the lateral surface in the region of the *M. brachialis* tuberosity. Maximum length = 250.0 mm.

Left Largely complete diaphysis from just distal of the *M. brachialis* tuberosity to just distal of the *M. pronator quadratus* crest (maximum length = 177.5 mm), and a portion of the coronoid process with about half of each of the trochlear and radial facets (maximum length = 20.0 mm).

SHANIDAR 6

Right Complete proximal epiphysis with the proximal half of the diaphysis. Maximum length = 158.0 mm.
Left Complete diaphysis from just distal to the M. *brachialis* tuberosity with the complete distal epiphysis. Maximum length = 189.2 mm.

Morphology

The Shanidar ulnae are the most complete of their long bones (Figures 45 and 46). Shanidar 1, 4, and 5 each possesses one largely complete ulna, and Shanidar 4 and 5 retain major portions of their other ulnae. Shanidar 6 preserves the majority of each ulna, and it has been possible to estimate the lengths of her ulnae from her radial lengths (Table 37). Reliable ulnar lengths are therefore available for four individuals. Shanidar 3 preserves only a few fragments of his ulnae.

The diaphyses of the Shanidar ulnae are relatively gracile, a characteristic of many Neandertal ulnae. The robusticity indices (minimum circumference/articular length) for the Shanidar 1, 4, 5, and 6 ulnae (12.5, 15.4, 13.7, and ca. 12.7, respectively) are comparable to or slightly less than those of most other Neandertals (Amud 1: ca. 15.1; Tabūn C1: 13.1; European Neandertals: 14.4 ± 0.5, N = 4), Skhūl–Qafzeh hominids (14.7 ± 0.6, N = 5), and Early Upper Paleolithic hominids (13.8 ± 1.2, N = 6), all of which are similar to those of recent humans (Europeans: 16.5 ± 1.4, N = 26; Melanesians: 13.3 ± 1.5, N = 18 [Fischer 1906]).

The Shanidar ulnar diaphyses tend to be relatively round, with the midshaft dorsovolar diameter slightly less than the transverse diameter. The midshaft indices (dorsovolar diameter/mediolateral diameter) for Shanidar 1, 4, 5, and 6 (90.7, 96.5, 84.1 & 85.1, and 70.8 & 84.8) cluster around the mean of a highly variable European Neandertal sample (86.6 ± 13.2, N = 10). Amud 1 and Tabūn C1 have relatively high indices (111.5, and 92.2 & 101.8, respectively). Early anatomically modern hominids tend to have similar or even higher midshaft indices (Skhūl–Qafzeh sample: 95.3 ± 7.9, N = 6; Early Upper Paleolithic sample: 105.6 ± 17.4, N = 8), whereas recent humans tend to have lower indices (Europeans: 77.7 ± 6.9, N = 26; Melanesians: 79.9 ± 7.7, N = 18 [Fischer 1906]). The significance of these variations is not entirely clear. The indices are partially affected by the development of the interosseus crest; the Shanidar ulnar interosseus crests, like those of other Neandertals, are not projecting, but they are clearly marked for the attachment of the ligamentous membrane (Figure 47).

The lenic indices of the Shanidar ulnae are highly variable because Shanidar 1 (94.4) is close to the mean of a European Neandertal sample (98.3 ± 6.5, N = 15), whereas Shanidar 4 (81.2) has one of the lowest indices and

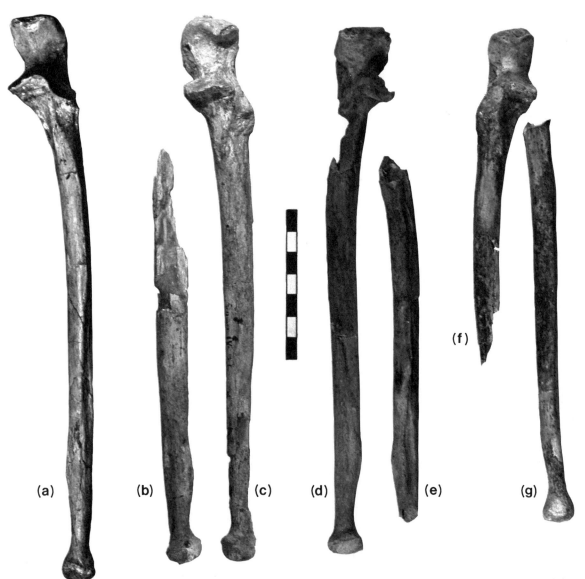

Figure 45 Anterior (volar) views of the ulnae. (a) Shanidar 1 left; (b,c) Shanidar 4 right and left; (d,e) Shanidar 5 right and left; (f,g) Shanidar 6 right and left. Scale in centimeters.

Shanidar 6 (116.0) has one of the highest for a Neandertal. Tabūn C1 has an index of 101.7. These values for the lenic index are not significantly different from those of a Skhūl–Qafzeh sample (95.0 ± 5.9, N = 7) and recent humans (Europeans: 87.8 ± 10.0, N = 26; Melanesians: 85.8 ± 8.5, N = 18 [Fischer 1906]). Although the lenic index may give a general idea of the degree of flattening of the proximal diaphysis of the ulna, the repeatability of the measurements is frequently uncertain. Furthermore, the morphology of the subsigmoid region, and hence its diameters, is influenced by the shapes of the di-

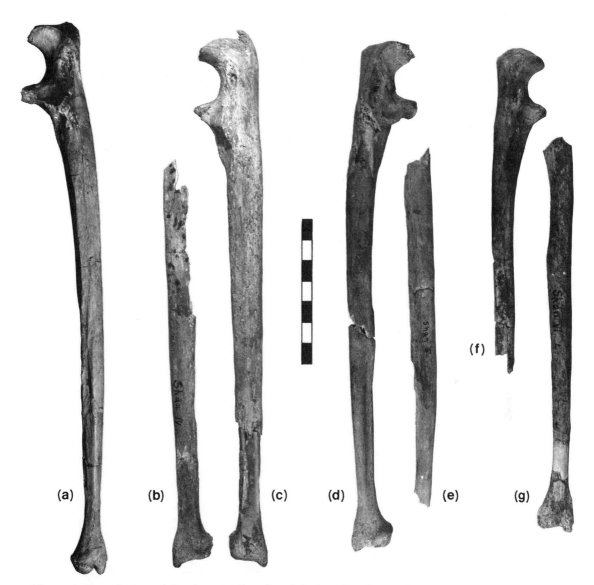

Figure 46   Lateral views of the ulnae. (a) Shanidar 1 left; (b,c) Shanidar 4 right and left; (d,e) Shanidar 5 right and left; (f,g) Shanidar 6 right and left. Scale in centimeters.

aphysis, coronoid process, radial facet, and *M. brachialis* tuberosity. The relative contributions of these features, and hence the significance of the index, are difficult to decipher.

One of the more striking aspects of the Shanidar ulnar diaphyses is the consistently large development of their *M. pronator quadratus* crests (Figures 44 and 45). On all the Shanidar ulnae, the insertion of *M. pronator quadratus* forms a distinct crest on the distomedial diaphysis that extends from the diaphyseal surface and curves slightly anteriorly. Shanidar 1, 3, 4, and 5 all have

TABLE 37
Measurements of the Ulnae (mm)

	Shanidar 1	Shanidar 3	Shanidar 4		Shanidar 5		Shanidar 6	
	Left	Left	Right	Left	Right	Left	Right	Left
Maximum length (M-1)	(272.5)	—	—	255.0	249.0	—	—	—
Articular length (M-2)	247.5	—	—	228.0	226.0	—	(212.0)	—
Dorsovolar diameter (M-11)	12.7	—	—	13.9	11.6	11.4	9.2	10.6
Mediolateral diameter (M-12)	14.0	—	—	14.4	13.8	13.4	13.0	12.5
Proximal dorsovolar diameter (M-14)	18.0	—	—	21.8	—	—	14.4	—
Proximal mediolateral diameter (M-13)	17.0	—	—	17.7	—	—	16.7	—
Proximal circumference[a]	53.8	—	—	59.0	—	—	51.0	—
Distal circumference[b]	31.0	—	35.0	—	31.0	31.5	—	27.0
Pronator quadratus maximum diameter[c]	13.6	—	15.3	—	14.0	13.4	—	10.3
Pronator quadratus minimum diameter[c]	9.4	—	9.7	—	8.9	9.0	—	8.0
Pronator quadratus circumference[c]	36.3	—	40.5	—	36.0	35.0	—	29.0
Olecranon height[d]	26.0	—	—	29.1	26.0	—	23.9	—
Olecranon breadth (M-6)	26.3	—	—	27.6	27.7	—	21.5	—
Olecranon thickness[e]	16.6	—	—	18.6	17.4	—	15.3	—
Trochlear notch height (M-7(1))	25.0	—	—	22.8	23.8	—	19.7	—
Trochlear notch depth[f]	12.0	—	—	12.9	9.6	—	(10.0)	—

236

Coronoid height[g]	30.2	—	32.8	30.4	27.2	—
Tuberosity position[h]	22.2	—	33.5	(40.9)	29.5	—
Olecranon length[i]	30.5	—	22.5	20.8	19.5	—
Head breadth[j]	17.0	18.0	17.0	17.0	—	15.3
Distal maximum depth[k]	—	25.0	21.5	21.5	—	18.3
Distal articular depth[l]	—	15.5	15.0	14.4	—	12.5
Proximal trochlear angle[m]	13°	—	12°	12°	15°	—
Midshaft trochlear angle[n]	8°	—	8°	4°	6°	—

[a]Circumference measured at the same point as the proximal (subsigmoid) diameters.

[b]Minimum circumference of the diaphysis between the M. pronator quadratus tuberosity and the distal epiphysis.

[c]Maximum and minimum diameters and circumference measured at the point of maximum development of the crest for the attachment of the M. pronator quadratus.

[d]Maximum dorsoventral dimension of the olecranon process (McHenry et al. [1976] measurement 9).

[e]Minimum dorsoventral distance from the middle of the trochlear notch to the dorsal surface of the proximal ulna (McHenry et al. [1976] measurement 7).

[f]Subtense from the trochlear notch height (the distance between the ventral tips of the olecranon and coronoid processes) to the deepest point on the central ridge of the trochlear notch.

[g]Maximum dorsoventral distance from the tip of the coronoid process to the dorsal surface of the proximal ulna (McHenry et al. [1976] measurement 8).

[h]Distance from the middle of the trochlear notch to the middle of the M. brachialis tuberosity (McHenry et al. [1976] measurement 11).

[i]Distance from the middle of the trochlear notch to the most proximal point on the olecranon process (McHenry et al. [1976] measurement 12).

[j]Mediolateral diameter of the distal articular surface (McHenry et al. [1976] measurement 3).

[k]Maximum dorsoventral diameter of the distal epiphysis.

[l]Maximum dorsoventral diameter of the distal articular surface.

[m]The angle between the line connecting the ventral tips of the olecranon and coronoid processes and the longitudinal axis of the proximal half of the diaphysis.

[n]The angle between the line connecting the ventral tips of the olecranon and coronoid processes and the longitudinal axis of the central region of the diaphysis.

[o]The articular lengths of the Shanidar 6 ulnae have been estimated from the articular length of the combined right and left radii (206.5 mm) using a least squares regression based on recent human paired radii and ulnae (r = 0.950).

Figure 47 Diaphyseal cross sections of
the ulnae of Shanidar 1 (1L), Shanidar 4 (4L),
Shanidar 5 (5L and 5R), and Shanidar 6 (6L).
The sections are taken at midshaft and viewed
in a proximal–distal direction. Anterior (volar) is above, and the arrows indicate the positions of the interosseus crests.

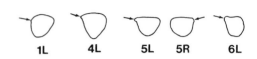

1L   4L   5L   5R   6L

exceptionally large crests, and Shanidar 6 has a smaller one. The relative development of the *M. pronator quadratus* crest can be quantified by the ratio of the
maximum to minimum diameters at the middle of the crest. These indices are
144.7, 157.7, 157.3 & 148.9, and 128.8, respectively, for Shanidar 1, 4, 5, and 6,
which span approximately the same range as those of other Neandertals (Amud
1: 144.9; Tabūn C1: 130.4; La Ferrassie 1: 167.0 & 159.3; La Ferrassie 2: 146.5;
Régourdou 1: 134.3). The Neandertal values for this index overlap with those of
more recent humans (Cro-Magnon–Skhūl–Qafzeh sample: 123.2 ± 13.6, N = 6;
recent humans: 123.4 ± 10.4, N = 40), but on the average the Neandertal
values, and especially those of Shanidar 1, 4, and 5, are greater than those of
more recent humans. This indicates a pronounced development of this muscle
among these individuals. Because *M. pronator quadratus* is one of the primary
pronators of the forearm, especially during rapid pronation (Basmajian
and Travill 1961), this implies that powerful rotation of the forearm was important among these early *H. sapiens*.

The proximal epiphyses of the Shanidar ulnae are moderately robust, with
fair-sized articular surfaces for the humeral trochlea and the radial head.
Shanidar 1 and 4 exhibit prominent exostoses on their olecranon processes for
the insertions of their *M. triceps brachii* tendons, and Shanidar 3 and 5 have
exostoses along the anterior margins of their coronoid processes, which extend
around the radial facet on the Shanidar 5 ulna. These exostoses are probably
related to irritation of the associated tendons and ligaments from activity
(Chapter 12).

The Shanidar 1 and 5 proximal ulnae have roughened pits along the lateral
margins of their articular surfaces for the attachment of the annular ligament.
The corresponding areas on the Shanidar 4 and 6 ulnae are roughened but do
not have the large pits present on those of Shanidar 1 and 5. And there are
prominent supinator crests leading distally from the distolateral margins of the
radial facets on the Shanidar 4 and 6 ulnae; the region is not preserved on the
Shanidar 1 and 5 ulnae. The size of these crests implies relatively large supinator muscles; such a hypertrophy of *M. supinator* would agree with the apparent
development of *M. pronator quadratus* among the Shanidar Neandertals because it is primarily *M. supinator*, along with *M. biceps brachii*, that is responsible for supination of the forearm (Travill and Basmajian 1961).

A feature that has been considered characteristic of Neandertal proximal
ulnae is the orientation of their trochlear notches (Fischer 1906; Thoma 1975).
The trochlear notches of Neandertal ulnae tend to face more anteriorly than
those of recent humans, which face proximoanteriorly. This feature can be

quantified by the ratio of the olecranon height to the coronoid height; a higher index indicates that the notch faces more anteriorly.

This index is 86.4, 88.7, 85.5, and 87.9, respectively, for Shanidar 1, 4, 5, and 6. These values are similar to those of European Neandertals (82.2 ± 3.8, N = 7) and below the very high index of 95.6 for Tabūn C1. The Shanidar indices and those of most of the other Neandertals, however, are above those of Skhūl 4, 5, and 7 (70.6, ca. 76.9 and 82.8, respectively), an Early Upper Paleolithic sample (70.0 ± 4.0, N = 6) and recent humans (Europeans: 71.4 ± 4.6, N = 26; Melanesians: 71.4 ± 3.8, N = 18 [Fischer, 1906]). These figures indicate that that Neandertal ulnae, including those from Shanidar, have trochlear notches that face more anteriorly than those of most more recent humans. It is uncertain whether this is a product of more anteriorly projecting olecranon processes, less anteriorly projecting coronoid processes, or both.

There is little of note concerning the Shanidar distal ulnar epiphyses. They have moderate-sized articular surfaces for the distal radius and the triangular articular disc. The styloid processes, which are preserved on at least one each of the Shanidar 3, 5, and 6 ulnae (the Shanidar 1 and 4 styloid processes have been reconstructed), are large but not particularly projecting.

The Shanidar ulnae therefore resemble those of other Neandertals in having moderately gracile diaphyses, strong crests for M. pronator quadratus and M. supinator, anteriorly oriented trochlear notches, and moderately-sized articular surfaces.

RADII

Inventory

SHANIDAR 1

Left Largely complete proximal epiphysis and complete diaphysis. Maximum length = 224.4 mm.

SHANIDAR 3

Left The bone consists of a proximal piece with the head, neck, and radial tuberosity that is damaged on the medial surface of the head (maximum length = 59.0 mm) and the volar half of the distal epiphysis and diaphysis (maximum length = 84.8 mm).

SHANIDAR 4

Right The bone is preserved from the head to the distal articulation, but a piece of volar and medial midshaft is missing, the dorsolateral third of the head is absent, only the dorsomedial corner of the carpal surface is preserved, and the region of the radial tuberosity is incomplete, especially dorsally and volarly. In addition, there is a tenuous contact between the head and neck and the proximal diaphysis in the region of the radial tuberosity. Maximum length = 227.3 mm.

Left   The bone is represented by two separate pieces: a complete proximal epiphysis with the proximal half of the diaphysis (maximum length = 134.3 mm), and a largely complete distal epiphysis with the adjacent distal diaphysis (maximum length = 80.0 mm).

SHANIDAR 5

Right   The bone consists of a proximal diaphyseal piece with the distal edge of the radial tuberosity and the proximal half of the interosseus crest (maximum length = 70.0 mm) and a complete distal epiphysis with the adjacent diaphysis (maximum length = 110.0 mm).

SHANIDAR 6

Right   Proximal epiphysis with portions of the proximal three-quarters of the diaphysis. The medial half of the head, the neck, and the radial tuberosity are complete; the diaphysis preserves primarily the medial and dorsal surfaces. The proximal epiphysis was previously assigned to Shanidar 8 (Trinkaus 1977b). Maximum length = 171.5 mm.

Left   The bone consists of two pieces, a proximal piece with the complete head and neck, and the proximal half of the radial tuberosity (formerly assigned to Shanidar 8 [Trinkaus 1977b]; maximum length = 31.4 mm), and the complete diaphysis and distal epiphysis (maximum length = 186.2 mm).

SHANIDAR 8

Right   Complete head and neck and the proximal two-thirds of the diaphysis (formerly assigned to Shanidar 6 [Stewart 1963; Trinkaus 1977b]). Maximum length = 159.6 mm.

Morphology

Shanidar 1, 3, 4, 5, 6, and 8 retain portions of their radii and provide considerable data on Neandertal radial morphology (Figures 48 and 49). Although no one radius is complete, each individual preserves at least one epiphysis largely intact, and all except Shanidar 3 retain major portions of their diaphyses. Only the Shanidar 4 radii sustained any significant amount of postmortem abrasion.

None of the Shanidar radii is sufficiently complete to provide a direct length measurement. However, it is possible to estimate the lengths of the Shanidar 1, 4, 5, and 6 radii. The lengths of the Shanidar 4 and 6 radii can be

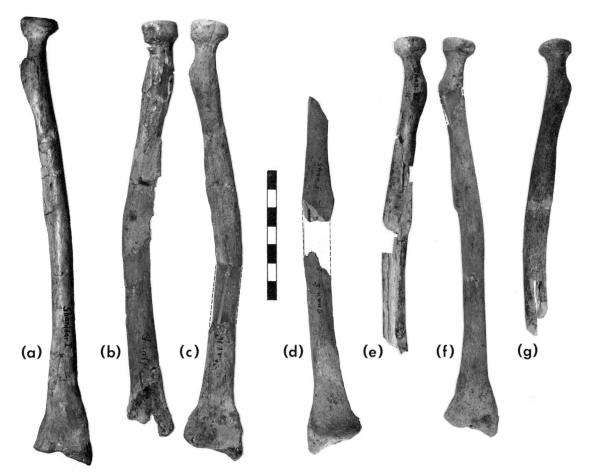

Figure 48 Anterior (volar) views of the radii. (a) Shanidar 1 left; (b,c) Shanidar 4 right and left; (d) Shanidar 5 right; (e,f) Shanidar 6 right and left; (g) Shanidar 8 right. The Shanidar 4 left, 5 right, and 6 right radii each consists of two separate pieces that have been joined or arranged relative to each other on the basis of the contralateral radius (Shanidar 4 and 6) or the ipsilateral ulna (Shanidar 5); the areas of reconstruction are indicated by dotted lines. Scale in centimeters.

estimated by aligning the preserved portions of their right and left radii according to anatomical landmarks. It has been possible to reconstruct the distal epiphysis of the Shanidar 1 left radius, at least for estimating lengths, using the left ulna as a guide. The two preserved pieces of the Shanidar 5 right radius are insufficient to permit a length estimate, but it is possible to approximate its length from the intact right ulna (Table 38).

The Shanidar radii exhibit the moderate diaphyseal robusticity apparent in their ulnae and other Neandertal radii. The robusticity indices (distal minimum circumference/articular length) for Shanidar 1, 4, 5, and 6 are about 16.6,

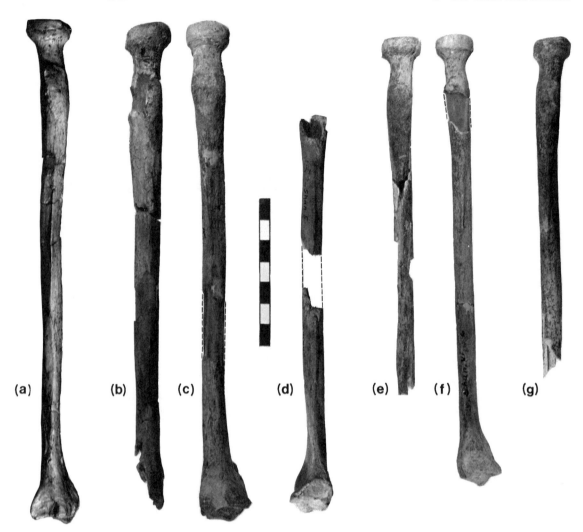

Figure 49 Medial views of the radii. (a) Shanidar 1 left; (b,c) Shanidar 4 right and left; (d) Shanidar 5 right; (e,f) Shanidar 6 right and left; (g) Shanidar 8 right (see Figure 48). Scale in centimeters.

about 18.4, about 16.7, and about 16.2, respectively. The Shanidar 4 index is slightly above a European Neandertal mean (18.1 ± 1.1, N = 5), whereas the other three Shanidar indices are below the European Neandertal mean. In this, Shanidar 1, 5, and 6 are similar to Amud 1 and Tabūn C1, both of whom have relatively low radial robusticity indices (ca. 16.7 and 15.2, respectively). The

Shanidar and most of the other Neandertal robusticity indices are nonetheless slightly greater than the means of Skhūl–Qafzeh (16.0 ± 0.6, N = 4) and Early Upper Paleolithic (15.9 ± 1.3, N = 6) samples, but all these indices fall within recent human ranges of variation (Europeans: 18.3 ± 1.6, N = 26; Melanesians: 15.9 ± 1.6, N = 18 [Fischer 1906]).

The Shanidar radial diaphyses exhibit the teardrop-shaped cross sections at the point of maximum interosseus crest development that are present on most Neandertal radii (Figure 50). Yet the relative development of the crest for the interosseus ligament is variable within the Shanidar sample, being extremely prominent on the Shanidar 5 radius and relatively small on the Shanidar 1 and 4 radii. The diaphyseal indices, computed from the diaphyseal diameters at the point of maximum projection of the interosseus crest, are 71.0, 81.9 & 70.0, 58.0, 61.6 & 61.2, and 66.4 for Shanidar 1, 4, 5, 6, and 8, respectively. The indices of Shanidar 1, 4, and 8 are well within the range of variation of other Neandertals (65.9–85.8, N = 15; Amud 1: 67.7; Bisitun 1: 68.9; Tabūn C1: 67.4; European Neandertals: 72.6 ± 7.7, N = 10). However, those of Shanidar 5 and 6 are below the Neandertal range, indicating that they had highly projecting interosseus crests. More recent humans tend to have indices either close to the Neandertal mean or slightly higher (Skhūl–Qafzeh hominids: 80.8 ± 3.1, N = 4; Early Upper Paleolithic hominids: 77.3 ± 6.4, N = 9; recent Europeans: 71.6 ± 5.9, N = 26 [Fischer 1906]; recent Melanesians: 77.8 ± 8.3, N = 18 [Fischer 1906]). The noticeable projection of the Shanidar 5 and 6, and to a lesser extent Shanidar 8, interosseus crests is interesting, especially given the small size of the interosseus crests on all of the Shanidar ulnae (Figure 47).

Neandertal radii have long been considered to have an exceptional lateral convexity of the diaphysis, which places them at or beyond the limits of more recent human ranges of variation (Boule, 1911–1913; Endo and Kimura 1970; Fischer 1906; Heim 1974). The index of radial diaphyseal curvature (subtense/chord for the lateral diaphyseal contour of the radius) provides values for Neandertals (Tabūn C1: 5.81, European Neandertals: 5.86 ± 0.97, N = 7) that are above those of most early anatomically modern humans (Skhūl–Qafzeh sample: 2.73 ± 1.49, N = 4; Early Upper Paleolithic sample: 2.59 ± 0.52, N = 8), and recent humans (Europeans: 3.27 ± 0.80, N = 26; Melanesians: 3.01 ± 0.72, N = 18 [Fischer 1906]). Shanidar 4 has a radial curvature index of 5.48, which is within the Neandertal range of variation and separate from those of more recent humans, but the radial curvature indices of Shanidar 1 and 6 (3.03 and 3.01, respectively) are below those of other Neandertals and within the range of means of recent human samples.

A less direct indication of radial curvature is the neck–shaft angle, as greater curvature will tend to produce a more lateral projection of the proximal radial diaphysis. The neck–shaft angles of Shanidar 1, 4, 6, and 8 are 13°, 15°,

TABLE 38
Measurements of the Radii (mm)

	Shanidar 1[h]	Shanidar 3	Shanidar 4[i]		Shanidar 5[j]	Shanidar 6[k]		Shanidar 8
	Left	Left	Right	Left	Right	Right	Left	Right
Maximum length (M-1)	(248.5)	—		(238.0)	(229.0)	(217.5)		—
Articular length (M-2)	(235.5)	—		(225.0)	(218.5)	(206.5)		—
Dorsovolar diameter (M-5)	11.0	—	14.0	11.2	10.5	9.8	9.3	9.3
Mediolateral diameter (M-4)	15.5	—	17.1	16.0	18.1	15.9	15.2	14.0
Circumference (M-5[5])	41.5	—	48.0	43.0	45.0	39.0	39.5	36.3
Midshaft dorsovolar diameter[a]	11.1	—	12.5	11.6	—	—	9.3	10.0
Midshaft mediolateral diameter[a]	14.5	—	15.0	15.1	—	12.6	13.1	13.3
Midshaft circumference[a]	40.0	—	43.0	41.5	—	—	35.0	37.0
Proximal dorsovolar diameter[b]	12.0	—	—	12.2	10.7	(10.0)	10.0	10.0
Proximal mediolateral diameter[b]	13.0	—	—	13.2	11.8	11.0	11.6	10.8
Proximal circumference[b]	40.5	—	—	40.0	36.5	(34.0)	33.0	35.0
Minimum circumference (M-3)	39.0	39.8	—	(41.5)	36.5	—	33.5	—
Head-neck length (M-1a)	34.0	25.0	—	31.0	—	33.4	—	30.6
Head dorsovolar diameter (M-5[1])	23.2	—	—	22.1	—	20.0	19.0	18.2
Head mediolateral diameter (M-4[1])	22.1		22.5	21.2	—	—	18.7	18.2
Head circumference (M-5[3])	72.0	(78.0)	—	69.0	—	—	60.0	59.0
Neck dorsovolar diameter (M-5[2])	12.8	13.1	—	13.7	—	10.4	9.4	11.3
Neck mediolateral diameter (M-4[2])	10.2	10.9	—	11.0	—	9.7	9.9	9.7

Neck circumference (M-5[4])	39.5	39.0	—	42.0	—	31.5	34.0	35.0
Radial tuberosity length[c]	26.0	26.0	—	24.4	—	22.7	—	23.4
Radial tuberosity breadth[c]	10.6	13.2	—	11.5	—	13.3	—	10.6
Neck-shaft angle (M-7)	13°	—	—	15°	—	17°	—	15°
Distal maximum breadth (M-5[6])	—	—	—	36.0	31.3	—	31.4	—
Distal maximum depth[d]	—	—	—	24.8	21.6	—	21.2	—
Distal articular breadth[e]	—	—	—	28.0	28.2	—	26.6	—
Distal articular depth[f]	—	—	—	15.3	17.0	—	17.9	—
Lateral curvature chord (M-6)	175.0	—	155.0	—	—	—	139.5	—
Lateral curvatuve subtense[g]	5.3	—	8.5	—	—	—	4.2	—

[a]Diameters and circumference measured at the midpoint of the diaphysis.

[b]Diameters and circumference measured midway between the radial tuberosity and the proximal end of the interosseus crest.

[c]Maximum proximodistal and transverse diameters of the *M. biceps brachii* tendon insertion area.

[d]Maximum dorsoventral diameter of the distal epiphysis.

[e]Maximum mediolateral diameter of the carpal articular surface.

[f]Maximum dorsoventral diameter of the carpal articular surface.

[g]Maximum subtense from the lateral curvature chord to the lateral surface of the radial diaphysis.

[h]Maximum length of the Shanidar 1 left radius has been estimated from its articular length using a least squares regression based on recent human radii ($r = 0.994$).

[i]The maximum and articular lengths of the Shanidar 4 radii were estimated by aligning the left distal epiphysis and diaphysis with the largely complete right proximal end and diaphysis.

[j]The articular length of the Shanidar 5 radius was estimated from the articular length of his right ulna using a least squares regression based on recent human paired radii and ulnae ($r = 0.950$); the maximum length of the Shanidar 5 radius was then estimated from its articular length using a least squares regression based on recent human radii ($r = 0.994$).

[k]The lengths of the Shanidar 6 radii have been estimated by aligning the largely complete right proximal radius with the complete diaphysis and distal epiphysis of the left radius.

Figure 50 Diaphyseal cross sections of the radii of Shanidar 1 (1L), Shanidar 4 (4L), Shanidar 5 (5R), Shanidar 6 (6L), and Shanidar 8 (8R), taken at the point of maximum projection of the interosseus crest. Anterior (volar) is above, and the cross sections are viewed in a proximal–distal direction.

17°, and 15°, respectively. These values are similar to those of other Neandertals (Tabūn C1: 15°; European Neandertals: 14.3° ± 1.3°, N = 11), which in turn are similar to the means of some more recent human samples (Skhūl–Qafzeh hominids: 10.5° ± 3.4°, N = 4; Early Upper Paleolithic hominids: 13.0° ± 2.3°, N = 7; recent Europeans: 8.7° ± 3.2°, N = 26 [Fischer 1906]; recent Melanesians: 14.0° ± 4.7°, N = 18 [Fischer 1906]). These angles suggest that the Shanidar radii are no more curved than those of most other Neandertals, which are not very different from those of more recent humans. Radial curvature indices, however, provide a more accurate quantitative assessment of radial lateral convexity, especially given the difficulties inherent in determining the midline axes of radial necks and proximal diaphyses.

Pronounced curvature of the radial diaphysis is an adaptation for powerful rotation of the forearm, especially pronation. Increased curvature moves the radial attachments of M. pronator quadratus and M. pronator teres laterally relative to the axis of rotation for pronation and supination, which runs through the radial and ulnar heads (Youm et al. 1979). It thus increases the mechanical advantages for M. pronator quadratus and M. pronator teres. The marked radial curvature of most Neandertal radii, and especially that of Shanidar 4, correlates with the exceptional development of the tuberosity for M. pronator quadratus on their ulnae. The lesser degree of radial curvature of Shanidar 1 and 6 suggests that this complex was not especially developed on them, an inference that is supported by the modest size of the M. pronator quadratus tuberosity on the Shanidar 6 left ulna.

Five Shanidar individuals preserve largely complete proximal epiphyses, including the head, neck, and radial tuberosity (Figures 44 and 48). Although their morphologies are within the ranges of variation of more recent humans, there are several aspects of their proportions that appear to be characteristic of the Neandertals.

Even though the Shanidar 3 and 4 humeri, but not those of Shanidar 1 and 6, exhibit a relative enlargement of their cubital articulations (see previous discussion), there is little difference between the relative head sizes of the Shanidar 1, 4, and 6 radii and those of more recent humans. The proximal articular indices (head dorsovolar diameter/articular length) of the Shanidar 1, 4, and 6 radii (ca. 9.85, ca. 9.42, and ca. 9.44, respectively) are similar to those of recent humans (Europeans: 9.87 ± 0.66, N = 50; Amerindians: 9.32 ± 0.53, N = 50), an early anatomically modern sample (9.24 ± 0.53, N = 5) and Tabūn C1 (9.33). A European Neandertal sample, however, has a rather wide range for this index (9.50–11.05, 10.32 ± 0.57, N = 6), and its mean is slightly above those of the Shanidar radii and more recent human samples.

The Shanidar radii and those of most other Neandertals give the impression of having small necks compared to their heads. The index formed from the ratio of their head and neck dorsovolar diameters, however, does not separate them from more recent humans. These indices are 55.1, 52.4, 64.6, 52.0 & 49.5, and 62.1 for Shanidar 1, 3, 4, 6, and 8, respectively. Those of Shanidar 1, 3, and 6 fall within a Neandertal range of variation (50.5–61.7, N = 13; Tabūn C1: 50.5, European Neandertals: 56.1 ± 3.5, N = 12), whereas those of Shanidar 4 and 8 are slightly higher. Early anatomically modern humans tend to have higher indices (63.1 ± 6.0, N = 6), but recent human samples vary with respect to this feature (Europeans: 56.1 ± 4.4, N = 26; Melanesians: 65.8 ± 5.5 [Fischer 1906]).

The impression of a constriction of the Shanidar radial necks may be a product in part of the medial projection of their radial tuberosities. Rather than projecting anteromedially, as do the radial tuberosities of most recent humans, the radial tuberosities of the Shanidar and other Neandertal radii project primarily medially, when the radii are oriented according to the interosseus crest and distal epiphysis (Figures 44 and 48). The significance of this pattern is uncertain, but it may be an adaptation to increase the moment arm of *M. biceps brachii* during supination. *M. biceps brachii* provides much of the power during supination (Travill and Basmajian 1961), and the more medial placement of the tuberosity would increase the moment arm between the *M. biceps brachii* tendon and the pronation–supination rotational axis through the middle of the radial neck (Youm *et al.* 1979).

Many Neandertal radii have relatively long head–neck lengths, as is indicated by the ratio of their head–neck lengths to their articular lengths. This ratio, expressed as a percentage, has a mean of 16.4 (± 1.1, N = 6) for a sample of European Neandertals; this index, however, is only 14.2 for Tabūn C1. The same ratio is somewhat less for samples of early anatomically modern humans (14.3 ± 0.8, N = 4) and recent humans (Europeans: 14.8 ± 0.8, N = 26; Melanesians: 13.6 ± 1.0, N = 16 [Fischer 1906]). Shanidar 6, similar to the European Neandertals, has a high ratio (ca. 16.3), indicating a relatively long head–neck length. However, Shanidar 1 and 4 have lower ratios (ca. 14.4 and ca. 13.8, respectively), which are in the middle of more recent human ranges of variation and similar to that of Tabūn C1.

It is not possible to compute this ratio for Shanidar 3 or 8, as neither one retains enough of its radii or ulnae to provide an accurate length estimate. However, their head–neck lengths (39.8 and 30.6 mm, respectively) are at either end of the Neandertal range of variation (Tabūn C1: 30.0 mm; European

Neandertals: 32.6–38.2 mm, N = 6). Because the Shanidar 3 humeral total length (ca. 314.5 mm) is well within the Neandertal range of variation (Tabūn C1: 284.5 mm; European Neandertals: 283.0–333.0 mm, N = 7), this suggests that Shanidar 3 probably had a relatively long radial head–neck length. It is not possible to assess, even indirectly, the relative length of the Shanidar 8 head and neck, but its small dimension and Shanidar 8's overall size similarity to Shanidar 6 suggest that it was probably relatively, as well as absolutely, short.

The length of the radial head and neck reflects the length of the moment arm for M. biceps brachii during flexion around the cubital joint (the full moment arm would include the head– neck length plus one-half the diameter of the humeral capitulum), whereas the articular length of the radius approximates the load arm relative to the elbow for objects held in the hand. A long head–neck length relative to the articular length of the radius therefore indicates an increased mechanical advantage for M. biceps brachii, one of the primary muscles used in elbow flexion (Basmajian 1974). Shanidar 6 and the majority of the other Neandertals appear to have had this increase in the mechanical advantage of M. biceps brachii as compared to more recent humans, even though Shanidar 1 and 4 do not exhibit the same accentuation.

There are no features of note on the Shanidar distal radial epiphyses. They are morphologically similar to those of other Neandertals and recent humans in their articular morphology and musculoligamentous markings.

In sum, the Shanidar radii are variable but nonetheless are similar to those of other Neandertals in most features. They exhibit the moderate diaphyseal robusticity and teardrop-shaped diaphyseal cross sections of other Neandertals, although there is considerable variation in lateral diaphyseal convexity and development of the interosseus crest. They all have, or appear to have, medially oriented radial tuberosities, and at least Shanidar 6 had the M. biceps brachii moment arm elongation characteristic of the Neandertals. The variation is as much within as between the earlier and later Shanidar subsamples.

HAND REMAINS

Inventory

OS SCAPHOIDEUM

Shanidar 3

Right Complete with minimal damage to the tuberosity. Maximum length = 27.6 mm.

Left Complete radial, capitular, and lunate articular surfaces, but the trapezium and trapezoid articulations and the tuberosity are absent. Maximum length = 19.0 mm.

Shanidar 4

> *Right*   Largely complete with damage to the radial distal margin. Maximum
>   length = 24.0 mm.
> *Left*   Intact, with exostoses on margins. Maximum length = 26.1 mm.

Shanidar 6

> *Right*   Complete bone. Maximum length = 22.0 mm.

Shanidar 8

> *Right*   Complete bone. Maximum length = 23.6 mm.

OS LUNATUM

Shanidar 3

> *Right*   Largely complete with some restoration of the dorsal distal edge.
>   Maximum breadth = 16.7 mm.
> *Left*   Complete bone. Maximum breadth = 17.8 mm.

Shanidar 4

> *Right*   Complete bone. Maximum breadth = 14.0 mm.

OS TRIQUETRUM

Shanidar 4

> *Left*   Complete bone, with exostoses on most surfaces. Maximum length =
>   17.7 mm.

Shanidar 5

> *Right*   Complete bone with abrasion on the palmar ulnar edge. Maximum
>   length = 15.9 mm.

Shanidar 6

> *Left*   Complete bone. Maximum length = 14.0 mm.

OS PISIFORM

Shanidar 4

> *Left*   Complete bone, with exostoses. Maximum length = 17.8 mm.

Shanidar 5

> *Right*   Complete bone. Maximum length = 14.0 mm.

OS TRAPEZIUM

Shanidar 3

> *Right*   Complete with minimal damage to the edges. Maximum breadth = 25.1 mm.

Shanidar 4

> *Right*   Largely present, but lacking the tubercle and the palmar margin of the metacarpal 1 surface. Maximum breadth = 24.8 mm.
> *Left*   Complete bone. Maximum breadth = 24.9 mm.

OS TRAPEZOIDEUM

Shanidar 4

> *Left*   Complete bone. Maximum dimension (dorsopalmar) = 18.5 mm.

OS CAPITATUM

Shanidar 4

> *Left*   Complete bone. Maximum length = 22.0 mm.

OS HAMATUM

Shanidar 3

> *Right*   The bone is complete on the radial side, but it lacks all of the ulnar side and the dorsal margin. Maximum length = 19.9 mm.

Shanidar 4

> *Left*   Complete bone. Maximum length = 20.5 mm.

Shanidar 5

> *Right*   Complete bone. Maximum length = 23.3 mm.

OS METACARPALE 1

Shanidar 4

Right Distal diaphysis and complete head. Maximum length = 27.9 mm.
Left Complete bone. Maximum length = 44.0 mm.

OS METACARPALE 2

Shanidar 3

Left Radial three-quarters of the head with the radial and dorsal surfaces of the distal diaphysis. Maximum length = 45.8 mm.

Shanidar 4

Right Incomplete diaphysis and separate fragments. Maximum length = 40.6 mm.
Left Complete base and diaphysis. Maximum length = 66.6 mm.

Shanidar 5

Right Complete bone. Maximum length = 68.8 mm.

Shanidar 6

Left Complete base and diaphysis. Minor damage to the palmar base. Maximum length = 48.1 mm.

OS METACARPALE 3

Shanidar 1

Left Complete diaphysis lacking the base and head. Maximum length = 39.8 mm.

Shanidar 3

Right Incomplete diaphysis with a complete midshaft cross section and the beginning of the proximoradial tubercles. Maximum length = 37.3 mm.

Shanidar 4

Right Complete base and proximal two-thirds of the diaphysis. Maximum length = 43.3 mm.
Left Complete bone. Maximum length = 66.8 mm.

Shanidar 6

> *Left* Complete bone with minor abrasion to the palmar base. Maximum
> length = 60.1 mm.

OS METACARPALE 4

Shanidar 1

> *Left* Complete diaphysis lacking the base and head. Maximum length =
> 33.4 mm.

Shanidar 3

> *Side Indeterminate* Left half of the head. Maximum length = 22.0 mm.

Shanidar 4

> *Right* Proximal half of the diaphysis. Maximum length = 29.2 mm.
> *Left* Complete bone with damage to the base. Maximum length = 56.6 mm.

Shanidar 5

> *Right* Complete bone. Maximum length = 56.4 mm.

Shanidar 6

> *Left* Diaphysis lacking the base and the head. Maximum length = 40.4
> mm.

OS METACARPALE 5

Shanidar 1

> *Left* Diaphysis lacking the base and the head. Maximum length = 32.9
> mm.

Shanidar 3

> *Left* Diaphyseal fragment with most of the distal two-thirds of the di-
> aphysis (maximum length = 30.9 mm), and an almost complete distal
> articulation (maximum height = 15.7 mm).

Shanidar 4

> *Right* Complete bone with damage to the ulnar side of the head. Maximum
> length = 52.2 mm.
> *Left* Complete base and diaphysis lacking the head. Maximum length =
> 43.0 mm.

Shanidar 5

   Right   Complete bone. Maximum length = 50.9 mm.

Shanidar 6

   Right   Largely complete diaphysis with the ulnar distopalmar tubercle.
        Maximum length = 31.3 mm.
   Left   Complete diaphysis and head. Maximum length = 39.7 mm.

PHALANX PROXIMALIS 1

Shanidar 4

   Right   Complete bone. Maximum length = 30.0 mm.
   Left   Complete bone. Maximum length = 30.1 mm.

Shanidar 5

   Right   Complete bone. Maximum length = 31.0 mm.

Shanidar 6

   Left   Complete bone. Maximum length = 29.8 mm.

PHALANX PROXIMALIS 2

Shanidar 3

   Left?   Distal half of the diaphysis and the complete head. Maximum length
        = 27.9 mm.

Shanidar 4

   Left   Complete bone. Maximum length = 39.4 mm.

PHALANX PROXIMALIS 3

Shanidar 3

   Left   Complete bone. Maximum length = 46.7.

Shanidar 4

   Right   Complete bone. Maximum length = 41.4 mm.
   Left   Complete bone. Maximum length = 42.5 mm.

Shanidar 6

> *Right*   Distal two-thirds of the diaphysis and the complete head. Maximum
>   length = 30.5 mm.
> *Left*   Complete bone. Maximum length = 38.1 mm.

PHALANX PROXIMALIS 4

Shanidar 3

> *Left*   Distal three-quarters of the diaphysis and the complete head. Max-
>   imum length = 33.1 mm.

Shanidar 4

> *Left*   Complete bone. Maximum length = 38.7 mm.

PHALANX PROXIMALIS 5

Shanidar 4

> *Right*   Complete bone with damage to the base. Maximum length = 32.9
>   mm.
> *Left*   Complete bone. Maximum length = 33.2 mm.

Shanidar 5

> *Right*   Complete bone. Maximum length = 33.9 mm.

PHALANX MEDIA 2

Shanidar 4

> *Right*   Complete bone. Maximum length = 27.5 mm.

Shanidar 6

> *Right*   Complete diaphysis and head. Maximum length = 17.5 mm.

PHALANX MEDIA 3

Shanidar 3

> *Side Indeterminate*   Complete bone. Maximum length = 28.9 mm.
> *Side indeterminate*   Complete bone. Maximum length = 29.4 mm.

Shanidar 4

> *Right*   Complete bone. Maximum length = 28.1 mm.

Left   Largely complete bone, lacking only the radial side of the distal half of the bone. Maximum length = 28.4 mm.

Shanidar 5

Right   Complete bone. Maximum length = 28.8 mm.

Shanidar 6

Right   Complete bone with damage to the radial corner of the base. Maximum length = 22.5 mm.
Left   Complete bone. Maximum length = 22.5 mm.

PHALANX MEDIA 4

Shanidar 3

Left?   Complete bone. Maximum length = 22.6 mm.

Shanidar 4

Left   Complete bone. Maximum length = 25.2 mm.

Shanidar 5

Right   Complete bone. Maximum length = 23.8 mm.

PHALANX MEDIA 5

Shanidar 3

Left?   Complete bone. Maximum length = 20.6 mm.

Shanidar 4

Right   Complete bone with abrasion of the base. Maximum length = 19.8 mm.
Left   Complete bone. Maximum length = 19.4 mm.

Shanidar 6

Left   Complete bone. Maximum length = 17.8 mm.

PHALANX DISTALIS 1

Shanidar 3

Left   Complete bone. Maximum length = 25.8 mm.

Shanidar 4

   Right   Complete bone. Maximum length = 25.5 mm.
   Left   Complete bone. Maximum length = 25.9 mm.

Shanidar 5

   Right   Complete bone. Maximum length = 25.5 mm.

Shanidar 6

   Left   Complete bone. Maximum length = 24.1 mm.

PHALANGES DISTALES 2–5

Shanidar 3

   3?: Side Indeterminate   Complete bone. Maximum length = 19.0 mm.
   5: Side Indeterminate   Complete bone. Maximum length = 18.6 mm.

Shanidar 4

   3?: Left?   Complete bone. Maximum length = 23.0 mm.
   4?: Left?   Complete bone. Maximum length = 18.8 mm.
   5: Side Indeterminate   Distal diaphysis with a slightly abraded tuberosity.
      Maximum length = 11.1 mm.

Shanidar 5

   2?: Right   Complete bone with damage to the radial side of the tuberosity.
      Maximum length = 20.9 mm.
   3?: Right   Complete bone. Maximum length = 21.6 mm.

Shanidar 6

   2?: Left?   Complete bone. Maximum length = 19.9 mm.

Hand Remains by Individual		
Right[a]	Indeterminate[a]	Left[a]
SHANIDAR 1		
		(Metacarpal 3)
		(Metacarpal 4)
		(Metacarpal 5)

Hand Remains by Individual (*continued*)

Right[a]	Indeterminate[a]	Left[a]
SHANIDAR 3		
Scaphoid		(Scaphoid)
Lunate		Lunate
Trapezium		
(Hamate)		
(Metacarpal 3)		(Metacarpal 2)
	(Metacarpal 4)	
		(Metacarpal 5)
		(Proximal phalanx 2)
		Proximal phalanx 3
		(Proximal phalanx 4)
Middle phalanx 3		Middle phalanx 3
		Middle phalanx 4
		Middle phalanx 5
		Distal phalanx 1
	Distal phalanx 3?	
	Distal phalanx 5	
SHANIDAR 4		
Scaphoid		Scaphoid
Lunate		Triquetral
(Trapezium)		Pisiform
		Trapezium
		Trapezoideum
		Capitate
		Hamate
(Metacarpal 1)		Metacarpal 1
(Metacarpal 2)		(Metacarpal 2)
(Metacarpal 3)		Metacarpal 3
(Metacarpal 4)		Metacarpal 4
Metacarpal 5		(Metacarpal 5)
Proximal phalanx 1		Proximal phalanx 1
		Proximal phalanx 2
Proximal phalanx 3		Proximal phalanx 3
		Proximal phalanx 4
Proximal phalanx 5		Proximal phalanx 5
Middle phalanx 2		
Middle phalanx 3		(Middle phalanx 3)
		Middle phalanx 4
Middle phalanx 5		Middle phalanx 5
Distal phalanx 1		Distal phalanx 1
		Distal phalanx 3?
		Distal phalanx 4?
	Distal phalanx 5	

(continued)

Hand Remains by Individual (continued)

Right[a]	Indeterminate[a]	Left[a]
SHANIDAR 5		
Triquetrum		
Pisiform		
Hamate		
Metacarpal 2		
Metacarpal 4		
Metacarpal 5		
Proximal phalanx 1		
Proximal phalanx 5		
Middle phalanx 3		
Middle phalanx 4		
Distal phalanx 1		
Distal phalanx 2?		
Distal phalanx 3?		
SHANIDAR 6		
Scaphoid		Triquetrum
		(Metacarpal 2)
		Metacarpal 3
		(Metacarpal 4)
(Metacarpal 5)		(Metacarpal 5)
		Proximal phalanx 1
(Proximal phalanx 3)		Proximal phalanx 3
(Middle phalanx 2)		
Middle phalanx 3		Middle phalanx 3
		Middle phalanx 5
		Distal phalanx 1
		Distal phalanx 2?
SHANIDAR 8		
Scaphoid		

[a]Bones in parentheses are missing major portions. The other bones are largely complete but they may have sustained minor damage.

Morphology

The Shanidar sample is remarkable in the extent to which hand bones have been preserved. Shanidar 1, 3, 4, 5, 6, and 8 retain part of at least one hand, and Shanidar 3, 4, 5, and 6 preserve sufficient portions of their hands to indicate overall proportions (figures 51–54). In fact, Shanidar 4 has the most complete hand skeleton known for a non–anatomically modern fossil hominid; its left hand lacks only the lunate and one ulnar distal phalanx, and the less complete right hand preserves the lunate. For almost every carpal, metacarpal, and phalanx, the Shanidar sample adds significantly to the Neandertal sample.

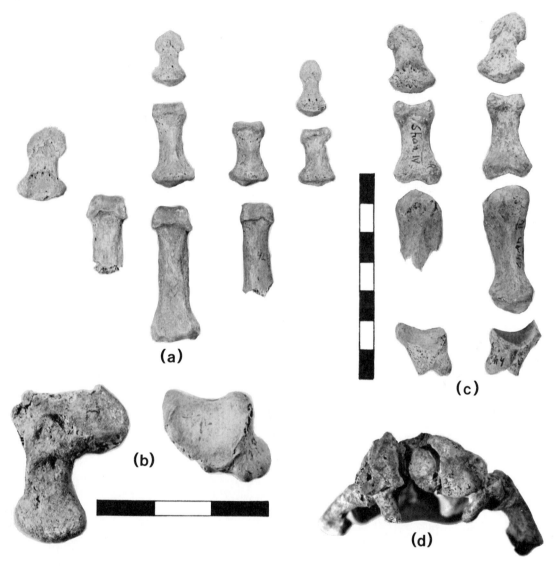

Figure 51 Shanidar 3 and 4 hand remains. (a) Palmar view of the Shanidar 3 phalanges, most of which are from the left hand. (b) Radial view of the right hamate bone (left) and distal view of the right trapezium (left) of Shanidar 3. (c) Palmar view of the Shanidar 4 right and left pollical remains. (d) Proximal view of the Shanidar 4 carpometacarpal skeleton, showing the enlargement of the carpal tunnel (the abnormal triquetral and pisiform are not included in the reconstruction). Scales in centimeters.

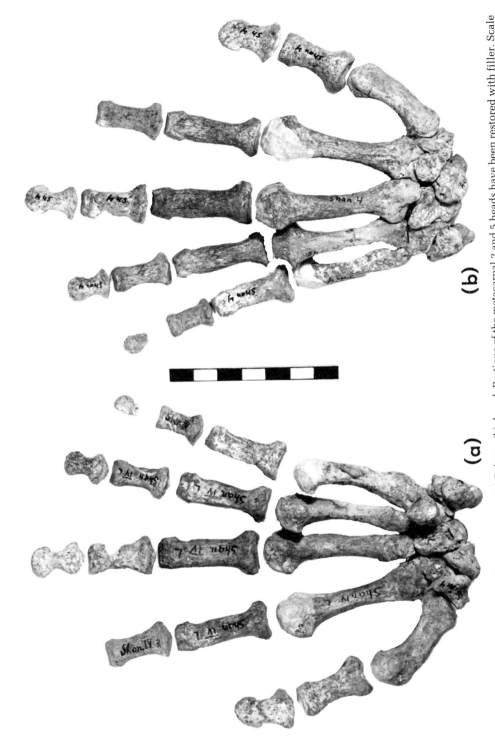

Figure 52 The Shanidar 4 left hand remains. (a) Palmar, (b) dorsal. Portions of the metacarpal 2 and 5 heads have been restored with filler. Scale in centimeters.

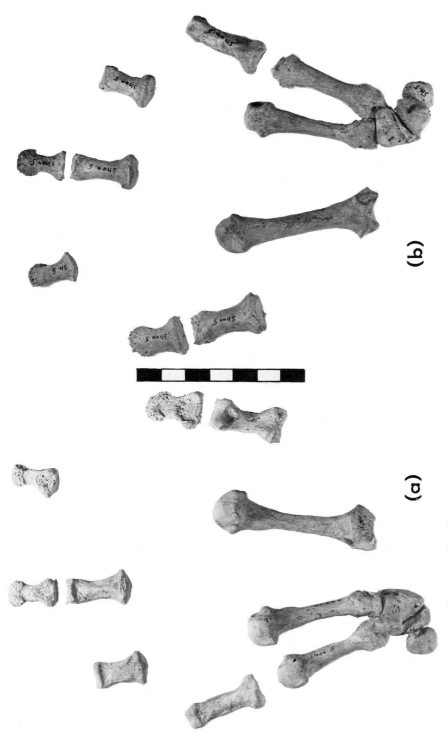

(b)

(a)

Figure 53 The Shanidar 5 right hand remains. (a) Palmar, (b) dorsal. Scale in centimeters.

261

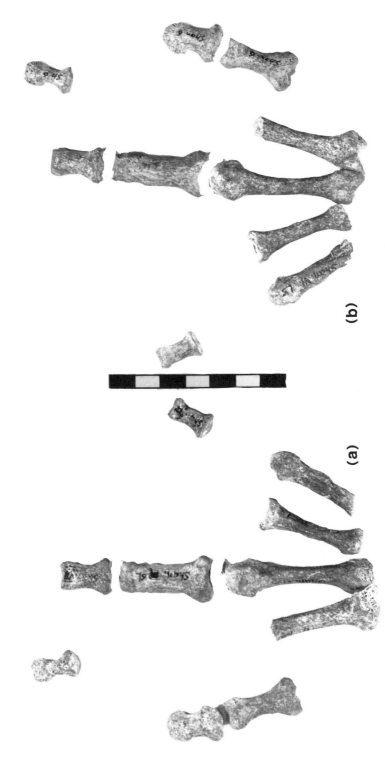

(b)

(a)

Figure 54 The Shanidar 6 left hand remains. (a) Palmar, (b) dorsal. Scale in centimeters.

The sorting of the Shanidar hand bones has presented few difficulties. There are no problems associated with the identification of the carpals, meta-carpals, and thumb phalanges that are sufficiently complete to provide mor-phological data. The sorting of the other phalanges as to digit and side has been done on the basis of relative size and morphology. The proximal phalanges of the four ulnar digits have distinctive base morphologies that permit their iden-tification as to digit (Landsmeer 1955). However, the diaphyses and heads of the proximal phalanges and all of the middle and distal phalanges have less distinctive morphologies and must be sorted largely on the basis of size.

The phalanges of the Shanidar 3 and 5 hand skeletons presented little difficulty in the determination of their digit numbers, but several of the side determinations for the Shanidar 3 phalanges are open to question. Because all the Shanidar 5 hand bones that are identifiable as to side are from the right hand, it is assumed that all of his phalanges also derive from the right hand.

The Shanidar 4, 6, and 8 hand bones, as with all of their other remains, were mixed *in situ*, and it has been necessary to sort the bones into individuals as well as digits and sides. The sorting of most of the carpals, metacarpals, and thumb phalanges by individual was straightforward because the Shanidar 4 hand bones are usually much larger than those of Shanidar 6. It is assumed that all of the smaller hand bones belong to Shanidar 6 except for the extra right scaphoid bone, which is assigned to Shanidar 8. It may be that some of the Shanidar 6 hand bones in fact came from Shanidar 8. The phalanges of the Shanidar 4 and 6 ulnar digits were sorted on the basis of size and morphology so as to provide the most reasonable arrangement. It is possible that some of the phalanges have been misidentified, but it is unlikely that any of the possible misidentifications will affect the interpretation of the Shanidar hand remains.

Recent years have seen the completion of a number of studies on Neandertal hand bones (e.g., Endo and Kimura 1970; Heim 1972, 1974; Kimura 1976; Musgrave 1970; Stoner 1981; Stoner and Trinkaus 1981; Vlček 1975), which have expanded greatly upon the previous descriptions of Neandertal hand bones (e.g., Bonć-Osmolovskij 1941; Boule 1911–1913; Gorjanović-Kramberger 1906; McCown and Keith 1939; Sarasin 1932). These studies have painted a picture of Neandertal hand morphology that appears to apply to most of the known Neandertal hand bones. The Shanidar hand bones largely follow the same morphological patterns.

RELATIVE HAND SIZE

It is possible to estimate the sizes of the Shanidar 4 and 6 hands relative to the lengths of their arms. Assuming that the length of the third metacarpal is representative of overall hand size, as it appears to be for most higher primates (Schultz 1930), the articular lengths of the Shanidar 4 and 6 third metacarpals have been compared to the summed articular lengths of their humeri and radii. This comparison provides indices of about 11.7 and about 11.6, respectively,

TABLE 39

Measurements of the Scaphoid Bones (mm)

	Shanidar 3		Shanidar 4		Shanidar 6	Shanidar 8
	Right	Left	Right	Left	Right	Left
Maximum length (M-1)	27.6	—	24.0	(26.0)	21.7	23.6
Maximum thickness[a]	17.1	—	(15.2)	16.4	13.9	14.7
Minimum thickness[b]	3.9	4.0	4.1	4.0	3.9	3.3
Radial articular length (M-4)	19.0	—	15.1	(13.5)	14.0	14.4
Radial articular height (M-5)	16.5	15.8	12.1	12.6	11.7	12.2
Capitate articular length (M-6)	16.0	—	(17.8)	17.9	15.6	15.8
Capitate articular height (M-7)	12.3	12.0	12.1	11.3	10.7	11.3
Capitate articular depth (M-8)	3.7	—	(3.8)	3.9	2.7	3.5
Tubercle projection[c]	13.5	—	(12.7)	13.4	11.3	11.3
Trapezium–trapezoid facet fusion	absent	—	(present)	present	present	present

[a]Maximum thickness across the radial margins of the radial and capitate articular surfaces.
[b]Minimum thickness across the midulnar margins of the radial and capitate articular surfaces.
[c]The direct measurement from the radial margin of the capitate articulation to the most radial point on the tubercle.

for Shanidar 4 and 6. These values are slightly lower than those of other Neandertals (La Ferrassie 1: 12.2; La Ferrassie 2: 12.4; Régourdou 1: 13.0; Tabūn C1:
12.3). However, all of the Neandertal indices are within the ranges of variation
of recent humans (Europeans: 11.9 ± 0.5, N = 11; Amerindians: 11.7 ± 0.5, N =
19), even though that of Régourdou 1 is relatively high. The Shanidar 4 and 6
hands are therefore similar to those of other Neandertals and recent humans in
overall size relative to arm length.

CARPALS

The four proximal carpals of the Shanidar Neandertals, the scaphoid, lunate, triquetral, and pisiform bones, are similar to those of more recent humans
in overall proportions and articular morphology (Tables 39–42). They appear
relatively large and robust, but they do not exceed the limits of more recent
human ranges of variation (Sarasin 1932). The only feature of note on them is
the development of the tubercle on the scaphoid. The tubercle projection measurements of the Shanidar scaphoid bones (13.5, ca. 12.7 & 13.4, 11.3, and 11.3
mm for Shanidar 3, 4, 6, and 8, respectively), and especially those of Shanidar 3
and 4, are toward the upper limits of the range of variation of a small Neandertal sample (Amud 1: 14.5 mm; La Ferrassie 1: 11.2 mm; La Ferrassie 2: 8.0 mm;
Régourdou 1: 11.2 & 11.0 mm); most of these Neandertal measurements are well
above the values for recent humans (Europeans: 8.0 ± 1.4 mm, N = 20; Amerindians: 9.0 ± 1.6 mm, N = 20 [Stoner 1981]). The tubercle of the scaphoid bone
provides part of the attachment for the flexor retinaculum, and its hypertrophy
among the Shanidar Neandertals implies a well-developed carpal tunnel. Further evidence for this interpretation is provided by their trapezia and hamate
bones.

TABLE 40
Measurements of the Lunate Bones (mm)

	Shanidar 3		Shanidar 4
	Right	Left	Right
Maximum length (M-1)	—	13.6	12.4
Maximum breadth (M-2)	17.3	18.0	14.0
Maximum depth (M-3)	—	19.9	16.0
Radial articular height (M-10)	—	18.0	14.5
Radial articular breadth (M-11)	16.8	17.8	14.0
Distal articular height (M-6)	—	14.3	12.5
Distal articular breadth (M-7)	11.6	13.0	10.3
Capitate articular breadth (M-7a)	—	6.7	7.3
Hamate articular breadth (M-7b)	—	6.3	3.0
Distal articular depth (M-12)	—	4.0	3.9
Triquetral articular height (M-8)	—	10.4	12.1
Triquetral articular breadth (M-9)	8.9	9.6	8.1

TABLE 41
Measurements of the Triquetral Bones (mm)

	Shanidar 4	Shanidar 5	Shanidar 6
	Left	Right	Left
Maximum length (M-1)	17.6	(16.5)	14.0
Maximum height (M-3)	p16.3	12.8	11.2
Hamate articular breadth (M-4)	15.2	14.6	12.2
Hamate articular height (M-5)	p8.9	9.7	8.8
Lunate articular breadth (M-6)	p8.0	7.9	6.4
Lunate articular height (M-7)	p11.5	10.8	9.5
Pisiform articular length (M-9)	10.2	—	6.4
Pisiform articular breadth (M-8)	7.8	(5.5)	5.2

Note: p = specimen altered by pathology.

In the intercarpal articulations of these and the distal row of carpals, the trapezium, trapezoid, capitate, and hamate bones are likewise similar to those of more recent humans, especially given the amount of variation present in detailed aspects of carpal articulations among recent humans (Pfitzner 1900). It is not possible to determine the degree of movement present between their carpals from the bones themselves.

The primary feature of note on the distal carpals is the hypertrophy of their processes for the attachment of the flexor retinaculum and the intrinsic flexor muscles of the hand, the tubercle of the trapezium and the hamulus (Tables 43 and 46).

The tubercles on the trapezia of Shanidar 3 and especially Shanidar 4 are prominent, relatively wide, and quite long, absolutely and relative to the size of the bones. The approximate cross-sectional areas of their tubercles (length $\times$ thickness of the tubercle) are 53.6 mm² and 83.2 & 94.0 mm² for Shanidar 3 and 4, respectively. These values are similar to those of other Neandertals (La

TABLE 42
Measurements of the Pisiform Bones

	Shanidar 4	Shanidar 5
	Left	Right
Maximum length (M-1)	p17.3	14.0
Maximum breadth (M-2)	p12.8	11.5
Maximum height (M-3)	p11.0	8.8
Triquetral articular length (M-5)	9.9	8.7
Triquetral articular breadth (M-4)	9.0	7.8

Note: p = specimen altered by pathology.

TABLE 43
Measurements of the Trapezium Bones (mm)

	Shanidar 3	Shanidar 4	
	Right	Right	Left
Maximum thickness[a]	14.5	15.9	16.0
Minimum thickness[b]	10.6	4.5	4.6
Dorsal breadth[c]	17.5	19.1	19.2
Maximum breadth[d]	24.9	25.0	25.0
Metacarpal articular breadth (M-4)	14.6	14.4	14.9
Metacarpal breadth subtense[e]	+2.2	—	+2.5
Metacarpal articular height (M-5)	13.0	—	10.8
Metacarpal height subtense[e]	−1.6	—	−0.6
Tubercle length[f]	11.4	14.6	16.2
Tubercle thickness[g]	4.7	5.7	5.8
Tubercle projection[h]	4.4	6.3	6.3

[a]Maximum distance across the ulnar margins of the scaphoid and metacarpal 1 articulations.

[b]Minimum distance across the radial margins of the scaphoid and metacarpal 1 articulations.

[c]Direct distance across the radial and ulnar margins, respectively, of the radial and ulnar dorsal ligamentous tubercles.

[d]Maximum distance from the metacarpal 2 articular facet to the most radial point on the tubercle.

[e]The maximum subtense from the chords formed by the metacarpal articular height and breadth to the metacarpal 1 articular facet. + = concave arc; − = convex arc.

[f]Maximum proximodistal dimension of the tubercle.

[g]Maximum radioulnar dimension of the tubercle.

[h]Maximum distance from the palmar surface of the tubercle to the floor of the sulcus for the M. flexor carpi radialis tendon on the ulnar side of the tubercle.

Ferrassie 2: 49.2 mm^2; Kiik-Koba 1: 113.5 mm^2; Régourdou 1: 98.0 mm^2) and above those of Qafzeh 9 (41.4 mm^2), Skhūl 5 (ca. 36.0 mm^2) and most recent humans (Europeans: 44.1 ± 9.3 mm^2, N = 20; Amerindians: 35.8 ± 6.7 mm^2, N = 20 [Stoner 1981]). An index of trapezial tubercle projection (tubercle projec-

TABLE 44
Measurements of the Shanidar 4 Left
Trapezoid Bone (mm)

Maximum length (M-1)	14.2
Maximum breadth (M-2)	13.0
Maximum height (M-3)	18.9
Metacarpal maximum breadth (M-10c)	11.9
Metacarpal minimum breadth (M-10b)	7.6
Metacarpal articular height (M-11c)	14.3
Scaphoid articular breadth (M-4)	9.6
Scaphoid articular height (M-5)	14.9
Trapezium articular breadth (M-6)	12.8
Trapezium articular height (M-7)	12.4

TABLE 45
Measurements of the Shanidar 4 Left Capitate
Bone (mm)

Articular length (M-4)	21.8
Maximum breadth (M-2)	16.8
Maximum height (M-3)	21.7
Proximal articular height (M-6)	p(17.2)
Proximal articular breadth (M-5)	11.0
Metacarpal articular height (M-7)	17.6
Metacarpal articular breadth (M-8)	15.5
Hamate–metacarpal 4 facet fusion	Absent

Note: p = specimen altered by pathology.

tion/metacarpal articular breadth; as an indicator of overall size of the bone) provides a similar distribution. Shanidar 3, with an index of 30.1, is close to the means of recent human samples (Europeans: 27.3 ± 5.0, N = 20; Amerindians: 22.6 ± 4.2, N = 20 [Stoner 1981]), whereas the indices of Shanidar 4 (43.8 & 42.3) and other Neandertals (La Ferrassie 1: 57.1; La Ferrassie 2: 52.8; Kiik-Koba 1: 54.8; Régourdou 1: 51.5) are considerably higher. Qafzeh 9 and Skhūl 5 have indices of 16.9 and about 17.1, respectively. These data indicate that Shanidar 4, the other Neandertals, and, to a lesser extent, Shanidar 3 have large and relatively projecting trapezial tubercles.

All three of the Shanidar Neandertals that preserve largely complete hamate bones, Shanidar 3, 4, and 5, have exceptionally large hamulae. The palmar ends

TABLE 46
Measurements of the Hamate Bones (mm)

	Shanidar 3	Shanidar 4	Shanidar 5
	Right	Left	Right
Articular length (M-1)	(18.5)	16.4	17.7
Maximum height (M-3)	(28.5)	28.2	25.2
Metacarpal articular height (M-7)	—	13.6	11.1
Metacarpal articular breadth (M-8)	—	15.3	15.3
Maximum capitate articular length (M-9)	10.9	16.7	17.7
Minimum capitate articular length[a]	10.4	12.6	10.5
Capitate articular height (M-10)	—	10.9	9.7
Triquetral articular length (M-11)	—	17.7	17.9
Triquetral articular height (M-12)	—	9.2	9.2
Hamulus length[b]	12.6	12.5	11.5
Hamulus thickness[c]	(6.3)	7.0	6.5
Hamulus projection (M-5)	13.6	12.9	10.9

[a]Proximodistal length of the main facet for the capitate bone.
[b]Maximum proximodistal dimension of the hamulus.
[c]Maximum radioulnar dimension of the hamulus.

of their hamulae are round and bulbous. Their approximate cross-sectional areas (hamulus length × thickness) are 79.4, 87.5, and 74.8 mm², respectively, all of which are at the upper end of a Neandertal range of variation (Amud 1: 98.0 mm²; La Ferrassie 2: 57.8 mm²; Régourdou 1: 82.8 mm²; Tabūn C1: 52.8 mm²). The dimensions of the Shanidar hamulae and those of Amud 1 and Régourdou 1 are well above the mean of a recent human sample (40.2 ± 9.2 mm², N = 23) and those of Qafzeh 8 and 9 (54.5 mm², and 54.5 & 53.5 mm², respectively). The hamulus projection indices (hamulus projection/maximum height of the hamate bone) of Shanidar 3, 4, and 5 (ca. 47.7, 45.7, and 43.3, respectively) are similarly above those of most more recent humans (Caviglione 1: 39.2; Qafzeh 8: ca. 36.9; Qafzeh 9: 40.5; recent humans: 36.3 ± 4.0, N = 23), as are those of other Neandertals (Amud 1: 45.4; La Ferrassie 2: 43.8; Régourdou 1: 43.0; Tabūn C1: 48.1). Shanidar 3, 4, and 5 therefore had relatively large and projecting hamulae.

The large sizes of the palmar tuberosities of the Shanidar scaphoid, trapezium, and hamate bones imply a hypertrophy of their flexor muscles. These processes provide attachment areas for the flexor retinaculum, which prevents bowstringing of the *M. flexor digitorum superficialis* and *M. flexor digitorum profundus* tendons and also provides attachment area for some of the intrinsic muscles of the hand. The large dimensions of the tips of these processes among the Shanidar Neandertals imply a strongly built flexor retinaculum for each of them. These processes also serve as origins for most of the intrinsic thenar and hypothenar musculature, as part of *M. abductor pollicis brevis* originates on the scaphoid tubercle, parts of *M. abductor pollicis brevis*, *M. opponens pollicis*, and *M. flexor pollicis brevis* originate on the trapezial tubercle, and *M. flexor digit minimi* and *M. opponens digiti minimi* originate on the hamulus. Not only do the large dimensions of these process reflect enlargements of the origins for these muscles, but the palmar projections of the processes increase the moment arms for the muscles around the carpometacarpal articulations. And finally, the noticeable projection of these processes (Figure 51) creates large carpal tunnels, which are probably related to the hypertrophy of the extrinsic digital flexors indicated by the Shanidar phalanges.

THE POLLEX

There are only four Neandertals that preserve all four bones of the thumb, and Shanidar 4 is one of those four (the others are La Ferrassie 1 and 2 and Régourdou 1). In addition, Shanidar 5 and 6 retain both phalanges of one thumb each, and Shanidar 3 preserves his trapezium and distal pollical phalanx (Tables 47–49).

Contrary to early claims (e.g., Boule 1911–1913; Sarasin 1932), Neandertal thumbs are neither absolutely nor relatively short. The Shanidar 4 first metacarpal length (43.3 mm) is similar to those of other Neandertals (Amud 1: 47.8 mm; Tabūn C1: 39.3 mm; European Neandertals: 43.5 ± 2.1 mm, N = 5) and

TABLE 47
Measurements of the Shanidar 4 First Metacarpals (mm)

	Right	Left
Articular length	—	43.3
Midshaft height	—	9.0
Midshaft breadth	—	12.6
Midshaft circumference	—	33.0
Maximum shaft breadth	15.3	15.2
Minimum shaft height	—	9.0
Minimum shaft breadth	—	10.7
Minimum shaft circumference	—	32.0
Proximal maximum height	—	16.1
Proximal maximum breadth	—	15.9
Proximal articular height	—	12.9
Proximal articular breadth	—	14.6
Articular height chord[a]	—	11.1
Articular height subtense[b]	—	0.0
Articular breadth chord[a]	—	12.4
Articular breadth subtense[b]	—	−3.1
Distal height	12.3	12.9
Distal maximum breadth	16.7	17.4
Distal articular breadth	13.8	14.2

[a]Chords used for determining the curvatures of the carpal surface in dorsopalmar and radioulnar directions. The chords are slightly smaller than the articular dimensions because the articular height and breadth include all of the subchondral bone, whereas the chords include only that subchondral bone involved in the primary articular curvature of the surface.
[b]The maximum subtenses from the chords to the middle of the carpal surface. − = convex arc.

recent humans (Europeans: 44.5 ± 2.7 mm, N = 20; Amerindians: 42.0 ± 2.7 mm, N = 20 [Stoner 1981]). The ratio of first metacarpal length to third metacarpal length (used as an indicator of ulnar digit size), expressed as a percentage, is similarly virtually the same for Shanidar 4 (70.0), other Neandertals (La Ferrassie 1: 67.2; La Ferrassie 2: 68.9; Régourdou 1: 68.0; Tabūn C1: 64.6), early anatomically modern humans (68.0 ± 2.5, N = 10), and recent humans (Europeans: 68.9 ± 3.2, N = 17; Europeans: 68.8 ± 3.1, N = 37; Amerindians: 68.8 ± 2.9, N = 19 [Stoner and Trinkaus 1981; Musgrave, personal communication, 1974]).

A similar pattern is seen when the summed lengths of the Shanidar 4 and other Neandertal pollical phalanges are compared to their first metacarpal lengths. The index formed by this comparison is 119.4 for Shanidar 4, which is similar to those of other Neandertals (La Ferrassie 1: 119.9 & 116.2; La Ferrassie 2: 115.2; Régourdou 1: 115.8). All of these indices fall within the ranges of variation of early anatomically modern humans (118.2 ± 4.9, N = 9), and recent humans (Europeans: 114.5 ± 3.1, N = 20; Europeans: 118.7 ± 5.1, N = 37; Amerindians: 111.9 ± 5.1, N = 20 [Stoner 1981; Musgrave, personal commu-

TABLE 48
Measurements of the First Proximal Phalanges of the Hand (mm)

	Shanidar 4		Shanidar 5	Shanidar 6
	Right	Left	Right	Left
Articular length	27.0	27.0	23.9	26.2
Midshaft height (M-3)	8.0	7.7	6.9	6.7
Midshaft breadth (M-2)	10.2	10.2	9.3	8.1
Midshaft circumference	28.0	28.5	27.0	24.0
Proximal maximum height	12.0	12.3	12.2	11.2
Proximal maximum breadth	17.3	17.7	17.0	15.9
Proximal articular height	10.1	10.1	10.1	10.0
Proximal articular breadth	12.6	13.0	12.9	11.5
Distal height	8.0	8.4	8.7	7.6
Distal maximum breadth	13.9	13.7	13.2	12.5
Distal articular breadth	13.5	13.3	13.0	12.3
Horizontal angle[a]	0°	0°	3°	0°

[a]The angle in the horizontal plane of the bone (coronal plane in anatomical position) between the transverse plane of the metacarpal surface and the transverse plane of the phalangeal surface. A positive angle indicates a radial deviation of the phalangeal surface.

TABLE 49
Measurements of the First Distal Phalanges of the Hand (mm)

	Shanidar 3	Shanidar 4		Shanidar 5	Shanidar 6
	Left	Right	Left	Right	Left
Articular length	23.7	24.2	24.7	24.3	23.6
Midshaft height	5.5	5.0	4.8	5.1	5.2
Midshaft breadth	9.9	10.0	9.9	9.7	9.0
Midshaft circumference	26.5	25.0	26.0	25.0	25.0
Proximal maximum height	10.8	9.1	9.6	9.3	8.5
Proximal maximum breadth	17.3	16.6	17.1	15.9	15.9
Proximal articular height	8.1	6.9	7.1	7.2	7.4
Proximal articular breadth	14.7	12.4	13.3	13.0	12.2
Distal height	3.8	4.0	4.2	4.3	4.5
Distal breadth	14.0	12.8	13.0	12.5	12.6
Flexor pit length[a]	8.8	10.2	10.4	9.1	8.4
Flexor pit breadth[a]	11.0	11.4	11.3	10.2	10.9
Flexor pit depth[a]	2.4	(1.7)	2.0	2.1	1.8
Horizontal angle[b]	84°	85°	80°	86°	85°

[a]Dimensions of the M. flexor pollicis longus tendon pit. The length and breadth are the proximodistal and radioulnar dimensions, respectively, of the tendon insertion area. The depth is measured from the proximal palmar tubercles to the deepest point on the tendon insertion area.

[b]The angle, measured in the horizontal plane of the bone (the coronal plane when in anatomical position), between the radioulnar transverse plane of the interphalangeal articulation and the proximodistal axis of the bone. An angle less than 90° indicates an ulnar deviation of the distal phalanx.

nication, 1974]). Clearly the overall proportions of the Shanidar 4 and other Neandertal thumbs are indistinguishable from those of more recent humans.

Despite these similarities in overall pollical proportions, the Shanidar and other Neandertals appear to have relatively long distal pollical phalanges and proportionately shorter proximal pollical phalanges. The ratio of the distal to proximal phalangeal lengths, expressed as a percentage, is 89.6 & 91.5, 101.7, and 90.1, respectively, for Shanidar 4, 5, and 6. These values are similar to those of other Neandertals (La Ferrassie 1: 89.3 & 85.2; La Ferrassie 2: 84.3; Régourdou 1: 102.1), but all of them are at or beyond the upper limits of the ranges of variation of early anatomically modern humans (66.9 ± 5.1, N = 9), and recent humans (Europeans: 74.9 ± 5.1, N = 20; Europeans: 75.8 ± 4.7, N = 37; Amerindians: 71.0 ± 3.5, N = 20 [Stoner 1981; Musgrave, personal communication, 1974]).

Phalangeal proportions of this nature would tend to increase the load arm between the interphalangeal joint and the finger tip and tend to decrease the load arm between the interphalangeal region and the metacarpophalangeal articulation. These would, in turn, decrease the effectiveness of the *M. flexor pollicis longus* when grasping objects at the finger tip and increase the effectiveness of the short thenar muscles (*M. flexor pollicis brevis, M. abductor pollicis* and *M. adductor pollicis*) when grasping larger objects with the whole thumb. Interestingly, the Shanidar 3, 4, 5, and 6 distal pollical phalanges all have extremely large insertions for their *M. flexor pollicis longus* tendons (Table 49; Figures 51–54), as do those of other Neandertals. This implies an exceptional development of this muscle, which may be a partial compensation for the elongation of their distal phalanges.

Shanidar 4 retains both the carpal and metacarpal surfaces of its left first carpometacarpal articulation, and Shanidar 3 preserves its right trapezium. Because it is primarily, although not exclusively, patterns of movement at the first carpometacarpal joint that permit human manipulative abilities, the configurations of these joint surfaces may have a direct bearing on the inferred manipulative abilities of the Shanidar Neandertals.

The carpal surface of the Shanidar 4 first metacarpal is evenly curved radioulnarly but it is straight dorsopalmarly. Among recent humans and most other anthropoids, this surface is radioulnarly convex and dorsopalmarly concave, extremely so in some anthropoids, and appears saddle shaped.

The cylindrical shape of the Shanidar 4 first metacarpal carpal surface is not unique, since La Ferrassie 2 has a similarly shaped first metacarpal surface. In addition, two Neandertals, La Chapelle-aux-Saints 1 and Kiik-Koba 1, have first metacarpal carpal surfaces that are convex both radioulnarly and dorsopalmarly. If the degree of dorsopalmar curvature of the articular surface is quantified using the index formed from the maximum subtense to the surface from its articular height chord divided by the articular height chord (a positive index indicates a concave surface), the Neandertals appear highly variable in their articular morphology (Amud 1: 4.7, European Neandertals: −9.7–8.2, 0.5

± 6.8, N = 6). All of them, however, are close to or below the lower limits of recent human ranges of variation (Europeans: 11.5 ± 2.0, N = 20; Amerindians: 11.4 ± 2.5, N = 20 [Stoner 1981]). Shanidar 4, with an index of 0.0, falls in the middle of the Neandertal range of variation and completely separate from the recent humans in this feature. The Shanidar 4 first metacarpal, therefore, along with those of most other Neandertals, has a carpal surface that is exceptionally flat dorsopalmarly. Interestingly, Qafzeh 9 and Skhūl 5 have relatively low indices (ca. 4.9 and 6.6, respectively).

The Shanidar 3 and 4 trapezia have saddle-shaped metacarpal surfaces that are radioulnarly concave and dorsopalmarly convex. Their general surface configurations are therefore similar to those of more recent humans. Yet their articulations are less curved than those of most recent humans. A similar dorsopalmar articular curvature index provides values of 12.3 and 5.6 for Shanidar 3 and 4, respectively (a positive index indicates a dorsopalmarly convex surface in this case), which are toward the lower limits of recent human ranges of variation (Europeans: 18.8 ± 6.9, N = 20; Amerindians: 20.7 ± 3.9, N = 20 [Stoner 1981]). Other Neandertal trapezia have relatively flat metacarpal surfaces as well (La Ferrassie 1: 13.9; La Ferrassie 2: 9.6; Kiik-Koba 1: 5.4; Régourdou 1: 14.5), but those of Qafzeh 9 (23.0) and Skhūl 5 (25.6) are highly curved.

This minimal development of a double saddle-shaped first carpometacarpal articulation among the Neandertals has suggested to others (e.g., Bonć-Osmolovskij 1941; Musgrave 1971; Vlček 1975) that the Neandertals lacked a full precision grip. Because Shanidar 4, and possibly Shanidar 3, lacked a full double saddle-shaped joint, this interpretation would imply that they too lacked full recent human manipulative abilities. Functional considerations, however, suggest the opposite. It is the deep, interlocking double-saddle articulation seen in African pongids and the Hadar australopithecines—AL333-58, AL333-80, and AL33w-39 (Bush et al. 1982)—that restricts rotational movement and hence fine manipulative abilities. The relatively open configuration of the Shanidar and other Neandertal first carpometacarpal articulations should indicate a greater range of thumb mobility than that commonly seen among recent humans (Cooney and Chao 1977; Kapandji 1972).

It has been suggested (Musgrave 1971) that Neandertal distal pollical phalanges deviate markedly ulnarly, and those of Shanidar 3, 4, 5, and 6 appear to do so (Figures 51–54). However, if one measures the angle of deviation (the angle between the midshaft axis and the transverse plane of the interphalangeal articulation), the Shanidar 3, 4, 5, and 6 angles (84°, 85° & 80°, 86°, and 85°, respectively) are little different from those of recent humans (Europeans: 84.4° ± 1.2°, N = 20; Amerindians: 86.2° ± 1.1°, N = 20 [Stoner 1981]) and early anatomically modern humans (Caviglione 1: 88°; Qafzeh 8: 88°; Qafzeh 9: 89°). Furthermore, the ulnar deviation angles of European Neandertal distal pollical phalanges (83.4° ± 2.3°, N = 8) are little different from those of the Shanidar and recent human phalanges.

Numerous investigators (e.g., Kimura 1976; Musgrave 1971; Sarasin 1932;

Vlček 1975, 1978) have remarked on the exceptional development among the Neandertals of the crest for the insertion of *M. opponens pollicis* on the distal radial margin of the first metacarpal. The Shanidar 4 left first metacarpal is no exception to this pattern (Figure 51). Beginning about midshaft, the dorsoradial margin of the diaphysis extends increasingly radially as one goes distally to the head. The radial margin of this crest is slightly roughened and curls slightly palmarly to receive the spread-out fibers of the *M. opponens pollicis*. Not only does this crest imply a large and powerful muscle, but it also increases the moment arm for the *M. opponens pollicis* relative to the longitudinal axis of the first metacarpal. Contrary to Vlček (1978), the morphology of the *M. opponens pollicis* insertions on the Shanidar 4 and other Neandertal first metacarpals is fully compatible with a flat and broad muscle, similar to those of recent humans.

The development of this crest can be indicated by the opponens pollicis index (maximum [distal] shaft breadth/minimum [proximal] shaft breadth). This index is 142.1 for Shanidar 4, which is virtually the same as a European Neandertal mean (142.6 ± 16.6, N = 5) and slightly above those of Amud 1 (134.8) and Tabūn C1 (136.0). It is well above those of recent humans (Europeans: 111.3 ± 6.1, N = 20; Amerindians: 114.5 ± 10.0, N = 20 [Stoner and Trinkaus 1981]). Qafzeh 9 (122.9) and Skhūl 5 (136.5) fall between the Neandertal and recent human means.

The large size of the *M. opponens pollicis* crests on the Shanidar 4 first metacarpals gives the impression that their heads are markedly asymmetrical. The actual articular surfaces for the proximal phalanges are evenly curved, although the processes for the radial sesamoid bones give the impression that the surface is obliquely oriented. None of the Shanidar pollical sesamoid bones survives, but the size of the surfaces for them on the Shanidar 4 first metacarpal heads suggests that they were relatively large.

The Shanidar proximal pollical phalanges are similar to those of recent humans, as are those of other Neandertals. Their bases have moderately large musculoligamentous attachment areas around the metacarpal articular surface, which are primarily for the insertions of the short thenar muscles, *M. flexor pollicis brevis*, *M. adductor pollicis*, and *M. abductor pollicis*.

The most noticeable aspect of the Shanidar distal pollical phalanges, in addition to their elongation and large *M. flexor pollicis longus* tendon insertions, is the expansion of their tuberosities. The tuberosity provides attachment area and support for the pulp of the finger tip and the nail (Shrewsbury and Johnson 1975), so that an enlargement of the tuberosity would imply a hypertrophy of the whole grasping region of the distal finger. The breadths of the Shanidar 3, 4, 5, and 6 tuberosities (14.0, 12.8 & 13.0, 12.5, and 12.6 mm) are in the middle of the European Neandertal range of variation (12.6 ± 1.6 mm, N = 8) and above those of most early anatomically modern humans (10.5 ± 1.7 mm, N = 5) and recent humans (Europeans: 9.5 ± 1.3 mm, N = 20; Europeans: 10.7

TABLE 50
Measurements of the Second Metacarpals (mm)

	Shanidar 3	Shanidar 4		Shanidar 5	Shanidar 6
	Side indeterminate	Right	Left	Right	Left
Articular length	—	—	(62.8)	66.4	—
Midshaft height	—	9.6	9.4	9.2	8.0
Midshaft breadth	—	8.7	8.4	7.2	7.1
Midshaft circumference	—	30.5	29.5	27.5	24.0
Proximal maximum height	—	—	18.8	17.0	—
Proximal maximum breadth	—	—	17.7	18.6	17.0
Proximal articular height	—	—	16.7	15.2	—
Proximal articular breadth	—	—	12.0	9.8	12.1
Distal height	19.0	—	—	15.0	—
Distal maximum breadth	—	—	—	15.6	—
Distal articular breadth	—	—	—	13.7	—

± 1.4 mm, N = 37; Amerindians: 9.3 ± 1.0 mm, N = 20 [Stoner 1981; Musgrave, personal communication, 1974]).

All of these features of the Shanidar pollical bones indicate that they have thumbs that were capable of the same manipulative movements as recent humans but were characterized by the robustness that is found elsewhere on their upper limb skeletons. This robustness is evident in attachments for their thumb muscles and ligaments, especially the *M. opponens pollicis* on Shanidar 4, the *M. flexor pollicis longus* on Shanidar 3, 4, 5, and 6, and the fingertips of the same four individuals. This is the same pattern of robustness that is evident on their carpal bones, and it is also present on their four ulnar digits.

TABLE 51
Measurements of the Third Metacarpals

	Shanidar 1	Shanidar 3	Shanidar 4		Shanidar 6
	Left	Right	Right	Left	Left
Articular length	—	—	—	61.8	57.5
Midshaft height	6.7	10.0	9.5	9.2	8.2
Midshaft breadth	6.9	8.5	9.0	8.4	7.3
Midshaft circumference	23.5	30.0	30.5	29.0	24.5
Proximal maximum height	—	—	16.8	18.2	—
Proximal maximum breadth	—	—	15.3	16.8	14.0
Proximal articular height	—	—	(16.0)	14.8	—
Proximal articular breadth	—	—	—	14.0	12.3
Distal height	—	—	—	14.5	13.0
Distal maximum breadth	—	—	—	16.2	13.8
Distal articular breadth	—	—	—	13.4	11.5

TABLE 52
Measurements of the Fourth Metacarpals (mm)

	Shanidar 1	Shanidar 3	Shanidar 4		Shanidar 5	Shanidar 6
	Left	Side indet.	Right	Left	Right	Left
Articular length	—	—	—	56.0	56.1	—
Midshaft height	6.2	—	7.9	8.1	7.3	7.3
Midshaft breadth	5.5	—	7.1	6.9	6.5	6.7
Midshaft circumference	19.0	—	25.0	25.5	23.0	22.0
Proximal maximum height	—	—	—	13.3	12.1	—
Proximal maximum breadth	—	—	—	13.5	12.0	—
Proximal articular height	—	—	—	12.6	12.0	—
Proximal articular breadth	—	—	—	10.3	11.9	—
Distal height	—	17.4	—	14.3	13.5	—
Distal maximum breadth	—	—	—	15.6	14.0	—
Distal articular breadth	—	—	—	13.0	12.3	—

THE FOUR ULNAR DIGITS

There are at least two, and frequently three or four, examples of most of the ulnar metacarpals and phalanges from the Shanidar Neandertals. In addition to the virtually complete set of metacarpals and phalanges from digits 2–5 of the Shanidar 4 left hand, Shanidar 5 and 6 each preserve several complete examples of these bones, and Shanidar 1 and 3 retain less complete but still valuable ulnar metacarpals and phalanges (Tables 50–62).

The second to fifth carpometacarpal articulations are indistinguishable from those of more recent humans. The Shanidar 4 and 6 third metacarpals

TABLE 53
Measurements of the Fifth Metacarpals (mm)

	Shanidar 1	Shanidar 3	Shanidar 4		Shanidar 5	Shanidar 6	
	Left	Left	Right	Left	Right	Right	Left
Articular length	—	—	52.2	52.0	50.4	—	—
Midshaft height	5.6	7.8	7.2	7.5	6.0	6.1	6.4
Midshaft breadth	7.7	7.4	8.1	8.0	7.0	7.3	8.2
Midshaft circumference	23.0	25.0	24.5	27.0	20.5	22.0	21.5
Proximal maximum height	—	—	10.7	12.0	8.8	—	—
Proximal maximum breadth	—	—	11.0	13.0	12.9	—	—
Proximal articular height	—	—	9.1	9.4	7.7	—	—
Proximal articular breadth	—	—	9.2	8.8	8.9	—	—
Distal height	—	—	11.3	—	12.0	—	10.8
Distal maximum breadth	—	—	12.5	—	13.4	—	11.9
Distal articular breadth	—	—	9.6	—	11.4	—	9.5

TABLE 54
Measurements of the Second Proximal Phalanges of the Hand (mm)

	Shanidar 3	Shanidar 4
	Left?	Left
Articular length	—	38.0
Midshaft height	7.5	6.4
Midshaft breadth	11.0	10.0
Midshaft circumference	29.5	27.5
Proximal maximum height	—	12.8
Proximal maximum breadth	—	15.5
Proximal articular height	—	11.0
Proximal articular breadth	—	12.7
Distal height	8.9	7.1
Distal maximum breadth	14.9	12.4
Distal articular breadth	13.0	11.2

have large and prominent styloid processes, as do those of other Neandertals. The Shanidar 4 and 5 hamate bones have evenly curved surfaces for the fourth and fifth metacarpals, which are separated by a low ridge. There is little to suggest that the degree of movement at their ulnar carpometacarpal joints was any more or less than is common among recent humans.

All of the metacarpals from Shanidar, but especially the second and third metacarpals of Shanidar 4, have well-marked dorsal crests for the *Mm. interossei dorsales*. In addition, Shanidar 1, 3, 4, and 6 have prominent crests on the ulnar aspects of their fifth metacarpal diaphyses for the insertion of *M. opponens digiti minimi*; a similar crest is absent from the Shanidar 5 metacar-

TABLE 55
Measurements of the Third Proximal Phalanges of the Hand (mm)

	Shanidar 3	Shanidar 4		Shanidar 6	
	Left	Right	Left	Right	Left
Articular length	44.3	40.0	40.6	—	36.0
Midshaft height	8.0	6.9	7.2	6.8	6.5
Midshaft breadth	10.6	11.4	11.6	11.4	11.7
Midshaft circumference	30.0	32.0	31.5	30.0	31.5
Proximal maximum height	14.4	13.4	13.9	—	12.6
Proximal maximum breadth	18.0	16.8	17.8	—	18.6
Proximal articular height	13.0	10.6	10.5	—	11.7
Proximal articular breadth	15.3	15.0	14.3	—	13.8
Distal height	9.3	8.0	8.3	8.0	8.0
Distal maximum breadth	14.8	13.7	13.4	13.3	12.5
Distal articular breadth	12.6	11.9	12.3	12.0	12.0

TABLE 56
Measurements of the Fourth Proximal Phalanges of the Hand (mm)

	Shanidar 3	Shanidar 4
	Left	Left
Articular length	—	37.5
Midshaft height	7.2	6.3
Midshaft breadth	10.3	9.5
Midshaft circumference	29.5	27.0
Proximal maximum height	—	12.0
Proximal maximum breadth	—	14.0
Proximal articular height	—	9.6
Proximal articular breadth	—	12.2
Distal height	8.8	7.0
Distal maximum breadth	13.0	12.3
Distal articular breadth	11.5	11.0

pal 5. Crests for *M. opponens digiti minimi* are present the Amud 1 and Tabūn C1 fifth metacarpals and on 66.7% (*N* = 6) of the known European Neandertal fifth metacarpals. However, they are relatively rare among more recent humans. The presence of such a crest implies a strongly developed *M. opponens digiti minimi*, an interpretation that agrees with the size and projection of their hamulae.

The ulnar sides of the Shanidar 4 and 5 fifth metacarpals present large tuberosities for the insertion of *M. extensor carpi ulnaris*. These tuberosities extend both ulnarly from the carpal surface and distally along the diaphysis, implying well-developed insertions.

TABLE 57
Measurements of the Fifth Proximal Phalanges of the Hand (mm)

	Shanidar 4		Shanidar 5
	Right	Left	Right
Articular length	31.1	31.0	32.7
Midshaft height	5.5	5.4	5.6
Midshaft breadth	9.8	9.8	8.4
Midshaft circumference	25.0	24.5	22.0
Proximal maximum height	10.4	11.1	10.1
Proximal maximum breadth	14.9	15.8	14.0
Proximal articular height	8.7	9.1	9.5
Proximal articular breadth	(11.1)	11.5	10.5
Distal height	6.4	6.3	6.3
Distal maximum breadth	10.2	10.7	10.0
Distal articular breadth	9.2	10.1	9.4

TABLE 58
Measurements of the Second Middle Phalanges of the Hand (mm)

	Shanidar 4	Shanidar 6
	Right	Right
Articular length	26.7	—
Midshaft height	6.0	6.0
Midshaft breadth	9.4	9.7
Midshaft circumference	26.0	—
Proximal maximum height	10.7	—
Proximal maximum breadth	15.1	—
Proximal articular height	7.5	—
Proximal articular breadth	13.4	—
Distal height	5.6	6.0
Distal maximum breadth	11.9	12.5
Distal articular breadth	11.4	11.4

The only other feature of note on the bones of the Shanidar hand digits 2–5 is the expansion of their distal tuberosities, especially on their second and third digits (Figures 51–54). Their tuberosities, rather than being long, narrow, and slightly pointed, are almost circular when viewed palmarly or dorsally. This configuration is characteristic of Neandertal ulnar distal phalanges, but it is relatively rare among more recent humans.

Comparisons of the distal tuberosity breadths of the Shanidar, other Neandertal, and recent human ulnar distal phalanges that can be reasonably assigned to a digit (Table 63) illustrate the large size of the Shanidar distal tu-

TABLE 59
Measurements of the Third Middle Phalanges of the Hand (mm)

	Shanidar 3	Shanidar 3	Shanidar 4	Shanidar 4	Shanidar 5	Shanidar 6	Shanidar 6
	Side indeterminate	Side indeterminate	Right	Left	Right	Right	Left
Articular length	27.0	27.6	27.0	26.8	27.4	21.8	21.5
Midshaft height	6.2	7.1	6.4	6.5	5.7	6.4	6.0
Midshaft breadth	8.3	8.9	9.4	10.2	7.8	9.3	9.6
Midshaft circumference	23.0	23.5	27.5	28.0	21.0	26.5	24.5
Proximal maximum height	11.0	11.5	11.2	11.0	9.6	10.3	10.0
Proximal maximum breadth	14.8	15.3	16.3	16.0	14.5	—	14.7
Proximal articular height	8.3	8.9	7.9	7.0	7.0	8.0	7.5
Proximal articular breadth	13.4	13.7	13.2	13.0	12.6	—	12.7
Distal height	6.1	6.6	6.4	6.5	5.8	5.7	5.6
Distal maximum breadth	11.8	12.6	12.1	12.1	12.5	11.4	11.4
Distal articular breadth	10.8	11.4	11.5	11.3	10.9	11.0	10.6

TABLE 60
Measurements of the Fourth Middle Phalanges of the Hand (mm)

	Shanidar 3	Shanidar 4	Shanidar 5
	Left?	Left	Right
Articular length	21.1	24.8	22.7
Midshaft height	6.6	5.2	5.5
Midshaft breadth	8.3	8.6	8.3
Midshaft circumference	24.0	24.0	22.0
Proximal maximum height	10.9	9.4	9.3
Proximal maximum breadth	14.3	13.6	13.9
Proximal articular height	8.8	6.2	7.2
Proximal articular breadth	12.8	11.1	12.5
Distal height	6.0	5.4	5.6
Distal maximum breadth	12.0	10.9	11.1
Distal articular breadth	10.7	10.1	10.3

berosities. Their breadths are all within Neandertal ranges of variation and above those of most recent humans (the 14 isolated distal phalanges from other Neandertals, which can not be assigned reliably to a digit, follow the same pattern). The distal phalanges of early anatomically modern humans in Europe and the Near East all exhibit the reduced tuberosities seen in recent human hands (Matiegka 1938; McCown and Keith 1939; Musgrave 1970; Vandermeersch 1981a). This tuberosity expansion, as with the enlargement of the pollical distal tuberosity, is probably an adaptation for increased levels of stress across the fingertip. The larger bony process would provide increased attachment area for the pulp and nail and general greater strength to the distal finger.

TABLE 61
Measurements of the Fifth Middle Phalanges of the Hand (mm)

	Shanidar 3	Shanidar 4		Shanidar 6
	Left?	Right	Left	Left
Articular length	19.0	19.4	19.0	17.4
Midshaft height	5.6	5.0	4.8	4.1
Midshaft breadth	7.9	8.0	8.2	7.3
Midshaft circumference	21.5	22.5	22.0	20.0
Proximal maximum height	9.5	—	8.6	7.9
Proximal maximum breadth	13.0	—	11.8	10.9
Proximal articular height	8.3	—	6.6	5.5
Proximal articular breadth	11.3	—	10.0	9.4
Distal height	5.3	4.7	5.0	4.2
Distal maximum breadth	11.8	—	9.6	9.0
Distal articular breadth	10.0	—	9.2	8.6

TABLE 62
Measurements of the Second to Fifth Distal Hand Phalanges (mm)

	Shanidar 3		Shanidar 4			Shanidar 5		Shanidar 6
	3? Side indet.	5 Side indet.	3? Side indet.	4? Side indet.	5 Side indet.	2? Right	3? Right	2? Left
Articular length	17.6	18.1	21.5	17.4	—	20.3	21.2	19.3
Midshaft height	4.1	3.8	4.0	4.1	—	4.3	4.0	4.5
Midshaft breadth	6.7	5.3	7.0	7.4	—	6.7	6.8	5.6
Midshaft circumference	20.5	15.0	19.5	20.0	—	19.0	19.0	17.5
Proximal maximum height	7.6	6.6	7.1	7.1	—	7.0	(6.5)	6.2
Proximal maximum breadth	12.1	(12.0)	13.5	12.2	—	12.9	12.6	11.4
Proximal articular height	6.5	5.3	6.8	5.5	—	5.8	(6.2)	5.0
Proximal articular breadth	10.9	(9.2)	11.5	10.5	—	11.0	10.5	9.4
Distal height	3.2	3.7	4.5	3.7	3.6	4.7	5.0	4.6
Distal breadth	10.8	7.9	12.2	10.3	(8.5)	(9.4)	11.0	10.4

Summary of Hand Remains

The hand remains from Shanidar exhibit a pattern that is characteristic of Neandertal hand bones. They have overall proportions and implied ranges of movement similar to those of more recent humans, but they differ in a few special characteristics. There are two features for which the significance is not entirely apparent. These are the relative dorsopalmar flattening of the first carpometacarpal articulation and the more proximal positioning of the pollical interphalangeal articulation. These features may imply slightly different habit-

TABLE 63
Comparisons of Distal Tuberosity Breadths of Hand Phalanges (mm)

	Digit 2	Digit 3	Digit 4	Digit 5
Shanidar 3		10.8		7.9
Shanidar 4		12.2	10.3	(8.5)
Shanidar 5	(9.4)	11.0		
Shanidar 6	10.4			
Amud 1	(12.0)	(12.4)		
La Ferrassie 1	10.6	12.2	9.8	7.6
Kiik-Koba 1	(13.0)	13.8		
Krapina 206.12				7.3
Régourdou 1	9.8	10.0		
Recent Europeans X̄ ± SD	7.9 ± 1.0	8.7 ± 1.2	8.3 ± 1.2	6.5 ± 1.0
(Musgrave 1973) N	38	37	37	37

ual patterns of thumb movement, within the range of manipulative abilities known for recent humans.

All the other significant features of the Shanidar hand bones are related to the general robustness that characterizes their upper limbs. The palmar processes of the carpals are large, implying a deep carpal tunnel, strong attachments for the flexor retinaculum and the thenar and hypothenar muscles and long moment arms around the carpometacarpal joints for the thenar and hypothenar muscles. The muscular insertion areas on all of the digits, but especially the first and fifth digits, are very prominent, and all of the distal phalanges have large, rounded tuberosities.

SUMMARY

The upper limb remains of the Shanidar adults depict a morphological pattern that is close to that evidenced by other Near Eastern and European Neandertals. They had strongly built shoulders, arms, and hands with especially well-developed muscles for grasping and rotating the limb. This hypertrophy is evident in the tuberosities and crests for various muscles on their arm and hand bones and in the increased breadths and axillary border morphologies of their scapulae. In addition, several of them show small differences in the proportions of their bones or the orientations of muscular attachments that would have increased the efficiency during powerful grasping of large or heavy objects.

The only differences in upper limb articular morphology or orientation between the Shanidar adults and more recent humans involve the superoinferior elongation of the Shanidar 1 and 4 scapular glenoid fossae, the anterior orientation of the Shanidar 1, 4, 5, and 6 ulnar trochlear notches, and the dorsopalmar flattening of the Shanidar 3 and 4 first carpometacarpal articulations. The actual significances of these variations, all of which predominate among Neandertals, is uncertain, but they probably indicate slightly different habitual patterns of arm movement rather than any inherent differences in their manipulative abilities.

Despite the conformity of the Shanidar upper limb remains to a general Neandertal morphological pattern, there is considerable variation within the sample. Unlike the cranial variation, most of these differences appear to be reflections of individual within-population variation rather than trends through time among the occupants of Shanidar Cave. Some of the variation may be due to sexual dimorphism, although there is no consistent pattern in which the females are less robust than the males. It is also possible that the relative gracility of some of the Shanidar 1 upper limb bones may have been due to his incapacitated state (Chapter 12). Although the Shanidar 1 left arm does not appear to have been directly affected by the abnormalities of his right arm, legs, and cranium, the inactivity that he undoubtedly experienced for many of his later years may well have led to some atrophy of his otherwise normal left arm.

CHAPTER 9

The Lower Limb Remains

The lower limb bones that have been preserved for the Shanidar Neandertals are less complete that their upper limb remains. Most of the long bones consist of diaphyses with incomplete epiphyses, and most of the innominate bones and pedal remains have been extensively damaged. Yet three of the individuals—Shanidar 1, 5, and 6—retain sufficient portions of the femora, tibiae, and/or fibulae to permit reasonable estimates of the proximal and distal lower limb segments. Shanidar 1 and 3 retain significant portions of their pedal skeletons, and Shanidar 2 preserves a virtually complete left tibia and fibula. Added onto these more intact pieces are numerous smaller pieces that provide morphological data.

The innominate bones, femora, patellae, tibiae, and fibulae are described in that order, followed by a description of the pedal remains. Their osteometric data are provided in Tables 64–90.

INNOMINATE BONES

Inventory

SHANIDAR 1

Right   The right os coxae consists of four separate fragments: a pubic bone with the complete superior ramus and the inferior half of the symphysis (maximum height = 75.0 mm; maximum breadth = 88.2 mm), a portion of the ischium with the internal surface of the ischium, the ischial spine, and the region of the acetabular notch (maximum height

= 88.4 mm; maximum breadth = 50.5 mm), and two fragments of the ilium, the anterior inferior iliac spine (maximum height = 71.7 mm) and the crushed and distorted posterior half of the ilium with the auricular area, the iliac tuberosity, the superior border of the greater sciatic notch, and part of the blade (maximum height = 108.0 mm; maximum breadth = 129.0 mm).

Left   The left os coxae is less complete than the right one. The identifiable fragments entail: the pubis with the medial three-quarters of the superior ramus, the dorsal rim of the symphysis and the complete inferior ramus (maximum height = 83.4 mm; maximum breadth = 78.6 mm), the lateral margin of the acetabulum with the superior surface of the sciatic notch (maximum height = 79.2 mm; maximum breadth = 81.0 mm), a small piece of the iliac crest with a portion of the iliac pillar (maximum height = 114.1 mm, maximum breadth = 66.1 mm), several fragments of the ischial tuberosity, and the majority of the iliac tuberosity (maximum dimension = 89.0 mm).

SHANIDAR 3

Right   The bone consists of six identifiable pieces: (1) the iliac blade with 65 mm of the iliac crest including the tubercle, a small portion of the external surface, and the internal surface extending posteriorly from the crest to the anterior margins of the iliac tuberosity and auricular surface (maximum height = 93.5 mm, maximum breadth = 101.0 mm); (2) the iliac margin between the anterior superior and anterior inferior iliac spines with the beginnings of each spine (maximum height = 50.8 mm); (3) the anterior corner of the auricular surface with the adjacent surface bone of the greater sciatic notch (maximum length = 29.1 mm); (4) a portion of the ischium with the ischial spine, the posterior obturator foramen border, the intervening pelvic surface and the acetabular notch (maximum height = 84.0 mm; maximum breadth = 46.5 mm); (5) a portion of the ischiopubic ramus from near the symphysis to the ischial tuberosity (maximum length = 45.8 mm); (6) and the superior pubic ramus with the ventral surface intact from the acetabulum almost to the pubic tubercle with an anterior superior portion of the acetabulum, a medial section of the pectineal line, and the superior medial border of the obturator foramen (maximum length = 71.5 mm; maximum height = 36.0 mm).

Left   The left innominate bone retains: a fragment of the pelvic surface of the ischium with part of the posterior obturator foramen border (maximum height = 34.7 mm), the superior and ventral margins of the middle of the superior pubic ramus (maximum length = 38.7 mm), and part of the pelvic surface of the inferior pubic ramus with 16.5 mm of the inferior symphyseal surface (maximum length = 44.7 mm).

SHANIDAR 4

Right   The right os coxae consists of a fragment of the iliac crest (maximum
        breadth = 41.6 mm), the superior edge of the pubic symphysis with a
        portion of the superior ramus (maximum breadth = 32.4 mm), and
        several fragments of the iliac blade.
Left   The left os coxae is more complete than the right one. It consists of: a
        distorted portion of the iliac blade with most of the iliac crest in the
        region of the iliac pillar (maximum height = 103.3 mm; maximum
        breadth = 117.6 mm); the inferior ilium with the superior surface of the
        sciatic notch (maximum breadth = 102.0 mm); a crushed portion of the
        ischium with the acetabular surface and the superior half of the ischial
        tuberosity fused postmortem to the left femoral head (maximum height
        = 102.4 mm); and the superior pubic ramus (maximum length = 54.0
        mm).

SHANIDAR 5

Side Indeterminate   Several pieces of the iliac blade, of which two are
        substantial: a piece of the external iliac surface (maximum height =
        42.0 mm), and a piece of the iliac blade with internal and external
        surfaces preserved (maximum height = 39.3 mm).

SHANIDAR 6

Side Indeterminate   A small fragment of the posterior acetabular rim (max-
        imum dimension = 23.6 mm), and a separate portion of the acetabular
        rim with the anterior inferior iliac spine (maximum dimension = 26.6
        mm).

Morphology

Although five of the Shanidar adults retain portions of their innominate
bones, only Shanidar 1, 3, and 4 preserve sufficient portions of their os coxae to
provide morphological data. Yet even these three individuals preserve only
isolated pieces of their innominate bones that are too incomplete or abraded
along the breaks to be reassembled accurately. The only region that is relatively
undistorted and can be reconstructed reliably is the pubic bones of Shanidar 1
and 3. Some aspects of the Shanidar 1, 3, and 4 iliac morphologies and a few
features of the Shanidar 3 ischium can also be discerned.

Figure 55 The Shanidar 1 innominate bones. (a) Superior and ventral views of the right and
left pubic bones, with a cross section of the right superior pubic ramus viewed in a lateral–medial
direction (ventral is to the right). (b) Pelvic view of the right pubis and ischium, arranged approximately in their original position. Portions of both symphyses have been restored in plaster. Scale
in centimeters.

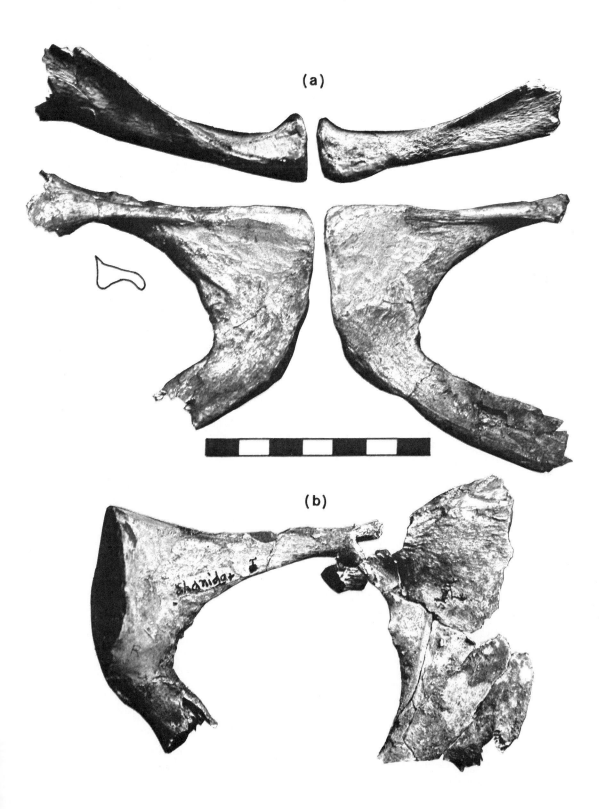

Largely complete superior pubic rami are preserved for Shanidar 1 and 3, and Shanidar 4 retains sections of both superior pubic rami (Figures 55–57; Table 64). Although portions of the Shanidar 1 pubic bones have been reconstructed, most of the restoration is in the region of the superomedial corner of the pubic symphysis. None of the pubic symphysis remains on the Shanidar 3 right pubic bone, so that the symphyseal region has been reconstructed. The subpubic angle was determined from a section of the left pubic bone that retains the inferior corner of the pubic symphysis, and the mediolateral breadth was estimated using the preserved morphology of the Shanidar 3 pubic bones and the dimensions of the Shanidar 1 pubic bones. It is possible that the mediolateral breadth of the Shanidar 3 symphyseal region (from the pubic symphysis to the medial margin of the obturator foramen) has been reconstructed too large, but it is unlikely that it was much less than that of the reconstruction. None of the pubic tubercle is preserved on the superior pubic ramus piece, so that all of it must have been accommodated in the missing portion. The orientation of the ischiopubic ramus piece has been determined by the left half of the subpubic angle and the dimensions of the right ischium.

The most striking feature of the Shanidar innominate bones is the configuration of their superior pubic rami. Shanidar 1 and 3 show a marked elongation of the superior pubic rami between the acetabulum and the pubic symphysis, and all three of them exhibit a superoinferior thinning of the ventral margin of the ramus (Stewart 1960, 1963; Trinkaus 1976b). Associated with this pubic elongation is an enlargement of their obturator foramina and an increase in their subpubic angles.

The acetabulosymphyseal lengths of Shanidar 1 and 3 (ca. 93.0 and 80.0–90.0 mm, respectively) are slightly below the only other Neandertal male for which this dimension can be determined (La Ferrassie 1: 98.0 mm) and slightly above the value of the only Neandertal female that provides this measurement (Tabūn C1: 79.5 mm). All of these measurements are well above the means of recent human males (Near Easterners: 67.7 ± 5.5 mm, N = 19; Amerindians: 67.2 ± 4.1 mm, N = 41), and even most females (Near Easterners: 70.4 ± 5.8 mm, N = 15; Amerindians: 69.6 ± 4.5 mm, N = 40). When an index is formed from the ratio of the acetabulosymphyseal length to the femoral bicondylar length (as an indicator of body size), the differences remain. This ratio is about 20.3 for Shanidar 1. If the mean estimate of 85.0 mm is used for the acetabulosymphyseal length of Shanidar 3 and his femoral bicondylar length is estimated from his humeral maximum length using a least squares regression based on other Neandertals (r = 0.873, N = 7) to be about 438.5 mm, this index is about 19.4 for Shanidar 3. (An estimate of 80.0 mm for the acetabulosymphyseal length would decrease the index to ca. 18.2.) These index estimates are similar to those of La Ferrassie 1 (ca. 21.4) and Tabūn C1 (ca. 19.4). However, they are above those of recent human males (Near Easterners: 15.1 ± 1.0, N = 19; Amerindians: 15.9 ± 1.0, N = 50 [Trinkaus 1976b] and at the upper limits of recent human female ranges of variation (Near Easterners: 16.8 ± 1.3, N = 15; Amerindians: 17.8 ± 1.1, N = 50 [Trinkaus 1976b]).

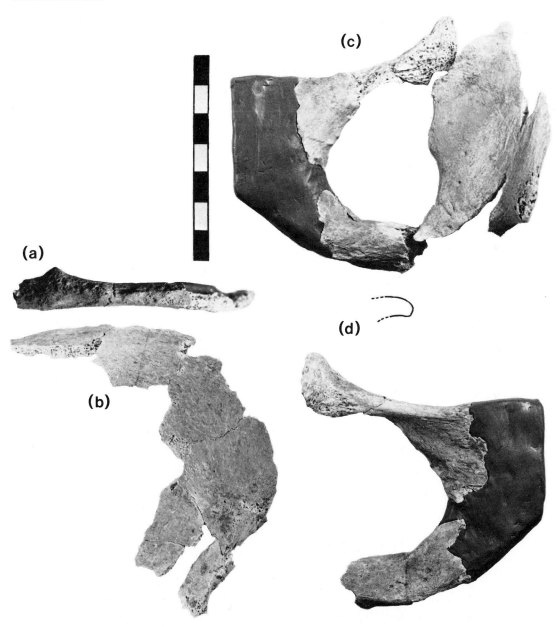

Figure 56 The Shanidar 3 right innominate bone. (a) Superior and (b) medial views of the ilium, showing the minimal development of the iliac tubercle. (c) Dorsal (pelvic) view of the pubis and ischium. (d) Ventral view of the pubis, with the midramal cross section of the superior pubic ramus. The mediolateral breadth of the symphyseal region was estimated from the preserved morphology of the superior ramus and the dimensions of the Shanidar 1 pubic bones. The orientation of the ischiopubic ramus was determined from the dimensions of the ischial fragments and the subpubic angle estimated from the left inferior pubic fragment. In the cross section, ventral is to the right. Scale in centimeters.

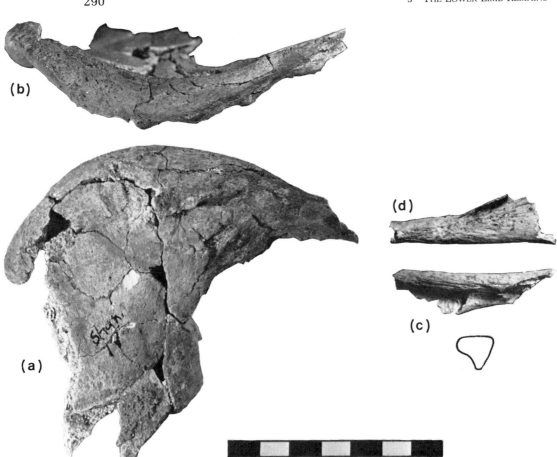

Figure 57   The Shanidar 4 left innominate bone. (a) Lateral and (b) superior views of the iliac piece, showing the development of the iliac pillar and tubercle. (c) Ventral and (d) superior views of the superior pubic ramus fragment, with the midramal cross section viewed in a lateral–medial direction (ventral is to the left). Scale in centimeters.

Associated with this mediolateral pubic elongation among the Shanidar Neandertals is a marked superoinferior thinning of the ventral margin of the superior pubic ramus. Rather than having a ventral margin that thickens steadily from the pubic tubercle to the acetabulum, the Shanidar pubic bones have ventral margins that remain thin and parallel sided along most of their rami. The superoinferior thicknesses of the Shanidar ventral margins (Shanidar 1: 5.3 & 5.0 mm; Shanidar 3: 6.5 & 6.8 mm; Shanidar 4: 7.8 mm) are similar to those of Amud 1 (♂; 5.5 mm) and Krapina 208 (♀; 7.5 mm), greater than that of Tabūn C1 (♀; 3.5 mm), and slightly less than those of La Ferrassie 1 (♂; 10.2 & 8.5 mm). All of these thicknesses except those of La Ferrassie 1 are below the ventral thicknesses of a recent Amerindian sample (males: 11.3 ± 1.5 mm, N =

TABLE 64
Measurements of the Innominate Bones (mm)

	Shanidar 1		Shanidar 3		Shanidar 4
	Right	Left	Right	Left	Left
Acetabulosciatic breadth[a]	—	33.0	—	—	—
Auricular surface breadth[b]	(56.0)	—	—	—	—
Iliac crest maximum breadth[c]	—	—	15.5	—	15.4
Iliac crest minimum breadth[c]	8.6	—	9.0	—	8.8
Acetabulosymphyseal length[d]	(93.0)	—	(80.0–90.0)	—	—
Superior pubic height[e]	7.0	7.0	—	—	—
Superior pubic breadth[f]	17.8	16.7	(16.5)	—	—
Ventral pubic thickness[g]	5.3	5.0	6.5	6.8	7.8
Symphyseal height (M-18)	—	50.8	—	—	—
Symphyseal breadth[h]	19.8	—	—	—	—
Subpubic angle (M-33)	(125°)l		(104°)l		—

[a]Minimum distance from the posterior border of the acetabulum to the inferoanterior margin of the greater sciatic notch (Olivier 1960).

[b]Maximum breadth of the auricular surface, measured perpendicular to the long axis of the surface.

[c]Maximum and minimum breadths of the iliac crest measured, respectively, at the iliac tubercle and between the iliac tubercle and the iliac tuberosity.

[d]The direct distance from the superior margin of the pubic symphysis to the nearest point on the anteromedial margin of the acetabulum (McCown and Keith 1939).

[e]Superoinferior height of the superior pubic ramus measured at the point of maximum depth of the obturator groove.

[f]Dorsomedial to ventrolateral breadth of the superior pubic ramus measured at the same point at the height.

[g]Superoinferior thickness of the ventral margin of the superior pubic ramus, measured at the middle of the obturator foramen margin.

[h]Maximum ventrodorsal breadth of the symphyseal surface.

42; females: 10.5 ± 1.9 mm, N = 40). The exact relationship between this ventral ramal thinning and the ramal elongation is not clear.

One product of the mediolateral pubic elongation is the enlargement of their subpubic angles. The subpubic angles of Shanidar 1 and 3 (125° and ca. 104°, respectively) are well above the ranges of variation of recent human females (range of means of eight samples: 74°–85° [Martin 1928]) and especially of recent human males (range of means of five samples: 56°–60° [Martin 1928]). They are also slightly above the rough estimates for La Ferrassie 1 (ca. 90°) and Tabūn C1 (ca. 100°).

In contrast to this configuration of the pubic bone among the Shanidar and other Neandertals, all of the early anatomically modern human pubic bones have morphologies identical to those of recent humans (Matiegka 1938; McCown and Keith 1939; Vandermeersch 1981a; Verneau 1906). Their acetabulosymphyseal lengths are within recent human ranges of variation (Qafzeh 9 [♀?]: ca. 59.0 mm; Skhūl 4 [♂]: 72.0 mm; Skhūl 9 [♂?]: ca. 83.0 mm; Caviglione 1 [♂]: 58.0 mm; Cro-Magnon 1 [♂]: ca. 73.0 mm; Předmostí 3 [♂]: ca. 68.0 mm;

Předmostí 4 [♀]: ca. 63.5 mm; Předmostí 10 [♀]: ca. 68.0 mm; Předmostí 14 [♂]: ca. 67.0 mm), and only that of Skhūl 9 is toward the upper limits of recent human ranges of variation. Their acetabulosymphyseal/femoral length indices are similarly identical to those of recent humans (12.3–16.4, 14.3 ± 1.5, N = 7). Likewise, their ventral pubic thicknesses (Qafzeh 9: 12.6 mm; Skhūl 4: 13.0 mm; Skhūl 9: 9.5 mm; Caviglione 1: 14.5 mm; Cro-Magnon 1: 17.5 mm) are around those of recent humans and separate from those of most Neandertals, especially those from the Near East. And finally, their subpubic angles are similar to those of most recent humans (Skhūl 4 and 9: ca. 80° each; Early Upper Paleolithic sample: 60.6° ± 9.4°, N = 5).

The Shanidar 1 obturator foramen appears to have been enlarged medio-laterally as a result of the pubic elongation. By aligning the preserved portions of the right pubic bone and ischium of Shanidar 1, its maximum obturator foramen length can be estimated at about 69.0 mm. This value is considerably greater than those of most recent humans (European males: 54.1 ± 3.6 mm, N = 128; European females: 50.0 ± 3.2 mm, N = 82 [Genovés 1959]) and early anatomically modern humans (52.3 ± 5.5 mm, N = 5).

The Shanidar 1 and 4 pubic bones exhibit prominent crests along their pectineal lines, and it appears as though the Shanidar 3 pubic bones possessed similar crests. Comparable crests are present on the La Ferrassie 1 and Krapina 208 pubic bones and on those of many recent humans. They indicate an ossification of the attachments of their lacunar and pectineal ligaments and probably imply a hypertrophy of the anterior abdominal musculature; an enlargement of *M. pectineus* may have also contributed to the formation of these crests.

The ilia and ischia from Shanidar 1, 3, and 4 are morphologically similar to those of other Neandertals and recent humans. No one of them is sufficiently complete and undistorted to determine whether features such as the iliac pillar are more anteriorly placed than those of more recent humans; they do not appear to have been significantly different in their positions or orientations.

The iliac crest of the Shanidar 4 left ilium is largely preserved near the iliac pillar. The crest widens gradually from its posterior point of minimum thickness to reach a maximum thickness of 15.4 mm above the iliac pillar, and then it thins slightly anteriorly as it approaches the anterior superior iliac spine. The crest is gently convex laterally along preserved portion. The preserved portion of the Shanidar 3 right iliac crest, in contrast, appears to be relatively thin along most of its length and possesses a distinct iliac tubercle rather than a gradual thickening of the crest above the iliac pillar. The thickness at the tubercle (15.5 mm) is nonetheless similar to the maximum thickness of the Shanidar 4 iliac crest.

The dimensions of the Shanidar 3 iliac fossa appear large by recent human standards. The minimum distance between the auricular surface and the crest at the iliac tubercle equals 99.0 mm. This measurement is 113.0 mm on the Neandertal 1 ilium but lower in a sample of recent Amerindians (males: 85.7 ± 4.8 mm, N = 40; females: 80.5 ± 5.6 mm, N = 37). However, Skhūl 4 and 5 have measurements (ca. 109.0 and 100.0 mm, respectively) that are similar to those of Shanidar 3 and Neandertal 1. If these measurements are normalized for body size by dividing them by the femoral bicondylar length (using the estimate of 438.5 mm for the Shanidar 3 bicondylar length), their indices are: Shanidar 3: ca. 22.6; Neandertal 1: 25.6; Skhūl 4: ca. 22.3; and Skhūl 5: ca. 19.4. The Neandertal 1 value is considerably above the indices of a recent Amerindian sample (males: 19.9 ± 1.4, N = 39; females: 20.6 ± 1.2, N = 37), but those of Shanidar 3 and the two Skhūl hominids are not significantly different from those of the recent humans. These data suggest that at least Shanidar 3 did not have an especially large ilium, although it must be kept in mind that this measurement is influenced by both the total iliac breadth and the relative position of the iliac tubercle along the crest.

The Shanidar 1, 3, and 4 pelvic remains are thus similar to those of other Neandertals in having ilia and ischia comparable to those of more recent humans and pubic bones that were significantly elongated and thinned along their ventral margins relative to the configuration of more recent human pubic bones. This mediolateral elongation of their pubic bones must have greatly increased in the anterior breadths of their pelves. This increase in pelvic dimensions, however, appears to have been solely in their pubic regions because their sacra (Chapter 7) and ilia are not particularly large relative to overall body size.

The greater relative breadths of the Shanidar and other Neandertal anterior pelves vis-à-vis those of more recent humans must have provided them with relatively large interacetabular distances. A larger interacetabular distance would increase the moment arm of the body's center of gravity around the hip articulation and, by extension, increase the gluteal abductor force necessary for stability and the joint reaction force at the hip (Lovejoy 1974; McLeish and Charnley 1970). Because a relatively greater interacetabular distance would be energetically less advantageous, the adaptive significance of this feature must lie elsewhere than in locomotor efficiency.

The dimensions of the pubic bone are largely under hormonal control and appear to be independent of most functional hypertrophy of the pelvis (Coleman 1969; Riesenfeld 1972). This suggests that the differences between Neandertal and modern human pubic morphologies may be related to differences in parturition or the developmental maturity of the newborn.

Neandertals and their early anatomically modern human successors had similar adult brain sizes (Chapter 5), and therefore their fetal and newborn head diameters should have been similar at equivalent stages of development (Leutenegger 1972). If the Neandertals had the same gestation length as modern humans, about 9 months, they should have been giving birth to similarly sized infants. Their larger anterior pelvic dimensions, and hence larger pelvic aperture diameters, should therefore have allowed the Neandertals to give birth more easily than is usually the case for modern humans. This implies, more accurately, that there was an increase in difficulties at birth with the advent of anatomically modern human pelves, problems for which cultural compensations in the form of improved obstetrical techniques and neonatal care for the mother and infant would have been necessary. The archaeological record indicates a number of social and cultural improvements at this time in the Upper Pleistocene, but it is uncertain to what extent they may have compensated for increased fetal constriction at birth. Furthermore, an improvement in obstetrical techniques would not necessarily have led to a consistent decrease in pelvic aperture diameters, even though it would allow some reduction of those dimensions.

An alternative explanation of the changes in anterior pelvic morphology from the Neandertals to early anatomically modern humans would see the primary shift as a decrease in gestation length, with anatomically modern humans having significantly shorter gestation periods than the preceding Neandertals. Estimates of pelvic aperture circumference from the generally incomplete Neandertal pelvic remains indicate that a sphere about 15 to 25% larger than one that could pass through most modern human pelves could have fit through a Neandertal pelvic aperture. The Neandertals could therefore have given birth to a full-term fetus with a head 15–25% larger than those of modern human newborns. Because most of the volume of a human neonatal head is neurocranium, this implies that the Neandertals could have given birth to infants with larger brains. Brain growth data from modern human infants (Boyd 1962) indicates that an additional 2–3 months postnatally is usually required to achieve an increase of 15 to 25% in brain size. This suggests that the Neandertals may have had gestation periods of 11 to 12 months, rather than the 9 months usual for modern humans. Interestingly, mammals with adult brain volumes of 1300 to 1500 cc should have gestation periods between 12.5 and 13.2 months (Sacher and Staffeldt 1974). It therefore appears as though the Neandertals had gestation periods close to those expected for mammals with their brain sizes, whereas anatomically modern humans have relatively short gestation periods.

As with the above suggested shift in pelvic constriction during parturition, a decrease in gestation length at the Neandertal to anatomically modern human transition would require cultural compensation because a reduction by 2 or 3 months in the gestation period would mean that the newborn was considerably more altricial, had less neuromuscular development, and was hence more dependent upon its mother for assistance. However, a decrease in gestation length would also expose the infant to environmental stimuli significantly earlier at a period of life when the brain is growing rapidly and is highly responsive developmentally to sensory input. The decrease in gestation length, despite the increased vulnerability of the neonate, may have been selectively advantageous in providing the infant with a headstart on neurological development.

Most of the preserved Neandertal pubic bones, including those from Shanidar 1, 3, and 4, probably derive from males, and they are as elongated as those known for Neandertal females (Trinkaus 1976b). Because the pubic morphology of these Neandertal males cannot be considered a direct response to the pressures of reproduction, it appears likely that this pattern was a general non-sex-linked trait, probably throughout most of human evolution. Unfortunately, pubic bones have not been preserved for earlier members of the genus *Homo* (among older hominid samples, only the *Australopithecus* AL-288-1 [Johanson *et al.* 1982], STS-14 [Robinson 1972], STS-65 [Robinson 1972], and SK-1590 specimens preserve pubic bones). However, the fact that the predicted gestation length for the Neandertals based on their pelvic dimensions approximates the gestation period indicated by their cranial capacities, and that a similar pattern is present in *Australopithecus africanus* (Leutenegger 1972), suggests that large pelves relative to brain size was the dominant pattern throughout most of human evolution.

FEMORA

Inventory

SHANIDAR 1

Right   Only the head and the medial condyle are missing from the bone, but all of the middle and distal diaphysis and much of the distal epiphysis have been crushed and distorted. In addition, the distal articulations were altered by degenerative joint disease. Maximum length = 437.5 mm.

SHANIDAR 3

Side Indeterminate   Eroded fragment of diaphysis. Maximum length = 39.0 mm.

SHANIDAR 4

Right   A largely intact section of diaphysis from the distal end of the gluteal tuberosity to the proximal end of the popliteal surface (maximum length = 291.5 mm), and a crushed head fused postmortem to the right acetabulum (maximum dimension = 49.2 mm).

Left   An eroded portion of the diaphysis from the middle of the gluteal tuberosity to midshaft (maximum length = 201.4 mm), and crushed portions of head fused postmortem to the left acetabulum.

SHANIDAR 5

Right   The disphysis is present from the spiral line to the supracondylar ligamentous surface, but most of it retains only the posterior and lateral

surfaces. The anterior and medial surfaces are present only along about
120.0 mm of the midshaft. Maximum length = 315.0 mm.

Left   The posterior half of the head and neck (maximum length = 66.0
mm), and the posterior diaphysis with portions of the medial and lateral surfaces from just distal to the gluteal region to the supracondylar
ligamentous surface (maximum length = 259.2 mm). Fragments of the
condylar surfaces are also preserved.

SHANIDAR 6

Right   Portions of the diaphysis are present from the greater trochanter to
the midpopliteal surface, but most of the surfaces are present only
distal to the gluteal tuberosity. In the region of the gluteal tuberosity,
only the lateral half of the bone is present, and distally most of the
anterior and anterolateral surfaces are absent. Maximum length = 306.9
mm.

Left   The bone retains three diaphyseal sections: a proximal diaphyseal
piece with the gluteal tuberosity and all of the surfaces preserved (originally assigned to Shanidar 4 [Stewart 1963]; maximum length = 147.2
mm), a distal piece with most of the anterior and lateral diaphyseal
surfaces (maximum length = 82.5 mm), and a piece of the posteromedial distal diaphysis (maximum length = 79.2 mm).

Morphology

Most of the Shanidar long bones consist of diaphyses with variably intact
epiphyses, and their femora are no exception to this pattern (Figures 58 and
59). Four individuals—Shanidar 1, 4, 5, and 6—retain significant portions of at
least one femur, but most of them consist of the diaphysis with or without
separate epiphyseal fragments.

The Shanidar 1 right femur is the most complete of the Shanidar femora
because it is the only one that retains most of the diaphysis and portions of both
epiphyses. However, it is also the most distorted. The trochanteric region and
the proximal third of the diaphysis are intact and undistorted. The distal two-
thirds of the diaphysis, however, were crushed anteroposteriorly in situ and
have been preserved in such a way that it is no longer possible to restore the
diaphysis to its original shape. The length of the bone has not been significantly
affected by the crushing, and the maximum and bicondylar lengths have been
estimated from its trochanteric length (Table 65). The distal epiphysis is incomplete and slightly distorted by postmortem crushing; it was further altered
by degenerative joint disease (Chapter 12).

The Shanidar 4, 5, and 6 femora consist primarily of diaphyses. The
Shanidar 4 maximum femoral length was measured by Stewart (1963) in situ,

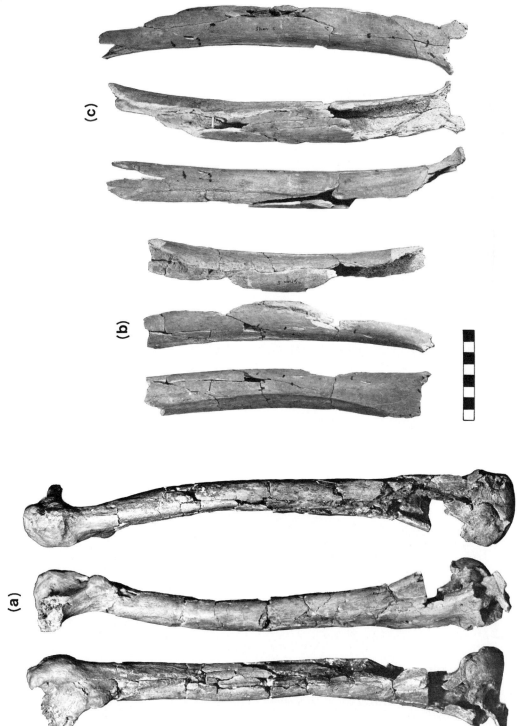

Figure 58 The Shanidar 1 and 5 femora. (a) Shanidar 1 right, (b) Shanidar 5 left, and (c) Shanidar 5 right. For each bone, the views, from left to right, are posterior, medial, and lateral. Scale in centimeters.

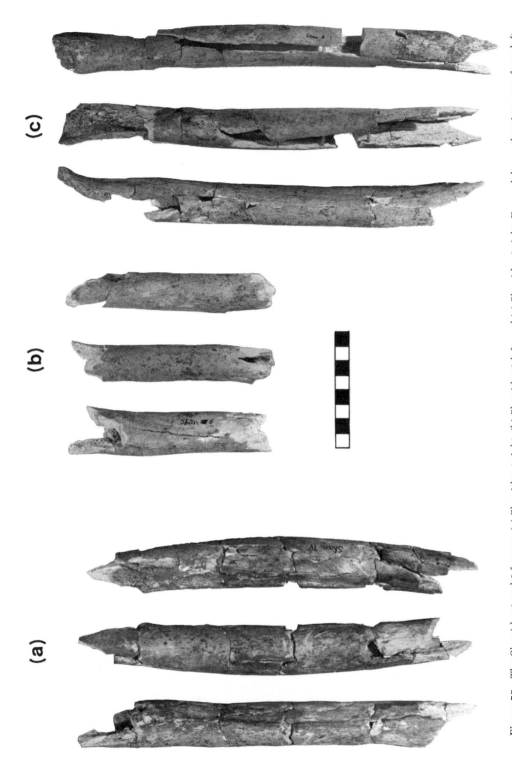

Figure 59 The Shanidar 4 and 6 femora. (a) Shanidar 4 right, (b) Shanidar 6 left, and (c) Shanidar 6 right. For each bone, the views are, from left to right, posterior, medial, and lateral. Scale in centimeters.

and its bicondylar length has been estimated from its maximum length (Table 65). The lengths of the Shanidar 5 and 6 femora were estimated from their preserved diaphyseal portions using regressions derived from samples of recent human femora (Table 65); it is possible that they were slightly underestimated because Neandertal femora tend to have relatively large articulations (Trinkaus 1980; Twiesselmann 1961), but any error in this regard should be small.

The Shanidar femoral diaphyses are similar to those of other Neandertals in being robust, roughly circular in cross section and lacking pilasters (Trinkaus 1976a). Their diaphyseal robusticity, in particular, places them at the limits of more recent human ranges of variation.

The Shanidar femora lack pilasters, even though each one has a strongly marked linea aspera (Figures 58–60). Associated with this absence of a pilaster are their roughly circular midshaft cross sections. The circularity of their diaphyses is best illustrated by their cross-sectional contours (Figure 60), but it can be quantified by the pilastric index. The Shanidar 4, 5, and 6 pilastric indices (114.1, 109.9, and 101.8, respectively) are slightly higher than those of most other Neandertals (Amud 1: 99.7; Tabūn C1: 87.6; Tabūn C3: 92.1; European Neandertals: 99.5 ± 7.7, N = 8) but at the lower end of the ranges of variation of more recent humans (Skhūl–Qafzeh hominids: 123.3 ± 9.8, N = 10; Early Upper Paleolithic hominids: 115.6 ± 14.3, N = 15; recent Europeans: 107.2 ± 7.6, N = 50; recent Amerindians: 116.3 ± 10.1, N = 50; recent Melanesians: 119.0 ± 9.1, N = 39). European Early Neandertal femora have similarly low pilastric indices (Ehringsdorf 5: 101.2; Sedia-del-Diavolo 1: 106.9), whereas the last interglacial Tabūn E1 femur has a pilastric index (92.9) towards the lower end of the known Neandertal range of variation. The Chou-kou-tien and Olduvai *H. erectus* femora have somewhat lower pilastric indices (84.7 ± 5.9, N = 6).

An absence of a pilaster is usually considered to be a sign of gracility among recent humans (Hrdlička 1934), but among the Neandertals and earlier hominids it is associated with increased robusticity (Trinkaus 1976a). In particular, an absence of a pilaster is usually associated with an increase in the relative breadth of the diaphysis (Trinkaus 1976a), which serves to reinforce the diaphysis against mediolateral bending stress. The relative mediolateral diaphyseal reinforcement is reflected in the shaft breadth index (midshaft breadth/bicondylar length) (Trinkaus 1976a). The Shanidar 1, 4, 5, and 6 femora have indices of about 7.64–7.86, about 7.37, about 7.43, and about 7.29, respectively. These indices are slightly greater than those of other Neandertals (Amud 1: ca. 6.72; Tabūn C1: 6.68; European Neandertals: 6.92 ± 0.16, N = 6). However, they are considerably greater than those of early anatomically modern humans (Skhūl–Qafzeh hominids: 5.65 ± 0.42, N = 4; Early Upper Paleolithic hominids: 6.12 ± 0.41, N = 7), and recent humans (Europeans: 6.21 ± 0.40, N = 50; Amerindians: 5.67 ± 3.9, N = 50; Melanesians: 5.65 ± 0.33, N = 39). They are even slightly above those of two *H. erectus* femora, Olduvai OH

TABLE 65
Measurements of the Femora (mm)

	Shanidar 1[d,e]	Shanidar 4[f]		Shanidar 5[e,g]		Shanidar 6[e,g]	
	Right	Right	Left	Right	Left	Right	Left
Maximum length (M-1)	(461.0)	(425.0)	—	(450.0)	—	(388.0)	—
Bicondylar length (M-2)	(458.0)	(422.0)	—	(447.0)	—	(384.0)	—
Trochanteric length (M-3)	437.5	—	—	—	—	—	—
Midshaft sagittal diameter (M-6)	—	35.5	—	36.5	—	28.5	—
Midshaft transverse diameter (M-7)	(35.0–36.0)	31.1	—	33.2	35.4	28.0	—
Midshaft circumference (M-8)	—	102.0	—	108.0	—	89.0	—
Proximal sagittal diameter (M-10)	28.6	—	(31.0)	—	—	—	24.6
Proximal transverse diameter (M-9)	35.3	49.2	(36.5)	—	47.5	—	30.5
Head diameter (M-19)	—	—	—	—	—	—	—
Vertical neck diameter (M-15)	32.1	—	—	—	—	—	—
Sagittal neck diameter (M-16)	(23.3)	—	—	—	—	—	—
Greater trochanter depth (M-26[1])	42.8	—	—	—	—	64.7	—
Gluteal tuberosity length[a]	90.0	—	—	—	—	11.5	—
Gluteal tuberosity breadth[a]	12.0	—	(14.0)	—	—	—	(12.5)
Hypotrochanteric fossa[b]	absent	—	—	—	—	present	present
Third trochanter[b]	absent	—	—	—	—	absent	absent
Lateral condyle breadth (M-21e)	25.6	—	—	—	—	—	—
Patellar surface absolute height (M-26[3a])	(33.3)	—	—	—	—	—	—
Patellar surface circumference[c]	(44.0)	—	—	—	—	—	—
Patellar surface breadth (M-26[3b])	(45.0)	—	—	—	—	—	—
Neck angle (M-29)	120°	—	—	—	—	—	—

[a] Maximum length and breadth of the M. gluteus maximus insertion area.

[b] Presence or absence of a distinct hypotrochanteric fossa or third trochanter.

[c] Length of the midsagittal arc from the proximal margin of the patellar surface to the intercondylar fossa.

[d] The bicondylar length of the Shanidar 1 right femur was estimated from the trochanteric length using a least squares regression based on recent human femora (r = 0.989). The trochanteric length of 437.5 mm provided here is considerably less than that published by Stewart (1977) of 470 mm but has been confirmed by reexamination of the specimen.

[e] The maximum lengths of the Shanidar 1, 5, and 6 femora were estimated from their bicondylar length estimates using a least squares regression based on recent human femora (r = 0.998).

[f] The maximum length of the Shanidar 4 right femur was measured in situ by Stewart (1977) as about 425.0 mm. The bicondylar length of the specimen was estimated from the maximum length using a least squares regression based on recent human femora (r = 0.998).

[g] The bicondylar lengths of the Shanidar 5 and 6 right femora were estimated from their preserved diaphyseal portions using least squares regressions based on recent human femora (r = 0.960 and r = 0.920, respectively).

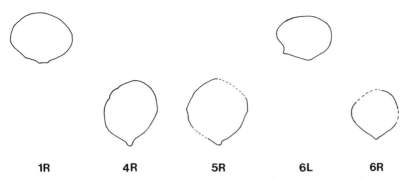

Figure 60 Diaphyseal cross sections of the femora of Shanidar 1 (1R), Shanidar 4 (4R), Shanidar 5 (5R), and Shanidar 6 (6L and 6R). Upper row: at the middle of the gluteal tuberosity. Lower row: at midshaft. Anterior is above, and the sections are viewed in a proximal–distal direction.

28 (ca. 7.17), and Chou-kou-tien femur IV (ca. 7.20). This index suggests that the Shanidar femoral diaphyses were hyperrobust.

It is possible that the Shanidar femoral lengths were slightly underestimated. If their bicondylar lengths are all increased by 5.0% and their shaft breadth indices are recalculated, their indices become about 7.28–7.49, about 7.02, about 7.07, and about 6.94 for Shanidar 1, 4, 5, and 6, respectively. These values are still high, even for Neandertals.

The proximal diaphyses of the Shanidar femora are likewise similar to those of other Neandertals. Their meric indices are relatively high (81.0, ca. 84.9, and 80.7 for Shanidar 1, 4, and 6, respectively). However, they are within the ranges of variation of other Neandertals (Amud 1: 83.0 & 79.7; Tabūn C1: 74.3; European Neandertals: 80.4 ± 4.8, N = 10), early anatomically modern humans (Skhūl–Qafzeh hominids: 83.1 ± 5.1, N = 5; Early Upper Paleolithic hominids: 74.3 ± 10.1, N = 18), and recent humans (Europeans: 78.4 ± 7.3, N = 50; Amerindians: 75.5 ± 5.9, N = 50; Melanesians: 82.8 ± 7.8, N = 39).

It is not possible to ascertain the degree of anterior femoral curvature in the Shanidar sample. The Shanidar 1 femur is too distorted, the Shanidar 4 femora are too incomplete, and the Shanidar 5 and 6 femora lack most of their anterior surfaces. However, the Shanidar 5 and 6 femora preserve much of their posterior surfaces without distortion (Figures 58 and 59). Although this does not permit the assessment of femoral curvature according to traditional methods (Anthony and Rivet 1907; Ried 1924), it suggests that Shanidar 5 had reasonably strong femoral curvature, whereas that of Shanidar 6 was considerably less.

The posterolateral aspects of the Shanidar proximal femora are marked by large gluteal tuberosities for their insertions of *M. gluteus maximus*. These tuberosities are especially well preserved on the Shanidar 1 and 6 femora (Figure 61). The Shanidar 1 gluteal tuberosity consists only of a large roughened area, but the Shanidar 6 tuberosities have clear depressions at their proximal ends that can only be identified as hypotrochanteric fossae. Similar fossae

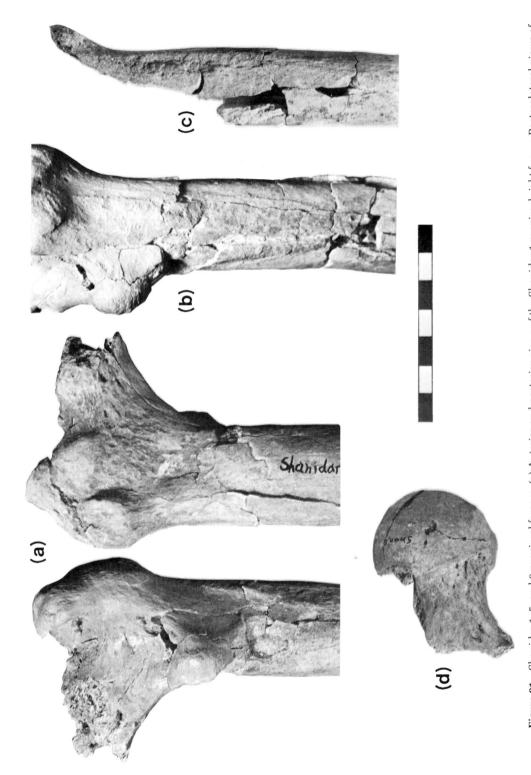

Figure 61 Shanidar 1, 5, and 6 proximal femora. (a) Anterior and posterior views of the Shanidar 1 proximal right femur. Posterolateral views of (b) the Shanidar 1 and (c) 6 right gluteal tuberosities. (d) Posterior view of the Shanidar 5 left femoral head and neck. Scale in centimeters.

are present on Amud 1 and 66.7% (N = 12) of European Neandertal femora; such a fossa is absent from the Tabūn C1 right femur. The Shanidar 4 left gluteal tuberosity is too poorly preserved to indicate its detailed morphology.

The midtuberosity breadths of the Shanidar 1 and 6 gluteal tuberosities (12.0, and 11.5 & ca. 12.5 mm, respectively) are similar to those of Amud 1 (12.0 mm) and Tabūn C1 (11.5 mm) but are slightly below a European Neandertal mean (13.1 ± 2.5 mm, N = 10), whereas the estimated tuberosity breadth for Shanidar 4 (ca. 14.0) is in the upper half of the Neandertal range of variation (10.0–17.5 mm, N = 12). More recent humans tend to have smaller tuberosity breadths, even though there is some overlap between the Neandertal and more recent human ranges of variation (Skhūl hominids: 9.1 ± 2.0 mm, N = 3; Early Upper Paleolithic hominids: 9.7 ± 2.1 mm, N = 6; recent Europeans: 8.4 ± 1.5 mm, N = 50; recent Amerindians: 7.0 ± 1.0 mm, N = 50).

The large dimensions and rugosity of the Shanidar gluteal tuberosities imply that they each had hypertrophy of the M. gluteus maximus. This muscle acts as a hip extensor during climbing and as a lateral thigh stabilizer during active locomotion, and its strong development implies that they were well adapted for active locomotion over rough terrain.

The proximal epiphyses of the Shanidar femora consist of the Shanidar 1 trochanteric area and neck and the Shanidar 4 and 5 femoral heads (Figure 61). The trochanteric area of the Shanidar 1 right femur is robust. On its anterior surface there is a prominent, rounded tubercle for the insertion of the M. gluteus minimus, which is separated from the anterior aspect of the greater trochanteric surface for the insertion of M. gluteus medius by a small sulcus. The intertrochanteric line is clear but not particularly strongly marked, and it blends distomedially with a modest spiral line. Posteriorly, the greater and lesser trochanters and the intertrochanteric crest are prominent, but all of their edges are rounded. Most of the insertions for the small hip muscles that insert on the trochanters are not readily discernible, except for that of M. obturator externus; its insertion is marked by small exostoses that are present in the trochanteric fossa.

The depth of the Shanidar 1 right greater trochanter equals 42.8 mm. This measurement is slightly below the mean of a small and predominantly male European Neandertal sample (44.8 ± 4.1 mm, N = 5) but above that of Tabūn C1 (35.7 mm). This suggests that the Shanidar 1 trochanters were moderately sized, at least for a Neandertal.

The Shanidar 4 and 5 femoral heads are not sufficiently intact to provide significant morphological information, but each retains enough of the articulation to permit determinations of their head diameters (49.2 and 47.5 mm, respectively). These diameters are quite similar to those of most other Neandertals (Amud 1: ca. 48.3 mm estimated from the acetabular height [Trinkaus 1980]), Tabūn C1: ca. 43.0 mm; European Neandertals: 49.3 ± 4.2 mm, N = 8). If their femoral head diameters are normalized for overall size using their femoral bicondylar lengths, the resultant indices are about 11.7 and about 10.6

for Shanidar 4 and 5, respectively. The Shanidar 4 value for this index is close to a European Neandertal mean (12.0 ± 0.6, N = 5), whereas that of Shanidar 5 is close to the lower indices of Amud 1 (ca. 10.0) and Tabūn C1 (ca. 10.5). There is considerable overlap between the Neandertal values, including those of Shanidar 4 and 5, and the ranges of variation of early anatomically modern humans (Skhūl–Qafzeh sample: 9.5 ± 0.2, N = 4; Early Upper Paleolithic sample: 10.4 ± 0.7, N = 11), and recent humans (Europeans: 10.4 ± 0.6, N = 50; Amerindians: 10.0 ± 0.6, N = 50). Therefore, Shanidar 4, but not Shanidar 5, had a relatively large femoral head, as do many other Neandertals, but they were not exceptionally large.

The Shanidar 1 neck angle (120°) is close to the mean of a European Neandertal sample (121.2° ± 5.2°, N = 7) and between those of Amud 1 (113°) and Tabūn C1 (122°). Because the neck angle decreases during development as a result of locomotor activity (Houston and Zaleski 1967), it provides a general indication of locomotor activity levels. The angles for the Neandertals, however, are not separable from those of Early Upper Paleolithic hominids (117.4° ± 7.7°, N = 7) and recent humans (Europeans: 128.5° ± 4.7°, N = 50; Amerindians: 126.8° ± 4.4°, N = 50 [Trinkaus 1976a]); curiously, a small Skhūl–Qafzeh sample has much higher indices (131.6° ± 6.6°, N = 4).

The incomplete nature of the Shanidar 1 and 5 distal femora and the diseased condition of the Shanidar 1 patellar and tibial articular surfaces prevent more than general observations of their distal femoral morphology. There does not appear to be anything in their condylar or patellar surface configurations that would distinguish them from relatively robust recent human and other Upper Pleistocene hominid distal femora. The Shanidar 1 lateral condyle has an even ellipsoid curve, and its patellar surface has a more projecting lateral margin than right margin.

The Shanidar femora are thus similar to those of other Neandertals in having epiphyses similar to those of more recent humans in relative size and morphology associated with considerably more robust diaphyses. The diaphyseal robusticity is reflected in their shaft breadth indices, their roughly circular cross sections, and the absence of a pilaster. In addition, they exhibit prominent gluteal tuberosities.

PATELLAE

Inventory

SHANIDAR 1

Right   Largely complete bone with damage to the superior posterior corner and the medial margin of the articular surface. Its morphology may have been altered slightly by degenerative joint disease. Maximum height = 44.5 mm; maximum breadth = 50.8 mm.

Left   Largely complete bone with damage and reconstruction on the superior and medial margins of the articular surface and on the posterior side of the inferior apex. Maximum height = 45.7 mm; maximum breadth = 45.5 mm.

SHANIDAR 4

Left   Damaged bone that retains the superior surface, the superior half of the anterior surface and the lateral half of the articular surface intact. Maximum height = 38.8 mm; maximum breadth = 48.1 mm.

SHANIDAR 5

Right   Fragment of the anterior surface and the adjacent superior surface and superolateral articular surface. Maximum height = 26.4 mm; maximum breadth = 23.3 mm.

Left   Incomplete patella that retains most of the anterior and superior surfaces, the complete medial articular surface but only the margins of the lateral articular surface, and a small part of the inferior surface. Maximum height = 39.3 mm; maximum breadth = 46.8 mm.

SHANIDAR 6

Right   Retains most of the anterior surface but lacks the medial and inferior margins. The articular surface is represented only by the lateral half of the lateral side. Maximum height = 34.0 mm; maximum breadth = 38.4 mm.

Morphology

Sufficient portions of at least one of the Shanidar 1, 4, and 5 patellae have been preserved to provide largely complete morphological and metric data, and enough of the Shanidar 6 right patella has survived to give an impression of its size and morphology (Table 66; Figure 62). Portions of the Shanidar 1 and 4 patellae have been restored with filler, but enough of these bones remains to give credibility to the restorations. The Shanidar 1 patellae are noticeably asymmetrical, with the right one being wider and shorter than the left one; this asymmetry is probably due to the degenerative joint disease that afflicted his right knee (Chapter 12). It is uncertain to what extent the various dimensions of the Shanidar 1 patellae were affected by the abnormalities in the lower limb, and it should be kept in mind that the proportions of the Shanidar 1 patellae may not be representative of their original configuration.

TABLE 66
Measurements of the Patellae (mm)

	Shanidar 1[e]		Shanidar 4	Shanidar 5	Shanidar 6
	Right	Left	Left	Left	Right
Maximum height (M-1)	(46.0)	(49.5)	(43.0)	39.3	—
Maximum breadth (M-2)	(51.1)	46.2	(47.7)	46.8	—
Maximum thickness (M-3)	25.5	—	25.5	(24.0)	19.5
Articular height (M-4)	(31.3)	—	36.0	(31.5)	(31.0)
Articular breadth[a]	47.5	(46.2)	47.0	45.1	—
Articular depth[b]	7.0	6.1	8.8	9.0	—
Point of maximum depth[c]	22.9	23.3	26.0	22.5	—
Medial facet height[d]	30.0	—	(32.4)	30.5	—
Medial facet breadth (M-5)	22.5	—	(22.5)	21.5	—
Lateral facet height[d]	(31.3)	—	36.0	—	—
Lateral facet breadth (M-6)	25.5	26.3	26.3	25.9	—
Vastus notch	present	absent	absent	present	present

[a]Maximum breadth of the femoral surface.

[b]Maximum subtense to the median articular ridge from the chord determined by the mid-medial and lateral margins of the articular surface.

[c]Distance of the depth subtense along the articular breadth chord from the lateral margin.

[d]Proximodistal dimensions of the medial and lateral halves of the articular surface.

[e]The right patella of Shanidar 1 was altered by degenerative joint disease, and the measurements of the bone, especially the overall dimensions, were affected by this abnormality.

The overall size and proportions of the Shanidar patellae are similar to those of other Neandertals and more recent humans, although those of Shanidar 1 and 4 especially are quite large. The maximum heights of the Shanidar 1 patellae (ca. 46.0 & ca. 49.5 mm) are toward the top of a Neandertal range (36.6–48.5 mm, N = 16, Tabūn C1: 37.7 mm, European Neandertals: 41.5 ± 2.9 mm, N = 15), whereas those of the Shanidar 4 and 5 patellae (ca. 43.0 and 39.3 mm, respectively) are closer to the Neandertal mean. The majority of the Neandertal values for this measurement fall within the range of means of 23 recent human samples (35.0–45.0 mm [Vriese 1913]). The maximum breadths of the Shanidar 1, 4, and 5 patellae (ca. 51.1 & 46.2, ca. 47.7, and 46.8 mm, respectively) are toward the upper end of a Neandertal range of variation (39.0–51.6 mm, N = 15; Tabūn C1: 39.0 mm; European Neandertals: 45.3 ± 3.5 mm, N = 14), but they are not exceptional for a Neandertal. The Neandertal mean is close to the upper end of a range of means for 23 recent human samples (35.0–45.5 mm [Vriese 1913]).

Height–breadth indices can be computed for the Shanidar 1, 4, and 5 patellae (ca. 90.0 & ca. 107.1, ca. 90.1 and 84.0, respectively). These values span the range of variation in this index present among other Neandertals (83.5–101.8, N = 13; Tabūn C1: 96.7; European Neandertals: 91.9 ± 4.5, N = 12), as the index for the Shanidar 1 left patella is the highest known for a Neandertal

Figure 62 The Shanidar patellae. (a) Shanidar 1 right, (b) Shanidar 1 left, (c) Shanidar 4 left, (d) Shanidar 5 left, (e) Shanidar 6 right. Above: anterior. Below: posterior. Portions of the Shanidar 1 and 4 patellae have been restored in filler. Scale in centimeters.

and the Shanidar 5 value is close to the lower limit of the Neandertal range. These Neandertal values are not different from those of an Early Upper Paleolithic sample (93.1 ± 6.7, N = 7), but they tend to be a little lower than those of Qafzeh 9 (ca. 98.3), Skhūl 4 (104.3), and most recent humans (range of means for 23 samples: 94.1–105.0 [Vriese 1913]). Contra Thoma (1975), most Neandertal patellae, including those of Shanidar 4 and 5 but possibly not those of Shanidar 1, tend to be relatively wider than those of recent humans.

It is possible to estimate the height of the Shanidar 1 and 5 patellae relative to their lower limb lengths (patella maximum height/ [femur bicondylar length + tibia maximum length]). This ratio provides indices of about 5.66 & about 6.09 for Shanidar 1 and about 4.87–4.93 for Shanidar 5. These values span the range of a small Neandertal sample (La Chapelle-aux-Saints 1: 5.32; La Ferrassie 2: 5.67; Spy 2: 5.92; Tabūn C1: 5.17); they suggest that Shanidar 1 might have had relatively high patellae, whereas Shanidar 5 had a relatively short one. For comparison, indices are available for Skhūl 4 (5.22), an Early Upper Paleolithic sample (4.97 ± 0.40, N = 7), and recent human samples (Europeans: 5.25 ± 0.39, N = 104; Amerindians: 5.33 ± 0.33, N = 60; Africans: 4.83 ± 0.40, N = 83 [Vriese 1913]). Although some of the Neandertals, such as Spy 2, La Ferrassie 2, and possibly Shanidar 1, appear to have relatively high patellae, all of their indices are within the range of variation for recent humans provided by Vriese (1913).

These data suggest that Shanidar 1, 4, and 5, along with those of most other Neandertals, had patellae that were fairly large, relatively and absolutely, although their overall sizes and proportions fall within the ranges of variation of more recent humans. Because the patella is merely a sesamoid bone within the *M. quadriceps femoris* tendon, its overall size and probably its proportions reflect the degree of development of the *M. quadriceps femoris*. A larger patella, and probably a relatively wider patella, would imply hypertrophy of this extremely important muscle for propulsion during locomotion.

Whereas the height and breadth of the patella reflect the size of the *M. quadriceps femoris* tendon, its thickness is related to the size of the moment arm for the *M. quadriceps femoris* at the knee during extension (Kaufer 1971). A thicker patella displaces the *M. quadriceps femoris* tendon and the patellar ligament anteriorly relative to the instant center of rotation through the femoral condyles, especially during the middle and later phases of knee extension (Smidt 1973). The maximum thicknesses of the three male Shanidar specimens (25.5, 25.5, and ca. 24.0 mm, respectively, for Shanidar 1, 4, and 5) are all at the upper end of the Neandertal range of variation (18.0–27.0 mm, N = 17; Tabūn C1: 18.0 mm, European Neandertals: 21.6 ± 2.1 mm, N = 16) and are exceeded only by that of the Kiik-Koba 1 patella (27.0 mm). The thickness of the Shanidar 6 right patella (19.5 mm), in contrast, is toward the lower end of the Neandertal range of variation. The thickness of the Shanidar 1, 4, and 5 patellae, but not those of Shanidar 6 and many other Neandertals, are above those of Qafzeh 9 (22.0 mm), Skhūl 4 (20.8 mm), Předmostí 3, 4, and 14 (22.0 mm, 21.0 mm, and

21.0 mm, respectively) and a recent European sample (19.8 ± 1.8 mm, N = 64 [O'Konski 1979]). This suggests that at least three Shanidar males had quite thick patellae.

If the thicknesses of the Shanidar patellae are compared to their tibial maximum lengths (as a measure of the load arm for *M. quadriceps femoris*), it becomes clear that all of them, including Shanidar 6, had relatively thick patellae, and hence enlargements of their *M. quadriceps femoris* moment arms. The resultant indices from the ratio of patellar maximum thickness to tibial maximum length are about 7.18, about 6.67–6.86, and about 6.50 for Shanidar 1, 5, and 6. These values are in the upper half of the Neandertal range of variation (La Chapelle-aux-Saints 1: ca. 6.13; La Ferrassie 2: 5.82; Kiik-Koba 1: ca. 7.80; Spy 2: 6.98; Tabūn C1: 5.64). All of these indices except those of La Ferrassie 2 and Tabūn C1 are well above those of Skhūl 4 (4.80), Caviglione 1 (4.47), Předmostí 3, 4, and 14 (5.20, 5.77, and 5.30, respectively) and a recent European sample (5.40 ± 0.37, N = 64 [O'Konski 1979]).

It is possible that these indices for the Shanidar and other Neandertal patellae are high as a result of the relative shortness of their tibiae, as reflected in low crural indices (Chapter 11; Table 96). However, the difference between most of the Neandertals and more recent humans remains if their patellar thicknesses are compared to their summed femoral and tibial lengths. The resultant indices are about 3.14, about 2.97–3.01, and about 2.85 for Shanidar 1, 5, and 6, respectively. These indices are similar to those of La Chapelle-aux-Saints 1 (ca. 2.71) and Spy 2 (3.06), above those of La Ferrassie 2 (2.52) and Tabūn C1 (ca. 2.47). Most of these Neandertal indices, and especially those from Shanidar, are greater than those of early anatomically modern humans (Skhūl 4: 2.26; Caviglione 1: 2.38; Předmostí 3: 2.42; Předmostí 4: 2.68; Předmostí 14: 2.47).

These data indicate that the Shanidar patellae contributed to the enlargement of their *M. quadriceps femoris* moment arms. A similar enlargement of this moment arm is evident in the proximal tibial proportions of Shanidar 2 and 5.

The Shanidar patellae have articular surfaces that are clearly divided into medial and lateral portions by a median vertical ridge. Their medial and lateral portions tend to be relatively flat or slightly concave, and in all of them that are sufficiently complete to be measured the lateral portion is distinctly wider than the medial portion. This is indicated by the indices formed from the ratio of the medial to the lateral articular breadths, which are 88.2, ca. 85.6, and 83.0 for Shanidar 1, 4, and 5, respectively. Other Neandertals are highly variable with respect to this index (78.8–107.6, N = 15; Tabūn C1: 102.6; European Neandertals: 92.6 ± 9.7, N = 14), with many having medial portions that are as wide or wider than their lateral portions. Early anatomically modern humans tend to have wider lateral than medial portions (Qafzeh 9: 81.7; Skhūl 4: 91.6; Předmostí 3, 4, and 14: 67.7, 67.9, and 66.7, respectively), but recent humans are highly variable with respect to the proportions of their medial and lateral portions (Reider *et al.* 1981; Wiberg 1941). The Shanidar patellae fall toward the lower end of the Neandertal range of variation but are within those of more recent humans with respect to this feature.

The significance of the relative sizes of the medial and lateral portions of the patellar articular surface is unclear, but it appears that their configuration is related to the patterns of stress through the patella and across the femoropatellar articulation (Minns *et al.* 1979; Reider *et al.* 1981). Patellae with a greater similarity of lateral and medial articular portions may be better adapted for tensile stress from *M. quadriceps femoris* and compressive stress across the femoropatellar articulation.

The Shanidar 6 patella has a deep vastus notch on its proximolateral corner, and smaller vastus notches are present on the Shanidar 1 right patella (but not on his left one) and on the Shanidar 5 patella. The Shanidar 4 patella does not exhibit a vastus notch. Full vastus notches are present on only 6.7% (N = 15) of European Neandertal patellae, and small notches are present on only 6.7% of them and on the Tabūn C1 patella. Frequencies of vastus notches may go as high as about 50.0% in samples of recent humans (Finnegan 1974).

The Shanidar 4 and 6 patellae exhibit prominent exostoses extending proximally from the medial halves of the proximoanterior margins of their patellae, and the Shanidar 1 right patella has smaller exostoses along the lateral half of its proximoanterior margin. These bony spurs are ossifications of the distal fibers of their *M. quadriceps femoris* tendons, and probably represent responses to considerable tensile stress in their tendons. Similar exostoses are present on the Shanidar 1 and 4 ulnar olecranons (Chapter 8). It is possible that the exostoses on the Shanidar 1 right patella are related to the degenerative joint disease of his right knee, but those on the Shanidar 4 and 6 patellae are probably from normal but accentuated tensile stress in the tendon insertion.

The Shanidar patellae are thus similar to those of other Neandertals in being moderately large and quite thick. These features are almost certainly related to their roles as sesamoid bones in the probably hypertrophied *M. quadriceps femoris* of the Shanidar Neandertals.

TIBIAE

Inventory

SHANIDAR 1

Right   The bone is represented by four separate pieces: a section of the proximal anterior and medial diaphysis (maximum length = 48.1 mm), a portion of the posterior proximal diaphysis with the soleal line (maximum length = 40.8 mm), a fragment of the tibial tuberosity (maximum dimension = 27.3 mm), and a complete distal epiphysis with arthritic alterations (maximum length = 74.5 mm).

Left   The bone retains most of the diaphysis from the tibial tuberosity to the distal epiphysis and the complete distal epiphysis. Some reconstruction of the diaphysis has been done, especially proximally. Maximum length = 333.0 mm.

SHANIDAR 2

Left   Largely complete bone with bone loss only on the anterior margins of the condyles and between the condyles and the tibial tuberosity. Some minor damage to the diaphysis has been restored. Maximum length = 337.5 mm.

SHANIDAR 3

Right   A fragment of the distal epiphysis with the anterior lateral corner of the talar articular surface. Extensive articular exostoses are present. Maximum breadth = 31.7 mm.

Left   A fragment of the distal epiphysis with the anterolateral corner of the talar trochlear articular surface with adjacent portions of the lateral and anterior surfaces of the epiphysis. Maximum breadth = 20.1 mm.

SHANIDAR 4

Right   Crushed and distorted portion of the lateral condyle and adjacent surface bone. Maximum length = 96.0 mm.

Left   Eroded and damaged portion of the distal epiphysis fused postmortem to the left talar trochlea and distal fibula.

Side Indeterminate   Six large diaphyseal sections, mostly fragmented lengthwise, that are primarily from the anterior and posterior margins. Maximum lengths of the pieces are: 47.3, 42.0, 38.5, 35.1, 31.8, and 24.8 mm, respectively.

SHANIDAR 5

Left   The bone consists of two separate segments: a proximal medial section with three-quarters of the medial condyle and the adjacent medial and posterior diaphyseal surfaces (maximum length = 140.7 mm), and a distal diaphyseal section with the medial diaphyseal surface from midshaft to the proximal end of the medial malleolus (maximum length = 175.6 mm).

SHANIDAR 6

Right   Midshaft section with all of the surfaces plus a section of posterior diaphysis extending proximally along the soleal line. Maximum length = 236.6 mm.

Left?   Midshaft section with the anterior margin and the anterolateral surface. Maximum length = 72.0 mm.

Morphology

The Shanidar tibiae vary from the virtually complete left tibia of Shanidar 2 to the few fragments of the Shanidar 3 and 4 tibiae. Although only the Shanidar 2 tibia presents a complete set of morphological and metric data, the Shanidar 1, 5, and 6 tibiae add to our appreciation of the Shanidar tibiae (Figure 63).

Both of the Shanidar 1 tibiae have been altered by the abnormalities of his lower limbs (Chapter 12). The distal epiphysis of his right tibia has exostoses around the talar articular surfaces, and the diaphysis of the left tibia exhibits a curious anterolateral concavity and posteromedial convexity. This abnormal bowing of the diaphysis does not seem to have affected the overall length of the bone, which is preserved from the tibial tuberosity to the distal articulations, or the cross-sectional morphology of the distal half of the diaphysis.

The lengths of the Shanidar 1 and 5 left tibiae have been estimated from their preserved portions. The estimate for Shanidar 1 should be quite accurate, given the amount of the diaphysis and distal epiphysis that remains. The length of the Shanidar 5 tibia is less certain because both the size of the distal epiphysis and a missing section of midshaft had to be estimated; a range rather than a single value is therefore given for its length. The length of the Shanidar 6 tibia has been estimated from its associated virtually complete left fibula using a least squares regression based on recent human paired tibiae and fibulae (Table 67).

The diaphyses of the Shanidar 2 and 6 tibiae are similar to those of other Neandertals in being relatively wide and amygdaloid in cross section (Figures 64 and 65). The cnemic index of the Shanidar 2 tibia (68.4) is close to a European Neandertal mean (70.0 ± 6.2, N = 6) and between those of Amud 1 (61.5) and Tabūn C1 (74.5). However, neither the Shanidar 2 cnemic index nor those of other Neandertals are distinct from those of early anatomically modern humans (Skhūl–Qafzeh sample: 65.4 ± 4.9, N = 6; Early Upper Paleolithic sample: 63.1 ± 5.9, N = 15), or recent humans (Europeans: 71.8 ± 6.0, N = 50; North Africans: 67.2 ± 4.7, N = 50; Amerindians: 64.2 ± 5.5, N = 50).

The midshaft indices of Shanidar 2 and 6 (71.1 and 72.2, respectively) are well above the value of 63.3 for Amud 1, slightly higher than the mean of a European Neandertal sample (68.9 ± 4.8, N = 5), and similar to that of Tabūn C1 (74.8). These data imply that the Shanidar specimens had slightly wider diaphyses relative to their anteroposterior dimensions than do most Neandertals. Yet again, these indices are not separate from those of early anatomically modern humans (Skhūl–Qafzeh sample: 69.7 ± 5.9, N = 6; Early Upper Paleolithic sample: 66.6 ± 6.4, N = 9) and well within recent human ranges of variation (Europeans: 78.2 ± 6.8, N = 50; North Africans: 72.2 ± 5.6, N = 50; Amerindians: 65.7 ± 5.1, N = 50).

Although the cnemic and midshaft indices of the Shanidar and other Neandertal tibiae are little different from those of more recent humans, the quantity and distribution of bone in their midshaft cross sections set them apart from

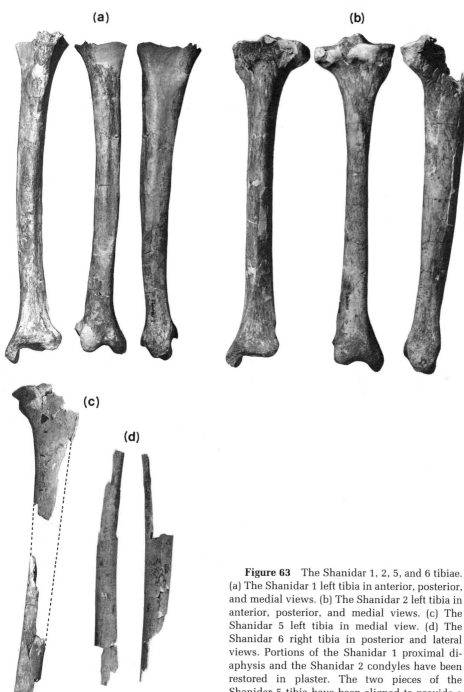

Figure 63 The Shanidar 1, 2, 5, and 6 tibiae. (a) The Shanidar 1 left tibia in anterior, posterior, and medial views. (b) The Shanidar 2 left tibia in anterior, posterior, and medial views. (c) The Shanidar 5 left tibia in medial view. (d) The Shanidar 6 right tibia in posterior and lateral views. Portions of the Shanidar 1 proximal diaphysis and the Shanidar 2 condyles have been restored in plaster. The two pieces of the Shanidar 5 tibia have been aligned to provide a maximum length of 350.0–360.0 mm. Scale in centimeters.

TABLE 67
Measurements of the Tibiae (mm)

	Shanidar 1[e]		Shanidar 2	Shanidar 5[f]	Shanidar 6[g]
	Right	Left	Left	Left	Left
Maximum length (M-1a)	—	(355.0)	337.5	(350.0–360.0)	(300.0)
Total length (M-1b)	—	—	325.0	—	—
Articular length (M-2)	—	(332.0)	309.8	—	(279.0)
Midshaft sagittal diameter (M-8)	—	p34.0	35.7	—	29.5
Midshaft transverse diameter (M-9)	—	p25.8	25.4	—	21.3
Midshaft circumference (M-10)	—	p93.0	98.0	—	80.0
Proximal sagittal diameter (M-8a)	—	—	42.1	—	—
Proximal transverse diameter (M-9a)	—	—	28.8	—	—
Proximal circumference (M-10a)	—	—	125.0	—	—
Proximal maximum breadth (M-3)	—	—	80.0	—	—
Medial condyle breadth (M-3a)	—	—	32.5	31.5	—
Medial condyle depth (M-4a)	—	—	—	(43.8)	—
Lateral condyle breadth (M-3b)	—	—	(29.0)	—	—
Tuberosity projection[a]	—	—	45.5	(45.0)	—
Distal breadth (M-6)	54.0	—	54.1	—	—
Distal depth (M-7)	39.0	—	36.9	—	—
Distal articular breadth[b]	31.4	32.0	31.3	—	—
Distal medial articular depth[b]	23.7	20.5	23.5	—	—
Distal lateral articular depth[b]	33.0	—	28.6	—	—
Medial retroversion angle (M-12)	—	—	14°	(14°)	—
Lateral retroversion angle[c]	—	—	15°	—	—
Medial inclination angle (M-13)	—	—	10°	—	—
Lateral inclination angle[c]	—	—	11°	—	—
Divergence angle[d]	—	—	4°	—	—
Torsion angle (M-14)	—	—	24°	—	—

[a]Distance from the middle of the intercondylar tubercles to the anterior margin of the tibial tuberosity, measured perpendicular to the diaphyseal axis.

[b]Dimensions of the articular surface for the talar trochlea. The articular breadth and lateral articular depth are maximum dimensions, whereas the medial articular depth is a minimum dimension.

[c]Retroversion and inclination angles measured on the lateral condyle, using the same techniques employed for measuring the angles on the medial condyle.

[d]The difference between the retroversion and inclination angles.

[e]The maximum length of the Shanidar 1 left tibia was estimated from the length of the preserved portion using a least squares regression based on recent human tibiae (r = 0.991), and the articular length was estimated from the maximum length estimate using a least squares regression based on recent human tibiae (r = 0.992).

[f]The maximum length of the Shanidar 5 left tibia was estimated from the approximated length of the preserved portion using a least squares regression based on recent human tibiae (r = 0.989). The preserved portions consist of a proximal half and a distal half (see inventory); the length of missing bone between the two segments was approximated from the in situ positions of the pieces, and the uncertainty of the amount of bone actually missing is indicated by the range of the length estimate.

[g]The maximum length of the Shanidar 6 tibia was estimated from the articular length of the left fibula, using a least squares regression based on recent human paired tibiae and fibulae (r = 0.979), and the articular length was subsequently estimated from the maximum length using a least squares regression based on recent human tibiae (r = 0.992).

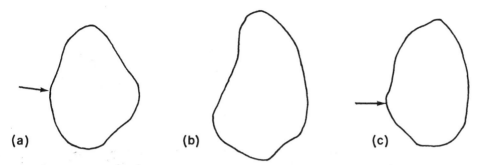

Figure 64 Diaphyseal cross sections of the Shanidar 1 and 2 left tibiae. (a) Shanidar 1 tibia at midshaft; (b) Shanidar 2 tibia at the distal margin of the nutrient foramen; and (c) Shanidar 2 tibia at midshaft. The sections are viewed in a proximal–distal direction, anterior is above, and the arrows indicate the positions of the interosseus crests. Sections kindly provided by T. D. Stewart.

recent humans. Because it is the geometric distribution and quantity of bone within a diaphyseal cross section that best indicates the adaptation of the bone to patterns and levels of biomechanical stress (Lovejoy *et al.* 1976; Ruff 1981), it is best to evaluate the structural characteristics of a diaphysis by examining, when possible, its cross-sectional geometry. Fortunately, the Shanidar 6 left tibia presented during reassembly a largely intact cross section of its midshaft region (Figure 65). Two other Neandertals, Amud 1 and La Chapelle-aux-Saints 1, present natural cross sections of their tibial midshafts, so that it has been possible to compare the biomechanical properties of these three Neandertal tibial diaphyses to those of recent humans (Lovejoy and Trinkaus 1980). Given variation in fossilization, it is not possible to take into account the original differences in bone density of the different tibial diaphyses, so that the analysis has assumed that all these individuals, Neandertals and recent humans, had similar densities of their tibial diaphyses; because the more robust Neandertals probably had denser cortical diaphyseal bone, given the tendency of bone to increase its density during hypertrophy (Tschantz and Rutishauser 1967), this assumption should minimize differences between the Neandertal and recent human tibiae.

Figure 65 Midshaft cross section of the Shanidar 6 right tibia, viewed in a proximodistal direction. Anterior is above and lateral is to the right. Both the medial and lateral borders are missing portions in the plane of the cross section, which were reconstructed for the purposes of the biomechanical analysis. Scale in centimeters.

The estimated minimum torsional, minimum bending, and maximum bending strengths of the Shanidar 6 tibia are similar to those of a recent human sample (10 Amerindians and 5 Euroamericans) and somewhat less than those of Amud 1 and La Chapelle-aux-Saints 1, both of whose estimated diaphyseal strengths are well above the recent human means (Table 68). However, the Shanidar 6 tibia was considerably shorter than the other two Neandertals and the recent humans in the comparative sample. If the estimated diaphyseal strengths are normalized for length (Table 68), the normalized minimum bending and minimum torsional strengths of the Shanidar 6 tibia are similar to those of Amud 1 and La Chapelle-aux-Saints 1 and 2.84 and 3.96 standard deviations from the recent human means. Only the normalized maximum bending strength of the Shanidar 6 tibia is noticeably lower than those of the other two Neandertals because it is intermediate between their values and the recent human mean and only 1.74 standard deviations from the recent human mean (Table 68). These data indicate that the amygdaloid cross-sectional shapes of the Shanidar and other Neandertal tibial diaphyses are associated with an exceptional robusticity.

Evidence of this robusticity can be provided for the other Shanidar tibiae and for those other Neandertals whose cross-sectional geometries can not be so readily analyzed with a robusticity index: (midshaft anteroposterior diameter $\times$ mediolateral diameter)$^{1/2}$/maximum length. The Shanidar 6 value for this index is about 8.36, which is exceeded by that of Shanidar 2 (8.92). It is also possible to compute a robusticity index for the Shanidar 1 left tibia if it is assumed that the anteroposterior and mediolateral diameters of its abnormal midshaft are close to what they would have been if the tibia had been normal; the resultant index (ca. 8.34) is essentially the same as that of Shanidar 6.

These Shanidar robusticity indices are at or beyond the upper end of a Neandertal range of variation (7.28–8.37, N = 7; Amud 1: ca. 7.91; Tabūn C1: 7.28; European Neandertals: 8.06 $\pm$ 0.32, N = 5). Most of these Neandertal indices, and especially those of the Shanidar individuals, are well above those of early anatomically modern humans (Skhūl–Qafzeh sample: 7.29 $\pm$ 0.66, N = 4; Early Upper Paleolithic sample: 6.84 $\pm$ 0.70, N = 7), and recent humans (Europeans: 7.01 $\pm$ 0.49, N = 50; North Africans: 6.20 $\pm$ 0.46, N = 50; Amerindians: 7.12 $\pm$ 0.44, N = 50). Even the Middle Pleistocene Ngandong 14 and possibly late Middle Pleistocene Broken Hill E691 tibiae have robusticity indices (ca. 6.72 and 7.02, respectively) below those of the Shanidar and other Neandertal tibiae. It is thus apparent that the Shanidar individuals, along with other Neandertals, had exceptionally robust tibial diaphyses.

The Shanidar 2 and 5 proximal epiphyses are relatively large but similar in morphology to those of other Neandertals and more recent humans. Their most salient feature is the retroversion of their condyles and the associated posterior positioning of their condyles (Figure 66). The retroversion angles of Shanidar 2 and 5 (14° and ca. 14°, respectively) are similar to those of other Neandertals (La Ferrassie 2: 15°; Kiik-Koba 1: ca. 16°; Spy 2: 18°; Tabūn C1: ca. 12°) and toward

TABLE 68

Geometrical Parameters and Relative Torsional and Bending Strengths of the Shanidar 6, Amud 1, and La Chapelle-aux-Saints 1 Neandertal Tibial Midshafts and Those of a Recent Human Sample[a]

	Maximum length (mm)	Area (mm^2)	Minimum torsional strength (mm^3)	Minimum bending strength (mm^3)	Maximum bending strength (mm^3)	Normalized minimum torsional strength	Normalized minimum bending strength	Normalized maximum bending strength
Shanidar 6	(300.0)	282	884	942	1349	982	1047	1499
Amud 1	(386.0)	510	1595	1556	3236	1070	1044	2172
La Chapelle-aux-Saints 1	(340.0)	439	1215	1359	2457	1051	1051	2125
Recent humans (N = 15)								
X̄	375	299	800	797	1420	564	564	999
SD	21	76	242	205	466	147	122	288

[a]All data from Lovejoy and Trinkaus (1980:469). The Shanidar 6 normalized strengths have been recomputed using an estimated maximum length of 300.0 mm rather than the 299.0 mm used previously. The strengths have been normalized by being divided by maximum length squared.

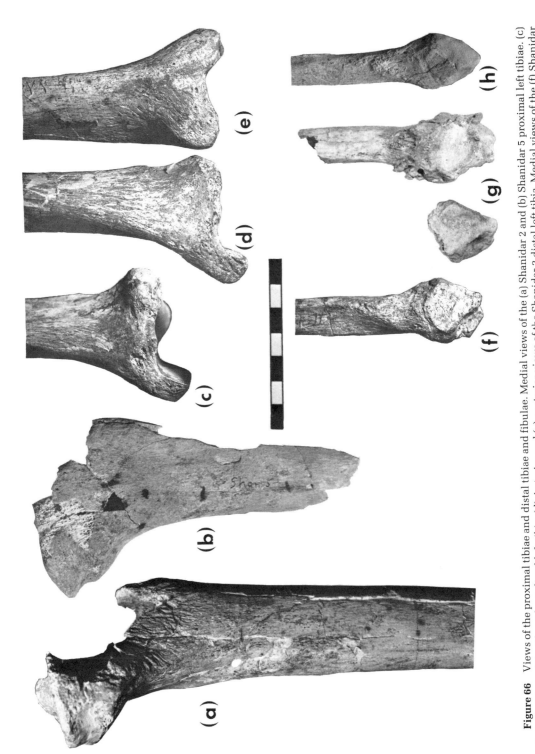

Figure 66 Views of the proximal tibiae and distal tibiae and fibulae. Medial views of the (a) Shanidar 2 and (b) Shanidar 5 proximal left tibiae. (c) Anterior view of the Shanidar 1 distal left tibia. (d) Anterior and (e) posterior views of the Shanidar 2 distal left tibia. Medial views of the (f) Shanidar 2 left, (g) Shanidar 3 right and left, and (h) Shanidar 6 left distal fibulae. Scale in centimeters.

the upper end of recent human ranges of variation (Europeans: 9.4° ± 3.7°, N = 109; North Africans: 14.7° ± 3.2°, N = 107; Melanesians: 14.9° ± 3.1°, N = 33 [Trinkaus 1975c]).

Tibial retroversion was once considered to indicate an habitually bent knee (Boule 1911–1913; Fraipont 1888). Not only is 10°–20° of retroversion fully compatible with completely erect posture, as indicated by its frequent occurrence among recent humans, but it is adaptive to high levels of joint reaction force at the knee during a normal striding gait. The peak joint reaction forces across the femorotibial articulations, from M. quadriceps femoris, M. gastrocnemius, and ground reaction forces, tend to occur when the knee is flexed between 10° and 20° (Bartholomew 1953; Eberhart et al. 1954; Kettlecamp et al. 1970; O'Konski 1979). The tibial retroversion of Shanidar 2 and 4, as well as that of other Neandertals and more recent humans, tends to minimize anteroposterior shear stress at the knee by orienting the main joint reaction force perpendicular to the plane of the tibial condyles.

The condylar retroversion present on the Shanidar 2 and 5 tibiae is associated with a posterior displacement of the tibial condyles relative to the anatomical axis of their diaphyses. This posterior displacement of the condyles can be quantified on the Shanidar 2 tibia by its divergence angle (4°), which is comparable to those of other Neandertals (Tabūn C1: 3°; La Chapelle-aux-Saints 1: 5°; La Ferrassie 2: 4°; Kiik-Koba 1: 6°; Spy 2: 5°) and slightly above those of most recent humans (Europeans: 2.3° ± 0.9°, N = 109; North Africans: 2.3° ± 0.7°, N = 107; Melanesians: 2.7° ± 0.9°, N = 33 [Trinkaus 1975c]). However, the primary effect of this posterior displacement is to increase the length of the moment arm for M. quadriceps femoris.

The length of the M. quadriceps femoris moment arm at the knee can be approximated on an isolated tibia with the tuberosity projection measurement (O'Konski 1979). If this dimension is compared to the maximum length of the tibia as an indicator of the load arm for M. quadriceps femoris during locomotion, the resultant tuberosity projection index provides an approximation of the mechanical advantage of M. quadriceps femoris. The tuberosity projection indices of Shanidar 2 and 5 (13.5 and ca. 12.5–12.9, respectively) are similar to those of other Neandertals (Tabūn C1: 10.4; La Chapelle-aux-Saints 1: 14.2; La Ferrassie 2: 12.3; Kiik-Koba 1: 13.9; Spy 2: 15.1). Furthermore, all of the Neandertal indices, except that of Tabūn C1, are at or above the upper limits of a recent European sample (7.8–11.8, 10.3 ± 0.9, N = 78 [O'Konski 1979]). The three available early anatomically modern humans—Caviglione 1, Cro-Magnon 1, and Skhūl 4—have indices (9.7, 10.4, and 10.2, respectively) close to the recent human mean, and the Broken Hill E691 tibia has a slightly higher index (11.2).

This information suggests that Shanidar 2 and 5 have relatively large moment arms for their M. quadriceps femoris. Another indication of this is provided by the absolute and relative thicknesses of the Shanidar patellae. Furthermore, among recent humans and fossil H. sapiens the tuberosity projection index is positively correlated with the retroversion angle (O'Konski 1979), which indicates that these are anatomically interrelated features. Their high values among the Shanidar Neandertals are undoubtedly part of the general robusticity of their lower limbs.

The Shanidar 2 tibia presents a relatively high degree of axial torsion, as indicated by its torsion angle of 24°. This value is at the top of the range of variation of a small Neandertal sample (La Ferrassie 2: 13°; Kiik-Koba 1: 20°; Spy 2: 23°; Tabūn C1: ca. 20°). However, it is well within the maximum range of variation recorded for normal recent humans (0°–39° [Martin 1928]), although it is at the upper limit of the range of means for 14 recent human samples (14°–23° [Martin 1928]). The torsion of the Shanidar 2 tibia indicates a normal human tendency toward toeing out.

The Shanidar 1 and 2 left distal tibial epiphyses are those of relatively robust bones with moderately large articulations (Table 67; Figure 66). Each bone has a faintly marked sulcus for the *M. tibialis posterior* tendon (the sulcus is marked on the abnormal Shanidar 1 right medial malleolus by an extensive ossification of the tendon sheath).

The Shanidar 1 left tibia and the fragment of the Shanidar 3 left tibia exhibit lateral squatting facets, but the Shanidar 2 tibia does not have one. Both the Shanidar 1 and 2 tibiae lack medial squatting facets (the region is not preserved for Shanidar 3). The Tabūn C1 tibiae both exhibit lateral squatting facets, but not medial ones; among European Neandertals, 66.7% (N = 6) exhibit lateral squatting facets, but none of them (N = 5) exhibits medial facets. Among recent humans, frequencies for lateral facets vary considerably (30.6–80.8% in six samples [Trinkaus 1975c]), depending upon the tendency of the individuals in the population to assume a squatting position.

The tibiae from Shanidar are thus similar to those of other Neandertals in having exceptionally robust diaphyses and proximal epiphyses adapted for the effective functioning of the *M. quadriceps femoris*.

FIBULAE

Inventory

SHANIDAR 1

Right Complete but abnormal distal epiphysis with the diaphysis in the region of the distal tibiofibular articulation. Maximum length = 78.8 mm.

Left Complete diaphysis from the neck to the region of the distal tibiofibular articulation. Maximum length = 275.0 mm.

SHANIDAR 2

Left Almost complete bone with damage only on the anterior medial head and the posterior malleolus. Maximum length = 417.1 mm.

SHANIDAR 3

Right Complete but abnormal distal epiphysis with a portion of the diaphysis in the region of the distal tibiofibular articulation. Maximum length = 85.3 mm.

Left Incomplete malleolus with damage to the posterior surface. Maximum length = 30.0 mm.

SHANIDAR 4

Right Section of damaged proximal and central diaphysis (maximum length = 80.8 mm), and a separate fragment of distal epiphysis (maximum length = 41.1 mm).

Left Heavily abraded malleolus and distal diaphysis fused postmortem to the left tibia and talus. Maximum length = 104.9 mm.

SHANIDAR 5

Left Posterior and medial surfaces of the head, neck, and proximal third of the diaphysis. Maximum length = 159.8 mm.

SHANIDAR 6

Right Complete diaphysis lacking the epiphyses. Maximum length = 252.8 mm.

Left Complete diaphysis with major portions of both epiphyses. Maximum length = 286.5 mm.

SHANIDAR 8

Right Proximal and central diaphyseal section. Originally assigned to Shanidar 4 (Stewart 1963). Maximum length = 42.6 mm.

Morphology

The fibula is the one bone for which each of the Shanidar adults retains a portion. Two of them—Shanidar 2 and 6—preserve at least one largely intact fibula, and three others—Shanidar 1, 4, and 8—retain major portions of their diaphyses (Figure 67). In addition, Shanidar 1 and 3, along with Shanidar 2 and

Figure 67   Anterior views of the fibulae. (a) Shanidar 1 left; (b) Shanidar 2 left; (c), (d) Shanidar 6 right and left; and (e) Shanidar 8 right. Portions of the Shanidar 2 and 6 left heads and the Shanidar 6 malleolus have been restored with filler. Scale in centimeters.

6, retain largely complete lateral malleoli. Only the Shanidar 5 fibula is too fragmentary to yield morphological or metric data.

The Shanidar 1 left fibular diaphysis experienced the same abnormal bowing as his left tibia; it is uncertain to what extent this curvature of the bone affected other aspects, such as the formation of muscular crests along the diaphysis. The Shanidar 1 and 3 right distal epiphyses experienced degenerative joint disease, which produced exostoses around their articular surfaces and along the distal tibiofibular ligamentous joint. Their measurements (Table 69) approximate the original dimensions of their malleoli and malleolar articular surfaces.

The lengths of the Shanidar 2 and 6 fibulae were measured directly on their fibulae, even though damage to the Shanidar 6 proximal epiphysis has required some estimation. For the purposes of comparative indices, the Shanidar 1 fibular maximum length has been estimated from its tibial maximum length of about 355.0 mm to be about 345.0 mm.

The Shanidar fibular diaphyses, like those of all other humans, are highly variable in morphology. Because the fibular diaphysis is primarily a non-weight-bearing muscular attachment bone in humans, its diaphyseal shape is affected by minor variations in the sural muscles. The Shanidar midshaft indices (minimum diameter/maximum diameter) illustrate some of this variation (73.0, 95.1, 80.8, 88.5 & 91.8, and 66.5 for Shanidar 1, 2, 4, 6, and 8, respectively). The Shanidar 2 and 6 indices are relatively high, but the other Shanidar indices are similar to those of other Neandertals (Tabūn C1: 81.8 & 85.5; European Neandertals: 63.2–82.4, 72.9 ± 6.5, N = 15). Furthermore, the indices of Shanidar 1, 4, and 8 fall within the ranges of variation of early anatomically modern humans (Skhūl–Qafzeh hominids: 66.5 ± 9.1, N = 4; Early Upper Paleolithic hominids: 72.4 ± 10.6, N = 6), and the range of means of 24 recent human samples (60.8–82.4 [Sprecher 1932]).

The Shanidar 1, 2, and 6 fibulae have relatively high robusticity indices (midshaft circumference/maximum length; ca. 13.0, 16.7, and ca. 14.0, respectively). These values are at or above the upper limits of the ranges of variation of other Neandertals (La Ferrassie 2: ca. 12.5; Kiik-Koba 1: 13.7; Tabūn C1: ca. 11.2), early anatomically modern humans (Cro-Magnon 1: 13.5; Skhūl 4: 10.6; Skhūl 5: ca. 10.3), and recent humans (range of means for seven samples: 11.4–12.6 [Sprecher 1932]). This fibular diaphyseal robusticity is undoubtedly part of their general lower limb robusticity, as seen in their femoral and tibial diaphyses.

Because all three of the preserved proximal epiphyses—those of Shanidar 2, 5, and 6—are incomplete, it is difficult to assess their morphologies. The preserved portions closely resemble their counterparts among recent humans.

The distal epiphyses of the Shanidar 1, 2, 3, and 6 fibulae appear to be relatively robust but otherwise morphologically similar to those of other humans. Their distal epiphyseal indices (maximum breadth/maximum depth; 78.9, ca. 69.6, 82.2, and ca. 69.6 for Shanidar 1, 2, 3, and 6, respectively) are

TABLE 69
Measurements of the Fibulae (mm)

	Shanidar 1[d]		Shanidar 2	Shanidar 3		Shanidar 4	Shanidar 6		Shanidar 8
	Right	Left	Left	Right	Left	Right	Right	Left	Right
Maximum length (M-1)	—	(345.0)	320.0	—	—	—	—	(301.0)	—
Articular length (M-1a)	—	—	312.0	—	—	—	—	(287.0)	—
Maximum midshaft diameter (M-2)	—	15.9	16.2	—	—	15.6	13.0	13.4	15.8
Minimum midshaft diameter (M-3)	—	11.6	15.4	—	—	12.6	11.5	12.3	10.5
Midshaft circumference (M-4)	—	45.0	53.5	—	—	46.0	40.0	42.0	43.5
Proximal maximum diameter[a]	—	12.6	15.0	—	—	—	12.1	10.4	—
Proximal minimum diameter[a]	—	10.2	10.9	—	—	—	8.5	9.0	—
Proximal circumference (M-4a)	—	36.5	45.0	—	—	—	33.0	33.0	—
Distal breadth (M-4[2])	21.3	—	(19.5)	23.5	—	—	—	(16.0)	—
Distal depth[b]	27.0	—	28.0	28.6	26.9	—	—	(23.0)	—
Distal articular depth[c]	21.4	—	20.1	27.8	29.3	—	—	—	—
Distal articular height[c]	28.3	—	26.3	22.3	20.7	—	—	—	—

[a]Maximum and minimum shaft diameters measured at the level of the proximal minimum circumference.
[b]Maximum anteroposterior dimension of the distal epiphysis.
[c]Maximum anteroposterior (depth) and proximodistal (height) dimensions of the articular surface for the talus.
[d]Maximum length estimated from the tibial maximum length using a least squares regression based on recent human paired tibiae and fibulae (r = 0.979).

similar to those of other Neandertals (La Ferrassie 2: 76.7; Hortus 40: 65.5; Kiik-Koba 1: 66.8; Tabūn C1: 69.0). Several of these Neandertals, including Shanidar 2 and 6, appear to have thin malleoli, according to these indices, relative to the range of means for 26 recent humans samples (77.2–90.1 [Sprecher 1932]). This is probably due to their tendency to have moderately large anteroposterior dimensions of their lateral malleoli, which is indicated by their distal robusticity indices (maximum depth/maximum length). These indices for Shanidar 1, 2, and 6 (ca. 7.82, 8.75, and ca. 7.64, respectively) are similar to that of Kiik-Koba 1 (8.44) and slightly above those of La Ferrassie 2 (ca. 7.40) and Tabūn C1: (ca. 7.00). Most of these Neandertal distal robusticity indices, including all three from Shanidar, are toward the upper limits of recent human ranges of variation (range of means for 26 samples: 6.0–7.8 [Sprecher 1932]). A small Early Upper Paleolithic sample has indices (7.11 ± 0.35, N = 4) closer to the middle of recent human values.

These two indices suggest that the Shanidar Neandertals had a moderate hypertrophy of their lateral malleoli. Because the lateral malleolus is important in maintaining the integrity of the talocrural joint during locomotion (Weinert et al. 1973), some enlargement of it would be in agreement with their lower limb robusticity.

The fibulae of the Shanidar adults thus have robust diaphyses and moderately robust distal epiphyses. In all other features, they fall within the large range of variation in fibular morphology present among more recent humans and other Neandertals.

FOOT REMAINS

Inventory

TALUS

Shanidar 1

   Right   Complete but abnormal bone. Maximum length = 55.6 mm; maximum breadth = 68.4 mm.
   Left   Complete bone with minor damage to the dorsolateral lateral neck. Maximum length = 55.4 mm; maximum breadth = 48.9 mm.

Shanidar 3

   Right   Complete bone with minor damage to the margins of the head and lateral malleolar surface. Extensively diseased bone. Maximum length = 60.9 mm; maximum breadth = 51.2 mm.

Left   Most of the lateral malleolar surface with adjacent portions of the trochlea and posterior calcaneal surface. Maximum height = 32.9 mm.

Shanidar 4

Right   Anterolateral fragment with portions of the lateral malleolar surface, posterior calcaneal surface, and sulcus tali. Heavily eroded and fused postmortem to the calcaneus. Maximum length = 28.4 mm; maximum breadth = 40.0 mm.

Left   A heavily eroded portion of the head, medial malleolar surface, and anterior calcaneal surface fused postmortem to the left calcaneus (maximum length = 31.4 mm; maximum breadth = 25.5 mm), and an eroded portion of the trochlea and lateral malleolar surface fused postmortem to the left tibia and fibula (maximum length = 27.5 mm; maximum breadth = 37.0 mm).

Shanidar 6

Right   Anterolateral fragment with small portions of the lateral malleolar, posterior calcaneal, and sulcus tali surfaces and of the trochlea. Maximum length = 16.3 mm; maximum breadth = 23.5 mm.

CALCANEUS

Shanidar 1

Right   Complete bone with minor abrasion on the articular surface margins. The lateral side of the body and the plantar sides of the tuber calcanei and cuboid surface have been partially crushed and distorted. Maximum length = 83.8 mm; maximum breadth = 46.6 mm.

Left   Largely complete bone with damage to the medial and lateral sides of the body and the lateral half of the tuber calcanei. Maximum length = 83.7 mm; maximum breadth = 45.8 mm.

Shanidar 3

Right   The bone retains much of the surface bone, although virtually all of the trabeculae have been lost. The portions preserved include most of the cuboid, anterior talar, and posterior talar surfaces, the medial body from the medial process of the tuberosity to the M. *flexor hallucis longus* sulcus, the plantar ligament surface and the dorsal half of the lateral surface (maximum length = 81.9 mm; maximum breadth = 50.5 mm). In addition, a fragment of the middle of the tuber calcanei has been preserved (maximum breadth = 28.2 mm).

Left   The major piece retains the anterior and medial talar surfaces and the dorsal half of the cuboid surface (maximum length = 38.0 mm; maximum breadth = 41.0 mm); there is also a fragment of the posterior talar surface with the cervical ligament attachment area (maximum length = 31.0 mm).

Shanidar 4

Right   A portion of the posterior talar surface fused to the right talus. Maximum length = 34.4 mm; maximum breadth = 39.2 mm.
Left   A small fragment of the anterior talar surface fused to the left talus. Maximum dimension = 21.3 mm.

OS NAVICULARE

Shanidar 1

Right   Complete bone with minimal dorsal damage. Maximum length = 29.0 mm; maximum breadth = 45.1 mm.
Left   Complete bone but partly crushed on the dorsal and plantar surfaces. Maximum length = 25.5 mm; maximum breadth = 48.5 mm.

Shanidar 3

Right   Complete body without the tuberosity. Maximum length = 18.0 mm; maximum breadth = 41.6 mm.
Left   Consists of the lateral half of the talar surface with parts of the lateral body and lateral cuneiform surface (maximum breadth = 27.0 mm) and a complete tuberosity (maximum length = 25.8 mm; maximum breadth = 25.0 mm).

Shanidar 4

Right   Complete bone with minor damage to the plantar margin of the cuneiform surfaces. Maximum breadth = 44.9 mm.

OS CUBOIDEUM

Shanidar 1

Right   Dorsal half of the bone with portions of the calcaneal, lateral cuneiform and metatarsal articular surfaces. Maximum length = 27.1 mm; maximum breadth = 19.1 mm.

Shanidar 3

> *Right* Complete bone with minimal abrasion. Maximum length = 35.3 mm; maximum breadth = 27.8 mm.
>
> *Left* A fragment of the dorsal lateral surface with the margins of the calcaneal and metatarsal 5 surfaces (maximum length = 23.7 mm); and a fragment of the M. *peroneus longus* sulcus with the margin of the metatarsal 4/5 surface (maximum breadth = 15.0 mm).

Shanidar 6

> *Left* Lateral dorsal surface of the bone with the dorsal third of the calcaneal and metatarsal 5 articular surfaces. Maximum length = 12.7 mm.

OS CUNEIFORME MEDIALE

Shanidar 1

> *Right* Complete but diseased bone. Maximum length = 27.1 mm; maximum breadth = 19.1 mm.
>
> *Left* Complete bone with minimal abrasion to the medial surface. Maximum length = 27.1 mm; maximum breadth = 18.0 mm.

Shanidar 3

> *Right* Central body fragment with portions of the navicular, intermedial cuneiform and metatarsal 1 surfaces. Maximum length = 23.8 mm; maximum breadth = 14.8 mm.
>
> *Left* Complete with minor damage to the plantar, medial and dorsal surfaces. Maximum length = 26.7 mm; maximum breadth = 18.8 mm.

OS CUNEIFORME INTERMEDIUM

Shanidar 1

> *Right* Largely complete bone with plantar damage. Maximum length = 16.9 mm; maximum breadth = 18.0 mm.
>
> *Left* Complete bone. Maximum length = 17.9 mm; maximum breadth = 19.5 mm.

Shanidar 3

> *Right* Complete bone with minimal damage to the dorsal edges. Maximum length = 17.6 mm; maximum breadth = 15.7 mm.
>
> *Left* Largely complete bone lacking the dorsal medial margin and part of

the lateral ligamentous surface. Maximum length = 16.9 mm; maximum breadth = 15.8 mm.

Shanidar 4

Right Dorsal surface with ca. 7 mm of the dorsal margin of the articular surfaces. Maximum length = 17.3 mm.

Left Dorsal surface with the dorsal margins of the articular surfaces. Maximum length = 17.3 mm.

Shanidar 6

Left Dorsal surface with the dorsal margins of the articular surfaces. Maximum length = 14.6 mm.

Shanidar 8

Right Dorsal surface with the dorsal margins of the articular surfaces. Maximum length = 15.5 mm.

OS CUNEIFORME LATERALE

Shanidar 1

Right Largely present with reconstruction on the plantar tuberosity. Maximum length = 23.1 mm; maximum breadth = 18.8 mm.

Shanidar 3

Right Dorsal two-thirds of the metatarsal articulation with a small portion of the dorsal surface. Maximum breadth = 19.9 mm.

Shanidar 4

Right Dorsal half of the bone with damage to the medial surface. Maximum length = 24.3 mm.

Left Largely complete, but the tuberosity is absent and the medial surface and the plantar half of the lateral surface are abraded. Maximum length = 23.3 mm.

OS METATARSALE 1

Shanidar 1

Right Largely complete bone with damage to the medial head. Maximum length = 61.9 mm.

Left   Largely complete bone with damage to the medial margin of the base and the lateral distal tuberosity. Maximum length = 64.1 mm.

Shanidar 3

Right   The medial three-quarters of the head. Maximum height = 20.4 mm.
Left   The base with the dorsal three-quarters of the articular and mus-culoligamentous surfaces (maximum length = 23.2 mm), and a frag-ment of the medial side of the head (maximum height = 18.5 mm).

Shanidar 8

Left   The bone consists of the complete base with the proximal diaphysis (maximum length = 40.0 mm), and a fragment of the distal articular surface (maximum breadth = 19.0 mm).

OS METATARSALE 2

Shanidar 1

Right   Complete base and diaphysis. Maximum length = 66.0 mm.
Left   Complete base and diaphysis with a portion of the distal ligamentous surface. Maximum length = 70.4 mm.

Shanidar 3

Right   Dorsal half of the base with the intermedial cuneiform surface and the adjacent dorsal ligamentous surface. Maximum length = 14.6 mm.

Shanidar 4

Left   Dorsal third of the base and proximal diaphysis. Maximum length = 32.4 mm.

Shanidar 6

Right   Diaphysis with the dorsal half of the base and the distal ligamentous surface. Maximum length = 63.0 mm.
Left   Complete diaphysis with the dorsal portion of the base and the distal ligamentous surface. Maximum length = 61.5 mm.

OS METATARSALE 3

Shanidar 1

Right   Complete bone with damage to the plantar base and the dorsal head. Maximum length = 73.2 mm.

Shanidar 3

Right   Complete base. Maximum length = 21.3 mm.

Shanidar 4

Left   Complete base with the adjacent diaphysis. Maximum length = 27.6 mm.

Shanidar 6

Left   Complete diaphysis and head and the dorsal surface of the base. Maximum length = 66.8 mm.

Shanidar 8

Right   Complete bone. Maximum length = 64.7 mm.

OS METATARSALE 4

Shanidar 1

Right   Complete base and diaphysis with the distal ligamentous surface. Maximum length = 69.8 mm.
Left   Complete diaphysis. Maximum length = 51.6 mm.

Shanidar 3

Left   Metatarsal 5 facet and the lateral margin of the cuboid surface. Maximum length = 16.8 mm.

Shanidar 4

Right   Metatarsal 3 facet with part of the dorsoproximal surface. Maximum length = 25.0 mm.
Left   Central and distal diaphysis and the head. Maximum length = 52.6 mm.

Shanidar 6

Right   Complete diaphysis and head, and the plantar half of the base. Maximum length = 65.3 mm.

Shanidar 8

Right   Complete diaphysis and head with the dorsal half of the base. Maximum length = 66.4 mm.
Left   Complete diaphysis and head. Maximum length = 56.1 mm.

OS METATARSALE 5

Shanidar 1

> *Right* Complete base and diaphysis plus the lateral two-thirds of the head. Maximum length = 79.5 mm.

Shanidar 3

> *Left* Complete base and the proximal two-thirds of the diaphysis. Maximum length = 54.6 mm.

Shanidar 4

> *Right* Largely complete bone lacking the medial half of the proximal diaphysis and epiphysis. Maximum length = 77.0 mm.
> *Left* Complete bone. Maximum length = 74.4 mm.

Shanidar 8

> *Right* Largely complete bone with minor damage to the articular surfaces and the proximal tuberosity. Maximum length = 67.9 mm.
> *Left* Complete base and diaphysis. Maximum length = 58.1 mm.

OSSA METATARSALE—NUMBER INDETERMINATE

Shanidar 3

> *3/4: Right* Plantar margin of a head with the plantar tubercles. Maximum length = 17.4 mm.

Shanidar 4

> *2/3: ?* Right side of a head and the adjacent tubercle. Maximum length = 21.9 mm.

OSSA SESAMOIDEA

Shanidar 3

> *Right: Medial* Complete bone. Maximum length = 14.6 mm.
> *Right: Lateral* Complete bone. Maximum length = 12.1 mm.

Shanidar 4

> *Left: Medial* Complete bone with minimal abrasion on the edges. Maximum length = 11.5 mm.

Shanidar 8

Right: Medial   Complete bone. Maximum length = 11.7 mm.

PHALANX PROXIMALIS 1

Shanidar 1

Left   Complete bone. Maximum length = 33.2 mm.

Shanidar 3

Right?   Complete base and the proximal plantar half of the diaphysis. Maximum length = 22.2 mm.

Shanidar 4

Right   Complete bone. Maximum length = 33.6 mm.
Left   Largely complete with bone loss on the plantar lateral base. Maximum length = 31.1 mm.

Shanidar 6

Right   Complete bone. Maximum length = 29.3 mm.

Shanidar 8

Right   Complete bone. Maximum length = 30.4 mm.

PHALANX PROXIMALIS 2

Shanidar 3

Right   Complete base, complete diaphysis with damage to the medial distal quarter, and a small part of the lateral distal articular surface. Maximum length = 28.8 mm.

Shanidar 4

Right   Medial side of the head and the adjacent diaphysis. Maximum length = 12.8 mm.
Left   Complete bone. Maximum length = 29.3 mm.

Shanidar 8

Right   Complete bone. Maximum length = 27.0 mm.

PHALANX PROXIMALIS 3

Shanidar 4

Right Complete bone. Maximum length = 27.7 mm.
Left Complete bone. Maximum length = 27.1 mm.

Shanidar 8

Left Complete base and diaphysis and the medial half of the head. Maximum length = 25.0 mm.

PHALANX PROXIMALIS 4

Shanidar 4

Right Complete bone. Maximum length = 26.5 mm.

PHALANX PROXIMALIS 5

Shanidar 4

Right Complete bone. Maximum length = 21.7 mm.
Left Diaphysis and head with the dorsal margin of the base. Maximum length = 19.5 mm.

Shanidar 8

Right Complete bone. Maximum length = 20.4 mm.

PHALANX MEDIA 2

Shanidar 4

Left Complete bone. Maximum length = 12.7 mm.

PHALANX MEDIA 3

Shanidar 4

Right Complete bone. Maximum length = 12.7 mm.
Left Complete bone. Maximum length = 13.0 mm.

PHALANX MEDIA 4

Shanidar 4

Right Complete bone. Maximum length = 10.4 mm.

PHALANX MEDIA 5

Shanidar 4

Right   Complete bone. Maximum length = 10.1 mm.

Shanidar 8

Side Indeterminate   Complete bone. Maximum length = 8.1 mm.

PHALANX DISTALIS 1

Shanidar 4

Left   Complete base and the adjacent diaphysis (maximum length = 14.5 mm), plus the separate but complete tuberosity (maximum length = 12.6 mm).

Shanidar 6

Right?   The lateral two-thirds of the base (maximum length = 8.8 mm) with the separate lateral half of the tuberosity (maximum length = 13.7 mm).

PHALANGES DISTALES 2–5

Shanidar 4

Numbers Uncertain and Sides Indeterminate   Five complete phalanges are preserved. They probably represent the right and left second distal phalanges, a third distal phalanx, a fourth distal phalanx, and a fifth distal phalanx. The assignment to digit is based on their relative lengths. Maximum lengths = 14.2, 14.2, 13.7, 11.1, and 9.5 mm.

Foot Remains by Individual

Right[a]	Indeterminate[a]	Left[a]
SHANIDAR 1		
Talus		Talus
Calcaneus		Calcaneus
Navicular		Navicular
(Cuboid)		
Medial cuneiform		Medial cuneiform
Intermedial cuneiform		Intermedial cuneiform
(Lateral cuneiform)		

(continued)

Foot Remains by Individual (*continued*)

Right[a]	Indeterminate[a]	Left[a]
Metatarsal 1		Metatarsal 1
(Metatarsal 2)		(Metatarsal 2)
Metatarsal 3		
(Metatarsal 4)		(Metatarsal 4)
Metatarsal 5		
		Proximal phalanx 1

SHANIDAR 3

Right[a]	Indeterminate[a]	Left[a]
Talus		(Talus)
(Calcaneus)		(Calcaneus)
(Navicular)		(Navicular)
Cuboid		(Cuboid)
(Medial cuneiform)		Medial cuneiform
Intermedial cuneiform		Intermedial cuneiform
(Lateral cuneiform)		
(Metatarsal 1)		(Metatarsal 1)
(Metatarsal 2)		
(Metatarsal 3)		
(Metatarsal 3/4)		(Metatarsal 4)
		(Metatarsal 5)
Medial sesamoid		
Lateral sesamoid		
(Proximal phalanx 1)		
Proximal phalanx 2		

SHANIDAR 4

Right[a]	Indeterminate[a]	Left[a]
(Talus)		(Talus)
(Calcaneus)		(Calcaneus)
Navicular		
(Intermedial cuneiform)		(Intermedial cuneiform)
(Lateral cuneiform)		(Lateral cuneiform)
	(Metatarsal 2/3)	
		(Metatarsal 2)
		(Metatarsal 3)
(Metatarsal 4)		(Metatarsal 4)
(Metatarsal 5)		Metatarsal 5
		Medial sesamoid
Proximal phalanx 1		Proximal phalanx 1
(Proximal phalanx 2)		Proximal phalanx 2
Proximal phalanx 3		Proximal phalanx 3
Proximal phalanx 4		
Proximal phalanx 5		(Proximal phalanx 5)
		Middle phalanx 2
Middle phalanx 3		Middle phalanx 3
Middle phalanx 4		
Middle phalanx 5		
		(Distal phalanx 1)
Distal phalanx 2		Distal phalanx 2
	Distal phalanx 3	

Foot Remains by Individual (continued)

Right[a]	Indeterminate[a]	Left[a]
	Distal phalanx 4	
	Distal phalanx 5	
SHANIDAR 6		
(Talus)		
		(Cuboid)
		(Intermedial cuneiform)
(Metatarsal 2)		(Metatarsal 2)
		(Metatarsal 3)
(Metatarsal 4)		
Proximal phalanx 1		
(Distal phalanx 1)		
SHANIDAR 8		
(Intermedial cuneiform)		
		(Metatarsal 1)
Metatarsal 3		
(Metatarsal 4)		(Metatarsal 4)
Metatarsal 5		(Metatarsal 5)
Medial sesamoid		
Proximal phalanx 1		
Proximal phalanx 2		
		(Proximal phalanx 3)
Proximal phalanx 5		
	Middle phalanx 5	

[a]Bones in parentheses are missing major portions. The other bones are largely complete but may have sustained minor damage.

Morphology

Even though pedal remains have survived for five of the Shanidar adults, only Shanidar 1 preserves a reasonably complete tarsometatarsal skeleton (Figures 68 and 69), and only Shanidar 4 retains most of the metatarsals and phalanges in reasonably good condition (Figure 71). Shanidar 3 retains most of the tarsals and fragments of metatarsals and phalanges (Figure 70), and Shanidar 6 and 8 preserve many of their metatarsals and phalanges. Together these pedal remains provide a good overall impression of the Shanidar pedal morphology.

In addition to their fragmentary condition, several of the Shanidar foot bones experienced antemortem alterations. The Shanidar 1 right foot had degenerative joint disease at its talocrural and first and second tarsometatarsal articulations and a fracture of the fifth metatarsal diaphysis (Chapter 12). The Shanidar 1 right talus appears to have changed shape as a result of the degenerative joint disease, perhaps from remodeling following an altered gait, so that many of its measurements cannot be used in comparative metric analyses; the

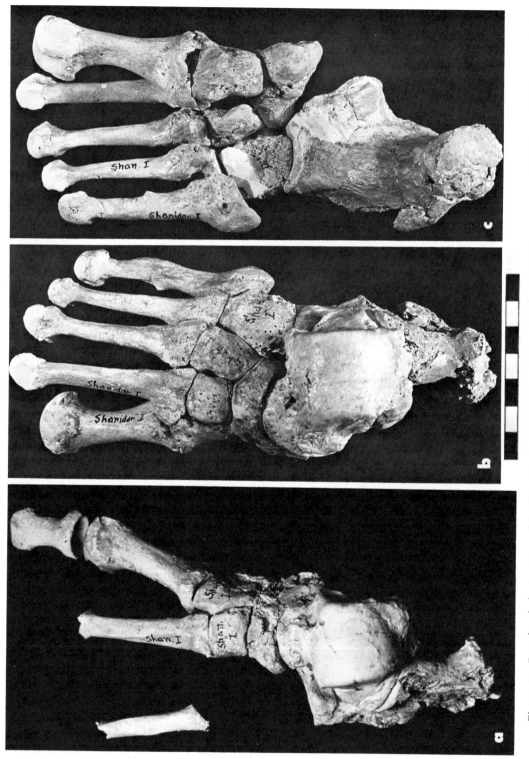

Figure 68 Dorsal and plantar views of the Shanidar 1 pedal skeletons. (a) Dorsal view of the left tarsometatarsal skeleton with the unattached fourth metatarsal and proximal hallucial phalanx. (b) Dorsal view of the right complete tarsometatarsal skeleton. (c) Plantar view of the right tarsometatarsal skeleton. Portions of the right cuboid and metatarsal heads have been restored with filler. Scale in centimeters.

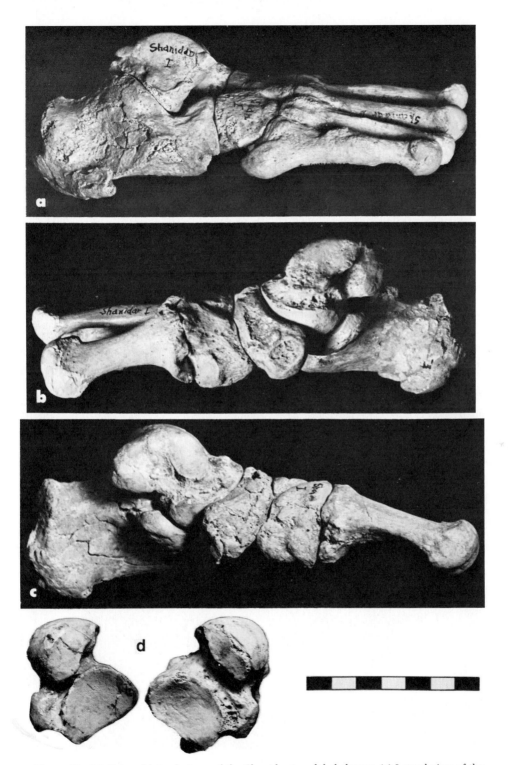

Figure 69 Medial and lateral views of the Shanidar 1 pedal skeletons. (a) Lateral view of the right tarsometatarsal skeleton. (b) Medial view of the right tarsometatarsal skeleton. (c) Medial view of the left tarsometatarsal skeleton. (d) Plantar views of the right and left tali. Scale in centimeters.

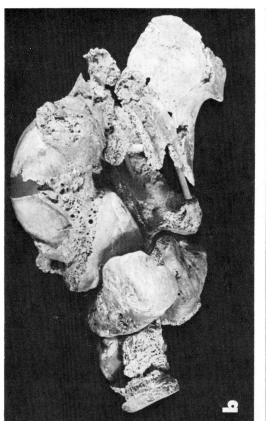

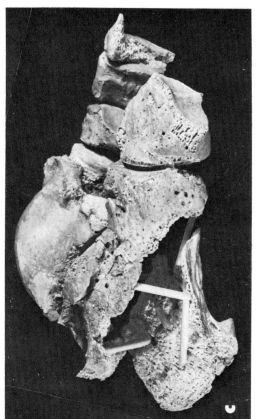

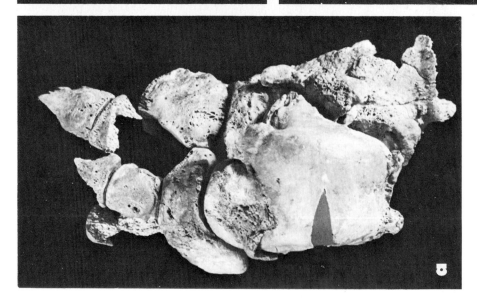

normal left talus is used for that purpose. The Shanidar 3 talocrural and talo-calcaneal articulations sustained extensive degenerative joint disease, and their margins are largely obscured but can be approximated (Chapter 12).

In order to provide impressions of the overall tarsometatarsal skeletons of Shanidar 1 and 3, the preserved tarsals and metatarsals of the Shanidar 1 right and left feet (Figures 68 and 69), and the Shanidar 3 right foot (Figure 70) have been articulated. Ideally, the articulated feet should be positioned in an intermediate position between full pronation and full supination. However, the need to maintain close contact between the bones to obtain a reasonably solid assembly has placed the tarsometatarsal skeletons in largely pronated positions. As a result of this, it is not feasible to estimate arch height (Heim 1972, 1974); because all pedal arches vary in height during normal locomotion (Hicks 1954), any measurement of arch height would be an approximation.

The individual Shanidar pedal bones and the reconstructions of the Shanidar 1 and 3 tarsometatarsal skeletons depict an overall foot configuration that is similar to those of other Neandertals (Trinkaus 1975a) and more recent humans. The tarsals and metatarsals form a compact structure with medial and lateral longitudinal arches and a transverse midtarsal arch. The metatarsals are in line with the long axis of the foot, and the hallux is fully adducted. The two most robust of the metatarsals are the first and fifth. And the bodies of the calcanei are located close to the midline of their feet, providing a strong posterior pedal segment.

There are nonetheless a few features that place the Shanidar pedal remains at the limits of recent human ranges of variation. All of these features relate to the robusticity that characterizes the Shanidar lower limbs and are fully compatible with a normal striding gait (Trinkaus 1975a).

Following a discussion of the Shanidar 1 overall pedal proportions, there are descriptions of the Shanidar 1 and 3 tali and calcanei. These are followed by descriptions of the anterior tarsals (navicular, cuboid, and cuneiform bones), the metatarsals, and the phalanges. Osteometric data for the pedal remains are in Tables 70–90.

OVERALL PROPORTIONS OF THE SHANIDAR 1 TARSOMETATARSAL SKELETON

The reassembly of the Shanidar 1 left tarsometatarsal skeleton permits an assessment of its overall proportions. In particular, it has been possible to determine the lengths of its anterior and posterior moment arms. The anterior moment arm extends from the midtalar trochlea to the distal surface of the first metatarsal head and approximates the moment arm for the ground reaction

Figure 70 The Shanidar 3 right tarsometatarsal skeleton. (a) Dorsal, (b) medial, (c) lateral. A wedge was removed from the medial margin of the talar trochlea for histological analysis (Constable 1973:64), and the contour of the trochlea has been restored with plasticene. Scale in centimeters.

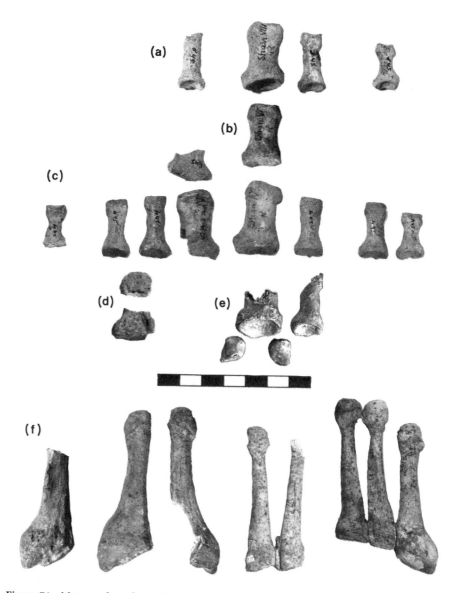

Figure 71 Metatarsals and pedal phalanges of Shanidar 3, 4, 6, and 8. All are in dorsal view except one view of the Shanidar 4 hallucial distal phalanx. (a) Shanidar 8 proximal phalanges 3 left and 1, 2, and 5 right. (b) Shanidar 6 proximal phalanx 1 right. (c) Shanidar 4 proximal phalanges 5, 3, 2, and 1 left plus the base of the hallucial distal phalanx, and proximal phalanges 1, 2, 4, and 5 right. (d) Plantar view of the Shanidar 4 hallucial distal phalanx. (e) The Shanidar 3 right proximal phalanges 1 and 2 plus the right medial and lateral hallucial sesamoid bones. (f) From left to right: the Shanidar 3 left metatarsal 5, the Shanidar 4 left and right metatarsals 5, the Shanidar 6 right metatarsals 3 and 4, and the Shanidar 8 right metatarsals 3, 4, and 5. Scale in centimeters.

force at heel-off around the talocrural articulation, whereas the posterior moment arm extends from the midtalar trochlea to the posterior margin of the calcaneal tuberosity and approximates the moment arm for M. *triceps surae* around the talocrural articulation. These moment arms are 125.5 and 57.5 mm, respectively, for the Shanidar 1 left foot.

The ratio of the Shanidar 1 posterior and anterior pedal moment arms, expressed as a percentage, is 45.8, which is similar to those of other Neandertals (La Ferrassie 1: 45.5; La Ferrassie 2: 42.9; Kiik-Koba 1: ca. 47.2; Tabūn C1: ca. 40.7). These Neandertal indices are within recent human ranges of variation (Amerindians: 38.7 ± 2.8, N = 40; North Africans: 43.0 ± 3.8, N = 25 [Trinkaus 1975a]), but most of them, including that of Shanidar 1, tend toward the upper limits of the recent human samples. This implies some elongation of the M. *triceps surae* moment arm relative to that of the ground reaction force. Interestingly, two early anatomically modern humans, Caviglione 1 and Skhūl 4, have very low (ca. 33.1) and high (ca. 53.8) indices, respectively.

In contrast, the Shanidar 1 tarsometatarsal skeleton, along with those of the other Neandertals, appears to be long relative to tibial length. The ratio of the medial subtalar length (sum of the anterior and posterior moment arms; 183.0 mm for Shanidar 1) to tibial articular length, expressed as an index, is about 55.1 for Shanidar 1. This value is slightly higher than those of the other Neandertals (La Ferrassie 1: ca. 52.7; La Ferrassie 2: 54.7; Kiik-Koba 1: ca. 55.9; Tabūn C1: ca. 53.0). These Neandertal indices, and especially that of Shanidar 1, are at or above the upper limits of recent human ranges of variation (Amerindians: 44.5 ± 1.7, N = 31; North Africans: 47.7 ± 2.7, N = 24). Skhūl 4 provides an index of 43.7, and Caviglione 1 has one of ca. 44.8. This suggests that Shanidar 1 had exceptionally long feet.

These large indices, however, may be a product of their relatively short tibiae. Most Neandertals, including those from Shanidar (Chapter 11), have relatively low crural indices (Trinkaus 1981); this would make their feet appear long if they are compared only to tibial length. If the medial subtalar length is compared instead to the summed femoral and tibial articular lengths, much of the difference disappears. The resultant indices for other Neandertals (La Ferrassie 1: ca. 24.2; La Ferrassie 2: 24.5; Tabūn C1: 22.4) are slightly greater than the mean of a recent North African sample (21.1 ± 1.1, N = 23) and those of Caviglione 1 and Skhūl 4 (ca. 20.9 and 19.6, respectively). Shanidar 1 has an index of about 23.2, which is slightly greater than those of most recent humans. Shanidar 1 may thus have had slightly longer feet than would be expected given his overall lower limb length, but not exceptionally so.

THE TALI

The Shanidar 1 left talus and the Shanidar 3 tali, despite the arthritic alterations of the Shanidar 3 right talus, provide considerable morphological and metric data (Table 70). Because the talus is primarily a cog in the universal joint

TABLE 70
Measurements of the Tali (mm)

	Shanidar 1		Shanidar 3	
	Right	Left	Right	Left
Length (M-1)	53.1	52.8	55.8	—
Maximum height (M-3a)	p32.6	33.2	—	—
Articular height (M-3b)	p27.3	28.2	29.1	—
Articular breadth (M-2b)	p52.9	48.9	(51.6)	
Medial total length[a]	p55.8	55.3	—	—
Lateral total length (M-1b)	p54.7	53.4	(59.5)	—
Trochlear length (M-4)	—	37.7	p(39.5)	—
Trochlear breadth (M-5)	p28.3	29.2	29.9	—
Trochlear height (M-6)	—	11.0	9.0	—
Lateral malleolar height[b]	p(24.6)	28.1	—	28.8
Lateral malleolar length[c]	p29.9	33.0	—	—
Lateral malleolar breadth (M-7a)	p9.5	10.2	—	(12.0)
Lateral malleolar oblique height (M-7)	p(25.8)	28.0	—	29.4
Medial malleolar breadth[d]	p15.1	9.5	9.7	—
Head–neck length (M-8)	—	16.2	p(22.0)	—
Head length (M-9)	35.6	39.0	(36.0)	—
Head breadth (M-10)	24.0	23.8	20.5	—
Head arc[e]	49.0	50.0	(47.0)	—
Posterior calcaneal length (M-12)	35.1	34.4	p(35.5)	—
Posterior calcaneal breadth (M-13)	23.5	23.9	—	—
Trochlear angle[f]	2°	3°	6°	—
Neck angle (M-16)	27°	26°	26°	—
Torsion angle (M-17)	39°	43°	34°	—
Posterior calcaneal angle (M-15)	45°	43°	—	—
Subtalar angle[g]	47°	48°	47°	—

Note: p = specimen altered by pathology.

[a]Maximum distance from the head to the tip of the medial posterior tubercle.

[b]Maximum dorsoplantar height of the lateral malleolar surface, measured perpendicular to the horizontal plane of the trochlea.

[c]Maximum anteroposterior dimension of the lateral malleolar surface.

[d]Maximum medial projection of the medial malleolar surface from the medial trochlear margin, measured perpendicular to the midline sagittal plane of the trochlea.

[e]Maximum arc of the navicular articular surface, measured parallel to the head length measurement.

[f]The angle between the medial and lateral margins of the trochlea, measured in the horizontal plane of the trochlea.

[g]The angle between the midline sagittal plane of the trochlea and the midline across the medial and posterior calcaneal surfaces.

between the leg and the foot (made up of the talocrural and subtalar joints), it is its articular configurations that are most relevant to its comparative morphology.

The Shanidar 1 and 3 trochlea exhibit the slight posterior narrowing that is characteristic of recent human tali and reflects the movement of the dorsiflexion–plantarflexion axis (Barnett and Napier 1952; Hicks 1953). This wedging is reflected by their trochlear angles of 3° and 6°, respectively. The Shanidar 3 angle is well within the ranges of variation of other Neandertals (Amud 1: 12°; Tabūn C1: 9° & 9°; European Neandertals; 7.0° ± 2.4°, N = 11), Skhūl hominids (7.7° ± 5.1°, N = 3), and recent humans (Europeans: 10.7° ± 4.1°, N = 50; North Africans: 7.9° ± 3.5°, N = 50; Amerindians: 9.4° ± 4.1°, N = 40 [Rhoads and Trinkaus 1977]). The Shanidar 1 angle is somewhat lower but nonetheless within other Neandertal and more recent human ranges of variation.

Similarly, contrary to early appraisals of Neandertal tali (e.g., Boule 1911–1913; Martin 1910), their necks deviate medially to about the same degree as those of more recent humans. The Shanidar 1 and 3 neck angles (26° each) are slightly above those of Amud 1 (20°) and Tabūn C1 (20° & 19°) and very close to the mean of a European Neandertal sample (26.5° ± 4.2°, N = 10). These Neandertal angles are similar to those of a Skhūl–Qafzeh sample (23.3° ± 2.7°, N = 6), an Early Upper Paleolithic sample (23.0° ± 2.2°, N = 6), and those of recent humans (Europeans: 24.1° ± 4.4°, N = 50; North Africans: 25.8° ± 4.1°, N = 50; Amerindians: 25.3° ± 3.7°, N = 40 [Rhoads and Trinkaus 1977]).

Finally, the Shanidar 1 and 3 talar torsion angles, which when large indicate a reinforcement of the midtarsal joint through realignment of the talonavicular and calcaneocuboid articular axes (Elftman 1960; Manter 1941), are comparable to those of contemporary and more recent humans. The Shanidar 1 and 3 torsion angles (43° and 34°, respectively) fall on either side of that of Amud 1 (38°), the mean of the Tabūn C1 right (33°) and left (39°) tali, and a European Neandertal mean (39.1° ± 6.0°, N = 10). The Neandertal mean is close to means of rather variable recent human samples (Europeans: 42.8° ± 7.1°, N = 50; North Africans: 42.3° ± 7.8°, N = 50; Amerindians: 40.3° ± 7.0°, N = 40 [Rhoads and Trinkaus 1977]).

These data illustrate the general similarity of the Shanidar talar articular orientations to those of more recent humans. There is nothing in the details of their articular surfaces to contradict this conclusion. Their trochlea are evenly convex anteroposteriorly and are slightly concave mediolaterally. Their heads are segments of spheres and grade smoothly onto the anterior and medial calcaneal surfaces. And their posterior calcaneal surfaces, inasmuch as they are preserved, present the mediolateral concavity oriented obliquely with respect to the long axis of the articular surface, which is associated with proper operation of the subtalar joint among recent humans (Hicks 1953; Manter 1941).

The one aspect of the Shanidar tali, and other Neandertal tali, that provides a contrast with recent human tali is the relative sizes of their talocrural articular surfaces. This is evident particularly in their head–neck and trochlear lengths and their lateral malleolar breadths.

The Shanidar trochleae are relatively long, which is reflected in their trochlear lengths and head–neck lengths; the length of the talar neck is inversely correlated with trochlear length because an expansion of the trochlea encroaches upon the nonarticular surface of the dorsal neck (Rhoads and Trinkaus 1977). The Shanidar 1 and 3 neck length indices (head–neck length/trochlear length) are 43.0 and about 55.7, respectively. The Shanidar 3 index is similar to a European Neandertal mean (55.1 ± 5.1, N = 10), but the Shanidar 1 index is considerably below that, near the minimum value for the European Neandertals (43.8–62.3, N = 10). The Amud 1 and Tabūn C1 tali, with indices of 50.0, and 59.3 & 55.2, respectively, have relative head–neck lengths similar to the Shanidar and European Neandertals. These Neandertal neck length indices are not significantly different from those of a Skhūl–Qafzeh sample (54.5 ± 6.4, N = 6), but they are largely below those of an Early Upper Paleolithic sample (60.2 ± 4.5, N = 6) and recent human samples (Europeans: 62.6 ± 5.2, N = 50; North Africans: 65.0 ± 6.3, N = 50; Amerindians: 65.5 ± 7.2, N = 40). The lower indices of the Shanidar and other Neandertals, as well as those of the Skhūl–Qafzeh hominids, indicate longer trochleae and proportionately shorter necks. This implies a relative enlargement of the tibiotalar articulation among these individuals.

Associated with this trochlear enlargement, the Shanidar tali had large lateral malleolar surfaces for articulation with the distal fibula. This is reflected in their lateral malleolar breadth indices (lateral malleolar breadth/trochlear breadth). The indices of 34.9 for Shanidar 1 and approximately 40.1 for Shanidar 3 (combined measurements from right and left tali) are similar to those of Amud 1 (40.7) and most European Neandertals (35.7 ± 5.7, N = 11). Tabūn C1, however, has lower indices (28.6 & 29.1). Although within recent human ranges of variation (Europeans: 27.0 ± 5.6, N = 50; North Africans: 28.6 ± 5.5, N = 50; Amerindians: 32.8 ± 6.0, N = 40), these indices for Shanidar 1 and 3 are toward the upper limits of the recent human ranges of variation. The enlargements of the talocrural articulations of the Shanidar tali indicate adaptations to habitually high levels of joint reaction force at this important articulation.

It is difficult to determine the variations of the anterior trochlear margin and dorsal neck on the Shanidar tali because two of the tali with this region preserved (Shanidar 1 and 3 right) are abnormal and the third (Shanidar 1 left) is damaged here. Yet it is clear that all three tali exhibit anterior extensions of their medial malleolar surfaces and lateral trochlear margins, as do Amud 1, Tabūn C1, and 100% (N = 15) and 93.3% (N = 15), respectively, of the European Neandertals. Nine recent human samples vary between 52.0 and 100% and between 17.0 and 95.3%, respectively, in the incidence of these features, with most samples having relatively high frequencies (Trinkaus 1975c). The Shanidar 1 left talus appears to lack a medial squatting facet, as do those of Amud 1, Tabūn C1, all European Neandertals (N = 13), and most recent humans (range of frequencies for 10 samples: 0.0–5.6% [Trinkaus 1975c]).

The Shanidar 1 right talus, along with the fragments of the Shanidar 4 and 6 tali, preserves the posterolateral surface of the sulcus tali adjacent to the posterior calcaneal facet. All three of these tali exhibit sulcus tali facets for articulation with the calcaneus during pronation and hyperflexion of the subtalar joint. These facets are relatively rare among other Neandertals because they are absent from the Amud 1 and Tabūn C1 tali and occur in only 25.0% (N = 12) of the European Neandertals. They vary between 14.2 and 46.9% in four samples of recent humans (Trinkaus 1975c).

The plantar surface of the Shanidar 1 left talus exhibits complete fusion of the anterior and medial calcaneal facets, as is usual for the Neandertals (Amud 1 and 92.3% [N = 13] of European Neandertals); the other Shanidar tali are insufficiently preserved to indicate the configurations of their calcaneal facets. This relatively high frequency of complete fusion of these facets (only 55.4–73.9% in four recent human samples [Trinkaus 1975c]) suggests an expansion of these articular facets, probably in response to high levels of joint reaction force.

The Shanidar tali therefore exhibit the same overall morphology as those of other Neandertals. They are morphologically similar to those of recent humans and differ only in their tendency to have large articular surfaces.

THE CALCANEI

The only reasonably well-preserved calcanei from Shanidar are those of Shanidar 1. The Shanidar 3 right calcaneus, although it is an incomplete shell of cortical bone and sustained degenerative joint disease around its talar surfaces, provides some information on overall proportions. Only the configuration of the anterior and medial talar surfaces is evident on the Shanidar 3 left calcaneal fragments, and the Shanidar 4 calcaneal pieces only document the existence of the two bones.

The morphology of the Shanidar calcanei is indistiguishable from that of other Neandertals and more recent humans. They have moderate-sized talar and cuboid articular surfaces, with the oblique orientation of the axis of curvature of the talocalcaneal articulation and the saddle-shaped configuration of the calcaneocuboid joint typical of recent human calcanei (Manter 1941). Their bodies are relatively large and robust for absorbing the stress from heel strike and they have moderately large tuberosities for the insertion of the M. triceps surae tendon.

In overall dimensions, the Shanidar calcanei follow the Neandertal tendency to have relatively long bodies (Table 71). The body length indices (body length/total length) of Shanidar 1 and 3 (82.6 & 83.3, and ca. 78.4, respectively) are similar to those of European Neandertals (La Chapelle-aux-Saints 1: 82.4; La Ferrassie 1: 84.2; La Ferrassie 2: ca. 77.3; Kiik-Koba 1: 81.3 & 84.5) but somewhat higher than that of Tabūn C1 (72.9). Skhūl 4 (75.9), and most recent humans (North Africans: 76.4 ± 2.0, N = 50; Amerindians: 73.9 ± 1.9, N = 40) tend to have lower indices. This suggests that the moment arms for M. triceps surae may have been slightly greater among these Neandertals, a pattern suggested by comparisons of their "pedal moment arms" (see earlier disussion).

TABLE 71
Measurements of the Calcanei (mm)

	Shanidar 1		Shanidar 3
	Right	Left	Right
Total length (M-1a)	80.0	78.0	(74.0)
Body length (M-5)	66.1	65.0	(58.0)
Medial breadth (M-2)	46.5	45.9	—
Sustentaculum tali breadth (M-6)	18.7	(21.0)	—
Tuberosity height (M-7)	(43.4)	50.8	—
Tuberosity breadth (M-8)	28.9	—	—
Medial process length[a]	29.6	29.3	(32.0)
Posterior talar length (M-9)	31.9	31.8	p(37.7)
Posterior talar breadth (M-10)	—	26.0	p(27.5)
Deflex angle (M-14)	—	48°	(42°)
Subtalar angle[b]	53°	47°	—

Note: p = specimen altered by pathology.

[a]Maximum distance from the posterior surface of the tuberosity to the anterior end of the medial process, measured parallel to the long axis of the calcaneum.

[b]The angle between the long axis of the calcaneum and the midline across the medial and posterior talar surfaces.

However, this posterior calcaneal elongation would also increase the moment arm for the ground reaction force at heel strike and require additional reinforcement of the longitudinal pedal arches.

Shanidar 1 preserves each sustentaculum tali, and it is possible to estimate the size of the Shanidar 3 sustentaculum tali. Both Shanidar individuals have high sustentacular indices (sustentacular breadth/median breadth) (40.2 & ca. 45.8, and ca. 42.1, for Shanidar 1 and 3, respectively, using estimates of 47.5 and 21.0 mm for the Shanidar 3 median and sustentacular breadths, respectively). These indices are at the top of the Neandertal range of variation (24.7–43.2, N = 9; Amud 1: 24.7; Tabūn C1: 38.6 & 38.9; European Neandertals: 35.1 ± 4.7, N = 7). However, they are still within recent human ranges of variation (North Africans: 35.9 ± 5.2, N = 50; Amerindians: 31.2 ± 4.1, N = 40), although they are clearly separate from those of early anatomically modern humans (Skhūl–Qafzeh sample: 32.2 ± 0.7, N = 4; Early Upper Paleolithic sample: 34.5 ± 1.6, N = 4). These figures indicate that the amount of medial projection of the Shanidar sustentaculi tali is generally similar to that of recent humans, implying that the pattern of weight distribution in their feet was comparable. This is actually only a reflection of the degree of medial positioning of the talar head, which their talar neck angles show to be similar to that of recent humans (see earlier discussion).

Each of the Shanidar 1 calcanei exhibits a sulcus for the *M. flexor digitorum longus* tendon, in addition to the main sulcus on the inferior surface of the sustentaculum tali for the *M. flexor hallucis longus* tendon. Similar sulci are found on 21.4% of European Neandertals (*N* = 7) and only 2.5% (*N* = 100) of a recent Amerindian sample. They are absent from the Tabūn C1 calcanei. Their presence on the Shanidar 1 calcanei is probably related to the relatively large size of his sustentacula talorum and normal variation in the positioning of the long flexor tendons.

The Shanidar 1 and 3 left calcanei have complete fusion of their anterior and medial talar surfaces, as do those of Amud 1, Tabūn C1, and 85.7% (*N* = 7) of European Neandertals. Between 47.5 and 73.1% of the individuals in six recent human samples have similar fusion of their calcaneal talar surfaces (Trinkaus 1975c). The Shanidar 3 right calcaneus, however, has a distinct anterior facet, which was separate from a medial facet if such was present originally. It is uncertain whether the morphology of the right talar facets was their original configuration, indicating an asymmetry in this feature (similar asymmetries occur between 4.5 and 14.0% in three recent human samples [Trinkaus 1978a]), or it was affected by the degenerative joint disease in the right foot. As with the fusion of the anterior and medial calcaneal surfaces of the talus, the fusion of these surfaces on the Shanidar 1 and 3 left calcanei indicates an expansion of these surfaces for high levels of joint reaction force.

The Shanidar 1 and 3 calcanei thus are robust bones that are otherwise within the ranges of variation those of other Neandertals and more recent humans.

THE ANTERIOR TARSALS

At least one of each of the anterior tarsals is preserved largely intact for the Shanidar Neandertals. However, most of their anterior tarsals consist of fragments of the dorsal surface or articular margins that indicate little more than the overall size of the bone or its general resemblance to those of other Neandertals and more recent humans (Tables 72–76).

Shanidar 1, 3, and 4 retain most of their navicular bones. Their articular morphologies are indistinguishable from those of recent humans, with segments of spheres for the articulation with the talar head and distinct facets for the three cuneiform bones. The Shanidar 3 right navicular and cuboid bones each has a distinct facet for an articulation with the other. Similar facets are absent from the Shanidar 1 and 4 navicular bones, but they are present on the Tabūn C1, Kiik-Koba 1, and Krapina 243/244 tarsals, absent from the La Ferrassie 1 and Petit-Puymoyen 7 tarsals, and present on between 24.0 and 64.6% of individuals in four recent human samples (Trinkaus 1975a). The Shanidar 3 naviculocuboid facets, like those of other Neandertals, are small ovoid surfaces rather than the large rectangular facets present on Plio-Pleistocene hominids (Latimer *et al.* 1982) and modern pongids.

The tuberosities of the Shanidar navicular bones are large projecting processes that grade evenly into the bodies of the bones, as they do among recent

TABLE 72
Measurements of the Navicular Bones (mm)

	Shanidar 1		Shanidar 3		Shanidar 4
	Right	Left	Right	Left	Right
Maximum thickness (M-8)	23.7	22.9	—	—	21.5
Minimum thickness (M-7)	8.0	8.6	7.5	(7.5)	9.8
Breadth (M-1)	43.6	44.0	(43.5)	—	43.0
Height (M-1)	(30.2)	27.7	29.0	—	28.5
Talar articular length (M-3)	30.4	32.5	32.0	—	28.2
Talar articular height (M-4)	23.0	22.8	21.3	—	22.6
Tuberosity length[a]	11.0	10.0	—	11.8	10.5
Tuberosity thickness[b]	24.1	23.2	—	24.8	23.2

[a]Maximum medial projection of the navicular tuberosity from the medial margin of the talar articular surface.
[b]Maximum anteroposterior dimension of the navicular tuberosity.

humans. The hypertrophy of their processes is partially indicated by the ratio of their tuberosity anteroposterior thicknesses to their minimum (lateral) thicknesses. The resultant indices are 303.3 & 269.8, about 330.7, and 236.7 for Shanidar 1, 3, and 4, respectively. The indices of Shanidar 1 and 3 are similar to those of other Neandertals (La Ferrassie 1: 317.5; La Ferrassie 2: 316.4; Kiik-Koba 1: 328.0; Tabūn C1: 267.5), whereas that of Shanidar 4 is closer to a recent Amerindian mean (212.3 ± 26.7, N = 39). Because the navicular tuberosity is the primary attachment area for the plantar calcaneonavicular (spring) ligament

TABLE 73
Measurements of the Cuboid Bones (mm)

	Shanidar 1	Shanidar 3	Shanidar 6
	Right	Right	Left
Medial length (M-1)	(27.7)	27.6	—
Lateral length (M-2)	17.9	12.2	7.9
Mean articular length[a]	(22.8)	19.9	—
Height[b]	—	28.9	—
Calcaneal articular height[c]	—	(22.5)	—
Calcaneal articular breadth[c]	—	27.4	—
Metatarsal articular height[d]	—	17.9	—
Metatarsal articular breadth[d]	23.4	25.3	—

[a]Average of the medial and lateral lengths.
[b]Maximum dorsoplantar dimension of the bone.
[c]The articular height is measured from the most dorsal point on the surface to the line between the medial and lateral plantar extensions of the surface, whereas the breadth is measured as the maximum dimension of the articulation perpendicular to the height.
[d]Maximum dorsoplantar and mediolateral dimensions of the combined metatarsal 4 and 5 articulations.

TABLE 74
Measurements of the Medial Cuneiform Bones (mm)

	Shanidar 1		Shanidar 3	
	Right	Left	Right	Left
Superior length (M-3)	22.6	23.3	—	24.5
Middle length (M-2)	22.8	21.9	22.7	23.5
Inferior length (M-1)	26.9	25.5	—	26.2
Proximal articular height (M-4)	21.7	22.1	—	21.9
Proximal articular breadth	16.0	(15.0)	—	15.1
Distal articular height (M-5)	32.4	33.5	—	32.2
Distal articular breadth	p13.6	13.7	—	(16.4)
Total breadth[a]	20.0	18.9	—	(19.0)

Note: p = specimen altered by pathology.
[a]Maximum mediolateral dimension of the bone across the plantar tuberosities.

and insertion for M. tibialis posterior, both of which are crucial to the maintenance of the medial longitudinal arch, its hypertrophy implies reinforcement of
this important locomotor structure.

An additional indication of this plantar musculoligamentous hypertrophy
is provided by the projection of the lateral cuneiform tuberosity of Shanidar 1.
The total height of the bone (tuberosity height) compared to the proximal
articular height provides an index of 172.8 for Shanidar 1. This index is in the
middle of the known range for other Neandertals (La Ferrassie 1: 172.2; Kiik-
Koba 1: 163.0; Tabūn C1: 180.3) and towards the upper limits of a recent
Amerindian sample (148.5 ± 12.3, N = 40). Because the tuberosity of the lateral
cuneiform receives fibers from M. tibialis posterior and several of the plantar
intertarsal and tarsometatarsal ligaments, its projection in the Shanidar 1 and
other Neandertal feet suggests an increased robusticity of their plantar musculoligamentous trusses for the pedal arches.

There are few other features of note on the Shanidar anterior tarsals. All of
their overall proportions and articular configurations are identical to those of
other Neandertals, which are similar to those of more recent humans (Trinkaus
1975a). They depict a compact set of bones that probably allowed little movement between them during normal locomotion.

THE HALLUX

Shanidar 1, 4, 6, and 8 preserve complete proximal hallucial phalanges, but
only Shanidar 1 retains a complete hallucial metatarsal and none of them
preserves a complete distal hallucial phalanx. However, Shanidar 4 retains
enough of his left distal hallucial phalanx to permit an estimate of its length. In
addition, Shanidar 3 and 8 have portions of their first metatarsals, Shanidar 3

TABLE 75

Measurements of the Intermedial Cuneiform Bones (mm)

	Shanidar 1		Shanidar 3		Shanidar 4		Shanidar 6
	Right	Left	Right	Left	Right	Left	Right
Superior length (M-1)	17.1	17.8	16.8	(16.8)	17.3	16.7	15.5
Middle length (M-2)	15.7	15.0	14.8	14.6	—	—	—
Mean articular length	16.4	16.4	15.8	15.7	—	—	—
Proximal articular height	—	18.9	19.2	—	—	—	—
Proximal articular breadth (M-4)	16.1	17.6	14.2	15.2	—	—	—
Distal articular height	—	20.2	21.0	20.7	—	—	—
Distal articular breadth (M-3)	15.5	17.5	14.0	15.0	14.3	—	12.7

TABLE 76
Measurements of the Lateral Cuneiform Bones (mm)

	Shanidar 1	Shanidar 3	Shanidar 4	
	Right	Right	Right	Left
Superior length (M-1)	22.7	—	22.9	22.8
Middle length (M-2)	20.8	—	—	21.9
Mean articular length	21.8	—	—	22.4
Proximal articular height	16.2	—	—	—
Proximal articular breadth (M-4)	12.4	—	—	—
Distal articular height	(19.2)	—	—	19.4
Distal articular breadth (M-3)	15.9	19.8	—	16.9
Tuberosity height[a]	28.0	—	—	—
Tuberosity length[b]	17.2	—	—	—

[a]Maximum distance from the dorsal surface of the bone to the plantar surface of the tuberosity.
[b]Maximum anteroposterior dimension of the tuberosity.

retains part of his proximal hallucial phalanx, Shanidar 6 preserves much of one distal hallucial phalanx, and Shanidar 3, 4, and 8 have at least one hallucial sesamoid bone each (Tables 77–79).

The orientation of the Shanidar halluxes was unquestionably in line with the other digits of their feet. This is evident in the tarsometatarsal reconstructions of the Shanidar 1 feet (Figure 68), but it is also confirmed by other aspects of their hallucial morphology.

Their first tarsometatarsal articulations, as evidenced by the medial cuneiform bones and first metatarsals of Shanidar 1, 3, and 8, exhibit an even mediolateral curvature that is convex distally. A mediolaterally curved first tarsometatarsal joint has been considered to indicate a mobile hallux (Boule 1911–1913; Jones 1929), although it has long been recognized that such a configuration is compatible with an adducted hallux (Leboucq 1882; Schultz 1950). Most recent humans possess curved surfaces between the medial cuneiform and first metatarsal, and furthermore, a curved articulation provides a stronger joint for resisting natural torsional stress on the hallux during locomotion (Trinkaus 1975a).

The Shanidar 1 left metatarsal 1 and 2, the Shanidar 6 right and left second metatarsals, and the Shanidar 8 left metatarsal 1 are complete enough to indicate whether an articular facet was present between their metatarsal 1 and 2 bases; all three of these individuals lacked such a facet. However, this does not indicate a divergent hallux because such facets are present in only 42.9% (N = 7) of European Neandertals, between 9.0 and 32.5% in five recent human samples (Trinkaus 1975a), and on the Amud 1 remains but not on those of Tabūn C1. Furthermore, the arthritic changes around the bases of the Shanidar 1 right first and second metatarsals indicate that they were next to each other during life.

TABLE 77
Measurements of the First Metatarsals (mm)

	Shanidar 1		Shanidar 3	Shanidar 8
	Right	Left	Left	Left
Articular length (M-1)	58.6	60.6	—	—
Midshaft height (M-4)	12.1	12.9	—	—
Midshaft breadth (M-3)	12.9	13.7	—	—
Midshaft circumference	40.0	41.5	—	—
Proximal maximum height (M-7)	—	33.3	—	26.5
Proximal maximum breadth (M-6)	—	22.2	—	20.4
Proximal articular height	30.1	31.1	—	25.3
Proximal articular breadth	—	15.9	16.0	14.4
Distal height (M-9)	22.0	23.8	—	—
Distal maximum breadth (M-8)	(25.2)	(23.3)	—	—
Distal articular breadth	(20.8)	19.6	—	—
Distal medial height[a]	19.0	20.1	—	—
Distal lateral height[a]	18.4	20.0	—	—
Distal circumference (M-10)	(36.0)	39.0	—	—
Torsion angle (M-11)	—	12°	—	—
Horizontal head angle[b]	3°	6°	—	—

[a]Minimum distance between the angles of the medial and lateral sesamoid sulci and the dorsal margin of the head.

[b]Angle between the long axis of the diaphysis and the line determined by the crest between the sesamoid sulci. A positive angle indicates a lateral deviation of the distal end of the intersesamoid crest.

The orientations of the Shanidar 1 first metatarsal heads and the distal articulations of the Shanidar 1, 4, 6, and 8 proximal hallucial phalanges indicate that they possessed the normal human valgus deviation of the hallux (Barnicot and Hardy 1955). The horizontal head angles of the Shanidar 1 first metatarsals (3° and 6°) are similar to those of other Neandertals (Tabūn C1: 8° & 12°; La Chapelle-aux-Saints 1: 4°; La Ferrassie 1: 3°; Kiik-Koba 1: 1° & 2°; Krapina 245: 9°) and a recent Amerindian sample (4.6° ± 3.4°, N = 40 [Trinkaus 1975a]), illustrating the slight lateral deviation of the sesamoid grooves on the Shanidar 1 and other Neandertal and recent human first metatarsals. And the

TABLE 78
Measurements of the Hallucial Sesamoid Bones (mm)

	Shanidar 3		Shanidar 4	Shanidar 8
	Medial right	Lateral right	Medial left	Medial right
Length	14.6	12.1	11.5	11.7
Breadth	11.1	10.8	9.6	8.8
Thickness	7.7	7.2	7.8	6.2

TABLE 79

Measurements of the First Proximal Pedal Phalanges (mm)

	Shanidar 1	Shanidar 3	Shanidar 4		Shanidar 6	Shanidar 8
	Left	Right(?)	Right	Left	Right	Right
Articular length (M-1)	28.1	—	27.2	27.7	24.5	24.5
Midshaft height (M-3)	10.2	—	11.1	11.4	8.3	9.0
Midshaft breadth (M-2)	12.4	—	14.1	14.0	12.6	13.4
Midshaft circumference	38.5	—	42.0	43.5	36.5	37.5
Proximal maximum height	18.9	18.1	18.6	—	16.9	16.3
Proximal maximum breadth	20.4	22.1	21.7	—	18.7	19.6
Proximal articular height	14.4	15.5	15.3	—	13.5	13.4
Proximal articular breadth	18.4	20.2	19.0	—	16.5	16.0
Distal height	10.2	—	9.2	9.5	9.5	8.8
Distal maximum breadth	18.2	—	17.2	17.8	16.0	16.9
Torsion angle[a]	4°	—	3°	—	2°	5°
Horizontal angle[b]	15°	—	18°	—	11°	13°

[a] The angle, in the coronal plane, between the mediolateral axes of the proximal and distal articulations. A positive angle, for the right side, indicates a clockwise twist of the bone when viewed in a proximal-distal direction.

[b] The angle, in the horizontal plane, between the coronal planes of the proximal and distal articulations. A positive angle indicates a lateral deviation of the distal articulation relative to the proximal one.

horizontal angles of the Shanidar 1, 4, 6, and 8 proximal hallucial phalanges (15°, 18°, 11°, and 13°, respectively) are all similar to or even greater than those of European Neandertals (12.1° ± 2.5°, N = 5) and a recent Amerindian sample (6.4° ± 3.7°, N = 40 [Trinkaus 1975a]). The Shanidar Neandertals clearly had the normal hallucial orientation of recent humans.

Even though the anterior segment of the Shanidar 1 tarsometatarsal skeleton is similar in relative size to those of recent humans (see earlier discussion), its proximal hallucial phalanx appears to be relatively short. An index that compares the proximal phalanx 1 articular length to the medial subtalar length is 15.4 for Shanidar 1. This value is below those Skhūl 4 (18.6) and most recent humans (North Africans: 17.6 ± 0.8, N = 15; Amerindians: 17.4 ± 1.0, N = 40). It is similar to the values for La Ferrassie 2 (13.6) and Kiik-Koba 1 (15.2).

This hallucial abbreviation may be a reflection of a shortness of the proximal phalanx relative to the distal phalanx. It is possible to compare proximal and distal hallucial phalangeal length only for Shanidar 4 among the Shanidar Neandertals, and the resultant index (ca. 97.5–99.3) is at the top of the known Neandertal range of variation (Kiik-Koba 1: 90.9 & 85.7; Krapina 250.1/252.1: 91.4; Krapina 250.4/252.3: 81.1) and quite distinct from those of Skhūl 4 (57.6) and a recent Amerindian sample (78.5 ± 6.2, N = 37). Interestingly, this is the same pattern of a relatively long distal phalanx and a proportionately short proximal phalanx that is present in the Shanidar and other Neandertal pollexes (Chapter 8), and they may be pleiotropically related. Assuming that Shanidar 1 had the same hallucial phalangeal length proportions as Shanidar 4 and the other Neandertals, his total hallucial phalangeal length relative to medial subtalar length was probably similar to that of recent humans.

The morphologies of the Shanidar hallucial metatarsals and phalanges are otherwise similar to those of recent humans. The Shanidar 1 and 8 first metatarsals have subtriangular diaphyseal cross sections that are flat laterally and more rounded medially. All of the proximal phalanges have ovoid diaphyseal cross sections, which have digitoscapial indices (shaft breadth/shaft height) similar to those of variable Neandertal and recent human samples (Table 88). And the configurations of their metatarsophalangeal and interphalangeal articulations are indistinguishable from those of recent humans.

The Shanidar halluxes exhibit only a moderate degree of robusticity. The Shanidar 1 first metatarsal robusticity index ([shaft height + shaft breadth]/articular length) is 42.7 & 43.9. These values are close to that for Tabūn C1 (44.8) but below those of a European Neandertal sample (49.3 ± 2.5, N = 7) and even a small Skhūl sample (50.7 ± 3.1, N = 3). They are only slightly above a recent Amerindian mean (42.2 ± 2.3, N = 40 [Trinkaus 1975a]). The proximal phalanx 1 robusticity indices of Shanidar 4 and 8 (92.6 & 91.7, and 91.4, respectively) are above a recent Amerindian mean (78.6 ± 6.4, N = 40 [Trinkaus 1975a]) and even a Neandertal mean (84.2 ± 6.6, N = 8), but those of Shanidar 1 and 6 (80.4 and 85.3, respectively) are not exceptional for a Neandertal and only moderately high for a recent human. It is possible that the relatively higher robusticity indices, at least of the Shanidar 4 and 8 proximal hallucial phalanges, are in part a product of their relatively shorter proximal hallucial phalanges. A similar pattern is seen in the proximal rugosity indices (Table 88) of the Shanidar proximal hallucial phalanges.

The Shanidar distal hallucial phalanges show some hypertrophy. Each of them has a large pit on the proximal plantar surface for the insertion of the M. *flexor hallucis longus* tendon. In addition, Shanidar 4 has an exceptionally wide tuberosity on its distal hallucial phalanx; its breadth (15.4 mm) is in the middle of a European Neandertal range of variation (12.9–19.8 mm, 15.6 ± 2.8 mm, N = 5) and separate from those of a recent Amerindian sample (11.6 ± 1.2 mm, N = 37). The distal breadth of the Shanidar 6 distal hallucial phalanx (ca. 12.0 mm), however, falls close to the recent human mean and below all of the other Neandertal breadths. This enlargement of the distal tuberosity, at least for Shanidar 4, is similar to that seen on the Shanidar distal hand phalanges, and probably implies an adaptation for higher levels of ground reaction force through the distal hallux.

Medial sesamoid bones have been preserved for Shanidar 3, 4, and 8, and Shanidar 3 retains a lateral sesamoid bone. Their volumes provide an indication of the sizes of the tendons of the intrinsic hallucial muscles—M. *flexor hallucis brevis*, M. *adductor hallucis*, and M. *abductor hallucis*—that contained them. Estimates of their volumes can be obtained by multiplying their three diameters (Table 78); for the medial sesamoid bones, these volumes are 1247.9, 853.6, and 638.4 mm³, respectively, for Shanidar 3, 4, and 8, and for the Shanidar 3 lateral sesamoid bone it is 940.9 mm.³ For comparison, a recent Amerindian sample provides values of 602.3 ± 247.8 mm³ (N = 19) and 558.7 ± 150.9 mm³ (N = 18) for the medial and lateral sesamoid bones, respectively, and the La Ferrassie 1 left medial sesamoid bone has a volume of 1417.5 mm³. The Shanidar 3 sesamoid bones, and to a lesser extent that of Shanidar 4, are enormous, being exceeded in volume only by that of La Ferrassie 1. They indicate exceptionally large tendons for these muscles. That of Shanidar 8, by comparison, is rather modest in size.

These various data indicate that the Shanidar halluxes were adapted for a normal human striding gait. They differ from those of more recent humans primarily in their relatively short proximal phalanges and tendency to have robust tendinous insertions.

THE FOUR LATERAL DIGITS

There are 49 metatarsals and phalanges preserved from the four lateral pedal digits of the Shanidar Neandertals. However, the majority of their metatarsals are incomplete, frequently consisting of a portion of the diaphysis with part of one epiphysis. Their phalanges are usually more complete, but only Shanidar 4 has a reasonably complete set of phalanges.

The identification of the metatarsals as to digit and side has been done in most cases with respect to size, proximal articular morphology, and diaphyseal cross-sectional shape. The proximal phalanges have been assigned to side on the basis of their distal articular orientation and to digit on the basis of their metatarsal articulation shape. The assignment of the middle phalanges to side also used the orientation of the distal articulation, but their location by digit has been based solely on their size. Except for some of the highly fragmentary pieces, mainly of the metatarsals, there was little difficulty in determining the side and digit of most of these pedal bones. The only complicating factor is the *in situ* mixing of the Shanidar 4, 6, and 8 remains; it is possible that some of these bones, especially those of Shanidar 6 and 8, have been misidentified as to individual, but it appears unlikely that any of them have been placed in the wrong digit. All of the tentative identifications are labeled in the inventory with a question mark.

The metatarsals of the four lateral digits from Shanidar are similar to those of recent humans, as are those of all other Neandertals (Trinkaus 1975a, 1978e; see Tables 80–83). All of their tarsal and intermetatarsal articulations are identical in shape to those of recent humans, and they are of similar absolute and relative size. The Shanidar 1, 3, 4, and 8 fifth metatarsals appear to have relatively large and projecting proximolateral tuberosities, which would imply a strongly developed *M. peroneus brevis* for each of them. However, their proximal rugosity indices, in which a smaller index indicates a large musculoligamentous area relative to the tarsal articulation (Table 88), are similar to those of a recent Amerindian sample (60.3 ± 7.6, N = 40 [Trinkaus 1975a]; 59.4, 66.8, 56.3, and 55.2 & 60.6, respectively, for Shanidar 1, 3, 4, and 8). Other Neandertal fifth metatarsals have proximal rugosity indices that are minimally lower, on the average, than those of the recent human sample (Tabūn C1: 58.6; European Neandertals: 52.6 ± 3.9, N = 6).

It is possible to compare metatarsal and proximal phalangeal lengths only for the Shanidar 4 fifth ray and the Shanidar 8 third and fifth rays (Tables 84–87). The metatarsophalangeal length index (ratio of articular lengths) for the Shanidar 8 third ray (33.4) is between those of La Ferrassie 2 (31.2) and Kiik-Koba 1 (34.9 & 35.7). It is relatively but not unusually low when compared to a recent human sample (36.0 ± 1.8, N = 40 [Trinkaus 1975a]). The Shanidar 4 and 8 fifth ray metatarsophalangeal indices (ca. 25.5 and 27.3, respectively) are below those of La Ferrassie 2 (30.4) and Kiik-Koba 1 (29.0 & 30.0), which are toward the lower end of a recent human sample's range of variation (32.9 ± 1.8, N = 40 [Trinkaus 1975a]). These three Shanidar indices suggest that they had relatively short lateral proximal pedal phalanges, as well as short hallucial proximal phalanges.

The diaphyses of the Shanidar lateral proximal pedal phalanges are all wider than they are high, as indicated by their digitoscapial indices greater than 100.0 (Table 88). This is the pattern present among other Neandertals; recent humans, in contrast, tend to have diaphyses of these phalanges that are higher than wide, at least for digits 2, 3, and 4 The significance of this is

TABLE 80

Measurements of the Second Metatarsals (mm)

	Shanidar 1		Shanidar 3	Shanidar 4		Shanidar 6	
	Right	Left	Right	Right	Left	Right	Left
Articular length (M-2)	(73.0)	—	—	—	—	(64.0)	(64.0)
Midshaft height (M-4)	8.3	10.4	—	—	—	8.0	7.7
Midshaft breadth (M-3)	9.5	9.0	—	—	—	7.4	8.2
Midshaft circumference	27.5	32.0	—	—	—	24.0	25.0
Proximal maximum height	22.4	23.7	—	—	—	—	—
Proximal maximum breadth	19.8	19.4	—	—	16.2	14.0	14.2
Proximal articular height	(19.5)	21.0	—	—	—	—	—
Proximal articular breadth	16.5	17.6	16.9	16.9	15.0	12.8	12.2
Distal maximum breadth	—	—	—	—	—	12.3	—
Horizontal angle[a]	78°	81°	—	—	—	80°	81°
Vertical angle[b]	94°	89°	—	—	—	—	—

[a] Angle between the long axis of the diaphysis and the transverse plane of the tarsal surface, measured in the horizontal plane of the bone.
[b] Angle between the long axis of the diaphysis and the transverse plane of the tarsal surface, measured in the parasagittal plane of the bone.

TABLE 81
Measurements of the Third Metatarsals (mm)

	Shanidar 1	Shanidar 3	Shanidar 4	Shanidar 6	Shanidar 8
	Right	Right	Left	Left	Right
Articular length (M-2)	71.1	—	—	65.3	63.2
Midshaft height (M-4)	9.2	—	—	7.5	8.5
Midshaft breadth (M-3)	7.7	—	—	7.5	6.8
Midshaft circumference	26.5	—	—	24.5	28.0
Proximal maximum height	—	(22.0)	21.8	—	20.0
Proximal maximum breadth	19.8	17.0	17.5	14.4	15.5
Proximal articular height	—	20.3	19.9	—	19.0
Proximal articular breadth	16.3	17.0	15.6	14.0	15.0
Distal height	(17.4)	—	—	14.3	15.5
Distal maximum breadth	14.6	—	—	10.8	11.4
Distal articular breadth	(11.5)	—	—	9.5	10.1
Torsion angle (M-11)	7°	—	—	11°	15°
Horizontal angle	73°	—	80°	78°	82°
Vertical angle	89°	—	—	—	—

TABLE 82
Measurements of the Fourth Metatarsals (mm)

	Shanidar 1		Shanidar 4	Shanidar 6		Shanidar 8	
	Right	Left	Left	Right	Right	Left
Articular length (M-2)	(71.0)	—	—	65.4	64.0	—
Midshaft height (M-4)	8.4	8.6	10.2	7.6	7.7	7.9
Midshaft breadth (M-3)	7.3	8.0	8.3	7.0	7.4	7.3
Midshaft circumference	25.0	28.0	32.0	23.5	25.0	27.0
Proximal maximum height	21.4	—	—	—	—	—
Proximal maximum breadth	16.1	—	—	—	—	—
Proximal articular height	19.0	—	—	—	—	—
Proximal articular breadth	11.0	—	—	—	—	—
Distal height	—	—	16.1	14.1	13.4	13.5
Distal maximum breadth	11.8	—	12.1	10.5	11.6	11.4
Distal articular breadth	—	—	11.3	9.6	10.6	10.5
Torsion angle (M-11)	(38°)	—	—	—	24°	—
Horizontal angle	81°	—	—	—	75°	—
Vertical angle	77°	—	—	—	—	—

TABLE 83
Measurements of the Fifth Metatarsals (mm)

	Shanidar 1	Shanidar 3	Shanidar 4		Shanidar 8	
	Right	Left	Right	Left	Right	Left
Articular length (M-2)	69.8	—	(69.0)	65.9	63.0	—
Midshaft height (M-4)	—	7.6	9.4	8.5	7.2	6.9
Midshaft breadth (M-3)	—	11.5	11.6	11.5	9.7	10.0
Midshaft circumference	—	35.0	34.5	34.0	31.0	29.5
Proximal maximum height	16.0	16.5	—	16.9	14.0	14.8
Proximal maximum breadth	24.3	23.8	—	26.7	20.7	20.3
Proximal articular height	15.4	16.4	—	15.4	12.5	14.0
Proximal articular breadth	15.0	16.0	—	16.5	12.8	13.0
Distal height	14.3	—	15.3	15.0	13.1	—
Distal maximum breadth	13.7	—	13.7	13.2	12.3	—
Distal articular breadth	(11.3)	—	11.3	11.6	9.4	—
Torsion angle (M-11)	31°	—	—	14°	11°	—
Horizontal angle	57°	56°	—	58°	60°	62°
Vertical angle	94°	96°	—	—	—	—

TABLE 84
Measurements of the Second Proximal Pedal Phalanges (mm)

	Shanidar 3	Shanidar 4		Shanidar 8
	Right	Right	Left	Right
Articular length (M-1)	(26.5)	—	25.0	23.0
Midshaft height (M-3)	7.6	—	8.1	6.6
Midshaft breadth (M-2)	9.3	—	8.7	8.1
Proximal maximum height	14.3	—	13.2	11.3
Proximal maximum breadth	15.3	—	15.4	12.9
Proximal articular height	12.3	—	11.3	9.7
Proximal articular breadth	13.6	—	13.0	11.5
Distal height	—	6.7	7.0	5.9
Distal breadth	—	—	11.0	9.9
Torsion angle	—	—	1°	−1°

uncertain, but it probably indicates an hypertrophy of the medial and lateral aspects of their diaphyses for reinforcement against mediolateral bending stress, such as would be prevalent on the toes of habitually unshod feet. Their phalangeal diaphyses are otherwise similar to those of recent humans in having ovoid cross sections and modest markings for the *M. flexor digitorum longus* tendon sheaths.

The proximal epiphyses of the Shanidar lateral proximal pedal phalanges exhibit the enlargement of the musculoligamentous area around the metatarsal surface relative to the size of the articulation. This is evident in their proximal rugosity indices (Table 88), most of which are close to Neandertal means and below recent human means. The hypertrophy of their plantar ligaments and muscles is thus apparent as well on their phalanges.

TABLE 85
Measurements of the Third Proximal Pedal Phalanges (mm)

	Shanidar 4		Shanidar 8
	Right	Left	Left
Articular length (M-1)	23.2	23.3	21.1
Midshaft height (M-3)	8.5	7.8	6.6
Midshaft breadth (M-2)	8.6	8.2	8.1
Proximal maximum height	13.4	13.0	11.7
Proximal maximum breadth	13.8	13.3	13.3
Proximal articular height	11.0	11.4	9.9
Proximal articular breadth	12.7	12.2	11.2
Distal height	8.4	7.3	6.9
Distal breadth	10.7	10.7	—
Torsion angle	3°	8°	—

TABLE 86
Measurements of the Shanidar 4 Right Fourth
Proximal Pedal Phalanx (mm)

Articular length (M-1)	22.5
Midshaft height (M-3)	7.6
Midshaft breadth (M-2)	8.2
Proximal maximum height	12.4
Proximal maximum breadth	14.0
Proximal articular height	9.9
Proximal articular breadth	12.2
Distal height	7.5
Distal breadth	10.3
Torsion angle	7°

The tuberosity breadths of the five distal phalanges 2–5 of Shanidar 4 (DP-2: 10.3 & 8.8 mm; DP-3: 8.4 mm: DP-4: 9.6 mm; DP-5: 7.7 mm) are within the range of variation of those from other Neandertals (Amud 1: 11.7 mm; European Neandertals: 9.2 ± 1.4 mm, N = 10) (Table 90). They are at or beyond the upper limits of the ranges of variation of a recent Amerindian sample (DP-2: 7.5 ± 0.8 mm, N = 14; DP-3: 7.0 ± 1.1 mm, N = 16; DP-4: 6.4 ± 0.7 mm, N = 11; DP-5: 5.2 ± 1.1 mm, N = 20), assuming that the longer phalanges from Shanidar 4 come from the more medial rays and the shorter ones come from the lateral rays. Thus, the distal tuberosities of at least the Shanidar 4 lateral pedal digits are enlarged relative to those of recent humans, as are those of the Shanidar 4 hallux, the Shanidar 3, 4, 5, and 6 hand phalanges (Chapter 8), and those of most Neandertal distal phalanges.

TABLE 87
Measurements of the Fifth Proximal Pedal Phalanges (mm)

	Shanidar 4		Shanidar 8
	Right	Left	Right
Articular length (M-1)	17.6	—	17.2
Midshaft height (M-3)	6.4	6.2	5.4
Midshaft breadth (M-2)	8.0	7.2	6.0
Proximal maximum height	10.9	—	9.8
Proximal maximum breadth	13.1	—	12.4
Proximal articular height	9.1	—	8.7
Proximal articular breadth	10.5	—	9.3
Distal height	7.5	6.9	6.1
Distal breadth	9.9	9.6	8.9
Torsion angle	4°	—	3°

TABLE 88
Proximal Pedal Phalangeal Comparisons

		Digitoscapial indices[a]					Proximal rugosity indices[b]				
		Digit 1	Digit 2	Digit 3	Digit 4	Digit 5	Digit 1	Digit 2	Digit 3	Digit 4	Digit 5
Shanidar 1	lt	121.6	—	—	—	—	68.7	—	—	—	—
Shanidar 3	rt	—	122.3	—	—	—	78.3	76.5	—	—	—
Shanidar 4	rt	127.0	—	101.2	107.9	125.0	72.0	—	75.5	69.6	66.9
	lt	122.8	107.4	105.1	—	116.1	—	72.3	80.4	—	—
Shanidar 6	rt	151.8	—	—	—	—	70.5	—	—	—	—
Shanidar 8	rt	148.9	122.7	—	—	111.1	67.1	76.5	—	—	66.6
	lt	—	—	122.7	—	—	—	—	71.3	—	—
Amud 1		—	—	—	—	—	—	—	74.0	—	—
Tabūn C1		—	114.8	116.1	110.7	—	89.2	86.3	77.0	78.1	—
European Neandertals X̄		130.9	119.3	116.7	110.4	109.9	74.9	73.2	67.8	74.7	68.0
SD		10.4	9.6	6.5	7.3	10.5	7.6	5.2	3.8	9.0	6.1
N		8	7	8	7	6	5	5	8	6	6
Recent Amerindians											
Libben (Ohio) X̄		130.6	97.1	95.1	93.9	101.5	81.6	82.9	83.5	83.9	74.1
SD		8.0	8.0	7.2	7.4	12.5	5.6	4.3	5.1	5.5	6.2
N		40	40	40	40	40	40	40	40	40	40
Pecos (N. Mex.) X̄		125.8	94.4	94.9	96.2	105.5	77.9	81.6	81.0	80.2	76.2
SD		9.4	9.1	10.5	8.7	12.2	6.3	5.0	5.7	6.1	7.1
N		40	47	43	46	35	40	47	43	46	35

[a] Digitoscapial index = (midshaft breadth/midshaft height) × 100. A higher index indicates a greater relative breadth of the midshaft.

[b] Proximal rugosity index = [(proximal articular height × proximal articular breadth)/(proximal maximum height × proximal maximum breadth)] × 100. A lower index indicates an expansion of the musculoligamentous attachment areas relative to the size of the metatarsal articular surface.

TABLE 89
Measurements of the Middle Pedal Phalanges (mm)

	Shanidar 4					Shanidar 8
	2 Left	3 Right	3 Left	4 Right	5 Right	5 Side indeterminate
Articular length	10.9	9.8	10.3	8.2	8.3	6.5
Midshaft height	5.1	5.5	4.9	4.7	4.6	4.3
Midshaft breadth	7.9	8.0	7.4	8.0	8.2	8.8
Proximal maximum height	9.3	9.0	8.3	8.5	9.0	7.3
Proximal maximum breadth	10.7	10.5	10.5	10.5	10.3	9.7
Proximal articular height	6.6	6.9	5.5	6.4	6.7	5.8
Proximal articular breadth	9.8	9.4	9.8	9.4	9.4	9.0
Distal height	6.4	5.0	5.0	5.9	6.9	4.7
Distal breadth	10.0	10.3	9.0	10.2	9.5	9.0

TABLE 90
Measurements of the Distal Pedal Phalanges (mm)

	Shanidar 4[b]	Shanidar 6	Shanidar 4	Shanidar 4	Shanidar 4	Shanidar 4	Shanidar 4
	1	1	2?	2?	3?	4?	5?
	Left	Right?	Side indeterminate	Side indeterminate	Side indeterminate	Side indeterminate	Side indeterminate
Articular length	(27.0–27.5)	—	11.2	11.2	11.1	10.5	8.7
Midshaft height	—	—	5.9	5.8	5.8	6.0	5.7
Midshaft breadth	—	—	6.6	6.1	6.0	6.8	5.6
Proximal maximum height	11.9	9.2	7.3	7.8	7.6	6.8	7.4
Proximal maximum breadth	(21.5)	(19.0)	12.0	11.8	11.1	10.9	10.4
Proximal articular height	9.5	7.0	4.6	4.5	5.0	4.1	5.3
Proximal articular breadth	(15.0)	(16.4)	9.2	8.2	7.6	9.2	8.0
Distal height	8.3	—	4.2	5.3	5.3	5.5	4.9
Distal breadth	15.4	(12.0)	10.3	8.8	8.4	9.6	7.7
Flexor pit breadth[a]	9.4	—					
Flexor pit depth[a]	2.4	—					

[a]Dimensions of the M. flexor hallucis longus tendon pit. The breadth is the mediolateral maximum dimension of the tendon insertion area. The depth is measured from the proximal plantar tubercles to the deepest point on the tendon insertion area.

[b]The bone is in two pieces. The length was estimated by aligning the two pieces in relation to each other using the contours of the pieces.

SUMMARY OF PEDAL REMAINS

The pedal remains from the Shanidar adults depict feet that were very similar to those of recent humans in overall structure and implied locomotor capabilities. Their primary differences with respect to more recent humans concern the general robusticity that characterizes all of the Shanidar lower limbs. This massiveness is evident primarily in modest articular enlargements, especially of the talus, and in the exaggeration of the attachments for muscles and ligaments involved in plantarflexion and maintaining the pedal arches. In addition, there is a tendency for them to have relatively short proximal phalanges and, at least for Shanidar 4, long distal phalanges.

SUMMARY

The rather abundant though characteristically incomplete lower limb remains from the Shanidar adult Neandertals describe a pelvic and locomotor anatomy that is similar to that of other known Near Eastern and European Neandertals and contrasts in several features with that of more recent humans. However, all of these fossil and recent humans exhibit the general proportions and articular morphologies that are in agreement with their having had normal human striding bipedal gaits.

The most pervasive aspect of the Shanidar lower limb bones is their robusticity. It is evident in their femoral and tibial diaphyses, in the anteroposterior dimensions of their patellae and proximal tibiae that provided them with large *M. quadriceps femoris* moment arms, in the enlargements of the attachment areas for several of the muscles involved with powerful acceleration during climbing or running, and to a lesser extent in the dimensions of their articular surfaces. In most of these features, the Shanidar specimens are similar to other Neandertals and are at or beyond the upper limits of more recent human ranges of variation.

The Shanidar 1 and 3 pelvic remains exhibit the mediolateral pubic bone elongation that was characteristic of the Neandertals, and Shanidar 1, 3, and 4 have the ventral thinning of the superior pubic ramus that was typical especially of the Near Eastern Neandertals.

There appears to have been less individual variation in lower limb morphology than in upper limb morphology among the Shanidar Neandertals. As with the upper limb remains, there are no consistent trends in which the later sample differs from the earlier sample. Most of the variation apparent in the sample appears to have been size related and probably reflects the considerable size difference among the Shanidar 1, 2, 3, 4, and 5 male specimens and the smaller Shanidar 6 and 8 females. Yet when size is taken into account, most of the differences disappear. The lower limb sample is, in fact, remarkably uniform, given its size and distribution in time.

CHAPTER 10

The Immature
Remains

The first and last of the Shanidar Neandertals to be discovered were infants. The first child was found in 1953 and consisted of a largely complete but crushed skeleton. This is the individual that was initially referred to as the "Shanidar child" but was later designated Shanidar 7 (Chapter 2). The second infant was part of the Shanidar 4, 6, and 8 multiple burial and bears the designation Shanidar 9. Although Shanidar 9 was excavated in 1960, its incomplete state (only nine vertebrae) postponed its identification until the Shanidar 4, 6, and 8 remains were cleaned and studied by Stewart in 1962.

Even though the Shanidar 7 and 9 remains are incomplete, they provide information on the skeletal morphology of Neandertal infants. There are relatively few immature Neandertals known, and most of them are fragmentary. Yet recent studies (e.g., Ferembach 1970; Smith and Arensburg 1977; Suzuki 1970; Tillier 1979; Vlček 1970, 1973) have made additional data on young Neandertals available, each of which adds to our understanding of the ontogeny of Neandertal morphology.

Shortly after their discovery, the Shanidar 7 remains were cleaned and studied by Şenyürek (1957a, 1957b, 1959). He discussed and illustrated most of the identifiable bones but concerned himself primarily with the virtually complete deciduous dentition. His study of the teeth will form part of their discussion here. The Shanidar 9 vertebrae were not cleaned until 1976, and they have previously received inventorial mention only (Trinkaus 1977b). As discussed in Chapter 4, Shanidar 7 and 9 were about 8 months old at death.

The Shanidar 7, other Upper Pleistocene, and recent human deciduous dental dimensions are in Tables 91 and 92. The Shanidar 7 and 9 vertebral dimensions are in Table 93, and the Shanidar 7 hand and foot bone dimensions are in Tables 94 and 95, respectively. Additional metric data are provided in the text for other, less complete bones of Shanidar 7.

CRANIAL REMAINS

Inventory

SHANIDAR 7

Several pieces of the cranial vault survive, all of which appear to derive from the frontal and parietal bones. There is a large piece with portions of the left frontal and partial bones (maximum length [anteroposterior] = 92.1 mm), a major piece of the right parietal bone, and about 20 smaller fragments of cranial vault bone. Of the last, 2 pieces (maximum lengths = 20.4 and 15.1 mm, respectively; maximum breadths = 17.0 and 10.9 mm, respectively) have sections of sutures, and 3 pieces (maximum lengths = 25.4, 24.3, and 23.6 mm, respectively; maximum breadths = 21.1, 21.7, and 19.5 mm, respectively) derive from the middle of either the parietal or frontal bones.

    Os Parietale: Right   The bone retains an anterior portion with 46.2 mm of the coronal suture. Maximum length (anteroposterior) = 41.1 mm; maximum breadth = 45.5 mm.

    Os Parietale: left   The central portion of the bone is preserved from the coronal to the lambdoid sutures, but nothing of either the sagittal or squamosal sutures is present. The posteromedial corner of the bone appears to be close to the position of lambda, 36.0 mm of the coronal suture and 28.6 mm of the lambdoid suture are preserved, and the parietal tuber is clearly evident in the middle of the piece. Maximum length (anteroposterior) = 69.5 mm; maximum breadth = 48.7 mm.

    Os Frontale   A section of the left frontal bone along the coronal suture, with 38.0 mm of the coronal suture, is preserved. Maximum length = 29.9 mm; maximum breadth = 44.1 mm.

Morphology

The fragmentary condition of the cranial vault bones permits few morphological observations. However, sufficient portions of the bones, especially of the left parietal bone, survive to enable an assessment of overall size, thickness, and a suggestion of shape.

The overall size of the neurocranium is indicated primarily by the anteroposterior length of 69.5 mm for the left parietal bone. Because this length measurement was determined laterally from the midline of the cranium, it is slightly less than the standard bregma–lambda measurement would have been.

It indicates that the original bregma–lambda chord was probably not much greater than about 80 mm. This suggests that Shanidar 7 had a relatively short parietal median sagittal arc because a sample of nine month-old Euroamerican males provide a mean parietal chord length of 109.0 mm (± 6. 0 mm, N = 15 [Young 1957]). Unfortunately, comparative data are not available from similarly aged Neandertal infants. Furthermore, it is uncertain what percentage of the original nasion–opisthion arc was made up by the parietal bones of Shanidar 7, and there is considerable variation in relative frontal, parietal, and occipital proportions among adults (Chapter 5). Nonetheless, it appears that Shanidar 7 probably had a relatively small neurocranium for its age.

It is possible to determine the thickness of the left frontal bone near its tuber as 2.3 mm and the thickness of the left parietal bone at its tuber as 2.2 mm. These thicknesses are similar to those of the slightly older (ca. 2 years) Pech-de-l'Azé 1 (2.0 and 2.0–3.0 mm for the frontal and parietal tubers, respectively [Ferembach 1970]), and they are within the ranges of variation of recent nine month-old Euroamericans for midline frontal thickness (males: 2.0 ± 0.3 mm, N = 14; females: 2.4 ± 0.5 mm, N = 18 [Roche 1953]) and midline parietal thickness (males: 1.8 ± 0.1 mm, N = 14; females: 1.7 ± 0.3 mm, N = 18 [Roche 1953]). The Shanidar 7 cranial vault bones are therefore similar in thickness to those of other Upper Pleistocene and recent human infants.

The cross-sectional morphology of the Shanidar 7 cranial vault bones is likewise similar to that of other recent human infants. The majority of the thickness is made up by the internal and external tables, and the diploë consists of large spaces separated by robust trabeculae. There is no evidence of any abnormal expansion of the diploic space.

On the endocranial surface of the right anterior parietal piece there is a deep sulcus about 1 mm wide along the preserved portion of the coronal suture. This is certainly the sulcus for the anterior, or frontal, branch of the middle meningeal artery. Although few of the details of the middle meningeal artery branching pattern can be discerned on the preserved pieces of the parietal bones, the configuration suggested here is within the ranges of variation of the branching patterns evident on other Neandertal and recent human infant crania (Ferembach 1970; Saban 1981).

The cranial vault bones are too incomplete to provide an accurate impression of their overall shape, especially as there may be small angular distortions in the joints between the preserved pieces. Yet what remains of the left parietal and frontal bones suggests that the anteroposterior curvature of the middle of the cranial vault was moderate, certainly within the ranges of variation of both Neandertal and recent human infants.

The posteromedial corner of the left parietal bone, however, curves slightly inward as it approaches where lambda would have been. This curvature suggests that Shanidar 7 may have had a supralambdoid flattening or depression, not unlike the ones associated with occipital buns on some fossil and recent human immature crania. Because the formation of an occipital bun, and an

associated supralambdoid flattening, is part of the normal growth and development of the posterior neurocranium (Trinkaus and LeMay 1982), it would not
be surprising if Shanidar 7 were to have had a small occipital bun.

DENTITION

Shanidar 7 retains one of the most complete deciduous dentitions known
for a fossil hominid (Tables 91 and 92; Figure 72). At least one of each of the
tooth crowns is preserved, and only one tooth, the dc_, does not retain a
complete, unworn crown. In the maxillary dentition, all of the left deciduous
teeth and the right di^1 to dc^- are represented by complete unworn crowns with
variable amounts of root formation. In addition, a major portion of the occlusal
surface of the incompletely formed left M^1 crown is present. In the mandibular
dentition, both di_1, the right di_2, both dm_1, and the left dm_2 preserve complete
crowns and variable amounts of their roots, and the right dc_ retains about
three-quarters of the crown, lacking the distolingual corner as a result of
postmortem damage. Because nothing remains of the maxilla or mandible, the
identification of the individual teeth is based entirely on morphology.

The degree of root preservation reflects the degree of development of each
tooth at the time of the death because several of the teeth, especially the incisors, exhibit partially formed roots with undamaged and open apices (Chapter 4). None of the teeth exhibits macroscopic occlusal wear facets, although the
degree of development of several of the teeth suggests that they had achieved at
least gingival eruption (Lunt and Law 1974).

Incisors

The maxillary central deciduous incisors have evenly curved labial surfaces
that are bounded mesially and distally by slight angulations in the crown. The
incisive edges are evenly curved mesiodistally, with their apices located a third
of the distance from the mesial to the distal margins of the crowns. There is a
blunt angle of almost 90° where each incisive edge meets its mesial margin,
whereas each incisive edge rounds evenly on to the distal margins. As a result,
the mesial margins are only slightly convex, whereas the distal margins are
noticeably convex in a cervicoocclusal direction.

The lingual surfaces of the teeth are bounded by clear marginal ridges that
are most prominent along the mesial margins but are also evident along the
occlusal and distal margins; these teeth are thus shovel shaped, as were at least
some of the Shanidar permanent incisors (Chapter 6). Both of the di^1 have large
lingual tubercles that merge imperceptibly on to the adjacent lingual, mesial,
and distal surfaces. The swelling of each tubercle continues predominantly

TABLE 91
Mesiodistal Lengths of the Shanidar 7 Deciduous Teeth and Those of Other Upper Pleistocene and Recent Humans (mm)[a]

	Shanidar 7 Right	Shanidar 7 Left	Near Eastern Neandertals	European Neandertals	Skhūl–Qafzeh sample	Early Upper Paleolithic sample	Recent Australians[b] Males	Recent Australians[b] Females	Recent Euroamericans[c] Males	Recent Euroamericans[c] Females
Maxilla										
di-1	7.5	7.4	7.8–9.1 (2)	7.6 ± 0.6 (7)	8.5 (1)	6.9–7.1 (3)	7.4 ± 0.5 (29)	7.2 ± 0.5 (18)	6.4 ± 0.4 (69)	6.5 ± 0.3 (64)
di-2	5.6	5.6	6.1 (1)	6.5 ± 0.6 (6)	—	5.4–5.8 (3)	6.0 ± 0.4 (54)	5.9 ± 0.4 (36)	5.2 ± 0.4 (69)	5.3 ± 0.4 (64)
dc	7.3	7.0	7.5 (1)	7.1 ± 0.9 (11)	7.0–7.1 (2)	7.2–7.6 (2)	7.4 ± 0.4 (113)	7.2 ± 0.5 (77)	6.8 ± 0.4 (69)	6.7 ± 0.4 (64)
dm-1	—	7.8	7.4–7.6 (2)	8.6 ± 1.2 (13)	8.5–8.9 (2)	7.3 ± 0.6 (10)	7.6 ± 0.5 (112)	7.3 ± 0.4 (74)	6.7 ± 0.5 (69)	6.6 ± 0.5 (64)
dm-2	—	8.9	9.1–10.2 (4)	9.8 ± 0.7 (16)	9.4–9.8 (2)	9.6 ± 0.8 (5)	9.7 ± 0.6 (113)	9.4 ± 0.5 (76)	8.8 ± 0.6 (69)	8.8 ± 0.5 (64)
Mandible										
di-1	4.6	4.6	5.0 (1)	4.7–5.3 (4)	5.0 (1)	4.0 (1)	4.5 ± 0.4 (18)	4.3 ± 0.4 (8)	4.0 ± 0.3 (69)	4.1 ± 0.3 (64)
di-2	5.2	—	5.1 (1)	4.6–6.0 (4)	5.0–5.5 (3)	4.8 (1)	5.0 ± 0.5 (34)	4.9 ± 0.4 (19)	4.6 ± 0.4 (69)	4.7 ± 0.4 (64)
dc	(6.8)	—	6.7–7.8 (2)	6.8 ± 0.7 (8)	6.2–7.0 (2)	5.3–5.9 (3)	6.3 ± 0.4 (109)	6.2 ± 0.4 (62)	5.8 ± 0.3 (69)	5.8 ± 0.3 (64)
dm-1	8.6	8.9	9.0 (2)	8.9 ± 0.5 (11)	8.8–9.5 (2)	8.1 ± 0.8 (12)	8.3 ± 0.6 (109)	8.1 ± 0.5 (70)	7.9 ± 0.4 (69)	7.7 ± 0.4 (64)
dm-2	—	10.0	10.1–11.2 (4)	10.5 ± 0.8 (19)	10.0–11.0 (3)	10.3 ± 0.8 (20)	10.9 ± 0.6 (115)	10.6 ± 0.5 (69)	9.9 ± 0.5 (69)	9.7 ± 0.5 (64)

[a]For samples ≥ 5, the mean, standard deviation and sample size are given; for samples < 5, the range and sample size are given.
[b]Margetts and Brown 1978.
[c]Black 1978.

TABLE 92
Buccolingual (Labiolingual) Breadths of the Shanidar 7 Deciduous Teeth and Those of Other Upper Pleistocene and Recent Humans (mm)[a]

	Shanidar 7 Right	Shanidar 7 Left	Near Eastern Neandertals	European Neandertals	Skhūl–Qafzeh sample	Early Upper Paleolithic sample	Recent Australians[b] Males	Recent Australians[b] Females	Recent Euroamericans[c] Males	Recent Euroamericans[c] Females
Maxilla										
di-1	6.0	5.7	6.0–6.3 2	6.0 ± 0.6 7	5.3 1	5.0–5.6 3	5.5 ± 0.4 29	5.3 ± 0.3 18	5.1 ± 0.4 69	5.2 ± 0.5 64
di-2	5.2	5.4	5.5 1	5.5 ± 0.5 6	5.8–6.3 2	4.8–5.4 3	5.2 ± 0.4 56	5.0 ± 0.4 36	4.7 ± 0.4 69	4.6 ± 0.4 64
dc	7.0	7.1	7.5 1	6.5 ± 0.6 11	4.9–6.3 2	6.5–6.8 2	6.6 ± 0.5 113	6.3 ± 0.4 77	6.1 ± 0.4 69	6.0 ± 0.4 64
dm-1	—	8.8	8.6–9.2 2	9.0 ± 0.8 13	8.6–9.1 2	8.7 ± 0.6 9	9.1 ± 0.6 114	8.8 ± 0.5 76	8.8 ± 0.5 69	8.6 ± 0.6 64
dm-2	—	9.8	10.1–10.7 4	10.5 ± 0.6 16	10.0–10.8 2	10.5 ± 0.5 10	10.7 ± 0.6 114	10.3 ± 0.4 76	9.5 ± 0.5 69	9.4 ± 0.5 64
Mandible										
di-1	4.7	4.5	4.8 1	4.0–5.1 4	4.3 1	3.6 1	4.3 ± 0.3 18	4.2 ± 0.4 8	3.9 ± 0.4 69	3.8 ± 0.3 64
di-2	4.7	—	4.8 1	4.5–5.6 4	4.8–5.0 3	4.1 1	4.8 ± 0.4 33	4.7 ± 0.4 18	4.4 ± 0.4 69	4.4 ± 0.3 64
dm-1	7.2	7.6	7.3–8.6 2	7.6 ± 0.5 11	7.5–7.7 2	7.1 ± 0.5 12	7.9 ± 0.5 112	7.5 ± 0.5 73	7.4 ± 0.5 69	7.3 ± 0.4 64
dm-2	—	9.1	9.2–9.5 4	9.5 ± 0.5 19	9.1–9.4 3	9.1 ± 0.6 20	9.9 ± 0.5 115	9.6 ± 0.5 75	8.9 ± 0.4 69	8.7 ± 0.4 64

[a]For samples ≥ 5, the mean, standard deviation, and sample size are provided; for samples < 5, the range and sample size are provided.
[b]Margetts and Brown 1978.
[c]Black 1978.

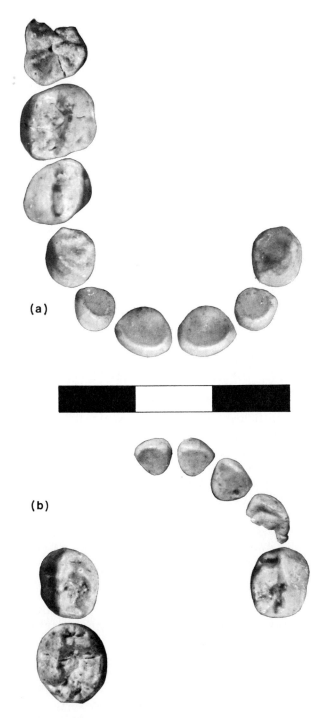

Figure 72 The Shanidar 7 deciduous dentition. (a) The maxillary deciduous dentition with the partial crown of the left M¹. (b) The mandibular deciduous dentition. Scale in centimeters.

mesially as one goes occlusally along the lingual surface of the crown. There is a slight excresence between the lingual tubercle and the distal marginal ridge on the left di^1 that is not present on the right di^1; it appears as a slight roughening of the enamel.

The roots of the two di^1 are flattened labiolingually, as are the roots of most recent human di^1.

The two upper lateral incisors are similar to the two di^1, although they are narrower mesiodistally. Their labial surfaces are evenly convex mesiodistally, but the points of maximum labial projection are located slightly mesially from the middles of the crowns. Their incisive edges are smoothly rounded, although they are more sharply curved than those of the di^1. Like the di^1, their points of maximum occlusal projection are located about a third of the distance from the mesial to the distal margins. The incisive margins curve evenly onto the slightly convex mesial margins, whereas the occlusal and distal margins blend into continuous and steeply sloping distal shoulders that end in angles about 2.0 mm above the distal cervical margins. From those angles, the distal margins angle sharply inward to the cervicoenamel junctions, so that the maximum lengths of the two di^2 are located about 2.0 mm above the cervicoenamel junctions.

The lingual surfaces of the di^2 are ringed by prominent marginal ridges mesially, distally, and to a lesser extent occlusally, and by lingual tubercles cervically. They are therefore shovel shaped. The marginal ridges of each tooth are clearest as projecting borders about 1.0 mm wide along the mesial edge of the lingual surface and along the distal edge above the angle in the distal surface of the crown. Below the distal angles, the left tooth has a distinct swelling that runs from the cervical margin to the distal angle, whereas the right tooth has a ridge similar to the rest of its marginal ridges. As a result, the lingual tubercle of the left di^2 is difficult to discern because it blends with the swelling along the distocervical margin of the lingual surface, but the lingual tubercle on the right tooth is clearly demarcated from adjacent structures.

Both of the mandibular central incisors are preserved, and they are mirror images of each other. Their labial surfaces are evenly and gently convex, and especially cervically curl around onto the mesial and distal surfaces. Their mesial surfaces are almost flat cervicoocclusally, but their distal surfaces are convex and curve evenly onto the distal two-thirds of the incisive edges. As a result, the highest points of the incisive edges are located two-thirds of the way mesially along the incisive edges. The mesial halves of their lingual surfaces are occupied by largely flat swellings that extend upwards from small lingual tubercles along the mesial margins almost to the incisive edges.

In contrast, the distal halves of the lingual surfaces each has a distinct marginal ridge 0.9 mm wide that runs all the way along the distolingual edge. These distal marginal ridges demarcate concave areas in the distal halves of the lingual surfaces that give a slight suggestion of shoveling. This lingual morphology is typical of human di_1.

The right lower lateral incisor is generally similar to the mandibular central incisors. The labial surface is smoothly convex mesiodistally, although the point of maximum projection is located slightly mesial of the middle of the tooth. The incisive edge reaches a blunt point that is also located somewhat mesially of the middle of the tooth. The mesial third of the incisive margin slopes slightly cervically and then forms a clear but blunt angle with the straight mesial margin of the tooth. In contrast, the distal two-thirds of the incisive edge and the distal margin blend into a continuous, convex curve that becomes relatively flat for only about the last 2.0 mm before it reaches the cervical margin. Both the mesial and distal margins are flat labiolingually as they approach the cervical margin.

The lingual surface of the di_2 gives the impression of being shovel shaped, although a clear marginal ridge is formed only along the distal margin. There is a suggestion of a marginal ridge near the mesioocclusal corner of the lingual surface, but most of the mesial margin of the lingual surface does not have a marginal ridge. A clear lingual tubercle is absent, but the mesial two-thirds of the lingual surface, especially close to the cervical margin, is gently convex.

Canines

Both of the maxillary deciduous canines are preserved, and they are mirror images of each other. They have continuously and evenly curved labial surfaces, each of which rises to a central, pointed cusp. The central cusps of these teeth are located in the centers of the ovoid surfaces demarcated by their cervicoenamel junctions. The two sides of each incisive edge are almost equal in length. They form the line between the smooth and convex labial surface and the irregular and largely concave lingual surface and include the central cusp. However, the mesial ridges are slightly longer, more as a result of the development of the lingual cingulum than from any off-center positioning of the cusp. The lingual surface of each of these teeth appears as a diamond-shaped surface with a central lingual ridge. The mesioocclusal and distoocclusal edges of the diamond are made up by the central mesiodistal ridge, and the mesiocervical and distocervical edges of the diamond are formed by marginal ridges of enamel. In addition, each tooth has a low but distinctly demarcated central lingual tubercle and a ridge of cingulum along side of the distocervical margin of the central diamond. The lingual tubercle and the distocervical ridge of cingulum have the effect of broadening the base of the crown lingually and distolingually by almost a millimeter.

What remains of the Shanidar 7 right dc_ suggests that it was morphologically similar to its maxillary deciduous canines. The labial surface is evenly convex, the single cusp appears to have been above the center of the cross section at the cerviocoenamel junction, the mesial and distal sides of the incisive edge are subequal with the mesial side being minimally longer, and the lingual surface appears to have been diamond shaped with a central lingual ridge. It is not possible to determine whether there was a lingual tubercle or a distolingual cingular ridge. However, at the distal end of the incisive edge there is a distinct tubercle of enamel projecting distoocclusally. Similar tubercles are rare but present among other Neandertals and recent humans (Şenyürek 1959; Tillier 1979).

Molars

The left maxillary first deciduous molar is a fully molarized tooth with four cusps clearly evident. As is usually the case, the paracone is the largest of the cusps, followed by the protocone, the metacone and the hypocone. The tip of the metacone protrudes only slightly from the distal slope of the paracone, but it is at least as high above the cericoenamel junction as the protocone. The hypocone, in contrast, is much lower, although it is clearly separated from the protocone by a small sulcus and from the metacone by a relatively large talon basin. The trigone basin is clearly delimited by the paracone, protocone, the mesial protocone–paracone crista, and the distal protocone–metacone crista. The last rises buccally up to the tip of the metacone but lingually only about half of the way up the buccal surface of the protocone. The trigone basin is relatively deep, being formed by a smooth, concave surface along the protocone and a crenulated, convex surface along the paracone. The presence of four distinct cusps on the dm^1 is common among Neandertals but relatively infrequent among recent humans (Hanihara 1963).

The line drawn across the tips of the paracone and protocone is obliquely oriented with respect to the mesiodistal axis of the tooth, here taken to be indicated by a line drawn midway between the paracone and protocone and the metacone and hypocone. This oblique arrangement is found among other Neandertals (Tillier 1979), but recent humans tend to have a more perpendicular orientation of the two lines.

The buccal and lingual aspects of the tooth present bulbous projections, especially in the region of the paracone. This is indicated by breadth of the trigone basin (4.1 mm), which is only 46.6% of the breadth of the tooth. The distal surface of the tooth is almost flat, but the mesial surface bulges slightly in the region of the paracone–protocone crista.

The left maxillary second decidous molar is similarly a tooth with a full complement of cusps. The protocone, paracone, and metacone are all clearly demarcated and subequal in size, and the hypocone is almost as large as the other three cusps. In addition, there is a small Carabelli's cusp separated from the protocone by a distinct sulcus; it most closely approximates type 5 of Hanihara (1963). As a result primarily of the presence of a Carabelli's cusp with its cingular development, the tooth is almost rectangular rather than rhomboidal. The region delineated by the four main cusps, however, is rhomboidal, and the midline drawn between the paracone and protocone and the metacone and hypocone is at an angle to the lines drawn between the tips of the paracone and protocone or metacone and hypocone. Both the buccal and lingual surfaces of the tooth extend considerably beyond the crests formed by the paracone and metacone and the protocone and hypocone.

The trigone basin is relatively deep, and it is bordered distally by a protocone–metacone crista that extends up to the tip of the metacone but only about half of the way up the buccal aspect of the protocone. At the mesial end of the trigone basin there is a small pit that is probably a small anterior fovea. The talon basin is similarly deep, even though the hypocone does not rise as high as the other three cusps. Both of the basin surfaces are moderately crenulated.

The two mandibular first deciduous molars are slightly asymmetrical in that the right one possesses five full cusps, whereas the left one lacks a hypoconulid. There is a slight suggestion of a nypoconulid on the left dm_1, but it is not sufficiently large to be called a cusp. Otherwise the two teeth are generally similar in having subrectangular areas between their cusps and prominent mesiobuccal shoulders for occlusion with the dc^-.

Each of the dm_1 has the protoconid as the most prominent cusp, followed by the metaconid, the hypoconid, and then the entoconid. The protoconid–metaconid ridge on each merges with the metaconid but only abuts against the lingual surface of the protoconid. Mesial to each metaconid there is a clear sulcus, but there is no suggestion of a cusp along the ridge extending mesially and then lingually from the protoconid. The surfaces of the left talonid basin are slightly crenulated, but those of the right talonid basin appear smoother. There are some slight crenulations on the buccal surfaces of each tooth, which appear to be the products of slight bulbous swellings at the base of each crown.

The single left second deciduous molar is a large tooth with a full complement of cusps, similar to the rest of the Shanidar 7 molars. It has five cusps, all of which are clearly demarcated from their adjacent cusps by sulci. There is no trace of a protostylid, although the base of the crown, especially buccally, is bulbous. There is a prominent central ridge on the metaconid, which extends across and abuts against the protoconid, but it is not especially high or thick. It sets off a deep but narrow trigonid basin from the large talonid basin of the tooth. All of the surfaces of the talonid basin are well crenulated.

In addition to the five preserved deciduous molars of Shanidar 7, there is an occlusal surface piece of the left maxillary first permanent molar. The fragment retains most of the trigone basin with all of the paracone and protocone and the mesial two-thirds of the metacone. The crown was only partially formed at the death of Shanidar 7, but it has also sustained some postmortem damage distally. The distance between the protocone and paratone tips and between the tips of the paracone and metacone are 6.7 and 4.8 mm, respectively.

The preserved portions of the M^1 depict a large tooth with prominent cusps

and a heavily crenulated occlusal surface. There is no evidence of crests between the three cusps because each one has a small ridge extending down into
the trigone basin. It is uncertain whether a hypocone was present, but the
morphology of the protocone–metacone region suggests that one would probably have been present in the fully erupted tooth.

The deciduous molars of Shanidar 7 are thus characterized by their large
numbers of cusps because all except the left dm_1 have the maximum number
normally found in recent human samples. In this, they resemble other Neandertal deciduous molars (P. Smith 1978; Tillier 1979).

Dental Dimensions

The dimensions of the Shanidar 7 deciduous teeth (Tables 91 and 92) are
relatively low for a Neandertal. Most of the dimensions, except those of the
dc^-, are close to or below the means of the European Neandertal samples and
towards the lower end of the Near Eastern Neandertal ranges of variation.
However, only the lengths of the di_1 are below the known range of variation for
other Neandertals, and the comparative sample is quite small. It is this small
size of the Shanidar 7 teeth that led to the suggestion (Şenyürek 1959) that
Shanidar 7 might be female, a suggestion that cannot be tested given the ranges
of variation of other Neandertal dental dimensions and the degree of overlap
between the sexes in deciduous dental dimensions in recent human samples.

The dimensions of the Shanidar 7 deciduous teeth are also largely within
the ranges of variation of those of more recent human deciduous dentitions.
This is due in part to the relatively small size of the Shanidar 7 teeth vis-à-vis
other Neandertals. It is also due to the fact that there has been relatively little
change in deciduous dental dimensions since the early Upper Pleistocene, so
that there is considerable overlap in deciduous dental dimensions between
Neandertal, early anatomically modern human, and recent human samples
(Smith 1978; Tables 91 and 92).

Summary

The well-preserved and unworn deciduous dentition of Shanidar 7 depicts
a morphological pattern similar to those known for other Neandertals (Legoux
1970; Smith and Arensburg 1977; Tillier 1979). The maxillary incisors are
shovel shaped and slightly bulbous labially. The maxillary canines have well-
developed lingual tubercles. The molars have the maximum number or close to
the maximum number of cusps known for recent human deciduous molars,
with considerable relief of the occlusal surfaces. In all of these features, the
Shanidar 7 teeth are similar to other Neandertal deciduous teeth and at the
limits of recent human ranges of variation. However, these morphological contrasts between the Shanidar 7 teeth and the usual patterns among recent humans are not accompanied by significant differences in dental dimensions.

AXIAL SKELETON

Inventory

SHANIDAR 7

Vertebrae

There are three vertebral centra preserved for Shanidar 7, all of which are probably lumbar. One is complete (maximum breadth = 15.8 mm), one preserves the dorsal and either the cranial or caudal surface (maximum breadth = 18.3 mm), and the third is a fragment of the dorsal surface (maximum breadth = 13.0).

Ribs

Central portions of two ribs are preserved. Maximum lengths = 22.4 and 25.4 mm.

SHANIDAR 9

Cervical Vertebrae

C5   Complete laminae, pedicles, and articular facets.
C6   Damaged centrum and separate laminae, pedicles, and articular facets with damage to the articular facets.
C7   Largely complete centrum, complete right lamina, pedicle, and articular facets, and damaged left lamina, pedicle, and articular facets.

Thoracic Vertebrae

The T1 was joined *in situ* to the C5–C7, but the remainder of the thoracic vertebrae, although articulated, were separate from the cervical vertebrae and T1. It is therefore uncertain which sequence of five thoracic vertebrae they represent; they are assumed to be the next five, T2–T6.

T1   Complete laminae, pedicles, and articular facets.
T2?   Centrum with damage to the dorsal margin.
T3?   Centrum with one surface preserved, plus the separate right lamina and articular facets and the left lamina, pedicle, and articular facets.
T4?   Complete right lamina, pedicle, and articular facets, and the left lamina and articular facets with damage to the transverse processes and the left articular facets.
T5?   Complete right lamina, pedicle, and articular facets, and the largely complete left lamina, pedicle, and articular facets with damage to the left superior articular facet and the left pedicle.
T6?   Left lamina and the pedicle with damage to the pedicle.

Morphology

There are few features of note on the Shanidar 7 and 9 axial skeletons (Figure 73; Table 93). They are morphologically similar to those of most recent human infants of similar developmental ages.

As mentioned in Chapter 4, the neural arches of the Shanidar 9 vertebrae were only partially fused dorsally. Those of the C5, T1, and T3? were unfused and those of the C6, C7, and T4?–T6? were partially joined but still clearly exhibited the lines of fusion. This is indicative of the young age of the individual.

The dimensions of the vertebral centra for Shanidar 7 and 9 are smaller than those preserved for Kebara 1 (Smith and Arensburg 1977), but this is probably a reflection of which vertebrae are preserved. However, like those from Kebara, the Shanidar 7 and 9 vertebral centra, and especially the lumbar centrum of Shanidar 7, appear to be short dorsoventrally relative to their breadths.

Little can be said of the two rib fragments from Shanidar 7 because their positions in the thorax cannot be determined.

UPPER LIMB REMAINS

Inventory

SHANIDAR 7

Ulna: right   Largely complete diaphysis damaged proximally and distally. Maximum length = 57.6 mm.

Metacarpal 1: right   Palmar and radial sides of the diaphysis and distal end and of the proximal epiphyseal surface. Maximum length = 13.0 mm.

Metacarpals 2–5: Side Indeterminate   Eight metacarpal or metatarsal diaphyses are preserved, although they are insufficiently developed to indicate from which limb they derive. Some of them are probably metacarpals.

Phalanges Proximales 2–5: Right?   Three diaphyses and associated proximal and distal surfaces are preserved. One is complete (maximum length = 14.1 mm), one is damaged on the proximopalmar margin (maximum length = 16.3 mm), and the third is broken distally (maximum length = 13.3 mm).

Phalanges Medies 2–5: Right?   Four diaphyses with their proximal and distal surfaces are preserved. Three are complete (maximum lengths = 9.3, 10.2, and 10.0 mm, respectively) and the fourth is damaged on its distopalmar margin (maximum length = 8.9 mm).

Phalanx Distalis ?: Right?   Complete bone. Maximum length = 6.4 mm.

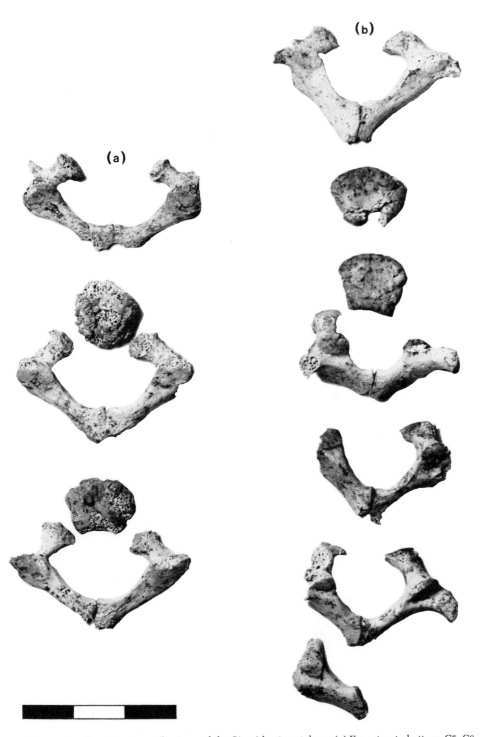

Figure 73 Superior (cranial) views of the Shanidar 9 vertebrae. (a) From top to bottom: C5, C6, and C7. (b) From top to bottom: T1, T2?, T3?, T4?, T5?, and T6?. Scale in centimeters.

TABLE 93
Measurements of the Shanidar 9 Cervical and Thoracic Vertebrae and of the Shanidar 7 Lumbar Vertebra (mm)

	Shanidar 9								Shanidar 7
	C5	C6	C7	T1	T2?	T3?	T4?	T5?	L?
Superior transverse diameter	33.7	33.3	—	30.4	—	(22.5)	(26.0)	(25.0)	—
Inferior transverse diameter	34.0	33.3	—	27.8	—	22.6	24.3	22.7	—
Canal transverse diameter (M-11)	21.9	19.8	—	16.4	—	(13.0)	14.3	14.5	—
Centrum medial height (M-3)	—	—	4.7	—	4.5	4.4	—	—	8.2
Centrum dorsoventral diameter	—	—	9.9	—	11.1	11.2	—	—	8.8
Centrum transverse diameter	—	—	13.6	—	14.6	13.3	—	—	15.8

Morphology

The upper limb remains from Shanidar 7, to the extent that they are preserved, appear to follow the same pattern of robusticity evident in the Kebara 1 (Smith and Arensburg 1977) and Kiik-Koba 2 (Vlček 1973) infants (Figure 74; Table 94). This is apparent primarily on the ulna and first metacarpal.

The right ulnar diaphysis presents a moderately robust midshaft region with a clear indication of the interosseus crest. The anteroposterior and mediolateral diameters at midshaft are both 5.5 mm. As with the Kiik-Koba 2 infant, the Shanidar 7 ulna has clear anteroposterior curvature. Furthermore, on the

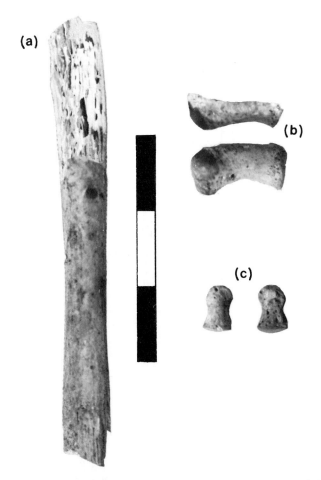

Figure 74 Upper limb remains of Shanidar 7. (a) Anterior (volar) view of the right ulna (the proximal end is at the top). (b) Dorsal (above) and radial (below) views of the right metacarpal 1, showing the development of the *M. opponens pollicis* insertion. (c) Dorsal (left) and palmar (right) views of the distal hand phalanx from digit 3 or 4. Scale in centimeters.

TABLE 94

Measurements of the Shanidar 7 Metacarpals and Hand Phalanges (mm)

	Metacarpal 1	Proximal phalanx ?	Proximal phalanx ?	Proximal phalanx ?	Middle phalanx ?	Middle phalanx ?	Middle phalanx ?	Middle phalanx ?	Distal phalanx ?
	Right	Right?	Right?	Right?	Side indeterminate	Side indeterminate	Side indeterminate	Side indeterminate	Side indeterminate
Length (w/o epiphyses)	13.0	14.1	16.3	—	9.3	10.2	10.0	—	6.4
Midshaft height	—	3.2	3.5	3.6	3.0	2.8	2.6	3.2	2.0
Midshaft breadth	—	5.5	5.5	5.8	5.2	4.7	4.7	5.2	3.2
Distal breadth	—	—	—	—	—	—	—	—	3.8

distal diaphysis there is a large roughened area for the attachment of the M. *pronator quadratus,* suggesting that even at this early age this muscle was strongly developed.

The radial half of the right first metacarpal is notable primarily for its attachment area for the *M. opponens pollicis.* There is a clear crest along the dorsoradial margin, which arises in the middle of the proximal half of the diaphysis and increases in size distally. It does not form an actual shelf as do those of older Neandertal children and Neandertal adults, but it unquestionably indicates the former presence of a hypertrophied *M. opponens pollicis.* In this, Shanidar 7 resembles the Kiik-Koba 2 infant, who also had an exceptional *M. opponens pollicis* crest given its young age (Vlček 1975).

It is difficult to assign the individual phalanges to digits. However, because all of them appear to derive from the right hand (following Şenyürek's notes), it is probable that digits 2, 3, and 4 are represented by the proximal phalanges, digits 2–5 are represented by the middle phalanges, and the single distal phalanx derives from either digit 3 or digit 4. If one assumes, for the sake of a general comparison, that the length of the proximal phalanx 3 is 16.3 mm, that of the middle phalanx 3 is 10.2 mm, and the distal phalanx with a length of 6.4 mm is from digit 3 (Table 94), these three bones make up 49.5, 31.0, and 19.5% of the summed skeletal length of the digit. These figures are similar to those of 50.1, 31.9, and 18.0%, respectively, for a recent human hand of the same developmental age (Pyle *et al.* 1971). The morphologies of the individual phalanges are similarly close to those of recent human infants. The tuberosity of the distal phalanx appears to be relatively large, but it is not unusual for recent humans of the same age.

The upper limb remains of Shanidar 7 are therefore generally similar to those of recent human infants. They differ only in the greater development of attachments for certain muscles, muscles that were hypertrophied among Neandertal adults (Chapter 8).

LOWER LIMB REMAINS

Inventory

SHANIDAR 7

Femur: Right?   The bone is represented by a diaphyseal fragment, which is probably a section of the proximal lateral diaphysis. Maximum length = 29.7 mm.

Tibia: Side Indeterminate   A diaphyseal fragment with one margin preserved, probably the lateral margin. Maximum length = 47.0 mm.

Metatarsal 1: Right   Proximal epiphyseal surface and most of the diaphysis. Maximum length = 15.3 mm.

TABLE 95
Measurements of the Shanidar 7 Metatarsals and Pedal Phalanges (mm)

	Metatarsal 1		Proximal phalanx 1	Proximal phalanx ?	Proximal phalanx ?
	Right	Left	Side indeterminate	Side indeterminate	Side indeterminate
Length (w/o epiphyses)	—	18.2	8.4	—	6.5
Midshaft height	4.0	3.9	3.9	2.8	2.8
Midshaft breadth	3.8	3.8	6.2	3.2	3.6

Metatarsal 1: Left   Complete bone. Maximum length = 18.2 mm.

Metatarsals 2–5: Side Indeterminate   Eight metatarsal or metacarpal diaphyses are preserved, some of which are probably metatarsals.

Phalanx proximalis 1: Side Indeterminate   Complete bone with damage to the distal end. Maximum length = 8.4 mm.

Phalanges proximales 2–5: Side Indeterminate   Two diaphyses with associated proximal and distal surfaces are preserved. One is complete, and the other is damaged on the distal surface. Maximum lengths = 7.9 and 6.5 mm, respectively.

Morphology

All of the Shanidar 7 pedal remains and its tibial fragment are indistinguishable from those of recent human infants of the same age. The diaphyseal fragment of one of the femora has a large roughened area, which is identified as the proximolateral muscle attachment area around the gluteal tuberosity. If this identification is correct (the incomplete state of the fragment makes it impossible to confirm), it indicates that Shanidar 7 had a well-developed *M. gluteus maximus*. As with the muscle markings on the Shanidar 7 upper limb remains, this foreshadows the hypertrophied condition apparent in Neandertal adults (Chapter 9).

SUMMARY

The remains of Shanidar 7 and 9 are generally similar to those of all *H. sapiens* of the same developmental age. However, Shanidar 7 has characteristics that place it at the limits of recent human ranges of variation and align it with other Neandertal infants. These features include the elaboration of cusp morphology on the deciduous teeth, especially the deciduous molars, and the indications of muscular hypertrophy in the attachments of the *M. pronator quadratus*, *M. opponens pollicis*, and *M. gluteus maximus*. The postcranial hypertrophy of Shanidar 7 and other Neandertal children suggests that the robusticity of the Neandertals was manifest at an early developmental age.

CHAPTER 11

Bodily Proportions
and the Estimation
of Stature

Six of the Shanidar adults, all except Shanidar 8, are sufficiently complete to permit the assessment of some aspects of their body proportions and have at least one long bone that is sufficiently intact to permit the estimation of their statures. Only 2 other Near Eastern Neandertals, Amud 1 and Tabūn C1, provide similar data; among the European Neandertals, only 6 individuals provide proportional data and 10 partial skeletons permit the estimation of their statures (Tables 96 and 97).

BODILY PROPORTIONS

A consideration of the overall body proportions of the Shanidar Neandertals involves four relatively separate comparisons: head to postcranial proportions, trunk to limb proportions, interlimb proportions, and limb segment proportions. Aspects of each of these have already been considered with reference to their regional anatomy. The data presented earlier will be reviewed here with the addition of aspects of body proportions not previously discussed.

It should be kept in mind that assessments of the body proportions of the Shanidar individuals involve comparisons between body segments, each of whose relative size is of interest. There is unfortunately no available independent standard reference measurement, such as body weight, that could be used

390

as a basis for assessments of the relative sizes of the individual body units. Therefore, similarities and differences among their body proportions and those of other hominid groups will be used to evaluate the relative sizes of each of the body segments employed.

The size of the neurocranium relative to stature of Shanidar 1 is similar to those of other Neandertals and early anatomically modern humans. The ratio of the cube root of cranial capacity to femoral length for Shanidar 1 is less than 1 standard deviation below the means of a Neandertal sample and an Early Upper Paleolithic sample, although it is almost 2 standard deviations above the mean of a small (N = 3) Skhūl–Qafzeh sample (Chapter 5).

In contrast, all of the Shanidar Neandertals appear to have had faces that were long anteroposteriorly compared to those of more recent humans, but ones that were similar in relative size to those of other Neandertals. This is indicated by comparisons of the Shanidar 1, 2, 4, and 5 mandibular superior lengths to their femoral and tibial lengths (Chapter 5). This difference between the Shanidar and other Neandertals and more recent humans probably reflects only their prognathism and not any difference in head to postcranium proportions.

It is difficult to obtain an accurate assessment of trunk size for fossil specimens as fragmentary as the Shanidar and other Pleistocene hominids. The best that one can do is to estimate their trunk lengths, or a value proportional to trunk length, and use those estimates in comparisons with long bones. It is simply not possible to obtain an accurate appreciation of trunk volume unless a specimen preserves a reasonably complete set of ribs and vertebrae, a condition not met by the Shanidar and other Neandertals. If the Shanidar individuals were indeed barrel chested in the way that most European Neandertals appear to have been (Chapter 7), then using only trunk length may underestimate their overall trunk sizes. However, although the state of preservation of the Shanidar specimens does not permit an assessment of their relative trunk volumes, they are the only Neandertals that allow comparisons of vertebral column segment lengths, other than those of the lower cervical vertebrae, to limb lengths.

Data presented in Chapter 7 show that the relative lengths of the Shanidar 1 and 3 lumbar and sacral regions are similar to those of recent humans. Furthermore, the relative lengths of the Shanidar 1 lower cervical and lumbar regions are within recent human ranges of variation, although they suggest that Shanidar 1 may have had a relatively shorter neck than most fossil and recent *H. sapiens* (Chapter 7). The data from the Shanidar 2 and 4 cervical vertebrae indicate that they had cervical regions whose relative lengths were similar to those of Shanidar 1 or even closer to the means of more recent human samples. It therefore appears reasonable to assume that the different segments of the Shanidar vertebral columns, especially in the lumbosacral region, made up similar percentages of the total C1–S5 length as among recent humans, and that one is justified in using the lengths of individual segments as indications of total trunk length.

In the discussions of the Shanidar 1, 2, 3, and 4 cervical vertebrae and sacra (Chapter 7), comparisons were made between their ventral body lengths and either femoral or tibial lengths. The resultant indices, especially those from comparisons of the Shanidar 2 C2–C7 length versus tibial length and the Shanidar 1 and 3 sacral length versus femoral length, indicated that their vertebral column segments were not particularly long or short relative to lower limb length. The same data also indicate that their lower limbs were approximately the lengths that one would expect for recent humans with their trunk lengths. It thus appears that the Shanidar individuals, given their trunk lengths, had lower limb lengths comparable to those of recent humans.

It is possible to estimate the lengths of the Shanidar 1 and 3 upper limbs relative to their trunk dimensions through their claviculohumeral indices. Because the clavicle is functionally part of the shoulder rather than of the axial anatomy, it may not be a very good indicator of overall trunk size. Yet its length is related to the breadth of the superior torso and therefore provides information on one aspect of trunk size. The estimated claviculohumeral indices of Shanidar 1 and 3 (Chapter 8; Table 96) are very similar to those of Tabūn C1 and the majority of more recent humans. Their indices, however, are below those of La Ferrassie 1 and Régourdou 1, both of whom have exceptionally high claviculohumeral indices. This indicates that these European Neandertals, but not the Shanidar individuals, had either exceptionally broad shoulders or short upper limbs; the intermembral indices of La Ferrassie 1 close to those of recent humans (Table 96) suggest that they probably had very broad shoulders.

The intermembral proportions of the Shanidar Neandertals can be assessed using an intermembral index for Shanidar 6, humerofemoral indices for Shanidar 4 and 6, and radiotibial indices for Shanidar 1, 5 and 6 (Table 96). The intermembral proportional indices of other Neandertals are all within the range of means of male and/or female recent human samples, but the Shanidar specimens tend towards the limits of the more recent human samples. The Shanidar 1 radiotibial index is relatively high, the Shanidar 4 humerofemoral index is moderately high, the Shanidar 5 radiotibial index is relatively low, and the Shanidar 6 indices are all near or slightly above the ranges of means of the recent human male and female samples. The significance of this range of intermembral, humerofemoral, and radiotibial indices among the Shanidar Neandertals is uncertain because all of them have indices that are within recent human ranges of variation. Some of the differences between individuals may be due to inaccuracies in the estimates of their limb bone lengths, but any such error is likely to be small.

The brachial indices (radial maximum length/humeral maximum length) of Shanidar 4 and 6, as well as those of most other Neandertals, including Tabūn C1, are within the range of means of more recent human samples (Table 96). The Shanidar 6 brachial index is relatively low, being close to the means of the recent human samples with the lowest average brachial indices. Yet it is still well within Neandertal ranges of variation because La Ferrassie 1 and 2 have

TABLE 96

Limb Segment Proportional Indices

		Claviculo-humeral index	Brachial index	Crural index	Intermembral index	Humero-femoral index	Radiotibial index
Shanidar 1		—	—	(77.5)	—	—	(70.0)
Shanidar 3		(46.7)	—	—	—	—	—
Shanidar 4		—	(78.0)	—	—	(72.3)	—
Shanidar 5		—	—	(78.3–80.5)	—	—	(63.6–65.4)
Shanidar 6		—	(74.2)	(78.1)	(74.6)	(76.3)	(72.5)
Neandertals							
Amud 1		—	—	(80.1)	—	—	(67.0)
Tabūn C1		(47.2–49.0)	77.4	(77.8)	(69.6)	(69.8)	(69.4)
La Chapelle-aux-Saints 1		—	(75.4)	(79.1)	(71.0)	(72.4)	(69.1)
La Ferrassie 1		(53.0)	(72.4)	(80.8)	(70.2)	(73.1)	(65.9)
La Ferrassie 2		—	(69.9)	76.4	(67.8)	(70.2)	64.3
Neandertal 1		—	76.1	—	—	70.9	—
Régourdou 1		(51.9)	75.2	—	—	—	—
Spy 2		—	—	78.2	—	—	—
Skhūl–Qafzeh sample	range	40.6–45.1	70.5–81.3	85.3–88.6	66.1–69.9	68.8–70.3	64.3–65.0
	N	2	3	2	2	2	2
Early Upper	X̄ ± SD	46.2 ± 1.6	77.5 ± 2.5	85.9 ± 1.8	69.3 ± 2.5	72.3 ± 2.7	66.0 ± 2.4
Paleolithic sample[a]	N	10	14	12	11	13	11
Recent humans[a]							
Male minimum mean	X̄ ± SD	46.3 ± 2.6	74.1 ± 2.6	81.1 ± 1.6	67.4 ± 1.6	69.8 ± 1.8	64.5 ± 2.0
Male maximum mean	X̄ ± SD	47.3 ± 1.3	78.8 ± 2.1	86.7 ± 2.6	72.1 ± 1.6	74.4 ± 2.2	69.2 ± 1.7
Number of samples		5	10	12	10	11	10
Female minimum mean	X̄ ± SD	44.8 ± 3.6	73.4 ± 2.8	81.2 ± 2.3	66.1 ± 2.1	69.2 ± 2.3	62.4 ± 2.3
Female maximum mean	X̄ ± SD	46.6 ± 1.8	78.6 ± 2.0	86.0 ± 2.8	70.1 ± 1.6	73.3 ± 2.0	67.4 ± 2.1
Number of samples		5	10	12	10	10	10

[a]Trinkaus 1981.

exceptionally low brachial indices. This suggests a slight tendency among the Neandertals, including Shanidar 6 but not necessarily Shanidar 4, to have relatively short distal segments of their arms.

This tendency towards relatively short distal limb segments is more strongly marked in the Shanidar and other Neandertal lower limbs (Table 96). The Shanidar 1, 5, and 6 crural indices (tibial maximum length/femoral bicondylar length), along with those of all other known Neandertals, cluster around the means of the recent human samples, Lapps and Eskimos, who have the lowest average crural indices (Trinkaus 1981; Table 96). Most impressively, the Neandertal crural indices, including those from Shanidar, are all lower than those of Near Eastern and European early anatomically modern humans.

Although the Shanidar 1, 5, and 6 legs and the Shanidar 6 arms have relatively short distal segments, which place them toward the lower ends of recent human ranges of variation, their hands and feet do not appear to be particularly different from those of recent humans with respect to their relative sizes. The Shanidar 4 and 6 third metacarpals, as indicators of overall hand length, have lengths relative to their summed humeral and radial lengths that are similar to those of other Neandertals and recent humans (Chapter 8). And the Shanidar 1 tarsometatarsal skeleton length, relative to his summed femoral and tibial lengths, is comparable to or minimally greater than those of other Neandertals and recent humans (Chapter 9).

These considerations of the proportions of the Shanidar partial skeletons demonstrate that there are relatively few features in which the proportions of their anatomical segments differ from the dominant pattern present among recent humans. The only proportional aspect that seems to separate the Shanidar specimens, along with other Neandertals, from more recent humans is the long lengths of their mandibles; this is merely a reflection of one of the best-documented features of the Neandertals, their prognathism. The only other proportional features that place the Shanidar individuals towards the limits of recent human ranges of variation are the possibly relatively short necks of Shanidar 1 and 4 and their low crural indices.

The significance of the possibly short necks of Shanidar 1 and 4 is uncertain, especially because Shanidar 2 did not have a particularly short neck and the ranges of variation of recent humans are poorly known. The implications of their low crural indices are clearer (Trinkaus 1981). They could be an adaptation for generating power in the lower limb at the expense of speed because a decrease in relative tibial length shortens the load arm of M. quadriceps femoris relative to its power arm at the knee. This interpretation would be in agreement with the analyses of the Shanidar knee proportions (Chapter 9) that indicate an accentuation of the power arm for M. quadriceps femoris. Alternatively, low crural indices could be seen as part of an adaptation for cold stress; they are positively correlated with mean annual temperature across recent human populations (Trinkaus 1981). The shortening of the lower limb segment would decrease the surface area of the leg and reduce appendicular heat loss (a variant of Allen's rule [Allen 1877]). Either or both of these interpretations could account for the low crural indices of the Shanidar individuals and other Neandertals.

ESTIMATION OF STATURE

If the length of one or more of the long bones of an individual is known, it is possible to estimate the living stature of that individual using regression formulae based on samples of modern humans. As a result of this, stature estimates are currently available for many Upper Pleistocene hominids and can be calculated for the Shanidar Neandertals.

A number of studies have calculated regression formulae relating long bone length to living or cadaver stature for a variety of recent human samples, primarily from Europe and North America (e.g., Dupertuis and Hadden 1951; Manouvrier 1893; Olivier 1963; Pearson 1899; Telkkä 1950; Trotter and Gleser 1952, 1958). Because there are populational differences in body proportions (Olivier 1960; Trinkaus 1981), each study has derived slightly different formulae; the stature of any one individual can therefore be estimated differently depending upon which reference sample is used. It is not possible to determine which of the many available formulae would be most appropriate for calculating the statures of Pleistocene hominids because we will never know the true living stature of any of these prehistoric individuals. It is therefore probably best to use the same reference sample for calculating the statures of all of the individuals whose statures are to be compared. In this way, any bias inherent in one set of regression formulae will influence all of the estimates equally.

In addition to variations across populations in body proportions, there are sexual and individual variations within populations. The sexual differences require the computation of separate regression formulae for each sex. Individual variations are accounted for by the standard errors of the stature estimates published with each of the formulae; these standard errors vary between about 3.0 cm and 5.0 cm, depending upon the reference sample and the bone used to estimate stature.

In order to estimate the statures of the six Shanidar adults with at least one long bone sufficiently intact to provide a length measurement, the regression formulae of Trotter and Gleser (1952) for Euroamericans have been used. The statures of the presumed males—Shanidar 1, 2, 3, 4, and 5—have been computed using the male Euroamerican formulae, and that of Shanidar 6 has been computed using the female Euroamerican formulae (Table 97). For comparison, the statures of other Neandertals, Skhūl–Qafzeh hominids and European Early Upper Paleolithic hominids have been computed, again using the Euroamerican regression formulae of Trotter and Gleser (1952) (Tables 98 and 99). The stature estimates provided here differ slightly from those that have been

TABLE 97

Stature Estimates for the Shanidar Neandertals (cm)[a]

	Humerus	Radius	Ulna	Femur	Tibia	Mean
Shanidar 1	—	(174.1)	176.2	(173.3)	(169.9)	173.4
Shanidar 2	—	—	—	—	165.0	165.0
Shanidar 3	(168.9)	—	—	—	—	168.9
Shanidar 4	(164.5)	(169.9)	169.6	(163.9)	—	167.0
Shanidar 5	—	—	167.3	(170.4)	(168.5–171.3)	169.2
Shanidar 6	(158.9)	(160.5)	—	(152.2)	(151.0)	155.7

[a] Using the male and female Euroamerican regression formulae of Trotter and Gleser (1952) for Shanidar 1, 2, 3, 4, and 5 and Shanidar 6, respectively. Statures were computed from the maximum lengths of the humeri, radii, ulnae, and tibiae and the bicondylar lengths of the femora.

TABLE 98
Stature Estimates for Near Eastern and European
Neandertals (cm)[a]

	Sex	Stature
Amud 1	M*	178.7 (3)
Tabūn C1	F*	158.5 (4)
La Chapelle-aux-Saints 1	M*	166.8 (4)
La Ferrassie 1	M*	173.5 (4)
La Ferrassie 2	F*	155.2 (4)
Fond-de-Forêt 1	M	164.4 (1)
Kiik-Koba 1	M	167.3 (1)
Neandertal 1	M*	168.3 (3)
La Quina 5	F	162.0 (2)
Régourdou 1	?	166.6 (2)
Spy 1	F	163.4 (1)
Spy 2	M	163.8 (2)

[a]For individuals with known or estimatable sex, the appropriate male or female Euroamerican regression formulae of Trotter and Gleser (1952) were used; for Régourdou 1, whose sex is uncertain, the mean of the male and female estimates is provided. An asterisk (*) after the sex indicates the sex determination is based on associated pelvic remains. The number in parentheses indicates the number of limb segments employed in the computation of mean stature.

published by Stewart (1977) for the Shanidar individuals and by other individuals for other Upper Pleistocene hominids (e.g., Endo and Kimura 1970; Heim 1974; Thoma 1975). The differences between my estimates and Stewart's are due to differences in our estimates of various Shanidar long-bone lengths. The variations in stature estimates for other Upper Pleistocene hominids are largely a product of using different regression formulae.

TABLE 99
Stature Estimates for Samples of European Neandertals, Combined European and Near Eastern
Neandertals, Skhūl–Qafzeh Hominids, and European Early Upper Paleolithic Hominids (cm)[a]

		European Neandertals	Neandertals	Skhūl–Qafzeh sample	Early Upper Paleolithic sample
Males	$\bar{X} \pm$ SD	167.4 ± 3.5	169.0 ± 5.3	184.7 ± 3.7	183.6 ± 5.1
	N	6	7	4	12
Females	$\bar{X} \pm$ SD	155.2–163.4	159.8 ± 3.7	169.1 ± 7.7	166.9 ± 1.6
	N	3	4	4	4
Total	$\bar{X} \pm$ SD	165.1 ± 4.8	165.7 ± 6.2	176.9 ± 10.0	178.4 ± 8.4
	N	10	12	8	19

[a]Statures computed as indicated in Table 96.

The mean stature estimates for the Shanidar individuals fall within the known ranges of variation of other Neandertals. The Shanidar 3 and 5 statures are extremely close to the Neandertal male mean, whereas that of Shanidar 1 is slightly above it and those of Shanidar 2 and 4 are below it. The low stature estimate for Shanidar 2 may be due in part to its being estimated solely from his tibial length; the low crural indices of the other Shanidar individuals and other Neandertals suggest that his other long bones, if preserved, might have provided a slightly higher stature estimate, probably close to that of Shanidar 4 (the ratio of the Shanidar 2 tibial length to the Shanidar 4 femoral length provides a crural index of 80.0, which is very close to those of other Neandertals). The only other Near Eastern male Neandertal, Amud 1, has exceptionally high stature, by far the greatest of any known Neandertal. The only estimate of stature for a female from Shanidar, that of Shanidar 6, is below the Neandertal female mean. Yet it is slightly above that of La Ferrassie 2 and not far below that of Tabūn C1.

Although the Shanidar stature estimates are similar to those of other Neandertals, they are considerably below the mean values for the same sex of the two early anatomically modern human samples. The Shanidar individuals thus follow the general Neandertal pattern of having modest statures and being considerably shorter, on the average, than the succeeding populations of early anatomically modern humans.

There appears to be a small but consistent difference in stature between the earlier Shanidar males, Shanidar 2 and 4, and the later Shanidar males, Shanidar 1, 3, and 5, with the later males being taller. This may reflect a real trend of increasing stature during the time that Shanidar Cave was occupied by Neandertals, it may be due only to sampling biases with regard to the individuals preserved, or it may be a product of which long bones have been preserved for each of the five individuals. It is difficult to determine which of these interpretations is most reasonable, especially given the standard errors of about 4.0 cm on the stature regression formulae. The large ranges of variation in stature present in most modern human populations suggest that considerably larger samples of Neandertals are required before any trend of increasing or decreasing stature can be established among the Shanidar or other Neandertals.

The Shanidar Neandertals thus have statures that are similar to those of other Neandertals. The Shanidar male statures cluster around the overall Neandertal male mean, even though they were slightly shorter than the other Near Eastern Neandertal male, Amud 1. The one Shanidar female for whom stature can be estimated, Shanidar 6, was relatively short for a Neandertal female. Yet her stature was within the known Neandertal female range of variation.

CHAPTER 12

The Paleopathology of the Shanidar Neandertals

In the foregoing discussions of the Shanidar adults, there have been numerous mentions of lesions on their bones. In the descriptive morphology chapters, the concern has been to determine whether the abnormalities significantly affected the morphology of the individual and to compensate for any possible bias that might be introduced by comparing diseased remains with those of normal individuals. Evidence of past trauma, degenerative joint disease, and other osteological lesions, however, provides positive evidence as to the behavior and adaptive patterns of the Shanidar Neandertals. The paleopathology of the Shanidar fossils therefore will be dealt with in detail as an aspect of their paleontology.

Previous descriptions of the Shanidar Neandertals by Stewart and me (see References) have noted most of the lesions present on the Shanidar specimens, although only a small portion of them have been described with any detail. These well-described abnormalities are those that were certainly or probably due to injuries sustained by the Shanidar individuals during their lifetimes (Stewart 1969; Trinkaus and Zimmerman 1979, 1982). The trauma-related abnormalities are the most impressive of their lesions: four of the adults—Shanidar 1, 3, 4, and 5—exhibit evidence of past trauma and two of them—Shanidar 3 and especially Shanidar 1—were partially incapacitated by their injuries.

Yet as with other fossil hominids (Dastugue 1960; Vallois 1935), the most common abnormality is osteoarthritis, or degenerative joint disease. It is usually evident in the form of exostoses around the margins of articular surfaces and less commonly in the deterioration of subchondral articular bone. In addition, there are frequent ossifications of tendon fibers at their insertions, especially of M. triceps brachii and M. quadriceps femoris, whose formation follows the same general etiology as the ossification of ligament fibers around articulations. These are the usual forms of osteological manifestation of these abnormalities among recent humans (Sokoloff 1972).

Most of the osteoarthritis on the Shanidar remains was undoubtedly due to excessive levels of biomechanical stress, which promoted collagen fiber ossifications at the insertions of tendons and ligaments and/or articular cartilage deterioration. However, much of the osteoarthritis on those individuals that exhibit traces of past trauma may have been secondary to the trauma. Severe sprains or fractures will frequently change the pattern of biomechanical stress transmission across a joint, which can lead to abnormally high stresses on articular capsules, associated ligaments, and portions of the articular cartilage. The diagnosis that a specific case of degenerative joint disease was secondary to trauma is frequently difficult to make because the resultant morphology is the same. In the lower limb, however, levels of biomechanical stress are usually relatively symmetrical, so that any degeneration of the lower limb articulations should be similar in both legs. If it is highly asymmetrical, it is reasonable to infer that stress other than high levels of normal biomechanical stress was responsible. In the upper limb, such an inference is not possible because most individuals use one arm more than the other.

The diagnosis of an injury in a fossil hominid can best be made if the trauma occurred some time before the death of the individual. Some evidence of healing, usually in the form of bony deposition, must be present to make a positive diagnosis of antemortem injury. Given the tendency of fossils to fragment in situ, it is often not possible to distinguish a fatal wound from postmortem breakage, a problem that has plagued human paleontology for much of the past century. Other changes, such as atrophy or infection, may be associated with trauma, but any connection between them and inferred injuries should be evaluated with respect to each case.

It is usually possible to diagnose accurately the cause of a specific abnormality, but it is seldom possible to determine the precise sequence of events responsible for several lesions on one individual. Such interpretations are invariably speculative and can seldom be established to the exclusion of alternative explanations. The interpretations provided here are those that appear to be the most reasonable; in the case of Shanidar 1, who sustained multiple injuries, alternative explanations are provided. Furthermore, the incomplete state of all of the Shanidar partial skeletons makes it impossible to assess the full extent of each individual's abnormalities. Negative evidence is inconclusive because individual lesions frequently affect only local regions. It is assumed that those

individuals, especially Shanidar 2, 6, and 8, that exhibit few abnormalities were generally healthy, but it should be kept in mind that their missing anatomical regions may have been seriously afflicted.

The evidence for skeletal abnormalities is presented for Shanidar 1, 2, 3, 4, 5, 6, and 8, in that order. For each individual, those lesions that appear to have been caused by trauma, directly or indirectly, are discussed first, followed by descriptions of those abnormalities that resulted from degenerative joint disease. The two Shanidar infants exhibit no evidence of disease or injury-related abnormalities and are not discussed in this chapter.

SHANIDAR 1

Trauma-Related Abnormalities

Shanidar 1 was one of the most severely traumatized Pleistocene hominids for whom we have evidence. He suffered multiple fractures involving the cranium, right humerus, and right fifth metatarsal, and the right knee, ankle, and first tarsometatarsal joint show degenerative joint disease that was probably trauma related.

THE UPPER LIMB

The preserved bones of the right arm—the clavicle, scapula, and humerus—are clearly abnormal at first inspection (Figures 75 and 76). They are much smaller than the corresponding bones of the normal left arm. Their small size is reflected in the measurements given in Table 100; they show a reduction on the right of 10–15% in clavicular shaft size, about 35% in scapular spine height, and about 45% in humeral shaft size. The decrease in clavicular shaft cross-sectional dimensions are relatively uniform with respect to cortical thicknesses and medullary cavity diameter, even though the cortical walls appear to have decreased slightly more than the medullary cavity. The changes in diaphyseal diameters of the humerus appear to have been, in contrast, largely a product of decreases in the medullary cavity diameters and the thicknesses of the anterior and lateral cortical walls; the posterior and medial cortical walls show some thinning, but far less than the other portions of the diaphyseal cross section (Table 100). The preserved portion of the right humeral diaphysis, which extends from the surgical neck to the mid olecranon fossa, measures 243.0 mm;

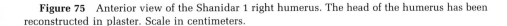

Figure 75   Anterior view of the Shanidar 1 right humerus. The head of the humerus has been reconstructed in plaster. Scale in centimeters.

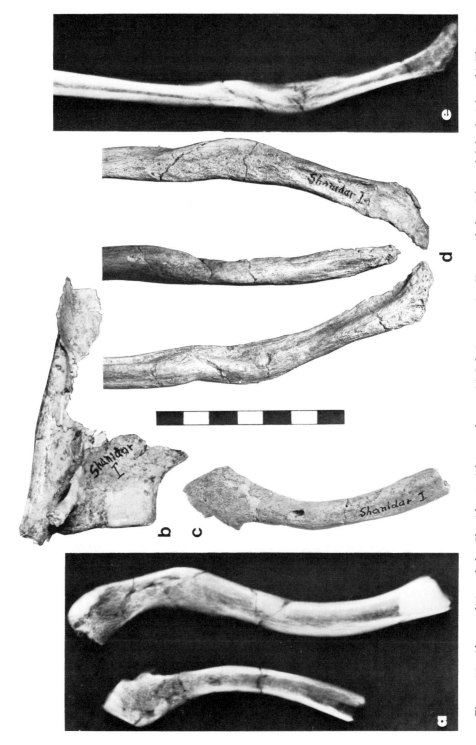

Figure 76 Abnormalities of the Shanidar 1 right arm bones. (a) Inferior–superior X rays of the right and left clavicles. (b) The atrophied–hypotrophied right scapula viewed anteriorly (ventrally). The (c) right clavicle viewed dorsally (note the cloaca and bone growth around the cloaca). (d) The distal end of the right humerus in anterior, lateral, and posterior views. (e) An anterior–posterior X ray of the distal right humerus. Scale in centimeters.

TABLE 100
Asymmetries in External Metrics and Diaphyseal Cross Sections of the Shanidar 1
Skeleton (mm)[a]

	Right	Left	Right/Left × 100
Cranium			
Orbital height (OBH)	36.0	36.0	100.0
Orbital breadth (OBB)	47.9	44.4	107.9
Cheek height (WMH)	25.5	28.0	91.1
Clavicle			
Vertical diameter (M-4)	8.3	8.7	95.4
Horizontal diameter (M-5)	11.4	13.8	82.6
Circumference (M-6)	32.5	37.2	87.4
Midshaft ant. cortical thickness	2.8	3.3	84.8
Midshaft post. cortical thickness	2.4	3.7	64.9
Midshaft medullary ant.–post. diameter	6.3	8.3	75.9
Scapula			
Spine height	25.0	38.2	65.4
Humerus			
Maximum diameter (M-5)	12.3	21.7	56.7
Minimum diameter (M-6)	8.9	17.0	52.4
Circumference (M-7a)	36.0	63.0	57.1
Proximal shaft ant. cortical thickness	2.9	5.3	54.7
Proximal shaft post. cortical thickness	4.3	5.9	72.9
Proximal shaft med. cortical thickness	3.9	4.4	88.6
Proximal shaft lat. cortical thickness	2.6	6.4	40.6
Proximal medullary ant.–post. diameter	3.6	10.0	36.0
Proximal medullary med.–lat. diameter	4.0	11.0	36.6
Patella			
Breadth (M-2)	51.1	46.2	110.6
Talus			
Length (M-1)	53.1	52.8	100.6
Articular height (M-3b)	27.3	28.2	96.8
Articular breadth (M-2b)	52.9	48.9	108.2

[a]The measurements of cortical thicknesses and medullary cavity diameters were taken from X rays of the paired clavicles and humeri and are only relative.

this is about 10% below the estimated surgical neck–olecranon fossa length of 270.0 mm for the normal left humerus.

The small size of these three bones was probably due to some form of nerve injury, leading to hypotrophy if it occurred during growth or to atrophy if it occurred during adulthood. The modest but clear asymmetry in humeral length would be in agreement with either of these interpretations (Fessard 1979; Turek 1967). However, the even reduction of the cortical thicknesses and medullary cavity diameter of the clavicle and the marked reduction of the medullary cavity diameters with variable reduction in cortical thicknesses of the humerus are at variance with the pattern frequently associated with paralysis in modern children. The long bones of modern children with congenital or acquired paralysis tend to exhibit a slight decrease in external diaphyseal diameters, a marked decrease in cortical thicknesses, and an increase in medullary cavity diameters (Fessard 1979; Glimcher personal communication, 1981). Yet a marked decrease in the transverse diameters of long bones is known to occur in posttraumatic atrophy (Sante 1961). Furthermore, Neandertals, as part of their general postcranial robustness, tend to have relatively thick diaphyseal cortical bone, and it is possible that their long bones would respond slightly differently to paralysis than would those of gracile modern humans. Paralysis with hypotrophy/atrophy therefore appears to be the most reasonable interpretation for the small size of the Shanidar 1 right arm bones.

In aspects other than its small size, the right scapula appears to be normal. The right clavicle and humerus, however, show additional abnormalities.

The right clavicle exhibits a moderately sized osteomyelitic lesion on the superior diaphyseal surface, slightly medial to the conoid tubercle (Figure 76). The opening for the pus, or cloaca, is surrounded by a callus of subperiosteal bone, or involucrum, which extends across the superior surface but does not go onto the inferior surface. The modest size of the involucrum suggests that the infection may have been largely healed at the time of death. It is unlikely that this was a hematogeneous osteomyelitis, given its location and the fully adult status of Shanidar 1 (Steinbock 1976); more likely it was produced by a soft tissue injury adjacent to the clavicle. The latter interpretation is in keeping with the condition of the other arm bones.

The Shanidar 1 right humerus shows two fractures in addition to its reduction in size. The more proximal fracture occurred about two-thirds of the way distally along the diaphysis. The bone exhibits in the region of this fracture a slightly sinuous curve, which was formed by the deposition of callus and the extensive resorption of diaphyseal cortical bone around the fracture site (Figure 76). In addition, the fracture produced an angular deformity, which turned the distal diaphysis about 20° medially. It is possible that the diaphysis was broken in more than one place along the 30–40 mm now covered by callus; postmortem damage and extensive healing prevent a determination of whether the bone was fractured at both the proximal and distal ends of the callus or was merely badly fractured towards the middle of the region. In any case, the abnormality was probably produced by a single injury to the diaphysis.

The other fracture of the right humerus was transversely across the olecranon fossa, perhaps at the margin of the distal articular capsule. The distal end of the humerus, as preserved, shows an irregular edge, flattened anteroposteriorly, with extensive exposure of trabecular bone. Even though the bone did sustain postmortem breakage, as evidenced radiographically, the distal end shows little or no damage. The exposed trabeculae are all rounded and show none of the angular edges associated with postmortem breakage. This irregular end is probably the proximal end of a fracture that did not subsequently reunite. It may be one side of a fracture nonunion, or pseudoarthrosis, it may be the end of an amputation of the arm just proximal to the elbow, or it may be the proximal side of an amputation performed to remove the useless forearm after the formation of a pseudoarthrosis. It is impossible to distinguish among these diagnoses. One side of a pseudoarthrosis can resemble the end of an amputation (Stewart 1974), and the absence of the distal humeral articulations, radius, ulna, and hand bones could be due to amputation or postmortem destruction. (Careful examination of the region around Shanidar 1 in Shanidar Cave failed to produce any trace of the right distal arm or hand [Stewart, personal communication, 1981]).

The right arm of Shanidar 1 clearly sustained a serious injury or injuries, resulting in the hypoplasia or atrophy of the preserved bones, multiple fractures of the distal humerus and osteomyelitis of the clavicle. It is impossible to ascertain in what order these abnormalities developed because all of them occurred long before death. A fuller consideration of this problem will follow the description of the other trauma-related lesions on Shanidar 1.

THE LOWER LIMB

The right foot of Shanidar 1 and its associated distal tibia and fibula show several abnormalities (Figures 68, 69, and 77). The partially preserved left foot, however, is normal, indicating a marked asymmetry in the incidence of these lesions.

The right fifth metatarsal exhibits a well-healed fracture near the middle of the diaphysis. There is a large callus, especially on the dorsal and dorsomedial surfaces, and the fracture produced a slight deformity in the diaphysis. The fracture was probably the product of trauma rather than a stress fracture due to abnormal locomotion because stress fractures usually involve the second or third metatarsal (Turek 1967). The break, once healed, does not appear to have produced a loss of function in the lateral longitudinal arch of the foot. Associated degenerative joint disease at the right talocrural, first tarsometatarsal, and first–second intermetatarsal articulations may have inhibited movement, or at least made it painful.

At the talocrural articulation, the degenerative joint disease is evidenced by the formation of exostoses around the tibiotarsal and fibulotarsal articular surfaces on all three bones and by the ossification of the connective tissues along the M. tibialis posterior sulcus on the posterior aspect of the tibial malleolus. Associated with these exostoses is a curious flattening and broadening of the right talus. These shape changes are partially indicated by the slightly smaller height and noticeably greater breadth of the right talus relative to the left one,

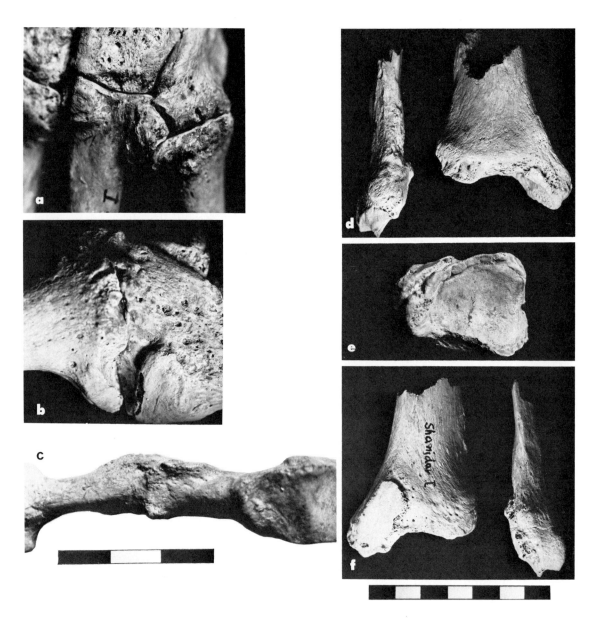

Figure 77 Abnormalities of the Shanidar 1 distal right tibia and fibula and right tarsometatarsal skeleton. (a) Dorsal view of the first and second tarsometatarsal articulations. (b) Medial of the first tarsometatarsal skeleton. (c) Medial view of the healed fracture of the fifth metatarsal diaphysis. (d) Anterior, (e) distal, and (f) posterior views of the distal tibia and fibula, showing the exostoses around the articulations and tendon sheaths. Scales in centimeters.

even though their lengths are similar (Table 100). The difference in articular breadth may be due in part to the exostoses on the right medial malleolar surface, but that does not account fully for the difference.

The articulations between the right medial cuneiform and first and second metatarsals have also been altered by degenerative joint disease. There are large exostoses across the dorsal margins of the articulations and along the dorsal half of the medial margin of the first tarsometatarsal articulation. The bone growths between the first and second metatarsal bases have produced an articulation, even though an intermetatarsal articular facet is absent from the normal left first and second metatarsals, as they are from most Neandertal and recent human first and second metatarsals (Trinkaus 1978e). In addition, there has been resorption of bone from the insertion of the M. tibialis anterior tendon on the medial cuneiform and first metatarsal and degeneration of the subchondral bone with the formation of bony cysts on the dorsolateral corner of the first tarsometatarsal articular surfaces. These features are all indicative of advanced degenerative joint disease (Sokoloff 1972).

Although advanced degenerative joint disease in the foot may occur as a result of normal but excessive wear and tear, it appears likely that the osteoarthritis of the Shanidar 1 right foot was trauma related. Not only is it associated with a fracture in the same foot, but the preserved portions of the left foot are normal (Figures 68 and 69). Such a degree of asymmetry in degenerative joint disease in the lower limb suggests that the articular degeneration followed disruption of the normal functioning of the joints by an injury.

A similar development of osteoarthritis can be seen at the right knee of Shanidar 1 (Figure 78). The right femoral condyles and patellar surface are surrounded by exostoses. Damage precludes determination of their extent on the medial side, but they extend as much as 7.5 mm from the articular margin along the lateral edge of the lateral condyle. The patellar surface appears to have been flattened and slightly broadened, but postmortem damage does not permit an accurate assessment of this on the distal femur. Both tibiae lack their proximal epiphyses and all of the left femur is missing, but both patellae are reasonably intact. The right patella exhibits exostoses, especially along the lateral articular margin, whereas the left patellar articulation, where preserved, is normal (Figure 62). In addition, the right patella is considerably wider than the left one (Tables 66 and 100), suggesting some remodeling of the bone after the onset of the degenerative joint disease. As with the feet, the degenerative joint disease appears to be unilateral and may well be trauma related.

Associated with these abnormalities of the right leg and foot is a curious curvature of the left tibial diaphysis (Figure 63). Instead of the usually straight diaphysis seem in other Neandertal and recent human tibial diaphyses, the Shanidar 1 left tibial diaphysis is anteriorly and laterally concave and posteriorly and medially convex. The diaphysis was damaged postmortem, and

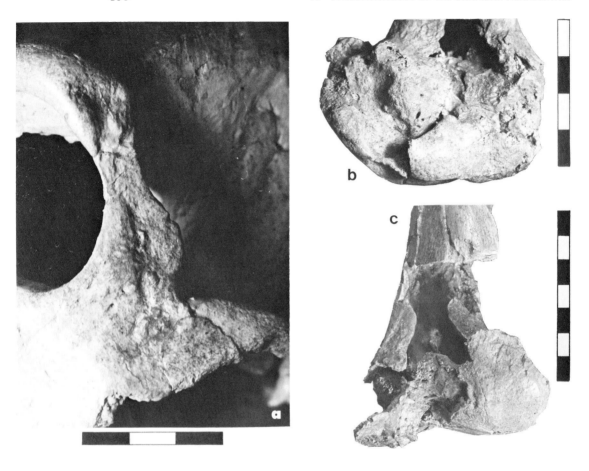

Figure 78   Abnormalities of the Shanidar 1 left orbit and femoral condyles. (a) anterolateral view of the left lateral orbit, with portions of the frontal, zygomatic, and temporal bones clearly evident. (b) Lateral view of the distal right femur. (c) Posterior view of the distal right femur. Scales in centimeters.

some distortion may have been introduced during its restoration; however, postmortem alteration was probably minimal and does not fully account for the curious curvature (Stewart 1977). Because the preserved portions of the left leg and foot are otherwise normal, this abnormality may have been produced indirectly by the multiple disorders of the right lower limb. An abnormal gait would alter the patterns of biomechanical stress within the tibial diaphysis and promote remodeling of the cortical bone (Tschantz and Rutishauser 1967). If the abnormal stress pattern persisted for a sufficient period of time, it could produce the type of deformity seen here.

THE CRANIUM

The injuries that Shanidar 1 suffered were not limited to his limbs. Traces of past injuries are also present on the cranium (Figures 9 and 78). There are healed scars on the external table of the right frontal, in the region of the tuber, suggesting scalp wounds that damaged the periosteum but did not fracture the frontal bone. Even though the internal table of much of the cranial vault was lost in situ, there is no evidence on the preserved internal surface of the right frontal to suggest that these wounds affected the cranial cavity.

The primary cranial injury that Shanidar 1 sustained was a crushing fracture to the lateral side of the left orbit, involving the frontal bone and the left zygomatic bone. This fracture healed over during the life of the individual, but it left a permanent deformation to the left side of the upper face. The lateral margin of the left orbit is flat, rather than being gently convex craniocaudally and anteroposteriorly. The external surface bone exhibits healing from about 10.0 mm above the frontozygomatic suture on the frontal bone and across all of the zygomatic bone. Although the right and left orbit heights are equal, the left orbit breadth is about 8.0% below that of the right orbit (Table 100), indicating the extent of the medial crushing of the frontal process of the zygomatic bone. The zygomatic bone was also broadened craniocaudally, largely by an extension of the maxillary process along the M. masseter insertion; this is indicated by the greater cheek height measurement on the left side (Table 100). This crushing fracture must have disturbed the contents of the orbital cavity, probably causing blindness in the left eye. However, the condition of the bone indicates that full healing of the fracture took place long before the death of Shanidar 1.

DIAGNOSIS

The exact interrelationship of these multiple injuries and injury-related abnormalities of Shanidar 1 is difficult to decipher. All of the fractures occurred some time before his death, probably years before, as indicated by the extensive healing and resorption of the calluses. Even the osteomyelitis on the right clavicle may have been largely healed and in the process of being resorbed when Shanidar 1 died. Yet it should be possible to interrelate these lesions so that they are not isolated entities, each with its own diagnosis.

Three general scenarios appear reasonable. These scenarios are not intended to be exhaustive of all possibilities, and details could be altered and still fit the available data; they are intended only as the most reasonable interpretations that account for all of the observed abnormalities of Shanidar 1.

Scenario 1

Shanidar 1 sustained a massive crushing injury to the right side of the body, primarily in the region of the arm and shoulder. A crushing injury, such as a rock fall, is more likely than an incised wound because an incised wound of this degree would probably have been associated with fatal hemorrhaging. A soft tissue injury would account for the evidence of infection (osteomyelitis) in the clavicle. The fractures of the distal humeral diaphysis and olecranon fossa region would have occurred at the same time, and the pseudoarthrosis/amputation would have developed subsequently. The small size of the right arm bones could be the product of hypoplasia or atrophy, depending upon when the injury occurred; either interpretation of the small size of the bones is consistent with a prolonged period of survival.

The fracture of the right fifth metatarsal probably occurred at the same time as the injury to the right arm. The extensive degenerative joint disease of the right lower limb and the abnormal curvature of the left tibial diaphysis were probably secondary to the trauma, resulting in part from soft tissue injury and in part from abnormal locomotion due to the injury.

In this interpretation, the cranial injuries would be seen as secondary to the crushing trauma to the right side of the body. They may have occurred at the same time from the individual falling away from the blow to the right side and striking a hard object, or they may have happened later as a result of the individual's inability to get around easily.

Scenario 2

The cranial trauma, especially the fracture of the left side of the upper face, could be seen as primary and the damage to the body secondary. The crushing fracture of the left lateral orbital margin undoubtedly caused blindness in that eye; it may also have damaged the left cerebral motor cortex, directly or indirectly through a localized disruption of cerebral circulation. Such an injury to the brain could cause hemiplegia to the right side of the body. It may well have affected the motor innervation to the upper limb primarily, for it is this portion of the motor cortex that is closest to the injured zygomatic bone, and affected the motor control to the lower limb to a lesser degree. The hypoplasia/atrophy of the upper limb would develop directly from this type of nerve injury, and the degenerative joint disease of the right lower limb and the abnormal curvature of the left tibial diaphysis could easily follow partial paralysis of the right lower limb and the resultant abnormal gait.

In this interpretation, the right frontal scalp wound, the osteomyelitis of the right clavicle, the fractures and pseudoarthrosis/amputation of the right humerus, and the fracture of the right fifth metatarsal would be seen as secondary to the cranial injury. Shanidar 1, once weakened by partial paralysis, would have been more susceptible to injury and infection.

Scenario 3

Shanidar 1 was subjected to a major injury to the brachial plexus that resulted in paralysis of the right arm and subsequent hypoplasia/atrophy of the various bones. A traction injury to the brachial plexus could have been responsible, in which case the clavicular osteomyelitis and the humeral fractures would be seen as having occurred subsequently. Alternatively, a penetrating wound to the shoulder or axilla could easily damage the brachial plexus and cause an infection that would lead to the osteomyelitis of the clavicle. In this case, the humerus could have been fractured at the same time that the shoulder was wounded.

In this scenario, the injuries to the cranium and right foot, the degenerative joint disease of the right leg and foot and the abnormal bowing of the left tibia would have to be seen as having developed independently, either prior or subsequent to the right arm lesions. If the various fractures are seen as having occurred independently, there are many different sequences that could be postulated.

These interpretations of the injuries to Shanidar 1 are clearly speculative. The first two scenarios suggest interrelationships between the various abnormalities, whereas the third one is more cautious and deals with them separately. The individual injuries are nonetheless obvious, however they might relate to each other.

Degenerative Abnormalities

In addition to the numerous trauma-related lesions, Shanidar 1 suffered several minor abnormalities, which may or may not have been etiologically related to one or more of his injuries.

As mentioned in Chapter 5, both of the external acoustic meatuses of Shanidar 1 are largely filled with exostoses. Auditory exostoses are a bony response to irritation of the external acoustic canal, which is age dependent and highly influenced by an individual's life history (Harrison 1962). They are known in most recent human populations (Gregg and Bass 1970; Roche 1964) and have been documented in La Chapelle-aux-Saints 1 (Boule 1911–1913) and even Chou-kou-tien "Skull X" (Weidenreich 1943). Their presence in the external auditory meatuses of Shanidar 1 is not particularly unusual, especially given his reasonably advanced age.

The left mandibular condyle of Shanidar 1 was partially remodeled by degenerative joint disease (Figure 15). This is evident primarily in the expansion of the condylar surface and flattening of its superior aspect. It is possible that this degeneration of the left temporomandibular joint was secondary to the injury to the left zygomatic region; the changes in zygomatic bone and possibly in the left M. *masseter* may have altered the stress patterns through the left temporomandibular joint.

As with most Pleistocene hominids, Shanidar 1 suffered minor osteophytosis or other degenerations of the vertebral column. The poor condition of most of his vertebral bodies prevents an adequate assessment of the extent of his osteophytosis. The anteroinferior margin of the C5 body exhibits minor exostoses, and the L3 body exhibits a large ossification of the left interior intervertebral ligament that extends about 13.7 mm from the original margin of the body (Figure 79). In addition, the left inferior articular facet of the L5 was partially remodeled and is surrounded by small exostoses as a result of degenerative joint disease.

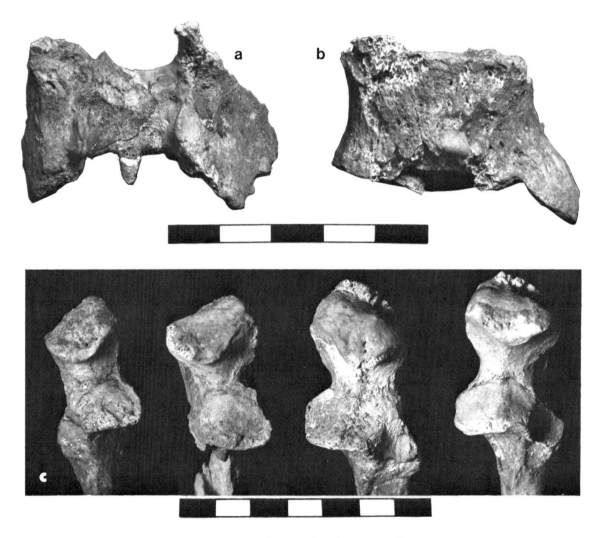

Figure 79 Anterior views of (a) the Shanidar 1 L5 and (b) L3, showing the exostosis formation on the L5 inferior left articular facet and the L3 left inferior body margin. (c) Anteroproximal views of the proximal ulnae of, from left to right, Shanidar 6, Shanidar 5, Shanidar 4, and Shanidar 1; Shanidar 1 and 4, but not Shanidar 5 and 6, exhibit large ossifications of the M. *triceps brachii* insertion. Scales in centimeters.

The only other abnormalities on the Shanidar 1 remains are ossifications of tendinous insertions. These include the insertion of *M. triceps brachii* on the left ulnar olecranon (Figure 79), *M. obturator externus* in the digital fossa of the right femur, *Mm. quadriceps femoris* on both patellae, and *Mm. triceps surae* on both calcaneal tuberosities. These bony spurs vary from being relatively small on the patellae to being quite pronounced on the left ulna. These ossifications of tendons at their attachments are generally indicative of high levels of strain on the tendons from hyperactivity of the muscles. To what extent this resulted from the other abnormalities of Shanidar 1 is not possible to determine.

These few degenerative abnormalities of Shanidar 1 are clearly noticeable, but they appear to be relatively minor when compared to his trauma-related lesions. And although they would not be unusual for an otherwise normal individual, it is highly possible that they are all somehow related in an indeterminate manner to the cranial and right side injuries and osteoarthritis.

SHANIDAR 2

Trauma-Related Abnormalities

In sharp contrast to Shanidar 1, Shanidar 2 exhibits no evidence of trauma-related lesions, although the incomplete state of his remains precludes knowing whether major portions of his limbs might have been injured.

Degenerative Abnormalities

The molar and premolar alveoli of the Shanidar 2 maxillae exhibit prominent alveolar exostoses (Figure 19). It is uncertain whether these exostoses are a discrete genetic trait, a result of functional hypertrophy, or periodontal inflammation, and they have therefore been discussed earlier (Chapter 5).

The only other abnormalities on the Shanidar 2 remains are minor exostoses on the lateral and posterior margins of the right occipital condyle and bony growths around the margins of the superior articular facets and the left inferior articular facet of the L4. The inferior L3 and superior L5 articular facets are not preserved, so it is uncertain to what extent they were involved. The right superior articular facet of the atlas is preserved, however, and it appears to be normal. These osteoarthritic degenerations on Shanidar 2 are quite minor, and their modest development probably reflects in part the relatively young age at death of Shanidar 2.

SHANIDAR 3

Trauma-Related Abnormalities

The fragmentary skeleton of Shanidar 3 displays evidence of antemortem trauma in two regions, on the left ninth rib and in the right talocrural and talocalcaneal articulations. The absence of the skull and most of the long bone diaphyses precludes knowing the full extent of this individual's injuries.

THE RIBS

The largely complete left ninth rib (portions of all 12 right ribs are preserved, so that the rib number is certain [Chapter 7]) exhibits a partially healed injury on the superior margin of the rib, about 60.0 mm distal to the angle (Figure 80). The injury consists of a parallel-sided groove, about 1.5 mm wide, which runs from external–distal to internal–proximal at an angle of 79° to the external surface and descends slightly from external to internal. The groove is clearly an antemortem injury, as there is a moderate reaction on the adjacent bone. This is indicated by exostoses along the margins of the groove, especially proximally, and an increased density of bone along the edges of the groove.

The parallel-sided nature of the groove and the lack of exostoses within the groove suggest that it was caused by a penetrating wound between the eighth and ninth left ribs. The instrument responsible cut across the top of the ninth rib, forming the groove, and probably remained in the cut until the individual died. The left eighth rib is insufficiently preserved to indicate whether it also was damaged in the process. The instrument responsible for the injury has not been recovered; it was probably lost postmortem when the rib broke below the groove.

The degree of reaction of the bone suggests that Shanidar 3 lived for at least several weeks after the wound was inflicted; the period of survival may have been considerably longer. A penetrating wound at this level would puncture the left pulmonary pleura and might penetrate the left lung, creating a pneumothorax. Secondary complications may have been responsible for the death of Shanidar 3, or the injury might have incapacitated him so that he was unable to avoid a later rockfall within Shanidar Cave. The remains of Shanidar 3 were displaced by a rockfall (Solecki 1960); whether the rockfall was responsible for his death is a matter of conjecture.

The angle and precision of the wound make it unlikely that the injury was self-inflicted. In fact, the angle and position of the wound are close to what one would expect if a right-handed individual were to have stabbed Shanidar 3 while they were standing face to face. If this interpretation is accurate, this

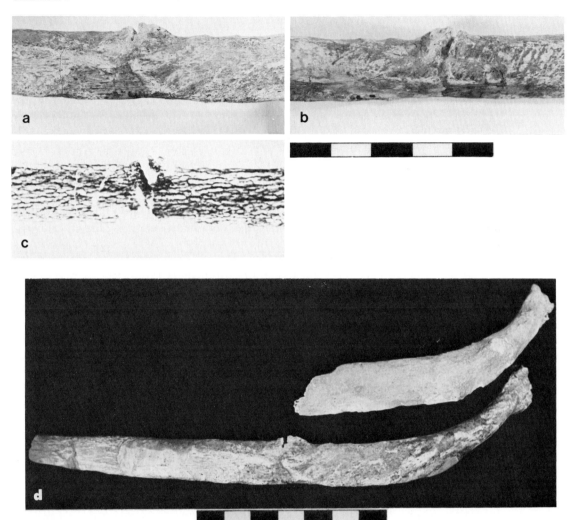

Figure 80 The injury to the left ninth rib of Shanidar 3. (a) External and (b) internal details of the partially healed injury with (c) an internal-external X ray of the region. (d) External view of the left eight and ninth ribs, positioned approximately in natural position. Scales in centimeters.

would be the oldest case of human interpersonal violence and the *only* possible one among known Neandertals. However, the possibility that this injury resulted from interpersonal violence by no means substantiates such a claim. It is possible that Shanidar 3 injured himself accidentally, or more likely, that another member of the social group wounded him accidentally. Regardless of the circumstances surrounding the wounding, Shanidar 3 was nursed for a period of at least several weeks and was intentionally buried after his death.

THE FEET

Sometime prior to his demise, Shanidar 3 developed severe degenerative joint disease in his right foot, primarily around the talocrural and talocalcaneal articulations (Figures 70 and 81). The right distal fibula has prominent bony spurs around its talar surface and in the region of the distal tibiofibular articulation. These bony spurs interlock with similar exostoses on the anterolateral fragment of the right distal tibia and meet similar bony growths on the right talus. The anterior margins of the talar trochlea and malleolar surfaces exhibit similar exostoses, which meet with those preserved on the tibial fragment when the bones are articulated in full dorsiflexion. The articular surfaces show no deterioration of the subchondral bone.

The plantar surface of the right talus exhibits bony growths in the sulcus tali, in the attachment of the talocalcaneal ligament, and along the anterior and medial margins of the posterior calcaneal surface. These are matched on the right calcaneus with growths surrounding the posterior talar surface and anterior to it where the lateral process of the talus articulates in full pronation of the subtalar joint. In addition, the posterior talocalcaneal articulations show degeneration of the subchondral bone with formation of extensive bony cysts. This degeneration eroded the lateral margin of the posterior calcaneal surface of the talus and thereby removed part of the posterolateral margin of the lateral malleolar surface. These arthritic changes, in conjunction with those at the talocrural joint, suggest a painful foot with restricted movement.

Although severe, this degenerative joint disease is limited to the talocrural and talocalcaneal articulations of the right foot. The left foot is fragmentary, but it is sufficiently complete to indicate a virtual absence of degenerative processes. As with the Shanidar 1 feet, this highly asymmetrical osteoarthritis implies that it was somehow related to trauma. It could have resulted from a fracture, subsequently healed, or a severe sprain, which altered the stress patterns within the proximal foot and promoted the arthritic changes.

Degenerative Abnormalities

Because relatively few of the Shanidar 3 articulations have been preserved, it is difficult to assess the extent to which he suffered from non-trauma-related degenerative joint disease. Both of the preserved ulnar coronoid processes have minor exostoses around their margins, and the right radial head has minimal exostoses formation along its medial margin. In addition, there is a slight lipping of bone along the superomedial acetabular margin, where it is preserved. All of these reactions of the capsular ligaments are minor and certainly did not affect movement.

Three of the Shanidar 3 upper thoracic vertebrae, T4 to T6, exhibit prominent ossifications of the ligaments flava attachments on the superior margins of their laminae (this region is preserved on Shanidar 3 from T1 to T7 and from

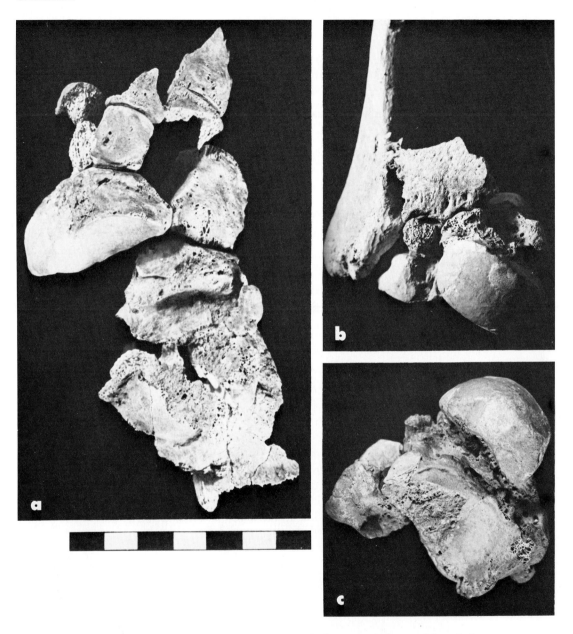

Figure 81 Degenerative joint disease of the Shanidar 3 right foot. (a) Dorsal view of the subtalar skeleton, showing the subchondral degeneration of the posterior talar facet of the calcaneus with exostosis formation around the facet. (b) Anterior view of the articulated distal tibia and fibula and talus, showing the interlocking exostoses. (c) Plantar view of the talus and fibula, showing the subchondral degeneration of the posterior calcaneal facet and the exostosis formation in the sulcus tali. Scale in centimeters.

T10 to L2). In addition, there is moderate osteophytosis between T12 and L1, especially on the right side, and between L1 and L2 on the right side, and L2 and L5 have small osteophytic growths on the inferior left margins of their bodies. The only articular facets that show any degeneration are the L2 and L3 inferior left facets and the L4 superior left facet, even though 32 of the 52 facets between T5 and L5 are preserved. The ligamenta flava ossifications and the osteophytosis represent reactions to biomechanical stress (Bourke 1967) and are found in the regions of the vertebral column where tensile stress on the ligaments would be greatest: the upper thoracic region dorsally and the lower thoracic and lumbar region ventrally. This distribution of exostosis formation along the vertebral column is similar to that seen in recent humans (Stewart 1966).

These data indicate that Shanidar 3 suffered a locomotor disability, experienced moderate to minor degenerative joint disease, and probably died a violent, if accidental, death. In fact, Shanidar 3 is the only Neandertal for whom we can reasonably speculate about the cause of death.

SHANIDAR 4

Trauma-Related Abnormalities

The only evidence of an injury on the largely complete though damaged partial skeleton of Shanidar 4 is a partially healed fracture of the right seventh or eighth rib (Figure 82). The rib was broken near the angle and healed without any deformity. The fracture is evidenced by a moderately large callus that extends around the rib and about 20.0 mm proximodistally. In the area of the callus, the cross section of the bone is filled with trabeculae, without any trace of the normal cortical bone. The fracture probably occurred a short while before death, but it was not necessarily debilitating.

Degenerative Abnormalities

The extremely fragmentary state of the Shanidar 4 vertebral column (Chapter 7) makes it difficult to assess the extent of his vertebral articular degenerations. It is merely possible to list to locations that exhibit bony growths, bearing in mind that they may or may not be representative of the column as a whole.

The cervical vertebral body identified as C4 possesses moderately pronounced osteophytosis along the ventral margins of its body, and one of the thoracic or upper lumbar body fragments has some osteophytosis. In addition, all three of the lumbar left superior articular facets and one of the two lumbar left inferior articular facets exhibit exostoses around their articular margins. Unfortunately, little more can be said of the incidence of osteoarthritis on the Shanidar 4 vertebrae.

The primary location of degenerative joint disease on Shanidar 4 is in his left wrist. The left distal radius has minor lipping around the margins of its carpal surface, and the left scaphoid, triquetral, and pisiform bones have been noticeably altered by exostosis formation around their articular surfaces and pitting of their ligamentous surfaces. The left capitate and hamate bones have small amounts of lipping around their metacarpal surfaces, but the three ulnar metacarpals do not show any articular changes. The preserved carpal bones of the right hand are all normal. These arthritic alterations of the left wrist of Shanidar 4 appear to be the product of use related degenerative joint disease. (Stewart [1963:19] stated that the left trapezoid bone of Shanidar 4 had been fused to the base of the second metacarpal; further investigation has shown that the bones were fused together postmortem and that their articulations were normal.)

Additional but minor degenerative joint disease is evident on the right scapula and the pedal phalanges of Shanidar 4. The posterior margin of the right scapular glenoid fossa exhibits secondary bony growths where the articular capsule attaches. Bony spurs, clearly ossifications of articular ligaments or long digital tendons at their insertions, are present on the plantar base of the right proximal pedal phalanx 3, on the dorsal base of the left middle pedal phalanx 2, around both articulations of the right middle pedal phalanx 4, around the head of the right middle pedal phalanx 5, and on the bases of four out of the five distal pedal phalanges from digits 2 to 5. In addition, the M. triceps brachii insertion on the left ulna and the M. quadriceps femoris insertion on the left patella have each formed large bony spurs (Figures 62 and 79) extending from the bones in the directions of the incoming tendon fibers. All of these changes represent responses to high levels of normal biomechanical stress.

SHANIDAR 5

Trauma-Related Abnormalities

The fragmentary skeleton of Shanidar 5 possesses only one trace of previous trauma, a surface scar on the left frontal squama (Figure 82). The scar is a roughened groove, about 5.0 mm wide, that runs from about 17.0 mm anterior to bregma to the left stephanion and causes a slight distortion in the arc of the

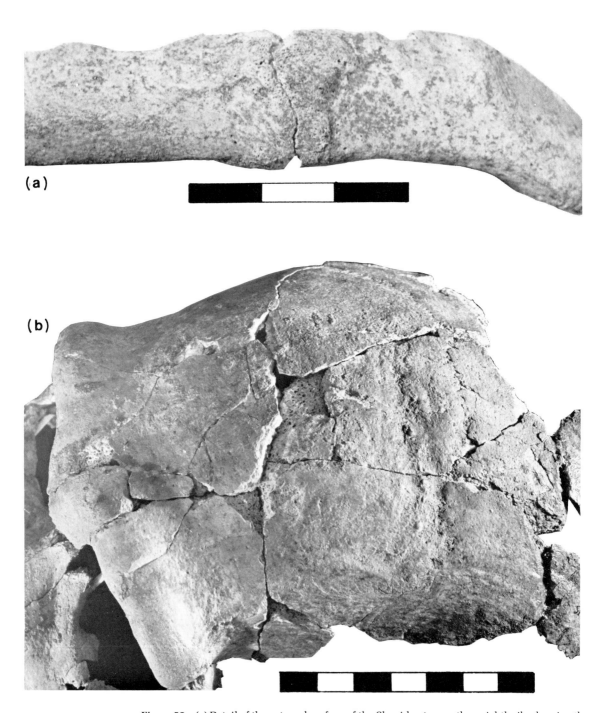

Figure 82   (a) Detail of the external surface of the Shanidar 4 seventh or eighth rib, showing the callus formation around the fracture. The break through the callus occurred postmortem. (b) Oblique left superolateral view of the Shanidar 5 frontal and adjacent bones, showing the scar extending from the left stephanion to slightly anterior of bregma. Scales in centimeters.

left temporal line. As with the scars on the right frontal bone of Shanidar 1, this abnormality appears to have been caused by a scalp wound that disturbed the periosteum. Postmortem breaks of the squama in the region of the scar show no disturbance of the diploë or internal table. The injury, like those of Shanidar 1, healed thoroughly.

Degenerative Abnormalities

The preserved remains of Shanidar 5 show relatively little evidence of osteoarthritis. The only articular abnormalities present are around the trochlear notch and radial facet on the right proximal ulna; the margins of the coronoid process and radial facet have prominent exostoses, and smaller ones appear to have been present along the anterior olecranon margin of the humeral articular surface. However, the proximal olecranon does not have any of the bony spurs for the *M. triceps surae* insertion seen on the Shanidar 1 and 4 ulnae. As with most of the degenerative joint disease on the Shanidar remains, there does not appear to have been any involvement of the articular cartilage and subchondral bone.

The only other evidence of osteoarthritis on Shanidar 5 is exostosis formation around the proximal articular facets on two of the right ribs, the ones identified as number 4 or 5 and number 5 or 6. In addition, there is a small alveolar exostosis above the left M^3, which may or may not be pathologic (Chapter 5).

In comparison to Shanidar 3 and 4 and especially to Shanidar 1, Shanidar 5 appears to have been relatively healthy, even though he probably lived about the same length of time as Shanidar 1, 3, and 4.

SHANIDAR 6

The numerous but fragmentary remains of Shanidar 6 do not possess any evidence of antemortem trauma and have relatively little evidence of degenerative processes. There is a slight amount of lipping along the preserved fragment of acetabular rim, and the right patella has very prominent bony spurs from the ossification of the *M. quadriceps femoris* tendon insertion (Figure 62).

SHANIDAR 8

None of the bones that have been attributed to Shanidar 8 exhibits any abnormalities. This may be a product of Shanidar 8's presumed young adult age at death and/or the incomplete state the partial skeleton.

SUMMARY

The Shanidar adults show a moderate degree of non-trauma-related degenerative joint disease, similar to the levels of incidence common among other fossil hominids (Dastugue and Lumley 1976; Vallois 1935) and in most recent human populations (Jurmain 1977). Because the frequency and anatomical distribution of osteoarthritis is related to the activity levels and patterns of the individuals involved (Jurmain 1977), the degenerative joint disease on the Shanidar specimens probably reflects the high activity levels indicated by their robusticity. None of the degenerative joint disease of the Shanidar specimens that cannot be interpreted as secondary to trauma appears to have been debilitating.

In contrast, the Shanidar adults show a high incidence of traumatic injury. Four of the six reasonably complete adult partial skeletons exhibit traces of past injury, and two of them—Shanidar 1 and 3—were at least partially incapacitated. The critical variable in evaluating the significance of the Shanidar traumatic injuries may be their ages at death. Shanidar 1, 3, 4, and 5 died at relatively advanced ages, whereas Shanidar 2 and 6 were young adults. It is the older individuals who exhibit severe trauma, and the high incidence of trauma among the Shanidar Neandertals may therefore be primarily a reflection of the number of elderly individuals in the sample.

This would imply that the risk of injury was high among the Shanidar Neandertals for those individuals who lived to a relatively old age. In fact, every reasonably complete partial skeleton of an elderly Neandertal known, as well as the remains of several other younger or less complete Neandertals, shows evidence of antemortem trauma. The original Neandertal 1 individual suffered a fractured proximal ulna that healed with a marked deformity (Schaafhausen 1858; Schaefer 1957). La Chapelle-aux-Saints 1 sustained a broken rib plus severe and probably trauma-related degenerative joint disease of the left hip (Dastugue and Lumley 1976; Trinkaus 1983). La Ferrassie 1 injured his right proximal femur (Dastugue and Lumley 1976). The individual from whom the Krapina 180 right ulna derives had a pseudoarthrosis or amputation of the ulna just proximal of the *M. pronator quadratus* crest (Gorjanović-Kramberger 1908). La Quina 5 suffered an injury to the left arm that produced hypoplasia or atrophy of the humerus, although not to the extent of the Shanidar 1 right arm (Martin 1923). The frontal bone of Šala 1 exhibits an injury to the right supraorbital torus (Vlček 1969).

This frequency of antemortem trauma among older Neandertals may not be surprising because evidence of trauma usually remains with an individual long after the injury was healed. However, such an incidence is still quite high compared to those of recent human populations (Angel 1974; Lovejoy and Heiple 1981; Steinbock 1976).

The elevated level of risk among the Shanidar Neandertals suggests that life among them was frequently dangerous. However, it also indicates that injured individuals were well cared for by other members of their social groups. All of these individuals show extensive healing of their injuries, with little or no evidence of infection, and Shanidar 1 and 3 lived for many years with disabling conditions that would have prevented them from contributing actively to the subsistence of the local group.

CHAPTER 13

Significant Aspects of the Shanidar Neandertals

Discussions of the Shanidar Cave Layer D human remains in the previous chapters provide descriptions of the individual fossil specimens and comparisons of their morphologies to those of other Upper Pleistocene human remains. From these comparisons of the disarticulated and incomplete skeletons there arises a picture of the Shanidar fossil human sample as a group of prehistoric people. In this chapter I summarize the significant aspects of their anatomy, place them morphologically within the known distributions of Upper Pleistocene human anatomy, and discuss the phylogenetic and behavioral implications of the Shanidar Neandertals.

THE SHANIDAR SAMPLE

The fossil human remains from Layer D of Shanidar Cave form two subsamples that should be considered both separately and together. They represent the inhabitants of Shanidar Cave during two periods of relatively intense occupation of the cave, one toward the middle of the Mousterian occupation and the other at the end of the long period during which makers of Middle Paleolithic implements took shelter there.

The first, and geologically older, subsample is the larger and demographically more diverse collection of partial skeletons. It includes two probable males, Shanidar 2 and 4, two probable females, Shanidar 6 and 8, and two infants of indeterminate sex, Shanidar 7 and 9. One of these individuals, Shanidar 4, was an elderly adult, whereas at least two of the other individuals, Shanidar 2 and 6, were relatively young adults. The infants were both less than one year old. Shanidar 8 is of indeterminate age but was probably closer in age to Shanidar 2 and 6 than to Shanidar 4.

The second and more recent subsample is smaller and demographically more homogeneous. All three of the individuals—Shanidar 1, 3, and 5—were elderly when they died, and all of them were probably male.

The paleontological value of the Shanidar Mousterian fossil human remains lies in their geographical location relative to other Upper Pleistocene human fossils, their distribution through time, and the number, anatomical diversity, completeness, and association in partial skeletons of the individual bones. In all of these aspects, the Shanidar remains contribute significantly to our understanding of Upper Pleistocene human evolution. And for several aspects of Neandertal morphology, the Shanidar specimens provide insights that were not previously possible, given the nature of other Near Eastern and European Neandertal remains.

The Shanidar sample is the only collection of reasonably complete adult human remains and associated but fragmentary immature human remains from western Asia east of the Levant. The only other archaic human remains from the eastern part of western Asia are the Azykh 1 partial mandible, the Bisitun 1 radius, and the Teshik-Tash 1 immature partial skeleton (Chapter 3). Early anatomically modern human remains from this region, such as the Darra-i-Kur 1 temporal bone, are even more rare, and Upper Pleistocene human remains from eastern Asia are few and generally fragmentary.

The Shanidar Layer D remains are also important because they provide glimpses of human morphology at two points in time during the Middle Paleolithic at one site. As discussed in Chapter 2, the precise geological ages of the two Shanidar Middle Paleolithic subsamples are not known. However, at least several millennia, and perhaps several tens of millennia, elapsed between the time of Shanidar 2, 4, 6, 7, 8, and 9 and the time of Shanidar 1, 3, and 5. Shanidar Cave is therefore the only site in the Near East, and possibly the only one in the Old World, where there are at least two groups of reasonably complete Mousterian-associated human fossils whose temporal relationships, at least on a relative scale, are securely known. It is therefore possible to examine trends through time with respect to a number of anatomical complexes with the Shanidar sample.

The Shanidar sample is also important for its size and representation of anatomical regions. With nine partial skeletons the Shanidar sample is approached, among single site collections of archaic human partial skeletons, only by that of La Ferrassie, which yielded eight individuals with associated remains (Heim 1976). Three Middle Paleolithic sites in Europe—Hortus (Lumley 1972), Krapina (Gorjanović-Kramberger 1906; Smith 1976b; Trinkaus 1975c; Wolpoff 1979), and La Quina (Martin 1910, 1912, 1923, 1926a, 1926b)—

have yielded more individuals than are known from Shanidar, but those samples consist primarily of disassociated bones. Only the samples of early anatomically modern humans from the sites of Předmostí (Matiegka 1934, 1938), Qafzeh (Vandermeersch 1981a) and Skhūl (McCown and Keith 1939), and more recent sites have larger collections of partial skeletons than Shanidar.

The completeness of the Shanidar partial skeletons varies from the largely complete Shanidar 1 remains to the fragments of Shanidar 8 and the nine vertebrae of Shanidar 9 (Chapter 2). Yet in each of the two Shanidar subsamples, at least one individual, and usually two or three individuals, retains substantial portions of most anatomical regions. Together, the Shanidar partial skeletons make up the majority of the Near Eastern individuals represented for most anatomical regions, and they contribute significantly to the sizes of the combined Near Eastern and European Neandertal samples for several regions of the body. This applies especially to the facial skeleton, dentition, vertebral column, hand skeleton, pubic region, and pedal skeleton. The 516 identifiable bones and the 112 teeth from the nine Shanidar individuals are clearly an important addition to the Upper Pleistocene hominid fossil record.

THE SHANIDAR FOSSILS AS NEANDERTALS

Throughout the foregoing descriptions and discussions of the fossil human remains from Layer D in Shanidar Cave, these prehistoric humans have been referred to as *Neandertals*. This biological designation was based initially on the preliminary morphological assessments of Stewart and me on various aspects of the Shanidar specimens and on their similarities to the Neandertal specimens from western Europe. These resemblances were most apparent in their facial skeletons (Stewart 1958, 1961b, 1963; Trinkaus 1977d), but subsequent analyses by Stewart (1960, 1961a, 1962a, 1962b, 1970), me (Lovejoy and Trinkaus 1980; Stringer and Trinkaus 1981; Trinkaus 1975a, 1976a, 1976b, 1978b, 1980, 1981, 1982f), and others (Brace 1979; Endo and Kimura 1970; Howells 1975; Ryan 1980; Suzuki 1970; Taylor 1968) of their skulls, their dentitions, and select aspects of their postcrania have supported the impression that they are indeed Neandertals. However, the presentation and analysis here of the Shanidar remains provides considerably more data on which to judge whether the Shanidar specimens are indeed morphologically close to the Neandertals.

There have been many and varied definitions of the Neandertals. Here, as discussed in Chapter 3, they are considered to be geographically limited to Europe and western Asia and to be identified by a cluster of anatomical traits that distinguishes them from earlier and later hominids and from their contemporaries in eastern Asia and Africa. Although no one of these features would necessarily identify a specimen as a Neandertal, especially if the fossil record for geologically older and non-European or non–western Asian hominids were more complete, the constellation of traits seen in western Asian and especially European Neandertals appears to be unique to them. It is in relation to this total morphological pattern that the Neandertal status of the Shanidar fossils is evaluated.

The Crania and Mandibles

The traditionally most diagnostic anatomical region for the Neandertals is their facial skeleton, and major portions of this region are preserved for four of the Shanidar individuals (Chapter 5). The Shanidar 1 and 5 faces exhibit remarkable similarity to those of their European contemporaries. Both have large, rounded supraorbital tori with frontal sinuses that fill the glabellar region but do not extend laterally of midorbit nor into the frontal squamous. Both have moderately inflated maxillary sinuses, and Shanidar 5, but not Shanidar 1, has an enormous nasal aperture. But most significantly, Shanidar 1 and 5 exhibit full Neandertal midfacial prognathism; this is reflected in their low zygomaxillary angles, their large molar alveolus–zygomaxillare radii differences, the large retromolar spaces on both of their maxillae and on the Shanidar 1 mandible, the anterior positions of their nasal apertures, their retreating zygomatic profiles, and the relative narrowness of the Shanidar 1 mandibular ramus. Despite some individual variation in details of facial morphology, there is little doubt that Shanidar 1 and 5 possess facial skeletons that fall within the known range of variation for Neandertals.

In contrast, the earlier Shanidar 2 and 4 specimens have facial skeletons that exhibit a mixture of Neandertal and non-Neandertal features. Their supraorbital tori, to the extent that they are preserved, exhibit the typical Neandertal external morphology and frontal sinus configuration and positioning. Their mandibular lengths indicate that they had the same degree of facial projection relative to leg length as did Shanidar 1 and 5 and other Neandertals. However, their zygomatic and anterior mandibular rami were positioned more anteriorly than those of Shanidar 1 and 5 and European Neandertals. As a result, they exhibit less midfacial prognathism; this is evident in their higher zygomaxillary angles, the small molar alveolus–zygomaxillare radii difference of Shanidar 2, their angled zygomatic regions and consequent flat or slightly concave anterior maxillae, their wide mandibular rami, and their small or absent mandibular retromolar spaces.

This configuration of the Shanidar 2 and 4 faces, associated with their greater facial robusticity, aligns them more with earlier Near Eastern and European specimens. The last interglacial Zuttiyeh 1 anterior cranium exhibits little projection of the superior nasal region, as indicated by its high nasofrontal angle, and has an angled and robust zygomatic bone. And several Middle Pleistocene European specimens, such as Petralona 1, Arago 21, and Steinheim

1, exhibit similar facial configurations. This suggests that the Shanidar 2 and 4 faces may be evidence of a continuation of an Early Neandertal facial configuration into the time period represented by the middle of Layer D in Shanidar Cave.

The three Levantine Neandertal facial skeletons, those of Amud 1 and Tabūn C1 and C2, appear in some respects to be intermediate between those of European Neandertals and Shanidar 1 and 5 on one hand, and those of Shanidar 2 and 4 on the other. Amud 1, and possibly Tabūn C1, may exhibit less midfacial prognathism than Shanidar 1 and 5. However, all three of these individuals possess features that are usually associated with Neandertal faces, such as the configuration of the supraorbital region, the large mandibular retromolar spaces, and a retreating zygomatic region (on Amud 1). If the evidence from Shanidar that midfacial prognathism increased during the Middle Paleolithic of the Zagros is applicable to the same time period in the Levant, however, it may be that the three Levantine Neandertal facial skeletons represent different phases of an evolutionary trend through time. Unfortunately, the paucity and incompleteness of the specimens and difficulties in determining the geological ages of these specimens (Jelinek, personal communication, 1982; Suzuki and Takai 1970; see following discussion) preclude a resolution of this problem at this time.

Archaic *Homo sapiens* facial skeletons from Africa and eastern Asia exhibit little of the midfacial prognathism evident in the Shanidar 1 and 5 specimens. The Dali 1 and Mapa 1 crania (Woo and Peng 1959; Wu 1981) probably had relatively flat facial skeletons, and the few African Upper Pleistocene archaic *H. sapiens* specimens known—Florisbad 1, Haua Fteah 1 and 2, Irhoud 1 and 3, and Laetoli 18 (Day *et al.* 1980; Ennouchi 1962; Hublin and Tillier 1981; Rightmire 1978; Tobias 1967)—also exhibit few if any of the morphological features or measurements associated with Neandertal midfacial prognathism. Only the probably Middle Pleistocene Broken Hill 1 cranium provides measurements of midfacial projection that fall within the Neandertal range, but the detailed morphology of its face is different from and more archaic than those of Neandertals.

The facial skeletons of the Shanidar 1 and 5 skulls therefore fully justify their inclusion with the Neandertal sample. The Shanidar 2 and 4 facial skeletons suggest a closer affinity to the Early Neandertals of the Near East and Europe.

The occipitomastoid region appears to be diagnostic of the Neandertals and their immediate predecessors, at least in Europe. The Shanidar crania, however, are variable with respect to this region. Shanidar 1 and probably Shanidar 2 exhibit wide, shallow suprainiac fossae. Shanidar 1 has tapering mastoid processes with anterior mastoid tubercles, whereas Shanidar 2 and 5 have parallel-sided mastoid processes without anterior mastoid tubercles. Shanidar 1 and 2 both have occipitomastoid crests, but the crest of Shanidar 2 is distinct from the transverse occipital torus, whereas that of Shanidar 1 is continuous with the torus. In addition, there is variation in the sizes of the transverse occipital tori and supramastoid crests, with Shanidar 2 and 4 having larger crests than Shanidar 1 and 5. The differences in torus development appear to be related to the lesser degree of robusticity present in the later Shanidar 1 and 5 crania as compared to the earlier Shanidar 2 and 4 crania. However, the variation in the other mastooccipital features does not appear to follow any temporal pattern; there is as much difference between Shanidar 1 and 5 in, for example, mastoid morphology as there is between Shanidar 1 and 2. The Shanidar 1 occipitomastoid region is probably the closest morphologically to the pattern described by Hublin (1978a, 1978b) and Santa Luca (1978) for the European Neandertals.

The Shanidar 1 and 5 tympanic regions and the Shanidar 5 external acoustic meatus closely resemble those of Amud 1 and various European Neandertals. They have clear tympanic crests oriented close to the coronal plane, and the Shanidar 5 external acoustic meatus is elongated and obliquely oriented.

Shanidar 1, 2, and 4 all lack the horizontal–oval pattern of the manidular foramen. However, the horizontal–oval configuration, although common among the Neandertals, is variable in both the European and Levantine samples.

The morphological affinities of the Shanidar cranial vaults are more difficult to assess. Those of Shanidar 2 and 4 are too incomplete to provide firm indications of their morphological affinities, although their shapes would be compatible with their inclusion in a Neandertal sample. Shanidar 1 and 5, in contrast, have frontal bones that are quite flat and parietal bones that are unusually curved for Neandertals. This combination of a flat frontal arc and a curved sagittal arc is unique among European and Near Eastern Pleistocene fossil hominids, whether archaic or anatomically modern. It suggests that they experienced some form of artificial cranial deformation as infants (Chapter 5). The shapes of their cranial vaults therefore can provide little indication of their biological affinities.

There thus appears to be little doubt that the Shanidar 1 and 5 crania and the Shanidar 1 mandible are morphologically closely aligned with the Neandertals. Their faces are remarkably similar to those known from western Europe, and only their unusual midsagittal cranial vault contours and high parietal regions are outside the known ranges of variation of other Neandertals. The Shanidar 2 and 4 skulls more closely resemble some of the Early Neandertals from the Near East and Europe, mainly in their combinations of large and robust faces associated with modest midfacial prognathism.

The Dentitions

The 112 teeth from six Shanidar adults and one infant provide a rather complete picture of their dental morphology and dimensions (Chapters 6 and

10). Morphologically, all of the Shanidar teeth, deciduous and permanent, are similar to those of other Upper Pleistocene hominid teeth. They have occlusal morphologies, to the extent that they are preserved, that are within recent human ranges of variation. However, they tend to have full complements of cusps on their molars and premolars, and their anterior teeth tend to have strong developments of the lingual margins associated with shoveling of the incisors. Although this morphological pattern is similar to that seen in Near Eastern and European Neandertals, it is also apparent in samples of early anatomically modern humans, non-European or western Asian archaic humans, and recent humans.

The dimensions of the Shanidar permanent premolars and molars and the Shanidar 7 deciduous teeth are largely undiagnostic. The individual diameters and areas of the teeth are within the ranges of variation of all known Upper Pleistocene hominid samples and many recent human samples. The permanent premolars and molars tend to be slightly larger than those of Amud and Tabūn C1, but they are similar to those of Tabūn C2 and most European Neandertals.

The one diagnostic aspect of the Shanidar dentitions is the large size of their anterior permanent teeth. The incisors and canines of all of the adults have exceptionally large breadths, both in absolute dimensions and relative to their posterior teeth. This is a pattern that is known primarily among the European and Near Eastern Neandertals, and it is remarkably consistent among them. Whether the Shanidar permanent anterior dental breadths are considered individually or as summations (for the Shanidar 1 and 2 maxillary anterior teeth and for the Shanidar 2 and 4 mandibular anterior teeth), they are within known Neandertal ranges of variation and largely separate from those of other human samples, especially more recent human samples. Furthermore, relative to the dimensions of their posterior teeth, the Shanidar 1 and 2 anterior teeth are similar to those of other Neandertals and larger than those of most more recent humans. Interestingly, although the Amud 1 and Tabūn C1 dentitions, but not the Tabūn C2 dentition, are relatively small compared to both the Shanidar teeth and those of European Neandertals, all of the Levantine Neandertal anterior–posterior dental proportions are very similar to those of the Shanidar fossils and European Neandertals.

In addition to having absolutely and relatively large anterior teeth, the Shanidar adults exhibit the extensive anterior occlusal wear seen on many Neandertal dentitions. For Shanidar 2 and 6, this anterior wear has resulted only in a horizontal planing off of the occlusal surfaces and the removal of about half of the anterior tooth crowns. Shanidar 1, 3, 4, and 5, on the other hand, had all or virtually all of their incisor and canine crowns removed by abrasion. Furthermore, and perhaps more diagnostically, their maxillary and mandibular anterior teeth exhibit pronounced labial rounding. Although similar types of wear are known from samples of recent humans and other fossil hominids, this characteristic type of abrasion appears to have been especially common among older Neandertals.

The dental remains from Shanidar thus indicate an affiliation with the Near Eastern and European Neandertals. It is primarily the dimensions of their permanent anterior teeth and their patterns of anterior dental wear that support this interpretation, but the dimensions and occlusal morphologies of their other teeth are in agreement with such a conclusion.

The Axial Skeleton

Even though the vertebrae, ribs, and sternal segment from the Shanidar fossils make up the largest known sample of archaic human axial remains (Chapter 7), there are few if any morphological features that indicate their affinities with other Upper Pleistocene hominid samples. This is a product both of the similarities among all known archaic *H. sapiens*, early anatomically modern human and recent human axial skeletons, and of the large ranges of variation of these bones across populations of recent humans.

The Shanidar 7 and 9 infant vertebrae and ribs are indistinguishable from those of recent human infants of the same developmental age. The vertebrae and ribs from the Shanidar adults, most of which appear to derive from Shanidar 1 to 5, are large and robust. They are generally more robust than those of the Tabūn C1 female, being comparable to those known for male European Neandertals.

The one feature of their axial skeletons that appears to align them with European Neandertals is the configuration of their caudal cervical vertebral spines. The Shanidar 1 and 2 C5–C7 have long, straight, horizontally oriented, and robust spines, which are similar to those known for European Neandertals. However, similar C5–C7 spines are known in more recent human samples and are merely indicative of a robust cervical region.

The Upper Limb Remains

Comparisons of the Shanidar upper limb remains have been limited to those of European and Near Eastern Neandertals and those of anatomically modern humans (Chapter 8). This is a product of the extreme scarcity and incompleteness of arm bones and absence of shoulder and hand bones among other archaic *H. sapiens*. Such bones are even rarer for *H. erectus*. It is therefore difficult to determine whether the similarities between the Shanidar postcrania and those of European and Near Eastern Neandertals are the result of a close phylogenetic relationship between them or are merely the reflection of a general archaic *H. sapiens* pattern possessed by both Neandertals and non-Neandertal archaic *H. sapiens*.

The shoulder girdles of the Shanidar specimens are similar to those of European and Near Eastern Neandertals primarily in the configurations of their scapulae. The Shanidar 1, 2, 3, and 4 scapulae show a predominance of the dorsal sulcus morphology, as do other Neandertals, and those of Shanidar 1, 3, and 4, and probably that of Shanidar 2 as well, exhibit the mediolateral enlargement relative to humerus length evident at least in the La Ferrassie 1 scapulae but not in those of more recent humans. Both of these patterns indicate hypertrophy of the rotator cuff muscles of the scapulohumeral joint. In addition, the Shanidar 1 and 4 scapulae have relatively narrow glenoid fossae, similar to those of Near Eastern and European Neandertals but unlike those of most more recent humans.

Although the Shanidar individuals have broad scapulae, the Shanidar 1 and 3 claviculohumeral indices are within recent human ranges of variation and are also similar to that of Tabūn C1. They are well below those of La Ferrassie 1 and Régourdou 1, which suggests that the western Asian specimens do not share an elongation of the clavicle with the European Neandertals.

Most of the features of the Shanidar humeri, ulnae, and radii that align them with the Neandertals and distinguish them from more recent humans are related to the hypertrophy of their arms. This is evident in the large sizes of the Shanidar 3, 4, and 6 *M. pectoralis major* tuberosities, the Shanidar 1, 3, 4, 6, and 8 radial tuberosities, and the Shanidar 1, 3, 4, 5, and 6 *M. pronator quadratus* crests. Even the Shanidar 7 infant ulna shows evidence of a marked *M. pronator quadratus* attachment. In addition, the Shanidar arm bones show the moderate diaphyseal and articular robusticity that characterizes the Neandertals but does not really distinguish them from more recent humans.

There are three other features that tend to distinguish Neandertal arm bones from those of more recent humans: pronounced radial diaphyseal curvature, radial neck elongation, and anterior orientation of the ulnar trochlear notch. The two aspects of the radius serve to improve the mechanical advantages of the pronator muscles and *M. biceps brachii,* respectively. Interestingly, the Shanidar radii are quite variable with respect to these features; Shanidar 4, unlike Shanidar 1 and 6, exhibits Neandertal-like radial curvature, and Shanidar 6, but not Shanidar 1 or 4, has the radial neck elongation. The significance of the anterior orientation of the trochlear notch of the ulna is not apparent, but those of Shanidar 1, 4, 5, and 6 clearly exhibit it.

The large number of hand bones preserved from Shanidar depicts a morphological pattern that is known only among the Neandertals. This complex of features includes their phalangeal length proportions, manual robusticity, and first carpometacarpal articular morphologies.

The overall proportions of the Shanidar hand remains, especially those of the largely complete Shanidar 4 left hand, are similar to the proportions of other Neandertals and recent humans. This involves overall hand length relative to arm length, thumb length relative to ulnar digit length, and thumb phalangeal length relative to first metacarpal length. The first relationship is ascertainable for Shanidar 4 and 6, whereas the latter two are known only for

Shanidar 4. However, within this framework, Shanidar 4, 5, and 6 exhibit a shortening of the pollical proximal phalanx and a proportionate elongation of the pollical distal phalanx relative to the proportions of these phalanges among more recent humans. This pattern is present among European Neandertals, but the Levantine Neandertals are insufficiently complete to indicate whether they exhibited it.

The pollical phalangeal length proportions of the Shanidar specimens and European Neandertals are probably an adaptation for generating strength during the power grip and are therefore related to their level of robusticity. In fact, the Shanidar hand bones exhibit exceptional robusticity. It is evident in the large dimensions of the Shanidar 3 and 4 trapezial tubercles, the exceptional sizes of the Shanidar 3, 4, and 5 hamulae, the large *M. opponens pollicis* crest on the Shanidar 4 first metacarpal, the large *M. flexor pollicis longus* tendon insertion pits on the Shanidar 3, 4, 5, and 6 pollical distal phalanges, the prominent *M. opponens digiti minimi* crests on the Shanidar 1, 3, 4, and 6, but not 5, fifth metacarpals, and the expansions of the tuberosities on the distal phalanges of Shanidar 3, 4, 5, and 6. Even the Shanidar 7 first metacarpal has a clearly identifiable *M. opponens pollicis* attachment, although it is still small. All these features bespeak exceptionally powerful grips for the Shanidar individuals, and they are seen on most of the known Neandertal hand bones. Only the Tabūn C1 hand bones, among those known for Neandertals (including those of Amud 1), show any reduction of these features approaching the usual configuration seen in early anatomically modern and recent human remains.

The third feature that tends to separate Neandertal hand remains from those of more recent humans is the morphology of their first carpometacarpal articulations. They tend to lack or have a minimal development of the double saddle-shaped articular configuration usual for recent humans. The Shanidar 4 trapezia and first metacarpal and the Shanidar 3 trapezium exhibit flattening of this articulation.

These aspects of the Shanidar upper limb bones illustrate their close morphological affinities with the Near Eastern and European Neandertals. The Shanidar shoulder and arm bones are variable in several features, but they tend to conform more to the pattern exhibited by the Neandertals than to that of early anatomically modern and recent humans. The Shanidar hand bones, however, are uniform in their morphology and follow the pattern evident in the Levantine and European Neandertal samples.

The Lower Limb Remains

As with the remains from the upper limbs, it is possible to compare most aspects of the Shanidar innominate, leg, and foot bones only to those of Neandertals and more recent humans (Chapter 9). There are considerably more lower limb remains preserved for non-Neandertal archaic *H. sapiens* and *H. erectus* than there are upper limb specimens from these samples, but they consist primarily of ilia and ischia and femoral and tibial diaphyses. Only those from Broken Hill are reasonably complete, but their association with the archaic cranium and Middle or early Upper Pleistocene materials from the site is uncertain (Clark *et al.* 1950). Therefore, as with the shoulder, arm, and hand bones from Shanidar, similarities between the Shanidar lower limb bones and those of Neandertals may only indicate that they are all archaic *H. sapiens*.

The ilia and ischia from Shanidar 1, 3, and 4 are sufficiently intact to demonstrate that these portions of their innominate bones fall within the ranges of variation of both Neandertals and anatomically modern humans, who are not distinct from each other with respect to these regions. However, all three of these Shanidar individuals exhibit the ventral thinning of the superior pubic ramus that is so far known only for the Neandertals, and especially the Near Eastern Neandertals. Furthermore, the Shanidar 1 and 3 pubic bones are sufficiently complete to reveal that they had the mediolateral elongation of the pubic region that is known only among the Neandertals. Relative to anatomically modern humans, this pubic morphology of the Shanidar fossils unquestionably aligns them with the Neandertals, especially the Levantine ones. However, the only geologically contemporaneous or older non-Neandertal hominid pubic bones currently known are from *Australopithecus*. This pubic morphology may be merely archaic for *H. sapiens*.

The Shanidar femora are likewise similar to those of Neandertals and at the limits of more recent human ranges of variation. The Shanidar 1, 4, 5, and 6 diaphyses are circular in cross section and lack pilasters. They are exceptionally broad relative to length, a pattern that places them at the robust end of the Neandertal range of variation. Those of Shanidar 1, 4, and 6 have large and rugose *M. gluteus maximus* insertions. The robusticity of the Shanidar proximal femora, as indicated by the Shanidar 4 and 5 relative head sizes and the Shanidar 1 neck–shaft angle, are in the zone of overlap between Neandertals and recent humans; however, they are separate from those of the Skhūl–Qafzeh hominids and imply considerably more robust hip regions than those of these Levantine early anatomically modern humans.

Femoral diaphyses are known for three Early Neandertals, including one from Tabūn (Chapter 9), and several *H. erectus* individuals (Day 1971; Weidenreich 1941). Neither the Shanidar femora nor those of the European and Levantine Neandertals are morphologically separable from the Early Neandertal specimens, but all of these early Upper Pleistocene femoral diaphyses show less anteroposterior flattening than those of *H. erectus*. This indicates that the morphological affinities of the Shanidar femora are primarily with those of other archaic *H. sapiens*, although to which sample of archaic *H. sapiens* is difficult to assess.

The Shanidar knees, which are represented by the Shanidar 1, 4, 5, and 6 patellae, the Shanidar 2 and 5 proximal tibiae, and the incomplete Shanidar 1 distal femur, show the exaggeration of the moment arm for M. quadriceps femoris evident on most Neandertal remains. This is apparent in the relative thicknesses of their patellae and the posterior displacement of the Shanidar 2 and 5 tibial condyles. In these features, the Shanidar specimens are most similar to European Neandertals because the only Levantine Neandertal with this region preserved, Tabūn C1, is relatively gracile in this complex. More recent humans and the Middle or Upper Pleistocene Broken Hill tibia only overlap the lower end of the Neandertal range and do not approach the Shanidar specimens in the enlargement of the M. quadriceps femoris moment arm.

Similarly, the Shanidar 1, 2, and 6 tibial diaphyses are as robust as those of Neandertals, and they are largely separate from those of more recent humans as well as from those from Ngandong and Broken Hill with respect to diaphyseal robusticity. All of them have the characteristically Neandertal amygdaloid midshaft cross section, which, however, may not be unique to these archaic humans.

The various pedal bones from the Shanidar individuals cannot be distinguished from these known for the Neandertals. But then, it would be difficult to separate morphologically most Neandertal foot bones from those of more recent humans. All of the Shanidar and Levantine and European Neandertal foot remains tend to be relatively robust, and this is reflected in their large articular surfaces, especially at the talocrural articulation, and in the hypertrophy of their musculoligamentous attachments, especially for the ligaments and tendons that provide support for the longitudinal pedal arches. This robusticity is evident particularly on the Shanidar 1, 3, and 4 pedal remains.

There are only two aspects of the Shanidar foot bones that appear to align them more with the Neandertals than with more recent humans. Compared to the proportions present among more recent humans, they have relatively short proximal hallucial phalanges and proportionately longer distal hallucial phalanges; this is indicated by the shortness of the Shanidar 1 proximal hallucial phalanx relative to medial subtalar length and by the shortness of the Shanidar 4 proximal hallucial phalanx relative to his distal hallucial phalanx. In addition, Shanidar 3, 4, and 8 have proximal pedal phalanges from digits two, three, and four that have relatively wide diaphyses. Probably related to an accentuation of mediolateral digital stress in their feet, this morphology is characteristic of these bones among the Neandertals but rare for more recent humans.

Even though the morphologies of the Shanidar lower limb remains may not be highly diagnostic for specifically aligning them with the Neandertals as opposed to other archaic humans, they do show remarkable similarities to those of the European and Levantine Neandertals. Although most of these features are related to general locomotor robusticity, their pattern of expression is similar to that seen in these European and Near Eastern archaic H. sapiens and different from that evident in remains of anatomically modern humans.

Summary

This review of the morphologically diagnostic aspects of the Shanidar fossils indicates their close morphological affinities to the Near Eastern and European Neandertals. This conclusion is supported by all diagnostic aspects of their postcranial skeletons, but it is confirmed primarily by their facial morphologies and anterior dental dimensions. There are differences between the early Shanidar 2 and 4 faces and those of the later Shanidar 1 and 5 individuals in midfacial prognathism and robusticity, with the later specimens closely resembling typical Neandertals and the earlier specimens more closely approximating an Early Neandertal morphology. However, this consideration does not appear to be sufficient to separate the earlier subsample from the Neandertals; they have many other similarities to the Neandertals, and they are probably very close to the arbitrary boundary that has been constructed in the evolutionary continuum from the Early Neandertals to the Neandertals in Europe and the Near East. It therefore appears reasonable to refer to the fossil human partial skeletons from Layer D of Shanidar Cave as Neandertals.

In light of these considerations, all of the Shanidar specimens should be included within the generally recognized subspecies of *Homo sapiens*, *H. sapiens neanderthalensis* (Campbell 1963). The evidence does not support the erection of a new subspecies, "H. sapiens shanidarensis" for the Shanidar sample, as proposed by Şenyürek (1959: 125) on the basis of the morphology of the Shanidar 7 infant; the proposed taxon "H. sapiens shanidarensis" should be considered synonymous with *H. sapiens neanderthalensis*.

EVOLUTIONARY TRENDS
IN THE SHANIDAR SAMPLE

Because the Shanidar fossil sample is really two subsamples separated by a number of millennia, it should be possible to determine whether significant human morphological change took place during the time that Layer D was formed in Shanidar Cave. Even though it is not possible at present to know how much time elapsed between Shanidar 2, 4, 6, 7, 8, and 9 and Shanidar 1, 3, and 5, the amount of change evident between these two subsamples should provide an indication of the degree of evolutionary stasis that occurred during this period at Shanidar.

The Shanidar remains provide a unique opportunity for examining evolutionary trends among the Neandertals because most aspects of adult morphology for at least one individual are represented in both of the subsamples. Despite the small sample sizes available, this means that the possible mosaic nature of any trends through time can be investigated. Furthermore, the presence of partial skeletons means that shifts in proportions, rather than merely differences in size, can be discerned.

Trends in the Postcrania

Discussions in previous chapters have tended to highlight the individual natures of the different Shanidar specimens, and this may have given the impression that there is considerable variation among them. However, in relation to the ranges of variation of other Neandertals or samples of anatomically modern humans, the Shanidar postcranial remains are relatively uniform (Chapters 7, 8, and 9).

There is a high degree of uniformity in both qualitatively evaluated aspects of morphology and comparative metrics throughout the Shanidar sample in most regions of the postcrania. The anatomical features in the axial skeleton and upper limb that exhibit this homogeneity include the elongate spines of the caudal cervical vertebrae, the breadths of the scapulae, the platybrachia of the humeral diaphyses but especially the configurations and accentuation of the muscle attachment areas on the diaphyses, the anterior orientation of the ulnar trochlear notches, and almost all aspects of the hand skeletons including the enlargement of the carpal tunnel, the relative flattening of the first carpometacarpal articulation, the proportions of the pollical phalanges, the expansion of the pollical and ulnar distal phalangeal tuberosities, and the accentuation of muscular attachments. In the pelvis and lower limb skeleton, this homogeneity is evident in the ventral thinning and cross-sectional morphology of their superior pubic rami, the robusticity and cross-sectional morphology of their femoral diaphyses, the expansion of their gluteal tuberosities, the relative thickening of their patellae, the posterior displacement of their tibial condyles, the cross-sectional morphology and robusticity of their tibial diaphyses, and several features of their pedal skeletons including the abbreviation of their proximal hallucial phalanges and the mediolateral expansion of their lateral proximal phalangeal diaphyses. The uniformity of all of these features across the Shanidar sample relative to the ranges of variation known for the Neandertals suggests that no discernible evolution took place in them between the earlier and later subsamples from Shanidar.

There are, however, several aspects of the Shanidar postcrania that show variation. These features are limited to the upper limb skeleton. There is variation in scapular axillary border morphology, with Shanidar 1 and probably 2 and 4 possessing the dorsal sulcus pattern and Shanidar 3 exhibiting the bisulcate pattern. Shanidar 1 and 3 differ in the degree to which their clavicles are curved. Shanidar 3 and 4 have relatively large distal humeral articulations, whereas those of Shanidar 1 and 6 are quite small. Shanidar 1, 4, and 5 have large *M. pronator quadratus* crests on their ulnae, whereas Shanidar 6 has a small one. The Shanidar 5 and 6 radii have large interosseus crests, whereas those of Shanidar 1, 4, and 8 are more modest in size. The Shanidar 4 radial diaphysis is strongly bowed laterally, whereas those of Shanidar 1 and 6 are straighter. And finally, Shanidar 1, 3, 4, and 6 have prominent M. *opponens digiti minimi* crests, whereas Shanidar 5 lacks one.

These features give the impression of considerable variability. However, the variation is as much within the subsamples as it is between them. It therefore does not indicate any pattern of morphological change between the two Shanidar subsamples, but rather a certain degree of variation within each. The actual source of the variation is probably a combination of sexual dimorphism, size variation, and random genetic differences between individuals.

These considerations should make it clear that considerable stasis was present in postcranial morphology among the populations that inhabited Shanidar Cave during the Mousterian.

Trends in the Dentition

It is possible to evaluate trends only with respect to the sizes of the permanent teeth for the Shanidar Neandertals (Chapter 6). Deciduous teeth are present only in the earlier subsample, and the occlusal morphologies of too many of the permanent teeth were obscured by antemortem occlusal wear.

In the posterior dentition, the summed areas for the Shanidar 1 dentition as compared to the Shanidar 2 and 6 dentitions give the impression that there was a reduction in dental size between the earlier and later Shanidar subsamples. Yet if the areas of the maxillary third molars are compared (as this tooth is preserved for Shanidar 1, 2, 3, 5, and 6), little if any difference is seen between the Shanidar 2 and 6 and the Shanidar 3 and 5 third molars, whereas that of Shanidar 1 is slightly smaller.

In the anterior dentition, there is not even a suggestion of dental reduction between the subsamples. The summed maxillary anterior breadths of Shanidar 1 and 2 are virtually identical, there is little or no change in either maxillary or mandibular canine breadths between the subsamples, and Shanidar 1 and 3 have slightly larger lateral mandibular incisors than those of Shanidar 2 and 4.

These data suggest that there was little or no change in dental size in Shanidar Cave inhabitants from the time of the earlier Neandertal subsample to the time of the later one.

Trends in the Skulls

In contrast to the postcrania and dentitions, the skull remains from the Shanidar individuals exhibited change during the deposition of Layer D. The earlier Shanidar 2 and 4 facial skeletons are reminiscent of those of Early Neandertals, and the later Shanidar 1 and 5 facial skeletons are similar to those of typical Neandertals. In the time between the Shanidar 2 and 4 individuals and the Shanidar 1 and 5 individuals, assuming a lineal relationship between their populations, there was an evolution of a typical Neandertal facial configuration from a more archaic facial form (Chapter 5).

This facial transformation can be seen primarily as an accentuation of midfacial prognathism with various associated changes, such as increased zygomatic flattening, maxillary convexity and retromolar space size, and decreased mandibular ramus breadth. However, it may be more accurate to view these alterations as part of a general pattern of decreasing masticatory robusticity. There was some reduction in masticatory massiveness between the earlier and later subsamples, which is evident in their mandibular surface reliefs and the rugosities of their M. masseter and M. pterygoideus medialis attachment areas. The other changes are probably related to this gracilization.

Because there is little difference in mandibular superior length (as an indicator of total facial prognathism) between the early and late Shanidar subsamples and no difference in mandibular superior length relative to femoral or tibial length between the subsamples, all of the differences in midfacial prognathism are probably due to the positionings of their masseteric attachments on the zygomatic bone and their anterior ramal margins relative to the rest of the face. In the later specimens, these two regions are located more posteriorly than they are in the earlier specimens. This had the effects of narrowing the mandibular ramus, increasing the size of the mandibular retromolar space, decreasing the angulation of the zygomatic bone, positioning the zygomatic region more posteriorly with respect to the dentition, decreasing the concavity in the anterior maxilla, and making the nasal region appear more projecting. These changes are all products of altered spatial relationships in the face, and they may have had little functional significance by themselves. However, the posterior retreat of the anterior portion of the M. masseter attachment on the zygomatic bone and of the M. temporalis insertion on the coronoid process and anterior ramal margin decreased the moment arms for these muscles during mastication. The increase in midfacial prognathism of the later Shanidar specimens was therefore associated with a reduction in the effectiveness of the masticatory apparatus for heavy and/or prolonged repetitive chewing.

It is possible that the anterior projection of the nasal aperture and the region around nasion in Shanidar 1 and 5 and other Neandertals is a biomechanical, as well as a spatial, consequence of this posterior placement of the zygomatic region. With a more posterior positioning of the zygomatic region vis-à-vis the arrangement present in Shanidar 2 and 4, the ability of the zygomatic bones and lateral supraorbital tori to resist bending moments on the upper facial skeleton from vertical incisal biting would have been reduced. An anterior positioning of the nasal aperture and the associated region around nasion would provide a more even arc of bone from the incisal alveoli to the anterior cranial vault, one that would be more effective in resisting and transmitting the bending moments in a sagittal plane.

These considerations suggest that the midfacial prognathism evident in the Shanidar 1 and 5 and other Neandertal faces was a product of a reduction of masticatory musculature massiveness and moment arms without any decrease in total facial projection. If different portions of the facial skeleton, such as the maxilla, the mandibular corpus, the dentition, and the zygomatic/ramal region, were under slightly different genetic and/or developmentally induced controls, it would not be surprising to see evolutionary reduction in one of these portions, such as the zygomatic/ramal region, prior to or independent of changes in the others. This would be possible as long as the different components still formed a functioning masticatory apparatus capable of generating and absorbing habitual levels of masticatory force.

The morphological change in facial form from the earlier Shanidar 2 and 4 to the later Shanidar 1 and 5 remains is probably representative of the changes that took place elsewhere in the Neandertal geographical range in the transition from an Early Neandertal morphology to that more usually recognized as Neandertal. The Shanidar sample thus provides both evidence of evolutionary change during the Mousterian in at least one region of the Near East and a model of how these alterations might have taken place throughout the Near East and Europe at various times in the early Upper Pleistocene (see following discussion).

The only other morphological shift evident on the Shanidar skull remains is an apparent reduction of nuchal robusticity, as the Shanidar 1 transverse nuchal torus is less pronounced than those of Shanidar 2 and probably Shanidar 4. Other regions of their crania, such as the mastoid process, are as variable within each subsample as between them or, as with the cranial vaults, are too altered and/or incomplete to permit an assessment of changes.

The Shanidar facial skeletons thus indicate evolutionary change between the two subsamples. It entails the development of a typical Neandertal facial configuration from that better known among their predecessors.

Trends in Body Proportions and Stature

It is possible to assess many aspects of body proportion among the Shanidar Neandertals (Chapter 11). However, few of the computable ratios permit comparisons among the Shanidar subsamples. The only ones for which at least one individual in each subsample provides data are relative facial size, relative neck length, and leg segment proportions (the crural index).

In the latter two cases, the individuals from both subsamples appear similar to each other. The Shanidar 1, 2, and 4 caudal cervical vertebral body heights are similar to each other, especially when they are normalized against femoral or tibial length. Similarly, the Shanidar 6 crural index of about 78.1 falls between the crural index of about 77.5 for Shanidar 1 and the range of about 78.3 to about 80.5 for the Shanidar 5 crural index. There does not appear to have been much, if any, change in body proportions through time among the Shanidar Neandertals.

There may have been a slight increase in stature from the earlier to the later subsample. If only the males are considered, so as to avoid biases from sexual dimorphism, the three later males—Shanidar 1, 3, and 5—have stature estimates that are above those of Shanidar 2 and 4 (Table 97). However, the difference between the two subsamples is less than 5% of their statures and is well within the margins of error of the regression formulae used to compute their statures.

Summary

In most aspects of their anatomy, the Shanidar Mousterian hominids exhibited stasis through time. Although there is variation across the sample in a number of features, most of that variation is as much within the two temporal subsamples as it is between them. And in most features, there is remarkable homogeneity of morphology for so large a hominid sample. The only region in which there is evidence for an evolutionary trend through time is in their facial skeletons. There is a development of midfacial prognathism from a flatter and more archaic midfacial region in the time from the early Shanidar subsample to that of the later one.

THE SHANIDAR NEANDERTALS AS NEAR EASTERN FOSSIL HOMINIDS

There have been numerous comments earlier on similarities and differences between the Shanidar specimens and the other Upper Pleistocene fossils from the Near East. Because the Shanidar sample is one of the largest known for the Upper Pleistocene of the Near East, it is of interest to assess where they fall chronologically, morphologically, and phylogenetically with respect to the other Near Eastern specimens.

The major problem in determining the evolutionary relationships of the various Near Eastern Upper Pleistocene fossil hominids, beyond morphological affinities, lies in uncertainties in their geological ages. Although a couple of the Levantine specimens have associated radiometric dates, most of the specimens or samples have only indirectly determined dates or relative ages.

The oldest Near Eastern Upper Pleistocene specimen is the Zuttiyeh 1 anterior cranium, which appears to date to the beginning of the last integlacial, or even slightly earlier (Gisis and Bar Yosef 1974; Schwarcz 1980). The Tabūn Layer E femoral diaphysis dates to the end of the last interglacial, and the Tabūn C2 mandible, from Layer C of Tabūn Cave, dates to around 50,000 to

60,000 years B.P. (Jelinek 1982). The Tabūn C1 partial skeleton probably derives from Layer C, but there is a possibility that it comes from Layer D of Tabūn Cave (Jelinek, personal communication, 1980). Its probable age could therefore be around 50,000 to 60,000 years B.P. or about 70,000 to 80,000 years B.P. (Jelinek 1982). The Tabūn Layer B remains are probably slightly less than 50,000 years old, and the Kebara 1 infant appears, on the basis of lithic comparisons (Jelinek 1982), to be about the same age. The Amud fossils are poorly dated and can only be referred to the Mousterian time period (Suzuki and Takai 1970); the same applies to the Bisitun 1 and Teshik-Tash 1 specimens.

The dates for the early anatomically modern human samples from Qafzeh and Skhūl are likewise difficult to determine. The Skhūl Layer B specimens, on the basis of comparisons of their associated lithics with those from the neighboring Tabūn Cave, appear to postdate the Tabūn Layer B material (Jelinek 1982).

Similar comparisons of lithics from the Qafzeh Mousterian levels (levels VII–XXIV) to those from Skhūl, Tabūn, and other Levantine sites suggest that the Qafzeh levels are either similar in age to those of Skhūl or even slightly younger (Jelinek 1982). However, earlier assessments of the Qafzeh lithics (Neuville 1951) and recent analyses of the Qafzeh microfauna, stratigraphy and sedimentology (Bar Yosef and Vandermeersch 1981; Farrand 1979; Haas, in Jelinek et al. 1973; Vandermeersch 1978b, 1981a) have suggested that the Qafzeh human remains may be considerably older, possibly 70,000–80,000 years B.P.

The microfaunal considerations consist primarily of the presence of two archaic rodents, *Arvicantis ectos* and *Mastomys batei*, in Qafzeh levels XV and XVII–XXIII and their absence from Tabūn Layer C and the absence of *Cricetalus migratorius* from the Qafzeh levels and its presence in Tabūn Layer C and more recent Levantine sites (Bar Yosef and Vandermeersch 1981). The question remains whether these faunal differences are due to chronological differences between the respective Qafzeh and Tabūn levels or are the result of different habitats being present at the coastal Tabūn and inland Qafzeh areas (Jelinek 1982). The stratigraphic considerations involve the correlation of the depositional hiatus between Layers C and D at Tabūn with the erosional event at the end of the Mousterian (top of level VIII) at Qafzeh (Bar Yosef and Vandermeersch 1981); it is uncertain whether these two events were the result of local climatic and/or karstic events or the products of a regional climatic shift (Bar Yosef and Vandermeersch 1981). The sedimentological data of Farrand (1979) has supported the earlier dates for the Qafzeh Mousterian levels, but it is not sufficient by itself to confirm the older age of these levels (Farrand personal communication, 1980). There have been several attempts to date the Qafzeh human remains by amino-acid racemization of both faunal and human material (Bada and Helfman 1976; Bar Yosef and Vandermeersch 1981; Masters 1982); however, the reliability of these amino-acid determinations is still uncertain (Masters 1982), especially given the lack of full consistency between the determinations and the relative stratigraphic positions of the samples. Clearly, further analyses, including radiometric dates, are needed to resolve this problem.

It is therefore possible to consider the Qafzeh hominids as either about 70,000 to 80,000 years B.P. in age or as somewhat less than 50,000 years old. The younger age would fit with the pattern known elsewhere in the Old World of anatomically modern humans always following archaic *H. sapiens* in time within any one region. It would also not require the coexistence of two distinct groups of *H. sapiens* in northern Israel for several tens of millennia, a situation that seems unlikely, given the biological and cultural similarities of these two groups. For these reasons, the younger date for the Qafzeh Mousterian remains will be used here, even though it is recognized that considerable data suggest an earlier date for them.

It is apparent that the chronological relationships of Near Eastern Upper Pleistocene fossils hominids are far from secure. Yet it is possible to arrange the remains into three samples: an Early Neandertal sample including Tabūn E1 and Zuttiyeh 1; a Neandertal sample consisting of Amud 1–5, Bisitun 1, Kebara 1, Shanidar 1–9, Tabūn B1–B4 and C1–C3 (Tabūn C4–C7 are part of Tabūn C1), and Teshik-Tash 1; and an early anatomically modern human sample consisting of the Qafzeh and Skhūl samples. It would be nice to know the ages of the Amud, Bisitun, Kebara, Tabūn, and Teshik-Tash remains relative to the two Shanidar subsamples, so as to determine whether the patterns of morphological change and stasis evident at Shanidar occurred elsewhere in the Near East. Unfortunately, that can only be done approximately and very tentatively.

The Postcrania

The many comparisons of the abundant Shanidar postcranial remains to those of other Near Eastern archaic *H. sapiens* have demonstrated a close resemblance between the limb remains of these individuals (Chapters 8 and 9). This morphological similarity is most evident in comparisons of the Shanidar postcrania to the Tabūn E1 femoral diaphysis, to the Bisitun 1 radial diaphysis, and especially to the Amud 1 limb bones. Whereas the Tabūn E1 and Bisitun 1 bones merely show a general resemblance to archaic *H. sapiens* postcrania, the Amud 1 partial skeleton exhibits a host of features that align it closely with the Shanidar specimens. These include the morphologies of the scapular axillary border, the *M. pectoralis major* and *M. pronator quadratus* attachments on the humerus and ulna, several features of the hand bones and especially of the first metacarpal, the pubic configuration, and the morphologies and robusticity of the femoral and tibial diaphyses.

In contrast, those of Tabūn C1 exhibit a mixture of differences and resemblances. (The Tabūn C3 femoral diaphysis is indistinguishable from those of Tabūn C1.) Most of the contrasts between the Tabūn C1 and Shanidar appen-

dicular skeletons involve robusticity; the general level of massiveness evident
in the Tabūn C1 remains is less than that of most Neandertals and approaches
that of early anatomically modern humans and recent humans in some anatomical regions. This is most evident in the sizes of the muscular attachment areas,
such as those of M. pectoralis major, M. pronator quadratus, and M. opponens
pollicis, in the relative sizes of the M. quadriceps femoris moment arms at the
knee, and in several diaphyseal robusticity indices. Yet the diaphyseal configurations of most of the Tabūn C1 long bones are similar to those of other Neandertals, the radius exhibits the characteristically Neandertal lateral bowing,
and at least one muscle attachment area, that of M. gluteus maximus, is quite
pronounced in size and rugosity. Furthermore, several of the distinctive aspects of the Shanidar and other Neandertal postcrania, such as the scapular
axillary border morphology, the superior pubic ramus thinning and elongation,
and the low crural indexes, are evident on the Tabūn C1 limb remains.

    The Tabūn C1 postcrania thus appear to be basically similar to those from
Shanidar in morphology, but they tend to be more gracile. Even though Neandertal females tend to be slightly less robust than the males (Trinkaus 1980), the
female nature of the Tabūn C1 remains does not fully explain its more gracile
condition; both Shanidar 6 and La Ferrassie 2 are almost as robust, if not just as
robust in most features, as known male Neandertals.

    There is the possibility that the relatively gracile nature of some of the
Tabūn C1 limb bones reflects part of an evolutionary trend not represented by
the other Near Eastern archaic H. sapiens postcrania. If this were so, the Tabūn
C1 specimen would have to postdate the Shanidar and Amud specimens; the
presence of the robust Tabūn E1 femur makes it unlikely that populations
preceding the Amud and Shanidar samples were less robust than these Neandertals. It is possible, given the uncertainties in the geological ages of all of the
Near Eastern archaic H. sapiens specimens, that Tabūn Layer C is more recent
than the Amud deposits and Shanidar Layer D. If so, the relative gracility of
Tabūn C1 could reflect a trend toward reduction in robusticity at the end of the
Neandertal period in the Near East. This hypothesis, however, is currently
untestable.

    Even though it is possible that the Tabūn C1 postcrania indicate the pres-
ence of a late, more gracile stage of the Neandertals in the Near East, the
morphological similarities between the Tabūn C1 postcrania and those from
Amud and Shanidar are much greater than the contrasts in robusticity between
them. Furthermore, aspects of the Tabūn C1 dentition and skull (see following
discussion) suggest that Tabūn C1 was more closely related to the other Near
Eastern Neandertals than to more recent humans. It therefore appears more
likely that Tabūn C1 was merely a Near Eastern Neandertal that experienced
less hypertrophy of the limbs than most of her contemporaries.

    The abundant postcranial remains of early anatomically modern humans
from the sites of Skhūl and Qafzeh contrast markedly with those of the preced-

ing Neandertals. The list of features that separate them morphologically from the Shanidar, Amud, Bisitun, and Tabūn remains is the suite of features that serve to distinguish Neandertal postcrania from those of more recent humans.

The initial impression of the Skhūl–Qafzeh postcrania is that they are considerably less robust than the Shanidar specimens. This is reflected in their diaphyseal and articular robusticity indices; in the modest breadths of their scapulae and the predominance of the bisulcate axillary border pattern; in the relatively small dimensions of their carpal tunnels, distal hand phalangeal tuberosities, and other musculoligamentous markings on their hand remains; and in the lack of enlargement of their M. quadriceps femoris moment arms at the knee. In addition, their femora exhibit exceptionally high neck–shaft angles, and their femoral diaphyses, although variable, tend to have large pilasters. Their pubic bones and their thumb proximal–distal phalangeal length proportions are indistinguishable from those of recent humans. And their crural indices are among the highest known for H. sapiens, comparable to those of European Early Upper Paleolithic hominids and equatorial recent humans.

It is apparent that in the period between the most recent of the Near Eastern Neandertals and the Skhūl–Qafzeh samples, there was a significant change in human postcranial morphology and proportions in the Near East. Most of the alterations reflect a general decrease in robusticity, but others, such as the changes in pubic morphology and limb segment proportions, may have been the products of other evolutionary shifts. It is not possible to determine how much time elapsed between the most recent Neandertals with postcrania and the Skhūl and Qafzeh samples, but it was certainly a small fraction of the period of postcranial morphological stasis among the Near Eastern Neandertals (Jelinek 1982). It therefore appears that in the Near East there was a long period during the early last glacial, and probably including much of the last interglacial, when there was little change in hominid postcranial morphology. This period was then followed by a considerably shorter span of time around the middle of the last glacial, during which a Neandertal, or archaic H. sapiens, postcranial morphological pattern was replaced by one that is within the ranges of variation of recent humans.

The Dentitions

All the Near Eastern earlier Upper Pleistocene dental remains, with the exception of the undiagnostic Tabūn E2 mandibular molar, derive from Neandertals and early anatomically modern humans. As with other comparative considerations of the Shanidar dental remains, it is primarily dental metrics that can be profitably compared.

The other Near Eastern Neandertal dental remains tend to be similar in size to those from Shanidar (Chapter 6). Tabūn B1 and C1 have slightly smaller

posterior teeth than those of the Shanidar individuals, especially those of
Shanidar 2 and 6, and both Amud 1 and Tabūn C1 have quite small second and
third molars. Yet other individuals, such as Tabūn BC2 and C2 and Teshik-
Tash 1, have larger posterior teeth, similar in size to those of Shanidar 2 and 6.
All of the Near Eastern Neandertals appear to have anterior teeth of sizes
comparable to those from Shanidar, and most important, three Levantine specimens, Amud 1 and Tabūn C1 and C2, exhibit the enlargement of the anterior
teeth relative to the posterior teeth that is characteristic of the Shanidar specimens and European Neandertals. The available data thus suggest that, despite
some variation in absolute size, all of the Near Eastern Neandertals exhibit the
pattern seen at Shanidar of having moderately-sized molars and premolars and
possessing relatively and absolutely enlarged incisors and canines. Even if it
were possible to arrange all of these Near Eastern specimens securely in chronological order, it is unlikely that any trends in dental size or proportions would
become evident.

The dental remains preserved for the Skhūl and Qafzeh human remains are
not greatly different from those of the preceding Near Eastern Neandertals in
overall size. The premolar and molar dimensions of the Skhūl–Qafzeh specimens are either similar to or even slightly larger than those of the Shanidar and
other Near Eastern Neandertal posterior teeth. The Skhūl–Qafzeh maxillary
anterior teeth likewise have diameters not greatly different from those of their
Near Eastern predecessors, although the mandibular anterior teeth from Skhūl
and Qafzeh, especially the mandibular incisors, are noticeably smaller than
those from Shanidar, Amud and Tabūn. Yet most of the Skhūl–Qafzeh individuals that preserve largely complete dentitions, Qafzeh 7 and 9 and Skhūl 4
and 5, have anterior to posterior dental proportions that are different from those
of Amud 1, Shanidar 1 and 2, and Tabūn C1 and C2. Only the Qafzeh 7
maxillary dentition exhibits the same relative enlargement of the incisors and
canines, whereas the Qafzeh 7 mandibular teeth and those from both jaws of
Qafzeh 9 and Skhūl 4 and 5 show the relative reduction of the anterior teeth
seen in European Early Upper Paleolithic specimens and more recent humans.
These data suggest that even though there was little change in dental dimensions across the archaic to anatomically modern *H. sapiens* transition in the
Near East, there was a shift in anterior to posterior dental proportions.

The Shanidar 7 deciduous teeth are likewise similar to those of other Near
Eastern Neandertals, primarily Kebara 1. The resemblance between the
Shanidar 7 and other Near Eastern Neandertal teeth lies mainly in their occlusal morphologies because the Shanidar 7 deciduous teeth tend to be slightly
smaller than those of Amud 3, Kebara 1, Teshik-Tash 1, and Tabūn B5. In
contrast, the few deciduous teeth from Skhūl and Qafzeh, although of similar
size to those of the Neandertals, exhibit simpler occlusal morphologies, closer
to the usual patterns evident among recent humans. Any change that might
have taken place across the archaic to anatomically modern human transition

in the Near East in deciduous teeth thus appears to be in terms of cusp morphology and not in size.

The Crania and Mandibles

Previous discussions have emphasized the morphological relationships among the facial skeletons of Shanidar 1, 2, 4, and 5 and those of other archaic *H. sapiens* from the Near East (Chapter 5). In the face, unlike the dentition and postcranial skeleton, there is an evolutionary trend through time between the Shanidar subsamples. Therefore, the other Near Eastern Neandertals and Early Neandertals can show considerable variation and still be morphologically close to at least a portion of the Shanidar sample.

The Zuttiyeh 1 remains appear to indicate a facial configuration similar to those of Shanidar 2 and 4, although the only features that can be compared are the lateral portions of the supraorbital tori, the zygomatic bones, the interorbital breadth, and the general curvature of the frontal bone. Basically, Shanidar 2 and 4 exhibit less midfacial prognathism than Shanidar 1 and 5 and the European Neandertals, a greater angulation of the zygomatic region, and generally more robust facial skeletons. The Zuttiyeh 1 specimen shares the same angulation of the zygomatic bone, although it is not possible to assess the spatial relationship of the Zuttiyeh 1 zygomatic bone to its now absent maxillae. It is also not possible to determine the degree of maxillary and mandibular prognathism on Zuttiyeh 1, but its high nasiofrontal angle suggests that nasal region and probably its lower midfacial regions were not as projecting. Other archaic *H. sapiens* specimens that do not show much midfacial prognathism, such as Arago 21, Irhoud 1, and Petralona 1, have relatively high nasiofrontal angles. Furthermore, among recent humans (17 samples) there is a low but positive correlation between nasiofrontal and zygomaxillary angles (average within-group correlation coefficients: males: 0.30, females: 0.32 [Howells 1973]), and a sample of archaic *H. sapiens* and early anatomically modern humans from Europe, the Near East, and Africa has an even stronger correlation between these two angles ($r = 0.48$, $N = 18$, $p < 0.025$). Shanidar 2 and 4 and Zuttiyeh 1 thus probably had similar degrees of midfacial projection.

Both Shanidar 4 and Zuttiyeh 1 have lateral supraorbital tori that are thick across to the region of the frontozygomatic suture and do not taper laterally, unlike those of Shanidar 1 and 5. On the other hand, the interorbital breadth of Zuttiyeh 1 is not as large as the estimate for the Shanidar 2 interorbital breadth, and the remaining pieces of the Shanidar 4 frontal bone appear to indicate a flatter nasion–bregma arc than that of Zuttiyeh 1. However, it is uncertain how reliable the estimates of these two features are for Shanidar 2 and 4, respectively. The available evidence thus suggests a basic similarity between the Zuttiyeh 1 and Shanidar 2 and 4 specimens.

The Amud 1 facial skeleton is clearly that of a Neandertal, and it approximates in many ways the configurations of the Shanidar 1 and 5 faces. In terms of overall robusticity, as indicated primarily by the relief on its mandibular corpus and rami and on its zygomatic bones, the Amud 1 face is less massive than either Shanidar 2 or 4 and does not differ significantly from Shanidar 1 and 5. The configuration of the Amud 1 supraorbital tori, especially, are reminiscent of those of Shanidar 1 and 5 and differ from those of Shanidar 4 and Zuttiyeh 1 because the different elements of the torus are marginally discernible and the lateral aspects of the tori taper slightly.

In terms of midfacial prognathism, Amud 1 gives the impression of having slightly less midfacial projection than Shanidar 1 and perhaps less than Shanidar 5. Its zygomaxillary angle of about 115° is the same as that of Shanidar 5 but above those of Shanidar 1 and the four European Neandertals that provide this measurement. And its molar alveolus–zygomaxillare radii difference of about 17.0 mm is below those of Shanidar 1 and 5 and four European Neandertals. It is possible that both of these measurements misrepresent the degree of midfacial prognathism of Amud 1; the nasal region of the Amud 1 cranium has been entirely reconstructed, and the position of the maxillary dentition relative to the zygomatic bones has been estimated by articulating the mandible with the temporal bones and placing the dentition in centric occlusion.

The configurations of the Amud 1 frontal and zygomatic bones suggest that he possessed Neandertal midfacial projection. His nasiofrontal angle of 129° is below those of all other Neandertals except La Quina 5, and his zygomatic bones are relatively flat and have a distinctly retreating profile. In addition, the rami of the Amud 1 mandible are narrow compared to its length, and there are large maxillary and mandibular retromolar spaces. It therefore appears that the Amud 1 face is morphologically close to those of Shanidar 1 and 5 and somewhat distinct from the flatter and heavier faces of Shanidar 2 and 4.

Despite these similarities with the Shanidar 1 and 5 faces, the superior length of the Amud 1 mandible relative to femoral or tibial length is shorter than those of any of the Shanidar specimens or European Neandertals; it approaches those of Near Eastern and European early anatomically modern humans. Is this merely a reflection of normal variation that is not otherwise indicated by the few sufficiently complete Neandertal partial skeletons, or is it an indication of a trend toward less facial projection in at least one of the Near Eastern Neandertal samples?

The morphological relationships between the Tabūn C1 and C2 facial skeletons and the Shanidar individuals are even more difficult to assess. Both exhibit several Neandertal features, but neither is sufficiently complete to resolve its morphological affiliation; Tabūn C2 is only a mandible, and Tabūn C1 lacks both zygomatic bones and much of the maxillae. The two Tabūn mandibles are also different from each other, with Tabūn C2 having a higher corpus, a more prominent mental trigone, and a relatively narrower rami than Tabūn C1; these differences could be considered either as normal or as sexual variation if they both derive from Layer C, or as reflections of an evolutionary trend if Tabūn C1 comes from Layer D.

The Tabūn C2 specimen is a large and robust mandible. Its surface markings, both in terms of structural features and muscle markings, are reminiscent more of the Shanidar 2 and 4 mandibles than of the Shanidar 1 mandible. Yet the size of the retromolar space and the relative narrowness of the rami imply a closer affinity to the later Shanidar subsample.

Subjective assessments of the Tabūn C1 reconstructed facial skeleton, in which the mandible is used to locate the position of the maxillary dentition, suggest that the degree of midfacial prognathism may have been less than that of Shanidar 1 and 5 and closer to that of Shanidar 2 and 4. This impression is supported by the relatively high (142°) nasiofrontal angle of Tabūn C1, which is at the top of the Neandertal range of variation, and by the large relative ramus breadth index (37.3) of the Tabūn C1 mandible, which is between those of Shanidar 2 and 4 and those of Shanidar 1, Amud 1, Tabūn C2, and most European Neandertals. In addition, the lateral portions of the supraorbital torus of Tabūn C1 lack the tapering seen in those of Shanidar 1 and 5 and Amud 1, but not of Shanidar 4 or Zuttiyeh 1.

These data imply that the morphological affinities of the Tabūn C1 face may be closer to the earlier Shanidar subsample than to the later one. If Tabūn C1 does indeed derive from Layer D of Tabūn Cave and date to the initial part of the early last glacial, these considerations might indicate that there was the same kind of evolution of the facial skeleton in the Levant as occurred around Shanidar during the same time period.

The last western Asian Neandertal specimen for whom the facial skeleton is sufficiently intact to indicate its overall configuration is the immature Teshik-Tash 1 skeleton. The remains of the 8- to 10-year-old individual retain a virtually complete skull, and the facial skeleton is remarkably similar to those of European Neandertal children of similar or slightly younger ages (Vlček 1970), especially La Quina 18 (Martin 1926b). There is an indication of midfacial prognathism and the beginning of supraorbital torus development. It appears likely that, if it had grown to adulthood, Teshik-Tash 1 would have had a facial configuration similar to those of Shanidar 1 and 5 and most European Neandertals (Alexeev 1981).

In contrast to these fine distinctions between the facial configurations of the few Near Eastern Neandertal specimens, some of which may not be evolutionarily meaningful, there is a clear morphological separation between their facial skeletons and those of the Qafzeh and Skhūl individuals. Their facial lengths (mandibular lengths) relative to femoral or tibial length are considerably below those of all Near Eastern Neandertals except that of Amud 1. Their zygomaxillary angles are all well above those of Shanidar 1 and 5, Amud 1, and European Neandertals, and those of Qafzeh 6 and 9 are even well above those of Shanidar 2 and 4. The molar alveolus–zygomaxillare radii differences of Qafzeh 6 and Skhūl 5 are below those of Shanidar 1 and 5 and Amud 1, although that of Qafzeh 9, largely as a result of its considerable alveolar prognathism, falls in the Neandertal range. And their zygomatic bones tend to be angled and lack the retreating profile of the later Shanidar specimens.

Despite these contrasts, the Qafzeh and Skhūl crania are quite robust. Skhūl 4, 5, and 9 have definite supraorbital tori, even though Qafzeh 3, 6, 7, and 9 and Skhūl 2 lack the full fusion of the supraorbital elements that defines a supraorbital torus. And the maxillae and mandibular corpori of at least the adult males are almost as robust as those of Shanidar 1 and Amud 1. In addition, the ramal breadths of the Skhūl–Qafzeh mandibles and very close to those of Shanidar 1, Amud 1, and Tabūn C1 and C2.

Most of the contrasts between the later Shanidar faces and those of the Skhūl–Qafzeh individuals may be primarily a result of their lesser total facial prognathism. Morphologically, it is possible to derive the Qafzeh and Skhūl facial configurations from that of the later Shanidar specimens by reducing total facial prognathism without moving the zygomatic and anterior ramal regions relative to the temporomandibular region. If that were done, the dentition and the associated mandibular corpus, anterior maxillae, and nasal region would move posteriorly relative to the zygomatic bones. Such a rearrangement of the midface would decrease midfacial prognathism and probably produce several of the other changes evident in the fossil record. The zygomatic bones would project more anteriorly relative to the maxillae, and there would be a greater angle between the zygomatic arch and the infraorbital region, producing a more angled zygomatic bone. In addition, the more posterior location of the dentition would decrease the moment arms for the bite force and thus reduce the amount of stress transmitted through the upper facial skeleton, especially by the masticatory musculature through the zygomatic and supraorbital regions; this could lead to the supraorbital torus reduction apparent in the Skhūl and especially Qafzeh specimens. Many of the other changes apparent between the Shanidar 1 and 5 faces and the Skhūl and Qafzeh faces could be seen as secondary consequences of changing spatial relationships in the face and alterations of the biomechanical stress patterns as a result of changing the position of the dentition relative to the masticatory musculature.

At present, it is not possible to determine whether these changes actually occurred across the morphological transition. Yet at least one of the Neandertal fossils, Amud 1, approaches the later sample in some features of the facial skeleton, and some of the later skulls, especially those of the Skhūl males, have features reminiscent of the earlier Neandertals. Thus, it provides a model for the transition from the Neandertal facial configuration to that of early anatomically modern humans. But at the same time, as with the postcrania, the amount of change evident in the time period between the most recent of the Neandertal facial skeletons and the earliest of the anatomically modern faces in the Near East was probably considerably more than occurred during equivalent amounts of time in the preceding period of gradual change in the Neandertal face.

The occipitomastoid regions of Amud 1 and Tabūn C1, the only other Near

Eastern adult Neandertals that retain this area, are generally similar to those of the Shanidar specimens. Amud 1 has a large mastoid process, whereas that of Tabūn C1 is small. Yet both of their mastoid processes appear to taper toward the tip and to exhibit anterior mastoid tubercles. Neither cranium has an external occipital protuberance, and both appear to have shallow suprainiac fossae. The Amud 1 occipitomastoid crest is relatively small and is dwarfed by its large mastoid process, whereas that of Tabūn C1 is large and extends inferiorly beyond the tip of the mastoid process; in this they resemble Shanidar 2 and 1, respectively. In addition, at least Amud 1 has a tympanic morphology close to those of Shanidar 1 and 5.

The Skhūl and Qafzeh occipitomastoid regions, on the other hand, are quite different and fall within the ranges of variation of robust recent humans. Again, the differences between the Shanidar and other Near Eastern Neandertals and the Skhūl and Qafzeh samples in this region parallel the contrasts between Neandertals and more recent humans in general.

The few and often incomplete archaic *H. sapiens* cranial and mandibular remains from the Near East are thus quite variable. They show differing degrees of morphological affinity to the two Shanidar subsamples, primarily in their developments of midfacial prognathism and overall facial massiveness. If one can be permitted to date the various specimens morphologically within the limits dictated by their archeological and geological contexts, it is possible to arrange the fossils in a reasonable and continuous sequence of morphological change. Obviously, such a scenario serves primarily to provide a hypothesis that concerns the evolution of the human face during the Upper Pleistocene in the Near East and that can be tested against future paleontological data.

The initial stage of the proposed sequence is represented by the Zuttiyeh 1 specimen, which is relatively robust and exhibits little midfacial prognathism. It is followed morphologically closely by the Shanidar 2 and 4 skulls. The next stage contains Tabūn C1, whose degree of midfacial prognathism appears to have been intermediate between those of Shanidar 2 and 4 and those of Shanidar 1 and 5, as suggested by her mandible, frontal bone, and remaining maxillary portions. The following stage, the one that includes the development of a Neandertal facial anatomy most like the contemporaneous European configuration, is occupied by Shanidar 1 and 5, Tabūn C2 and Teshik-Tash 1. The positioning of the Amud 1 specimen depends upon how one evaluates its midfacial and total facial prognathism in relation to the expected ranges of variation among the Near Eastern Neandertals in these features. Its affinities are closest to such individuals as Shanidar 1 and 5 and Teshik-Tash 1, but it may be considered as falling slightly to the anatomically modern side of them. The final stage is represented by the Skhūl and Qafzeh samples, with the Skhūl sample possibly being slightly earlier in the sequence than the Qafzeh specimens.

If one accepts this sequence of facial evolution in the Near East from the last interglacial to the middle of the last glacial, a regular pattern of facial changes through time can be seen to have occurred. The sequence starts with populations having large, robust, projecting faces; yet they exhibit little midfacial prognathism because their masticatory muscles are placed relatively anteriorly with respect to the dentition. This is a basically Middle and early Upper Pleistocene human facial pattern, even though the Zuttiyeh 1 and Shanidar 2 and 4 specimens do not have faces as robust as those of the earlier Middle Pleistocene fossil hominids. During the early last glacial, from the time of Shanidar 2 and 4, through the time of Tabūn C1, to the period of Shanidar 1 and 5, Teshik-Tash 1, and Tabūn C2, there is a reduction in facial robusticity accompanied by a retreat posteriorly of the masticatory muscles. This reduction of the face is not, however, accompanied by any decrease in total facial prognathism. This produces the Neandertal-like faces of these individuals, with their projecting midfacial regions, retreating zygomatic bones, and relatively narrow mandibular rami. Subsequently, there is a reduction in total facial prognathism, without any further posterior migration of the masticatory musculature. This results in the reduction of midfacial prognathism and associated features evident in the Skhūl and Qafzeh samples; the Amud 1 individual may represent the beginning of this last transition from an archaic human facial morphology to an anatomically modern one in the Near East.

This scenario does not assume, even as a hypothesis, that these changes necessarily took place continuously and/or gradually. It merely provides an evolutionary construct that permits the derivation of the Near Eastern Neandertal face from that of the Early Neandertals and the derivation of the Near Eastern robust early anatomically modern face from that of the Neandertals.

Summary

The detailed comparison of the Shanidar Neandertals to the other Upper Pleistocene Near Eastern fossil hominids provides an overall picture of human evolution during this time period in this region of the Old World. There appears to have been stasis from the late Early Neandertals through the Neandertals in postcranial morphology, despite some individual variation in overall robusticity. At least among the Neandertals of the Near East, there was little change in proportions within the dentition through time, although there was considerable variation in absolute dental dimensions. In both of these features and in morphological details of the posteroinferior cranium, there was a marked shift in morphology with the advent of anatomically modern humans. In contrast, the facial skeleton of Near Eastern Upper Pleistocene hominids appears to have gone through a series of changes from the Early Neandertal to the Neandertal to the anatomically modern human phases that can all be seen as parts of a shift from a robust Middle Pleistocene face and masticatory apparatus to a more gracile one close to those of recent humans.

PHYLOGENETIC IMPLICATIONS OF THE SHANIDAR NEANDERTALS

The data on all aspects of human skeletal anatomy that derive from the Shanidar Layer D fossils provide new insights into the phylogenetic relationships among Near Eastern archaic *Homo sapiens* and between them and more recent humans. Primarily, the much larger sample sizes furnished by the Shanidar specimens, and the associations of the bones in partial skeletons, permit the assessment of long-term trends in human morphology during the Upper Pleistocene of the Near East and of their implications for the possible evolution of Neandertals from Early Neandertals and of anatomically modern humans from Neandertals.

The Shanidar fossil remains, as discussed in the previous two sections, provide considerable support for local continuity of human populations in the Near East from the beginning or middle of the last interglacial to the middle of the last glacial. No matter how one arranges chronologically the various fossil specimens from Amud, Bisitun, Kebara, Shanidar, Tabūn, Teshik-Tash, and Zuttiyeh, as long as one follows the constraints placed on their dates by their proveniences, a pattern of postcranial and dental stasis and relatively gradual craniofacial change emerges. Although gene flow certainly existed between these populations and contemporaneous populations in Europe, Africa, and more eastern portions of Asia, it is not necessary to invoke an increase in the level of gene flow into the Near East to account for the evolution of the Neandertals from more archaic members of *H. sapiens* in the Near East.

It is assumed here, as discussed earlier, that the Qafzeh specimens were roughly contemporaneous with the Skhūl Layer B sample and postdated the Near Eastern Neandertals. Yet even if the earlier date for the Qafzeh sample (Bar Yosef and Vandermeersch 1981; Vandermeersch 1978b, 1981a; see earlier discussion) were correct, it would not be necessary to derive the Neandertal pattern from outside the Near East. It would only be necessary to explain how Neandertals and anatomically modern humans, as morphologically distinct members of the same species, remained genetically separate within a restricted geographical range for many millennia.

The major morphological shift in the Near Eastern sequence exists between the later Neandertals and the early anatomically modern Qafzeh and Skhūl samples. Despite the model just given for the transformation of the Near Eastern Neandertal face into an anatomically modern one, there were pronounced alterations across the transition in postcranial morphology and proportions, anterior to posterior dental proportions, and occipitomastoid morphology. Moreover, there was at least an acceleration of the rate of change of facial shape. These alterations must have been produced by a shift in selective pressures resulting in a marked shift in gene frequencies, and probably involving the introduction of new genetic material into populations in the Near East. The alterations appear to be too marked and anatomically pervasive to have been produced merely by environmentally induced changes during development. The probable genetic and populational complexity of such a suite of changes and the paucity of well-dated, roughly contemporaneous fossil hominids from neighboring areas of eastern Europe, Africa, and Asia precludes the determination of what types of genetic changes could have been responsible for this evolutionary shift.

Even though it is necessary to evaluate the European, African, and eastern Asian regional sequences of Upper Pleistocene human evolution each in its own terms, the phylogenetic patterns elucidated for the Near East by the Shanidar and other western Asian fossil hominids may provide useful models for interpreting the other Old World sequences.

The central and western European fossil record provides evidence of a similar series of morphological forms through time, even though some of the transitions may have taken place at different times than in the Near East. The lack of associated partial skeletons for European individuals with Early Neandertal facial configurations prevents the development of a model of facial evolution similar to that put forth here for the Near Eastern sequence using only European data. However, the available fossils from Europe make it likely that a similar evolutionary trend in facial anatomy took place in Europe (Smith 1982; Smith and Ranyard 1980; Wolpoff 1980a, 1980b). Likewise, the European dental and postcranial remains from the last interglacial to the middle of the last glacial suggest the same stasis in postcranial morphology and anterior to posterior dental proportions until the transition to anatomically modern humans. At that transition, similar changes in relative anterior dental size, pubic morphology, limb segment proportions, and robusticity appear to have taken place. It may well be that, despite the expected minor regional morphological variations, the evolutionary patterns among European and Near Eastern Upper Pleistocene humans were similar.

The Upper Pleistocene fossil evidence from Africa and eastern Asia is too incomplete to determine their sequences of morphological forms to the extent that is possible for the Near East and Europe. This situation is aggravated by the poor geological dating of the majority of the African and eastern Asian specimens. The scarcity of reasonably complete fossils applies especially to the postcranium and, to a lesser extent, to the dentition. However, the preserved facial remains indicate that the midfacial prognathism of Shanidar 1 and 5 and other Near Eastern and European Neandertals never evolved in Africa or eastern Asia.

In Africa, and possibly in eastern Asia, it appears that the transition from a large Middle Pleistocene human face to a shorter and more gracile anatomically modern human one involved a relatively early and possibly gradual reduction of robustness and total facial prognathism. In other words, as the masticatory musculature migrated posteriorly in conjunction with the decreasing facial massiveness evident in all of the Upper Pleistocene human fossil sequences, the position of the dentition relative to the temporomandibular region appears to have receded concurrently. As a result, the projection of the dentition and nasal region in front of the zygomatic and orbital region seen in the Neandertals is not in evidence among eastern Asian or African Upper Pleistocene archaic *H. sapiens*. Only the probably late Middle Pleistocene Broken Hill 1 cranium shows any evidence of midfacial prognathism, whereas its probable contemporary, the Bodo 1 cranium, merely has a large and robust Middle Pleistocene human face.

These reconstructions of evolutionary trends in different regions of the Old World and their phylogenetic implications derive in part from the insights into Upper Pleistocene Near Eastern human evolution provided by the Shanidar fossil human remains. Although the Shanidar specimens, in conjunction with other Near Eastern fossils, can provide models against which to evaluate the other regional sequences, the ultimate elucidation of specific regional patterns of *H. sapiens* evolution must depend upon the other fossil samples. The significance of the Shanidar fossils lies largely in the perspective they provide on the mosaic nature of *H. sapiens* anatomical evolution and the functional explanations of morphology they furnish for the evaluation of alternative phylogenetic reconstructions.

BEHAVIORAL IMPLICATIONS OF THE SHANIDAR NEANDERTALS

The paleontological implications of the Shanidar Layer D human remains do not lie entirely in the insights they provide into *H. sapiens* phylogeny. They also contribute significantly to our understanding of the behavioral patterns of the Neandertals. Because human anatomy is adapted to habitual behavior patterns, consistent differences between samples, and especially between temporally separated samples in a regional sequence, can provide information on shifts in behavior during human evolution. Because the Shanidar specimens greatly enlarge our samples of several anatomical regions for both the Near Eastern Neandertals and the total Neandertal group, they permit new insights into the habitual activity patterns of the Neandertals.

The Crania and Mandibles

The primary behavioral inference from the Shanidar skulls derives from the morphological changes between the earlier Shanidar 2 and 4 faces and those of the later Shanidar 1 and 5 individuals. Almost all of the differences between the faces of the two subsamples are products of a general decrease in robusticity and biomechanical effectiveness of the masticatory musculature. This implies that there was a relaxation of the selection that was responsible for maintaining the robust faces of Middle Pleistocene hominids, and that, as a consequence, the facial skeletons of these archaic *H. sapiens* gradually reduced. The relaxation of selection to maintain a large and robust face could involve decreases in the levels of biomechanical stress placed upon the facial skeleton and/or reductions in the amount of repetitive chewing of the kind that can lead to fatigue fractures. Either one is commensurate with the interpretations that food preparation techniques improved and paramasticatory dental use decreased during this time period.

Because there may be considerable time lag in the reduction of structures under conditions of relaxed selection, the actual behavioral shifts responsible for the reduced load on the Shanidar faces may have preceded the period of decreasing robusticity documented by the Shanidar fossils. The archeological materials associated with the Shanidar human remains are not sufficient to indicate whether there was a general improvement in human technology at Shanidar during this time period. However, analyses of the Levantine Middle Paleolithic sequence by Jelinek (1982) indicate that at least in the Levant there was a gradual increase in human technological abilities during the Mousterian; a similar shift may have occurred in the neighboring Zagros Mountains.

Other features of the Shanidar crania and mandibles that appear to have phylogenetic implications are of uncertain functional significance. Either they indicate a pattern that cannot be distinguished from that of more recent humans, such as the absolute and relative brain size of Shanidar 1, or their associations with behavioral patterns have yet to be ascertained, such as the various occipitomastoid and temporal traits.

In addition to these morphological features of the Shanidar skulls and their functional implications, the configurations of the Shanidar 1 and 5 cranial vaults provide insights into their behaviors. Both of these individuals appear to have experienced artificial cranial deformation as infants, which is reflected primarily in their flat frontal bones, their curved parietal bones, and the elevated position of lambda on Shanidar 5. This inferred presence of intentional body modification among the later Shanidar Neandertals implies a sense of personal esthetic among these people. The associated evidence for intentional burial of the dead (Chapter 2) and prolonged survival of the infirm (Chapter 12), together with this evidence for modification of personal appearances, indicate a heretofore poorly documented level of social cohesion for these prehistoric humans.

The Dentitions

The dental remains from the Shanidar adults furnish considerable information on how they used their teeth. Their posterior teeth appear to have been employed in mastication, much as most humans use theirs. Their incisors and canines, however, were utilized for extensive manipulation of the environment. This is apparent from their relative dimensions and their degrees and patterns of occlusal wear (Chapter 6).

The large dimensions of the Shanidar anterior teeth, both absolutely in relation to other hominid samples and relatively in relation to their molars and premolars, imply that they were using their anterior teeth for more than just chewing thoroughly cooked food. The large sizes of the teeth may indicate that they were applying considerable force through them. Alternatively, and more probably, the dimensions of the teeth may have been primarily an adaptation for high attrition; a larger tooth will wear down more slowly and remain functional longer, and it is not necessary to exert high levels of bite force in order to wear a crown down rapidly. This is especially relevant in light of the inference from their facial skeletons that their levels of bite force were lower than those of their predecessors.

Extensive wear of the Shanidar anterior teeth is evident in most of the Shanidar adult dentitions. Shanidar 1, 3, and 5 had each worn at least one incisor down to below its neck, Shanidar 4 had worn his incisors to the bases of their crowns, and Shanidar 2 had worn his anterior teeth considerably more than he had worn his cheek teeth. Furthermore, the Shanidar anterior teeth that have been examined microscopically exhibit traces of heavy wear, more than would normally be produced by chewing fully cooked and/or reasonably grit-free food.

The large dimensions of and heavy wear on the Shanidar anterior teeth suggest that they employed their teeth as a vise for manipulating various aspects of their natural and cultural environments. This is a behavior pattern that has been inferred for European Neandertals (Koby 1956; Ryan 1980). It is supported among the Shanidar Neandertals by the presence of transverse scratches on the labial surfaces of the Shanidar 2 incisors and the marked labial rounding of the incisors of Shanidar 1, 3, 4, and 5. They were apparently pulling at and cutting a variety of substances held in the teeth to an habitual extent that exceeded that known ethnographically for recent humans.

The Postcrania

The most pervasive aspect of the Shanidar postcrania is their massiveness. Although slightly reduced from that of Middle Pleistocene hominids, the robusticity of the Shanidar specimens equals that of their contemporaries and exceeds that known for anatomically modern humans. Even the Shanidar 7 infant shows traces of postcranial hypertrophy, suggesting that this was a pattern that started early in life. In addition, evidence of it persisted in the elderly Shanidar 3, 4, and 5 individuals and even in the partially incapacitated Shanidar 1 individual. The ubiquity of this robusticity in their axial and appendicular skeletons implies that it was an important part of their biological adaptation.

The diaphyseal, articular, and musculoligamentous hypertrophy of the Shanidar individuals' postcrania would have permitted them to generate and sustain considerably more strength and higher levels of activity on an habitual basis than most anatomically modern humans. However, the development, maintenance, and operation of such a hypertrophied body must have had significant energy costs that would have had to have been outweighed by the advantages conferred by the greater strength and durability. It therefore seems likely that the massiveness of the Shanidar individuals and other Neandertals was necessary for their survival in a way that it was not for early anatomically modern humans and subsequent human populations. The robusticity of the Shanidar Neandertals thus suggests that their cultural systems were less effective than those of the subsequent anatomically modern humans in promoting the survival of the individuals.

As with the facial skeleton, the postcranial robusticity of the Shanidar Neandertals could have been adapted for frequently elevated levels of biomechanical stress and/or persistent and repetitive stressful activities. It is not possible to determine which, if either, of these sources of stress was primarily responsible for the hypertrophy of their bodies; either one would fit with the foregoing interpretation that their massiveness was a biological compensation for deficiencies in the effectiveness of their culturally based subsistence technology. It is possible that the robusticity of the Shanidar Neandertals was primarily a pattern inherited from earlier Pleistocene human populations and was in the process of reduction under conditions of relaxed selection. However, the lack of evidence of reduction in the appendicular skeleton during the period from the last interglacial to the middle of the last glacial, its relative uniformity across the Shanidar and other Neandertal fossils, and its responsiveness to levels of biomechanical stress suggest that the appendicular skeleton was indeed a response to Neandertal behavioral patterns.

The phalangeal length proportions of the Shanidar 4, 5, and 6 thumbs and the relative flatnesses of the Shanidar 3 and 4 first carpometacarpal articulations suggest that the Shanidar individuals used their thumbs in slightly different ways than do more recent humans. This does not imply that they were incapable of the manipulative tasks performed by recent humans, but rather it suggests that the frequencies with which they performed different tasks varied from those common among more recent humans. The pollical phalangeal length proportions indicate that they probably used the power grip a greater percentage of the time than do more recent humans. This is an aspect of their general postcranial robusticity, and the same behavioral inferences would apply. The precise functional implications of their first carpometacarpal articular configurations are less clear, but they probably indicate that the Shanidar individuals had slightly greater mobility of their thumbs.

The low crural indices of Shanidar 1, 5, and 6 may also have been an adaptation for generating strength because the abbreviation of the distal limb segment would increase the leverages of the muscles acting around the knee, especially *M. quadriceps femoris.* However, among recent humans and probably the European Neandertals, this distal shortening of the leg reflects a thermoregulatory response for minimizing heat loss through the distal extremities in cold climates (Trinkaus 1981; see Chapter 11). Given the probably temperate climate of the Shanidar region during the period it was occupied by the Shanidar Neandertals, it is difficult to determine whether this pattern should be considered as part of their general robusticity or as a reflection of cold adaptation. If it was a product of the latter, it would imply that the Shanidar Neandertals had considerably less protection from the cold during growth and development than their early anatomically modern successors, as represented by the Skhūl and Qafzeh samples (Trinkaus 1981).

Two of the Shanidar individuals, Shanidar 1 and 3, exhibit an elongation of the superior pubic ramus. It is uncertain whether the other Shanidar individuals possessed similar pubic elongations, but the morphological similarities between the Shanidar 4 superior pubic rami and those of Shanidar 1 and 3 suggest that at least he had the same pubic enlargement. This mediolateral enlargement of the pubic bone relative to those of anatomically modern humans, without any associated relative increase in iliac and sacral breadths, indicates that these Shanidar individuals had exceptionally broad anterior pelves. The same pattern of pubic elongation is or probably was present in the Tabūn C1 and Krapina 208 females and the La Ferrassie 1 male.

As discussed in Chapter 9, this large size of the Neandertal anterior pelvis provided Neandertal females with larger pelvic aperture diameters than are present among anatomically modern humans. This relative enlargement of the pelvis would have permitted the Neandertals to have easier parturition and/or to have longer gestation periods and give birth to more mature infants than is possible for modern appearing humans. However, since the Neandertals preceded anatomically modern humans, this means that early anatomically modern humans had more difficult births and/or less mature neonates; both of these consequences of the pelvic changes in the transition from the Neandertals to modern appearing humans would have required more effective cultural practices in birth assistance and/or neonatal care to guarantee successful reproduction.

The lack of a selective advantage for greater difficulty with the birth process among anatomically modern humans and the obvious advantage provided by the earlier neurological development associated with a shorter gestation period suggests that the differences in pelvic diameters produced by the large anterior pelves of the Shanidar individuals and other Neandertals were indicative of differences in gestation length between these two human groups. The Shanidar and other Neandertals closely approximated the general mammalian pattern of gestation length relative to brain size, whereas anatomically modern humans were able to shorten gestation and provide their infants with a headstart on neurological development.

Summary

The fossil human remains from Shanidar thus imply that the Shanidar Neandertals had axial and appendicular skeletons and anterior dentitions that enabled them to perform through biological means many of the tasks that are accomplished through cultural practices in more recent human populations. This suggests that the level of cultural efficiency of these prehistoric humans was significantly less than that of recent humans and even early anatomically modern humans. Yet the evidence for facial reduction during this time and for artificial cranial deformation of the later Shanidar specimens indicates that they had made considerable cultural advances over their Middle and early Upper Pleistocene ancestors.

CONCLUSION

The large cave that overlooks the Shanidar Valley in northeastern Iraq thus provided shelter and a final resting place for nine individuals that have become known to us as the Shanidar Neandertals. The skeletal remains of these seven adults and two infants have been variably preserved in the deposits of the cave and were subsequently discovered during archeological excavations. They supply us with a window onto their anatomy, their biological relationships to previous, contemporaneous, and subsequent human populations, and their general behavioral patterns. Through the detailed descriptions of their individual bones and the comparisons of their morphologies to those known for other Pleistocene and recent humans, an image emerges of a group of prehistoric humans that closely resemble us in many ways but differ from us in others. As such, they furnish a perspective on that period of human existence that provided the background for the evolutionary emergence of modern humanity.

CHAPTER 14

Some Thoughts on the Evolution of the Neandertals

The descriptions and discussions of the Shanidar Cave Layer D human remains in the preceding chapters provide information and interpretations that have relevance to our understanding of the Shanidar sample and of Upper Pleistocene human evolution in the Near East. They are also relevant to our perception of the general patterns of evolution of the Neandertals across Europe and western Asia and their relationships to temporally and spatially neighboring samples of later Pleistocene humans. It therefore appears appropriate to conclude this monograph with a few thoughts on the evolution of the Neandertals.

The term *evolution* has slightly different meanings to various researchers. Here it is taken to include the relationships among samples of fossil humans as a reflection of original populational relationships, patterns of change within perceived lineages of humans, and the changes in behavior (or adaptations) of the humans in question. The first two aspects of evolution are discussed in the section on Phylogenetic Relationships and the last is considered in the section on Neandertal Behavior; both discussions follow a consideration of the history of scientific thought on Neandertals.

HISTORICAL BACKGROUND

The position of the Neandertals in human evolution, especially their phylogenetic relationship to anatomically modern humans, has remained a topic of controversy for more than a century (e.g., Boule 1911–1913; Brace 1964, 1981; Spencer and Smith 1981; Trinkaus 1982e; Vallois 1958). This is due in part to their chronological position as the immediate predecessors of modern-appearing humans in Europe and western Asia and in part to their status as the first, and for a long time the only, recognized group of archaic fossil humans. It is also a product of the wealth of fossil material that is available for the Neandertals; many of the evolutionary questions that can be evaluated for the Neandertal to anatomically modern human transition cannot be answered even tentatively for earlier periods of human evolution. As a result, much of what has been written about the Neandertals in recent years can be seen as reactions, in the light of new data and insights, to previous statements on their place in human evolution.

The Neandertals have been recognized as a prehistoric human group since the middle of the nineteenth century (Fuhlrott 1857; King 1864; Schaafhausen 1858), but it was not until there was a series of spectacular discoveries of their remains in central and western Europe around the turn of the century (e.g., Spy [Fraipont and Lohest 1887], Krapina [Gorjanović-Kramberger 1906], Le Moustier [Klaatsch and Hauser 1909b], La Chapelle-aux-Saints [Boule 1911–1913], La Quina [Martin 1910, 1912, 1923, 1926a, 1926b], and La Ferrassie [Boule 1911–13; Heim 1972]) that an assessment of their total morphological pattern was possible. The research of several workers, but especially that of Boule (1911–1913), established at this time that the Neandertals were incompletely human in a number of important functional anatomical complexes and, given their chronological proximity to early anatomically modern humans, could not have had anything to do with the ancestry of modern populations (Keith 1915; Boule 1921; Hooton 1931). It is this view that has dominated popular conceptions of the Neandertals and has served as a starting point for many recent evaluations of them (e.g., Brace 1964; Trinkaus and Howells 1979).

During the 1950s, this view of the Neandertals as an archaic human group that had nothing to do with the ancestry of modern humans was revised. By that time, earlier and more archaic human remains (e.g., *Homo erectus* and species of *Australopithecus*) were well represented in the fossil record and were recognized as generally ancestral to later humans. The Neandertals, in contrast to these earlier hominids, appeared surprisingly modern. As a result, most of the misconceptions of their functional anatomy were corrected (e.g., Arambourg 1955; Koenigswald 1958; Schultz 1955; Straus and Cave 1957; Toerien 1957), and they were included within *Homo sapiens* rather than being placed in their own species, "Homo neanderthalensis", as a recognition of their morphological and, by inference, phylogenetic proximity to modern humans (Dobzhansky 1944; Mayr 1951). These changes in interpretations of the Neandertals were in part a product of the evolutionary synthesis during the 1940s (Mayr and Provine 1980) that led to both the more rational taxonomy of the hominids currently used and more populational and adaptational approaches to the fossil record (e.g., Howell 1951, 1952; Coon 1962).

During the 1960s and the early 1970s, interest in the Neandertals waned, largely as more attention was given to discoveries of Lower Pleistocene and Pliocene hominids in Africa. However, research on the Neandertals continued, consisting of descriptions and analyses of new fossil discoveries in Europe and the Near East, reevaluations of previously known fossils, and occasional syntheses of Neandertal morphology with interpretations of their position in human evolution (e.g., Brace 1964; Bordes 1972; Brose and Wolpoff 1971; Coon 1962; Heim 1972, 1974; Howells 1975; Lumley 1973; Piveteau 1963–1965; Stringer 1974a; Suzuki and Takai 1970; Trinkaus 1975a; Twiesselmann 1961). The descriptions and analyses of the Shanidar fossils by Stewart (see References) formed part of this research and contributed to our knowledge and understanding of the Neandertals.

In recent years, there has been a resurgence of interest in the Neandertals, both as a sample of Upper Pleistocene humans to be understood in their own right and as a background for the origins of modern-appearing humans. This research has been complemented by new discoveries and analyses of Middle Pleistocene *H. sapiens* fossils (the Early Neandertals in Europe and western Asia), African and east Asian contemporaries of the Neandertals, and anatomically modern human successors of the Neandertals in the Near East and Europe. It is therefore possible, as in the foregoing discussions of the Shanidar Layer D human remains, to evaluate the morphology of the Neandertals reasonably well with respect to those of their temporal and spatial neighbors and to draw phylogenetic and behavioral implications from these comparisons.

PHYLOGENETIC RELATIONSHIPS

The evaluation of the phylogenetic relationships of the Neandertals to neighboring groups involves considerations of their morphological, and by inference genetic, affinities to their predecessors (the Early Neandertals of Europe and western Asia), their African and east Asian contemporaries, and their anatomically modern human successors. The evaluation of their relationship to the last group requires a discussion of the patterns of change through time within the Neandertal sample.

The Neandertal sample, as discussed in Chapters 3 and 13, is defined by a total morphological pattern that is known only from Europe, the Near East, and central Asia from approximately the end of the last interglacial (roughly 75,000–80,000 years B.P.) to the middle of the last glacial (roughly 35,000–40,000 years B.P.). (For a description of Neandertal morphology, see Chapter 13.) The exact ages for the oldest and youngest Neandertal samples vary, depending upon the accuracy of available dates, individual variation in evaluating the morphological affinities of certain fragmentary fossils, and what region of Europe and western Asia is being considered.

Recent years have seen the expansion of the sample of European *H. sapiens* specimens that antedate the Neandertals, primarily from western Europe (Lumley and Lumley 1971, 1979; Piveteau 1976; Vandermeersch 1978a) and the reevaluation of most of the previously known specimens (Hublin 1978a; Stringer 1974a, 1974b, 1981; Stringer *et al.* 1979; Trinkaus 1982c; Wolpoff 1980a). Despite problems of relative dating of a number of the specimens (Cook *et al.* 1982; Stringer 1981), it is now apparent that all of them can be seen as part of a lineage that leads from the earliest inhabitants of Europe (late *H. erectus* or early *H. sapiens*, depending upon where one places the boundary between these chronospecies) to the Neandertals of the early last glacial. All of the specimens that have been considered to be morphologically closer to modern humans than to the Neandertals (e.g., the "Pre-sapiens" specimens from Fontéchevade and Swanscombe [Vallois 1958]) have been shown to be well within the ranges of variation of their Middle or early Upper Pleistocene contemporaries (Cook *et al.* 1982; Hublin 1978a; Stringer 1974a; Trinkaus 1973).

In this lineage, there was a gradual reduction in overall cranial massiveness, which appears to have been associated with a steady increase in endocranial capacity. Even though there are no sufficiently complete partial skeletons that would permit the formulation of a model of facial reduction and midfacial prognathism development such as that derived from the Near Eastern archaic *H. sapiens* specimens (Chapters 5 and 13), the preserved mandibles and upper facial skeletons suggest that a similar pattern of continued pronounced total facial prognathism associated with a posterior migration of the zygomatic and anterior ramal region occurred in the transition from Early Neandertals to Neandertals in Europe. This transition in facial morphology appears to have been relatively gradual since some specimens that date to around the time of the last interglacial (e.g., the Krapina and Saccopastore specimens) exhibit facial features that are, in some respects, intermediate between earlier and later samples.

Associated with these shifts in cranial morphology and robustness is a reduction in dental dimensions (Wolpoff 1979). The anterior teeth of these predecessors of the Neandertals exhibit the same absolute and relative enlargement seen among the Neandertals, suggesting that the relatively large anterior teeth of the later sample may be primarily a continuation of a previously existing pattern.

Postcrania are rare and generally fragmentary for European Early Neandertals. However, the few diagnostic elements (primarily the Ehringsdorf 5 femoral diaphysis [Weidenreich 1941] and various lower limb remains from Arago [Lumley and Lumley 1979]) suggest that there was little morphological difference between European Early Neandertal and Neandertal postcranial morphologies. There is only a suggestion of a modest gracilization between these two samples.

In the Near East, as discussed in Chapter 13, only the Zuttiyeh 1 and Tabūn

Layer E remains antedate the Neandertals and provide diagnostic morphological information. Although the Zuttiyeh 1 specimen has recently been seen as
distinct from the Neandertals and morphologically closer to early anatomically
modern humans from Qafzeh and Skhūl (Vandermeersch 1981b), it is probably
best considered as a late Early Neandertal that is similar to the Shanidar 2 and 4
specimens (Chapter 13).

It therefore appears that the evolution of the Neandertals from their predecessors can be seen as a relatively gradual process that occurred around the
time of the last interglacial across Europe and western Asia. It is not necessary
to invoke any increase in the levels of gene flow across this area to explain the
sequence of morphological changes evident in the fossil record.

The African and eastern Asian contemporaries of the Neandertals are still
poorly known, and it is primarily their crania and mandibles that provide
indications of affinities. Despite serious problems of geological dating, it is
possible to say that there were groups of humans during the first half of the
Upper Pleistocene in Africa and eastern Asia that were of a similar evolutionary grade as the Neandertals (more likely the same grades as the later Early
Neandertals and the Neandertals) (Day et al. 1980; Ennouchi 1962; Hublin and
Tillier 1981; Rightmire 1978, 1981; Tobias 1967; Wei 1979; Woo and Peng
1959). This is indicated primarily by the general level of robustness of their
crania and mandibles and their platycephaly. These specimens do not, however, appear to have possessed the suite of occipitomastoid traits common among
the Neandertals (Hublin 1978a; Santa Luca 1978), and they do not exhibit, or do
not appear to have exhibited, the midfacial prognathism of the Neandertals.
Even though there undoubtedly was considerable gene flow between these
African and eastern Asian archaic H. sapiens populations and the Neandertals
(especially those in western Asia), they are probably best viewed as the evolutionary products of semi-independent lineages during the late Middle and early
Upper Pleistocene.

There are a few specimens of anatomically modern humans from Africa that
appear to have been contemporaneous with the Neandertals. These are the
fossils from Dar-es-Soltane 2 (Ferembach 1976), Omo-Kibish (Day 1969),
Klasies River Mouth (Rightmire 1981; Singer and Wymer 1982) and perhaps
Border Cave (Beaumont et al. 1978). Even though there are difficulties in determining the exact ages of some of these fossils, they clearly indicate that modern-appearing humans were present in Africa by at least 40,000 years B.P. and
probably more than 50,000 years B.P., well before they existed in Europe or
western Asia.

Throughout the history of Neandertal studies, the primary research question has been whether they can justifiably be considered as direct ancestors of
the subsequent populations of modern-appearing humans. The majority of research has been directed at determining whether the observed anatomical differences between the Neandertals and their successors are sufficiently pro-

nounced to have prohibited the transformation of Neandertal morphology into that of early anatomically modern humans in the time available between the most recent Neandertal populations and the oldest modern-appearing human individuals. A brief review of the recent literature on the Neandertals (e.g., Smith 1982; Stringer 1982; Trinkaus and Howells 1979; Vandermeersch 1981a, 1981b; Wolpoff 1980b) makes it evident that human paleontologists are far from reaching a consensus on this issue.

Considerations of the evolutionary relationships between the Neandertals and their successors should take into account the amount of morphological change that took place across the transition, the time available for the anatomical shift, and whether there were previously existing trends that could allow the transition to be seen merely as a continuation with acceleration of established evolutionary trends.

The anatomical alterations across the transition between the Neandertals and their early anatomically modern human successors are described in detail in Chapters 5–11 and are summarized in Chapter 13. Briefly, the alterations include a reduction in total facial prognathism with associated changes in midfacial prognathism, maxillary morphology, zygomatic curvature, and supraorbital torus morphology. There is frequency shift toward less platycephaly without any change in endocranial capacity. The Neandertal occipitomastoid configuration largely disappears. There is a reduction in anterior dental dimensions without any change in posterior tooth size. The pubic bone shortens mediolaterally, thereby decreasing the size of the pelvic aperture relative to body size. There is a generalized reduction in postcranial robusticity, which is evident primarily in the appendicular skeleton, and there is a marked increase in crural indices, which may be related to the decrease in robusticity and/or patterns of cold adaptation.

In both Europe and the Near East, there is a trend through time among the Neandertals toward less robust facial skeletons and neurocrania. This is reflected in the general dimensions of the facial skeleton and cranial vault thicknesses (Wolpoff 1981; Chapters 5 and 13) and in reductions of the supraorbital torus (Smith and Ranyard 1980). However, there does not appear to have been any reduction in the amount of total facial or midfacial prognathism until the transition to modern-appearing humans (Chapter 5). The craniofacial gracilization is accompanied, at least in Europe, by a gradual decrease in overall dimensions of permanent teeth (Wolpoff 1981), even though the proportions of the anterior–posterior dental dimensions do not appear to have altered significantly until the appearance of anatomically modern humans (Brace 1979; Chapter 6). Interestingly, deciduous teeth do not appear to share this trend (Wolpoff 1980b; Chapter 10).

The postcranial skeletons of the Neandertals, in contrast, exhibit no discernible trend towards the more gracile condition of more recent humans. This is apparent in both the Near East (Chapter 13) and in Europe. It is evident in their pubic morphologies (Trinkaus 1976b; Chapter 9), their axial and appendicular robusticity (Stoner 1981; Trinkaus 1975a, 1976a, 1977a, 1980; Chapters 7–9), their thumb morphologies (Musgrave 1971; Stoner 1981; Chapter 8), and their limb segment proportions (Trinkaus 1981; Chapter 11).

There was therefore a mosaic of evolutionary trends through time among the Neandertals. Some features, such as craniofacial massiveness and permanent tooth size, changed in the direction of more recent humans, whereas anterior–posterior dental proportions, deciduous tooth size, and postcranial morphology exhibited stasis. It is not possible, given the genetic and developmental complexities of all of these features, to say which aspects of their anatomy are most important in indicating the general pattern; it is most likely that no one feature is, and therefore all of them have to be taken into consideration to evaluate the patterns of change through time among the Neandertals.

One of the primary reasons that many researchers have excluded the Neandertals from recent human ancestry has been the apparent lack of sufficient time between the most recent Neandertal specimens and the oldest anatomically modern human ones to permit the transformation of the total morphological pattern of the Neandertals into that of their temporal successors. Revisions and refinements in the geochronology of the last glacial, reanalyses of previously excavated sites, and studies of new sites with human remains are constantly altering the exact dates of the transition, and it is unlikely that its age and duration will be securely known for some time. It is possible, however, to approximate the age of the transition for regions of western Europe (mainly southwestern France), central Europe (mainly the Pannonian Basin), and western Asia (mainly the Levant).

The most recent Neandertal remains from western Europe are those from Saint-Césaire, recently discovered in association with a Châtelperronian industry (Lévêque and Vandermeersch 1980, 1981; Vandermeersch 1981c). Although exhibiting some gracilization of the facial skeleton, the total morphological pattern of the Saint-Césaire 1 partial skeleton falls clearly within the Neandertal range of variation and is separate from that of anatomically modern humans (Vandermeersch 1981c). The hominid level at Saint-Césaire has not yet been dated radiometrically, but dates for Châtelperronian levels in other western European sites range from about 31,000 to about 35,000 years B.P. (Harrold 1981). It therefore appears unlikely that the Saint-Césaire Neandertal is older than about 35,000 years, and it may be much younger.

The oldest anatomically modern humans remains in western Europe are those associated with the Aurignacian, an industry that has yielded the remains only of modern-appearing humans (the Combe-Capelle 1 skeleton, originally attributed to the Châtelperronian [Klaatsch and Hauser 1909a], almost certainly derives from more recent [probably Aurignacian] levels). The Aurignacian begins in western Europe about 34,000 years B.P. (Movius 1969), and it is unlikely that the oldest anatomically modern skeletal material is much younger than about 32,000 years B.P. (Movius 1969). It thus appears that the transition, at least in western Europe, was relatively rapid, taking place in less—probably considerably less—than 5000 years.

The timing of the transition is less well known for central Europe, but recent excavations and analyses allow some precision (Smith 1982). The most recent Neandertals, which are probably those from Vindija (Wolpoff et al. 1981), are at least 40,000 years old. Although Neandertal in their total morphological pattern, they show some reduction of facial massiveness, especially in the supraorbital torus and the mandibular corpus. They are followed in time by Aurignacian-associated specimens from the sites of Brno, Hahnöfersand, Mladeč, and Velika Pećina, all of which date to around 34,000 years B.P. (Bräuer 1980; Smith 1982). These early anatomically modern specimens from Aurignacian contexts are generally robust, especially the males, and approach or match earlier Neandertal specimens in a number of craniofacial dimensions (Bräuer 1980; Smith 1982; Wolpoff 1981); however, their total morphological patterns (cranial and postcranial) are distinct from those of the Neandertals. It therefore appears that the transition in central Europe, although occurring about the same time or slightly earlier than the shift in western Europe, may have had a slightly longer duration.

The dating of the transition in the Near East is considerably more complicated than in western or central Europe (Chapter 13). The Neandertals with the most recent dates are probably Shanidar 1 and 5 (Chapter 2) and Kebara 1 (Jelinek 1982); they appear to date to between 40,000 and 50,000 years B.P. The Skhūl specimens are slightly younger than these specimens (Jelinek 1982). The Qafzeh remains, however, are more difficult to date. Considerations of the microfauna and geology of the hominid levels at Qafzeh suggest a date in the vicinity of 70,000 to 80,000 years B.P. (Bar Yosef and Vandermeersch 1981), whereas analysis of the associated lithic antifacts suggests that the hominids are of an age similar to or more recent than those from Skhūl (Jelinek 1982; Chapter 13). Acceptance of the older date for the Qafzeh specimens would imply that there was a period of 20,000 to 30,000 years during which both Neandertals and anatomically modern humans occupied a relatively small region of the Levant, a situation that appears improbable. Acceptance of the younger date would eliminate the need to account for the coexistence of two closely related human groups in a local area for so long a period of time. However, even assuming that the younger date for the Qafzeh remains is more accurate, none of these determinations is sufficiently precise to indicate whether the period of transition in the Levant was a few or many millennia.

These considerations suggest that the morphological shift from a Neandertal morphology to a robust but anatomically modern one occurred in a relatively short period of time in western Europe, a slightly longer time in central Europe, and an uncertain but perhaps longer period of time in the Near East. It should be kept in mind that these estimates for the length of the transition are probably maximum figures; the actual amount of time between the two groups may be less in these or other portions of their geographical distribution. Regardless of the actual amount of time involved in the transition, it is apparent that this was a period of an accelerated rate of change in human morphology. This is especially true for those aspects of the postcrania and dental proportions that exhibit stasis among the Neandertals, but it applies as well to the craniofacial morphology and dental dimensions that appear to have changed during the early last glacial.

What do these considerations mean for the phylogenetic relationships between the Neandertals and their modern-appearing successors? They indicate that there were a considerable number of morphological changes in most regions of the anatomy, and that it is unlikely that they could have all been produced by environmentally induced changes during development and/or minor shifts in gene frequencies. It therefore seems that there must have been an appearance of new genetic material in the gene pools of Neandertal populations, probably as a result of gene flow, between Neandertal populations and/or from non-Neandertal human groups in neighboring geographical areas. Similar gene flow undoubtedly took place throughout the Middle and Upper Pleistocene, but the increased rate of change at the time of the Neandertal-to-anatomically-modern-human transition suggests that there was a marked elevation in the level of gene flow throughout this region at this time in human evolution. This conclusion is supported by the relative uniformity of the total morphological pattern of the early anatomically modern humans across Europe and the Near East; in the absence of an elevated level of gene flow at this time, greater variation would be expected between the samples from the ends of the geographical range under consideration here immediately following so marked a morphological shift.

This interpretation does not mean that the same pattern of gene flow or the same rate of change occurred throughout Europe and western Asia at this time in human evolution. The natural complexity of human population dynamics, combined with the geographical diversity and size of the Neandertal range, makes this unlikely. It merely means that even though there was undoubtedly some population continuity across this transition, it is improbable that the anatomical changes evident in the fossil record took place without an elevation in the rate of exchange of genetic material between populations.

It is difficult to specify the exact sources of the new genetic material that appear to have been necessary for this transition to occur. Some of it undoubtedly arose within Neandertal populations. Other aspects were probably derived from outside the Neandertal range, perhaps in Africa where anatomically modern humans arose prior to their appearance in the Near East or Europe. The actual sources of the new variations may remain indeterminate, given the fragmentary nature of the human fossil record and the impossibility of determining the manner of genetic control of most of the morphological features observable in the fossil record. However, it should be evident that the evolutionary transition from the Neandertals to their modern-appearing human successors was both a rapid shift in human morphology and one that was undoubtedly the result of evolutionary processes far more complicated that most explanations of it would have us believe.

NEANDERTAL BEHAVIOR

The morphological patterns of the Neandertals and their evolutionary neighbors do not merely contain information about the phylogenetic relationships among these human groups. They also provide insights into changes in patterns of behavior through time. Because morphology reflects habitual behaviors, changes in human anatomy through time should reflect shifts in the behavioral or adaptive modes of these humans. Once the behavioral implications of the observable anatomical alterations have been deciphered, it should be possible to combine them with the more complete data from the contemporary archeological record to create a composite picture of human adaptive evolution during the latter half of the Pleistocene.

The descriptions and discussions of the Shanidar specimens in Chapters 5 to 12 have included a number of interpretations as to the behavioral implications of their morphological patterns, and these interpretations have been summarized in Chapter 13. Because the Shanidar sample includes specimens of virtually all portions of the skeleton that are known for the Neandertals, these considerations have contained comments on most aspects of Neandertal behavior as discernible from their fossils. The comments here will therefore merely summarize the general behavioral implications of the changes that occurred across the Early Neandertal to Neandertal transition, during the evolution of the Neandertals, and at the transition to anatomically modern humans.

The anatomical changes from the European and Near Eastern Early Neandertals to the Neandertals, to the extent that they can be determined, given the incomplete nature of most Early Neandertals, appear to consist primarily of a slight gracilization of the entire anatomy. This is reflected in an apparent, but difficult to confirm, slight decrease in postcranial robusticity, and in similarly modest shifts in craniofacial massiveness and dental dimensions. The single marked shift, and the one usually used to differentiate Neandertals from their predecessors (Chapter 13), is the increase in midfacial prognathism produced by a posterior migration of the zygomatic and anterior ramal region without any change in total facial prognathism. All of these changes imply that the biomechanical loads habitually placed upon their skeletons were slightly and gradually decreased during the relatively long period of transition from one group to the other. The archeological record for this same general time period (late Middle and early Upper Pleistocene) suggests that a similar gradual shift in technology took place, at least across most of Europe and the Near East (Jelinek 1982; Ronen 1982; Tuffreau 1979).

During the evolution of the Neandertals themselves, a mosaic of behavioral change and stasis appears to have taken place. Behaviors directly involved with food preparation, especially those that would have reduced the load on the facial skeleton and indirectly on the rest of the cranium, appear to have increased gradually in effectiveness among the Neandertals. This is probably the reason for the modest reductions in craniofacial size and massiveness and the decrease, at least in Europe, of overall dental dimensions. Paramasticatory use of the anterior dentition does not appear to have decreased, given the persistence of relatively large incisors and canines and high levels of wear on those teeth. In addition, the variety of behaviors involved with food acquisition, most of which would involve primarily the postcranial, and especially the appendicular, skeleton, do not appear to have altered significantly during this time period. Otherwise, there would not have been the stasis in postcranial robusticity evident in the Neandertal fossil record; this is especially true given the tendency of the appendicular skeleton to atrophy under conditions of reduced biomechanical loads (Tschantz and Rutishauser 1967; Turek 1967). The well-known associated archaeological record (mostly Middle Paleolithic) suggests a similar pattern, with most aspects of the technology and subsistence pattern apparently changing little despite the existence of some gradual improvements in technology (Binford 1982; Bordes 1981; Jelinek 1982).

In marked contrast to these implied gradual improvements in human adaptive patterns among the Early Neandertals and Neandertals, there was a major shift in many aspects of human behavior around the time of the transition from the Neandertals to modern-appearing humans. Although some anatomical regions, such as the neurocranium and posterior dentition, changed little if at all, implying no significant shift in the associated behaviors, many regions altered noticeably. These include: (1) anterior dental size and attrition reductions, which imply a decrease in paramasticatory dental use; (2) decreased prognathism, which suggests a lowering of the loads placed upon the facial skeleton; (3) changes in thumb morphology, which imply shifts in the habitual patterns of use of the hand; (4) generalized reduction in postcranial robusticity, which indicates a significant decrease in the levels of biomechanical stress on the anatomy; (5) increase in crural indices, which are part of the general postcranial robusticity reduction and/or indicate increased protection from cold stress, especially during development; and (6) a reduction in pelvic aperture size, which indicates a reduction in gestation length and, as a consequence, increased abilities to deal with more immature neonates. All of these anatomical changes strongly suggest that there was a marked improvement in human abilities to deal with adaptive pressures through nonbiological (cultural) means. This interpretation is supported by the archeological record (e.g., Binford 1982; Harrold 1980; Jelinek 1982; Klein 1973; Marshack 1972; White 1982), which indicates that there were major changes in most aspects of the human cultural repertoire at this time and that most of these cultural alterations served to improve human adaptive abilities.

The behaviors inferred from the anatomical changes evident in the human fossil record thus are similar to those implied by the archaeological record, with periods of slow or rapid change in each occurring about the same times during the late Middle and Upper Pleistocene. This suggests that there was a close interrelationship between these cultural and biological alterations. The precise natures of the possible feedback relationships between culture and biology cannot be determined at this time, and it is likely that they were quite varied (Trinkaus 1982b). Each, however, provides its insight into the behavioral evolution associated with the Neandertals and the origin of anatomically modern humans.

These interpretations of changing behavior patterns derived from the shifts in human anatomy during the latter part of the Pleistocene in Europe and the Near East suggest that Neandertals were the most recent participants in a level of cultural adaptation that was significantly less complex and efficient than that of anatomically modern humans.

CONCLUSION

The fossil record for the Neandertals and their temporal and spatial neighbors from the Middle and Upper Pleistocene indicates a mosaic of evolutionary change and stability. From the Middle Pleistocene to the middle of the last glacial, there was relatively slow change in human anatomy and the associated behavioral patterns. Some functional complexes, particularly those associated with mastication, changed gradually toward a more gracile condition, whereas others, especially those concerned with manipulation and locomotion, changed very little. This period, characterized by archaic *Homo sapiens* morphology and paleocultural behavioral patterns, was replaced relatively rapidly approximately 35,000–40,000 years ago by an anatomical and behavioral complex that was close to those of recent hunter–gatherers. The Neandertals therefore represent the end of the period of human evolution that provides the background for the emergence of modern humans. It is from them and their adaptive patterns that the morphology and behavioral patterns of our own immediate predecessors evolved.

References

Akabori, E.

    1934   Septal apertures in the humerus in Japanese, Ainu and Koreans. *American Journal of Physical Anthropology* **18**:395–400.

Akazawa, T.

    1975   Preliminary notes on the Middle Palaeolithic assemblage from the Shanidar Cave. *Sumer* **31**:3–10.

Alexandersen, V.

    1967   The pathology of the jaws and the temporomandibular joint. In *Diseases in antiquity*, edited by D. R. Brothwell and A. T. Sandison. Springfield: Thomas, Pp. 551–595.

Alexeev, V. P.

    1981   Fossil man on the territory of the USSR and related problems. In *Les processus de l'hominisation*, edited by D. Ferembach. Paris: Éditions du C.N.R.S. Pp. 183–188.

Allen, J. A.

    1877   The influence of physical conditions in the genesis of species. *Radical Review* **1**:108–140.

Anderson, D. L., G. W. Thompson, and F. Popovich

    1977   Tooth, chin, bone and body size correlations. *American Journal of Physical Anthropology* **46**:7–12.

Angel, J. L.

    1972   A Middle Paleolithic temporal bone from Darra-i-Kur, Afghanistan. In Prehistoric Research in Afghanistan (1959–1966), edited by L. Dupree. *Transactions of the American Philosophical Society* **62**:54–56.

    1974   Patterns of fractures from Neolithic to modern times. *Anthropologiai Kozlemenyek* **18**:9–18.

Anthony, R., and P. Rivet

    1907   Contribution à l'étude descriptive et morphologénique de la courbure fémorale chez l'homme et les anthropoïdes. *Annales des Sciences Naturelles: Zoologie.* Série 9, 6:221–261.

Arambourg, C.

    1955   Sur l'attitude, en station verticale, des néanderthaliens. *Comptes Rendus de l'Académie des Sciences, Paris.* Série D, **240**:804–806.

473

Bada, J., and P. Helfman
  1976   Application of amino-acid racemization in paleoanthropology and archaeology. *Colloque du Union Internationale des Sciences Préhistoriques et Protohistoriques. IXe Congres* **1**:39–62.
Bar Yosef, O, and B. Vandermeersch
  1981   Notes concerning the possible age of the Mousterian layers in Qafzeh Cave. In *Préhistoire du Levant*, edited by P. Sanlaville and J. Cauvin. Paris: Éditions du C.N.R.S. Pp. 281–285.
Barnett, C. H., and J. R. Napier
  1952   The axis of rotation at the ankle joint in man. Its influence upon the form of the talus and the mobility of the fibula. *Journal of Anatomy* **86**:1–9.
Barnicot, N. A., and R. H. Hardy
  1955   The position of the hallux in West Africans. *Journal of Anatomy* **89**:355–361.
Bartholomew, S. H.
  1953   The Pattern of Muscular Activity in the Lower Extremity during Walking. *Prosthetic Devices Research Project, University of California at Berkeley*. Series II, **25**:1–41.
Bartucz, L.
  1940   Der Urmensch der Mussolini-Höhle. In Die Mussolini-Höhle (Subalyuk) bei Cserépfalu. *Geologica Hungarica. Series Paleontologica* **14**:47–105.
Basmajian, J. V.
  1974   *Muscles Alive: Their Functions revealed by Electromyography.* 3rd ed. Baltimore: Williams and Wilkins.
Basmajian, J. V., and A. A. Travill
  1961   Electromyography of the pronator muscles in the forearm. *The Anatomical Record* **139**:45–49.
Beaumont, P. B., H. de Villiers, and J. C. Vogel
  1978   Modern man in Sub-Saharan Africa prior to 49,000 years B.P.: A review and evaluation with particular reference to Border Cave. *South African Journal of Science* **74**:409–419.
Benfer, R., and T. W. McKern
  1966   The correlation of bone robusticity with the perforation of the coronoid–olecranon septum in the humerus of man. *American Journal of Physical Anthropology* **24**:247–252.
Berry, A. C.
  1978   Anthropological and family studies on minor variants of the dental crown. In: *Development, Function and Evolution of Teeth*, edited by P. M. Butler and K. A. Joysey. New York: Academic Press. Pp. 81–98.
Berry, A. C., and R. J. Berry
  1967   Epigenetic variation in the human cranium. *Journal of Anatomy* **101**:361–379.
Billy, G.
  1972   L'évolution humaine au paléolithique supérieur. *Homo* **23**:2–12.
Billy, G., and H. V. Vallois
  1977   La mandibule pré-Rissienne de Montmaurin. *L'Anthropologie* **81**:273–312, 411–458.
Binford, L. R.
  1982   Comment on R. White: Rethinking the Middle/Upper Paleolithic transition. *Current Anthropology* **23**:177–181.
Black, T. K. III
  1978   Sexual dimorphism in the tooth-crown diameters of the deciduous teeth. *American Journal of Physical Anthropology* **48**:77–82.
Blackwood, B., and Danby, P. M.
  1955   A study of artificial cranial deformation in New Britain. *Journal of the Royal Anthropological Institute* **85**:173–191.

Blumberg, J. E., W. L. Hylander, and R. A. Goepp
1971   Taurodontism: a biometric study. *American Journal of Physical Anthropology* **34**:243–255.

Bonč-Osmolovskij, G. A.
1941   Kist' iskopaemogo cheloveka iz grota Kiik-Koba (The hand of the fossil man from Kiik-Koba). *Paleolit Kryma*. Vol. 2.

Bordes, F.
1954–
1955   Les gisements du Pech-de-l'Azé (Dordogne). *L'Anthropologie* **58**:401–432; **59**:1–38.

Bordes, F.
1972   (editor) *The Origin of* Homo sapiens. Paris: UNESCO.
1981   Vingt-cinq ans après: le complèxe moustérien revisité. *Bulletin de la Société Préhistorique Française* **78**:77–87.

Boule, M.
1911–
1913   L'homme fossile de La Chapelle-aux-Saints. *Annales de Paléontologie*. **6**:111–172; **7**:21–56, 85–192; **8**:1–70.
1921   *Les Hommes Fossiles: Éléments de Paléontologie Humaine.* Paris: Masson et Cie., Éditeurs. (First edition).

Bourke, J. B.
1967   A review of the palaeopathology of the arthritic diseases. In *Diseases in antiquity*, edited by D. R. Brothwell and A. T. Sandison. Springfield: Thomas. Pp. 352–370.

Boyd, E.
1962   Organ weights from birth to maturity: Man, North American. *In Growth, including Reproduction and Morphological Development*, edited by P. L. Altman and D. S. Dittmer, Washington: Federation of American Societies for Experimental Biology. Pp. 346–348.

Brabant, H., and I. Kovacs
1961   Contribution á l'étude de la persistence du taurodontisme dans les race modernes et de sa parenté possible avec la racine pyramidale des molaires. *Bulletin du Groupement International pour la Recherche Scientifique en Stomatologie* **4**:232–286.

Brace, C. L.
1962   Cultural factors in the evolution of the human dentition. In *Culture and the Evolution of Man*, edited by M. F. A. Montagu. New York: Oxford University Press. Pp. 343–354.
1964   The fate of the classic Neanderthals: A consideration of hominid catastrophism. *Current Anthropology* **5**:3–43.
1967   Environment, tooth form, and size in the Pleistocene. *Journal of Dental Research* **46**:809–816.
1979   Krapina, "Classic" Neanderthals, and the evolution of the European face. *Journal of Human Evolution* **8**:527–550.
1981   Tales of the phylogenetic woods: The evolution and significance of evolutionary trees. *American Journal of Physical Anthropology* **56**:411–429.

Brace, C. L., and P. E. Mahler
1971   Post-Pleistocene changes in the human dentition. *American Journal of Physical Anthropology* **34**:191–203.

Brace, C. L., A. S. Ryan, and B. H. Smith
1981   Tooth wear in La Ferrassie man: Comment. *Current Anthropology* **22**:426–430.

Bräuer, G.
1980   Die morphologischen Affinitäten des jungpleistozänen Stirnbeines aus dem Elbmündungsgebiet bei Hahnöfersand. *Zeitschrift für Morphologie und Anthropologie* **71**:1–42.

Broecker, W. S., and J. L. Kulp
      1957   Lamont natural radiocarbon measurements IV. *Science* **126**:1324–1334.
Brose, D. S., and M. H. Wolpoff
      1971   Early Upper Paleolithic man and late Middle Paleolithic tools. *American Anthropologist* **73**:1156–1194.
Brothwell, D. R.
      1975   Possible evidence for a cultural practice affecting head growth in some late Pleistocene East Asian and Australasian populations. *Journal of Archaeological Science* **2**:75–77.
Brown, P.
      1981   Artificial cranial deformation: A component in the variation in Pleistocene Australian Aboriginal crania. *Archaeology in Oceania* **16**:156–167.
Bush, M. E., C. O. Lovejoy, D. C. Johanson, and Y. Coppens
      1982   Hominid carpal, metacarpal and phalangeal bones recovered from the Hadar Formation: 1974–1977 collections. *American Journal of Physical Anthropology* **57**:651–667.
Campbell, B. G.
      1963   Quantitative taxonomy and human evolution. *In* Classification and Human Evolution, edited by S. L. Washburn. *Viking Fund Publication in Anthropology* **37**:50–74.
Campbell, T. D.
      1925   Dentition and palate of the Australian Aboriginal. *University of Adelaide: Keith Sheridan Foundation Publications.* **1**:1–123.
Carbonell, V. M.
      1963   Variations in the frequency of shovel-shaped incisors in different populations. In *Dental anthropology*, edited by D. R. Brothwell. Oxford: Pergamon Press. Pp. 211–234.
Carlson, D. S., and D. P. VanGerven
      1977   Masticatory function and post-Pleistocene evolution in Nubia. *American Journal of Physical Anthropology* **46**:495–506.
Clark, J. D., K. P. Oakley, L. H. Wells, and J. A. C. MacClelland
      1950   New studies on Rhodesian Man. *Journal of the Royal Anthropological Institute* **77**:7–32.
Coleman, W. H.
      1969   Sex differences in the growth of the human bony pelvis. *American Journal of Physical Anthropology* **31**: 125–152.
Constable, G.
      1973   *The Neanderthals.* New York: Time-Life.
Cook, J., C. B. Stringer, A. P. Currant, H. P. Schwarcz, and A. G. Wintle.
      1982   A review of the chronology of the European Middle Pleistocene Hominid record. *Yearbook of Physical Anthropology* **25**:19–65.
Coon, C. S.
      1951   Cave explorations in Iran 1949. *Museum Monographs, University Museum.*
      1962   *The Origin of Races.* New York: Knopf.
      1975.   Iran. In *Catalogue of Fossil Hominids Part III: Americas, Asia, Australasia,* edited by K. P. Oakley, B. G. Campbell and T. I. Molleson. London: British Museum (Natural History). Pp. 117–120.
Cooney, W. P., III, and E. Y. S. Chao
      1977   Biomechanical analysis of static forces in the thumb during hand function. *Journal of Bone and Joint Surgery* **59-A**:27–36.
Costa, R. L., Jr.
      1977   Dental Pathology and Related Factors in Archeological Eskimo Skeletal Samples from Point Hope and Kodiak Island, Alaska. Ph.D Thesis, Department of Anthropology, University of Pennsylvania, Philadelphia.

Cunningham, D. J.
    1886   The neural spines of the cervical vertebrae as a race-character. *Journal of Anatomy
            and Physiology* **20**:637–640.
    1908   The evolution of the eyebrow region of the forehead, with special references to the
            excessive supraorbital development in the Neanderthal race. *Transactions of the
            Royal Society of Edinburgh* **46**(2):283–311.
Dastugue, J.
    1960   Pathologie de quelques Néandertaliens. *VIᵉ Congrès des Sciences Anthropologiques
            et Ethnologiques Paris* **1**:577–581.
Dastugue, J., and M. -A. de Lumley
    1976   Les maladies des hommes Préhistoriques du Paléolithique et du Mèsolithique. In *La
            Préhistoire Française*, edited by H. de Lumley (Vol. 1). Paris: Éditions du C. N. R. S.
            Pp. 612–622.
Day, M. H.
    1969   Early *Homo sapiens* remains from the Omo River region of south-west Ethiopia: Omo
            human skeletal remains. *Nature* **222**:1135–1138.
    1971   Postcranial remains of *Homo erectus* from Bed IV, Olduvai Gorge, Tanzania. *Nature*
            232:383–387.
Day, M. H., M. D. Leakey, and C. Magori
    1980   A new hominid fossil skull (L. H. 18) from the Ngaloba Beds, Laetoli, northern
            Tanzania. *Nature* **284**: 55–56.
Delsaux, M. -A.
    1976   *Caractères mesurables de l'humérus humain, humérus fossiles, humérus modernes.*
            Thèse de Doctorat, Faculté Libre des Sciences de Lille.
Dembo, A., and J. Imbelloni
    1938   Deformaciones intencionales del cuerpo humano del carácter étnico. In *Humanior,
            Biblioteca del Americanista Moderno*, edited by J. Imbelloni. Sección A. **3**:1–348.
Dieulafé, R.
    1933   Le coccyx, Étude ostéologique. *Archives d'Anatomie, d'Histologie et d'Embryologie*
            16:41–91.
Dingwall, E. J.
    1931   *Artificial Cranial Deformation: A Contribution to the Study of Ethnic Mutilations.*
            London: Bale, Sons and Danielsson.
Dittner, C.
    1977   *The Morphology of the Axillary Border of the Scapula with Special Reference to the
            Neandertal Problem.* M.A. Thesis, Department of Anthropology, University of Ten-
            nessee, Knoxville.
Dobzhansky, T.
    1944   On species and races of living and fossil man. *American Journal of Physical An-
            thropology* **2**:251–265.
Doyle, W. J.
    1977   Functionally induced alteration of adult scapular morphology. *Acta Anatomica*
            99:173–177.
Dupertuis, C. W., and J. A. Hadden, Jr.
    1951   On the reconstruction of stature from long bones. *American Journal of Physical
            Anthropology* **9**:15–53.
Eberhart, H. D., V. T. Inman, and B. Bresler
    1954   The principle elements in human locomotion. In *Human Limbs and their Substitutes*,
            edited by P. E. Klopsteg and P. D. Wilson. New York: McGraw-Hill Book Company.
            Pp. 437–471.
Edens, C.
    1980   A critical review of Upper Paleolithic studies in the Zagros and the Levant. Un-
            published M.S.

Eickstedt, E. F. von
    1925   Variationen am Axillarrand der Scapula (Sulcus axillaris teretis und Sulcus axillaris subscapularis). *Anthropologischer Anzeiger* **2**:217–228.

Elftman, H.
    1960   The transverse tarsal joint and its control. *Clinical Orthopaedics and Related Research* **16**:41–46.

Endo, B., and T. Kimura
    1970   Postcranial skeleton of the Amud Man. In *The Amud Man and his Cave Site*, edited by H. Suzuki and F. Takai. Tokyo: Academic Press Pp. 231–406.

Ennouchi, E.
    1962   Un Néandertalien: L'Homme du Jebel Irhoud (Maroc). *L'Anthropologie* **66**:279–299.

Evins, M. A.
    1981   *A study of the Fauna from the Mousterian Deposits at Shanidar Cave, Northeastern Iraq.* M.A. Thesis, University of Chicago, Department of Anthropology, Chicago, Illinois.

Farrand, W. R.
    1971   Late Quaternary paleoclimates of the eastern Mediterranean area. In *The Late Cenozoic Glacial Ages*, edited by K. K. Turekian. New Haven: Yale University Press. Pp. 529–564.
    1979   Chronology and palaeoenvironment of Levantine prehistoric sites as seen from sediment studies. *Journal of Archaeological Science* **6**:369–392.

Fenner, F. J.
    1939   The Australian Aboriginal skull: Its non-metrical morphological characters. *Transactions of the Royal Society of South Australia* **63**:248–306.

Ferembach, D.
    1970   Le crâne de l'enfant du Pech-de-l'Azé. In *L'Enfant du Pech-de-l'Azé. Archives de l'Institut de Paléontologie Humaine* **33**:13–51.
    1976   Les restes humains de la Grotte de Dar-es-Soltane 2 (Maroc) Campagne 1975. *Bulletin et Mémoires de la Société d'Anthropologie de Paris*, Série 13, **3**:183–193.

Fessard, C.
    1979   Neurologic diseases. In *Bone Diseases of Children*, edited by P. Marotaux. Philadelphia: Lippincott Pp. 305–328.

Finnegan, M.
    1974   Discrete non-metric variation of the post-cranial skeleton in man. *American Journal of Physical Anthropology*. **40**:135–136. (Abstract).

Fischer, E.
    1906   Die Variationen an Radius und Ulna des Menschen. *Zeitschrift für Morphologie und Anthropologie* **9**:147–247.

Fraipont, C.
    1927   Sur l'omoplate et le sacrum de l'homme de Spy. *Revue Anthropologique* **37**:189–195.

Fraipont, J.
    1888   Le tibia dans la race de Néanderthal. *Revue d'Anthropologie*, Série 3, **3**(2):145–158.

Fraipont, J., and M. Lohest
    1887   La race humaine de Néanderthal ou de Canstadt en Belgique: Recherches ethnographiques sur des ossements humains, découverts dans les dépôts quaternaires d'une grotte à Spy et détermination de leur âge géologique. *Archives de Biologie* **7**:587–757.

Frayer, D. W.
    1977   Metric dental changes in the European Upper Paleolithic and Mesolithic. *American Journal of Physical Anthropology* **46**: 109–120.
    1978   Evolution of the Dentition in Upper Paleolithic and Mesolithic Europe. *University of Kansas Publications in Anthropology* **10**:1–201.

1980   Sexual dimorphism and cultural evolution in the late Pleistocene and Holocene of
         Europe. *Journal of Human Evolution.* **9**:399–415.

1981   Body size, weapon use, and natural selection in the European Upper Paleolithic and
         Mesolithic. *American Anthropologist* **83**:57–73.

Frey, H.
1923   Untersuchungen über die Scapula, speziell über ihre äussere Form und deren Ab-
         hängigkeit von der Funktion. *Zeitschrift für Anatomie und Entwicklungsgeschichte*
         68:277–324.

Fuhlrott, J. C.
1857   Theilen des menschlichen Skelettes im Neanderthal bei Hochdal. *Verhandlungen
         des naturhistorischen Vereines der preussischen Rheinlande und Wastfalens*
         14:50–52.

Gabuniya, L. K., D. M. Tushabramashvili, and A. K. Vekua
1961   The first discovery of remains of Mousterian Man in the Caucasus. *Voprosy
         Antropologii* **8**:156–162. (In Russian).

Garrod, D. A. E.
1930   The palaeolithic of southern Kurdistan: Excavations in the caves of Zarzi and Hazar
         Merd. *American School of Prehistoric Research Bulletin* **6**: 8–43.

1957   Notes sur le paléolithique supérieur du moyen orient. *Bulletin de la Société Pré-
         historique Française* **54**:439–446.

Genovés, S.
1954   The problem of the sex of certain fossil hominids, with special reference to the
         Neandertal skeletons from Spy. *Journal of the Royal Anthropological Institute*
         84:131–144.

1969   Sex determination in earlier man. In *Science in Archaeology*, edited by D. R. Broth-
         well and E. Higgs. New York: Praeger. Pp. 429–439. (Second edition).

Genovés, S., and M. Messmacher
1959   Valor de los patrones tradicionales para la determinacion de la edad por medio de las
         suturas en craneos mexicanos (indigenas y mestizos). *Cuadernos del Instituto de
         Historia (Universidad Nacional Autonoma de Mexico)*, Serie Antropológica,
         7:1–53.

Giles, E., and O. Elliot
1963   Sex determination by discriminant function analysis of crania. *American Journal of
         Physical Anthropology* **21**:53–68.

Gisis, I. and O. Bar Yosef
1974   New excavation in Zuttiyeh cave, Wadi Amud, Israel. *Paléorient* **2**:175–180.

Gonda, K.
1959   On the sexual differences in the dimensions of the human teeth. *Zinruigaku Zassi
         (Journal of the Anthropological Society of Nippon)* **67**:151–163.

Gorjanović-Kramberger, D.
1906   *Der diluviale Mensch von Krapina in Kroatien: Ein Beitrag zur Paläoanthropologie.*
         Wiesbaden: C. W. Kreidel's Verlag.

1908   Anomalien und pathologische Erscheinungen am Skelett des Urmenschen aus Kra-
         pina. *Korrespondenz-Blatt der Deutschen Gesellschaft für Anthropologie, Ethnologie
         und Urgeschichte* **39**:108–112.

Gregg, J. B., and W. M. Bass
1970   Exostoses in the external auditory canals. *Annals of Otology, Rhinology and
         Laryngology* **79**:834–839.

Gremyatskij, M. A., and M. F. Nesturkh (editors)
1949   *Teshik-Tash.* Moscow: Moscow State University. (In Russian).

Guth, C.
1963   Contribution à la connaissance du temporal des néandertaliens. *Comptes Rendus de
         l'Académie des Sciences de Paris*, Série D, **256**:1329–1339.

Hanihara, K.
  1963   Crown characters of the deciduous dentition of the Japanese–American hybrids. In *Dental Anthropology*, edited by D. R. Brothwell. Oxford: Pergamon Press. Pp. 105–124.
Harrison, D. F. N.
  1962   The relationship of osteomata of the external auditory meatus to swimming. *Annals of the Royal College of Surgeons of England* **31**:187–201.
Harrold, F. B.
  1980   A comparative analysis of Eurasian Palaeolithic burials. *World Archaeology* **12**:195–211.
  1981   New Perspectives on the Châtelperronian. *Ampurias.* **43**:35–85.
Hasebe, K.
  1912   Die Wirbelsäule der Japaner. *Zeitschrift für Morphologie und Anthropologie* **15**:259–380.
Heim, J. -L.
  1972   *Les Néandertaliens adultes de La Ferrassie (Dordogne). Études anthropologique et comparative.* Thèse de Doctorat d'État, Université de Paris VI.
  1974   Les hommes fossiles de La Ferrassie (Dordogne) et le problème de la définition des Néandertaliens Classiques. *L'Anthropologie* **78**:81–112, 321–378.
  1976   Les hommes fossiles de La Ferrassie I: Le gisement. Les squelettes adultes (crâne et squelette du tronc). *Archives de l'Institut de Paléontologie Humaine* **35**:1–331.
  1978   Contribution du massif facial à la morphogenèse du crâne Néanderthalien. In *Les Origines Humaines et les Époques de l'Intelligence.* Paris: Masson et Cie. Pp. 183–215.
Henry, D. O., and A. F. Servello
  1974   Compendium of carbon-14 determinations derived from Near Eastern prehistoric deposits. *Paléorient* **2**:19–44.
Hicks, J. H.
  1953   The mechanics of the foot I: The joints. *Journal of Anatomy* **87**:345–357.
  1954   The mechanics of the foot II: The plantar aponeurosis and the arch. *Journal of Anatomy* **88**:25–30.
Hinton, R. J.
  1979   *Influence of Dental Function on Form of the Human Mandibular Fossa.* Ph.D. Thesis, Department of Anthropology, University of Michigan, Ann Arbor, Michigan.
Hole, F., and K. V. Flannery
  1967   The prehistory of southwestern Iran: A preliminary report. *Proceedings of the Prehistoric Society* **33**:147–206.
Hooton, E. A.
  1931   *Up from the Ape.* New York: Macmillan.
Horsley, V.
  1892   On the topographical relations of the cranium and surface of the cerebrum. *Royal Irish Academy "Cunningham Memoirs"* **7**:306–355.
Houghton, P.
  1974   The relationship of the pre-auricular groove of the ilium to pregnancy. *American Journal of Physical Anthropology* **41**:381–390.
Houston, C. S., and W. A. Zaleski
  1967   The shape of vertebral bodies and femoral necks in relation to activity. *Radiology* **89**:59–66.
Howell, F. C.
  1951   The place of Neanderthal man in human evolution. *American Journal of Physical Anthropology* **9**:379–416.
  1952   Pleistocene glacial ecology and the evolution of "classic Neandertal" man. *Southwestern Journal of Anthropology.* **8**:377–410.

1957 The evolutionary significance of variation and varieties of "Neanderthal" Man. *Quarterly Review of Biology* **32**:330–347.

Howells, W. W.

1970 Mount Carmel Man: Morphological relationships. *Proceedings of the VIIIth International Congress of Anthropological and Ethnological Sciences, Tokyo 1968* **1**:269–272.

1973 Cranial Variation in Man. *Peabody Museum Papers* **67**:1–259.

1975 Neanderthal Man: Facts and figures. In *Paleoanthropology: Morphology and Paleoecology*, edited by R. H. Tuttle. Paris: Mouton Pp. 389–407.

1978 Position phylétique de l'homme de Néanderthal. In *Les Origines Humaines et les Époques de l'Intelligence*. Paris: Masson et Cie. Pp. 217–237.

Hoyte, D. A. N.

1966 Experimental investigations of skull morphology and growth. *International Review of General and Experimental Zoology* **2**:345–408.

Hrdlička, A.

1920 Shovel-shaped teeth. *American Journal of Physical Anthropology* **3**:429–465.

1927 The Neanderthal phase of man. *Journal of the Royal Anthropological Institute* **57**:249–274.

1930 The skeletal remains of early man. *Smithsonian Miscellaneous Collections* **83**:1–379.

1932a The humerus: Septal apertures. *Anthropologie (Prague)* **10**:31–96.

1932b The principal dimensions, absolute and relative, of the humerus in the white race. *American Journal of Physical Anthropology* **16**:431–450.

1934 Contributions to the study of the femur: the crista aspera and the pilaster. *American Journal of Physical Anthropology* **19**:17–37.

1940 Mandibular and maxillary hyperostoses. *American Journal of Physical Anthropology* **27**:1–55.

Hublin, J. -J.

1978a *Le Torus Occiptal Transverse et les Structures Associées: Évolution dans le Genre Homo*. Thèse de Docteur du Troisième Cycle. Université de Paris VI.

1978b Quelques caractères apomorphes de crâne néandertalien et leur interprétation phylogénique. *Comptes rendus de l'Académie des Sciences de Paris, Série D,* **287**:923–925.

Hublin, J. -J., and A. -M. Tillier

1981 The Mousterian juvenile mandible from Irhoud (Morocco): A phylogenetic interpretation. In *Aspects of Human Evolution*, edited by C. B. Stringer. London: Taylor and Francis. Pp. 167–185.

Hylander, W. L.

1975 The human mandible: lever or link? *American Journal of Physical Anthropology* **43**: 227–242.

1977 Morphological changes in human teeth and jaws in a high-attrition environment. In *Orofacial Growth and Development*, edited by A. A. Dahlberg and M. Graber. World Anthropology. Hague: Mouton, Pp. 301–331.

Jelinek, A. J.

1975 Some current problems in Lower and Middle Paleolithic typology. Conference on Lithic Typology, Les Eyzies. Unpublished manuscript.

1982 The Tabun cave and paleolithic man in the Levant. *Science* **216**:1369–1375.

Jelinek, A. J., W. R. Farrand, G. Haas, A. Horowitz, and P. Goldberg

1973 New excavations at the Tabun cave, Mount Carmel, Israel, 1967–1972: A preliminary report. *Paléorient* **1**:151–183.

Johanson, D. C., C. O. Lovejoy, W. H. Kimbel, T. D. White, S. C. Ward, M. E. Bush, B. M. Latimer, and Y. Coppens

1982 Morphology of the Pliocene Hominid partial skeleton (A.L. 288–1) from the Hadar Formation, Ethiopia. *American Journal of Physical Anthropology* **57**:403–451.

Jones, F. W.
  1929   The distinctions of the human hallux. *Journal of Anatomy* **63**:408–411.
Jurmain, R. D.
  1977   Stress and the etiology of osteoarthritis. *American Journal of Physical Anthropology*
            46:353–366.
Kallay, J.
  1963   A radiographic study of the Neanderthal teeth from Krapina, Croatia. In *Dental An-
            thropology*, edited by D. R. Brothwell. Oxford: Pergamon Press. Pp. 75–86.
  1970   Komperativne napomene o čeljustima Krapinskih Praljudi s obzirom na položaj mec-
            tu Hominidima (Comparative observations on the mandible of a Krapina Neanderthal
            man in respect to its position among Hominids). In *Krapina 1899–1969*, edited by M.
            Malez. Zagreb: Jugoslavenska Akademija Znanosti i Umjetnosti. Pp. 153–164.
Kapandji, I. A.
  1972   La rotation du pouce sur son axe longitudinal lors de l'opposition. *Revue de Chi-
            rurgie Orthopédique et Réparatrice de l'Appareil Moteur* **58**:273–289.
Kaufer, H.
  1971   Mechanical function of the patella. *Journal of Bone and Joint Surgery* **53-
            A**:1551–1560.
Keiter, F.
  1934   Unterkeifer aus Australien und Neuguinea as dem Nachlasse Rudolf Pöchs.
            Zeitschrift für Morphologie und Anthropologie **33**:190–226.
Keith, A.
  1913   Problems relating to the teeth of the earlier forms of prehistoric man. *Proceedings of
            the Royal Society of Medicine and Odontology*. Section 6:103–124.
  1915   *The Antiquity of Man*. London: Williams and Norgate.
  1927   A report on the Galilee skull. In *Researches in Prehistoric Galilee*, edited by F.
            Turville-Petre. London: British School of Archaeology in Jerusalem. Pp. 53–106.
  1931   *New Discoveries relating to the Antiquity of Man*. New York: Norton.
Kelley, M. A.
  1979   Parturition and pelvic changes. *American Journal of Physical Anthropology*
            51:541–546.
Kettelcamp, D. B., R. J. Johnson, G. L. Smidt, E. Y. S. Chao, and M. Walker
  1970   An electrogoniometric study of knee motion in normal gait. *Journal of Bone and Joint
            Surgery* **52-A**:775–790.
Kimura, T.
  1976   Correction to the *Metacarpale I* of the Amud Man. A new description especially on
            the insertion area of the *M. opponens pollicis*. *Journal of the Anthropological Society
            of Nippon* **84**:48–54.
King, W.
  1864   The reputed fossil man of Neanderthal. *Quarterly Journal of Science* **1**:88–97.
Klaatsch, H., and O. Hauser
  1909a   Homo Aurignacensis Hauseri ein paläolithischer Skeletfund aus dem Aurignacien
            der Station Combe-Capelle bei Montferrand (Périgord). *Praehistorische Zeitschrift*
            1:273–338.
  1909b   Homo mousteriensis Hauseri. Ein altdiluvialer Skelettfund im Departement Dor-
            dogne und seine Zugehörigkeit zum Neandertaltypus. *Archiv für Anthropologie*
            7:287–297.
Klein, R. G.
  1973   *Ice-Age Hunters of the Ukraine*. Chicago: University of Chicago Press.
Kleinschmidt, O.
  1938   Unausrottbare falsche Behauptungen II. Die Halswirbel des Neandertalmenschen.
            Beilage zu Falco **34**:1–4.

Kobayashi, K.
  1967   Trend in the length of life based on human skeletons from prehistoric to modern times in Japan. *Journal of the Faculty of Science, University of Tokyo. Section V.* **3**:107–162.

Koby, F. E.
  1956   Une incisive néandertalienne trouvée en Suisse. *Verhandlungen der Naturforschers Gesellschaft in Basel* **67**:1–15.

Kochetkova, V. I.
  1978   *Paleoneurology.* Washington, D.C.: Winston and Sons.

Koenigswald, G. H. R. von (editor)
  1958   *Hundert Jahre Neanderthaler.* Utrecht: Kemink en Zoon N.V.

Krogman, W. M.
  1962   *The Human Skeleton in Forensic Medicine.* Springfield, Illinois: Thomas.

Landsmeer, J. M. F.
  1955   Anatomical and functional investigations of the articulation of the human fingers. *Acta Anatomica* **25**:1–69. (Supplement 24).

Lanier, R. R. Jr.
  1939   The presacral vertebrae of american white and negro males. *American Journal of Physical Anthropology* **25**:341–420.

Larnach, S. L.
  1974   Frontal recession and artificial deformation. *Archaeology and Physical Anthropology in Oceania* **9**:214–216.

Larnach, S. L., and N. W. G. Macintosh
  1966   The craniology of the Aborigines of coastal New South Wales. *The Oceania Monographs* **13**:1–94.
  1971   The mandible in Eastern Australian Aborigines. *The Oceania Monographs* **17**:1–34.

Latimer, B. M., C. O. Lovejoy, D. C. Johanson, and Y. Coppens
  1982   Hominid tarsal, metatarsal, and phalangeal bones recovered from the Hadar Formation: 1974–1977 collections. *American Journal of Physical Anthropology* **57**:701–719.

Leboucq, H.
  1882   Le développement du premier métatarsien et de son articulation tarsienne chez l'homme. *Archives de Biologie* **3**:335–344.

LeDouble, A. F.
  1903   *Traité des Variations des Os du Crâne de l'Homme et de leur Signification au point de vue de l'Anthropologie Zoologique.* Paris: Vigot Frères.

Legoux, P.
  1970   Étude odontologique de l'enfant néandertalien du Pech-de-l'Azé. *Archives de l'Institut de Paléontologie Humaine* **33**:53–87.

LeGros Clark, W. E.
  1964   *The Fossil Evidence for Human Evolution.* Chicago: University of Chicago Press. (Second edition).

LeGros Clark, W. E., and B. G. Campbell
  1978   *The Fossil Evidence for Human Evolution.* Chicago: University of Chicago Press. (Third edition).

LeMay, M.
  1976   Morphological cerebral asymmetries of modern man, fossil man, and non-human primate. *In* Origins and Evolution of Language and Speech, edited by S. R. Harnad, H. D. Steklis, and J. Lancaster. *Annals of the New York Academy of Sciences* **280**:349–360.
  1977   Asymmetries of the skull and handedness. *Journal of the Neurological Sciences* **32**:243–253.

Leroi-Gourhan, A.
  1968   Le Néanderthalien IV de Shanidar. *Comptes Rendus de la Société Préhistorique Française* **65**:79–83.
  1975   The flowers found with Shanidar IV, a Neanderthal burial in Iraq. *Science* **190**:562–564.

Leutenegger, W.
  1972   Newborn size and pelvic dimensions of *Australopithecus*. *Nature* **240**:568–569.

Lévêque, F., and B. Vandermeersch
  1980   Découverte de restes humains dans un niveau castelperronien à Saint-Cèsaire (Charente-Maritime). *Comptes rendus de l'Académie des Sciences de Paris*, Série D, **291**:187–189.
  1981   Le néandertalien de Saint-Césaire. *La Recherche* **12**(119):242–244.

Liau, S. -C.
  1956   On the position of the mental foramen and the mandibular foramen in the mandible in Formosan residents. *The Quarterly Journal of Anthropology* **3**:46–54. (In Chinese).

Limbrey, S.
  1975   China. In K. P. Oakley, B. G. Campbell and T. I. Molleson (eds.) *Catalogue of Fossil Hominids* (Part 3): *Americas, Asia, Australasia.* London: British Museum (Natural History). Pp. 49–87.

Loth, E.
  1938   Beiträge zur Kenntnis der Weichteilanatomie des Neanderthalers. *Zeitschrift für Rassenkunde* **7**:13–35.

Lovejoy, C. O.
  1974   The gait of Australopithecines. *Yearbook of Physical Anthropology* **17**:147–161.

Lovejoy, C. O., A. H. Burnstein, and K. G. Heiple
  1976   The biomechanical analysis of bone strength: A method and its application to platycnemia. *American Journal of Physical Anthropology* **44**:489–506.

Lovejoy, C. O., and K. G. Heiple
  1981   The analysis of fractures in skeletal populations with an example from the Libben site, Ottowa County, Ohio. *American Journal of Physical Anthropology* **55**:529–541.

Lovejoy, C. O., and E. Trinkaus
  1980   Strength and robusticity of the Neandertal tibia. *American Journal of Physical Anthropology* **53**: 465–470.

Lukacs, J. R.
  1981   Crown dimensions of deciduous teeth from prehistoric India. *American Journal of Physical Anthropology* **55**: 261–266.

Lumley, H. de, and M. -A. de Lumley
  1971   Découverte de restes anténéandertaliens datés du début du Riss à la Caune de l'Arago (Tautavel, Pyrénées-Orientales). *Comptes Rendus de l'Académie des Sciences de Paris*, Série D, **272**:1739–1742.
  1979   L'homme de Tautavel. *Dossiers de l'Archéologie* **36**:54–59.

Lumley, M. -A. de
  1972   Les Néandertaliens de la grotte de l'Hortus. In: H. de Lumley (ed.) *La Grotte de l'Hortus (Valflaunès, Hérault).* Études Quaternaires **1**:375–385.
  1973   Anténéandertaliens et néndertaliens du bassin méditerranéen occidental européen. *Études Quaternaires*, Université de Provence **2**:1–626.

Lunt, R. C., and D. B. Law
  1974   A review of the chronology of calcification of deciduous teeth. *Journal of the American Dental Association* **89**:599–606.

Macgillivray, J.
  1852   *Narrative of the Voyage of the H. M. S. Rattlesnake.* London: Boone.

Manouvrier, L.
    1893   La détermination de la taille d'après les grands os des membres. *Mémoires de la Société d'Anthropologie de Paris*, Sèrie 2, **4**:347–402.
Manter, J. T.
    1941   Movements of the subtalar and transverse tarsal joints. *Anatomical Record* **80**:397–410.
Margetts, B., and T. Brown
    1978   Crown diameters of the deciduous teeth in Australian aboriginals. *American Journal of Physical Anthropology* **48**:493–502.
Marshack, A.
    1972   Cognitive aspects of Upper Paleolithic engraving. *Current Anthropology* **13**:445–477.
Martin, H.
    1910   Astragale humain du Moustérien moyen de La Quina. Ses affinités. *Bulletin de la Société Préhistorique Française* **7**:391–397.
    1912   Position stratigraphique des ossements humains recueillis dans le Moustérien de la Quina de 1908 et 1912. *Bulletin de la Société Préhistorique Française* **9**:700–709.
    1923   *Recherches sur l'Évolution du Moustérien dans le Gisement de La Quina (Charente) III: L'Homme Fossile.* Paris: Librairie Octave Doin.
    1926a   Machoire humaine Moustérienne trouvée dans la station de La Quina. *L'Homme Préhistorique* **13**:3–21.
    1926b   *Recherches sur l'Évolution du Moustérien dans le Gisement de La Quina (Charente) IV: L'Enfant Fossile de La Quina.* Paris: Librairie Octave Doin.
Martin, R.
    1928   *Lehrbuch der Anthropologie.* Jena: Verlag von Gustav Fischer. (Second edition).
Masters, P.
    1982   An amino acid racemization chronology for Tabun. In *The Transition from the Lower to Middle Palaeolithic and the Origin of Modern Man*, edited by A. Ronen. Oxford: British Archaeological Reports, International Series. **151**:43–54.
Matiegka, J.
    1934   *Homo Předmostensis: Fosilní Člověk z Předmostí na Moravě I. Lebky (L'Homme Fossile de Předmostí en Moravie (Tchécoslovaquie) I. Les Crânes).* Prague: Česka Akademie Věd a Umění.
    1938   *Homo Předmostensis. Fosilní Člověk z Předmosti na Moravě II. Ostatní Části Kostrové (L'Homme Fossile de Předmostí en Moravie (Tchécoslovaquie) II. Autres parties du squelette).* Prague: Česka Akademie Věd a Umění.
Mayr, E.
    1951   Taxonomic Categories in Fossil Hominids. *In* Origin and Evolution of Man, edited by K. B. Warren. *Cold Spring Harbor Symposia on Quantitative Biology* **15**: 109–118.
Mayr, E., and W. B. Provine (editors)
    1980   *The Evolutionary Synthesis: Perspectives on the Unification of Biology.* Cambridge: Harvard University Press.
McCown, T. D., and A. Keith
    1939   *The Stone Age of Mount Carmel II: The Fossil Human Remains from the Levalloiso-Mousterian.* Oxford: Clarendon Press.
McHenry, H. M., R. S. Corruccini, and F. C. Howell
    1976   Analysis of an early hominid ulna from the Omo basin. *American Journal of Physical Anthropology* **44**:295–304.
McKern, T. W., and T. D. Stewart
    1957   *Skeletal Age Changes in Young American Males.* Natick, Massachusetts: Quartermaster Research and Development Command, Technical Report EP-45.
McLeish, R. D., and J. Charnley
    1970   Abduction forces in the one-legged stance. *Journal of Biomechanics* **3**:191–209.

Miles, A. E. W.
 1963   Dentition in the assessment of individual age in skeletal material. In *Dental An-thropology*, edited by D. R. Brothwell. New York: Pergamon Press. Pp. 191–209.
Minns, R. J., A. J. M. Birnie, and P. J. Abernethy
 1979   A stress analysis of the patella and how it relates to patellar articular cartilage lesions. *Journal of Biomechanics* **12**:699–711.
Molnar, S.
 1971   Human tooth wear, tooth function and cultural variability. *American Journal of Physical Anthropology* **34**:27–42.
Mongini, F.
 1975   Dental abrasion as a factor in remodeling of the mandibular condyle. *Acta Anatomica* **92**:292–300.
Moorrees, C. F. A.
 1957   *The Aleut Dentition*. Cambridge: Harvard University Press.
Moorrees, C. F. A., E. A. Fanning, and E. E. Hunt, Jr.
 1963   Formation and resorption of three deciduous teeth in children. *American Journal of Physical Anthropology* **21**:205–213.
Morant, G. M.
 1927   Studies of Palaeolithic man. II. A biometric study of Neanderthaloid skulls and of their relationships to modern racial types. *Annals of Eugenics* **2**:318–381.
 1930   Studies of Palaeolithic man. IV. A biometric study of the Upper Palaeolithic skulls of Europe and of their relationships to earlier and later types. *Annals of Eugenics* **4**:109–214.
Movius, H. L. Jr.
 1969   The Abri de Cro-Magnon, Les Eyzies (Dordogne), and the probable age of the con-tained burials on the basis of the evidence of the nearby Abri Pataud. *Anuario de Estudios Atlánticos* **15**:323–344.
Musgrave, J. H.
 1970   *An Anatomical Study of the Hands of Pleistocene and Recent Man*. Ph.D. Thesis, Churchill College, University of Cambridge, Cambridge.
 1971   How dextrous was Neanderthal Man? *Nature* **233**:538–541.
 1973   The phalanges of Neanderthal and Upper Paleolithic hands. In *Human Evolution*, edited by M. H. Day. London: Taylor and Francis. Pp. 59–85.
Nemeskéri, J., and L. Harsányi
 1962   Das Lebensalter des Skelettes aus dem Neandertal (1856). *Anthropologischer Anzeiger* **25**:292–297.
Neuville, R.
 1951   Paléolithique et mésolithique du dèsert de Judée. *Archives de l'Institut de Paléon-tologie Humaine* **24**:1–271.
Oakley, K. P., B. G. Campbell, and T. I. Molleson (editors)
 1971   *Catalogue of Fossil Hominids* (Part 2) Europe. London: British Museum (Natural History).
 1975   *Catalogue of Fossil Hominids* (Part 3) Americas, Asia, Australasia. London: British Museum (Natural History).
 1977   *Catalogue of Fossil Hominids* (Part 1) Africa. London: British Museum (Natural History). (Second edition).
Ogawa, T., T. Kamiya, S. Sakai, and H. Hosokawa
 1970   Some observations on the endocranial cast of the Amud Man. In *The Amud Man and his Cave Site*, edited by H. Suzuki and F. Takai. Tokyo: Academic Press. Pp. 407–420.
O'Konski, M.
 1979   *The Proximal Tibia in Homo sapiens and Neandertal Man: Adaptations to Locomo-tor Stress*. B.A. Thesis, Department of Anthropology, Harvard University, Cambridge, Massachusetts.

Olivier, G.
  1951–
  1956   Anthropologie de la clavicule. *Bulletins et Mémoires de la Société d'Anthropologie de Paris*, Série 10, **2**:67–99, 121–157; **3**:269–279; **4**:90–100; **5**:35–56, 144–153; **6**:283–302; **7**:225–261, 404–447.
  1960   *Pratique Anthropologique.* Paris: Vigot Frères, Éditeurs.
  1963   L'estimation de la stature par les os longs des membres. *Bulletins et Mémoires de la Société d'Anthropologie des Paris*, Série 11, **4**:433–449.

Ossenberg, N. S.
  1976   Within and between race distances in population studies based on discrete traits of the human skull. *American Journal of Physical Anthropology* **45**:701–716.

Ossenfort, W. F.
  1926   The atlas in whites and negroes. *American Journal of Physical Anthropology* **9**:439–443.

Oyen, O. J., R. W. Rice, and M. S. Cannon
  1979   Browridge structure and function in extant primates and Neanderthals. *American Journal of Physical Anthropology* **51**:83–96.

Parsons, F. G.
  1917   On the proportions and characteristics of the modern English clavicle. *Journal of Anatomy* **51**:71–93.

Paterson, A. M.
  1893   The human sacrum. *Scientific Transactions of the Royal Dublin Society*, Series II, **5**:123–204.

Patte, E.
  1955   *Les Néanderthaliens.* Paris: Masson et Cie., Éditeurs.
  1959   La dentition des Néanderthaliens. *Annales de Paléontologie* **45**:221–305.
  1960   Découverte d'un Néanderthalien dans la Vienne. *L'Anthropologie* **64**:512–517.

Pearson, K.
  1899   On the reconstruction of stature of prehistoric races. *Philosophical Transactions of the Royal Society*, Series A, **192**:169–244.

Perkins, D. Jr.
  1964   Prehistoric fauna from Shanidar. *Science* **144**:1565–1566.

Pfitzner, W.
  1900   Beiträge zur Kenntnis des menschlichen Extremitätenskeletts VIII: Die morphologischen Elemente des menschlichen Handskeletts. *Zeitschrift für Morphologie und Anthropologie* **2**:77–157, 365–678.

Phenice, T. W.
  1969   A newly developed visual method of sexing the *os pubis. American Journal of Physical Anthropology* **30**:297–302.

Piveteau, J.
  1963–
  1965   La grotte du Régourdou (Dordogne), paléontologie humaine. *Annales de Paléontologie (Vertébrés)* **49**:285–305; **50**:155–194; **52**:163–194.
  1976   Les Anté-Néandertaliens du Sud-Ouest. In *La Préhistoire Française* (Vol. 1), edited by H. de Lumley. Paris: Editions du C.N.R.S. Pp. 561–566.

Poirier, P., and A. Charpy
  1931   *Traité d'Anatomie Humaine.* Paris: Masson et Cie, Éditeurs. (Fourth edition).

Poulhés, J.
  1947   La branche ischio-pubienne; ses caractéres sexuels. *Bulletins et Mémoires de la Société d'Anthropologie de Paris*, Série 9, **6**:191–201.

Puech, P. -F.
  1981   Tooth wear in La Ferrassie Man. *Current Anthropology* **22**:424–425.

Pyle, S. I., A. M. Waterhouse, and W. W. Greulich
  1971   *A Radiographic Standard of Reference for the Growing Hand and Wrist.* Cleveland: The Press of Case Western Reserve University.

Radlauer, C.
  1908   Beiträge zur Anthropologie des Kreuzbeines. *Gegenbaurs Morphologisches Jahrbuch* **38**:323–447.

Reed, C. A., and R. J. Braidwood
  1960   Toward the reconstruction of the environmental sequence in northeastern Iraq. *In* Prehistoric Investigations in Iraqi Kurdistan, edited by R. J. Braidwood and B. Howe. *Studies in Ancient Oriental Civilization* **31**:163–173.

Reider, B., J. L. Marshall, B. Koslin, B. Ring, and F. G. Girgis
  1981   The anterior aspect of the knee joint. *Journal of Bone and Joint Surgery* **63**A:351–356.

Rhoads, J., and E. Trinkaus
  1977   Morphometrics of the Neandertal talus. *American Journal of Physical Anthropology* **46**:29–44.

Ried, A. H.
  1924   Die Schaftkrümmung des menschlichen Femur. *Anthropologischer Anzeiger* **1**:102–108.

Riesenfeld, A.
  1956   Multiple infraorbital ethmoidal and mental foramina in the races of man. *American Journal of Physical Anthropology* **14**:85–100.
  1966   The effects of experimental bipedalism and upright posture in the rat and their significance for the study of human evolution. *Acta Anatomica* **65**:449–521.
  1972   Functional and hormonal control of pelvic morphology in the rat. *Acta Anatomica* **82**:231–253.

Rightmire, G. P.
  1978   Florisbad and human population succession in southern Africa. *American Journal of Physical Anthropology* **48**:475–486.
  1979   Cranial remains of *Homo erectus* from Beds II and IV, Olduvai Gorge, Tanzania. *American Journal of Physical Anthropology* **51**:99–116.
  1981   Later Pleistocene Hominids of Eastern and Southern Africa. *Anthropologie (Brno)* **19**:15–26.

Robinson, J. T.
  1972   *Early Hominid Posture and Locomotion.* Chicago: University of Chicago Press.

Roche, A. F.
  1953   Increase in cranial thickness during growth. *Human Biology* **25**:81–92.
  1964   Aural exostoses in Australian aboriginal skulls. *Annals of Otology, Rhinology and Laryngology* **73**:82–91.

Ronen, A. (editor)
  1982   *The Transition from the Lower to the Middle Palaeolithic and the Origin of Modern Man.* Oxford: British Archaeological Reports, International Series **151**.

Rubin, M., and C. Alexander
  1960   U.S. Geological Survey Radiocarbon Dates V. *American Journal of Science Radiocarbon Supplement* **2**:129–185.

Rubin, M., and H. E. Suess
  1955   U.S. Geological Survey Radiocarbon Dates II. *Science* **121**:481–488.

Ruff, C. B.
  1979   Right-left asymmetry in long bones of California Indians. *American Journal of Physical Anthropology* **50**:477–478. (Abstract).
  1981   *Structural Changes in the Lower Limb Bones with Aging at Pecos Pueblo.* Ph.D. Thesis, Department of Anthropology, University of Pennsylvania, Philadelphia.

Ryan, A. S.
    1980   *Anterior Dental Microwear in Hominid Evolution: Comparisons with Humans and Nonhuman Primates.* Ph.D. Thesis, Department of Anthropology, University of Michigan, Ann Arbor, Michigan.

Saban, R.
    1981   Modifications des empreintes des veines méningées moyennes sur la voûte du crâne humain au cours de la croissance. *Comptes Rendus de l'Académie des Sciences de Paris*, Série III, **292**:817–820.

Sacher, G. A. and E. F. Staffeldt
    1974   Relation of gestation time to brain weight for placental mammals: Implications for the theory of vertebrate growth. *American Naturalist* **108**:593–615.

Santa Luca, A. P.
    1978   A re-examination of presumed Neandertal-like fossils. *Journal of Human Evolution* **7**:619–636.
    1980   The Ngandong fossil Hominids: A comparative study of a far Eastern *Homo erectus* group. *Yale University Publications in Anthropology* **78**:1–175.

Sante, L. R.
    1961   *Principles of Roentgenological Interpretation.* Ann Arbor: Edwards.

Sarasin, F.
    1932   Die Variation im Bau des Handskeletts verschiedener Menschenformen. *Zeitschrift für Morphologie und Anthropologie* **30**:252–316.

Schaafhausen, D.
    1858   Zur Kenntnis der ältesten Rassenschädel. *Archiv für Anatomie, Physiologie und wissenschaftliche Medicin* **25**:453–478.

Schaefer, U.
    1957   Homo neanderthalensis (King). I. Das Skelett aus dem Neandertal. *Zeitschrift für Morphologie und Anthropologie* **48**:268–297.

Schulter, F. P.
    1976   A comparative study of the temporal bone in three populations of man. *American Journal of Physical Anthropology* **44**:453–468.

Schultz, A. H.
    1930   The skeleton of the trunk and limbs of higher Primates. *Human Biology* **2**:303–438.
    1949   Sex differences in the pelves of primates. *American Journal of Physical Anthropology* **7**:401–423.
    1950   The physical distinctions of man. *Proceedings of the American Philosophical Society* **94**:428–449.
    1955   The position of the occipital condyles and of the face relative to the skull base in primates. *American Journal of Physical Anthropology* **13**:97–120.

Schwalbe, G.
    1901   Der Neanderthalschädel. *Bonner Jahrbücher* **106**:1–72.
    1914   Kritische Besprechung von Boule's Werk: "L'homme fossile de la Chapelle-aux-Saints" mit einigen Untersuchungen. *Zeitschrift für Morphologie und Anthropologie* **16**(3):527–610.

Schwarcz, H. P.
    1980   Absolute age determination of archaeological sites by uranium series dating of travertines. *Archaeometry* **22**:3–24.

Şenyürek, M. S.
    1957a   A further note on the palaeolithic Shanidar infant. *Anatolia* **2**:111–121.
    1957b   The skeleton of the fossil infant found in Shanidar cave, northern Iraq. *Anatolia* **2**:49–55.
    1959   A study of the deciduous teeth of the fossil Shanidar infant. A comparative study of the milk teeth of fossil men. *Publications of the Faculty of Languages, History and*

Geography, University of Ankara, Publications of the Division of Palaeoanthropology **2**:(128):1–174.

Sergi, S.
  1947   Sulla morfologia della "facies anterior corporis maxillae" nei paleantropi di Saccopastore a del Monte Circeo. *Rivista di Antropologia* **35**:401–408.
  1974   *Il Cranio Neandertaliano del Monte Circeo (Circeo I)*. Rome: Accademia Nazionale dei Lincei.

Shrewsbury, M., and R. K. Johnson
  1975   The fascia of the distal phalanx. *Journal of Bone and Joint Surgery* **57-A**:794–788.

Simonton, F. V.
  1923   Mental foramen in the Anthropoids and in man. *American Journal of Physical Anthropology* **6**:413–421.

Singer, R.
  1953   Estimation of age from cranial suture closure: Report of its unreliability. *Journal of Forensic Medicine* **1**:52–59.

Singer, R. and J. Wymer
  1982   *The Middle Stone Age at Klasies River Mouth in South Africa*. Chicago: University of Chicago Press.

Skinner, J. H.
  1965   *The Flake Industries of Southwest Asia: A Typological Study*. Ph.D. Thesis, Department of Anthropology, Columbia University, New York.

Skinner, M. F.
  1977   *Dental Maturation, Dental Attrition and Growth of the Skull in Fossil Hominids*. Ph.D. Thesis, Christ's College, University of Cambridge, Cambridge.

Smidt, G. L.
  1973   Biomechanical analysis of knee flexion and extension. *Journal of Biomechanics*. **6**:79–92.

Smith, F. H.
  1976a   The Neandertal Remains from Krapina: A Descriptive and Comparative Study. *Department of Anthropology, University of Tennessee, Report of Investigations* **15**:1–349.
  1976b   The Neandertal remains from Krapina northern Yugoslavia: An inventory of the upper limb remains. *Zeitschrift für Morphologie und Anthropologie* **67**:275–290.
  1978   Evolutionary significance of the mandibular foramen area in Neandertals. *American Journal of Physical Anthropology* **48**:523–532.
  1980   Sexual differences in European Neanderthal crania with special reference to the Krapina remains. *Journal of Human Evolution* **9**:359–375.
  1982   Upper Pleistocene hominid evolution in South-Central Europe: A review of the evidence and analysis of trends. *Current Anthropology* **23**:667–703.

Smith, F. H., and G. C. Ranyard
  1980   Evolution of the supraorbital region in upper Pleistocene fossil hominids from south-central Europe. *American Journal of Physical Anthropology* **53**:589–610.

Smith, P.
  1976   Dental pathology in fossil hominids: What did Neanderthals do with their teeth? *Current Anthropology* **17**:149–151.
  1978   Evolutionary changes in the deciduous dentition of Near Eastern populations. *Journal of Human Evolution* **7**:401–408.

Smith, P., and B. Arensburg
  1977   A Mousterian skeleton from Kebara cave. *Eretz-Israel* **13**:164–176.

Sokoloff, L. S.
  1972   The pathology and pathogenesis of osteoarthritis. In *Arthritis and Allied Conditions*, edited by J. L. Hollander and D. J. McCarty Jr. Philadelphia: Lea and Febiger. Pp. 1009–1031. (Eighth edition).

Solecki, R. S.
  1952   Notes on a brief archaeological reconnaissance of cave sites in the Rowanduz district
            of Iraq. *Sumer* **8**:37–48.
  1952–
  1953   A palaeolithic site in the Zagros mountains of northern Iraq. Report on a sounding at
            Shanidar cave. *Sumer* **8**:127–192; **9**:60–93.
  1953   The Shanidar cave sounding, 1953 season, with notes concerning the discovery of the
            first palaeolithic skeleton in Iraq. *Sumer* **9**:229–232.
  1954   The Shanidar child. *Iraq Petroleum* **3**:4–9.
  1955a   Shanidar cave, a paleolithic site in northern Iraq, and its relationship to the Stone Age
            sequence of Iraq. *Sumer* **11**:14–38.
  1955b   Shanidar cave, a paleolithic site in northern Iraq. *Annual Report of the Smithsonian
            Institution for 1954.* Pp. 389–425.
  1955c   The Shanidar child, a paleolithic find in Iraq. *Archaeology* **8**:169–175.
  1957a   The 1956 season at Shanidar. *Sumer* **13**:165–171.
  1957b   The 1956–1957 season at Shanidar, Iraq: A preliminary statement. *Quarternaria*
            4:23–30.
  1957c   Shanidar cave. *Scientific American* **197**(5):58–64.
  1957d   Two Neanderthal skeletons from Shanidar cave. *Sumer* **13**:59–60.
  1958a   The 1956–1957 season at Shanidar, Iraq: A preliminary statement. *Sumer*
            14:104–108.
  1958b   *The Baradostian Industry and the Upper Palaeolithic in the Near East.* Ph.D. Thesis,
            Department of Anthropology, Columbia University, New York.
  1959   Early man in cave and village at Shanidar, Kurdistan, Iraq. *Transactions of the New
            York Academy of Sciences* **21**:712–717.
  1960   Three adult Neanderthal skeletons from Shanidar cave, northern Iraq. *Annual Report
            of the Smithsonian Institution for 1959.* Pp. 603–635.
  1961   New anthropological discoveries at Shanidar, northern Iraq. *Transactions of the New
            York Academy of Sciences* **23**:690–699.
  1963   Prehistory in Shanidar valley, northern Iraq. *Science* **139**:179–193.
  1964   Shanidar cave, a late Pleistocene site in northern Iraq. VIᵉ *Congrès de l'INQUA.*
            6:413–423.
  1971a   Neanderthal is not an epithet but a worthy ancestor. *Smithsonian* **2**(2):20–27.
  1971b   *Shanidar, the First Flower People.* New York: Knopf.
  1975   Shanidar IV, a Neanderthal flower burial in northern Iraq. *Science* **190**:880–881.
  1977   The implications of the Shanidar cave Neanderthal flower burial. *Annals of the New
            York Academy of Sciences* **293**:114–124.
  1979   Contemporary Kurdish winter-time inhabitants of Shanidar cave, Iraq. *World Archae-
            ology* **10**:318–330.
Solecki, R. S., and A. Leroi-Gourhan
  1961   Palaeoclimatology and archaeology in the Near East. *Annals of the New York Acade-
            my of Sciences* **95**(1):729–739.
Spencer, F., and F. H. Smith
  1981   The significance of Aleš Hrdlička's "Neanderthal phase of man": A historical and
            current assessment. *American Journal of Physical Anthropology* **56**:435–459.
Sprecher, H.
  1932   *Morphologische Untersuchungen an der Fibula des Menschen unter Berücksich-
            tigung anderer Primaten.* Zürich: Anthropologischen Institut der Universität Zürich.
Steinbock, R. T.
  1976   *Paleopathological Diagnosis and Interpretation.* Springfield: Thomas.
Stewart, T. D.
  1958   First views of the restored Shanidar I skull. *Sumer.* **14**:90–96. (Reprinted in *Annual
            Report of the Smithsonian Institution,* 1958. Pp. 473–480.)

1959   Restoration and study of the Shanidar I Neanderthal skeleton in Baghdad, Iraq. *Year Book of the American Philosophical Society for 1958.* Pp. 274–278.

1960   Form of the pubic bone in Neanderthal Man. *Science* **131**:1437–1438.

1961a A neglected primitive feature of the Swanscombe skull. In *Homenaje a Pablo Martínez del Río*, edited by I. Bernal, J. Gurría, S. Genovés and L. Aveleyra. Mexico City: Instituto Nacional de Antropología e Historia. Pp. 207–217.

1961b The skull of Shanidar II. *Sumer* **17**:97–106. (Reprinted in *Annual Report of the Smithsonian Institution for 1961.* Pp. 521–533.)

1962a Neanderthal cervical vertebrae with special attention to the Shanidar Neanderthals from Iraq. *Bibliotheca Primatologica* **1**:130–154.

1962b Neanderthal scapulae with special attention to the Shanidar Neanderthals from Iraq. *Anthropos* **57**:779–800.

1963   Shanidar skeletons IV and VI. *Sumer* **19**:8–26.

1966   Some problems in human palaeopathology. In *Human Palaeopathology*, edited by S. Jarcho. New Haven: Yale University Press. Pp. 43–55.

1969   Fossil evidence for human violence. *Trans-action* **6**(7):48–53.

1970   The evolution of man in Asia as seen in the lower jaw. In *VIIIth International Congress of Anthropological and Ethnological Sciences, Tokyo 1968* **1**:263–266.

1974   Nonunion of fractures in antiquity, with descriptions of five cases from the New World involving the forearm. *Bulletin of the New York Academy of Medicine* **50**(8):875–891.

1977   The Neanderthal skeletal remains from Shanidar cave, Iraq: A summary of the findings to date. *Proceedings of the American Philosophical Society* **121**(2):121–165.

Stewart, T. D., and R. S. Solecki
1975   Iraq. In *Catalogue of Fossil Hominids* (Part 3), *Americas, Asia, Australasia*, edited by K. P. Oakley, B. G. Campbell, and T. I. Molleson. London: British Museum (Natural History). Pp. 121–124.

Stoner, B. P.
1981   *A Statistical Analysis of the Neanderthal Thumb: Functional Adaptations for the Transmission of Force.* B.A. Thesis, Department of Anthropology, Harvard University, Cambridge, Massachusetts.

Stoner, B. P., and E. Trinkaus
1981   Getting a grip on the Neandertals: Were they all thumbs? *American Journal of Physical Anthropology* **54**:281–282. (Abstract).

Straus, W. L. Jr., and A. J. E. Cave
1957   Pathology and the posture of Neanderthal man. *Quarterly Review of Biology* **32**:348–363.

Stringer, C. B.
1974a *A Multivariate Study of Cranial Variation in Middle and Upper Pleistocene Human Populations.* Ph.D. Thesis, Department of Anatomy, University of Bristol, Bristol.

1974b Population relationships of late Pleistocene hominids: A multivariate study of available crania. *Journal of Archaeological Science* **1**:317–342.

1978   Some problems in Middle and Upper Pleistocene Hominid relationships. In *Recent Advances in Primatology*, edited by D. J. Chivers and K. A. Joysey. London: Academic Press. **3**:395–418.

1981   The dating of European Middle Pleistocene Hominids and the existence of *Homo erectus* in Europe. *Anthropologie* (Brno) **19**:3–14.

1982   Towards a solution to the Neanderthal problem. *Journal of Human Evolution* **11**:431–438.

Stringer, C. B., F. C. Howell, and J. K. Melentis
1979   The significance of the fossil hominid skull from Petralona, Greece. *Journal of Archaeological Science* **6**:235–253.

Stringer, C. B., and E. Trinkaus
   1981   The Shanidar Neanderthal crania. In *Aspects of Human Evolution*, edited by C. B. Stringer. London: Taylor and Francis. Pp. 129–165.
Suzuki, H.
   1970   Skull of the Amud man. In *The Amud Man and his Cave Site*, edited by H. Suzuki and F. Takai. Tokyo: Academic Press. Pp. 123–206.
Suzuki, H., and F. Takai (editors)
   1970   *The Amud Man and his Cave Site*. Tokyo: Academic Press.
Tappen, N. C.
   1973   Structure of bone in skulls of Neanderthal fossils. *American Journal of Physical Anthropology* **38**:93–98.
Taylor, J. V.
   1968   *The Neanderthal Tibia*. Ph.D. Thesis, Department of Anthropology, Columbia University, New York.
Telkkä, A.
   1950   On the prediction of human stature from the long bones. *Acta Anatomica* **9**:103–117.
Terry, R. J.
   1932   The clavicle of the American Negro. *American Journal of Physical Anthropology* **16**:351–379.
Thoma, A.
   1975   Were the Spy fossils evolutionary intermediates between classic Neanderthal and modern man? *Journal of Human Evolution* **4**:387–410.
Thompson, D. D.
   1978   *Age Related Changes in Osteon Remodeling and Bone Mineralization*. Ph.D. Thesis, Department of Anthropology, University of Connecticut, Storrs.
Thompson, D. D., and E. Trinkaus
   1981   Age determination for the Shanidar 3 Neanderthal. *Science* **212**:575–577.
Tillier, A.-M.
   1974   Contribution à l'étude des hommes fossiles Moustériens du Moyen Orient: La pneumatisation de la face. *Paléorient* **2**:463–468.
   1979   La dentition de l'enfant moustérien Châteauneuf 2 découverte à l'Abri de Hauteroche (Charente). *L'Anthropologie* **83**:417–438.
Tobias, P. V.
   1967   The hominid skeletal remains of Haua Fteah. In *The Haua Fteah (Cyrenaica) and the Stone Age of the South-east Mediterranean*, edited by C. B. M. McBurney. Cambridge: Cambridge University Press. Pp. 338–352.
Toerien, M. J.
   1957   Note on the cervical vertebrae of the La Chapelle man. *South African Journal of Science* **53**:447–449.
Travill, A., and J. V. Basmajian
   1961   Electromyography of the supinators of the forearm. *Anatomical Record* **139**:557–560.
Trinkaus, E.
   1973   A reconsideration of the Fontéchevade fossils. *American Journal of Physical Anthropology* **39**:25–36.
   1975a   *A Functional Analysis of the Neandertal Foot*. Ph.D. Thesis, Department of Anthropology, University of Pennsylvania, Philadelphia.
   1975b   The Neandertals from Krapina, northern Yugoslavia: An inventory of the lower limb remains. *Zeitschrift für Morphologie und Anthropologie* **67**:44–59.
   1975c   Squatting among the Neandertals: A problem in the behavioral interpretation of skeletal morphology. *Journal of Archaeological Science* **2**(4):327–351.
   1976a   The evolution of the hominid femoral diaphysis during the Upper Pleistocene in Europe and the Near East. *Zeitschrift für Morphologie und Anthropologie* **67**:291–319.

1976b   The morphology of European and southwest Asian Neandertal pubic bones. *American Journal of Physical Anthropology* **44**:95–104.

1977a   A functional interpretation of the axillary border of the Neandertal scapula. *Journal of Human Evolution* **6**:231–234.

1977b   An inventory of the Neanderthal remains from Shanidar cave, northern Iraq. *Sumer* **33**:9–33.

1977c   A note on the dental remains from Mugharet es-Skhūl in the Peabody Museum, Skhūl II, V, VI, and VII. Unpublished manuscript.

1977d   The Shanidar 5 Neanderthal skeleton. *Sumer* **33**:35–41.

1978a   Bilateral asymmetry of human skeletal non-metric traits. *American Journal of Physical Anthropology* **49**:315–318.

1978b   Dental remains from the Shanidar adult Neanderthals. *Journal of Human Evolution* **7**:369–382.

1978c   Functional implications of the Krapina Neandertal lower limb remains. In *Krapinski Pračovjek i Evolucija Hominida*, edited by M. Malez. Zagreb: Jugoslavenska Akademija Znanosti i Umjetnosti. Pp. 155–192.

1978d   Hard times among the Neanderthals. *Natural History* **87**(10):58–63.

1978e   Le métatarsiens et les phalanges du pied des Néandertaliens de Spy. *Bulletin de l'Institut Royal des Sciences Naturelles de Belgique (Biologie)* **51**(7):1–18.

1978f   A preliminary description of the Shanidar 5 Neandertal partial skeleton. In *Recent Advances in Primatology*, (Vol. 3) edited by D. J. Chivers and K. A. Joysey. London: Academic Press. Pp. 431–433.

1980   Sexual differences in Neanderthal limb bones. *Journal of Human Evolution* **9**:377–397.

1981   Neanderthal limb proportions and cold adaptation. In *Aspects of Human Evolution*, edited by C. B. Stringer. London: Taylor and Francis. Pp. 187–224.

1982a   Artificial cranial deformation of the Shanidar 1 and 5 Neandertals. *Current Anthropology* **23**:198–199.

1982b   *Behavioral implications of human postcranial changes at the Middle to Upper Paleolithic transition.* Paper presented at the 47th meeting of the Society for American Archaeology, Minneapolis, Minnesota.

1982c   Evolutionary continuity among archaic *Homo sapiens*. In *The Transition from Lower to Middle Palaeolithic and the Origin of Modern Man*, edited by A. Ronen. Oxford: British Archaeological Reports, International Series **151**:301–314.

1982d   Evolutionary trends in the Shanidar Neandertal sample. *American Journal of Physical Anthropology* **57**:237. (Abstract).

1982e   A history of *Homo erectus* and *Homo sapiens* paleontology in America. In *A History of American Physical Anthropology, 1930–1980*, edited by F. Spencer. New York: Academic Press. Pp. 261–280.

1982f   The Shanidar 3 Neandertal. *American Journal of Physical Anthropology* **57**:37–60.

1983   Pathology and posture of the La Chapelle-aux-Saints Neandertal. *American Journal of Physical Anthropology* **60**:262 (Abstract).

Trinkaus, E., and W. W. Howells
1979   The Neanderthals. *Scientific American* **241**(6):118–133.

Trinkaus, E., and M. LeMay
1982   Occipital bunning among later Pleistocene hominids. *American Journal of Physical Anthropology* **57**:27–35.

Trinkaus, E., and T. D. Stewart
1980   The Shanidar 3 Neanderthal: A fragmentary skeleton from Shanidar cave, northern Iraq. *Sumer* **36**:9–39.

Trinkaus, E., and M. R. Zimmerman
1979   Paleopathology of the Shanidar Neanderthals. *American Journal of Physical Anthropology* **50**:487. (Abstract).

1982   Trauma among the Shanidar Neandertals. *American Journal of Physical Anthropology* **57**:61–76.

Trotter, M.
1934a   Septal apertures in the humerus of American whites and negro. *American Journal of Physical Anthropology* **19**:213–228.
1934b   Synostosis between manubrium and body of the sternum in whites and negroes. *American Journal of Physical Anthropology* **18**:439–442.

Trotter, M., and G. C. Gleser
1952   Estimation of stature from long bones of American whites and negroes. *American Journal of Physical Anthropology* **10**:463–514.
1958   A re-evaluation of estimation of stature based on measurements of stature taken during life and of long bones after death. *American Journal of Physical Anthropology* **16**:79–124.

Trotter, M., and P. F. Lanier
1945   *Hiatus canalis sacralis* in American whites and negroes. *Human Biology* **17**:368–381.

Tschantz, P., and E. Rutishauser
1967   La surcharge mécanique de l'os vivant. Les déformations plastiques initiales et l'hypertrophie d'adaptation. *Annales d'Anatomie Pathologique* **12**:223–248.

Tuffreau, A.
1979   Les débuts du paléolithique moyen dans la France septentrionale. *Bulletin de la Société Préhistorique Française* **76**:140–142.

Turek, S. L.
1967   *Orthopaedics: Principles and their Application*. Philadelphia: Lippincott. (Second edition).

Turner, C. G. II
1969   Microevolutionary interpretations from the dentition. *American Journal of Physical Anthropology* **30**:421–426.

Twiesselmann, F.
1961   Le fémur Néanderthalien de Fond-de-Forêt (Province de Liège). *Mémoires de l'Institut Royal des Sciences Naturelles de Belgique* **148**:1–164.
1973   Évolution des dimensions et de la forme de la mandibule, du palais et des dents de l'Homme. *Annales de Paléontologie* (Vertébrés) **59**:171–277.

Twiesselmann, F., and H. Brabant
1967   Nouvelles observations sur les dents et les maxillaires d'une population ancienne d'âge Franc de Coxyde. *Bulletin du Groupement de la Recherche Scientifique en Stomatologie* **10**:5–180.

Ubelaker, D. H.
1978   *Human Skeletal Remains*. Chicago: Aldine.

Ullrich, H.
1955   Paläolithische Menschenreste aus der Sowjetunion II. Das Kinderskelett aus der Grotte Teschik-Tasch, *Zeitschrift für Morphologie und Anthropologie* **47**:99–112.

Vallois, H. V.
1928–
1946   L'omoplate humaine: Étude anatomique et anthropologique. *Bulletins et Mémoires de la Société d'Anthropologie de Paris*, Série 7, **9**:129–168; **10**:110–191; Série 8, **3**:3–153; Série 9, **7**:16–100.
1935   Les maladies des hommes préhistoriques. *L'Anthropologie* **45**:476–478.
1958   La Grotte de Fontéchevade II: Anthropologie. *Archives de l'Institut de Paléontologie Humaine* **29**:1–164.
1960   Vital statistics in prehistoric population as determined from archaeological data. In *The Application of Quantitative Methods in Archaeology*, edited by R. F. Heizer and S. F. Cook. *Viking Fund Publication in Anthropology* **28**:186–222.

1961   The social life of early man: The evidence of skeletons. In *Social Life of Early Man,*
            edited by S. L. Washburn. Chicago: Aldine. Pp. 214–235.

1965   Le sternum néanderthalien du Régourdou. *Anthropologischer Anzeiger* **29**:273–
            289.

1969   Le temporal néanderthalien H 27 de La Quina: Étude anthropologique. *L'An-
            thropologie* **73**:365–400, 525–544.

Vandermeersch, B.

1965   Position stratigraphique et chronologique des restes humains du paléolithique moyen
            du sud-ouest de la France. *Annales de Paléontologie (Vertébrés)* **51**:69–126.

1972   Récentes découvertes de squelettes humains à Qafzeh (Israël): Essai d'interprétation.
            In *The Origin of* Homo sapiens, edited by F. Bordes. Paris: UNESCO. Pp. 49–54.

1978a   Le Crâne Pré-Würmien de Biache-Saint-Vaast (Pas-de-Calais). In *Les Origines Hu-
            maines et les Époques de l'Intelligence,* edited by J. Piveteau. Paris: Masson et Cie.
            Pp. 153–157.

1978b   Quelques aspects du problème de l'origine de l'homme moderne. In *Les Origines
            Humaines et les Époques de l'Intelligence.* Paris: Masson et Cie. Pp. 251–260.

1981a   *Les Hommes Fossiles de Qafzeh (Israël).* Paris: Éditions du C.N.R.S.

1981b   Les premiers *Homo* sapiens au Proche-Orient. In *Les processus de l'hominisation,*
            edited by D. Ferembach. Paris: Éditions du C.N.R.S. Pp. 97–100.

1981c   A Neandertal skeleton from a Châtelperronian level at St. Césaire (France). *American
            Journal of Physical Anthropology* **54**:286. (Abstract).

Verneau, R.

1906   *Les Grottes de Grimaldi (Baoussé-Roussé)* III. Anthropologie Monaco: Imprimérie de
            Monaco. **2**:1–212.

Vlček, E.

1967   Die *Sinus frontales* bei europäischen Neandertalern. *Anthropologischer Anzeiger*
            30:166–189.

1969   *Neandertaler der Tschechoslowakei.* Prague: Verlag der Tschechoslowakische
            Akademie der Wissenschaften.

1970   Étude comparative onto-phylogénétique de l'enfant du Pech-de-l'Azé par rapport à
            d'autres enfants Néandertaliens. In *L'Enfant du Pech de l'Azé. Archives de l'Institut
            de Paléontologie Humaine* **33**:149–178.

1973   Postcranial skeleton of a Neandertal child from Kiik-Koba, U.S.S.R. *Journal of Human
            Evolution* **2**:537–544.

1975   Morphology of the first metacarpal of Neanderthal individuals from the Crimea.
            Bulletins et Mémoires de la Société d'Anthropologie de Paris, Série 13, **2**:257–276.

1978   Transformation of the metacarpal bones and some short hand muscles of the Nean-
            derthal man. *XIXth Morphological Congress Symposia.* Charles University, Prague.
            Pp. 89–99.

Vogel, J. C., and H. T. Waterbolk

1963   Groningen radiocarbon dates IV. *Radiocarbon* **5**: 163–202.

Vriese, B. de

1913   La signification morphologique de la rotule basée sur des recherches anthropologi-
            ques. IIᵉ partie. La rotule au point de vue anthropologique. *Bulletins et Mémoires de
            la Société d'Anthropologie de Paris,* Série 6, **4**:306–369.

Wallace, J. A.

1975   Did La Ferrassie I use his teeth as a tool? *Current Anthropology* **16**:393–401.

Warren, E.

1897   An investigation on the variability of the human skeleton: with especial reference to
            the Naqada race. *Philosophical Transactions of the Royal Society,* Series B,
            189:135–227.

Warwick, R., and P. L. Williams

1973   *Gray's Anatomy.* Philadelphia: W. B. Saunders. (Thirty-fifth British edition).

Washburn, S. L.
  1947   The relation of the temporal muscle to the form of the skull. *Anatomical Record*
          99:239–248.
  1948   Sex differences in the pubic bone. *American Journal of Physical Anthropology*
          6:199–207.
Wei, C.
  1979   Ricerca dei discendenti dell'uomo di Pechino. *Minerva Medica* **70**:2723–2728.
Weidenreich, F.
  1936   The mandibles of *Sinanthropus pekinensis:* A comparative study. *Palaeontologia
          Sinica*, Series D, **7**:1–162.
  1940   The *Torus occipitalis* and related structures and their transformation in the course of
          human evolution. *Bulletin of the Geological Society of China* **19**:379–558.
  1941   The extremity bones of *Sinanthropus pekinensis. Palaeontologia Sinica*, Series D,
          5:1–82.
  1943   The skull of *Sinanthropus pekinensis:* A comparative study on a primitive hominid
          skull. *Palaeontologia Sinica*, New Series D, **10**:1–298.
  1945   The brachycephalization of recent mankind. *Southwestern Journal of Anthropology*
          1:1–54.
Weinert, C. R. Jr., J. H. McMaster, and R. J. Ferguson
  1973   Dynamic function of the human fibula. *American Journal of Anatomy* **138**:145–150.
Weinert, H.
  1925   *Der Schädel des Eiszeitlichen Menschen von Le Moustier in Neuer Zusammen-
          setzung.* Berlin: Verlag von Julius Springer.
Weiss, K. M.
  1972   On the systematic bias in skeletal sexing. *American Journal of Physical Anthropology*
          37:239–250.
White, R.
  1982   Rethinking the Middle/Upper Paleolithic transition. *Current Anthropology*
          23:169–192.
White, T. D.
  1974   Body, mandible, tooth and temporalis size in a prehistoric Amerind population.
          American Journal of Physical Anthropology **41**:509. (Abstract).
  1977   *The Anterior Mandibular Corpus of Early African Hominidae: Functional Signifi-
          cance of Shape and Size.* Ph.D. Thesis, Department of Anthropology, University of
          Michigan, Ann Arbor, Michigan.
Wiberg, G.
  1941   Roentgenographic and anatomic studies on the Femoropatellar joint, with special
          reference to *Chondromalacia patellae. Acta Orthopedica Scandinavica* **12**:319–410.
Wolpoff, M. H.
  1971a   Interstitial wear. *American Journal of Physical Anthropology* **34**:205–228.
  1971b   Metric Trends in Hominid Dental Evolution. *Case Western Reserve University Stud-
          ies in Anthropology* **2**:1–244.
  1975   Some aspects of human mandibular evolution. In *Determinants of Mandibular Form
          and Growth*, edited by J. A. McNamara Jr. Ann Arbor: Center for Human Growth and
          Development. Pp. 1–64.
  1976   Some aspects of the evolution of early hominid sexual dimorphism. *Current An-
          thropology* **17**:579–606.
  1979   The Krapina dental remains. *American Journal of Physical Anthropology* **50**:67–114.
  1980a   Cranial remains of Middle Pleistocene European hominids. *Journal of Human Evolu-
          tion* **9**:339–358.
  1980b   *Paleoanthropology.* New York: Knopf.
  1981   Evolutionary changes in European Neandertals. *American Journal of Physical An-
          thropology* **54**:290. (Abstract).

Wolpoff, M. H., F. H. Smith, M. Malez, J. Radovčić, and D. Rukavina
    1981   Upper Pleistocene human remains from Vindija cave, Croatia, Yugoslavia. *American Journal of Physical Anthropology* **54**:499–545.

Woo, J. K., and R. C. Peng
    1959   Fossil human skull of Early Paleoanthropic stage found at Mapa, Shaoquan, Kwangtung Province. *Vertebrata PalAsiatica*, **3**:176–182.

Wright, H. E.
    1962   Pleistocene glaciation in Kurdistan. *Eiszeitalter und Gegenwart* **12**:131–164.

Wu, X.
    1981   A well-preserved cranium of an archaic type of early *Homo sapiens* from Dali, China. *Scienta Sinica* **24**(4):530–539.

Youm, Y., R. F. Dryer, K. Thambyrajah, A. E. Flatt, and B. L. Sprague
    1979   Biomechanical analyses of forearm pronation-supination and elbow flexion-extension. *Journal of Biomechanics* **12**:245–255.

Young, R. W.
    1957   Postnatal growth of the frontal and parietal bones in white males. *American Journal of Physical Anthropology* **15**:367–386.
    1959   The influence of cranial contents on postnatal growth of the skull in the rat. *American Journal of Anatomy* **105**:383–415.

Zito, R. J.
    1981   *A Study of Serial Changes in the Size and Shape of Hominoid Post-Diaphragmatic Vertebrae.* B.A. Thesis, Department of Anthropology, Harvard University, Cambridge, Massachusetts.

Index